D1610002

BLACKPOOL AND THE FYLDE COLLEGE

3 8049 00085 161 1

Other Plays by Joyce Carol Oates

Three Plays (1980)
Twelve Plays (1991)
The Perfectionist and Other Plays (1995)

NEW PLAYS

Joyce Carol Oates

Ontario Review Press • Princeton

Copyright © 1998 by The Ontario Review, Inc.
All rights reserved.
Printed in the U.S.A.

Ontario Review Press
9 Honey Brook Drive
Princeton, NJ 08540

Distributed by George Braziller, Inc.
171 Madison Avenue
New York, NY 10016

Library of Congress Cataloging-in-Publication Data
Oates, Joyce Carol, 1938–
    [Plays. Selections]
    New plays / Joyce Carol Oates.
        p.   cm.
    Contents: Bad girls — Black water — The passion of Henry David Thoreau —
Here I am — Duet — Good to know you — Poor Bibi — Homesick — The adoption
— No next of kin — When I was a little girl and my mother didn't want me.
    ISBN 0-86538-089-9
    ISBN 0-86538-090-2 (pbk.)
    I. Title.
PS3565.A8A6 1998
812'.54—dc21   97-46802
                                                                                      CIP

First Edition

Caution: Professionals and amateurs are hereby warned that these plays, being
fully protected under the Copyright Laws of the United States of America and all
other countries subscribing to the Universal Copyright Convention, are subject to
royalty. All rights are strictly reserved. Written permission must be obtained from
The Ontario Review, Inc., 9 Honey Brook Dr., Princeton, NJ 08540.

These plays are dedicated, with heartfelt gratitude and much affection, to the directors who helped shape them for the theater—

August Staub, Ed Herendeen, Gordon Edelstein, Carol Rocamora, Susana Tubert, Karin O'Connell, Kevin Confoy, Curt Dempster

CONTENTS

NEW PLAYS

I

Bad Girls
A Play in Two Acts

CHARACTERS:
THE MURCHISONS:
  ORCHID, 20 years old, as narrator; 15, in the past
  CRYSTAL, 13 years old
  MARIETTA, 36 years old
  ISABEL, "Icy," 16 years old
ISAAK DRUMM, mid-40s

PLACE: Yewville, a small city of 30,000 in upstate New York

TIME: the near-present
  Act I, March
  Act II, April
  Epilogue, May, five years later

ACT I

Scene 1

Darkness. The sound of a train whistle, faint and melancholy at first; gradually increasing in volume. Lights rush past a window stage left. (The MURCHISON living room/kitchen, in shadows, is partly illuminated.) Rumbling of a locomotive and freight cars.

Lights up on ORCHID, *aged 20, in a nurse's uniform. She stands in a space or on a platform stage left, addressing the audience.*

ORCHID: That day, the world began to break into pieces for us. But we didn't know at the time. *(Pause)* We were living in half a rented woodframe house on South Niagara Street, Yewville, New York...the slipping-down side of the street, on a hill. The New York Central railroad tracks were just below, running practically through our back yard. Got so we hardly even heard the trains.

As lights come up in the MURCHISON *living room. (The kitchen remains in shadows.) Initial lighting has a sepia cast to suggest that this is the past. A window and a door facing us, in the living room, lead to the unseen street; a kitchen area, stage right, is at the rear of the house, overlooking the railroad tracks. Vases and glassware vibrate with the train's passing.*

The living room is modestly furnished, with some romantic touches: peacock feathers in a vase, a colorful handknit afghan draped over the back of a sofa, needlepoint pillows. A shag rug. A lamp with a tasseled shade. A glitzy gilt-framed mirror on the wall.

CRYSTAL *in jeans and snug sweater is dancing to an MTV video and simultaneously devouring handfuls of a sugar-coated cereal. She is a softly pretty, slightly plump girl of 13, physically mature for her age. The sound of the MTV music comes up as the sound of the train subsides.*

ORCHID: That's my "baby" sister Crystal. Doing her math homework, I believe. Waiting for our mother to come home. I— Orchid—am on my way home. Seems like another lifetime... That evening in March five years ago.

ORCHID *unobtrusively exits as lights come up further on* CRYSTAL *who looks around as if her name has been called.*

CRYSTAL *is alert, having heard someone coming; clumsy but quick, she switches off the TV; hides the cereal box behind a pillow on the sofa; sprawls out on the rug to resume her homework, spread out messily before her.*

CRYSTAL *(muttering, taking up a compass and pencil)*: "Isos-ce-les tri-angle"—"trap-e-zoid"—

MARIETTA *enters though the kitchen door, stage left. Quickly removes her coat, an attractive, inexpensive cloth coat with "stylish" features, as she hurries into the living room.*

MARIETTA *(breathless)*: Oh Crystal!—didn't you and your sisters pick up in here? I begged you—

CRYSTAL *(looking up from homework as if distracted)*: Oh hi Momma.

MARIETTA: What time *is* it? That shithead boss of mine kept me late again—tonight of all nights. He does it deliberately, I just know. *(Lets her purse fall onto the sofa; kicks off shoes to carry them with her toward the hallway, stage right, which leads to the unseen bedrooms; glancing around distressed, annoyed)* This place is the identical pigsty it *was*! You girls! Didn't I tell you that Isaak Drumm— *(pronouncing the name almost reverently)* —is coming in— *(checks watch, voice rises)* —oh my God: it's ten to eight already! Isaak is coming in ten minutes! No time to shower, shampoo my hair—

CRYSTAL *(as if deeply immersed in her homework, loudly)*: "Isos-ce-les tri-angle"—"trap-e-zoid"—"sum-of-the-sides-is-equal-to-the—" Oh shit! *(Shoving at papers, textbooks)*

MARIETTA pauses in her haste to kiss the top of CRYSTAL's head, but can't help scolding.

MARIETTA: Crystal, honey, I've told you and *told* you—a nice girl doesn't use profane language. At least, not that anybody can hear.

CRYSTAL: Why not, Momma? *You* do.

MARIETTA: But not so anybody can *hear*. *(Exiting, calling over her shoulder)* Where the hell are those sisters of yours?

CRYSTAL *(whining)*: How the hell should I know?

MARIETTA *(voice offstage)*: Did anybody call?

CRYSTAL scrambles over to get another handful of cereal from the hidden box.

CRYSTAL: Huh?

MARIETTA *(voice)*: —Anybody call?

CRYSTAL: I don't know, I've been working. *(Picking up compass)*

MARIETTA returns, in her stocking feet, with a dress over her head, arms flailing. She wears a lacy white slip.

MARIETTA: Crystal, help me, please!

CRYSTAL *leaps up, glad to help* MARIETTA. *The dress is a bit tight.*

MARIETTA: Oh damn! The dry cleaners must've shrunk this. *(Smoothing material over hips)* Wouldn't you know!—everything happens at once.

CRYSTAL: Momma, you look real nice. I love that color!

MARIETTA *(lifting arms)*: Well, I'm perspiring. In fact—sweating. Right through my "lightly scented" deodorant. *Not* the note I want for tonight! *(Moving about distractedly tidying up the room;* CRYSTAL *helps)* You girls! I thought *you* liked to vacuum, Crystal.

CRYSTAL: Momma, I *do*. But the damn ol' thing's broke—the hose is all stuffed solid with yucky-fuzzy stuff. *(Shivers)*

MARIETTA: Oh hell, I forgot. Meant to get it repaired. But the car broke down . . . *(Pause, sighs)* Thank God, Isaak wants to take me *out*. *(Glances in mirror)* Damn, my hair! Looks like I used an eggbeater on it.

CRYSTAL *(hugging her)*: Momma, you look *beautiful*.

MARIETTA *(hugging her in return, warmly)*: Baby, if only you were Isaak Drumm!

CRYSTAL *(wrenching away, hurt)*: Why does *he* matter, and I don't?

MARIETTA: You matter—but he's a man. *(Exiting, calling over shoulder)* See where your sisters are—it's late.

CRYSTAL *(undertone)*: "*You* matter—but *he's* a man!" La-dee-dah! *(Plops back down on the floor, in front of TV)*

ORCHID *enters noisily, through kitchen. Wears running shoes, a denim jacket, jeans; tosses the jacket at a chair.* ORCHID *is a tall, skinny, defiant, ironic girl of 15—the "brains of the Murchisons," though she doesn't always show it.*

ORCHID: What's going on?

CRYSTAL *(sullen)*: Oh—some guy's taking Momma out to dinner and she's kinda uptight. She's been waiting for Friday all week.

ORCHID *(sardonic)*: Momma's been waiting for Friday all *winter*. This the same bozo stood her up last week?

CRYSTAL: I wish Momma was happy with just us. *(Pause, eating cereal dreamily)* Y'know what I love best, Orchid?—we're all home here, at night, Momma and me and you and Icy, and outside it's dark, real dark, windy, maybe snowing— *(Shivers with pleasure)* A train coming through— "Whooooooo—"

ORCHID *(in her own thoughts)*: This the same bozo keeps promising he's gonna "drop by after work"—and never does? Jeez, you'd think Momma would give up on men, at her age.

CRYSTAL *(with dread)*: What's Momma's age?

ORCHID *(dramatically)*: Thirty-six.

CRYSTAL: Oh! She is not.

ORCHID: She *is*. What's wrong with you?

CRYSTAL *(hands over ears)*: I don't like to hear personal things about Momma. My stomach gets queasy.

ORCHID *(clinical detachment)*: Jeez!—thirty-*six*. Years *old*. Ever think you'll get that old?

CRYSTAL *(blankly)*: Me?

ORCHID: 'Course if Momma was to marry the right guy, our "standard of living" just might improve.

CRYSTAL: We're O.K. just like we are! We don't need anybody else.

ORCHID: This graph they were showing on TV the other night?— "median income"—remember Momma switched channels? That's 'cause our household is in the lowest five percent before you hit the poverty line.

CRYSTAL: How do *you* know?

ORCHID *(secretively)*: I got ways.

CRYSTAL: You been looking through Momma's papers!

ORCHID: Hey: Momma marries this guy, he's insured for one million, he drops over dead, *we* collect. Whooee! *(Pause)* Make that ten million. *(On way to refrigerator)* Except he's probably too smart to show up tonight. *(Opens refrigerator)* Wow, what's this?

CRYSTAL: Orchid, no! *(As ORCHID reaches for an appetizer)* Momma got up at six this morning to make that—*we're* not s'posed to touch any.

ORCHID (*eating a tiny sandwich on a toothpick*): Mmmm! This stuff is good. (*Brings a handful of appetizers to the living room, eating; retains a toothpick to suck on*) You think this guy is really coming?

CRYSTAL *eats hungrily, though guiltily.*

CRYSTAL (*mouth full*): Momma said—eight o'clock.

ORCHID (*peering out window*): Jeez, it's almost eight now. Last Friday she really crashed when he didn't show. Poor Momma!

CRYSTAL: *Somebody's* coming, for sure. They're going to the Lobster Shanty.

ORCHID: Again? That's where they didn't go last week. (*Pause*) Jeez—you think this guy maybe doesn't *exist*? It's all in Momma's *head*?

CRYSTAL: Icy says she saw him—Momma and him together in his car driving downtown.

ORCHID (*skeptically*): When was that? (*When* CRYSTAL *shrugs*) Hell, it might not even be the same guy. You know how Momma is—

CRYSTAL: Real picky.

ORCHID: —desperate. (*Picking up magazine*) I found this *Cosmopolitan* she's been reading—"How to Keep Your Man Perpetually Aroused: New Tricks for Older Women." Half of it's underlined in Magic Marker. (*Turns pages*) "Aphrodisiac Appetizers"— yuck!

CRYSTAL: "Afro-"—what?

ORCHID (*tossing down magazine*): It'd be comic, it wasn't so *sad*.

CRYSTAL (*new idea, claps hands*): Oh, Orchid—*we* can take Momma out. Like we did on her birthday?—a nice surprise for her? I got six dollars saved from babysitting—

ORCHID (*takes out wallet, checks*): Not great. Four bucks seventeen lousy cents.

CRYSTAL: It's O.K. We can go to the Italian Villa.

ORCHID: Oh, no—we're going to the House of Wong. We went to the Italian Villa last time.

CRYSTAL *(childish)*: We did not! We went to House of Wong last time.

ORCHID *(in a sober tone)*: Look, if this bozo doesn't show again, Momma isn't going to want Italian *or* Chinese. Or us. You know what Momma's going to want. *(Gestures as if drinking from bottle)*

CRYSTAL *(biting thumbnail)*: Momma promised *no*, never again. I believe her.

ORCHID: Last Friday—that was kind of scary. *(Pause)*

CRYSTAL: Momma's going to be all right. Whether this guy shows or not. She's got us, hasn't she?

ORCHID *(cruel mimicry of her mother)*: "Never again! Swear to God never again get bombed out of my skull and puke all over the bathroom!"

CRYSTAL *(hearing MARIETTA returning)*: Shhh!

MARIETTA enters the living room, now in slinky high-heeled shoes; glamorously dressed; wearing prominent costume jewelry. She is putting finishing touches on her makeup with a compact and lipstick. We see that she is a very attractive woman, if a bit feverish at the moment.

MARIETTA: Orchid, honey—where've you been? *(Hugs ORCHID who seems embarrassed at MARIETTA's affection)* I was getting worried.

ORCHID: Oh Momma—one of us is five minutes late, you think we've been kidnapped, raped, and murdered. Or—kidnapped, murdered, and raped. *(Laughs)*

MARIETTA: Damn, Orchid, don't talk like that! That is not funny.

ORCHID *(seeing MARIETTA is upset)*: Jeez, Momma—

MARIETTA: *That is not funny.*

ORCHID: O.K., I'm sorry.

MARIETTA: Just pray to God none of us ever knows what those words actually *mean*.

ORCHID *(sullen)*: I *said* I was sorry, Momma. *(Pause)* Anyway, since "Dad" Murchison took a walk, we're all pretty safe.

MARIETTA: Now *that* is truly not *funny*.

CRYSTAL *(humming loudly, hands over ears)*: I don't want to hear. Lalalalalala!

ORCHID *(cruelly)*: Good ol' "Dad" was *your* father, baby!

CRYSTAL: He wasn't, he *wasn't*. I hate you!

MARIETTA *(losing temper)*: Stop! Just—STOP! *(Girls are abruptly silent.)* That's all over and done with, years ago. You know better, both of you. *(Regarding ORCHID)* Oh, Orchid—is that a toothpick in your mouth? *(She tries to snatch it away, but ORCHID is too quick for her.)* That's not what nice girls—women—*do!*—suck toothpicks. *(Pause)* And *that's* what you're wearing, to meet Isaak Drumm for the first time?

ORCHID *(preening, to make CRYSTAL giggle)*: Real sexy, eh?

MARIETTA: You wore that to school today?

ORCHID: If you're so ashamed of me, Momma, I can hide in the cellar when this guy comes.

MARIETTA *(holding ORCHID by the shoulders, trying to adjust her posture)*: If you'd just stand up *straighter*, sweetie! I hope you're not, uh, self-conscious or anything—growing breasts. A woman should take pride in her body— *(Strokes her own breasts as if to bolster her ego)*

ORCHID *(embarrassed, trying to squirm away)*: Jeez, Momma!

MARIETTA: And you've got your father's eyes—nice thick lashes— real striking.

ORCHID *(fiercely)*: I don't want that asshole's eyes! Or anybody's eyes!

MARIETTA: Orchid, watch your mouth. I've told you: profanity is *not* your upbringing. Any of you.

ORCHID: Where'd I get it from, then?

MARIETTA: You never even knew your father. You were just three weeks old when he—left Yewville.

ORCHID: I remember him anyway.

MARIETTA: You do not.

ORCHID: I remember lots of things. From past lives, maybe.

MARIETTA (*wiping at eyes*): Don't remember! Please.

ORCHID *has wandered into the kitchen and returns with a plastic bag which she slips over her head, clowning.*

ORCHID: How's this? An improvement, eh? (*Chasing after* CRYSTAL *who rebuffs her, giggling*) Kissy-kiss!

MARIETTA (*hears something outside*): Oh! He's here.

ORCHID (*now smooching at her mother through the bag*): Guaranteed AIDS protection! (*MARIETTA pushes her away, annoyed;* ORCHID *yanks off the bag and hands it to* MARIETTA.) You take it—you can wear it on your "date."

MARIETTA (*snatches the bag and crumples it in her fist*): Shhhh! (*Listening; there's a dull thud off-stage*) Oh, damn—somebody next door. (*Pause, regarding* ORCHID, *hurt, yet coercive*) I named you "Orchid" because it was the absolutely most beautiful name in the Baby Book—and look how you act! It breaks my heart.

ORCHID: Should've named me "Skunk-Cabbage," then. "Stink-weed." (*Airily*) I'm not to blame for your female delusions of grandeur, Momma.

MARIETTA (*sudden thought*): Where *is* Isabel? She gets off work at six-thirty.

ORCHID: If you mean *Icy*, I don't know.

MARIETTA (*dreading*): She was in school today—wasn't she? (*As* ORCHID *shrugs evasively*) I saw you both waiting for the bus.

ORCHID: Sure. (*Pause, can't resist*) I was, anyway.

MARIETTA (*upset*): Orchid, tell me the truth: did Isabel cut school today? The principal said they'd have to fail her— automatically—if she misses any more days. Oh she's *got* to graduate—

CRYSTAL (*to divert attention*): "Isos-celes"—"rhom-boid"—"equi-lat-eral"—"ob-tuse"— Who made up these things? My brain is *hurting*!

MARIETTA (*tidying room, out of nervous energy*): If Isabel is running around with that juvenile delinquent—that awful Reardon girl— after she *promised*—

ORCHID (*coolly*): Momma, Icy does what she wants to do. You know Icy.

MARIETTA (*deflecting this; dismayed*): Oh, look at the time!

ORCHID: When is this Dumm—Dumbo—expected?

MARIETTA: "Drumm." His name is "Isaak Drumm" and he's about the nicest kindest most gentlemanly man I've ever met in my life.

ORCHID (*cruelly*): That's not saying much, Momma, with your track record.

MARIETTA (*breathless, telling a now-familiar story*): It was freezing sleet when I left the Safeway—pitch black *night* at six-thirty P.M.— and my grocery bag got soaked and the bottom went out and all my groceries fell to the pavement and I was sobbing, I was so *defeated*, having dealt all day on the phone with Mr. Mack's disgruntled customers—and out of nowhere comes this man, this gentleman—"Let me help you, ma'am," he said. And handed me his umbrella and gathered up the things on the pavement— (*Dreamily*) And there's these broken runny *eggs* leaking down his coat sleeve—and he's getting completely soaked—and never once swore, nor even made a crude comment as any other man would at such a time. Later confiding in me, when we had coffee, he'd been wounded some years ago in Beirut, Lebanon—he was a Marine officer stationed there and has a Purple Heart and a, I think it's a, Silver Star medal. "When I woke up in the hospital and saw I wasn't dead, I vowed to Jesus Christ that I would take my life as a blessing and never complain about anything again." Isaak's exact words.

ORCHID (*adolescent sarcasm*): Wow, Momma—that's real wisdom.

MARIETTA (*ignoring sarcasm*): Yes. I think it is. Compared to certain men I have known and their philosophies of life—it *is*.

ORCHID: So? When's this dreamboat due?

MARIETTA (*a bit vaguely*): Isaak *said* he'd drop by—on the way home from work—he's not the kind of man you can pin down to exact times but he said—sort of—*I* suggested—around eight.

ORCHID: Yeah? It's past "around eight" now, Momma. Like, fifteen minutes past.

CRYSTAL: It's only *twelve* minutes past!

MARIETTA *(fluffing hair, regarding herself critically in the mirror)*: Isaak is his boss's right-hand man at O'Mara Construction—practically the manager. He can't just shut up shop and walk away on a dime. *(Pause)* He's the kind of man who doesn't like to be boxed into a specific time—I can respect that.

ORCHID: Or a day. Like last Friday.

MARIETTA *(quickly)*: Last Friday, Isaak had word of a sudden family crisis in Buffalo he had to attend to. He called right away Monday morning and apologized and was so sweet—

ORCHID: Grandma's funeral, I bet. Unless that's gonna be tonight.

CRYSTAL *(shoving book, papers)*: NOBODY CARES ABOUT MY FUCKING BRAIN THAT'S BREAKING INTO FUCKING PIECES.

MARIETTA: Crystal, shame on you! What if somebody heard you?

CRYSTAL: I DON'T CARE WHO HEARS ME I'M IN A CRISIS!

ORCHID: Overgrown baby just wants attention.

MARIETTA stoops to pick up papers, as CRYSTAL seizes them, tears a sheet of paper into pieces.

CRYSTAL: The hell with "rhom-boyds"—"crap-zoyds"! I'm gonna watch MTV. *(Goes to TV to switch on)*

MARIETTA *(preventing her)*: No, girl, you are *not*. Not till you've finished your homework—no, not even then. That's trash TV, and no good for your mind. Oh, honey—d'you want to turn out like your Momma? Not *knowing* a goddamned thing?

ORCHID *(sisterly contempt)*: Biggest baby in eighth grade! Crystal Murchison's bra size is catching up with her I.Q.

CRYSTAL: Ohhh!

MARIETTA: Orchid, that's cruel. That isn't worthy of you. You and Crystal and Isabel love one another, you know that. You're not like other sisters who can't get along.

CRYSTAL *(thumb in mouth, angry and hurt)*: 'Cause I'm not her sister really. I don't belong here really. Her and Icy—they hate me.

MARIETTA (*hugs* CRYSTAL *to calm her*): Hush! That's the most—ridiculous, hurtful thing—I've ever heard! You know that *is not so*, Crystal. (*Hands math text to* ORCHID) Help Crystal, will you? You're the brains of the Murchisons.

ORCHID (*flattered, though pretending otherwise*): Wow. *That* wouldn't be any big deal. (*Scanning the page, sniffily*) See—the answer to number one is "2576 oranges"—the answer to two is "17 feet by 39 yards"—number three is—

CRYSTAL (*plaintively*): But how d'you *get* the answers, Orchid? Our teacher says we got to have *steps*.

ORCHID (*shrugging*): *I* never bother with steps. In my geometry class, either. I just know the answer right away.

MARIETTA (*sighing*): A head for figures like—

ORCHID: My old man. Sure.

MARIETTA: Well, Miles did have a mind like some kind of machine. Except about fifty percent of the time it added up wrong.

ORCHID: He was real handsome, wasn't he?

MARIETTA: That's snapshots you're thinking of—not him.

ORCHID: Nah, you ripped all the snapshots up, Momma. I *remember* him like—like it was a dream—a dream I have all the time—but can't get clear. (*Pause; this is a familiar question*) Momma, where *is* he? I'm old enough to know.

MARIETTA (*evasively*): Your father and I went our separate ways fifteen years ago. *He* skipped town refusing to pay child support for you and Isabel—County Services traced him for me as far as Fairbanks, Alaska—then— (*a wild giggle*) —the trail got *cold*. And that's that. (*Stroking her jaw, her breasts, as if she'd been struck and feels again some of the pain*) Bless us all.

ORCHID: "Miles Shurts." What a name to get stuck with! No wonder my father exhibited "sociopathetic tendencies"—

MARIETTA: How'd you know about *that*?

ORCHID (*shrugs*): Telepathy.

MARIETTA: You've been looking through my *papers*— !

ORCHID (*a gesture to indicate its unimportant*): Anyway it's O.K. "Dad" Murchison adopted Icy and me—we don't need to be "Shurts." (*Laughs*)

MARIETTA (*defensively*): Well, it makes it easier for filling out forms: everybody's got the same last name.

CRYSTAL (*leaning against MARIETTA like a small child*): Momma, you don't think Dad is ever coming back, do you?

MARIETTA (*as if knowing something the girls don't*): Mmmm—I wouldn't worry about it if I was you.

ORCHID: Don't tell me "Dad" Murchison is up in Alaska, too?—the state's gonna get gridlock.

MARIETTA: I don't know where either of them is at the present time and that's fine with me. As long as it isn't Yewville. And it isn't.

ORCHID (*seeing that MARIETTA is getting upset*): Hell, Momma, what do *we* care? We're O.K.

MARIETTA (*wiping her eyes*): Well, I guess. I pray so. Long as I don't lose my job. Or my looks. (*Frowning into mirror*) Being a receptionist at a place like Mack's Motors isn't easy. You're expected to look good all the time. Mr. Mack's always scrutinizing me like it's the Miss America contest and I'm on the ramp. Every guy walks into the showroom does the same thing. "There's a sweet chassis!" (*Pause*) Is that a car?

ORCHID, CRYSTAL hurry to the window.

CRYSTAL (*excitedly*): Looks like!

ORCHID (*flatly*): Gone past.

MARIETTA has been tidying quickly, has discovered the cereal box.

MARIETTA (*blank*): Gone past... ?

CRYSTAL (*innocently*): I could go for a pizza tonight, I sure could.

MARIETTA (*nibbling from box*): Look, Orchid, Crystal: if—Isaak Drumm inquires into our—background—ever—I'd rather you didn't—exactly—

ORCHID, CRYSTAL *(murmuring)*: Yeah yeah, Momma.

MARIETTA: For sure, I intend to tell him myself—sometime. But—

ORCHID, CRYSTAL *(overlapping)*: O.K., Momma.

MARIETTA: Some men get scared off… *(Pause)* Not that I'm ashamed of anything—I am not. I did my best but I married young the first time—crazy in love—and the second time—never mind. *(Pause)* Stricken with bad luck, that's all!

ORCHID *(teasing)*: Bad luck, Momma?—hey, you had *us*.

MARIETTA *(emotional)*: Oh, not you! You girls are all that's kept me going over the years.

CRYSTAL *(thumb in mouth, childlike)*: Me, too, Momma?—you're counting me, too?

MARIETTA *(smoothing CRYSTAL's hair back from forehead)*: For sure I'm counting you, Crystal. Don't be silly.

ORCHID *(worldly)*: Two husbands isn't anything these days, Momma. At least you were *married*, not a *single mother*.

MARIETTA: Look, there's nothing wrong with being a "single mother." I respect those women—they've got guts. When I was a girl you *had* to get married to have a baby. And if you were having a baby, you had to get married. No way out! *(Pause; excited)* Is that a car—?

CRYSTAL, ORCHID peer out the window.

ORCHID: Gone past.

MARIETTA has taken out her compact and lipstick to re-apply makeup. Too restless to remain in one place for long. Goes into the kitchen where she also peers out a window.

ORCHID *(calling over)*: Momma, relax. It's only eight twenty-eight. Last time it was nine-thirty before you freaked.

MARIETTA *(hotly)*: Tonight Isaak *is* coming.

MARIETTA prepares a tray: glasses, napkins, bowl of peanuts, the large platter of canapés from the refrigerator. Carries it into the living room and sets it on the coffee table.

CRYSTAL: Wow, Momma—that looks *super*.

ORCHID: Who's going to eat all *that*?

MARIETTA: It's "appetizers." Before going out to dine, people have "appetizers."

CRYSTAL *(blankly)*: To make you *hungry*?

MARIETTA, ORCHID, CRYSTAL begin to nibble from the tray. Their movements are discreet and furtive at first.

CRYSTAL *(mouth full)*: Mmmm, Momma—these are *good*.

MARIETTA: That's ham slices stuffed with dill cream cheese—*fresh* dill. *(Licking fingers)* Made fresh from a recipe.

CRYSTAL *(innocently)*: "Afro—?" "Afri-*can*?"

MARIETTA stares at her blankly.

ORCHID *(doubtfully)*: Momma, this Sergeant Dumdum *does* exist, doesn't he?

MARIETTA *(offended)*: Orchid, I resent that! That's calling your own mother a liar, or worse. *(Pause)* And Isaak Drumm was a Marine major—he was *Major Drumm*.

A noise at the front door; all are alerted. MARIETTA gets to her feet excitedly; the girls sneak one or two final snacks from the tray.

MARIETTA *(undertone)*: Now be good, will you, girls? Please!

But before MARIETTA can get to the door, it swings open—it's ISABEL, "ICY." A striking girl of 16. She wears jeans, boots, a short rib-hugging black leather jacket; her hair is cut jaggedly short, punk style, platinum blond streaked with purple and green. Her face is pale; her eyes shadowed, as if from lack of sleep. No evident makeup or lipstick. There are several glittering studs in her earlobes and a thin gold ring in her nose. ICY's appearance and manner are androgynous; her body is lean and compact; she is both an exhibitionist and, oddly, rather shy. Her character is fueled by a subterranean rage ICY herself done not fully comprehend, though, on the surface, she is capable, at times, of a childlike candor and charm.

ICY: What're *you* all looking at?

MARIETTA *(hand to chest, breathless)*: Isabel, honey—you surprised us.

rapport with them; but ORCHID, CRYSTAL *shrink back, colliding with each other and giggling harder.*

ISAAK, *his feelings a bit ruffled, shrugs, and stoops to devour two or three of the canapés.*

MARIETTA *enters, breathless. It is clear that this "date" is of enormous significance to her, but she isn't in control and seems to be doing everything wrong. She crosses quickly to* ISAAK *and they touch hands almost shyly.* MARIETTA *is carrying her coat which she lays across the back of a chair— it begins to slide to the floor and she and* ISAAK *stop it.* MARIETTA *giggles nervously.*

MARIETTA: Isaak, you're—here! I'm so—glad you—could find the house. I—I'm sorry to—

ISAAK *(overlapping)*: Marietta, I hope I'm not—barging in—

MARIETTA: Oh no oh no!—just a, a minor family emergency—

ISAAK *(alarmed)*: Emergency?

MARIETTA: Oh no oh no!—everything's under control. Please—sit down.

ISAAK: Am I—barging in?

MARIETTA: Not at all! You're, er—expected, Isaak! Do have a seat—

ISAAK: —I, uh, happened to be in the neighborhood and I—thought maybe I'd—drop in— What's this? *(As* ISAAK *is about to sit down, he discovers a blood-stained tissue on the sofa, or on the floor at his feet.)*

MARIETTA *stares aghast at the blood-stained tissue, which* ICY *must have dropped. Quickly, with a mother's expert hand, she snatches it up, crumples it in her fist, hides it in a pocket or in her purse.*

MARIETTA: Oh—it's nothing!

ISAAK: It looked like a—Kleenex stained with blood?

MARIETTA: Oh no! Just some paint—red paint—nothing. Please do sit down, Isaak. May I get you a drink?

ISAAK *(as if things are going too rapidly for him)*: I, uh, happened to be in the neighborhood—Marietta?—and, uh, like we sorta planned—thought maybe I'd drop in—see if you'd like a bite to eat—uh, if it isn't too late, I mean— *(Stares at watch)*

MARIETTA *(urging ISAAK to sit):* Of course it isn't too late, it's *early.* What would you like, Isaak? Wine, beer—

ISAAK *(suppressing belch, as if he'd been drinking on the way over):* I'll—uh—stick with beer. Thanks!

MARIETTA: And these lovely roses!—are they for me?

ISAAK: Sure!

MARIETTA: Thank you so much, Isaak. That's so thoughtful of you. *(Examining glass that contains the roses)* Except—this isn't the best vase! *(MARIETTA takes the roses into the kitchen. Shakes her fist at ORCHID, CRYSTAL who are giggling there. Pokes ORCHID to find a more suitable vase for the roses, which ORCHID does, though still giggling. MARIETTA opens the refrigerator and calls out to ISAAK.)* And do help yourself to some appetizers, Isaak! You must be starving.

ISAAK is sitting self-consciously on the sofa, having checked to make sure he isn't sitting on any more bloody tissues.

ORCHID *(undertone):* That guy was a Marine *major*? He looks like one of those Mideast terrorists. *Wei-rd!*

CRYSTAL *(whining):* Momma, I don't feel well.

MARIETTA *(furious undertone):* You girls just *stop.* Both of you! *(Calling out, cheerful, to ISAAK)* Isn't this weather just—more of the same? Winter just goes on and *on.*

ISAAK *(calling back):* You're, uh, sure I'm not barging in—?

MARIETTA *(laughing sharply, gaily):* Isaak, I've been expecting you.

ISAAK *(almost alarmed):* You have—?

MARIETTA has poured two glasses of beer and sets them on another tray. The roses are now in a larger and more attractive vase, and she sets this on the tray, too. Turns to ORCHID, CRYSTAL.

MARIETTA: Come on—and be *good.*

ORCHID, CRYSTAL: Aw, we already met him.

MARIETTA: You did *not.* Not properly.

CRYSTAL: Momma, I'm serious. My stomach is upside-*down.*

MARIETTA herds the girls back into the living room, where ISAAK awkwardly stands. He is making an effort to be well-mannered.

MARIETTA hands a glass of beer to ISAAK, and sets the vase down on the coffee table.

ISAAK *(murmuring)*: Thanks!

MARIETTA: These roses are just so, so— *(smells them)* —beautiful.

ISAAK *(awkward joke)*: I, uh—didn't grow 'em myself. *(Laughs)*

MARIETTA: Still, it's so thoughtful. *(Pulling at ORCHID, CRYSTAL to come forward)* My girls probably didn't introduce themselves when they let you in, Isaak—they're shy. This is Orchid— *(Poking her to come forward)* And this is Crystal. *(Poking CRYSTAL)*

ISAAK and the girls regard one another for a beat or two.

ISAAK *(heartily)*: H'lo, Orchid! H'lo, Crystal! Pretty names for— pretty girls.

ORCHID, CRYSTAL *(mumbling)*: H'lo.

MARIETTA *(urging)*: "Hello, Mr. Drumm."

ISAAK: Nah—"Isaak" is good enough.

But there is silence. An awkward beat.

MARIETTA *(happily if a bit feverishly)*: My girls *are* pretty, I think so, too. And I have a third daughter, too— *(glancing around, but ICY is not present)* —my eldest.

ISAAK *(drinking beer thirstily)*: Mmmm.

MARIETTA sits, ISAAK sits as before. ORCHID, CRYSTAL would back off, but MARIETTA pointedly addresses them. (She is passing peanuts, the canapé platter, napkins, etc., to ISAAK.)

MARIETTA *(to girls)*: Isaak served in the Marines, a major, weren't you, Isaak?

ISAAK *(a brisk salute, attempt to be comic)*: Yes ma'am!

ORCHID: You already told us, Momma.

MARIETTA: Imagine!—*Major* Drumm. It sounds so—military!

ISAAK: Well, that was a while back. I'm just what you'd call a regular citizen now.

MARIETTA: I think the Marines have the handsomest uniforms. If I were a man, I'd want to be a Marine. But it's the most strenuous branch of the armed services, isn't it?—the most demanding—

ISAAK: Once a Marine, always a Marine. In uniform, or out. For life. *(Eating)* This is *good!*

ORCHID *(clearing throat, summoning up courage to be cheeky)*: Momma says you were fighting in Beirut, Lebanon. We didn't have any war there, did we?

ISAAK *(genially)*: No war, no, but a peacekeeping mission. I was shipped in October 1983.

ORCHID *(adolescent cynicism)*: Peacekeeping? I bet.

MARIETTA *(warning)*: Orchid—

ISAAK *(with dignity, curtly)*: Two hundred sixty of us—Marines, I mean—died there. Two of my real close buddies. *(Pause)* It wasn't any official war, maybe—but it *was* death, for some. *(Pause)*

ORCHID *appears rebuffed;* CRYSTAL *is impressed, staring.*

MARIETTA *(genuinely sympathetic)*: Oh dear, it must have been just— oh just so terrible—

ISAAK *(overlapping, awkwardly)*: I was one of the lucky ones. I mean *am.* I feel kinda guilty about it and I, uh— *(pause, as he seems not to know what to say)* —I'd just as soon change the subject, Marietta, I guess.

A pause.

MARIETTA *(softly)*: I understand, Isaak. I'm sorry to bring the subject up.

ISAAK *(unaccustomed to articulating his thoughts, speaking in a groping, brusque manner)*: I guess—anything *you* survive—and somebody else doesn't—you kinda keep remembering. *(Pause, drinks beer, eats)* Uh—this is *good.*

MARIETTA: Thank you! They're from a new recipe in *Cosmo!*—I mean *Good Housekeeping.*

ORCHID, CRYSTAL, *also nibbling, laugh together.*

ICY appears. In jeans, black T-shirt. A fresh white bandage wrapped around her right hand. When ISAAK sees this striking girl he does a double take.

MARIETTA *(cheerfully, nervously)*: Oh!—here's my eldest daughter Isabel. *(As ICY hangs back, seemingly shy)* Isabel dear, come meet my friend Isaak Drumm.

ICY approaches slowly; ISAAK rises, extends his hand for a handshake; then sees ICY's bandaged hand.

ISAAK: H'lo, Isabel! Did you—hurt your hand?

ICY *(coolly, ignoring the proffered handshake)*: Yeh. H'lo.

MARIETTA: Isabel had a little accident but she's fine now, aren't you, Isabel?

ISAAK *(awkwardly)*: "Isa-bel"—another pretty name for a, uh— pretty girl.

ICY sniggers at the absurdity of this remark. ORCHID, CRYSTAL join in.

MARIETTA *(hurt, tries to gloss over ICY's rudeness)*: Isabel is of that age, Isaak, she's what you might call self-absorbed.

ISAAK *(friendly)*: And what age is that, Isabel?

ICY *(cupping a hand to her left ear)*: Say what?

ISAAK: I was asking—what age is that?

ICY: What age is what?

MARIETTA: Isaak is asking how old you are, Isabel.

ICY: What the fuck for? I'm not asking *him* how old he is, am I?

MARIETTA *(mortified)*: That's rude, Isabel. You know better.

ISAAK is shocked, a bit; yet, at the same time, ICY's candor and profanity strike a chord with him.

ISAAK *(laughing)*: Hell, Marietta, the girl's right. None of my goddamn business, is it?

ICY is surprised by ISAAK's remark; casts him an assessing smile as if to say Hey: you're not so bad. *Snatches up an appetizer to eat and would saunter off, but MARIETTA seizes her wrist.*

MARIETTA (*firm, suppressing anger*): I'd like you please to apologize to *our guest*, Isabel.

ICY stands mute and stubborn, staring at MARIETTA. *It's a duel of nerves and each is strong-willed.* ORCHID, CRYSTAL *poke each other in delight;* ISAAK *shifts in his seat uncomfortably. A beat, two beats.*

ISAAK: Nah, it's O.K. *I* don't mind. (*Joking*) I'm a Marine, after all, eh?

MARIETTA *has won the war of nerves, for* ICY *suddenly looks away, at the floor.*

ICY (*mumbling*): Sorry.

MARIETTA (*still gripping* ICY's *wrist*): And *why* are you wearing that ridiculous ring through your nostril! It's ugly ugly *ugly*! Isn't it, Isaak?

ISAAK (*sipping beer*): Ummm, it's—different.

ICY *disengages her wrist from* MARIETTA's *grasp and makes a show of rubbing it.*

MARIETTA: They don't allow nose rings at school so Isabel slips it on, and slips it off. I've begged her to dispose of it, but—no! She came home one day and scared the life out of me, I swear—a daughter of mine looking like a savage! an African cannibal!

ICY (*laughing*): Oh hey, Momma—can'tcha see I'm *white*?

ISAAK (*laughing heartily, hoping to win over* ICY): These "nose rings"— all the earrings kids wear in their ears—the "punk hair"—it's kinda kinky, sexy—eh? Takes getting used to, for sure. Where d'ya get them, Isabel?

ICY (*blankly*): Say what?

MARIETTA (*quickly*): Isabel is just a little hard of hearing in her left ear.

ISAAK (*raising voice, jovial and awkward*): I'm asking where you purchased your "nose ring," Isabel? Maybe I'll get one, too. (*Laughs*)

ICY *shrugs, and says nothing.*

MARIETTA (*forced smile*): Well! It's going on nine-thirty, Isaak. They'll be waiting for us at the Lobster Shanty.

ISAAK (*finishes his beer, wipes mouth with napkin, gets to his feet smiling broadly*): Right! Time to be shovelin' on.

MARIETTA (*cheery undertone*): You girls do me a big favor, will you?—and put these things away?

ISAAK: It's real nice—a pleasure—to make you girls' acquaintance—Orchid, and Christabel— (*he has confused the two girls*) —and, um, Isabel.

ORCHID: I'm "Orchid," but she isn't "Christabel."

MARIETTA (*quickly intervening*): My youngest girl is "Crystal," Isaak.

ISAAK: "Crystal"—that's what I meant to say.

ICY is unexpectedly helpful, taking up glasses, putting them on the tray, etc.; but she lets the tray tilt, so that at least one of the glasses topples against the front of ISAAK's trousers, wetting him.

ISAAK: Hey!

MARIETTA (*overlapping*): Oh, Isabel!

ICY (*overlapping*): Jeez—sorry.

Fortunately, there wasn't much left in the glass, and the trousers are only dampened. ORCHID, CRYSTAL press their knuckles against their mouths to keep from giggling hysterically.

MARIETTA (*dabs at him with napkin*): Isaak, I'm so sorry—oh, dear!—

ISAAK (*embarrassed, but tries to gloss it over*): Nah, it's nothing.

ICY (*disingenuous*): My hand sorta got weak and *slipped*. I'm real sorry.

ISAAK: Nah, it's nothing. (*Takes napkin from MARIETTA and dabs at himself*)

MARIETTA (*flashing ICY a furious look*): Isabel, really! I'll speak to you later.

ICY saunters off into the kitchen. ORCHID, CRYSTAL remain behind. ISAAK helps MARIETTA put on her coat, a bit awkwardly; she has trouble getting her arms in the sleeves.

MARIETTA *(nervous gaiety, kissing ORCHID, CRYSTAL)*: 'Bye! Momma won't be gone long! Be good!

ISAAK *(at door)*: G'night!

MARIETTA, ISAAK exit. As soon as the door closes behind them, ICY returns, bounces about the room discharging her pent-up nervous energy. She is wound tight as a rubber band. ORCHID, CRYSTAL are her fascinated audience.

ICY: "Isaak Drumm"—man, he's the weirdest, the scariest yet! You see those eyes? Boring right into you? I know serial killer eyes when I see them. *Rapist* eyes. *Pederast* eyes.

ORCHID, CRYSTAL: "Pederast"—? What's that?

ICY takes a switchblade knife out of her pocket, clicks open the blade, snatches up one of the roses out of the vase and cruelly shreds its petals with the knife, letting them fall scattering on the floor as ORCHID, CRYSTAL look on gaping.

ICY *(backing off to exit dramatically)*: Ask "Isaak."

Lights out.

Scene 3

Lights up. MURCHISON living room, but it is dimly lit and so altered to suggest another, more general time. (The roses, the tray, glasses and canapés, etc. are gone from the coffee table.)

Funky-popular music with a strong, sentimental beat.

ORCHID takes up a narrator's position, stage left. She addresses the audience with an air of protest, though there is a mischievous current beneath.

ORCHID: We *were not* jealous of Momma's boyfriends!

CRYSTAL appears, sucking on a thumbnail.

CRYSTAL *(vehemently)*: I sure wasn't.

ORCHID *(self-righteously)*: We just wanted Momma to be happy. A self-respecting and independent woman. To "date" men worthy of her. And of us.

CRYSTAL *(overlapping)*: —and of us.

ORCHID *(hooting laugh)*: Remember ol' "Open Wider, Please"?

CRYSTAL *(shuddery giggle)*: Oh! Dr. Prick—

ORCHID: -chard—

CRYSTAL *(trying to get it right)*: Dr. Pri-chard—

ORCHID: Prick-head—

CRYSTAL: Oh! was that one *gross*!

ORCHID *(incensed)*: Our own *dentist*, for God's sake. That asked Momma for a date right in the dentist *chair*.

CRYSTAL: —Having three wisdom teeth removed. Yuck!

ORCHID: The way ol' Prickhead would examine your teeth with this nasty little pick—"Open wider, please"—

CRYSTAL: "Open wider, please"— YUCK!

ORCHID: —and "rinse, please"—

CRYSTAL: —bloody spit—swirling around in the drain—

ORCHID: —and take hold of your tongue, your actual tongue in some kind of creepy-gauzy cloth—

CRYSTAL *(deeply revulsed, near-hysterical giggle)*: —And pull it—!

ORCHID: —And sort of bump his potbelly against you—

CRYSTAL: DOUBLE YUCK!

ORCHID *(snapping her fingers, with satisfaction)*: At least—we don't go to the dentist anymore.

CRYSTAL *(snapping fingers)*: Anymore *ever*.

ORCHID: But a worser creep yet was John Calvin—

CRYSTAL: Potty!

ORCHID: Pot*ter*.

CRYSTAL: Momma's boss at Potty's Realtors—

ORCHID *(sarcastic)*: *We* gotta "be nice, be sweet" to this fat-ass—

CRYSTAL: —'cause Momma's working for him, she says it's the best job she's had in years—

ORCHID: —so this John Calvin Potter—

CRYSTAL *(overlapping)*: Potty!—

ORCHID: —he's paying Momma a "real generous" salary she says—

CRYSTAL: —except, is *he* gross! That whatdayacallit pretend-hair on his head—

ORCHID *(a derisive tootling sound)*: TOO-PAY!

CRYSTAL *(loud giggling)*: TOO-PEE! TOO-PEE! POTTY!

ORCHID: His hands all over everything like a creepy-sticky *octopus*—

CRYSTAL: Calling Momma and us "gurls"—

ORCHID *(imitating)*: "Oh you GURLS are so pret-ty"—

CRYSTAL: Must've been fifty years old—some nasty old grand-pappy—

ORCHID: —trying to act like Burt Reynolds—

CRYSTAL: —trying to act like somebody'd want to kiss *him*—Yuck!

ORCHID: Just 'cause he had MONEY to spend—

CRYSTAL: Just 'cause he was Momma's BOSS—

ORCHID: Just 'cause he could FIRE her if he got pissed—

CRYSTAL: Nasty *cruel* ol' thing!

ORCHID *(shrugging)*: So?—Potty did fire Momma. One week's pay, and *out.* *(Gesturing with thumb)*

CRYSTAL: That's O.K. We don't want our Momma who we love working for such a creep, do we?

ORCHID, CRYSTAL: N-O. *NO.*

ORCHID *(continuing)*: We *were not* jealous of Momma's "boy-friends"—we just wanted to protect her.

CRYSTAL: *I'm* not jealous of any goddamn "boyfriend." I hate men!

ISAAK: Jeez, did I hurt you?—I'm such a clumsy ox.

MARIETTA: You're not clumsy, you're doing fine. You just need to take it slow.

ISAAK goes to get his drink, and offers MARIETTA *her glass, which she hesitatingly accepts.* MARIETTA *is warmly flushed, very pretty; she lifts her hair from the nape of her neck to cool herself.*

ISAAK *(embarrassed)*: I guess there must be some people not meant to dance. And me with my bad knee—

MARIETTA: Everybody is meant to dance!—everybody that's got two feet. *(Giggles)* Or even an artificial foot, these days. We're all born with an instinctive sense of rhythm— *(swaying, snapping her fingers)* —and a love of just *doing it.*

ISAAK *(staring at her)*: —A love of just *doing it. (Drinks)* Yeah!

MARIETTA: The weird dances kids do these days—I don't even know what they are. That "heavy metal" sound—ugh! I grew up on disco—in the Seventies—but later I got into this kind of dancing, which I'm crazy about. *(Graceful dance steps, arms lifted toward* ISAAK*)* So romantic, tender—the music—the beat—what music should be. Music should make you happy you're alive. *(*ISAAK *returns to dance with* MARIETTA*; as they start, he grips her a little too tightly and they stumble.)* Oops!

The song ends. Abrupt intrusion of radio announcer.

RADIO ANNOUNCER *(loud, bright voice)*: This is your Golden Oldies Hour, folks, station WBBW-FM Radio Wonnnderrfull, your host Richie Ryan here to the wee hours of—

ISAAK *(turning volume down)*: Jezuz!

MARIETTA, *fanning herself, moves about* ISAAK's *living room examining his things with a genuine appreciation. In a sense she is eluding the man's embrace (it's clear he is sexually aroused) even as, seemingly unconsciously, she is presenting herself.* ISAAK *stares at her.*

MARIETTA: Isn't this *nice!* I always wondered what these Riverside Townhouse Condos looked like inside—now I know. Everything so clean and white and modern—

ISAAK: Huh. Don't look too close. This is the kind of "luxury" condo, the doorknobs come off in your hand.

MARIETTA: At my place, I'm lucky to *have* doorknobs. *(Glancing around, runs fingertips over videos and paperbacks on a shelf)* I see your tastes run to Clint Eastwood, Bruce Willis, hmmm—*The Triumph of the Night*—

ISAAK *(embarrassed)*: That stuff's just for diversion. Actually I'm reading— *(He picks up a paperback book from the coffee table, shows the cover to* MARIETTA.*)* —Stephen Jay Gould. *Wonderful Life.*

MARIETTA: *Wonderful Life*—what's that?

ISAAK: Fossils.

MARIETTA: Huh?

ISAAK *(trying hard)*: Uh—basically fossils are little squiggly things embedded in rock, from five million years ago—unless it's five hundred million. Species of animals long gone. *(An admission made with a smile)* Actually, I'm only on chapter one.

MARIETTA *(examining book)*: "Pal-e-on-tol-ogy." My daughter Isabel used to be interested in, uh, science—when she was younger.

ISAAK: She's the one with the—? *(Gesturing at nose)*

MARIETTA *(quickly)*: My oldest girl. *(Glances around appreciatively)* So!—this *is* nice. I remember when I was first married—um— we drove out River Road here—pretending we'd be going to build our dream house— *(somewhat awkwardly)* —and all this, this land here—where we are right now—was the most beautiful farmland. Who'd have thought—

ISAAK *(trying for a philosophical, hearty tone)*: Well—like our bootcamp sergeant used to say, "Some things happen, and then other things happen."

A beat. MARIETTA *looks at* ISAAK *expectantly.*

MARIETTA: That's all?

ISAAK: Huh?

MARIETTA: "Some things happen, and then other things happen"— is that all there's to it?

ISAAK: To what?

MARIETTA: I don't know—life?

ISAAK (*running hand through hair, a bit blankly*): Actually, that's how it was with the fossils, too. The ones that got extinct.

MARIETTA: You were saying in the restaurant—you don't feel at home here?

ISAAK (*shrugging*): These condos, they're O.K., but ... kind of lonely. (*Pause*) There's mainly single people here—ex-married people. Like me.

MARIETTA (*seeing photos*): Mmmm. Isn't he handsome! Major Isaak Drumm in his Marine dress uniform. How old were you—?

ISAAK (*embarrassed*): Thirty ... Just before I was shipped to Beirut.

MARIETTA (*another photo*): And this is you with?—your ex-wife?

ISAAK (*roughly*): Nah, my sister. I don't have any pictures of— Audrey. (*Pause; to mitigate harshness of his words*) I mean, sure I do. But they're put away.

MARIETTA (*shifting subject*): My, what a wonderful big family! What— (*trying to be diplomatic*) —striking faces.

ISAAK: Some of us have moustaches, and some don't. That's the main difference.

MARIETTA: Oh, this is you, isn't it?—so *sweet*.

ISAAK (*pointing*): Nah, this is me, the fat kid with the eyebrows. That's my cousin Ezra. I was maybe eight years old here.

MARIETTA: Oh, my—eight? You were mature for your age.

ISAAK: Yeah. I was fat.

MARIETTA (*not wanting to pry*): You, um—you and your former wife—didn't have any children?

ISAAK (*trying for a joke*): Not that *I* know of.

MARIETTA (*not getting it*): What's that mean?

ISAAK: No, we didn't. (*Pause*) We didn't, and we don't. Maybe that's why I don't feel one hundred percent real sometimes.

MARIETTA: Hey, *I* have kids, and I'm lucky if I feel eighty percent real lots of times. That's got nothing to do with it.

ISAAK: What's it got to do with, then?

MARIETTA: I sure as hell don't know. I used to think when I grew up I'd be, y'know, more *solid*. More *certain*. But having kids—the two oldest are mine and Crystal is adopted—I mean, she came with my second husband after his wife died, she's *his* kid—or was— *(shakes her head, rolls her eyes)* —it's all confused but never mind—having kids right out of your own body, you'd think, my God, you should be real enough, you should know all the answers—but you don't.

ISAAK: *You* feel that way? A woman feels that way?

MARIETTA *(laughing)*: Why shouldn't a woman feel that way?

ISAAK *(refilling glasses, speaking slowly)*: It isn't just you're a woman, Marietta, you're a—beautiful woman. *(Pause)* Actually, I'd seen you around town some before that time in the parking lot—like at Friday's, and the Cloverleaf—saw you dancing with some guy—I would've been afraid to come up to you except, at the Safeway, I didn't actually know it was *you* having trouble with your groceries—until I got up close, and saw your face— *(Pause, embarrassed)* Jeez, why am I telling you this now!

MARIETTA *(almost shy)*: Why, I—don't know what to say, Isaak.

Both begin to laugh or giggle almost wildly.

ISAAK: Damn good thing I didn't know it *was* you—I'd been too scared to approach you.

MARIETTA *(overlapping)*: Good thing you didn't know it *was* me—

MARIETTA *(continuing)*: —I'd've really been out of luck!

ISAAK: Nah, some other guy'd be coming right along to help.

MARIETTA: Hmmm. *(Pause)*

ISAAK: Marietta, I—

MARIETTA seems not to hear; she has gone to the radio, to turn the volume up experimentally. But now an advertisement is playing—bright and brassy.

RADIO AD: YOU DON'T NEED TO TRUST YOUR LUCK
>AT AL MACK'S PONTIAC-BUICK-GMC TRUCK!
>WHERE A SALES FORCE OF HONESTY, ZEAL, AND SKILL
>IS SHARPENING THE PENCIL JUST FOR *YOU!*

MARIETTA *(turning volume down)*: Yuck!—as my girls would say. Speak of the devil. My boss.

ISAAK: You don't like your job?

MARIETTA *(quickly)*: I love my job. It's a damn sight better than being a waitress.

ISAAK: I was a waiter once, age twenty, at a hotel in Lake Placid. I quit after four days—I was lousy at being "subservient."

MARIETTA: Well, I'm pretty practiced at being "subservient." It's my feet and legs that couldn't make it.

ISAAK: Waiting on tables, the whole game is angling for tips. I figured it was like, um, hooking—not for *me.*

MARIETTA *(dryly)*: Well, believe it or not, women figured that out a long time ago.

ISAAK: So—?

MARIETTA: So—what?

ISAAK: So they figured it out, so—?

MARIETTA: So waitresses get tips.

ISAAK *(perplexed)*: I guess I don't know much about women, actually. Like every other guy I know.

MARIETTA: But you were married!—for seven years.

ISAAK *(harsh laugh)*: What's that got to do with it? *(Pause)* I've been divorced for eight years. *(Pause, brooding)* One day Audrey decides she "just doesn't want to be married any longer." She says— *(mimicry, wide-eyed)* —"It's nothing to do with *you*, Isaak."

MARIETTA *(sympathetic)*: Well, sometimes that's just how it works out—

ISAAK *(dryly)*: Who it had to do with was another guy she'd met— Reebok salesman out of New York, supplying the shoe store at the mall she worked in. That's who—not "Isaak."

MARIETTA: Gee, Isaak, I'm sorry—

ISAAK *(shrugging)*: Hell, it's like it happened to somebody else. I'm not bitter or anything. Water under the bridge.

MARIETTA: After a divorce there's always a transition time. It can last a long time…

ISAAK: A guy's "transition time" starts at age twelve and goes on till his prostate is removed.

MARIETTA: Oh, don't talk that way!

ISAAK, moved by MARIETTA's sympathy, approaches her as if to take hold of her and kiss her. MARIETTA turns aside as if suddenly shy or frightened; as if unaware of his arousal, and pursuing her own thoughts.

MARIETTA *(turning abruptly)*: I will admit, Isaak, I have a hard time comprehending men. Or trusting them.

ISAAK *(trying for an expansive, hearty tone)*: You can trust me.

MARIETTA *(lightly)*: Well, we'll see!

Pause.

ISAAK *(a sudden admission)*: Actually, I don't blame you. Guys I know, they're not bad guys, but—I wouldn't trust them—us— either. If I was a woman. It's like the truth is confused.

MARIETTA: What truth?

ISAAK: About how you're supposed to act toward your fellow man—if she's a woman. *(Pause)* If she's a man, you know how to act.

MARIETTA *(dryly)*: That's nice to hear confirmed.

ISAAK *(earnestly)*: The thing is, a guy never feels what a woman says is what she means—exactly.

MARIETTA: Oh, is that it!

ISAAK: Well—sometimes it *is*; and sometimes it's the opposite. But you never know which is which.

MARIETTA: And that's *our* fault, huh?

ISAAK: It's nobody's fault but like I say it's confusing. *(Pause, a slightly aggrieved air)* Like at the Lobster Shanty you offered to pay half the bill. And the waiter was listening. Shit, you got to know I'm not gonna let any woman pay for her dinner—unless it's my sister. *(Laughs)*

MARIETTA: Why shouldn't I pay half?—I ate half. I'm a working woman.

ISAAK: Nah, come on. You don't mean that.

MARIETTA: What? I'm not a working woman?

ISAAK: Sure, but it's the principle of the thing. *I* asked *you* out—that's understood.

MARIETTA: What's understood? These are modern times, not the Fifties. I'm a divorced woman, I support my family, I'm proud of making it on my own. *(Pause)* Well, up to a point.

ISAAK: O.K. But there are four of you in your family—and only one of me. And I make more money than you, probably.

MARIETTA *(laughs, startled by his frankness)*: Oh yes!—probably.

ISAAK *(doggedly)*: So? It's the principle of the thing.

MARIETTA: Well, I weakened; I let you pay. But next time—

ISAAK *(eagerly)*: Yeah? Next time?

MARIETTA: Maybe I'll make dinner.

ISAAK: I'd like that.

MARIETTA goes to turn up the radio volume. A livelier dance tune is being aired. (Suggested: "Taking a Chance on Love.")

MARIETTA: C'mon, Isaak, you said you wanted to learn! *(They resume their positions, and MARIETTA urges ISAAK into cautious motion.)* Like this—

ISAAK: But it's faster now—

MARIETTA *(laughing)*: Right, hon! You got it.

A few smooth steps; a turn; ISAAK stumbles.

ISAAK *(sudden temper)*: Shit!

MARIETTA: Oh, come on. Who's watching?

ISAAK: With a fucking knee like mine—you don't dance.

MARIETTA: Isaak, you're doing real well. C'mon— *(Tugging at arm)*

ISAAK: That's enough.

A pause. Music continues. Isaak limps away. MARIETTA *turns to audience, brooding, sipping her drink. During this pause of perhaps three or four beats, it seems that* ISAAK *has destroyed the tender mood between them. But, after a moment,* ISAAK *unexpectedly returns to* MARIETTA.

ISAAK *(rueful smile)*: O.K. I'll try.

They embrace but don't quite dance.

ISAAK: I told myself when I met you, Marietta—it was going to change my life.

A kiss. Tentative at first, then with growing passion.

Lights dim.

Lights out.

ACT II

Scene 5

Darkness. Heavy-metal rock music.

Lights up on ICY *in "punk" clothes; boots, ear studs, nose ring; hair spiky. Her thin body moves to the music in a manic, jerky way as if the music controls it; her expression is one of rapt, ecstatic concentration. She is oblivious of her surroundings until the music begins to subside.*

The background set is the MURCHISON *living room, with the kitchen stage right. The space* ICY *inhabits is private and interior.*

ICY *addresses the audience in a feisty, arrogant manner. During this monologue she moves restlessly and twitchily about, dancing, feinting, moving her head like a boxer slipping punches. Beneath her facade she is anxious, doubtful; wanting very much to be liked.*

ICY *(an air of protest, outrage)*: I'm walking downtown yesterday minding my own business—I got a right, don't I, to walk in the public street?!—you assholes cutting your eyes at me like I'm freaky or something well FUCK THAT SHIT—take a look in the mirror see who's freaky!—and I'm feeling O.K. I'm feeling real good it's the end of winter, blue sky and a warm sun and icicles dripping and I'm not high either like half the kids at school guzzling beer in the parking lot or smoking weed—popping diet pills which is what the cheerleaders do—huh, not ICY MURCHISON!—ICY WALKS ALONE!—so this happens: these two men walking along the sidewalk I'm crossing South Main to Video Village so what I cut my last-period class American Fucking History, there's these two staring at me like I'm NAKED or something!—older guys like somebody's father for Chrissake you expect better of, the Good Fart Suit and Necktie, the Good Fart Shined Shoes and Haircut, one of these bozos wearing glasses for Chrissake you don't expect a Good Fart With Glasses to be a pervert but they're giving me the eye that way that's dirty and angry and blaming you for it and I'm seeing they're not gonna step aside to let me pass so I duck to the side— *(ICY demonstrates)* —I don't look at them exactly but for sure I'm aware of them, so one of them says in a low singsong voice "Better take care girlie bouncing your titties like that" and the other one showing his wet slimy teeth like a panting dog "Mmmmm baby want to suck my dick?" so— *(ICY is breathless, worked up)* —I go, "Pigs, your time is now!" *(ICY whips out her switchblade knife, the blade shoots up)* —right to the fuckers' throats— *(laughing)* —"Oh oh oh! don't hurt me!"—"Oh no oh no don't slash my throat!"—

ICY *holds the switchblade up at throat level; freezes for a beat; then withdraws it, shuts up the blade and returns it to her pocket. Her posture reflects her deflated tone.*

ICY: Nah, shit, I didn't. Nothing like that. Just walked on by, hearing them laugh. *(Self-mockery)* ICY MURCHISON BULLSHIT ARTIST.

ICY *turns on her heel to exit, slamming off stage left.*

ICY *(regained arrogance)*: Still, you pigs're gonna *pay.*

Lights out.

Scene 6

Lights up. MURCHISON *living room where* ORCHID *and* CRYSTAL *are watching TV.* ORCHID *is flicking through the channels. Both girls wear glittering ear studs now, and* CRYSTAL's *hair has been luridly streaked with green and purple. They wear jeans and shirts or sweaters, and socks. School books and homework papers are scattered on the rug.*

It is an evening in April, immediately following Scene 5.

CRYSTAL *(as* ORCHID *restlessly flicks the channel)*: Oh, Orchid, wait—that looked kinda interesting—

ORCHID *(flicking back to the previous channel; disdain)*: This —? "Christian Youth Chorus"—?

We hear the CHORUS, *their voices sentimental, sweet, and earnest.*

CHORUS: This little light of mine,
   I'm going to let it shine!
   Let it shine all over God's moun-tain!
   I'm going to let it shine!

   This little light of mine—

ORCHID: Crap! *(Flicking past, to a talk show)*

CRYSTAL: Oh, Orchid, you hadn't oughta be so—*hard*—about stuff like that.

ORCHID: Y'think Big Daddy up in the sky is going to strike us dead? Like, with lightning?

CRYSTAL *(glancing upward)*: He could if He wanted...

ORCHID: So, let Him. *(Pause, as* ORCHID *continues flicking through channels)*

ORCHID, CRYSTAL *jump hearing a loud banging in the kitchen.*

ICY *has come home. She bangs into the kitchen, swoops into the living room bearing a gift—a pizza in a large cardboard box.* ICY *is high-strung and prancing like a young horse, basking in her younger sisters' adulation.*

ICY *(high-pitched drawl)*: HERE'S IIII-CCCCY! BRINGIN' THE GOODS!

ORCHID, CRYSTAL: Oh, Icy! Hey!

ICY *lets fall the pizza onto the coffee table. Stoops to give* CRYSTAL *a rough hug and a kiss. Ruffles* ORCHID's *hair, as* ORCHID *fondly aims a gentle punch at her leg.* ICY *tears off her leather jacket and tosses it. Flying high, in a good mood.*

ORCHID *(switching off TV)*: Icy, gee! Thanks!

CRYSTAL *(overlapping)*: Oh wow, Icy!—pizza! You're my heart! *(Tearing open the box to reveal a large, gross pizza; she is almost in tears)* Oh—the Villa *Special!*

ORCHID: Uh—where've you been, Icy? It's almost eleven.

ICY: That's for Icy to know and you to wonder, kid.

ORCHID: Momma made us a tuna casserole—

ICY *(mimicry of vomiting)*: Yeccchh!

ORCHID: —before she went out. She just called a few minutes ago— I told her you were *in*, taking a bath.

ICY *(laughing)*: Momma didn't believe *that*, did she?

ORCHID: I was pretty convincing.

ICY *(prancing about, brooding)*: 'Course, if Momma *didn't* believe you she'd maybe feel obliged to come home early for once. Which ain't what she wants to do, I guess—if she can fuck The Mustache instead.

ORCHID *sniggers, though discomforted.*

CRYSTAL *has picked up a slice of pizza and has taken a bite, in such haste that a string of mozzarella hangs down her chin.*

CRYSTAL *(wincing)*: Icy, you hadn't ought to talk about Momma like that.

ICY *(lightly mimicking CRYSTAL)*: Hadn't oughta talk like what about who?

CRYSTAL *(hesitantly)*: Oh, you know—saying bad things about Momma.

ICY *(cupping hand to ear)*: Mad things about Wawa?

CRYSTAL: Oh, Icy, you can hear good as anybody, you're just pretending.

This sets ICY *off. We see how fragile her control is.*

ICY *(losing temper)*: Yeh? Pretending *what*? Somebody's scumbag-Daddy didn't coldcock me upside the head, break my fucking eardrum? *(In a fury* ICY *threatens to do the same to* CRYSTAL: *she rushes to her, straddles her on the floor, puts one hand flat against* CRYSTAL's *ear, palm outward, and slams her fist into her palm several times in rapid succession, as* CRYSTAL *shrieks and tries to escape.)* Yeh? yeh? yeh?

ORCHID *deftly intervenes to protect* CRYSTAL; *knowing enough not to further antagonize* ICY.

ORCHID *(pulling* ICY *away)*: Don't pay Baby Tits any heed, Icy—she thinks with her pisser.

ICY *(a bit manic)*: Just "pretending" to be freaky-deaf in one ear, oh yeh! Wow! Man! Somethin to get off on, yeh!

CRYSTAL *(crawling away, in tears)*: Icy, I'm sorry. I didn't mean it.

ICY *(still mocking but beginning to relent)*: "Icy I'm sorry I didn't mean it"—FUCK THAT CRAP!

ORCHID: Aw c'mon Icy. Here—

ORCHID *tears a slice of pizza out of the pie which she hands to* ICY; *tears another for herself, and bites in. The three girls devour the pizza hungrily.*

ORCHID, ICY, CRYSTAL *murmur variously "Jeez, this is good!" "Oh, wow!" "Ter-rific!" etc.*

ICY *(jumping up, chewing with mouth full)*: Y'know what we need with this— *(Saunters into kitchen, opens refrigerator)* Shit! Only one? *(Takes out the single can of beer, deliberates opening it)*

ORCHID: Hey Icy, better not. Momma's sure to miss that.

ICY: How come she's down to *one*? Big Prick guzzled 'em all? *(Yanks the ring-top from the can, tosses it down nonchalantly; takes a thirsty swig; wipes her mouth like a man)* Mmmm!—just what the doctor ordered.

CRYSTAL *(giggling)*: Momma's gonna be mad.

ICY swaggers back into the living room. Drinks. Offers the can to ORCHID, *who declines; and to* CRYSTAL, *who shakes her head No, then changes her mind; with a big grin, takes the can from* ICY *and drinks.*

CRYSTAL *(choking, sputtering)*: Oh!—

ICY, ORCHID *regard their baby sister with amusement.* ICY *slaps her between the shoulder blades and she seems to recover.*

CRYSTAL: —it's kinda *strong.*

ICY *(to* ORCHID, *coolly)*: So where'd they say they were going?

ORCHID *(shrugging)*: Cloverleaf. Dancing.

ICY *(sneering)*: Big Prick in action! *(Demonstrates her cruel vision of* ISAAK *dancing with a pronounced limp and a goofy grin)* "Just happened to be in the neighborhood and thought I'd limp in!"

ORCHID, CRYSTAL *dissolve in giggles.*

ICY *(sudden mood shift)*: The Mustache ask about *me*?

ORCHID: Yeah. Said he hadn't seen much of "Isabel" lately—

CRYSTAL: —asked us please to "say hello"—

ICY *(sweet smile)*: Why h'lo, Major Dumdum! Farts a lot for your sol-lic-i-tude! Next time no see, have a shit on me, GOO'NIGHTY NIGHT! *(Gives him the finger)*

ORCHID, CRYSTAL *dissolve in giggles.*

ICY: What'd Momma say?

ORCHID *(evasively)*: Oh you know Momma, she's always worrying about you...

ICY *(little-girl, hurt)*: Fuck she is! She don't give a shit about me.

CRYSTAL *(emphatically)*: She said be sure to save some supper for you—

ICY *(laughs contemptuously)*: Tuna Sucking Casserole! *(Pause)* How'd she look when she asked about me?

ORCHID: Aw, you know Momma—she's got one kind of look when *he's* around and another kind when it's just us. Like, she's always *smiling* for The Mustache.

ICY: What I said: she don't give a shit about me. *(Pause)* Uh—anything about the 7-Eleven?

ORCHID: That you don't work there anymore, or—it was broke into?

ICY *(shrugging)*: Either.

ORCHID: Well, Momma assumes you're still working there after school—

CRYSTAL *(quickly)*: —nobody told her *not.*

ORCHID: She knows Doris Reardon got her sentence at Red Bank—Mrs. Reardon told her.

ICY *(a bit anxiously)*: Yeah—?

ORCHID *(shrugging)*: Doris never talked, so nobody knows about you. *(Laughs)* Huh!—Mrs. Reardon told Momma *she* was lucky she had such "good girls"—

ORCHID, ICY, CRYSTAL giggle. (CRYSTAL is still eating pizza.)

ORCHID: Momma said Mrs. Reardon said— *(mimicry)* —"Now Doris is in custody maybe I can get some peace"—

ICY *(appalled)*: Doris's mother said that?

ORCHID: Well, you can't blame her—

ICY: The bitch!

CRYSTAL: Doris is *crazy,* Icy! What if she'd burned down their house like she tried and it spread *here*!

ICY *(pacing about)*: Mrs. Reardon really said that? To Momma? *(Pause, brooding)* The bitch must've gone to Family Court, *she* got Doris sentenced. 'Cause nobody saw us, and nobody blabbed.

CRYSTAL: How long's Doris gonna be at Red Bank?

ICY: Eight months minimum but could be three fucking years if she maxes out, like for "bad behavior." That's more than some guys get for manslaughter, for Chrissake.

ORCHID *(to CRYSTAL)*: They got to release you from Juvie when you're eighteen. That's the law.

CRYSTAL: I hope Doris stays *in*! I'm scared of her!

ICY *(suddenly threatening)*: *You* keep out of it, Baby Tits. You don't know shit about Doris Reardon or anybody else.

CRYSTAL *cringes before* ICY's *waved fist.*

ORCHID *(an effort to restore calm)*: Anyway, Momma thinks you still got your job, you're working late. And you're in school. It's cool.

ICY: Yeah, well—you two don't clue her in, got it?

ORCHID, CRYSTAL *(protesting)*: Oh no, Icy, we won't—

ICY: Momma's so out of it, she's pathetic. Every time she "falls in love" with some bozo, it's like her brains are all in her cunt.

CRYSTAL *(shocked)*: Icy!

ICY: You think Momma doesn't have a cunt? You think she doesn't use it—her and Big Prick? Like, right now?

ORCHID, CRYSTAL *(hands over ears, overlapping)*: Stop! Icy—

ICY *(continuing, cruelly)*: Right at this very second? The two of them fucking away, in Big Prick's bed?

ORCHID: Oh Icy, the things you say!

ICY: Every time Momma starts "dating," it's like a smell is released around here. *(Sniffs)* Smell it?

CRYSTAL: That's pepperoni sausage!

ICY: That's *cunt*. Juiced-up *cunt*. *(Puritanical)* Makes me sick, and I'm gonna tell Momma.

ORCHID, CRYSTAL *giggle, shocked.*

ICY: Momma met The Mustache— *(counting on fingers)* —seven weeks ago. Been out with him fifteen times—that I know of. *This* week, tonight's the third time they've been together. That's an insult to us.

ORCHID *(disagreeing)*: Well, Wednesday they had supper here. We all had supper here—except you, Icy. Then Dumdum just went home.

CRYSTAL *(quivering with the memory)*: Momma made spaghetti and meatballs and garlic bread with parmesan cheese. It was *so good*.

ICY: Fuck that! You know it's an insult to us, Momma's behavior. When Baby Tits' Daddy got kicked out of here—

CRYSTAL: He wasn't my Daddy—

ICY: Momma promised us it'd be just the four of us from now on, remember? "No man will ever get power over me again—I promise," Momma said. Right here! In this room! *(Stamping on floor)* I hold the woman to that promise.

CRYSTAL *(almost in tears)*: He *wasn't*. We *said*. That isn't fair!

ICY *(pacing, brooding—or is she inventing?)*: The other night I heard them out in his car and they were quarreling for sure and when Momma came in she was crying. I heard her.

ORCHID: Crying? How come?

ICY: How the hell do I know? It's fucking insulting, she's always thinking of *him*. Like when she's happy, too—it's 'cause of *him*, the man. Not us.

CRYSTAL *(eagerly, accusingly)*: This morning Momma was up by seven and singing in the kitchen, she made French toast for us and it wasn't even Sunday— *(licking her lips)* —and she sees me and says don't *I* look pretty— *(rolls eyes, self-contempt)* —Pffff!— and wasn't it a nice day, Momma says, and it *wasn't*—it was raining!

ICY *(brooding)*: A woman falls in love with a man, near as I can figure out, *he's* got the power to make her happy, or miserable; *he's* got the power to make her think she's hot shit, or just plain shit. Fucking insulting!

ORCHID: Yeah, but look: last year Momma was crying all the time, and drinking. Remember? And there wasn't any man then.

ICY: That's 'cause she wanted a man, asshole. *We* aren't enough for her.

CRYSTAL *(plaintive)*: *Why* aren't we? I'd die for Momma, I love her so.

ICY *(stalking about)*: *This* guy's the worst yet. I get psycho-vibes for sure—the way he eyes you up and down— *(Shudders)*

CRYSTAL: He *does*?

ICY: "Pretty names for pretty girls"—

ICY, ORCHID, CRYSTAL laugh in derision.

ICY: Hey, I got it: y'know what he *is*?

ORCHID, CRYSTAL: What?

ICY: I betcha—a "serial killer." Yeah! Preying on women—girls—strangling and raping and cutting out body parts—*eating them*—

CRYSTAL *(frightened, disgusted)*: Oh, Icy!

ORCHID *(skeptically)*: The Mustache?

ICY: Serial killers never look like who they are. That's how they get away with a rampage of bloodlust.

ORCHID: So, who's missing? Where are his victims?

ICY: Lots of victims, nobody even knows they're gone. And their bodies are never found.

ORCHID: But wouldn't somebody be missing? Like—Connie Markson, people were scared she was kidnapped, then it turns out she ran away with her sister's husband—

ICY: What the fuck's that got to do with it?

ORCHID: Well, *somebody* would be missing, if The Mustache was killing them.

ICY: A serial killer's got to start somewhere, right?

ORCHID: I can't stand the jerk either, but—he can't be *that* bad.

ICY: How the fuck do you know? You can read minds or something? A pervert makes you think he's harmless—that's his first step. He gets you to trust him—that's his second. *(Sadistically)* Then— *he gets you alone.*

CRYSTAL *(thumb to mouth)*: I'm scared for Momma, she's so trusting!

ICY: That TV movie we saw about Ted Bundy? Remember?

ORCHID *(shaking head)*: I don't want to remember.

ICY *(jubilantly)*: Here's a man killed thirty women and girls—the youngest your age— *(points at CRYSTAL)* —tied them up and raped them and beat their brains out and stuck curtain rods up inside them and tore at them with his teeth—their *nipples!*—like a wild animal—

CRYSTAL *(horrified)*: Oh, stop!

ICY: —and chopped 'em up with a meat cleaver—taking the *heads* away for trophies. Whooeee! *(Grabbing her own hair at the top of her head as if she is holding her own head aloft)*

CRYSTAL, ORCHID *squeal in revulsion.*

ICY: And Bundy was *a whole lot less weird than "Isaak Drumm."*

ORCHID: Icy, c'mon!

ICY: You got to be initiated into real life sooner or later, you two.

CRYSTAL *(shivering, nervously nibbling at a pizza crust)*: I g-guess I don't like "real life."

ICY: This is "real life" right here, dummy! Our own mother is involved with a man just possibly a serial killer.

ORCHID *(challenging ICY)*: O.K., look: if Momma married Isaak Drumm, our standard of living would sure be improved.

ICY *(speechless for a moment)*: M-Married? Are you nuts? We're talking serial killer!

ORCHID: *You're* talking serial killer.

ICY *(anxious, threatening)*: Who's talking about married? Her? *Him?*

ORCHID *(backing down a bit)*: Isn't that what people do?—grown-ups?

ICY: You heard them talking about it?

ORCHID: No, but—

ICY *(whirling on CRYSTAL)*: *You* heard 'em?

CRYSTAL *(blankly)*: Me?

ICY *is relieved; but disguises it with boastful swaggering as she moves dancer/boxer-like to exit stage right. Opens switch blade.*

ICY: NO WAY Marine Major Mustache-Asshole is gonna marry Momma, babes. NO WAY. Icy Murchison *swears.*

ICY *exits dramatically.* ORCHID *and* CRYSTAL *stare after. A beat of silence.*

CRYSTAL: You think he m-maybe *is?*—some kind of a—?

ORCHID *has begun tidying up, flattening the cardboard box. She notices something written on it.*

ORCHID *(peering at box)*: Uh-oh! "S. Richards, 872 Genesee"—

ORCHID, CRYSTAL *(laughing)*: Oh, Icy!

Lights out.

Scene 7

Lights up dimly. MURCHISON *living room/kitchen. It is hours later. A freight train passes outside, flashing light, sounding its whistle; brief rattle of cars.* ICY *is sitting in the darkened living room, awaiting* MARIETTA, *but we are not aware of her presence yet.*

MARIETTA *and* ISAAK *enter by way of the rear door, extreme stage left, into the kitchen. They are stealthy, giggling and whispering. Someone collides with a chair.*

MARIETTA: Shhh! *(Switches on a light—not a bright light)* Hon, thanks!—now you better go back home to bed.

ISAAK *(amorous, hugging her around the hips)*: Mmmm maybe I'll just crawl into bed *here.*

MARIETTA: Wish you could!…

ISAAK: —time's it?

MARIETTA: Oh, dear!—four-twenty.

ISAAK *(thin whistle)*: How'd that happen? *(Pause)* Those trains going by the back yard here—don't they bother you? Keep you awake?

MARIETTA: Oh, no—we almost don't hear them, any longer. *(Laughs)* We'd miss them, I guess, if they didn't run on schedule. If they stopped.

ISAAK: Guess it's like an artillery range, or war—you get used to what's *there.* *(Laughs)* But I sure don't miss gunfire, bombs—

MARIETTA: Oh, it makes me so—sad—to think of *you*—in some scary situation—being shot at, hurt—

ISAAK: Then don't think of it, honey. Think of— *(murmuring in her ear, nuzzling her neck)* —eh?

The lovers murmur together, arms around each other's waist. MARIETTA opens the refrigerator to offer ISAAK something to drink and ISAAK selects a quart container of orange juice. They share it, drinking straight from the container, MARIETTA first and then ISAAK who thirstily drains it.

ISAAK: I needed that. *(Nuzzling MARIETTA again, whispering in her ear and both laughing, muffled)*

MARIETTA *(pushing ISAAK gently away)*: Isaak, you'd better get back home—to *sleep.* You've got to get up in two hours!

ISAAK *(ebullient)*: Hell, I could go straight to work now.

MARIETTA *(hugging him)*: Call me tonight?

ISAAK: You bet, darling.

A final kiss as ISAAK leaves. MARIETTA shuts the door and latches the chain, sighing. Quickly she tidies up the kitchen, turns off the light. Removes her shoes to walk in stocking feet into the living room.

MARIETTA *(singing)*: "—taking a chance on lov-ve—!"

MARIETTA makes her way through the darkened living room without needing to switch on a light. When she sees ICY sitting ramrod straight in a prominent position, facing her, she recoils in fright.

MARIETTA: Oh!—God! *(Hurriedly switches on a lamp, almost over-turning it)*

ICY, waxen-faced, grave, sits silent and unblinking staring at MARIETTA, arms folded tight across her chest. She wears pajamas and is barefoot.

MARIETTA *(hand to breasts)*: Isabel, is something wrong? Honey—?

ICY remains silent; MARIETTA draws near to touch her—shoulder, forehead, hair.

MARIETTA: Why are you sitting here in the dark, Isabel? Are you waiting up for me? I've asked you girls please not to. *(Pause)* Why are you looking at me like that? *(Pause, nervously brushes at hair, checks clothing)* Isabel, I'm speaking to you. Answer me. *(Steps back)* God damn you, Isabel, answer me. *(Guilty, defensive)* Look, I have a right to stay out as late as I please; to stay out all night if I please. *(Pause)* Well—I'm going to bed.

MARIETTA starts to leave; then returns. She confronts ICY who remains composed as a Buddha, staring unblinking at her.

MARIETTA *(voice rising)*: How dare you judge me! I'm more than your goddamned "Momma"! I was a woman—I was *me*—before I was ever "Momma"! *(Pause)* You don't know the first thing about me. I have my own life, and I want my own life, and I'm going to have my own life, *do you understand*? *(Pause)* He isn't like the others—he isn't! He's a good, decent man! *(Pause; MARIETTA seizes a cushion from the sofa, tosses it onto the floor at ICY's feet, half-sobbing in frustration.)* You—blackmailer! I want this to work with Isaak and I'm not going to let you ruin it!

ICY remains stubbornly still, silent. MARIETTA begins to shake her, sobbing furiously. At the door to the hall, ORCHID and CRYSTAL appear, in pajamas; CRYSTAL is biting her thumbnail.

MARIETTA *(seeing them)*: Blackmailers! What right have you! Leave me alone! I deserve some happiness! I'm more than just your goddamn "Momma"! I'M A WOMAN, I'M MORE THAN JUST "MOMMA"!

MARIETTA sobs and sinks to the floor. CRYSTAL would run to her, but ORCHID restrains CRYSTAL.

A beat or two as the girls watch MARIETTA.

ICY *(coolly, uncoiling from her chair to gaze down upon MARIETTA)*: Momma, you're drunk. Better let us help you to bed.

Lights out.

Scene 8

Rock music with a heavy, sultry beat. (Not to be confused with ICY's *heavy-metal music.)*

Lights come up on ORCHID. *She is moving with the music, excited, elated, reckless.*

ORCHID: What's a "bad girl"—"bad girl"—"bad girl"—? *(Pause)* What's a "bad girl"—"bad girl"—"bad girl"—?

ORCHID begins to express agitation, her body moving against the music.

ORCHID: When you know you're making a mistake—you *know* you're making a mistake—and you do it anyway! *(Pause)* And you know ahead of time you're going to be sorry later—you *know* you're going to be sorry later—AND YOU DO IT ANYWAY. *(Pause)* That's a "bad girl"—"bad girl"—"bad girl"—

Music ceases suddenly. ORCHID *hides her face in her hands.*

Lights out.

Scene 9

Lights up. A few days later. In a mood of bravado, ICY *is leading her sisters to* ISAAK DRUMM's *condominium.* ICY *and* CRYSTAL *walk ahead,* ORCHID *lags a bit behind.* CRYSTAL *more resembles* ICY *now, her hair more luridly streaked, and more studs in her ears; but she does not wear a nose ring like* ICY. ICY *is dressed as usual, and has fingerless leather gloves on; she is enlivened, reckless, defiant.*

The girls are surreptitiously approaching the condo unit from the rear, making their way along a high river bank.

ICY *(singsong)*: Who's gonna pay?—PIGS IS GONNA PAY! *(Pause, turning to her sisters)* Who's gonna pay!—

CRYSTAL: Pigs is gonna pay!

ORCHID *(less certainly, overlapping)*: Pigs is gonna pay—

ICY *(squinting ahead)*: "Riverside Townhouse Luxury Condos"—
pffft! From the back like this it's pretty crappy. Yeah and look
down there, what's it?— *(pointing in another direction)* —a body?
Jezuz—floating in the river!

CRYSTAL *(giving a little shriek, clutching at ICY)*: Ohhh!

ICY clamps her hand over CRYSTAL's mouth.

ORCHID: It's an old rotted *tire*, for God's sake.

ICY *(pretending she holds a microphone)*: "The site of the badly
decomposed female bodies…!"

CRYSTAL: Oh, I'm scared, Icy *don't*.

ICY *(an arm around CRYSTAL's shoulder)*: Nah, baby, you're not. That's
"adrenaline rush." Baby Girl is primed to *fight*.

CRYSTAL *(frightened giggle)*: M-Me?

ICY: Like, our ancestors, male *and* female, a million million years
ago, had these real cool coordinated *instincts* in the presence of
the enemy: to fight to fight TO FIGHT. To the DEATH. If they
didn't—we'd all be extinct like—whatd'yacallem—

ORCHID: Fossils?

ICY: Adrenaline's the sweet hot juice that pumps you up.

ORCHID *(ironic)*: What if we get caught?

ICY *(to CRYSTAL)*: Hey, who's that? Y'hear somebody whining?—
some jerk-off coward?

ORCHID: Who's a coward? Just 'cause I got some *sense*.

ICY: So—go on back home, then. Who needs you? *(To CRYSTAL)*
Right, baby?

CRYSTAL *(not certainly, but loudly)*: Right!

ORCHID: *What if we get caught?*

ICY: Nobody's gonna get caught, shithead. Ain't Big Prick always
boasting he works *late*?

ORCHID: What the hell d'you think we're going to find?

ICY: I told you: evidence.

ORCHID: Evidence of what?

ICY *(lofty, passionate)*: Of what the man *is*.

They are below the condo now. Icy takes stockings from her jacket pocket to fit over their heads. ICY *puts hers on, as* CRYSTAL *and* ORCHID *watch wide-eyed; she helps* CRYSTAL *put hers on; the girls' faces are ludicrously flattened.* CRYSTAL *begins to giggle.* ICY *silences her with a quick slap.*

ICY *(pointing)*: Number 9—see?—nobody's home, no car.

ORCHID: So what if he comes back early? *(Pause; she is ignored)* What if somebody calls the cops? *(Pause)* I'm going home, I'm not crazy. *(Pause)*

ICY *and* CRYSTAL *move toward stage left,* ICY *with her arm around* CRYSTAL's *shoulders.* ORCHID *watches; suddenly changes her mind and hurries to catch up with them.*

ORCHID: Icy, wait! I'm coming.

ICY *grins in triumph and tosses a stocking at* ORCHID, *catching her in the face.*

ICY: PIGS IS GONNA PAY!

Lights out.

Scene 10

Lights up. ISAAK DRUMM's *living room/bedroom. Shortly following Scene 9. A light suggestive of late afternoon. As* ICY *squirms through a narrow window into the bedroom.*

ICY *tiptoes to the doorway, peers excitedly about, is satisfied that no one is home; returns to the window to help* ORCHID *squirm through; then both she and* ORCHID *help* CRYSTAL. *(*CRYSTAL *is wider-hipped than her sisters and has some trouble getting inside.)*

CRYSTAL *(flustered, frightened, panting, discomforted)*: Oh!—oh!—I can't—

ICY, ORCHID: Shhh!

ICY and ORCHID tug at CRYSTAL and pull her inside; she falls to the floor. ICY and ORCHID suppress laughter.

CRYSTAL *(clutching at their hands, big-eyed)*: Oh, I'm so afraid—I don't want to be here—

ICY *(slapping lightly at her hands)*: Too late for that, babe. We're here! *(Sauntering about, excited, apprehensive)* WE'RE HERE AND NOBODY KNOWS.

ORCHID: Shh!

ICY: WE'RE HERE AND NOBODY CAN STOP US.

ICY signals her sisters to follow her into the living room. ORCHID is hesitant, and CRYSTAL stands for a beat frozen with fear, her thumb to her mouth.

CRYSTAL: Oh!—my heart's going like one of them tiny hummingbirds—

ORCHID takes hold of CRYSTAL and pulls her along.

ICY *(sniffing)*: Smell that?—you'd know we're in the right place, eh?

ORCHID: Yeah!—The Mustache's after-shave.

ICY *(over-reacting)*: Lookout!—

ICY has sighted a sweater or jacket of ISAAK DRUMM's tossed onto a chair. She springs back, crouching; collides with her sisters; for a moment they clutch panicked at one another.

ICY: Shit!—it's nothing.

CRYSTAL: Oh!—I peed my pants ...

ORCHID: You didn't!

CRYSTAL: Just a little ... *(Tugging at crotch of jeans)*

ICY, ahead, leading the way on tiptoe, hasn't heard. She pulls off her stocking-mask, stuffs it in her pocket, and the other girls follow suit. They move about the living room with exaggerated caution, almost in slow motion, staring at quite ordinary objects. ICY snatches up the piece of apparel on the chair, twirls it around her head, lets it fly to land where it will.

ICY *(elated)*: Big Prick's secret life! *We're* in it!

ORCHID *unobtrusively picks up the piece of apparel and replaces it.*

CRYSTAL *(begging)*: I'm s-scared—I'm *wet*—let's go home!

ICY *(sniffing suspiciously)*: There's a real *weird* smell in here.

ORCHID *(quickly)*: Stale beer. Like, spilled on the rug.

ICY: Yeah?

ORCHID: Remember—"Dad" Murchison smelled like that.

ICY *(surprised, seeing photos atop the TV)*: Isaak Drumm's got *family*?

ORCHID: Wow!—lots of them.

CRYSTAL *(indicating Marine photo)*: That's him? Gee, he's kinda handsome...

ICY *(snatching up photo, studying it)*: Nah, it's the same psycho eyes, only younger. *(Spits on photo)*

ORCHID, CRYSTAL *(shocked)*: Icy!

ICY: I kinda like the uniform, though. Yeah! I was a guy, maybe I'd be a Marine. They knock the shit out of you if you're not tough enough.

ICY *tosses the framed photo aside, moving restlessly on. (ORCHID wipes the glass with her sleeve and replaces the photo atop the TV.) She and CRYSTAL continue to look at the photos.*

ORCHID *(wistfully)*: S'pose these are all his *family*? These old people, and all these kids— Two dogs!— *(Pause)* 'Course, a rat's got family, too.

CRYSTAL: Gee, it'd be nice, wouldn't it, so many relatives...they'd all know your name, and love you.

ORCHID: Your ol' drunk Dad knew your name, babe, but he sure didn't love you.

CRYSTAL *(reacting with a little hurt cry)*: Oh!—he wasn't my Dad!— not really. You *stop*.

ORCHID: You *do* smell. Don't stand so close to me.

CRYSTAL: I can't help it, I'm scared!

ICY has been pawing through newspapers, magazines, and paperback books on the coffee table, so carelessly that some fall to the floor. She lifts a copy of Playboy *and waves it triumphantly.*

ICY *(elated)*: See, what'd I tell you? Porn! *(Opens to centerfold, which she holds up for her sisters to see) This,* Isaak Drumm hides from Momma when she's here.

ORCHID, CRYSTAL regard the centerfold.

ORCHID: *We're* s'posed to look like *that*? *(Angry incredulous laugh)*

CRYSTAL: I'd be scared to look like that... *(Pause)* Momma does, though.

ICY, ORCHID: What! Momma?

CRYSTAL: When she's...bare. Or if you can sort of...see through...her nightie. *(Vague gesture indicating her own breasts, hips)* She's *pretty*.

ICY *(puritanically)*: Our mother would never shame herself so, for money. That's why women like this do it—for money.

CRYSTAL: How much money?

ICY: How the fuck should *I* know? I'm not a whore! *(Tears out centerfold, rips into pieces)*

ORCHID, CRYSTAL: Icy!

ICY *(fierce)*: It's disgusting. A woman exposing herself like raw meat, so guys can jerk off looking at her. Ugh!

ICY tosses the magazine down, moves on restlessly.

CRYSTAL *(naive, serious)*: Why *do* men like to see bare women?—I don't want to see no bare *men*. *(Shudders)*

ICY: 'Cause they're pigs, that's why.

CRYSTAL: Yeah, but *why*?

ORCHID has made an effort to pick up the pieces of torn paper, and replaces the copy of Playboy *on the coffee table; tries to tidy up.*

ICY *(elated, chanting)*: Pigs is gonna pay!

ICY *next goes to the shelves of videos and books; paws through these carelessly; snatches up a thick paperback book.*

ICY: *The Triumph of the Night*—what's this shit? *(Reads, with dramatic revulsion)*: "The silver-haired gentleman seized his beauteous screaming prey and tore open his three-piece pinstripe suit and too late she saw that he was—*protoplasm.* She was helpless to resist as he pushed her bare feet into his midriff—eased her struggling legs, hips, torso, and last of all her head—into the core of his ravenous being. She screamed and screamed as she was dissolved into—"

ORCHID, CRYSTAL *(begging)*: Icy, shh! Stop!

ICY *(giggling, revulsed)*: See? He's a sicko, what'd I tell you?

CRYSTAL: Oh, is that yucky!

ORCHID: C'mon, Icy, is that *evidence*? Some dopey *book*?

ICY *has tossed the book down;* ORCHID *hurriedly replaces it on the shelf.* ICY *drifts into the adjoining room (a kitchen) as* ORCHID *and* CRYSTAL *cower together.*

CRYSTAL: Orchid, I want to go home. I keep hearing noises like somebody's *coming.*

ORCHID *(listening)*: Maybe it's just...rats.

CRYSTAL, *hearing something, pushes into* ORCHID's *arms.*

ORCHID *(pushing her away)*: Damn it, you smell! G'wan.

CRYSTAL *(whimpering)*: It's just a little pee...it's almost dry.

ICY *returns with a can of beer from which she's drinking; offers the can to* ORCHID *and* CRYSTAL *who both accept.* ORCHID *drinks thirstily and wipes her mouth on her sleeve;* CRYSTAL *drinks thirstily and clumsily, and beer dribbles down her chin.*

ICY: Hits the spot, eh? There's plenty more where that came from.

ORCHID: Icy, c'n we go home?—please—

ICY *(making a mock judo chop at* ORCHID, *but laughing)*: Yeah? Traitor? Y'want to go home?—*go. (As* ORCHID *cringes)* We're not leaving here till we get the evidence.

CRYSTAL (*dabbing at herself*): I, uh—wet myself, kind of. This damn beer—

ICY (*kisses* CRYSTAL *with a smack*): Shit, kid, you'll catch on!

ORCHID: Icy, *please*—

ICY *swaggers back into the bedroom, clicking open her switchblade dramatically.* ORCHID *and* CRYSTAL *follow haltingly.*

ICY (*ebullient, somewhat manic*): PIGS HAS GOT TO PAY!

ICY *dislodges the pillows on* ISAAK DRUMM's *bed with the switchblade; lifts the bedclothes to peer under. (The bed has been neatly made; the bedspread is a gaudy, shiny material.)*

ICY (*sniffing, crinkling her nose*): Ugh!—Big Prick's crotch and smelly feet! Dis-gusting! Die! (*Jabs with the knife*)

ORCHID: Hey Icy, c'mon—

ICY: You hiding in here, sucker? Huh? You hiding in here? (*Jabs with the knife*)

ICY *drifts off into an adjoining room, the bathroom (offstage);* ORCHID *and* CRYSTAL *stare after her.*

CRYSTAL: Icy scares me with that knife—

ORCHID (*seeing bedside clock*): Jesus! it's after six. We better get out of here.

ORCHID *tries hurriedly to tidy up the bed;* CRYSTAL *helps.*

CRYSTAL: If Momma ever finds out about this—

ICY *returns holding aloft a pink plastic shampoo container, a woman's deodorant, and the tube of lipstick* MARIETTA *was using in Scene 1. A beat.*

CRYSTAL: That's Momma's!

ORCHID: Where'd you find them?

ICY (*disgusted*): In the bathroom. Right beside *his* crap.

CRYSTAL (*blinking*): But—why's Momma's stuff *here*?

ICY (*contemptuous laugh*): 'Cause Momma spends time here,

dummy. When she's gone from us, nights, she's here—sleeping with that bastard.

CRYSTAL *(hands over ears)*: She does *not*.

CRYSTAL *bolts from room into kitchen (offstage).*

ORCHID: She's scared, we shouldn't have brought her.

ICY: "We"? I shouldn't have brought *you*. *(Opening closet)* Wow, lookit the fancy wardrobe! For a guy so weird, so ugly— *(ICY limps around, holding a necktie, sweater or shirt against her chest.)* Ain't we hot shit! *(Locates a pair of boxer shorts, puts over her head)*

ORCHID *laughs wildly.* ICY *snatches the shorts off and slaps them at her playfully.*

ORCHID: Icy, let's go? It's after six—

ICY: Y'know what I'd like to do?—burn this fucking place down.

ORCHID: Well, we're not.

ICY *(pawing through closet)*: Oh Christ! *(She has discovered* MARIETTA's *robe.)*

ORCHID: Oh.

ICY *(hurt, in a serious voice)*: Momma's birthday present *we* gave her. Thirty-two dollars ninety-eight cents—*I* paid twenty of it!—the bitch. Betraying *us*. *(Slashes at robe with knife)*

ORCHID: Icy, for Christ's sake—

ICY *(wide-eyed, whirling on her)*: Y'want me to stick *you*?

A beat.

ORCHID: Icy, come *on*.

ICY *(near tears)*: I hate Momma! I hate them both! Pigs!

ORCHID *(touching* ICY's *shoulder gently)*: Hey Icy, it's O.K.

ICY *stands in physical anguish, no longer play-acting.*

ICY: It's not O.K. It's never gonna be O.K. again.

ORCHID *(trying to be reasonable)*: Momma's got a right, doesn't she, to see a guy if she wants?

ICY: No!

CRYSTAL reappears, carrying boxes of sugar-coated cereal and swigging from a bottle of beer.

CRYSTAL: Ooooh I got this weird *buzzing* right here— *(Indicates the back of her skull)* Wow!

ICY *(abrupt mood change)*: Ter-rific, babe!

ICY drinks from CRYSTAL's bottle, as does ORCHID. All three devour handfuls of the cereal. A beat or two, as they eat.

ORCHID *(an odd look, chewing frantically)*: Never know I'm hungry till I start eating this stuff—then I can't stop.

ICY: WHO'S GONNA PAY? *(Leaps on bed, jumps about)*

ORCHID, CRYSTAL *(jumping on bed, spilling beer, cereal, etc., laughing)*: PIGS IS GONNA PAY!

ICY jumps down, goes to a bureau and yanks open drawers.

ICY *(pawing in top drawer)*: Uh-huh! Big Prick's junk jewelry! *(She waggles a wristwatch at crotch level.)* Ain't worth shit, but— *(She pockets it anyway.)* What's this? *(Military medal)* "Silver Star—Distinguished Service—ISAAK J. DRUMM, MAJOR U.S. MARINES"—worse shit! *(She pockets the medal.)* Say what?! M O N E Y. *(Brandishes a wad of bills)* —Twenty! *(Hands to ORCHID who stares in dismay)* —Forty! *(Hands to CRYSTAL who grins drunkenly)* Sixty, eighty, hundred—WOW! *(Pockets most of the money, some bills flutter to floor)* Say what? *(Has opened another drawer, and removes a handgun)*

ORCHID, CRYSTAL freeze.

ICY *(deep throaty growl, reverently)*: MMMMMM! Here's Icy's BABY!

A beat.

ORCHID: Icy, geez—

CRYSTAL: Is that real?

ORCHID: —what if that's loaded?

CRYSTAL *(shakily, grinning)*: Wow! Cool!

ICY struts about, staring at the gun as if hypnotized.

ICY *(strange voice)*: I'm holding Death in my hand. This is Death…I'm holding in my hand.

ORCHID: Icy, I said, what if that's loaded?

ICY *(teasing)*: Y'want me to pull the trigger, and see? *(She swings the gun around in an arc, not quite aiming it at her sisters, but close enough to throw them into a panic.)*

ORCHID, CRYSTAL *squeal, clutching at each other.*

ICY *(regards herself in a mirror, aiming the gun)*: Death in my hand. Yeah.

ORCHID *(pleading)*: Icy, you're scaring us. *I* just about peed my pants.

ICY: I'm scaring myself. *(Pause)* I like it.

CRYSTAL *(tugging at crotch of jeans)*: I'm wet worse. Oh!

ORCHID, CRYSTAL *have climbed down from the bed and watch* ICY *with trepidation.*

ORCHID: Icy, please put that back, huh?—and let's get the hell out of here—

CRYSTAL *(overlapping)*: Icy, please—I'm about freaked—

ICY *(strange, mystical voice)*: All things are meant to be. This— *(as she waves the gun)* —me—us.

A sudden noise which only ORCHID *and* CRYSTAL *hear.*

ORCHID: Oh God—what's that?

CRYSTAL: Oh!

ICY *(straining to hear)*: What's what?

ORCHID: Sounded like a car door slamming.

ORCHID, CRYSTAL *listen, tense.*

ORCHID, CRYSTAL *(panicked)*: Somebody's coming!

ICY *(cupping a hand to her good ear)*: I don't hear anything—

ISAAK DRUMM *is unlocking his front door as the girls stand paralyzed.*

ICY *peers through the doorway, sees* ISAAK *entering his living room, leaps back out of sight.*

ISAAK wears workclothes and a cloth cap and appears quite different from the man we've seen. At first he seems unaware of the disarray in the room; then he freezes, staring.

ISAAK: What the hell—?

ICY has pushed her sisters to the window, and has thrust the gun into her jacket pocket.

ICY *(hoarse, panicked)*: Go on! GO—

A mad scramble. CRYSTAL whimpers in terror as ICY and ORCHID push her roughly through the window; again it's a tight fit, but they manage to shove her through. ORCHID, leaner and quicker, has less trouble. Next is ICY who is about to escape when ISAAK DRUMM bounds into the room.

ISAAK: Hey! You! Stop!

A struggle. ISAAK grabs ICY's ankle, then her leg, yanking her back inside the room.

ISAAK: God damn! I got you!

ICY *(overlapping)*: Let me go!

ISAAK: Jesus—*Isabel?*

ICY: Fucker! Let me go!

ICY has the gun in her hand; ISAAK tries to wrench it from her; it goes off—a sharp, deafening crack. The bullet skims ISAAK's hair to lodge in the ceiling.

ISAAK *(losing control)*: You little bitch! You almost killed me!

As ICY screams and struggles, ISAAK overpowers her. He turns her over onto his knee and, clumsily, panting, spanks her.

ISAAK: I'll teach you!—breaking in my place!—stealing from me!— God damn bitch!—brat!—take this! this! this!

Lights out.

A police siren sounds briefly.

Scene 11

Lights up. A neutral space. Days later. MARIETTA *in a suit and white blouse, hair modestly tamped down and makeup minimal, is being interrogated; gazing out, now and then blinking, into the light. Her eyes glisten with tears which she wipes with a tissue. Her manner is anxious, placating, passionate.*

MARIETTA: No, Your Honor, I had no idea!...didn't know...I was working at the time...my daughters are good girls...Yes, I have been seeing Mr. Drumm... No, they had not ever been to his place before... Yes, we did all "get along"...I thought... Yes, we *are* close... I love my girls and I, I am very close to...yes to Mr. Drumm too... Yes, I have been there...frequently... No, I did not...Isaak never told me... No, I don't think it is a good idea for a private citizen to have a gun...permit or not...but I respect the opinion that some people have...that a gun might be needed...in case of break-ins, burglars... *(Hands to face)* Oh! *(Pause)* ...Your Honor, I've told you *yes*...very close... *(Pause, embarrassed)* Well, no, I...guess I did not, Your Honor...Isabel must have intercepted the letters from school... *(Pause, wipes at eyes)* You see, Your Honor, the PTA meetings are seven o'clock Thursdays and I work late Thursdays so it's hard to... *(Pause, listens)* Well, maybe not *every* meeting... *(Pause)* Well, I did sort of wonder...about her report card...so many things on my mind... I'm so ashamed, I...I love them, but I'm damned angry with them... *(Pause)* Totally out of contact. Miles Shurts. The father of Isabel and Orchid. Yes. No. *(Bitterly)* Never paid child support and the court didn't make any effort...didn't give a damn. Miles's place of residence I can't swear to, might be Alaska. *(Pause)* Reginald Murchison. Now deceased, Your Honor. *(Pause)* My youngest girl, Crystal. Yes, she's adopted. No, her birth mother is dead. Died of cancer when Crystal was eight. Came to live with her father and me. Yes we *were* married at the time. No! I mean yes, I love Crystal like my own daughter...Crystal *is* my own daughter. *(Pause)* The one thing I know, is *I love my girls.* That's the one thing I know, Your Honor.

Lights down on MARIETTA.

Lights up on ISAAK DRUMM. *He too is dressed soberly, in a suit, white shirt, dark necktie; his manner earnest, hopeful, placating, now and then "humorous." He is nervous and visibly sweating.*

ISAAK: No, Your Honor, I sure did not. I just walked in and...saw the place'd been broken into...went into the bedroom and there's this kid...I see it's a girl, Jesus I see it's Isabel, Marietta's daughter, I didn't know what was going on but I acted fast and pulled her back and...that's when the gun went off: *she* had it. *(Pause, wiping face with tissue)* No, Your Honor. I already made a statement to the police. Thirty-eight caliber Smith & Wesson. No, I do not have a homeowner's gun permit... No, I...don't know why. *(Pause)* I realize that, Your Honor. I am very sorry, Your Honor. I sure meant to but I...guess I didn't get around to it. *(Pause, uncomfortably)* When I was in the Marines. In a poker game. No, I never used it...against any, uh, human object... *(Shakes head, frowns)* Yes, Your Honor, I am pleading guilty to that. I am sorry, and I...I'll pay the fine, and... *(Pause, vehemently)* No, of course not, Your Honor. I don't want to press charges against them. They're Marietta's daughters and they're basically good kids, they were just maybe...curious...about me... *(Pause, grinning)* I'm the kind of guy loses his temper sometimes but I don't hold a grudge. All I can think of...Jesus I'm dreaming about it, every night since it happened...is I'm goddamned lucky the bullet went like this— *(a gesture, skimming the top of his head)* —and not like this— *(ramming his knuckles against his forehead)* I'd be in some other space right now, eh, Your Honor? *(Laughs)*

Lights dim on ISAAK DRUMM.

Lights up center stage. MARIETTA *stands holding a tissue to her eyes;* ISAAK *comes to comfort her. They confer;* MARIETTA *leans against* ISAAK, *who embraces her; after a beat,* MARIETTA *breaks hurriedly away, compelled to leave. She looks back at him as she exits, as* ISAAK *looks after her, holding out his hand.*

ISAAK: I'll call you tonight, MARIETTA, O.K.?—it's still O.K.? *(Smile)* No hard feelings on my part, I promise!

MARIETTA *nods, quickly exiting stage right.*

Lights out.

Scene 12

Lights up. MURCHISON *living room/kitchen. Evening, a few days later.* MARIETTA, ORCHID, *and* CRYSTAL *are eating supper in the kitchen; lights in the living room are dim. A fourth place is set at the table.*

MARIETTA *(incensed)*: Orchid, go get Isabel! I'm not calling her again.

ORCHID: Momma, I already tried. She won't even look at me.

MARIETTA: Is she still in bed?—I refuse to be manipulated.

ORCHID: She's *on* the bed. She just lays there.

MARIETTA *lays down her fork, goes to the doorway, calls.*

MARIETTA: Isabel! Supper! Come and *eat!*

A beat. MARIETTA *waits, but* ICY *does not appear.* MARIETTA *returns to the table and sits heavily. Pours herself a glass of beer from a can on the table.*

MARIETTA: This is just a, a new game of hers—now she's not *eating.* God damn that girl! *(To* ORCHID*)* But she *was* in school today?

ORCHID: I guess so. She went to all her classes if that's what you mean.

MARIETTA: What else would I mean?

CRYSTAL *(shivery)*: Momma, Icy's gotten real weird. I say something to her and she doesn't hear me.

ORCHID: She doesn't *see* me.

MARIETTA: It's a new game of hers and I refuse to be manipulated.

A beat. CRYSTAL *eats hungrily,* ORCHID *eats slowly;* MARIETTA *passes a hand over her eyes, drinks.*

MARIETTA: Almost I don't trust myself, I'm so goddamned angry! Isaak says "forgive and forget"—"no hard feelings" on his part— *(Pause)* I'm so ashamed, my own daughters—common thieves. *(Pause)* That's what you are, aren't you?

ORCHID, CRYSTAL *look down.* CRYSTAL *wipes at her eyes.*

MARIETTA *(demanding)*: That's what you are, aren't you?

ORCHID: *(squirming)*: Icy wanted to get evidence, she said—

MARIETTA: What "evidence"?

ORCHID: I don't know.

CRYSTAL: I don't know.

MARIETTA: What kind of crazy talk?—"evidence"?

ORCHID: Icy said—

MARIETTA: —"Isabel" is the name!—

ORCHID: —"Isabel"—it was her idea—

CRYSTAL: —We just went along, Momma—

MARIETTA: No more sense than that! Aren't you ashamed?

ICY has appeared, stage right; crosses the living room slowly, like a sleepwalker. She is very pale, disheveled in jeans and T-shirt, wearing no earrings or nose ring. Her manner is much changed, almost vacuous, catatonic in affect. Weakened from hunger, she has to support herself as she walks.

ORCHID: Momma, we're sorry...

CRYSTAL *(almost in tears)*: Momma, don't be mad anymore!

MARIETTA: Goddamn idiots! Making fools of yourself *and* you also might've gotten killed.

CRYSTAL: When that gun went off!—jeez, I almost died, I thought *I* was shot. *(Wild giggle)* I v-vowed to Jesus Christ I would take my life as a blessing if I wasn't—forever. *(Begins to cry)*

MARIETTA *(hugging CRYSTAL)*: Honey, it' O.K. Somebody *was* maybe watching over you—all of you. *(To ORCHID, tone shift)* God damn that sister of yours! I'll never forgive her.

ICY, in the kitchen doorway, has heard. She withdraws, to reappear again a moment later, wraith-like, almost fainting. ORCHID points her out to MARIETTA.

MARIETTA *(forgetting her anger, maternal)*: Isabel! Thank goodness. *(Leads ICY into the kitchen, to the table; ICY moves haltingly)* I've been so worried about you. Here—this is still warm. I can heat this up... *(Fusses, moving bowls on table)*

ICY *sits stiffly at her place; staring toward* MARIETTA *without seeming to see her.*

MARIETTA *(trying to be hearty)*: Isabel, honey, you know you have to eat. You're already too thin…

CRYSTAL *(pushing a bowl toward* ICY*)*: This mac'roni-and-cheese is real good.

A beat. ICY *sits unmoving.*

MARIETTA: Isabel, what is it? *(Pause)* I'm sorry I yelled at you yesterday… *(Losing patience)* Isabel, God *damn*. Look at me.

ICY *hides her face in her hands.*

MARIETTA: Orchid, Crystal—leave us alone, will you? Just go—shut the door—please.

CRYSTAL *(protesting)*: Momma, I'm not done eating yet—

ORCHID *(pulling at* CRYSTAL*)*: C'mon!

CRYSTAL *heaps more food on her plate to take with her.*

ORCHID, CRYSTAL *leave the kitchen;* ORCHID *shuts the door, and* MARIETTA *rises to make sure that it is shut tight. (*ORCHID *and* CRYSTAL *move to exit stage right.)* MARIETTA *returns to* ICY, *anxious and exasperated.*

ICY *has lowered her hands but will not look at* MARIETTA.

MARIETTA *(stroking* ICY's *forehead)*: You've got a little fever—I hope it isn't the flu. I'll give you some vitamin C. *(Pause)* Orchid says you were in school today. That's two days in a row. That's *good*. *(Pause)* I hope you do more in school than just sit like a zombie. *(Pause, exasperated)* Isabel, damn you! This is some new game of yours and I refuse to be manipulated!

ICY *(hoarsely)*: I'm s-sorry, Momma.

MARIETTA: Isabel? What?

ICY *seems about to speak, but does not. She is visibly shivering.*

MARIETTA: Honey, don't scare me. Don't you think, these last few days, since that call came from the—the police—I've been scared enough? *(Pause)* What if Isaak Drumm wanted to press charges!

You'd have been *arrested*, Isabel—you'd have to go to court—
(Suddenly furious) And wind up in Red Bank like your friend
Doris Reardon!

ICY *(haltingly)*: Momma, before the police came...when it was just
the two of us...there...he d-did something to me...

MARIETTA: What?

ICY: *Him*—D-Drumm. He did things to me.

MARIETTA: What are you saying?

ICY *(runs her hands slowly, roughly over her body)*: He...hurt me.

MARIETTA: Isabel—!

*ICY speaks slowly, almost as if in a trance; there is no doubt that she is
speaking the truth, as she remembers it. Tears well up in her eyes and
spill onto her cheeks. This is an ICY we have never seen before.*

ICY: Oh Momma he hit me...punched me...pulled down my
jeans...*spanked* me...I'm so ashamed Momma he *saw* me...my
panties down...he *touched* me... *(revulsed)* ...poked his thing
against me...

MARIETTA *(hugging her)*: Isabel, honey—no!

ICY *(rocking from side to side, slowly and haltingly as before)*: —His
p-penis, he poked against me...so hard!...he hit me...my
head... *(dazedly rubbing her right ear)* ...oh Momma he hurt me...

MARIETTA: Not Isaak—

ICY: He was real mad, like he hated me...wanted to k-kill me...he
said he would kill me if I told.

MARIETTA *(frightened)*: No, Isabel—no—

ICY: I'll show you, Momma!—he *spanked* me...*punched* me...my
bare skin... *(ICY stands, undoes her jeans and lowers them so that
MARIETTA can see purplish bruises on her upper buttocks and thighs.)*
He said he would kill me if I told...you.

MARIETTA stares aghast at ICY's bruises; then embraces her, weeping.

MARIETTA: Not Isaak! Not Isaak! Not Isaak—

Lights out.

Scene 13

Lights up. Neutral space. ISAAK DRUMM *is again being interrogated; he is anxious, sweating.*

ISAAK: No, I did *not*. I did *not* "molest" that girl. I'm not a man who does things like that—I'm not a man who needs to do things like that! Look, I caught the kid in my apartment, what the hell?—she'd broken in, she'd stolen from me—had my gun for God's sake almost blew my head off—I pulled her back from the window, sure, I kind of lost my temper, maybe—I spanked her, I admit—so what? I didn't take down her jeans, I didn't "sexually assault" her, didn't even touch her bare s-skin—*I did not.*

Lights down on ISAAK.

Lights up on MARIETTA. *As* ISAAK *approaches her.*

ISAAK: Marietta, please—at least listen to me. I—

MARIETTA *(grim, curt, cold)*: Get away. Get out of here. I told you I never want to see you again and I never want to talk to you again.

ISAAK: But, Marietta, your daughter isn't telling the truth—

MARIETTA *(hands over ears)*: Get away! Go to hell! I'll call the police if you don't get out of here!

ISAAK: Jesus, I can't believe this. Marietta—we love each other.

MARIETTA: Who "loves each other"— ! What a joke! You bastard!

ISAAK: But Isabel is *lying*. You must know she's *lying*.

MARIETTA: Shut up!

ISAAK: She's *crazy* if she's saying—

MARIETTA: My daughters don't lie to me. Go to hell!

ISAAK *(trying to touch her)*: —God damn it she's *lying*. I'm not a, a—sex pervert—

MARIETTA *(slapping at him, turning away)*: I believe Isabel. I saw the bruises. You!—pretending to be so *nice*. Not like the others—*nice*.

ISAAK *(distressed)*: Marietta, for God's sake—look at me.

MARIETTA: No! Get away from me! *(Sobbing)* It was my fault—I trusted you. Oh, my God!

ISAAK: You *can* trust me, Marietta. Didn't we promise always to be honest with each other?

MARIETTA: I believe my daughter! Isabel doesn't lie to me! I love her! I love *her*!

MARIETTA *slaps* ISAAK *in the face—hard. He backs off, defeated, limping.*

MARIETTA *(face glistening with tears)*: I believe Isabel. This time—I know she's speaking the truth. Oh God! *(Voice lifts in a wail, she is almost doubled over in grief)*

Lights down on MARIETTA.

Lights up on ICY, *speaking to a police matron or a social worker. She is breathless; shivering, occasionally hugs herself, rocking from side to side; clearly traumatized. She is surprised by and enjoys the sympathy and attention; the more her story is believed, the more she has to tell. She is childlike and ingenuous, not calculating or vindictive. This is the truth as* ICY *now recalls it.*

ICY *(nodding eagerly)*: —Yeah I was trying to get out the window I was scared shitless!—this guy coming at me, yelling—I never seen him look like that before!—he grabs me by the ankle— *(demonstrates)* —yanks me back inside the fucking window and I'm on the floor and he's like straddling me—this big, heavy guy—he punches me upside the head— *(she demonstrates, bringing her fist against her right ear)* —so I just about go out—I'm scared my brains is leaking out— *(laughs)* —he's crazy like a maniac calling me bitch! cunt!—"I'm gonna teach you a lesson, cunt!"—puts his hand over my mouth so I almost choke—saying he's gonna strangle me if I don't shut up—then he's squeezing me— *(squeezing gesture at her breasts)* —oh! it hurt!—he's got my jeans down—my panties—he's squeezing like he's gonna tear me apart— *(her hands shaped like claws, kneading and tearing gestures at her own flesh)* —he took out his thing—his penis—out of his pants—it was big, and red, and wet-looking—he didn't stick it in, just poked—jabbed—'till he came. *(Pause, breathless)* Like they do—men. So there's no evidence. If you're examined—like I was at the hospital—no evidence. *(Pause)* "Nobody will believe you, cunt," he said. "If you tell I'll kill you, cunt." *(Pause)* Yeah, ma'am. Lots of times. I lost track how many times. *(Pause)* He'd put his hand on me, or sort of...rub...like they do. Like you're going through a doorway, y'know?—and they push through, too. "Baby want to suck my dick?" he asked, me and my sister Crystal too. She's young, she don't know no better, she's real trusting. *(Pause)* How long?—jeez, how many weeks I don't know— *(counting on fingers, gets confused)* —five, six—no, maybe it was a lot longer— it's hard to remember— *(her face creases with the effort of remembering, as if in pain)* —"Isaak Drumm"—that's his name. Momma brought him home.

Lights down on ICY.

Lights up on ISAAK DRUMM. *In conference with his attorney.* ISAAK *has been drinking and is smoking a cigarette in quick, short puffs. His face appears sallow, swollen. His manner ranges from belligerent to incredulous to pleading to anguished, defeated.*

ISAAK: You're my fucking lawyer and you're advising me to plead guilty? "Sexual misdemeanor"—? *(Pause)* I told you a hundred times I DIDN'T DO ANYTHING! *(Pause, breathing hard)* O.K. I admit I spanked her. She deserved it! *(Pause)* I didn't spank her *hard*—I didn't want to *hurt* her—I DIDN'T TAKE DOWN HER JEANS LIKE SHE'S SAYING. *(Pause, wiping face with tissue)* No I did not threaten to s-strangle her—I AM NOT THAT KIND OF MAN. *(Pause, more subdued)* No, I can't explain that. Why she turned against me...Marietta...won't talk to me. *(Pause, listlessly)* No, we hadn't made any plans. Anything formal... *(Pause)* So— that's the deal? "Sexual misdemeanor" instead of "sexual assault"—two years' probation instead of seven years' jail time— but I'm innocent, God damn it! *(Pause, breathing hard)* I'll be down on the record as guilty. It'll be in the paper, on TV—already everybody's talking about it. Guys I thought were my friends. My boss—looks at me like I'm shit, for sure he's gonna fire me soon as this job is over we're doing, laying foundation for a parking garage. *(Flexes his fingers; pause, angry and resolute)* O.K., I'll plead guilty. What the fuck choice do I have? *(Reaches out as if to accept a sheet of paper from his attorney, bitter smile)*

Lights down on ISAAK DRUMM.

Lights up on ORCHID and CRYSTAL, standing close together, as ICY approaches them. ICY wears her earrings and nose ring again and has regained some of her former bravado.

ICY: What's with you two? You avoiding me?

ORCHID, CRYSTAL regard their sister silently. ORCHID appears skeptical, CRYSTAL a bit fearful.

ICY *(incensed)*: You don't believe me?—fuck off.

A beat.

ICY *(hyped up, breathless, as if moving to interior music)*: Yeah! well! it's true! That fucker put his hot-meat hands on me—his *thing*—lots of times. And he'd look at *you*—both of you. When Momma wasn't around he'd get this weird look in his face, yeah and his mouth— *(she pulls roughly at her lips)* —like it's filling up with blood. Yeah!—lots of times! *(Pause, advancing upon her sisters; making a mock-threatening gesture from which they flinch)* Don't believe me, huh?—the hell with you!—*they* believe me—*they're* taking it down on tape—*they* know I'm telling the truth—*they* respect me, *they're* my friends. *(Proudly)*

CRYSTAL *(shyly)*: Icy, I'm your friend.

ICY: He touched you, too, didn't he!—c'mon, Baby Tits, tell the truth.

CRYSTAL *(a long pause)*: I—don't remember.

ICY: "Isaak Drumm"—that's his name. They ask you his name and there's a picture of him you got to identify—"Isaak Drumm." Got it? *(Snaps her fingers as if to say, "It's easy!")*

A train approaches. In the near distance, a whistle; sound of locomotive, freight cars.

ICY: Orchid—you, too. Cut the shit, you know the things he did.

ORCHID shakes her head, baffled, scared.

ICY takes out her switchblade knife, in a cocky stance flicks the blade open. She is both teasing and threatening, advancing upon her sisters who back away.

ICY: You remember, huh? You two? Huh? Huh? Huh?

The sound of the train becomes louder, drowning out ICY's words. The knife in her hand, ICY freezes; ORCHID, CRYSTAL freeze in place.

Lights down on ICY, ORCHID, CRYSTAL.

Lights up on MARIETTA. She sits alone at the kitchen table, in her blue flannel robe; her skin is sallow, her eyes tired. She is now drinking gin which she pours with exaggerated care into a glass, and sips.

MARIETTA: The one thing I know is, I love my girls. That's the one thing and that's everything.

Lights out.

Epilogue

Lights up. MARIETTA remains seated at the kitchen table. ORCHID, aged 20, in her student nurse's coat, addresses the audience.

ORCHID: It's five years later. A lifetime later. I live in another place now. I'm another person now. *(Pause)* "Orchid Murchison" is still my name—but I'm not the "Orchid" that was.

During this speech, ICY appears in jeans, leather jacket, boots; wearing a backpack. She is pale, stubborn, inscrutable, as MARIETTA seems to be appealing to her; then, giving in, kisses her goodbye. ICY hugs MARIETTA, then pushes quickly away, exits.

ORCHID *(wistful tone)*: After what happened, seems like the Murchisons just—fell apart. In the neighborhood, in school, at where Momma worked—people *looked* at us, and people *knew*. Icy's name didn't get in the paper 'cause she was the "victim" and a minor but everybody knew this "16-year-old girl" Isaak Drumm pleaded guilty to "committing a sexual misdemeanor" against was Icy Murchison. Oh yeah! *(Pause)* Icy couldn't take it—cut classes, disappeared for days—then one day she announces to us she's going to Alaska to look for her father! *(Pause)* Sure, Momma tried to talk her out of it, but—you can't talk to Icy. So she left. Said she'd take buses, hitch rides—she'd get there if it killed her. *(Pause)* She sent a few postcards—from Wyoming, from Oregon, from Vancouver, from Fairbanks, Alaska. Then—nothing. The last card came four years ago. *(Pause)*

Momma keeps waiting to hear from her—but there's no way to trace where Icy might be. No way to know whether she ever found "Miles Shurts," our father. *(Pause)* No way to know if she's even alive. *(Pause)* Damn you, Icy! *I loved you . . .*

MARIETTA now says goodbye to CRYSTAL, now attractively dressed, her hair conventionally styled. She too kisses MARIETTA goodbye—MARIETTA hugs her tight—crosses the stage to exit.

ORCHID: Our baby sister changed almost overnight! Joined this church up the block called Apostles of Christ Risen—got engaged to the minister's son—got *married*, aged 18. Crystal! *(Pause)* She's having a baby in a few weeks—is that fast, or is that fast? She's a "good girl" now, for sure. *(Pause)* I'm happy for her, *she's* so happy. *(Pause)* The person I feel sorry for is Momma. She sees Crystal pretty often but she's lonely—you can't blame her. Her three girls all grown up and gone. *(Pause; a thin wail of loss)* Momma—!

Lights down on MARIETTA.

ORCHID *(regaining poise)*: I'm 20 years old. A nursing student at the University of Rochester. I'd say I've come pretty far from Niagara Street, Yewville, New York. I'm not a "bad girl" now—except sometimes in my thoughts.

ISAAK DRUMM approaches. His hair is no longer a sleek, oily black but threaded with gray, and combed flat; his moustache is gone; he wears a nondescript jacket, khaki pants. His limp is perceptible. Seeing ORCHID, he freezes.

ORCHID *(breathless)*: Momma doesn't know!—the other day I ran into Isaak Drumm on the street. I didn't recognize him at first— this strange man staring at me. I'd have walked away, but—

ISAAK *(uncertainly)*: Orchid—?

ORCHID *(cautious)*: Yes?

ISAAK: You're Orchid Murchison—aren't you?

ORCHID *(now recognizing him)*: Oh!—God!— *(About to turn away)*

ISAAK: Wait, don't go away, Orchid—

ORCHID: I, I have a class now—

ISAAK: It's Isaak Drumm—remember?

ORCHID: No—yes—I'm s-sorry, I can't—

ISAAK *(forced smile, nervous, almost pleading)*: Wait, please—do you remember me?

ORCHID *(a deep breath)*: I, uh—yes, sure—

ISAAK *(putting his hand out to her)*: "Isaak Drumm"—

ORCHID *(shying away from the handshake)*: Y-yes, "Isaak"—

ISAAK *(trying to relax)*: I *thought* that was you, crossing the street. Orchid Murchison—grown up! *(Glancing around)* You're a nurse?

ORCHID: A student nurse.

ISAAK: Well!—that's something to be proud of, eh?

ORCHID *(a bit stiffly)*: I guess.

ISAAK: How long—?

ORCHID: I'm finishing up my second year. It's pretty hard work. *(Pause, backing off)* —I, uh, have a biology lab right now—

ISAAK *(distressed that she might leave, wanting to touch her but not daring to do so)*: Orchid, wait—maybe we could have coffee somewhere?

ORCHID: Thanks, but—I have my biology lab—

ISAAK: Afterward, then? I'll be in the neighborhood—

ORCHID: Then I go straight to my cafeteria job. I'm sorry—

ISAAK *(embarrassed)*: Well, I won't keep you. I—know how it is.

ORCHID *(relenting a bit)*: You—live in Rochester now?

ISAAK: Yeah, great place, isn't it? A real city, not like—Yewville. I'm with Ross Myer Builders—heard of us? *(ORCHID has not.)* Second-biggest construction firm in the area. Real high quality.

ORCHID *(murmuring)*: That's—good.

ISAAK: I left Yewville as soon as the—probation time was up. Lived in Watertown for a while. Now—here. *(Pause)* How is—Marietta?

ORCHID *(quickly)*: My mother is fine.

ISAAK: Does she still have that job?—

ORCHID *(overlapping)*: No—

ISAAK *(overlapping)*: —she didn't like, much.

ORCHID *(overlapping)*: She's—married now.

ISAAK *(struck by this)*: Married. *(A beat, then quickly)* Well—that's good news, I guess. She's happy?

ORCHID: Very happy.

ISAAK *(forcing it, sadly)*: That's the main thing, then. That's what she deserves. A good woman... *(Pause)* Would you say "hello" to her, from Isaak?

ORCHID *(evasively)*: Maybe.

ISAAK: I still think of her, sometimes—I mean, a lot. Sometimes, a lot. *(Laughs awkwardly)* And you girls.

ORCHID laughs self-consciously.

ISAAK *(heartily)*: There was Orchid—there was Christabel—no Crystal—there was— *(a beat: the name is hard for him to say)* — Isabel. *(Pause)* How are your sisters?

ORCHID: Crystal is married.

ISAAK: Married! But she's just a girl—

ORCHID: And Icy—"Isabel"—joined up with the military. The Navy.

ISAAK: The Navy!

ORCHID *(wildly inventing)*: She's stationed in Alaska. In the—Bering Sea.

ISAAK: The Bering Sea...

A beat.

ORCHID: Well! Guess I'd better—

ISAAK *(overlapping; suddenly appealing to her)*: Orchid, I—was hurt so bad, the way it ended—it took me a long time to get over it— except I'm not, I guess. Seeing you just now— *(hand against his heart)* —went through me like a knife! *(Pause, short of breath)* I had to leave Yewville, I was so shamed in everyone's eyes. Sometimes even now I can't believe it. I wake up in the night and I'm, like, crying—how my life changed, so fast. I was so happy and then—you all turned against me—so fast.

ORCHID *(backing off, embarrassed)*: Well, I'm—I'm sorry—

ISAAK: Your mother who I loved so—believing that girl, that "Icy"—the story she told, just to hurt me! Marietta wouldn't give me a chance to tell my side—just shut me out. Like she didn't want to know—your sister *was* making it all up—couldn't you tell? You must've! Didn't you *care*? Didn't any of you like me, or trust me? *(Pause)* Jesus, I loved you so much. I was crazy about you all. I wanted to— *(faltering)* —marry your mother. You'd have been my family, her and you girls—

A beat. ORCHID *is shocked, yet can't respond emotionally; she stares at* ISAAK, *backing off.*

ISAAK *(embarrassed)*: Shit, I'm sorry, Orchid. I—

ORCHID: I guess I have to l-leave now—

ISAAK: Maybe we can get together some other time? Can I call you at the nursing school?

ORCHID: I don't know, maybe—

ISAAK *(a rush of words)*: Tell your mother hello and best wishes and I'm thinking of her and would like to hear from her—sometime—will you? You remember my name?—Isaak—

ORCHID: Yes, "Isaak"—

ISAAK: Here— *(takes a slip of paper from his pocket, writes)* —my telephone number. Maybe give me a call?

ORCHID *(no choice but to take the paper from him, even as she edges away)*: M-Maybe—

ISAAK: Goodbye, Orchid!

ORCHID *walks out of the scene, as* ISAAK *looks yearningly after her.*

Lights down on ISAAK.

ORCHID *(guiltily, wonderingly, to herself)*: Can a man have such feelings, like a—woman? Can a man be hurt? *(Pause)* Can a man really love you? Can a man tell the truth?

A beat. ORCHID *tears the slip of paper into several pieces and lets them fall.*

ORCHID: No! No! I can't believe it—can I?

A beat. ORCHID *changes her mind, kneels to gather up the pieces and fit them together.*

Lights down.

Lights out.

THE END

Black Water
A Dramatization in Two Acts

CHARACTERS:

KELLY KELLEHER, 26

THE SENATOR, early 50s

BUFFY ST. JOHN, mid-20s

LUCIUS SMITH, late 20s

ROY ANNICK, early 50s

SARAH CONNOR, mid-20s

MICHELLE RAVEL, mid-20s

JENNIFER O'BRIEN, mid-20s

GRAEME WINTHROP, late 20s

DWIGHT MURPHY, late 20s

PLACE: Mt. Grayling Island, off the coast of Maine

TIME: July 4th, a few years ago

Overture

Darkness. The sound of an approaching car. Glaring lights towards edge of stage. Brakes, scream, tires skid.

The sound of a crash: a car swerving off the road into a body of water.

The sound of water.

CHORUS *(incantatory)*
> You're an American girl; you love your life.
> You're an American girl; you believe you have chosen it.
> You're an American girl; you will live forever.
>
> As the black water filled her lungs, and she died.
>
> In the night, in the swamp, nocturnal creatures in their frenzy
> > of copulation and procreation—
> So many! You would not think that God would make so many!
> And forget so many!
>
> As the black water filled her lungs, and she died.

KELLY *(voice)*
> No! I'm here Senator! Senator don't leave me! Senator, Senator
> > take my hand!
> Senator, Senator, Senator, Senator—

Lights up (dimly) on THE SENATOR *at a telephone booth.*

SENATOR *(a low voice, agitated)*
> Roy, it's me—and I'm in bad trouble.
> There's been an accident—

ROY *(voice)*
> You! An accident!
> Where are you?

SENATOR
> A terrible accident— The girl, The girl, The girl—
> The girl—she's dead—

KELLY *(voice)*
> NO!

ROY *(stunned)*
> Dead!

SENATOR
> She was drunk, she got emotional,
> she grabbed at the wheel and—

ROY *(overlapping)*
> Don't tell me over the phone!

Just tell me where you are for Christ's sake,
and I'll come get you!

Lights down on THE SENATOR.

CHORUS
You're an American girl; you love your life.

ACT I

Scene 1: The Anticipation

Fourth of July at a luxurious summer cottage on Mt. Grayling Island, Maine. Mid-afternoon of a bright, gusty day. A terrace overlooking the beach, breakers. A sound of waves, gulls. Enter KELLY, *in a summer shift, sandals. She looks toward the sea with romantic anticipation.*

KELLY
All night, all night, last night the bellbuoy rang of fog and
    danger—
Now, the light breaks everywhere, there are no shadows.
How the breakers sound— I want! I am! I want! I am! I want!
    I am!
How light comes over the sea, afire!

Waves, sing to me—under the sea-wind sing to me!
Bring love to me! Bring love to me!
The secret of love is the secret of the sea:

every moment is now—
we live only now—
rejoice in now—
God is now. Is now!

(In a different tone, rueful)
No!— what am I saying?
Who is this speaking?
I want to do all I can do.
I want to give all I can give.
I want to be all I can be.
A woman today controls her own destiny.

No excuse now—"You're a woman."
History's caught up with us now—
"You're a woman." There's no turning back now, you're a
   woman.
I want to be all I can be.

A woman today controls her own destiny.

(Yet, as if unable to resist)

KELLY *(joined by* BUFFY *and* SARAH, *in background)*
All night last night the bellbuoy rang of fog and danger—
Now, the light shines everywhere, there are no shadows.

All night all night last night the bellbuoy rang of fog and
   danger—
Now, the light breaks everywhere, there are no shadows.

Waves, sing to us under the sea-wind sing to us!
Bring love to me! Bring love to me!
The secret of love is the secret of the sea:
every moment is now—
we live only now—
rejoice in now—
God is now. Is now.

BUFFY *and* SARAH *enter, to lay out picnic things on a table. They are
dressed like* KELLY *for the beach,* BUFFY *most strikingly; her finger- and
toenails are boldly painted bronze. The young women join* KELLY *looking
toward the sea.*

KELLY & SARAH *(abrupt change of tone)*
Do you think the Senator will come?

BUFFY *(shrugs, barely controlling excitement)*
I don't know!—I don't expect him, really.
Roy invited him last year, and he couldn't make it.
He sent his "regrets"—he couldn't make it.
This year—who knows?

KELLY & SARAH
Do you think he will come?
Do you think he won't come?
Last year he sent his "regrets" and this year—

BUFFY
I don't expect him really.

Enter other guests with picnic things including a portable barbecue. ROY, LUCIUS, DWIGHT, GRAEME, JENNIFER and MICHELLE. (All are young except for ROY who is middle-aged—though vigorous and attractive. ROY is matched with BUFFY, LUCIUS with KELLY, DWIGHT with SARAH.)

CHORUS *(playful, but acknowledging a genuine hope)*
> Do you think the Senator will come?
> Do you think the Senator won't come?
> Can he have been delayed?
> Can he have changed his mind?
> From Washington to Portland—by air;
> from Portland to Boothbay Harbor—by car;
> from Boothbay Harbor to Mt. Grayling Island—by ferry.
> So far!
> Is that the Senator now? Oh—

A car passes up on the road, invisibly; a disappointment.

ROY *(with authority)*
> The Senator told me—he hoped to.
> The Senator told me—he wanted to.
> He has no other place to go, he truly wants to go—he told me.
> He's so much in demand, he's such a lonely man—he told me.
> He never makes promises he can't keep—I know him.
> He knows he must never light a flame only to blow it out.
> A great man must never disappoint.
> A great man must never disappoint.

CHORUS
> The Senator! The Senator!
> A great man must never disappoint.
> Politics is the American religion,
> politics is the only religion.
> Is that him now? Is that him now?

Another car passes invisibly. CHORUS expresses disappointment.

BUFFY *(airily)*
> I don't think he will—
> I'm not expecting him.
> We don't really need him.
> The Senator!—at my party!

KELLY (*gaily*)
    I think he will—
    I have a premonition.
    The moon already in the sky— (*Pointing*)
    My horoscope for July—

BUFFY & SARAH (*laughing*)
    Kelly's horoscope!
    Oh, Scorpio!

KELLY
    We don't believe in the stars,
    the stars we see are extinct.
    We're free of old superstitions,
    we believe in ourselves.
    Yet, we have our premonitions.

LUCIUS (*with sly meaning*)
    And it's the Fourth of July.
    What more auspicious occasion?
    For a man with his eye on the prize,
    for a man of such noble ambition,
    what more auspicious occasion?

CHORUS
    Do you think he will come?
    Do you think he won't come?
    Mt. Grayling Island off the coast of Maine,
    on the Fourth of July—
    what more auspicious occasion?
    a great man must never disappoint.

    Is *this* him? Is he here? Is this him? Is he here? Is this him? Is
    he here? Is this him? Is he here? The Senator— The Senator—
    Senator— Here!

BUFFY (*straightening cushions on chairs, setting a vase of flowers on
    the table, behaving with controlled mania*)
    I don't know—I'm not expecting him—
    I'd die if—
    The Senator, here—at my party! Oh!
    Where's the camera? Where's the camera? Where's the
    camera? Where's the camera? Where's the camera? Where's
    the camera? Where's the camera? Here!

BUFFY brandishes a Polaroid camera which, when THE SENATOR actually arrives, she discreetly sets aside.

ROY
>A good man must never compromise. Here!

CHORUS
>The Senator—here!

(All are looking eagerly stage right.)

The scene fades.

Scene 2: The Arrival

THE SENATOR appears, stage right, elevated and spotlighted; the rest of the stage is darkened. He speaks with impassioned sincerity and a youthful vigor: an actor wholly identified with his role.

SENATOR
>My friends! My friends! My friends!
>I believe in the principle of Democracy,
>I believe in the integrity of the individual,
>I believe in the nobility of the individual,
>and in the compassion and the charity of the American people.
>I believe there is no political leadership without
>moral conviction, I believe
>there is no moral conviction without vision,
>and there is no vision without sympathy.

(To himself, appalled)
>It's all true. Yet why
>do my words taste like wetted ashes?

SENATOR
>I believe that "Love thy neighbor as thyself"
>is the bedrock of all human community.
>For the individual is in the community, and
>the community is in the world.
>And the greatness of the one is inherent in the greatness
>of the other.
>And there is no one without the other.

I believe in protecting our priceless American environment
through taxation.
I believe in raising the taxes of the wealthy—the "privileged"—
though I am of that class.
I believe in—I have myself proposed, in Congress—a compre-
    hensive reform of the welfare system, and I have brought
    into being through my three terms in Congress legislation
    involving expanded medical coverage for the indigent,
    and the Women, Infants, and Children's Protection
    Agency, and—

(To himself)
Words! The art of politics is the art of words!
These words point to the truth, or did; yet why
do they taste like wetted ashes in my mouth, like
my own death, a black water rising
out of this sun-blazoned summer day?
Why do the seagulls grin at me and jeer
with such brotherly
rapacity?

(In his public voice, preparing to join the others)
My friends, today is a holiday from politics— Thank God.
I'm not a public man today.
I'm not a household word—a "Presidential candidate"—today.
I'm one of you today.
Away from the buzzing hive of Washington, today.
My friends! My friends! My friends! My friends! My friends!
    My friends!

In a flare of lights simulating fireworks, scene fades.

Scene 3: The Arrival II

THE SENATOR *arrives deep in apparently serious conversation with* ROY
*who has gone to greet him; we see that the two men (who are of an age
significantly older than the other guests) are intimate friends.* THE
SENATOR *carries a seersucker sport coat over his shoulder; he is dressed
more formally than the others; he has loosened his necktie. His manner is
not at all self-important or pompous; on the contrary, he makes a very*

favorable impression by his smiling, even boyish demeanor though he is fatigued by traveling. He seems eager to please, for each episode of his life among strangers is a challenge: he is an actor subsumed by his role. (He carries a bottle of champagne as a gift for his hostess.)

ROY leads THE SENATOR forward to be introduced. First, BUFFY.

SENATOR

    How kind of you to invite me to your beautiful house,
    Buffy St. John! To make a stranger welcome,
    on the Fourth of July!

(Shaking hands, giving her the champagne)

BUFFY

    Senator, you're hardly a stranger: we all know you.
    And Roy has told me so much.

SENATOR *(a clap on ROY's shoulder)*
    Not too much, old buddy, I hope?

ROY *(a crafty smile)*
    Only the truth.

Next are introduced SARAH, KELLY, LUCIUS, DWIGHT, JENNIFER, GRAEME, MICHELLE; THE SENATOR shakes hands vigorously and happily. Each character states own name, THE SENATOR responds with "hello."

SENATOR

    Sarah! Hello! Michelle! Hello! Jenny! Hello! Kelly! Hello!
    Graeme! Hello! Lucius! Hello! Dwight! Hello! Hello!

(Glancing upward)

    That flag—is a landmark. Highest on the island.
    I had no trouble finding your place, Buffy.

BUFFY

    It isn't my house, it's my father's, Owen St. John, surely you
        know him?
    Thirty-five years in the CIA, and you couldn't catch him.

SENATOR *(a genial laugh)*
    Not for lack of trying.

The following testimonials overlap slightly.

SARAH

> Senator, I do admire you. Senator, I love your policies. Senator, I love your policies. Senator, I do. Senator, I do. Senator, I do. Senator, I do.

DWIGHT

> I'm from your home state of Connecticut—Mr. Senator. Connecticut, Mr. Senator. I'm from your, I'm from your home state of Connecticut. I'm from your, I'm from your home state of Connecticut.

LUCIUS *(in a cooler tone, as if restraining enthusiasm)*

> I heard you at Harvard. I heard you at Yale. Mr. Senator, I heard you at Yale. Mr. Senator, I heard you at Harvard. I heard you at Harvard.

SENATOR

> Thank you. Thank you. Thank you. Thank you. Thank you. My friends. Thank you my friends.

ROY

> Easy guys, easy girls. Easy guys, easy girls. Easy guys, easy girls. Easy guys, easy girls. Give the Senator some space. Give the Senator some space.

MICHELLE & JENNIFER

> Senator, we heard you at Brown, five years ago— Do you remember?

KELLY

> You spoke so powerfully, many of us were in tears. "Our Invisible Americans: The Underclass" was your topic. Remember?

SENATOR

> Brown University! Of course.

BUFFY *(slyly)*

> Kelly did her honors thesis on you.

SENATOR

> You don't say! I hope it was worth it.

KELLY *(shyly)*

> Of course it was worth it, Senator. *(Pause)*
> May I get you a drink?

SENATOR

(As KELLY *moves away, looking after, to himself)*
> That face!—those eyes!
> Such trust! So young, *she* believes.

(Pause)
> Seeing myself so in eyes like hers—
> *(A sweeping gesture taking in all who listen)*
> I can respect myself again.

ROY

> Time to celebrate! You've come a long way
> and it's early in the day,
> so let's begin.

SENATOR *(removing his necktie)*
> I feel like a pilgrim. Every journey should be a pilgrimage,
> and every destination sacred.
> I've never been on Mt. Grayling Island till now—
> I swear I've never smelled such clean clear air till now—
> never really seen and felt the ocean till now—
> the beat, beat, beat of the waves till now.
> Washington's a hive of maddened bees and I among them
> except—not here, not today.

They all drink, toasting THE SENATOR, *who deflects their homage by touching their glasses, each in turn.*

CHORUS
> Welcome, Senator, to Mt. Grayling Island
> on the Fourth of July!

SENATOR
> To us all, Americans—on the Fourth of July.

BUFFY *sneaks out the Polaroid camera and takes a picture.*

Scene fades.

Scene 4: Rosa Virginiana

Later that afternoon. Stage left, KELLY, BUFFY, SARAH *confer in girlish undertones; stage right,* THE SENATOR *(now dressed in white shorts, T-shirt, tennis shoes) and* ROY *confer. The men have beer cans in hand, as does* BUFFY.

KELLY, BUFFY & SARAH
> He isn't as you'd expect, is he!
> He's warm, really nice—
> really *really* nice
> truly interested in other people—
> truly listens to other people
> oh and *sweet*—
> oh isn't he—
> such a surprise—
> not at all vain—
> not at all condescending—
> and so smart, you can tell—
> smart men are the sexiest—
> and handsomer than his photos—isn't he!

KELLY
> But he's married?—isn't he?

BUFFY *(airily)*
> Oh, Kelly.
> Yes—but *no.*

KELLY
> Yes—but *no?*

BUFFY *(forefinger to lips)*
> It's like with Roy and his marriage.
> Purely pro forma.
> One of those sad old dead old marriages some of our parents—

SARAH
> Most of our parents have. You know?

BUFFY
> Eighty-six years married, or twenty-six years married, what's
>   the difference!

The Senator and his wife lead totally separate lives;
they don't divorce because of her pride and his career.
And who cares?
Someday he may be President.
And to think he came *here*.

KELLY & SARAH
    To think he came *here*!

THE SENATOR *and* ROY *speak together too in guarded undertones.*

SENATOR
    Which one is yours, Roy?—Buffy?

ROY
    The black-haired one, yes.
    Isn't she gorgeous?

SENATOR
    God, yes.
    How long have you been—

ROY
    Screwing her?

SENATOR
    Yes!

ROY
    When I'm in town, and she's free.

SENATOR
    What about Miriam?

ROY *(shrugs)*
    What about Miriam?
    What about Vivien?

SENATOR *(shrugs)*
    She's at the Cape. Talking divorce.

ROY
    Think of the party. Think of your future.
    Think of the White House, you're in politics.
    You gotta be an optimist. You're no longer an optimist,
    you're no longer in politics, you're dead.

SENATOR
    I'll drink to that.

Men drink. BUFFY, *raising her beer can, signals flirtatiously to them and drinks, too.*

Lights alter subtly as scene shifts.

LUCIUS *mimes instructing* KELLY *in her serve. The two have a playful relationship.*

LUCIUS *(displaying excellent tennis form)*
    Hit it! Hit it! Hit it! Hit it!
    Try it again girl.
    Don't be afraid to hit—
    the ball, girl. Again. Again. Again. Again. There you go, girl.
    What did I tell you. Don't be afraid to hit the ball, girl.

KELLY *tries again, improving a bit.*

KELLY *(laughing)*
    Thank you, Lucius.

(Shakes LUCIUS' *hand with playful formality, retains her hand)*

LUCIUS *(change of tone)*
    Kelly, let's play a real game.

KELLY *(drawing back)*
    Now?

LUCIUS
    Yes!

(As KELLY *hesitates)*

(Pause)
    When I called you last week, Kelly, you said, "Lucius, I look
        forward to seeing you."

KELLY *(quickly)*
    There's always tomorrow—

LUCIUS *(drily)*
    There's always tomorrow.
    There's always next year.
    Remember *last* year, Kelly,
    here?

KELLY *(conflicted)*
> Lucius, yes!
> I wasn't ready for—
> your friendship.

LUCIUS *(hurt but retaining playful tone)*
> "Friendship"—
> Oh.

KELLY
> I never misled you—

LUCIUS
> I must've misread you—

KELLY *(embarrassed, awkward)*
> It's just I'm not ready—

LUCIUS
> I mustn't be greedy—

KELLY
> Oh Lucius, please—
> It's not the time.

LUCIUS *(hurt with dignity)*
> It's the time but
> I'm not the man.

LUCIUS walks off. BUFFY and SARAH, who've been looking on, hurry over to him, and put their arms through his. THE SENATOR has been watching. KELLY is unaware of his presence. (ROY slips away.)

KELLY *(earnestly, passionately)*
> I don't know who I am—
> what I am—
> what the answer to the riddle is!
> Our lives are riddles, but who can know the answers?

(Pause)
> Why am I so happy?—I'm not in love.
> I only know the waves cry *I want! I am!*
> I only know I want to live forever and ever!

(Pause)
> Am I greedy, I want so much!

It frightens me, how much!
I want—all I can get.
I want to do all I can do.
I want to give all I can give.
I want to be all I can be.
There's no excuse now:
"You're a woman."
History's caught up with us now. You're a woman.
Politics?—a career in law?
history? journalism?—foreign service?
public health? teaching?
It frightens me to want so much!

(Pause)

No,
This *is* happiness,
to be a woman, living now,
and to want so much.

THE SENATOR *walks toward the water, sees a wild beach rose and takes one.*

SENATOR

How raw and beautiful this northern island—
how fierce the light, the salt air
and the bright fresh Atlantic stinging the eyes
and the white capped waves notched like sharks' teeth
and the beat! beat! beat! of the surf—
so brotherly, this world you want to sink your teeth into
and suck, and suck, and suck—
the bone's sweet marrow—
thrust yourself up to the hilt in it,
Oh Christ, Oh Christ, Oh Christ!

KELLY *(passionately)*

Why am I so happy, I'm not in love.
I only know the waves cry *I want, I am!*
I only know I want to live forever and ever.

THE SENATOR *now approaches* KELLY *directly. He is shy, or gives that impression.*

SENATOR

Kelly, is it?—Callie? *Kelly.*

KELLY (*a little coolly at first)*
>Elizabeth Anne Kelleher, Senator.
>Kelly's my schoolgirl name.

SENATOR
>But a name that suits you.

KELLY
>Yes? Why?

SENATOR
>Your eyes. Green?

(They gaze frankly at each other.)

KELLY
>And yours are blue—like washed glass.
>Bluer than your photographs.

SENATOR
>And bloodshot. Kelly, I'm so tired
>of traveling, of where I've come from
>and where I'm going. Here, there, up and
>down with the turning of the wheel,
>the wheel turning, always in motion
>both forward and back—
>like those gulls: when you first see them you see freedom,
>beauty in their wide wings' arc, later you see raw appetite,
>lashed to a wheel.
>And what loneliness raw ambition.

KELLY
>Lonely? You?

SENATOR
>Nothing is so lonely as the sound
>of your own words in your own ear.
>And the taste of wetted ashes.

KELLY
>Senator, what are you saying? you?

SENATOR
>Oh, you come to despise yourself—a little.
>When your words have changed so little.
>You despise yourself for your "celebrity"

for the reason others adore you.

KELLY
> You're joking?—that's it.

SENATOR
> I'm joking—that's it.

(He hands her the wild rose sprig.)
> This wild rose, it grows everywhere on the island.
> Isn't it beautiful! I saw it
> from the ferry, everywhere along the beach amid the dunes,
> *Rosa Virginia.* My heart lifted like a kid's.
> These little berries are rose hips.
> My grandmother used to make rose hip tea from them,
> at our family place on Cape Cod.

KELLY takes the wild rose sprig, winces and laughs as a thorn pierces her skin.

KELLY
> Oh—a thorn.

SENATOR
> Is your finger bleeding? God, I'm sorry—

THE SENATOR takes KELLY's hand as if to kiss away the blood; KELLY instinctively resists.

KELLY
> No I'm fine.

A sound of raised voices, hilarity close by. LUCIUS calls to KELLY.

LUCIUS *(voice)*
> Kelly? Kelly? Kelly?

KELLY hurries off; THE SENATOR looks after her.

SENATOR *(to himself)*
> Every journey should be a pilgrimage, and every destination
> sacred.

The scene fades even as a sound of voices and laughter comes up.

Scene 5: The Match

A doubles tennis match between THE SENATOR *and* ROY, LUCIUS *and* DWIGHT. *The others look on. The older men are the better, more strategic players; the younger men have more energy.* BUFFY, KELLY, SARAH *and others of the* CHORUS *watch attentively, and are quick to applaud, cheer, whistle, emit "Ohh's and Ahhhh's." (*CHORUS *in this scene is only women.)*

ROY
    We'll spin to see who serves, eh?

They spin a racket, and the older men get the serve. THE SENATOR *begins. He is an excellent player who places the ball so shrewdly in a corner of* LUCIUS's *court that* LUCIUS *misses wildly.*

CHORUS
    Fifteen-love!

LUCIUS & DWIGHT
    Damn! Damn! Damn! Damn!

CHORUS
    Thirty-love!
    Ball out! Looked in! Out—in—in—out—out—in—

There is a brief, fierce volley. ROY *slams the ball just across the net.*

LUCIUS
    Ball out.

ROY
    Looked in to me, kid.

CHORUS
    In? Out?
    Did you see—?
    Looked in/out to *me*.

SENATOR *(magnanimous)*
    Let's say out.

(Signaling to ROY, *"We'll concede."* ROY *irritably shrugs.)*

CHORUS
    Thirty-fifteen!

Game continues, with increasing ferocity. THE SENATOR's *serve is a furious one.*

BUFFY, KELLY & SARAH
   Men! Men! Look at them—men!
   The difference between us and them—
   the legs! the muscles! the thrust! the slam!
   Oh! Ow! Wow! Score!
   Slam! Bam! Thank you ma'am!
   They're out for blood. We play for fun.

THE SENATOR *makes the final point.* BUFFY *takes a photograph.*

The men wipe their faces with towels, drink thirstily from cans of beer, while the young women speak together sotto voce.

BUFFY
   Isn't the Senator terrific? For a guy his age.
   I mean, like, *wow.*
   He's a killer, you know? *Wow.*

KELLY & SARAH
   And a gentleman.

BUFFY
   And a gentlemen.

CHORUS
   A killer *and* a gentlemen.

The men change courts and continue the game, with increasing ferocity. LUCIUS *serves: his first serve is reckless, flamboyant, and it goes out of bounds; his second serve is more tentative, and* ROY *returns it with a hard drive.* LUCIUS *almost falls down trying to return it. Dialogue and* CHORUS *should be counterpoint.*

LUCIUS
   Damn!

DWIGHT
   C'mon, get hot, guy.

CHORUS
   Love-fifteen!

SENATOR
   Great shot, Roy.

LUCIUS *serves again, and again his serve is flamboyant—but it's in;* THE SENATOR *returns the ball into the net.*

CHORUS *(dramatically)*
> Fifteen-all!

DWIGHT
> That's more like it, man!

LUCIUS preening, serves again. A fierce rally.

CHORUS
> Mmmmm men, men. Look at them—men!
> They're out for blood.

LUCIUS makes his point. The older men are getting winded.

LUCIUS *(boyish fervor, elation)*
> Hah!

CHORUS
> Forty-fifteen!
> Set!

DWIGHT
> Fantastic!

LUCIUS
> Man, see them run, yeah!

ROY
> Damn! Damn! Damn! Damn!

DWIGHT serves and there is another fierce rally. THE SENATOR strikes the ball desperately and it sails out of bounds.

The young men celebrate tactlessly by clapping each other on the back; the older men are panting, sweating.

SENATOR
> Hell, it's only a game.

As the third game begins the CHORUS moves away. ROY serves, his anger impeding his skill; the ball slams into the net.

ROY
> Damn! Damn!

LUCIUS *(almost, not quite, mocking)*
> Man, it's only a game.

The tennis match continues in a stylized manner; the older men are increasingly winded, uncoordinated. The young men preen, strut, grin.

Lights dim on the tennis court and come up strongly on the young women who are setting things out on the picnic table; and as they do so, drink from cans of beer.

BUFFY
>They'll keep it up till they drop.
>I've seen Roy play way past dark.
>It's like making love—just keeping it up.
>Keeping it *up up up* till you scream.

KELLY (*laughing, lightheaded from beer*):
>Oh Buffy! The things that you say!

BUFFY
>I speak the truth.

KELLY
>Such as—

BUFFY
>The Senator's got his eye on you.

KELLY
>Don't be silly. It's—only a game.

BUFFY
>Life and death—and only a game.

(On the court)

LUCIUS
>Point! Point! Point! Point!

DWIGHT
>Forty-fifteen, forty-fifteen, forty-fifteen, forty-fifteen.

LUCIUS & DWIGHT
>Game! Set! Match!

ROY
>Damn! Damn! Damn! Damn!

The scene fades with KELLY's *somewhat wild laughter (as, light-headed, she sinks onto a bench) and from the tennis court (where lights might blaze up suddenly)* LUCIUS's *cry "Point!" and* DWIGHT's *cry "forty-fifteen!" in gloating, boyish triumph over the panting older men.*

Scene 6: The Secret Kiss

Lights up on KELLY *alone. She lies on a bench dozing in the sun.* THE
SENATOR *appears at stage left, wiping his face and head with a towel; he
has just come from the tennis court and defeat. He observes the sleeping
young woman through a scrim.*

SENATOR
> It seems that I have come this long way
> for a purpose—
> for her?
> To be cleansed—
> to be chastened—
> reborn.
> God grant me guilt, but also forgiveness.
> God help me, I can't help myself.

THE SENATOR *pushes through the scrim decisively; leans over* KELLY *and
kisses the hollow of her neck. He then backs off and watches her as she
stirs, wakes, glances up, doesn't see him.*

KELLY *rises unsteadily, hugging herself, shivering. Then she smiles.*

KELLY
> I feel as if a spell has come upon me—
> I'm so frightened,
> and so happy.
> I'm not in love—yet I'm happy.
> Or am I in love?—and so happy.

KELLY *hides her face in a girlish gesture, laughs.*

As KELLY *exits,* THE SENATOR *exits with her, behind the scrim. He is
observing her closely but she doesn't see him.*

Scene fades.

Scene 7: Barbecue

*Early evening. A barbecue supper, with a good deal of drinking (wine,
beer, scotch). A gay, festive atmosphere. Everyone is present, with* ROY
overseeing the barbecue and BUFFY *playing hostess (though rather giddily);*

THE SENATOR holding forth, perhaps inadvertently. Questions are being directed at him. (LUCIUS is jealously attentive of KELLY, who stares at THE SENATOR as if mesmerized by him.)

BUFFY

> More, more, more, more, more, more,
> more? more Tex-mex, more ribs, more
> chicken, more good red carnivore meat?
> More corn, more potato salad, more
> coleslaw beet salad, curried rice and hot dogs.
> More wine? champagne? more beer, cocaine. There's more,
> lots more, and Häagen-Dazs to follow. More.

LUCIUS *(aggressively, overlapping with BUFFY)*

> What I fail to see, Senator, is why you
> agreed to give aid to the Contras—

SENATOR

> I've explained my position many times—

BUFFY

> Not politics, please!
> Not today!

ROY *(overlapping)*

> Hey kid, give the Senator a break:
> he's on your side, and you know it.
> Cut the shit—you know it.

LUCIUS

> What do you mean, "he's on my side."
> Spell out to me, sir, what you mean.

ROY

> Give us all a break, it's the Fourth of July.
> Anyway, you know what I mean.

BUFFY, SARAH & OTHERS *(overlapping with ROY)*

> No politics, please!
> Not today, please!
> Not here, please!

SENATOR

> Damned if I do,
> and damned if I don't.

(Trying for a genial tone: as he becomes increasingly intoxicated his emotions swing from boyish-sweet to masculine-aggressive with little transition; always, he is an actor striving to milk the most from a situation, win his listeners' hearts)

LUCIUS
> "You know what I mean"—no I don't
> "know what you mean."
> I do know what you mean:
> and I resent it.

KELLY
> Lucius, that's rude.

LUCIUS
> So I am rude,
> I'm crude.
> Not like whitey—
> who's so subtle.

BUFFY, SARAH & OTHERS
> Oh no.
> Not today, please!
> Politics at our party—
> that's death.

LUCIUS *(standing off from the others, impassioned)*
> Senator, that Affirmative Action crap in which
> you liberals believe—
> I resent, and I despise. I may be "black"
> in your eyes, but I am "Lucius Smith" in my own.
> My father is a doctor, and my mother's a professor
> at Vassar and I do not need, nor do I want, your
> liberal condescension.
> I do not need, nor do I want,
> your privileged-Caucasian charity.
> I am a research chemist at MIT and I made my own way and
> I did it and not my fucking *skin.*

SENATOR *(miming applause)*
> Young man, you belong in Washington.
> As a most eloquent voice of your generation.

KELLY *(passionately, but not adversarial)*
>Senator, there is no such thing as "our generation."
>Not for us.

LUCIUS and the others murmur agreement.

SENATOR *(staring at KELLY)*
>Well, then—Kelly Kelleher!
>I stand corrected.

BUFFY
>Let's change the subject,
>our minds will follow.

BUFFY & CHORUS
>No more politics, please!
>Not today, please!
>It's a glorious Fourth of July
>we celebrate without remembering why— *(DWIGHT's aside)*
>Who's for more barbecue? more drink? more wine? more beer?
>>more champagne?

Everyone except KELLY takes more to eat and drink. THE SENATOR has pulled his chair up close to hers, drink in hand.

BUFFY
>Oh!—terrific photo opportunity!
>Everybody SMILE PLEASE!

BUFFY brandishes the camera. THE SENATOR stiffens.

BUFFY
>Oh, Senator, smile please.
>Do smile, please.
>Such a handsome man
>can't be camera-shy!

ROY deftly straightens THE SENATOR's hair, removes a bottle of beer from his hand as BUFFY snaps a picture. All smile.

BUFFY
>Now *me* me me. Don't forget me. Now me Now me Now me.

BUFFY hands the camera to ROY and squeezes between THE SENATOR and KELLY, sitting on the ground, hugging her knees. ROY peers through the viewfinder. All smile, even THE SENATOR—though smile is forced.

ROY
>Smile please.

ROY & SENATOR
>We love the public eye,
>but not public censure.
>We all want our picture in the papers
>but we want to write the story.

Blinding camera flash as of cosmic magnitude.

BUFFY
>More wine, more beer, more champagne, who's for more
>>barbecue?
>It's a glorious Fourth of July!

Scene fades.

Scene 8: The Seduction

THE SENATOR *and* KELLY *are walking along the beach at sunset. Sand dunes, wild beach rose, stunted jack pine, the break of the waves. And wind.* THE SENATOR *wears a sweater over his T-shirt,* KELLY *wears a coarse-knit tunic or a shawl over her flimsy summer clothes.* THE SENATOR *is an ardent suitor, but takes care not to overwhelm* KELLY *too quickly.*

SENATOR
>How young you are, Kelly Kelleher!—
>to have spoken so wisely as you did.

KELLY
>Young? I'm not young, Senator, at all.
>I don't feel young, at all.

SENATOR *(tenderly, surprised)*
>Why do you say that?
>Has someone hurt you? A man?
>Are you in love, or—

KELLY *(with dignity)*
>I never speak of it.

SENATOR
>That young black man Lucius—
>he isn't—?

KELLY
My lover?
No. I have no lover.

SENATOR
But tell me anything about yourself, Kelly!—
Kelly with the sea-green eyes—

KELLY *(laughing)*
They're more pebble-green, Senator—

SENATOR
Kelly who has done a thesis on—me?
What could you have found to say?

KELLY
"Jeffersonian Idealism and New Deal Pragmatism:
American Liberalism in Crisis—"

SENATOR *(taken just slightly aback)*
"Jeffersonian Idealism"—yes—
"—In Crisis"—yes—

(Pause)
Well, I hope you earned an A.

KELLY
In fact, an A+.

SENATOR
What a coincidence, then!
You...here. In this wild, beautiful place.
And me.

(Pause)
Tell me who you are, Kelly,
so that I may know who I am,
and why I've come here,
today.

KELLY
What can I say?
My background is like Buffy's—
my father is a good man, but conservative—
resentful of change. So frightened of change!
He gives money to politicians to do his hating for him.

SENATOR
>   Poor deluded man!—and yet,
>   he loves you.

KELLY
>   He loves Daddy's girl
>   who is these days, Senator
>   not quite me.

SENATOR
>   And your mother, Kelly?

KELLY
>   My mother loves me—as a daughter.
>   Her baby.
>   She doesn't know *me*.
>   She doesn't always approve of *me*.

SENATOR
>   And why is that?

KELLY *(recklessly)*
>   Because I'm not her.

(Pause)
>   I live in Boston—alone.
>   I write for *The American Way*—*The Nation*—
>   I've been a paralegal—
>   a Crisis Center administrator—

(Laughs)
>   Sometimes, I even earn a salary.

SENATOR
>   Kelly, how would you like
>   to come to Washington, and work for me?
>   work *with* me?

KELLY *(startled)*
>   With—you?

SENATOR
>   On my staff—
>   research committee preparing for the upcoming primaries—

KELLY *(covering her confusion with a gay, flirtatious air)*
>   Well, Senator—that depends.

SENATOR
    "Depends"—?

KELLY
    On the terms.

SENATOR
    Dear, you're cold!—are these goose bumps?

THE SENATOR draws his fingers lightly along KELLY's arm. She shivers the more at his touch, but does not draw away.

KELLY
    No. I'm fine.

SENATOR
    Would you like to—turn back?

KELLY
    Turn back? NO.

(Suddenly hiding her face, laughing)

SENATOR *(smiling)*
    What's so funny, dear?

KELLY *(giddy as a child)*
    "Goose bumps"—the word!—
    it used to make me laugh when I was a little girl—

SENATOR
    "Goose bumps"—dear Kelly!

THE SENATOR caresses her arms as if to warm them; suddenly takes hold of her shoulders and kisses her. After a moment's hesitation, KELLY slips her arms around his neck in a mutual passionate embrace.

Scene fades.

Scene 9

At the cottage, as dusk comes on, the others are dancing. The beat is erotic and suggestive. LUCIUS cuts in upon BUFFY and ROY, to sweep BUFFY laughingly away.

THE SENATOR and KELLY return from their walk on the beach. KELLY moves apart from THE SENATOR as if she's shy of being seen with him so intimately; but, with the others paired off, and the mood of the dance so erotic, she has no choice but to return to THE SENATOR's *company.*

BUFFY
>Just in time!—come join us.

ROY *(sly innuendo)*
>Just in time, Senator!
>Tide's out, moon's up.

SARAH
>What's your favorite music, Senator?
>We have all kinds.

LUCIUS
>All ages,
>all persuasions.
>All rhythms and rhymes.

THE SENATOR *joins* SARAH *at the tape deck. He chooses a selection and turns to* KELLY *who, hesitantly at first, then decisively, moves into his arms.*

Music. All dance, with THE SENATOR *and* KELLY *at the center. A romantic-erotic moment in which it seems that* THE SENATOR *and* KELLY *are very well matched.*

Lights fade upon dancing.

ACT II

Scene 10

Lights up on ROY *outside the St. John house. He speaks as if addressing* THE SENATOR *in a pleading, reproachful tone.*

ROY
>Senator where are you going so soon?
>Senator why are you leaving so soon?
>This isn't like you, This isn't like you, This isn't like you.
>The greater part of our profession is, after all, discretion.
>Senator, a great man must never disappear.

At the St. John house. Dusk. In the distance, at Brockden's Landing, fireworks have begun. A shift in tone.

KELLY *(breathless)*
> How the breakers sound—I *want*, I *am*! I want, I am! I want I am!
> How light comes over the sea, afire!
> The secret of love is the secret of the sea:
> *every moment is now—*
> *we live only now—*
> *rejoice in now*, rejoice in now—
> *God is now*, is now, is now, is now, is now, is now!

KELLY moves off, to enter the house; LUCIUS waylays her. (THE SENATOR observes.)

LUCIUS
> Kelly, I've been looking for you.
> You aren't—leaving?

KELLY *(quickly)*
> Lucius,
> I can't talk now, I'm sorry.

LUCIUS
> Is it with *him*?
> You're leaving the island with him?
(Accusing)
> I came here because you were going to be here
> and now—you're leaving with *him*?
> Mr. Senator?

KELLY
> I'm sorry you don't understand—
> I can't talk now.

LUCIUS
> You're leaving Mt. Grayling Island?—with *him*?
> Going where?

KELLY
> Is my life your business, Lucius?
> We're friends, but—

LUCIUS
> Friends but—

(Impulsively tries to restrain her)
> Kelly, the man's been drinking all day.
> Don't you care, don't you see?
> —I'll go talk to him.

KELLY *(excited)*
> You have no right, Lucius! You
> aren't my lover, Lucius. You don't know me. You don't own
>> me.
> Let me go!

KELLY *pulls free of* LUCIUS, *hurries into the house.*

LUCIUS *(calling after, hurt and angry)*
> That's for damn sure: I don't
> know you, you don't know me.
> You never gave me a chance.
> I'm not a U.S. Senator.

LUCIUS *turns to see* THE SENATOR, *extreme stage right. The men stare at each other wordless for a beat or two.*

THE SENATOR *comes forward;* LUCIUS *confronts him, with nervous bravado. Their exchange is staccato and rapier-like. At first,* LUCIUS *holds his own; then, as if beaten back by the force of the older man's personality, he begins to weaken and retreat.*

LUCIUS
> Senator!
> You and Kelly are leaving us
> and going—where? Sir?

SENATOR
> Where?
> What's that to you?

LUCIUS
> You don't know Kelly—and
> you don't deserve Kelly, Senator.

SENATOR
> And you're thinking, Lucius,
> you do?

LUCIUS
> I'm thinking—yes, I do.

SENATOR *(as if reasonably, but with authority)*
>But, that's up to Kelly,
>isn't it?

LUCIUS *(beginning to waver)*
>Kelly doesn't know!
>Kelly doesn't know *you*.

SENATOR
>And you're thinking, Lucius—
>you do?

LUCIUS
>I'm *thinking*, Senator—
>what you are.

SENATOR
>No, you don't know me.
>But that's up to Kelly
>And not to you.

The men stare at each other. LUCIUS *retreats. Lights fade slowly.*

Lights up in the guest room that is KELLY's. *She has hastily changed into a white summer dress that shows her shoulders and part of her back. Regarding herself in an old-fashioned dressmaker's mirror. (THE SENATOR observes, unseen.)*

KELLY
>How the breakers sound—I *want*, I *am*! I want, I am! I want, I
>   am!
>How light comes over the sea, afire!
>The secret of love is the secret of the sea:
>*every moment is now*— Every moment is now—
>*we live only now*—rejoice in now.
>*God is now*, is now—

(Pause)

>Don't expect anything, Kelly—really.
>Nothing will come of it, Kelly—probably.
>It's an—adventure.

BUFFY *enters the room. She is both excited for her friend, and apprehensive. Perhaps, too, slightly jealous.*

BUFFY

> He told me—you're leaving? you and him? now?
> for the 8:20 ferry? for Boothbay Harbor?
> Oh but Kelly, why now?
> it's late, there's tomorrow—
> he's been drinking all day—

KELLY

> Don't be silly, he's fine,
> I'm fine, I'll call you tomorrow,
> I might be back, and there's Sunday—
> Oh Buffy—it's an adventure!
> I can't say no.

BUFFY

> But why *now*, Kelly? *tonight*?
> It's almost eight—

KELLY hastily throws things into a small suitcase.

KELLY

> He's asked me, and I want to go.

BUFFY

> No, Kelly.
> Wait for tomorrow! wait, wait, wait!
> Wait for tomorrow, wait, wait, wait for tomorrow!
> Don't let the man rush you,
> don't let the man push you. Don't let him push you, Kelly.
> Wait, wait, wait!

KELLY *(an almost gay, defiant fatalism)*

> If I don't do as he asks, Buffy
> there won't be any tomorrow.
> You know that, Buffy, I can't wait. I can't wait.

Stage right, THE SENATOR appears, prepared to leave. He has changed back into his original clothes, but is tieless and carries his seersucker coat over his shoulder, a drink in hand.

SENATOR

> Kelly, Kelly, come with me.
> Kelly don't be late. Kelly come with me. Kelly we'll be late.

LUCIUS appears, stage left, looking on in angry disapproval.

LUCIUS

Kelly, Kelly, don't trust him!
Kelly, Kelly, be careful, don't trust him, Kelly—Mr. Senator.
Kelly, Kelly, don't trust the Senator.

SENATOR

Kelly of the sea-green eyes—
Come with me, Kelly. Come with me. Come with me, Kelly.

KELLY

I'm coming—Senator, Senator. I'm ready Senator, I won't be
late.
Senator, I want to live forever and ever, Senator. I'm coming,
Senator.

SENATOR

Kelly, come with me.
It's time!—we'll be late.

LUCIUS

You don't know the man, Kelly—
"The Senator"—
Don't trust him!

KELLY *(to THE SENATOR)*

I'm here, I'm coming—
I won't be late!

KELLY and BUFFY embrace, in farewell. As KELLY hurries to THE SENATOR:

BUFFY *(looking after KELLY)*

You're the one, the one he has chosen—
tonight.
You're the girl, the girl he has chosen—
tonight, I know.
Tomorrow's too late.

(Pause)

A woman makes a man want her—she can't turn back.

(Pause)

Oh Kelly!—
you—and *the Senator!*—
What an adventure!

LUCIUS
> It's a mistake, a mistake, a mistake.

SARAH & BUFFY
> Oh, Lucius.
> We'll find you another girl tonight.
> Kelly's the one he has chosen. Let's be happy for her.
> An adventure, an adventure.

LUCIUS
> A mistake, a mistake.

LUCIUS has retreated. Lights down on BUFFY.

KELLY has run to join THE SENATOR, carrying her overnight case; THE SENATOR seizes her hand, kisses it.

Scene fades.

Scene 11: Lost

KELLY and THE SENATOR in his rented car, which he drives fast, and erratically. He is holding a plastic cup of Scotch from which, awkwardly, he sips from time to time. It is dark now, and the moon is prominent. Only the car's lurching headlights illuminate the narrow road. KELLY gripping a strap of her seat belt, is both exhilarated and frightened.

Stage left, rear, through a scrim, a CHORUS of women.

We hear laughter: THE SENATOR's louder than KELLY's.

We hear jazzy radio music. THE SENATOR fiddles with the radio dial even as the car swerves.

SENATOR
> We're losing the station—
> Damn—Damn.
> You try—

KELLY tunes the radio, there's a burst of jazz, then static.

SENATOR
> Damn.
> Turn it off.

KELLY does so. She is thrown to one side as THE SENATOR *makes a sharp turn.*

KELLY
>This road—
>oh be careful—

SENATOR *(an annoyed chuckle)*
>Relax, dear.
>I've been driving since I was fifteen.

KELLY
>Yes, yes, but I think—

SENATOR *(reaching out to squeeze* KELLY's *knee, thigh)*
>Dear girl just relax.
>We'll get there, and
>we'll get there on time.

KELLY *(to herself)*
>I'm the one, the one
>he has chosen—I can't turn back.
>The spell is upon me, I've made him love me—
>I can't turn back.
>In a speeding Toyota
>in the night in the marshland
>on the way to the ferry and Boothbay
>Harbor and—Washington?—

(Breathless pause)
>Except is this the way?
>this terrible road?
>no lights, no other cars—
>will I anger him if I say the word "lost"?

CHORUS
>You don't want to anger them
>you don't want to upset them
>you don't want to challenge them
>you don't want to undermine them
>even the nice ones
>even the really really really, really nice ones
>you don't want to make them doubt
>their MASCULINITY.

A man can turn mean if he is made to doubt
his MASCULINITY.
It's the DEATH OF LOVE if a man is made to doubt
his MASCULINITY—
even the nice ones.

KELLY *(to herself)*
Don't anger. Don't upset. Don't
ask. It's fine. You know it's fine.
An adventure. Why not an adventure. Why not you,
for once. *You're* the one—
tonight.

The car swerves suddenly.

SENATOR
Damn! Damn! Damn! Damn! God damn!

KELLY *(overlapping)*
Oh!—watch out—

SENATOR *(annoyed, words slurred)*
No problem, just relax,
for Christ's sake, relax.
Kelly, is it—relax.
We'll get there, and
we'll get there on time.

KELLY *(hesitantly)*
Yes, Yes, Yes
but the road is
so—
rutted and narrow
narrow and twisted and rutted
and dark, dark, dark, dark.

SENATOR
This is the right road—I'm certain.
This is the way I came—I'm certain.
Just relax, will you?—I'm certain.
We'll get there, and
we'll get there on time.

KELLY
Oh yes!—I'm not worried

except the road, no
lights, no
other cars—
the swamp,
the trees—
so many dead trees—

(Pause)

Oh Senator I think
I think
I wonder if, if
we're—lost?

SENATOR *(impatiently)*

Lost?—we're not lost.
It isn't a habit of mine to get lost.
We're not lost, we're not lost, we're not lost, we're not lost,
we're not—

*Another sharp turn. THE SENATOR loses control of the car which crashes
through a low guard rail and overturns in a deep stream.*

Lights out as KELLY screams.

Scene 12: The Escape

*As the car sinks further in a deep, fast-running stream, THE SENATOR
and KELLY struggle to free themselves. Action is confused, neither is fully
conscious. The car has listed to its passenger's side which means THE
SENATOR must force his door open against the weight of gravity and the
weight of the water; while KELLY, at a disadvantage, is beneath. She clings
to him, his arm, his sleeve. THE SENATOR strains to lift himself free by
way of the steering wheel and KELLY herself.*

SENATOR *(moaning)*

Oh God, oh God—

KELLY

Don't leave me!
Help me!
Wait, wait, wait, wait—

THE SENATOR *shoves her desperately away; in order to get out of the car, he steps on her, kicks her head, as she grabs frantically at his leg, his ankle, his foot. His shoe comes off in her hand.*

THE SENATOR *escapes the car. (He manages to swim to land, and collapses exhausted, water in his lungs, on the bank amid the tangled vegetation.)* KELLY *remains, trapped.*

KELLY
>Help me, help me, help me, help me,
>help me, help me, help me, help me—

(To herself)
>Will I die—like this?

The scene fades to black amid a delirium of roaring churning water.

Scene 13: Black Water I

While THE SENATOR *lies (in darkness, and motionless) on the bank,* KELLY *alternately struggles to free herself and rests. Water has begun to seep into the car from numerous fissures in the windshield and elsewhere. A pocket of air remains in the car since the windows and doors are shut.*

At the rear, beyond a scrim, the CHORUS *seems to observe.*

CHORUS
>He's gone, he's gone, but will dive back to save you.
>He's gone, he's gone, but will dive back to save you.
>Unless he's gone for help—to save you.
>Have faith!

KELLY *(to herself)*
>He's gone, but—
>he'll be back—
>he won't leave me—
>he didn't mean to hurt me—
>my head, my shoulder—
>oh what is this—
>*(Brandishing his shoe, with a wild near-hysterical laugh)*
>Is this his shoe!

KELLY loses control and cries out in terror.

KELLY
>Help! I'm here!
>Help me! I don't want to die.
>I'm here—!
(To herself, panicked but calm)
>Yes but where is here,
>upside down in a car
>in water, black water—
>yes but no—
>there's air—
>I can breathe—
>I'll be all right,
>he's gone for help,
>it will be only a matter of minutes.

CHORUS
>Only a matter of minutes.
>Don't doubt. Never doubt.
>Have faith.
>He'll be back to save you, save you, save you—
>You're an American girl, what's to fear?
>YOU'RE THE ONE HE HAS CHOSEN. THE ONE HE HAS
>CHOSEN.

THE SENATOR crawls on hands and knees; manages to rise to his feet unsteadily. He is coughing, choking, vomiting; in a delirium of his own. Panic, terror, guilt and an instinct for sheer self-survival contend in him in this moment of crisis.

SENATOR
>Where am I, what
>has happened—
>where is this—
>black water rising—
>wetted ashes—
>a river?—
>the car?—
>the girl?—
>the girl—

A look of horror. THE SENATOR *stands frozen.*

Lights fade on THE SENATOR *and come up on* KELLY.

KELLY
> Help me—
> I'm here, help me I'm here—
> Help me, help me, help me, help me, help me, help me—

(Silence)

KELLY *(to herself)*
> What is it that holds me, this
> tight band, this
> band around my chest that holds me—
> my shoulder—
> it's broken?
> my forehead, my head where
> he kicked me—
> is it blood?
> my leg is pinned, my knee
> is crushed—
> but no pain—
> pitch black—
> or am I blind?
> I've soiled myself—
> this water seeping,
> trickling—
> am I upside down?
> and where is up?
> where is the air?
> where is the moon?
> if I can see the moon
> I'm still alive—

(Voice rising)
> Where is the moon? moon? moon? moon? moon? moon?

Lights out to blackness.

Scene 14: Black Water II

KELLY is trapped in the car as the water level rises. She struggles fitfully, exhausts herself and rests; struggles again. The atmosphere is increasingly hallucinatory and threatening.

CHORUS
> She should not have angered him—you know how men are.
> She should not have said the word "lost."
> You know how men are. It's the death of love if a man is made
> > to doubt his MASCULINITY—

> As the black water filled her lungs, and she died.

KELLY *(fiercely)*
> No!—I can hold myself up,
> like this,
> there's air, a pocket of air—
> air-bubble—
> precious, floating—
> if I lift, lift myself—
> But—where is the moon?
> Where is the moon?

Abrupt change of mood. BUFFY and SARAH appear.

BUFFY & SARAH
> No!—it hasn't happened yet.
> It's blazing noon, the wind just right,
> one of those days in Maine the light so clear
> it hurts—
> *You know you want to live forever*, and ever and ever.
> So we're teasing Kelly, she's sort of—
> old-fashioned, shy around men—
> shy about sex—

BUFFY and SARAH retreat in peals of girlish laughter.

KELLY *(in a bright, enthusiastic voice)*
> and then I met—The Senator!—on the Fourth of July.
> At Buffy's house—you know, it's gorgeous!
> He seemed to—like me. We were sort of—
> attracted to one another.
> Oh, I didn't expect anything!—

just an adventure!—
He asked me would I come work for him in Washington.
I said, I said—
(*Voice rises wildly*)
"Senator, that depends on the terms!"

CHORUS (*echoing, overlapping*)
Senator, that
—depends on the terms!
As the black water filled her lungs,
and she died.

KELLY (*defiantly*)
No! I'm strong,
my heart is strong,
he called me young, I *am* young,
I mean to put up a damn good fight!

(*Tone changes, anecdotal*)
Yes it was an adventure—turned into a nightmare.
So fast!
I was trapped in the car—the car was submerged—
water seeping in I was blind, I was panicked my knee was
pinned but thank God *he* was able to escape and pull me out—

SENATOR (*voice*)
Kelly?—Kelly, Kelly—
Kelly?—come to me!
Kelly of the sea-green eyes! I'm here, come to me.

KELLY
Senator, Senator, here I am!
I'm so frightened,
yet so happy.
I'm so frightened, here's my hand.

SENATOR (*voice*)
Come to me, here's my hand. Never, never doubt me.
Kelly of the sea-green eyes. Kelly of the sea-green eyes.

KELLY
Senator, I would never, never doubt you!

MOTHER & FATHER (*voices*)
Kelly?—Kelly?—Kelly?

(Repeated)

KELLY *(excitedly)*
>Mother?—Father?—Mother?—Father?—Mother?—Father?
>Where are you?

MOTHER *and* FATHER *appear in the shadows stage right.*

FATHER *(jagged, atonal)*
>Kelly my daughter
>my daughter my baby—

KELLY
>Mommy, Daddy, Mommy, Daddy—
>Mommy, Daddy please forgive me.
>He tried to save me,
>oh many times
>to save me, oh many times to save me,
>it was an accident, nobody's fault—

FATHER
>Kelly my daughter, my daughter,
>my baby—Kelly, my daughter,
>my daughter, my baby—

MOTHER *(weeping)*
>—love you, Kelly—
>my little girl—
>when they brought you to me—
>in the hospital—
>they said, they said, they said—"a baby girl"—
>never so happy in all my—

KELLY
>Mommy, Daddy, Mommy, Daddy, Mommy, Daddy
>please take me home—
>don't let me die—Mommy, Daddy
>I love you—

MOTHER *and* FATHER *retreat.*

CHORUS
>As the black water filled her lungs,
>and she died.

KELLY
>NO!

(Eager, pleading)
>Senator?—my hand—
>here!
>I would never doubt *you*! I'm the one. The one you have
>>chosen. I can't turn back.
>The spell is upon me. I've made you want me, I can't turn
>>back.
>Senator?—Senator here?
>I would never doubt you.

CHORUS
>As the black water filled her lungs,
>and she died.

KELLY *(resisting)*
>No!
>I can see now—
>he's here—
>diving to rescue me—
(Lifting her arms)
>Senator, here—
>Here I am, here—

THE SENATOR *has reached a highway. There he cowers in a ditch to avoid being seen; runs limping across a road to a telephone booth. Panting and desperate as he fumbles to dial the phone.*

SENATOR
>God have mercy—
>my hour of need—
>You have broken
>me.
>I can hear my enemies now
>I can see the headlines now
>vultures feeding on me
>a great man cast down never redeemed
>never exalted
>never nominated by my party
>never President of the United States
>no!

God help me.
God help me, help me, help me, help me, help me, help me—

THE SENATOR *has dialed* BUFFY's *house. We see guests on the terrace;* SARAH *has answered, amid a good deal of party noise, and calls* ROY *to the phone.*

THE SENATOR *and* ROY *speak in rapid, conspiratorial tones.*

SENATOR
Roy, it's me—and I'm in bad trouble.
There's been an accident—

ROY
You! an accident!
Where are you?

SENATOR *(agitated, pleading)*
A terrible accident—
The girl, the girl, the girl, the girl, she's dead—

ROY *(stunned)*
Dead!

SENATOR
She was drunk, she got emotional,
she grabbed at the wheel—

ROY *(overlapping)*
Don't tell me over the phone—

SENATOR *(overlapping)*
No one must know, no one must see me—
what can we do—
the scandal, the papers—
my enemies—
"manslaughter"—

ROY *(with authority)*
Stop! Someone might see you! Someone might hear you!
Just tell me where you are for Christ's sake
and I'll come and get you!

KELLY
Senator, Senator
never doubted—

I believe!
All night last night the bellbuoy rang of fog and danger
now the light breaks everywhere.
There are no shadows.
I can see the moon—

CHORUS
You're an American girl, you love your life.
You're an American girl, you believe you have chosen it.
You're an American girl.
You *are* the one he has chosen.

As the black water filled her lungs, and she died.

Scene fades.

THE END

The Passion of Henry David Thoreau

A Play in Two Acts

"Life too near paralyzes Art. Long these matters refuse
to be recorded, except in the invisible colors of Memory."
—Ralph Waldo Emerson

CHARACTERS:
Henry David Thoreau (1817–1862)
John Thoreau (1815–1842)
Ellen Sewall, several years younger than Thoreau
Rachel, Ellen's age
Lidian Emerson, several years younger than Emerson
Ralph Waldo Emerson (1803–1882)
Margaret Fuller (1810–1850)
Bronson Alcott (1799–1888)
James Russell Lowell (1819–1891)
Sam Staples, youthful middle-age
John Brown (1800–1859)
Prisoner, no specific age
Anonymous Man, Anonymous Woman (voices)
Dancers

*The play can be cast with eight actors, with the suggested doubling of
John/Lowell, Alcott/Staples, Prisoner/Emerson, and Staples/Brown. The
dancers of Scene 2 may be merely suggested.*

PLACE: Concord, Massachusetts

TIME: 1838–1862

ACT I

Prologue: "When I Died..."

Lights up. Very bright, in a blindingly white space. Center-stage, HENRY DAVID THOREAU lies on his deathbed. A curtain partway around the bed. This is no clearly defined room but has the disorienting look of a dream. A door, stage right, unobtrusive in the wall; an unusually tall, narrow window stage left, to the rear of the bed, with a filmy white curtain. Beside the bed is a plain wooden table with an enamel basin, a wadded white towel, a vase with a single dwarf iris in it, and an untidy pile of manuscript pages and books. THOREAU is pale, with a hectic flush in his cheeks; clean-shaven and gaunt; his large, dark eyes glisten with fever. He wears trousers and a long-sleeved white undershirt; his feet are bare. White light illuminates his body. A filmy curtain stirs in the breeze.

Silence. Then THOREAU's hoarse, irregular breathing (amplified). In this fever dream everything is exaggerated. THOREAU is writing fiercely in a journal on his lap, with a yellow pencil.

THOREAU *(an air of self determination)*: "I think it will be today— May 6, 1862. When I died. 259 Main Street, Concord, Massachusetts—where I died. Forty-four years, ten months. All accounts paid." *(Interrupted by coughing)*

The curtain stirs with an ominous life of its own. The Universal Lyre is heard. This is an exquisitely sweet but elusive melody, atonal, mysterious; a vibratory, bell-like hum. [See appendix.]

THOREAU: Am I dreaming?—
   I'm *not* dreaming—
   This is my brother John's former bed, and this is my brother
      John's former room.
   I am Henry David, I am at peace, I am unafraid.
   Death is—nothing to me.

As the Universal Lyre rises, THOREAU becomes more agitated.

THOREAU: No—I'm going to M-Minnesota.
   I have no plans to die, I'M GOING TO MINNESOTA.
   THREE HUNDRED MILES UP THE MINNESOTA RIVER BY
      STEAMER...
   (Pause) Unless I've already been.

THOREAU has dropped his pencil, which falls to the floor beside the bed and rolls. He leans over to retrieve it and begins coughing. THOREAU covers his mouth with the towel and when he brings it away we see a spot of bright blood. THOREAU wads the towel up roughly and tosses it down in disgust.

THOREAU *(fevered, writing in journal)*:
   "I stand in awe of my body, this matter to which I am bound
      has become so strange to me.
   Talk of mysteries!—Think of our life in Nature!—
   The *solid* earth! the *actual* world! *Who* are we?
   Where are we? Am I—Henry Thoreau—to deliquesce and
      scatter like milkweed seed blown by the wind?
   Except *my* seed has found no fertile soil." *(Pause)*
   No: strike that. Damned self-pity. *(Tearing page
   out of the journal and crumpling it.)*
   "When a man dies, he bites the dust." *That's* so.
   (Writing in journal, inspired)
   "There is as much comfort in perfect disease
      as in perfect health." *That's* so—almost.
   "To die, you must first have lived." *That's* so.
   But have I lived? And what is life…?
   (Squinting at the window)
   A cruel jest, to die in May. The light so piercing—
   I feel such yearning, such desire!
   A boy of fourteen mad to mate with—anything!
   (Pause)
   I *did* go to Minnesota, last June. I remember.
   I *did* journey three hundred miles up the Minnesota River.
   But there was no cure for my lungs. My trip was cut short.
   And now I am home. *(Pause)*

The wind blows the door open. Lights quiver.

THOREAU *(trying to contain terror)*: Who—? Is someone—?

The doorway is empty, darkness lies beyond.

THOREAU *(on his feet, defensive and angry)*: It's too soon!
   I have work to do, I am not ready.
   I am unafraid of that other shore but I will pass to it WHEN I
      AM READY.

The Universal Lyre rises hauntingly.

Lights out.

Scene 1: "Woods-Burner"

The Universal Lyre of the Prologue shifts to a fire alarm. A lurid red light illuminates the stage.

JOHN THOREAU, HENRY's elder brother, a youth of twenty in this scene, is squatting extreme stage left.

JOHN *(laughing):* His first public act—by accident, playing with fire, he sets ablaze three hundred acres of forest!

As HENRY THOREAU, a lanky adolescent, runs crouching, slapping at smoldering clothing, to hide extreme stage right as if behind a bush. He watches the fire with terror and fascination. Siren, men's shouts.

JOHN: *This,* you can be sure he won't write about in *Walden.*

Lights out.

Scene 2: Animal

Darkness. Bright, lively music. Lights up on young dancers in contredanse, or square dance, formation. (This is a folk dance in which couples face one another in two lines or in a square. Dancing is animated, good-spirited. Music may be provided by a fiddle, concertina, fife, small drums.) Of the young men dancers, one is JOHN THOREAU; of the young women, one is ELLEN SEWALL. They are not paired in the dance.

Stage right, HENRY DAVID THOREAU appears. In his early twenties. Lean, sinewy-muscular, plainly clothed, with long, ragged, windblown hair. Not conventionally handsome but striking; childlike with eagerness and passion; critical; at once shy and aggressive; "mystical" yet hot-blooded, impulsive, and erotic. When excited, he stammers slightly. He is staring at ELLEN SEWALL.

ELLEN SEWALL glances around as she dances. THOREAU, outside the dance hall, is invisible to her.

Lights down as dance continues.

Lights up on JOHN THOREAU as he leaves the dance to seek out his brother. JOHN is a handsome young man in his mid-twenties, respectably dressed and groomed. There is a distinct family resemblance between the two brothers.

JOHN: Henry!—where on earth have you been? Come inside!

THOREAU: No.

JOHN: We thought you were camping on the Sudbury tonight.

THOREAU: I changed my mind.

JOHN *(wiping face with handkerchief, smiling)*: Come join the dance! *(Lowered voice)* Ellen has been missing you.

THOREAU *(eagerly)*: She has—? But no.

JOHN: It's clear she has. I can read the girl's eyes.

THOREAU *(hotly)*: What are Ellen Sewall's eyes, to *you*?

JOHN *(laughing away his brother's rudeness as if accustomed to it)*: Brother, come! Don't look so dour. We'll teach you the Highlander. *(Hand on THOREAU's arm)*

THOREAU *(pulling away)*: No. *(Removing a much-folded sheet of paper from his pocket)* Give this to her.

JOHN *(as if to open the note and read it, teasing)*: Not another of your obscure poems...

THOREAU *(flaring up)*: I said give it to Ellen, not read it.

JOHN: The young lady would rather see you, my friend, than another of these. *(Thrusting the note back at THOREAU)* Give it to her yourself.

THOREAU *(vulnerable)*: John, please—

JOHN: Damn it, Henry, you make yourself ridiculous!—and that reflects on all the Thoreaus. Come inside, you needn't dance. Speak with Ellen yourself.

THOREAU: I c-can't—

JOHN: Why not?

THOREAU: The crowd, their eyes—

JOHN: Henry, everyone in there is a friend, a neighbor, a former classmate, a relative! How can you call us a "crowd"?

THOREAU *(striking his fist against his chest)*: The air will be overheated, stale. I can't breathe...

JOHN: Henry, the Sewalls are well aware of your undeclared courtship of Ellen. Don't you know you compromise the girl's reputation by refusing to acknowledge her publicly—skulking about like this.

THOREAU *(alarmed, angry)*: Who knows? Who's talking about me?

JOHN: Henry, it's obvious.

THOREAU: Has *she* told?

JOHN: For God's sake, Henry, calm yourself. (Laughs, lays a hand on his shoulder) You've never been in love before, that's clear.

THOREAU *(pummeling him)*: D-D-Damn you! To s-speak that w-way!

JOHN, still laughing, shoves THOREAU; THOREAU shoves him more forcibly in turn; their brotherly wrestling almost gets out of hand. THOREAU's folded note falls to the ground, and JOHN kicks at it. THOREAU hastily snatches it up and returns it to his pocket.

JOHN *(incensed)*: Graduated from Harvard College twelve days ago, and a fine fool you're making of yourself. Go back on the river with your muskrats and loons! *They* will thrill to your verse.

JOHN strides back into the dance hall as THOREAU looks after. Loud, bright music resumes. Lights up inside dance hall.

As if against his will, THOREAU is drawn to the doorway to watch the dancers. JOHN, happily rejoining the group, ignores him. ELLEN SEWALL and a young woman friend, RACHEL, who are not dancing at the moment, whisper together stage left; they are covertly aware of THOREAU. He is awkward and self-conscious, making a belated attempt to adjust his clothes, brush back his hair with wetted fingers. He discovers clotted mud on his boots which he tries to kick off.

RACHEL laughs, seeing him. ELLEN is stricken with embarrassment.

RACHEL *(in ELLEN's ear)*: Henry Thoreau is in love with you, Ellen! Mr. Thoreau's *strangest* son!—look at him.

ELLEN *(shyly turning aside)*: No! (Pause; wraps her shawl about her shoulders) Oh, Rachel, I wish he would not *stare* at me. His eyes are so—hurtful.

RACHEL: They say Henry Thoreau is a changeling. A forest creature. His eyes are lynx eyes—they penetrate the dark.

ELLEN *(looking away)*: Is he—still there?

RACHEL: He's coming inside!—

THOREAU has taken a tentative step inside; hesitates; and retreats.

RACHEL *(giggling)*: —No.

The dancers are well aware of THOREAU, exchange glances, and look toward ELLEN, smiling. JOHN continues to ignore him.

RACHEL *(a bit cruelly)*: Your suitor, Ellen—I wonder he isn't ashamed of himself. No man should expose himself—his heart on his sleeve—so! *(Laughs)*

ELLEN *(moving abruptly from RACHEL)*: You would admire him, if it were you he came for.

ELLEN crosses to HENRY, who is surprised, and gratified, when she joins him. As the others stare, they step outside together. By degrees lights down on the dancers; music subsides.

ELLEN SEWALL is a sweet-faced, ravishingly pretty but conventional girl of 17. She is both attracted to, and fearful of, THOREAU, whose desire for her is direct and candid. Of course, ELLEN is accustomed to the circumlocutions of her time, place, and class. (This is a genteel, religious village society, by no means affluent.)

THOREAU tries to take both ELLEN's hands, and ELLEN draws away.

During this brief scene, THOREAU and ELLEN slowly and awkwardly circle each other, like dancers; THOREAU advances upon the girl, seemingly unaware of frightening her.

THOREAU: I—couldn't stay away. I've thought of you—dreamt of you—

ELLEN *(quickly, trying to smile, in a "social" manner)*: Henry, how are you? I have not seen you since last week—

THOREAU: I meant to stay away—

ELLEN *(laughing)*: Oh, but that's not very—flattering—

THOREAU: —after your letter—

ELLEN *(quickly, rattled)*: My letter?—oh, I write so many—receive so many—

THOREAU: —your father is r-right to disapprove—

ELLEN *(trying to be gay, light)*: If only you *would* accompany us to church, just once!—it would not kill you, you know—

THOREAU *(strange, stern)*: Yes. It would kill me.

ELLEN *(nervous laughter, attempt to be chiding)*: Henry Thoreau, the things you say!—not all the Thoreaus are free thinkers, surely?

THOREAU *(intense, unsmiling)*: I am not all the Thoreaus.

ELLEN: Were you not born and baptized Unitarian?—in the First Parish Church of Concord, which is my family's church, too?

THOREAU: I was born a naked, braying thing—too innocent for any "original sin" to be washed from me. *(Laughs, a bit awkwardly)* Surely, Ellen, you were, too?

ELLEN *(blushing)*: I—?

THOREAU: Naked we come into the world, and naked we leave— it is only the interim, where our clothes encumber us.

ELLEN: Henry, the things you—

THOREAU: Come, walk with me!—out of *here*— *(He pulls at ELLEN's arm, and she resists.)*

ELLEN *(uneasy)*: Where—?

THOREAU: To the Mill Brook—

ELLEN: No, that's too far. It's too—dark.

THOREAU *(laughing)*: Too far? A mere mile—?

ELLEN: I am not dressed for one of your woodland excursions. And it is hardly the proper time.

THOREAU: All time is the "proper" time!—d'you think we existed, before this moment? *(Snapping his fingers, smiling)*

ELLEN: I don't understand.

THOREAU: D'you think there is any "history," any "past"—indeed, any "future"—that is not *now*? *(As ELLEN stares uncomprehending at him, THOREAU takes her wrist, presses his thumb against her pulse; speaks urgently.)* Your pulsebeat, Ellen—and mine—are they not *now*?

ELLEN *detaches herself from* THOREAU; *firmly, though gently. It is clear that she is very much attracted to him; virtually hypnotized by him.*

ELLEN: I—don't understand.

THOREAU *(marveling)*: You are so beautiful, Ellen. Even more in person than in my fever-dreams.

ELLEN *(turning slightly away, recovering some of her equanimity)*: Henry, your last letter was most upsetting. You said that you "entertained a serious doubt" of the divinity of our Lord Jesus Christ—

THOREAU: —oh, humbug!—did I say that?—I, so timorous?—in fact, I am not a man to "entertain" any degree of doubt, as the world will discover.

ELLEN: What does that mean?

THOREAU: I have no "doubt" at all: I know. That God is here, now, in *us*, and in the night that surrounds us, in the owl's cry—d'you hear him?—a screech owl?—in the stars, in the soil—in that horse dung in the road— *(pointing)* —God is all, everywhere. And so, as I put it to the Reverend William Channing himself, at Harvard— what need we of a *savior*? From what, and to what, in a world of such infinite riches, can we be *saved*?

ELLEN *(a bit overwhelmed by this)*: I, I—but—God Himself has—sent His Only Begotten Son to us—hasn't He?

THOREAU: If I see Him, I shall ask Him. If He insists so, I shall believe Him—maybe. *(Laughs)*

ELLEN *(reproving)*: It's as everyone says—you make light of the most serious things. Surely your teachers at Harvard College had answers for your questions?

THOREAU *(youthful swaggering)*: Ellen, I have lived some twenty-one years on this planet, and I have yet to hear the first syllable of valuable or even earnest advise from my seniors. They have told me nothing, and probably cannot tell me anything, to the purpose.

ELLEN *(shocked)*: Henry! For shame! —What "purpose"?

THOREAU: That, I admit, I have yet to discover. Perhaps you, Ellen, might help me?

ELLEN: I?—how?

THOREAU *(reaching for her hand)*: Come with me! I promise, I will bring you back safely to your friends, before the dance is over.

ELLEN *(nervously, putting him off)*: They are your friends, too, Henry Thoreau. Why do you not rather join *us*? We've been having the happiest time. Your brother John is *such* a dancer—

THOREAU *(arrogantly)*: I had rather be an ant in an anthill, in a frenzy of copulation, than join that crowd.

ELLEN *(protesting)*: Henry!—our friends and neighbors—our families—are hardly an *anthill*.

THOREAU: So too the ants proclaim, but we, of a higher consciousness, know better.

ELLEN: Is this the wisdom you have brought home to Concord, from Harvard College?

THOREAU: It is the wisdom with which I was born.

ELLEN *(boldly, wrapping her shawl tightly around her)*: Really! Why are you here tonight at all, then?

THOREAU *(a level look)*: You know why, Ellen.

ELLEN *(nervously, recklessly)*: And why is that?

THOREAU: Because you're here.

A beat. ELLEN *turns shyly away, biting her lip.*

THOREAU *(suddenly vulnerable)*: You know that I love you. *(Pause)* I h-had not intended to—m-marry— *(Pause, trying not to become agitated)* Can I support a wife?—a family?—I will be a village schoolteacher—I will work in my father's pencil-making shop— I will, must be, a poet— *(Pause)* But my love for you, Ellen, sweeps all else away.

ELLEN *(moved)*: Oh, Henry, I—

ELLEN *has to resist the childlike impulse to hide her face.* THOREAU *is an overwhelming presence.*

THOREAU: Ellen, do you—could you—love m-me? *(Pause)* I bare my soul to you now, I have never spoken to anyone so, in my life—Ellen? Could you love me?—m-marry me?

ELLEN: I must go back—

THOREAU *(restraining her)*: I love you so! I think of you constantly!—awake, asleep—I'm haunted—I've lost my soul—Ellen?

ELLEN *(wiping at her eyes)*: If—you would come to me at home, Henry, if you would speak with my father and mother—

THOREAU *(forcibly)*: What do I care about *them*! It's you I love. Do you love me?

ELLEN *(dazed)*: I—love you—

THOREAU: Ellen—!

THOREAU embraces ELLEN, kisses her wildly; in an instant he seems out of control, like a starving animal; ELLEN is terrified. They struggle and ELLEN pushes out of THOREAU's arms; her shawl falls to the ground, and a coil of her hair has come loose. The two young people stare wide-eyed and breathless at each other.

ELLEN *(tearful, backing away)*: You—are an animal.

THOREAU: Ellen, I'm sorry—I love you—

ELLEN *(sobbing)*: No! You are crude, you disgust me!

ELLEN runs away. (Not back into the dance but presumably toward her home.) THOREAU takes a few steps after her, then stops, staring.

Lights out.

Scene 3: The Red Slayer

A room in Bush House, the Concord home of RALPH WALDO EMERSON and his wife LIDIAN. In the semi-darkness we hear a woman singing. [See appendix, "The Fairy Ship."] LIDIAN is dressed in black, kneeling on a carpet and putting a child's things away in a little brightly painted trunk. (These include items of clothing, a small stuffed animal, toys, etc. and a "tower" constructed of thread spools, cards, a flour-box top, balanced upon one another.) Close by, a vase containing a single purple dwarf iris.)

LIDIAN: "I saw a ship a-sailing
      A-sailing on the sea
      And oh! it was a-laden
      With pretty things for me:

> There were comfits in the cabin,
> And apples in the hold;
> The sails were made of satin,
> And the masts were made of gold..."

EMERSON enters. Carrying writing materials.

EMERSON *(uneasily)*: I was looking for you, my dear, in the hope you might copy out some new poems for me. My friend William Wordsworth has sent me several of *his*, and... Why do you remain on the *floor*, Lidian? When I am addressing you?

LIDIAN slowly pushes herself to her feet, resisting EMERSON's proffered arm; but then she leans heavily on it. A coil of her hair is loosened. We see she is in her stocking feet.

EMERSON: Your hair, Lidian... *(As LIDIAN mechanically tidies her hair)* Your *feet*! *(Shocked)* Where are your shoes? *(LIDIAN picks up her shoes, which have been hidden behind the trunk.)* If the servants should see...!

LIDIAN *(in her own thoughts; not aggrieved but rather in wonder)*: Eighteen months. Since God called him back. *(Mechanically putting her shoes on)*

EMERSON *(wincing)*: My dear, haven't I asked you not to speak in such...primitive terms. God is not a *person*, still less a *personality*, to whom we can ascribe human motives. "Calling back" an innocent child as if it were a sort of cruel whim... *(Shaking head soberly)* It's absurd.

LIDIAN: But if God called Waldo back, it must be for a reason; and we shall know that reason someday. *(Pause)* I prefer to believe in such a "reason" than in...nothing.

EMERSON: "Nothing"—? Lidian! A conviction of our own boundless *human* integrity—our spiritual strength, self-reliance—our freedom to define ourselves after centuries of churchly, superstitious oppression—is not, after all, *nothing*.

EMERSON eases away from LIDIAN. He becomes brisker and more confident now that the subject is not a dead child, but philosophy.

LIDIAN *(vague, weak echo)*: "Nothing"...

EMERSON *(as if lecturing, eloquently)*: A belief in the essential benignity of Nature, of God *in* Nature, is not, after all, nothing!

(Quoting himself) "Nature is not fixed but fluid. Spirit alters, moulds, makes it." *(Pause)* I hope, Lidian, you would not prefer the old notions of heaven-and-hell, "salvation" and "damnation," "original sin"—these burdensome chains we are casting off! *(Pause)* My lecture for the Hartford Lyceum, this Friday, is on precisely this subject.

LIDIAN: Hartford?—Friday? You will want your serge suit cleaned and pressed; and two changes of linen—

EMERSON: And this new poem... *(Reads from a much-scribbled sheet of paper)*

If the red slayer thinks he slays,
   Or if the slain think he is slain,
They know not well the subtle ways
   I keep, and pass, and turn again.

LIDIAN *(blankly)*: "Red"—"slayer"?

EMERSON: The title is "Brahma," do you see. Title, and theme.

LIDIAN: But—what is the "red slayer"?

EMERSON: I...have not worked it out yet. Some sort of beast, perhaps.

LIDIAN *(apologetically)*: Poetry is too difficult for me now. Though, as a girl, I had loved it.

EMERSON: You loved the simplicity of your own thoughts, reflected back to you in cloying ladies' verse. *My* verse is quite different.

LIDIAN: Oh yes! I rejoice that I am married to the greatest poet of our day; but I do confess, Mr. Emerson,* your poetry is incomprehensible to me.

EMERSON: It is the nature of poetry, my dear, to be incomprehensible. If it were comprehensible, it would be prose.

A sound of wind outside.

LIDIAN: Oh!—listen to the wind.

---

* Through their entire married life, Lidian never addressed her husband as other than "Mr. Emerson" or "husband" in public or in private.

EMERSON: There is a somber beauty to the wind.

LIDIAN: Over *his* grave. Such a small grave! *(Pause)* I visited the cemetery this morning. Quite early—just past dawn—as the church bell rang—as it had rung *then*. *(Pause, lifts vase of iris)* Somebody came by, and picked dwarf iris out of the woods— gave some to me, for Waldo's grave. Here is one I saved out: isn't it beautiful?

EMERSON *(glancing at iris, struck by a thought)*: Flowers! One never really sees them, yet they are *there*. Like the wind. *(Scribbles down this thought)*

LIDIAN: It was John Thoreau's youngest son, the one people call strange. Out of nowhere he came—sudden and silent as a deer.

EMERSON: —As the vast Over-Soul, the eternal One—surrounds us. *(Scribbles down this thought)*

LIDIAN: In an instant seeing me, and Waldo's grave, he understood; and made no mention of it... Save with his eyes. *(Pause)*

EMERSON: David Henry Thoreau, is it?—the boy who burnt down the woods. I was asked to write a letter for him, for a scholarship at Harvard. He was awarded the scholarship, I believe—but never wrote to thank me.

LIDIAN: He has changed his name: it is now Henry David Thoreau.

EMERSON: Changed his name? But why?

LIDIAN: *You* changed my name, when we were married, didn't you?—perhaps it was for a like motive.

EMERSON: But that was different, surely. "Lydia" grated harshly on the ear—"Lidian" glides. *(Testing the sounds, with a poet's sensibility)* "Lydia"—"Lidian": d'you hear the distinction?

LIDIAN *(pursuing her own thought)*: But how odd, how bold—to name *oneself*.

EMERSON: "David Henry Thoreau"—"Henry David Thoreau"— *(Laughing condescendingly) Much* more melodic, isn't it!

LIDIAN: Perhaps it is not the melodic the young man wishes, but something more profound.

The wind rises again.

LIDIAN *(suddenly emotional, reaching out to touch EMERSON)*: Oh husband, will we ever recover from our grief?

EMERSON: R-Recover?—*our*—?

LIDIAN: *My* grief, then—

EMERSON: None of us is a stranger to death, thus to grief. You must not fix so morbidly on *yourself*, dear.

LIDIAN: I know, I know—yet I want him back, I dream of him—I see him—more clearly than I see you— *(Begins to cry)* Tell me there is God, and Waldo is with Him!—and we shall see him again someday—

EMERSON *(in dread of surrendering to his own emotion)*: We will— speak of this another time, Lidian. When you are yourself again.

EMERSON exits.

Lights out.

Scene 4: The Whip

Darkness. The sound of a cane or small whip striking a bundle of clothing on the floor. This WHUP! WHUP! WHUP! might be amplified.

Lights up. A room in the THOREAU house. Some time later. THOREAU is "whipping" a bundle of clothing on the floor, grimly and without much zest. (The room need be only a suggestion of a room. Books and papers scattered about on the floor. A pair of muddy boots.) THOREAU is plainly dressed, in his shirt sleeves which are rolled up to reveal his distinctly "hairy" arms; his expression is ironic.

THOREAU: "—MUST learn—MUST learn—MUST learn to WIELD the WHIP—"

JOHN THOREAU enters. He too is plainly dressed but wears a jacket and is handsomely groomed. He carries an armload of books which he lets fall to the floor.

THOREAU *(angry humor, for JOHN's benefit)*: "—MUST learn to LOVE the WHIP—or— *(panting)* NO PLACE FOR YOU IN OUR SCHOOL—MR. THOREAU—"

JOHN *(laughing):* You need not learn to love the whip, Mr. Thoreau, but only to administer it when required.

THOREAU flings down the whip.

THOREAU: John, I *can't* do it. Am I a Southern slaveowner, am I a tyrant, a madman—to be an agent of *pain* to another's living *flesh*? Ugh!

JOHN: As always, Henry, you make too much of the simplest things. All teachers must use the whip, occasionally; even the females. It *is* loathsome, but—

THOREAU: If one could whip with *love*—and not merely to *punish*—

JOHN: Brother, recall that you yourself were regularly whipped, in our very school, for idleness, "vacancy of mind," truancy—

THOREAU: John, that's just it: now I am a teacher, I sympathize with the idlers, daydreamers, and truants. The Keyes boy stares out the window at great cumulus clouds blown westward from the ocean—just as I did, ten years ago, in that very desk. The Shepard boy no more knows or cares if the Emperor Augustus preceded Tiberius, or followed him; if Caligula was Nero's son, or his own grandsire—his lips recite by rote but his mind remains vacant, exactly like my own at his age. *(Pause)* D'you know, John: I don't recall being whipped. I doubt it ever happened.

JOHN: It was Mr. Hedge who whipped you most. You must recall Hedge—? *(JOHN makes a gesture to indicate a tall, husky man.)*

THOREAU: Violence is abhorrent to me—another's, or my own. If I cannot control another's, I must control my own.

JOHN picks up the whip and hands it back to THOREAU who accepts it reluctantly.

JOHN *(reprovingly):* You mustn't allow bullies and louts to take advantage of your good nature—or your pusillanimity.

THOREAU *(uneasily):* What have you heard of my classes—?

JOHN: Henry, I believe I have sometimes *heard* your classes, all the way to my side of the school. Mr. Pickard spoke with me today, to appeal to you: if discipline doesn't improve in your classes—

THOREAU: —my contract will not be extended beyond the new year.

JOHN: He reported to me your remarks to him, and your attitude. Henry, really! To speak so—arrogantly—to the very man who hired you—

THOREAU: Hired me to *teach*, and to convey a love of language, poetry, truth—not to *whip* human flesh—

JOHN: Your fellow teachers are not sympathetic with you. Including me. *I* don't want a spirit of anarchy in my classrooms.

THOREAU: Who has complained?

JOHN: Mr. Pickard has told you, surely. And, in Father's shop yesterday, Sophia waited on Mrs. Sewall, Edmund's mother: Mrs. Sewall is most upset that her boy is tormented by the bullies in your class, who ridicule him because his eyes are weak. It seems to me—

THOREAU *(overlapping)*: The Sewalls! *Her* aunt! I can't bear it, the family talking of *me*.

JOHN: The Sewalls are not the only family in Concord who talk of you, Henry. Father hears a good deal of it, and so does Mother. It is embarrassing to us all. Father says, it was a mistake to send Henry off to Harvard; now he thinks he is too good to manufacture pencils, but he is incapable of doing anything else.

THOREAU paces about, slapping his opened palm with the whip; not hard, but emphatically.

JOHN: Father asked me again if your decision is final? *(Pause, as THOREAU paces about)* Your invention of that new grinding mill for the graphite has made such a difference in the quality of Thoreau Pencils—it's remarkable. For the first time, Father says, we can compete with the German market. *(Pause)* I would be proud to work with Father, if I had half your genius for—

THOREAU *(interrupting)*: I am happy that pencil sales are up, and that the business will not go bankrupt immediately. But I am not proud of my invention: it adds not one whit to the spiritual growth of mankind. In fact, as it heightens market competition—

JOHN: —it heightens "Thoreau & Sons" profits! And well done, I say.

THOREAU: Father! He waits for me... *(Imagining an elevated sign)* "Thoreau & Sons, Pencil Manufacturers of Concord, Mass." I dream of my fate, with millstones grinding *me*; the sheds out behind the house, my coffin. Lead-dust—so fine as to be invisible—lethal. *(Coughs)* No. I've told Father I *will not.*

JOHN *(tapping his chest)*: Well, we Thoreaus have "weak" chests— But lead-dust is no worse than chalk-dust, surely?

THOREAU: Yes, I think it may be worse. I have been exposed to it much more than you.

JOHN: It is cold and damp and exhaustion you expose yourself to, in the woods. Your marathon hikes—surely they are not good for your lungs?

THOREAU *(quickly, to change the subject)*: It is not our bodies that are "weak"; but our wills. A body, I think, may be perfect—a wonder of Nature. But human *will* ... As Mr. Emerson has said, "Man is a god in ruins."

JOHN *(skeptically)*: On what authority does Mr. Emerson say so?

THOREAU *(pursuing his own thought)*: It's obvious—most men and women are blind, cloaked in ignorance and superstition; they *will* not see the truth. *(Slapping palm with whip)* Imagine: a religion, Christianity, where *meekness* is extolled, and the conformity of sheep led by a "Good Shepherd"—! *(Contemptuous laughter)*

A beat. JOHN has picked up one of his books and leafs distractedly through it.

JOHN whistles.

THOREAU: You have...heard f-further...of...?

A beat. JOHN shuts the book.

JOHN: Henry, why bring up the subject? In your heart, you don't want to know.

THOREAU: ...that means the engagement *is*...a fact?

A beat. JOHN shrugs and strolls about, stretching.

THOREAU: No one will tell me anything! Our own sister Sophia says she fears my "turning savage"—

JOHN *(laughs)*: Well, Sophia exaggerates. But—at times—if you could see your own eyes.

THOREAU *(in control)*: Be it life or death, I crave only reality—the unsparing truth. *(Pause)* Ellen is to marry the Reverend Osgood?

JOHN *begins to whistle.*

THOREAU *(calmly):* John, you mistake me. I am quite recovered from that…fever of last spring.

JOHN *(nodding, a smile):* Well, good!

THOREAU: "To sigh under the cold, cold moon for a love unrequited, is to put a slight upon Nature; the natural remedy would be to fall in love with the moon and the night, and find our love requited."

JOHN: Really? Who said that?

THOREAU: I did. *(Pause)* It's an observation I made in my journal the other night. I have begun to write, not haphazardly as in the past, but daily. I believe I will be a *writer.*

JOHN: Is this some new decision? For years, you've been writing verse, haven't you?

THOREAU *(a dismissive gesture):* Mere juvenalia. Now, at age twenty-two, I declare myself a writer of prose: poetry *in* prose. There has never been such a prose style yet. An American shaping the English tongue to suit *him*—the world will see.

JOHN *(laughing good-naturedly):* My dear Henry! About to be dismissed from a county school, yet confident of a brilliant future.

THOREAU: "Each generation must write its own books"—Mr. Emerson has declared. At the Phi Beta Kappa address, at Harvard, he appeared to be looking straight at *me*—out of the many hundreds in the chapel. *(Pause)* The engagement *is*…a fact?

JOHN: I wonder Ellen has not written you, herself. I would think, caring for you as she had, she—

THOREAU *(roughly):* We can never plumb the depths of others' emotions, John. Even when those emotions are shallow as a barnyard puddle. *(Pause)* One day soon, I intend to walk out to Bush House; I will introduce myself to Ralph Waldo Emerson. For it may be, John, Mr. Emerson is lonely in this country village for someone with whom he might converse.

JOHN *laughs good-naturedly, shaking his head.*

THOREAU: You think I lack the courage? That I would tremble outside the great man's gate, and slink away like a dog?

JOHN: Brother, not you!

THOREAU (*with a shrug*): Yet I've already done so.

JOHN: Done what?

THOREAU: Trembled outside the gate of Bush House, and after a half-hour slunk away like a dog.

JOHN (*exasperated, seizing* THOREAU *by the arm and shaking him*): Enough of these fancies! You are in a serious predicament, brother. There have been complaints of your teaching, as you well know.

THOREAU: I allow that my classes are sometimes—rowdy. There is much laughter, for I believe that learning springs from joyous spirits.

JOHN: Some learning, Henry, can only spring from pain.

THOREAU: John!

JOHN: When I first whipped a boy, I was ill with self-disgust for days. But, what a cleansing of the atmosphere in my classroom!

THOREAU (*stubbornly*): I still think I will win them over, even the worst of them. In the spring, I will lead a "nature excursion" out to Walden Pond. Botany, biology, and local history need not be lifeless subjects, but—

JOHN (*cutting in*): "In the spring"—? There will be no spring for you!

THOREAU (*handing* JOHN *the whip*): Whip me, then. Then I will know to what degree I administer hurt.

JOHN: What?

THOREAU (*holding out his hands*): Brother, do it.

JOHN: Of course I won't do it!

THOREAU: If you love me—

JOHN: —what has love to do with it? (*Throwing down whip, turning aside*) Henry, goodnight.

THOREAU (*picking up whip, pressing it into* JOHN's *hands again*): John, I insist. If you walk out that door, I hand in my resignation to Mr. Pickard tomorrow morning.

JOHN: Why, on earth?

THOREAU: Because there is no future for me as a schoolmaster. You have told me as much.

JOHN *(increasing exasperation)*: Talking to you is like talking to the accursed Sphinx!

THOREAU: I must know what pain is, to administer it exactly. And if it is administered with love...

JOHN: You're joking.

THOREAU: I never joke. Even my laughter is dead serious. *(Forcing JOHN to confront him, gripping his muscled arm)* I think this arm is capable of good, vigorous punishment—eh, John?

JOHN: Yes!

JOHN strikes THOREAU's extended hands with the whip. THOREAU falls to his knees with a muffled whimper but doesn't shrink away as JOHN raises the whip to strike again, and again.

Lights out.

Scene 5: The Visitor

Darkness. EMERSON's sermonizing voice.

EMERSON: "...I am born into the great, the universal mind. I, the imperfect, adore my own Perfect. I am receptive of the Great Soul. More and more the surges of everlasting nature enter into me. So I come to live in thoughts and act with energies which are immortal." ACHOO! *(A violent sneeze)*

Lights up during this speech. EMERSON is pacing before his desk in his study, pince-nez on his nose, composing a lecture. EMERSON's study is book-lined; his desk is appropriately large, and heaped with books and manuscripts. A chair behind the desk, and a chair for visitors. We note handsome leatherbound books, a tall kerosene lamp, a quill pen and inkwell, a number of bright yellow pencils atop the desk. EMERSON is in his shirt-sleeves, but his shirt is starched and white, and he wears a necktie. He blows and wipes his nose with a dazzling white handkerchief.

EMERSON: Sometimes I feel like a God in nature—sometimes like a weed by the wall.

Lets fall his writing materials onto his desk.

A knock at the door.

EMERSON *(annoyed)*: Yes?

LIDIAN appears. Dressed less severely than in Scene 3, but her manner is sober and deferential.

LIDIAN: Forgive me for interrupting you, but—the young man is back.

EMERSON: Which young man?—there are so many, plaguing me with requests for visits. And all carrying manuscripts!

LIDIAN: It is Henry Thoreau, who was by yesterday morning.

EMERSON: Yesterday, scarcely past dawn! "Henry David"—the pencil-maker's son. Belated thanks, no doubt, for my letter of recommendation to Harvard—four years late. *(Laughs, goes to put on his coat, which gives him a stiffly formal appearance)* Well, show him in, Lidian.

LIDIAN: Show him in? Now?

EMERSON: I am curious to know him. Such things are said of him.

LIDIAN turns to usher THOREAU into the room. THOREAU is dressed as usual, tieless, with badly scuffed boots. He carries a wide-brimmed hat and a duffel bag, which he lets fall onto the floor in front of EMERSON's desk.

LIDIAN exits unobtrusively. THOREAU, self-conscious, looks after her; but the focus of his attention is EMERSON.

THOREAU *(extending hand awkwardly, boldly)*: Mr. Emerson.

EMERSON: Mr.—Thoreau.

THOREAU: Mrs. Emerson warns me I cannot stay long—you are preparing a lecture for the Boston Lyceum. And I would not wish to, for I have obligations of my own.

EMERSON: Ah, yes: you teach at the Center School, in the village.

THOREAU: No longer. Since January, the Center School and I have gone our separate ways.

EMERSON *(gravely)*: I'm sorry to hear that.

THOREAU: Why should you be sorry, Mr. Emerson, if I am not?

EMERSON: Please, Mr. Thoreau, be seated—

THOREAU: I hope you will call me "Henry"—"Mr. Thoreau" was the name my students called me, which I found fit me badly, like an outgrown pair of britches.

EMERSON sits behind his desk, THOREAU in the visitor's chair. THOREAU is ill at ease, self-conscious; yet has affected a haughty air. EMERSON stares at him, not knowing what to make of him.

EMERSON: You are—teaching elsewhere?

THOREAU: I should like to become a teacher of humankind—like you, Mr. Emerson.

EMERSON: Ah, a writer! Yes—there are many of us in New England.

THOREAU *(frowning)*: No, sir, indeed not; not many of *us*. Many of *them*, perhaps.

EMERSON *(just remembering)*: Mr. Thoreau—I mean Henry—did I not hear that you are the Thoreau son responsible for this remarkable new pencil? *(EMERSON picks up several of the pencils on his desk.)* It marks so *clearly*—does not tear the page—and is erasable, as well. Yankee ingenuity! I congratulate you. *(Awkward, well-meaning condescension)* No wonder you have quit school-teaching—your fortune will be in *pencils.*

THOREAU: Not at all. I have nothing to do with pencils. I would not do again what I have done once.

EMERSON *(taken aback)*: Indeed.

THOREAU: *You* would not reiterate a shopworn idea, Mr. Emerson, would you? Even if it were one of your own.

EMERSON: Hmmm!—I hope not. *(Pause)* And so—you're a graduate of Harvard College, my alma mater?—a lively center of learning, with many excellent instructors, is it not? Our "American Oxford"!

THOREAU: I did not find it so.

EMERSON: But—

THOREAU: My most memorable intellectual experiences as a student were solitary tramps along the Charles, at dawn; and days of truancy, hiking and climbing Mt. Greylock and Monadnock. I have found that one is never oppressed, still less bored, in one's own company. *(Pause; in a ringing voice)* "Why should we grope among the dry bones of the past, or put the living generations into masquerade out of its faded wardrobe?"

EMERSON *(surprised)*: Who said that?

THOREAU: You, Mr. Emerson. Your preface to "Nature."

EMERSON: Oh yes…

THOREAU: Memorable lines that strike to the heart.

EMERSON: Thank you.

THOREAU: A pity, though, they're surrounded, in that essay, by so many others.

EMERSON *(clearing throat)*: I…see. *(Pause, strokes chin)* But you *do* have a bachelor of arts diploma from Harvard?

THOREAU: I am a "bachelor of arts"—for whatever that is worth; but, of course, I have no diploma. *(Indicating EMERSON's diploma on the wall)* No heraldic "sheepskin" of that sort.

EMERSON: But why not? You have earned the honor.

THOREAU *(snorting with bemused derision)*: And pay an extra five dollars? Let every sheep keep but his own skin, I told the registrar.

EMERSON *(laughing suddenly, as if surprising himself)*: Yes, indeed! I think you must be right, young man. These honors, these proud possessions— *(indicating his books, etc.)* —what are they but the intellectual's visible signs of grace?—as our Puritan ancestors grimly sought visible signs of God's grace, to assuage their terror of damnation.

THOREAU: The Puritans were not *my* ancestors, Mr. Emerson. My father's father, Jean Thoreau, emigrated to Massachusetts from the Isle of Guernsey, in the 1750s. He was an adventurer, with no interest in "salvation."

EMERSON *(stubbornly)*: Yet there is a Puritan streak in all of us in New England—we imbibe it with the very air.

THOREAU: A repugnance for the showy, the meretricious, the impure—yes. But the Puritans were of that sick mentality that must always be judging others' lives; *I* can hardly summon up the interest to judge my own.

EMERSON: And what *is* your life, Henry, may I inquire?

THOREAU: Outwardly, I live with my parents, my brother John and my sister Sophia, in the white frame dwelling on Main Street with the sign JOHN THOREAU & CO. on the front. Inwardly, I am, I must confess, a hovering *question*—which, I seem to believe, Mr. Emerson, you will have a hand in answering.

EMERSON: Well! That's very flattering...

THOREAU: I don't mean it to be: I am not a man to flatter.

EMERSON *(laughing)*: Somehow, my young friend, I have sensed that.

THOREAU *(earnest, boyish)*: "My young friend"—do you mean it, Mr. Emerson?

EMERSON: Why, I—of course, I—

THOREAU: I have long fantasized, that since you have moved to Concord, to the home of your paternal ancestors, there was a— significance to it. That we were destined to be f-friends—

EMERSON *(drawing back, stiffly)*: Hmmm! Indeed.

THOREAU: In the exchange of ideas, of course. For I am of the generation of whom you spoke in your Phi Beta Kappa address— "Each age must write its own books." How your vivid, piercing eyes, Mr. Emerson, seemed to single out *me*—!

EMERSON: Hmmm.

THOREAU *(excited, on his feet)*: And so, you see, Mr. Emerson, I count myself born in the most estimable place in all the world— Concord, Massachusetts. And in the very nick of time.

EMERSON *(dryly)*: It is well, to think so well of oneself.

THOREAU: I *am* very pleased with myself, I confess. *(Laughing)* I am all I have, after all. *(Goes to examine a bookshelf)* Ah, the new translation of Plotinus! *(Takes book from shelf and leafs through it)* I hope I may borrow it for a day or two, Mr. Emerson? I am having a damnably difficult time borrowing books out of the Harvard College Library—now I am no longer a student, the librarian claims I have no privileges.

EMERSON: But—you *are not* a student, are you?

THOREAU *(excitedly)*: And these volumes of Pascal, Kant, Hegel—the Scripture of Zoroaster—ah! Carlyle's *Sartor Resartus* in a single volume— *(Takes down book, examines it)* With an inscription from Carlyle himself: "to my brave Emerson." *(Gazing at EMERSON reverently)* What riches!

EMERSON *(proudly)*: Yes. Carlyle was kind enough to see that I received an early copy, inscribed in his hand.

THOREAU: I shall treat the book reverently, you can rest assured, Mr. Emerson. *(He has an armful of books which he transfers into his duffel bag.)*

EMERSON: Excuse me, Mr.—, I mean Henry—

THOREAU: I own but few books myself. A library of such riches is, to me, like a landscape of infinite beauty: one need not own it, to partake of it. *(Shaking EMERSON's hand more animatedly than EMERSON is accustomed to)* I am so grateful to you, sir! And to think that I cowered out by your gate like a d-dog—for everybody says of you that you are chill as the northeast wind, a man *on stilts.*

EMERSON: Wind—? Stilts—? Who has said—?

THOREAU: So any full-formed man would appear, among the Lilliputians. *I* admire you the more, that you don't bend to be merely *liked*. *(THOREAU has slid several books into his duffel bag, removed a manuscript, and now shuts the bag up again.)*

THOREAU *(placing a manuscript on EMERSON's desk)*: This—an account of a winter hike to Wachusett—I leave for your perusal, and whatever criticism you may wish to offer. *(Pause)* And now, Mr. Emerson, let me take you for a walk.

EMERSON: A walk? Now?

THOREAU *(a hand to his chest)*: It is very warm in here, airless. I wonder you can breathe.

EMERSON: A *walk*? In this wind?

THOREAU *(extending a hand)*: Come, let's go to Walden Pond. *There*, you shall find your lecture for the Boston Lyceum.

A beat. EMERSON regards THOREAU with astonishment at his audacity.

THOREAU: *My* finest ideas are blown to me by the wind, flung in my face. To execute words, one must flee them. *(THOREAU takes up his duffel bag, which he slings over his shoulder and carries easily.)*

EMERSON (*rising slowly to his feet*): Well. I suppose I can spare an hour... (*Shakes head, bemused*) The lecture is progressing very poorly, I must confess.

As the men prepare to leave the study, LIDIAN appears at the door, as if she has been waiting close outside.

LIDIAN: Husband, where are *you* going?

EMERSON: For a walk, dear. Mr. Thoreau—that is, *Henry*—has convinced me to come out with him to Walden Pond.

THOREAU: Come with us, Mrs. Emerson!

LIDIAN stares at THOREAU as if he were mad.

LIDIAN (*to EMERSON*): All the way out there, to that wild place?—in this blustery wind? You will catch pneumonia.

EMERSON: Nonsense, Lidian. It's over-warm in here.

LIDIAN: But what of your lecture?

EMERSON (*an attempt at gaiety*): It is waiting for me at Walden Pond. *Here* is a stalled and polluted pond.

LIDIAN: What are you saying? (*Looking from EMERSON to THOREAU, as if both are mad*)

THOREAU (*warmly*): Do come with us, Mrs. Emerson. If you do not resist the wind, your soul is cleansed by it.

LIDIAN: My soul, Mr. Thoreau, is my own business. (*To EMERSON*) At least let me get your muffler, your vest, your gloves—and you must wear your high boots.

LIDIAN hurriedly exits.

EMERSON (*embarrassed*): Since our little boy Waldo died of scarlet fever, two years ago, Mrs. Emerson fusses over me inordinately. You know how women are!

THOREAU: No. I'm pleased to say, I do not.

Lights out.

Scene 6: In Walden Woods

An hour or so later. In darkness, and as green-tinctured lights come up, we hear the Universal Lyre. The atmosphere is dreamlike, eerie.

THOREAU *and* EMERSON *are walking in the woods above Walden Pond,* THOREAU *in the lead. He wears his oddly-shaped hat pulled down tight over his forehead;* EMERSON *is bulkily dressed, in hat, vest, gloves, boots.*

EMERSON *(slightly winded)*: What...is that sound?

The Universal Lyre rises in pitch; then subsides, but continues for several beats, just audibly.

EMERSON *(unnerved)*: It must be the wind? In the pine trees? *(Pause)* But it has voices in it...

THOREAU: It is the music of these woods. Why give it a name?

EMERSON: Could—it be church bells? From Concord, or Acton? *(Pause)* Or voices—the souls of Indians, banished by our Puritan ancestors?

THOREAU *(with Yankee practicality)*: It's a vibratory hum of pine needles, the highest branches of these hickory trees sawing together in the wind, giant rushes on the pond's shore that shiver so finely in the wind, one would swear they are living souls. To this, we supply "voices"—in our heads.

EMERSON: Nature is a riddle—to be solved by man. *(Stumbling in underbrush)* Oh—!

THOREAU *(extricating him)*: These briars!—

EMERSON: Thank you. *(Urgent voice)* One day, Henry, the vast riddle of Nature *will*—*must*—be solved by human cognition. We will give names, and we will assign causes. The twentieth century will soar to heights of scientific knowledge—and control. Man shall no longer be a "god in ruins," but God. *(Pause, glancing about)* Henry, I hope we are not lost? This is such a wild place...

THOREAU *(laughing with youthful disdain)*: The "vast riddle of Nature" to be solved by *man*? More likely, man will be "solved" by Nature.

EMERSON: What do you mean?

THOREAU: We shall be extinguished if we are too bold. Made extinct. *(He makes a grinding gesture with the heel of his boot.)* And all this— *(a gesture taking in the woods)* —will survive, and flourish.

EMERSON: But if mankind does not *see* Nature, does Nature exist?

THOREAU laughs as if this is a very funny question.

THOREAU *(excited)*: Look! Lactarius deliciosus!

EMERSON: Yes? What?

THOREAU: A mushroom rare in these woods. *(THOREAU breaks off one of the cluster of mushrooms at its stem, and nibbles at it.)*

EMERSON: But—what if it's poisonous?

THOREAU: Lactarius deliciosus is not poisonous.

EMERSON: But—it may be wormy.

THOREAU *(shrugging)*: If I eat a worm or two, as surely I have done in my life, where's the harm? Are we not all *meat-protein*?

EMERSON: Ugh!

THOREAU laughs. He may be teasing or goading the older man. He holds out the mushroom, but EMERSON refuses even to touch it.

THOREAU: *I* am never squeamish. In the woods, my appetite grows. I could sometimes eat a fried rat with a good relish.

EMERSON *(revulsed)*: Henry!—oh, I see you are joking.

THOREAU: Many a rat has thought so, prematurely.

EMERSON laughs, awkwardly; is short of breath.

EMERSON: I must confess, I've heard many…mixed…things about you, Henry Thoreau.

THOREAU *(happily)*: Mr. Emerson, I would far rather be mixed than smooth: a gnarly, chewy substance than a pulpy pablum to be swallowed down and easily digested—and shat.

EMERSON *(wincing at this crudeness)*: Y-Yes. *(Pause. He glances about, tugging at his collar and tight-buttoned vest.)* It *is* beautiful here… if wild, and…strange. *(Alarmed)* What is that sound?

THOREAU: "Sound"?—there are thousands of sounds here.

EMERSON: A voice...

We hear the liquid call of a wood thrush.

THOREAU immediately answers the call, whistling gently. A beat. The wood thrush calls again, and again THOREAU answers.

EMERSON: How wonderful! What is the bird?

THOREAU: A wood thrush. Very common in these woods. They are just slightly smaller than robins, with rusty heads and brown-spotted breasts. You have heard them all your life, Mr. Emerson.

EMERSON: I have?

Another, fainter call of the wood thrush.

EMERSON tries gamely to whistle, but the sound is mainly hissing.

EMERSON: How d'you do it—?

THOREAU whistles again, perfectly; EMERSON peers closely at the way his lips are shaped; EMERSON tries again, without success.

THOREAU: It's very easy, if you are born to it.

EMERSON *(startled laugh)*: A cruel observation, young man!

THOREAU: Is it? I had thought it an honest one.

EMERSON *(regarding him uneasily)*: You seem...different...here, Henry Thoreau. Altered from the person you were in my study.

THOREAU: And you, Mr. Emerson, as well.

EMERSON *(stiffly)*: No, I am always the same. *(Pause, not very convincingly)* You must learn to call me "Waldo"...

THOREAU: No. "Mr. Emerson" must do, for the present. We are not yet equals.

EMERSON *(taken a bit aback by the youth's egotism)*: Hmm!—I see. May I inquire, why did you change your name?

THOREAU: Because I wanted to.

EMERSON: Hmm! Yes... And you intend, you say, to be a writer?

THOREAU: I *am* a writer, only not yet published. I am a poet of the *real*; the *actual*. I hope to take all of life for my subject; yet to place it here in Concord.

EMERSON: Hmmm! *(Uneasily)* Do you think we might be—lost?

THOREAU *(laughing)*: Lost! In *my* company?—in these woods I've been tramping since the age of twelve? *(Pointing)* Rest assured, Mr. Emerson: as the crow flies, Bush House is but three miles in that direction.

EMERSON: Only three miles! *(A touch of stubbornness)* I would have sworn *this* direction. *(Pointing vaguely outward)*

THOREAU: Come!

THOREAU leads EMERSON in the direction in which EMERSON has just pointed. We surmise that THOREAU spreads pine boughs to show EMERSON an unexpected view of Walden Pond. (The two men are at front center-stage gazing out into the audience.)

A blue-tinctured light comes up.

EMERSON *(dazzled)*: Ah!—a mountain lake.

THOREAU: No. Walden Pond.

EMERSON: *This*?

THOREAU: Why are you so surprised, Mr. Emerson?

EMERSON: It...disorients me, it is so perfect.

THOREAU *(lyric, animated)*: When I first saw Walden Pond, with the eyes of a young boy, alone, unaccompanied by any adult, I felt that I was blinded—its pure, chill waters penetrated my soul. And this is the spot I love best, of all the world—where someday I will build a hut, and retire from the world.

EMERSON: Retire from the world!...yes...in such a place... *(Peering at the pond)* Is it...unnaturally deep?

THOREAU: Local legend is it has no bottom, at its center.

EMERSON: No bottom!...like Infinity itself.

THOREAU: No. This is a real pond, not a Transcendental idea of a pond. *I* have measured it, from my rowboat, at one hundred two feet at its deepest.

EMERSON: One hundred two feet! A vertiginous depth! Are you sure?

THOREAU *(coolly)*: I never speak carelessly about things that matter, Mr. Emerson.

EMERSON: But it's more a lake than a pond, surely! Four or five miles in circumference...

THOREAU: Not quite two miles. Sixty-one water acres.

EMERSON: You've measured that, too?

THOREAU *(proudly)*: I've measured all of Concord's ponds.

EMERSON: But—why?

THOREAU: I am Concord's secret chronicler of waterways, weather, trees, beasts and birds.

EMERSON *(stiffly)*: I'm afraid I know little of local geography. To inhabit a place is somehow not to see it. *(Pause)* But—Walden Pond! It seems to float in the depths of the sky. It shimmers with invitation. *(Pause)* Yet a man like myself, drawn to it, would sink like a stone—drown.

THOREAU *(disbelieving)*: You don't swim?

EMERSON: I? Swim?

THOREAU: This summer, I will teach you.

EMERSON: This summer...I travel to England, and the Continent.

THOREAU: Any warm day will do, then. When I am alone, especially by moonlight, I swim naked. Perch, shiners, pickerel join me— slide up my sides—tickle me. *(He laughs, making upward stroking gestures against his body.)*

EMERSON: Naked...! *(Pause; a sudden thought)* Does no one own this property?—we must be trespassing.

THOREAU: "Property"!—the word is vile.

EMERSON: Still, one could be, if not arrested, chided... I should be terribly embarrassed.

THOREAU: You, Mr. Emerson, of all men?—"embarrassed"?

EMERSON: Surely embarrassment—shame—help to define us as human, and not beasts.

THOREAU: You are thinking, only beasts go *naked*?

EMERSON: I am not th-thinking—*naked*—at all.

THOREAU: Such ignoble scruples—emotions of any weak kind, I sometimes think—occur only in houses. Where women reign. In Nature, there are events, and there are facts; but there are no *emotions*.

EMERSON: Are you not rather young, Henry, to have eschewed the world of women—emotions?

THOREAU: Not young enough!

EMERSON: But do you not wish to marry? To claim your place as a citizen of Concord? To...father children?

THOREAU (*laughs*): There is no dearth of children hereabouts, as I see.

EMERSON: But—what are the wishes of your father and mother?

THOREAU (*quoting, firmly*): "I shun mother and father, wife and brother, when my genius calls me."

EMERSON: Eh?

THOREAU: Did you not make such a claim yourself, Mr. Emerson?

EMERSON: You must not quote me out of context. I meant—

THOREAU (*cutting in, youthful audacity*): My father and mother were but the *means* by which I entered this world. I owe them thanks, yes!—but no sentiment attaches. They were not thinking of *me*, after all, at the time of my conception, any more than I was thinking of them.

EMERSON: Really, Henry Thoreau!—you speak disrespectfully. And crudely.

THOREAU: Why?

EMERSON: There are matters of which gentlemen do not speak.

THOREAU: *I* am not a gentleman, I hope! Why then should I falsify the truth? Nature bids us propagate our kind, whether shoats, milkweed, fungi, *Homo sapiens*, and Nature cares not a whit for individuals. My seed would do as well for me—I, Henry Thoreau, need scarcely be involved in the act, at all.

EMERSON (*shocked*): What—!

THOREAU: Shall I tell you a confidence, Mr. Emerson? I hope you won't be repulsed.

EMERSON: If you don't tell it, there's no danger of my being repulsed.

THOREAU has been pacing about elatedly; his passionate lyricism may verge upon mania. EMERSON listens with appalled fascination.

THOREAU: Sometimes, in these wild places, I do strip naked!—to have nothing between my skin and the air!—I know not my own name, nor care to know! Talk of mysteries! Look at *us*! I stand in awe of my body, this Titian that possesses me! My seed wells up in me terrible, piercing—sweet— *(A gesture of stroking his genitals)* One could mate with female or male—any living thing!—has it but the blood-pulse, the leap of life...

EMERSON turns away, shutting his eyes; a hand to his brow.

THOREAU *(not very apologetic)*: I have offended you, Mr. Emerson! I'm sorry. *(Pause)* I am called coarse. My own brother shrinks from me sometimes. As if all *men* are not in thrall to the identical sex-hunger—

EMERSON *(overlapping)*: Excuse me!—please—

THOREAU: —yet will not speak of it.

(A beat)

EMERSON *(trying to regain authority)*: You are very—innocent, Henry.

THOREAU: Not so innocent as my elders should like me. *(A beat)*

EMERSON: Such—physical—thoughts are degrading. What I think, I am.

THOREAU: What I *do*, I am. *(A beat)*
(Gaily) Well—no swimming today. Instead, I'll row us in my boat. Come, Mr. Emerson!

EMERSON: Boat—? In this wind?

THOREAU: *Come*! Take care of the path. *(He leads EMERSON down an incline. The Universal Lyre rises hauntingly. EMERSON stumbles, and THOREAU supports him.)*

EMERSON *(recoiling, fearful)*: Ugh! What is that!

THOREAU goes forward to investigate.

THOREAU: Only the decaying carcass of a doe. (*Grimacing from the smell, but peering curiously*) Pregnant, I would guess—a creature, perhaps a fox, has torn out her belly.

EMERSON too is drawn forward to look, as if against his will; he then recoils, appalled.

EMERSON: I feel ill... Ugh! (*Puts his handkerchief over his nose and mouth, gagging*)

THOREAU: My rowboat is just down there. Beyond those rocks...

EMERSON (*backing off unsteadily*): I have never looked upon such a...hideous sight. (*Almost vomiting*)

THOREAU: Yet death is all around us in Nature.

EMERSON (*weakly*): I am familiar with Death; I write of Death often. But of *deadness*...the stench, maggots...ugh!...I know nothing.

THOREAU (*assisting him*): Mr. Emerson—

EMERSON (*throwing off THOREAU's hands, panicked*): I n-never told Lidian: I had the child's body exhumed upon the first anniversary of his death. The cemetery keeper did not wish to oblige me. But I insisted. I wanted to *see*...my son Waldo.

THOREAU (*sympathetic, frankly curious*): And what did you see, Mr. Emerson?

EMERSON moans as if he's been struck, hiding his face in his hands.

THOREAU: I'm sorry!—

THOREAU makes a gesture to comfort the older man, but EMERSON stumbles away from him.

EMERSON exits.

THOREAU looks after him, surprised. EMERSON has left behind a glove which THOREAU picks up; THOREAU follows him.

Lights out.

Scene 7: The Predestined Marriage

Lights up on LIDIAN, *stage left. During this scene, Lidian completes her toilette, coiling her luxuriant, lustrous dark hair into a prim, unflattering bun affixed with numerous hairpins and, at the scene's end, outsized mother-of-pearl combs.*

LIDIAN *speaks matter-of-factly at first, then with growing emotion. This is a woman at the very edge of emotional control.*

LIDIAN: *I?*—I had no hand in the matter.
    God seared my vision, in *his* form.
    A woman does not WANT.
    A woman does not CHOOSE.
    (Pause)
    I?—I have always been unworthy of my marriage.
    I know what people say, and they are correct.
    Yet: to love where one is unworthy,
    that is my penance.
    I am a Christian woman.
    My secret sin is pride.
    (Stroking her breast, a surreptitious gesture)
    Ah!—the ache of it.
    The shame.
    (Pause)
    All of Boston murmured—buzzed—*raged*
    at our engagement.
    Even my family was bewildered.
    Lydia Jackson?—*her*?
    What principle of Transcendentalist logic
        guided the great man to choose *her*?
    (Pause, fearful)
    I was Lydia Jackson, of Plymouth, Massachusetts.
    I came of age in the great Winslow mansion
        overlooking the Atlantic, and Plymouth Rock.
    I was plain, serious, good, "spiritual"—
        on my knees in prayer at dawn, and dark.
    And the Holy Bible close at hand.
    I had a dowry, but it was a modest one.
    My family had given up hope even before
        I was twenty-one.

For no man had ever looked upon me with love.
Nor even upon my dowry, and my family name, with love.
I expected nothing—of course.
I was a virgin at age thirty, and beyond.
(Pause)

Lights up on EMERSON, *stage right. A golden glow as of one beatified.* EMERSON *is dressed for the pulpit; we see (but do not hear) him preaching. He is younger than we have seen him.*

LIDIAN *(with girlish ardor)*: Oh, how Mr. Emerson soared—
   like an eagle—
   in the pulpit of the Twelfth Congregational Church!
   I gazed up—mesmerized.
   (Pause)
   I did not want the *man*
   As the coarseness of appetite *wants.*

Lights down on EMERSON.

LIDIAN: I was a virgin and had never examined my own body.
   I had never looked upon my own body directly.
   Not even in the bath. I swear, I had not.
   For we were taught to bathe ourselves clothed
      in thin muslin.
   And never to *look*, still less to *touch.*
   Save where it could not be avoided...
   (An expression of repugnance; pause)
   They said that I was "peculiar."
   They said I was "dull."
   Yet, that Sunday morning,
      I KNEW.
   Afterward I was wordless for hours except to say—
      I have forgotten, but my sister recalls—
   "That man is certainly my predestined husband."
   (A wild laugh)
   I!—Lydia Jackson!—to speak *thus!*
   (Pause)
   I had no hand in the matter.
   A woman does not WANT.
   A woman does not CHOOSE.
   As a woman does not have a vote in any election.

As a woman does not own property but is the property
   of her father, brother, husband, or son.
As a woman does not own her name.
As a woman does not own her body.
Of course, I loved him.
(Pause)

Lights up on EMERSON. *An air of stiff, dutiful formality.*

EMERSON: Can I resist the impulse, Miss Jackson, to beseech you
   to love me?

LIDIAN *laughs wildly.*

EMERSON: My love for you, Miss Jackson, is of a type different
      from that of my love for my first wife.
   I offer you a mature love. I offer you a noble love.
   If it cannot be that the identical *tenderness* of first passion
      resides in my bosom, I hope you will forgive me.
   For youth, and youth's hopes, cannot be repeated.

LIDIAN *(to audience; a wide smile, almost gaily)*:
   I said, in some surprise—
(speaking now to EMERSON, *across the width of the stage)*
   "Why, Mr. Emerson, should you have imagined,
   I would expect otherwise?"

EMERSON *smiles weakly—in perplexity, or in relief.*

EMERSON: Miss Jackson—Lydia—I thank you.

(A peal of wild laughter from LIDIAN*)*

EMERSON: Miss Jackson—Lydia—I love you...

Lights fade on EMERSON.

LIDIAN *(brightly)*: Upon that note it was understood
   that we should marry.

LIDIAN *is now finished with most of her toilette, and may be affixing a
lace collar and cuffs to her dress. Her movements are brisk.*

LIDIAN: *I?*—I did not want him.
   I did not choose him.
   This "Henry David Thoreau"—to live beneath our roof.
   I am not a woman who WANTS.
   I am not a woman who CHOOSES.

Lights up on EMERSON, *stage right, in his study. It is present time.* EMERSON *is animated, excited, writing in his journal.*

Lights up on THOREAU, *rear center-stage, seen through a scrim. He is in his shirtsleeves, sleeves rolled up, chopping firewood. His actions are rhythmic and performed with zest; we hear a thunk! thunk! thunk! of the long-handled ax on wood, but it should be a stylized and non-naturalistic sound, like a musical downbeat. Sun pours down upon* THOREAU's *bare head.*

EMERSON *(as he writes):* "Henry Thoreau gives me, in flesh and blood
   and pertinacious Saxon belief, my own belief, my own ethics. He
   is far more real than I…"

LIDIAN: Mr. Emerson simply informed me—
   "Henry Thoreau is coming to live with us.
   He will be handyman, copyist, proofreader—"

EMERSON *(overlapping, inspired):*
   "He will be legs and feet for me—
   Arms, eyes, spirit—
   The woodgod who goes where I cannot—or will not.
   My creature!"

LIDIAN: No matter how Concord whispers.
   Over the years. Decades.
   Till we are all mummified skeletons
   in Sleepy Hollow Cemetery.

EMERSON *(writing):* "A strong, healthy youth, village-born.
   Solitary as the wood thrush.
   Elusive as the wildcat." *(Pause; laughing)*
   I will not tell them he once, as a boy, set a forest ablaze!
   "A celibate bachelor of thought and Nature.
   The woodgod-poet!"
   Henry Thoreau!—*my* creature. *(Pause)*

LIDIAN: There is no forgiveness where there is MEMORY.
   I have forgotten, and will forget, much.

EMERSON: "I have been a skeleton all this year until
   I have been ashamed…
   Now this young man is beneath my roof I *work! work! work!*
   Suddenly I am well and strong."

LIDIAN: Mr. Emerson will live another forty-one years.
   I to outlive them all. *(Laughs)*

EMERSON: My arrow aimed at your hearts, my friends!
　　How he will burst upon the literary scene
　　like very milkweed scattering his seed.
　　(Laughs, elated)
　　Ah, but he *is* crude.

Lights down on EMERSON.

THOREAU comes forward, carrying a load of firewood in his arms. LIDIAN *encounters him.* THOREAU *regards* LIDIAN *shyly, as they ease past each other.*

LIDIAN *(brightly)*: Good morning, Henry.

THOREAU *(a murmur)*: Good m-morning, Mrs. Emerson.

Lights out.

Scene 8: The Transcendentalists

As lights come up, an animated babble of voices. The scene is EMERSON's *parlor where MARGARET FULLER, JAMES RUSSELL LOWELL, and BRONSON ALCOTT (just arriving, short of breath) are visitors.* EMERSON *is a regal, gracious, somewhat reserved host.* LIDIAN *is self-effacing in a dark silk dress; she moves among the company with few words, then retires to a chair extreme stage left where she takes up her handiwork (knitting or needlepoint). A fire burning in a fireplace at the rear.*

Overlapping and contrapuntal dialogue. These are vigorous, highly verbal individuals.

FULLER *(early 30s but a mature, full-bodied, forceful young woman)*: Ah, Mr. Emerson!—

EMERSON *(taking her proffered hand, to shake)*: Miss Fuller—

FULLER *(coquettishly)*: Now, now!—you must call me "Margaret."

EMERSON: Y-Yes of course: "Margaret"—

FULLER: In your last letter, you did so: don't you recall?

EMERSON *mumbles a vague, startled reply.*

ALCOTT *(early 40s but middle-aged, plump, avuncular)*: Oh dear, am I late? I own no carriage, of course—had to walk—two-thirds of a mile, and in this snow!

LOWELL *(mid-20s, precocious, patrician, smartly dressed)*: Walk? But why?

ALCOTT: We eschew all luxury at our house. We Alcotts are plain-living folk. I think it ethically dubious, you know, to shackle horses to carriage or plow. *(Earnestly)* What if *Equus caballus* shackled *us*?

LOWELL: We should have to put a stop to it, sir, at once. *(Turning to* EMERSON, *shaking hands)* Mr. Emerson!—an honor, as always.

EMERSON: James!—a delight, as always. How smart you look!

FULLER *(pushing in)*: Mr. Emerson, I bring you greetings from our great reformer—Harriet Martineau.

EMERSON: Ah, yes—and how is Miss Martineau?

FULLER is aggressive and coquettish, and stands closer to EMERSON *than* EMERSON *likes; he is forced to step back, or to ease himself around her.*

FULLER: Miss Martineau is one of our saints. She scarcely sleeps night or day and wears herself out, I fear. She asks me to inquire of you when we can expect a public pronouncement from Ralph Waldo Emerson, on the subject of slavery in the South, and female suffrage in all the states.

EMERSON: *I!*—a "public pronouncement"!—but I am not a minister any longer, Miss—Margaret—I am a private citizen who ekes out a living by lectures, essays, and poetry.

FULLER: Nonsense. Ralph Waldo Emerson is our leading American *voice*. If you speak, all will listen.

EMERSON *(cordially)*: As you know, I am an Abolitionist in principle, and opposed to all forms of slavery. But my Transcendentalist instinct is to resist politics; I place my faith in individual conscience.

FULLER *(passionately)*: Nonsense! We must educate and spiritualize the multitudes, to bring them to our level of insight. The Negroes must be freed, and we women must have the vote, or—

LOWELL: These matters, Miss Fuller, are best dealt with, as Mr. Emerson says, by the individual. Where politics intrudes— thought grows crude.

FULLER *(protesting)*: We Transcendentalists have been criticized for our elitism. A great upheaval awaits this nation, and—

EMERSON: Not before our tea, I hope. Will you all be seated? Lidian, my dear—

The guests are seated, with much buzzing. LIDIAN pushes a heavily laden tea cart, glittering with silver and china.

ALCOTT *(sweetly gracious, as if addressing a child)*: Lidian, thank you! *My* wife sends you her greetings, and inquires if you are well?

LIDIAN *(impassively)*: Very well, thank you.

ALCOTT: And you are looking very well.

LOWELL: Indeed, yes. *My* wife sends her greetings, Mrs. Emerson.

LIDIAN makes no reply.

ALCOTT: Have you, um, a little message for Mrs. Alcott?

LIDIAN seems not to have heard, now serving FULLER and EMERSON. ALCOTT and LOWELL exchange startled looks.

FULLER: Lidian!—my, how handsome you are! What a flattering shade of—is it blue?—and how lovely your tea, as always!— how *perfect* everything looks! *(As LIDIAN hands her a teacup and saucer, etc.)* Thank you!

EMERSON: Thank you, dear.

As LIDIAN turns away, FULLER to EMERSON sotto voce, clearly meant to be heard by LIDIAN.

FULLER: What an ideal wife Mrs. Emerson is!—I do envy you such an alliance, quite unknown to *my* sex! She is tender-hearted, submissive, and knows one language only: the language of home.

ALCOTT *(loudly, genially)*: And where is your young disciple, Mr. Emerson?

FULLER: Yes, this "raw young poet" of whom you wrote so glowingly to me?

EMERSON *(wincing)*: Henry Thoreau is not my disciple. I hope I am not the sort of man who encourages disciples!

FULLER: He is the son of an artisan, I believe?

ALCOTT: "Thoreau"—I know them well. Pencil-makers, of modest success.

LOWELL: Pencil-makers! Well, I suppose someone must do it: or we would have no pencils.

EMERSON: Lidian, my dear—where *is* Henry? He knows he's expected... *(Pause; LIDIAN, fussing with the tea cart, seems not to hear)* Lidian? Would you call Henry?

Lights up dimly on THOREAU, extreme stage right. He is sitting on the floor, scribbling in a ledger-journal, by candlelight. A book or two, papers, close about him. THOREAU glances up as if he can hear EMERSON and his guests; his expression is severe.

ALCOTT: One of my sons said he saw Henry Thoreau out on the Assabet alone this morning, ice-skating. In this wind and cold! *I* should freeze to death.

LOWELL: I thought the young man was your servant, Mr. Emerson? How has he time for ice-skating?

EMERSON: No, no—Henry is nobody's servant!

LOWELL: Then what does he do for you?

EMERSON: He is a *presence*. These past ten months, for his room and board and the use of my library, he has helped me with writerly chores—what an eagle eye the young man has, for printers' errors!—and with the upkeep of Bush House, and the grounds. He razed our old, decaying apple trees and planted thirty new ones. *(Pause)* Lidian: do fetch Henry; and make sure he brings his manuscript.

LIDIAN impassively crosses to stage right, where THOREAU sits writing. Though THOREAU is well aware of her approach, he does not look up at first. Then, his eyes narrowed as if he is looking into a blazing light, he looks up. For a moment LIDIAN and THOREAU regard each other wordlessly.

Simultaneously, the others continue their dialogue.

FULLER: And do you think, Mr. Emerson, his work is of a quality for us to publish in *The Dial*?

EMERSON: I am certain. He has promised to read us a new piece tonight. *You* shall judge.

ALCOTT: I know *I* will like it. After that heavy snowstorm of last week, when damp, clotted snow lay on the evergreens on our property, Henry Thoreau happened by to "save" them, as he said, before their limbs cracked. He did this service for any number of neighbors! He says a tree is capable of feeling pain; it has nerve endings like a human being.

LOWELL *(eating)*: Hmmm! On what authority does he say so?—have the trees confided in him?

FULLER *(waving her forefinger in an exaggerated manner, as if she's just made a discovery)*: Ah-HAH!

All look at FULLER, *who basks in their attention.*

EMERSON: Miss— Margaret?—what is it?

FULLER *(coquettishly, to EMERSON)*: The Upanishads.

EMERSON: What of the Upanishads...?

FULLER: Your young disciple obviously purloined the idea—*All sentient things have consciousness*—from the Upanishads, out of your library, Mr. Emerson.

EMERSON: Really Margaret, I doubt it—

FULLER *(shutting her eyes, shaking her head, an overbright school-girl)*: Yes, yes! When first you were so kind as to reply to my letters and guide *me*, two years ago, you suggested that I complement my vast knowledge of European philosophy with an exploration of the Indian sacred scriptures, and so I did, promptly; and so, no doubt, this "Through" has, too.

EMERSON, ALCOTT: "Thoreau" is the name...

FULLER: Yes, I would wager on it!

EMERSON *(slightly annoyed)*: I really don't think—

LIDIAN leads THOREAU into the parlor. THOREAU is both diffident in this company, and brash; a bit disheveled; frowning. EMERSON and his guests turn to gaze at him expectantly. FULLER is wide-eyed.

FULLER *(an undertone, to LOWELL)*: Why—it's a *faun*.

EMERSON *(on his feet, warmly genial, drawing THOREAU in)*: Why, Henry! At last. We have visitors from Boston—Margaret Fuller, editor of *The Dial*— *(FULLER and THOREAU exchange murmured greetings, shake hands)* —and James Russell Lowell— *(greetings, handshake)* And of course you know our dear neighbor Bronson Alcott—

ALCOTT *(shaking* THOREAU's *hand heartily):* Good to see you, lad!

EMERSON: —My friend Henry David Thoreau, of Concord. *(Pause, an attempt at uncharacteristic ebullience)* A young man who attended Harvard College—and yet is a poet.

FULLER, LOWELL, ALCOTT laugh as if this is very witty. THOREAU stares glumly at his feet. LIDIAN retreats to the edge of the gathering; takes up her knitting or needlepoint; but she is keenly aware of THOREAU and his ordeal.

FULLER: Henry David!—may I inquire—

THOREAU sees that the fire needs tending, and goes to put another log in the fireplace. He is wordless, brusque.

FULLER, LOWELL react with raised brows.

EMERSON: Very good, Henry! Thank you.

FULLER *(beginning anew):* Henry David!—may I inquire: You have read the sacred Indian scripture, the Upanishads, yes?

THOREAU *(a bit overwhelmed):* Y-Yes...

FULLER: Out of Mr. Emerson's library, yes?

THOREAU: —Some, not much. I—

FULLER *(to EMERSON, triumphant):* Yes, YES?—you see, Mr. Emerson?

EMERSON *(embarrassed):* Well. A trifle, I'm sure. —Henry, do be seated.

FULLER: I think we must always acknowledge our spiritual mentors. Whether they are living persons, or books.

ALCOTT: Have some tea, son! And these little cakes—or whatever— are delicious.

LOWELL: Yes, delicious. Indeed. Are these—raisins?

FULLER: Raisin *bread!* How very droll! *(Calling over)* Lidian, you have invented a new bread, have you?—new, at least, to me.

LIDIAN: It is not my invention, but Henry Thoreau's. *He* is the baker in this house. *(Continuing with her knitting or needlepoint)*

FULLER: No! Amazing.

LOWELL *(bemused)*: Indeed. Amazing.

ALCOTT *(chewing)*: It is a very *poem* in one's mouth. Far tastier than most.

EMERSON: Henry, you must introduce yourself to my friends. I have told them only a little of you.

FULLER: Teasingly little!

THOREAU sits silent, frowning at the floor. A beat.

EMERSON: Or, you might read us something. That account of your winter hike to Wachusett, which I found so promising—have you revised it yet?

FULLER *(encouraging, enthusiastic)*: As editor of *The Dial*, I am most anxious to hear your work, Henry. *(Pause; THOREAU fails to respond, shifting self-consciously in his chair)* You know that Mr. Emerson spurred us into starting a magazine—we Transcendentalists must express ourselves to the multitudes.

ALCOTT: Otherwise, we should be misunderstood. Dismissed as mere dreamers and Utopianists!

LOWELL *(making an effort to be sympathetic)*: Henry, Mr. Emerson has said you attended Harvard? What do you wish to make your life's vocation?

THOREAU *(with a glance at EMERSON, whom he does not want to embarrass)*: To live, and write of what I see, and love.

LOWELL: "Love"?—here in Concord?

THOREAU *(more aggressively)*: Why not Concord, since Concord gave birth to me?

FULLER *(as one might speak to a child)*: But have you traveled abroad, Henry? To Italy?—France?

LOWELL: England? Germany?

THOREAU *(defensively)*: I've t-traveled a good deal in Concord.

FULLER and LOWELL laugh condescendingly.

EMERSON *(quickly)*: Henry is our newest species of American poet— a poet who is a naturalist. He uses facts as material to the mythology which he is writing, I believe. Yes, Henry? *(Pause; a bit boldly)* His genius is for the Cosmos, in a grain of sand.

FULLER *(smiling, skeptical)*: "Genius!" Mr. Emerson rarely praises any of us, Henry. I hope you are duly grateful.

THOREAU *(haughtily)*: If Mr. Emerson is correct, there's no need for gratitude. And if he is not—there's no need.

This is the first indication of THOREAU's *arrogance, and it is received with surprise by the visitors.* EMERSON *laughs.* LIDIAN *glances over, with approval.*

LOWELL *(combative)*: You seem not to comprehend, Mr. Thoreau, that "genius" is nothing but consensus of opinion. Shakespeare is a genius, and Poet So-and-So—no names to be uttered!—is not, because the majority of us *say so.*

THOREAU: No. Genius exists in and of itself.

ALCOTT *(sagely)*: I like that! Genius resides with the Divine, I believe.

LOWELL: And do you truly believe, Mr. Thoreau, that *you* are a literary genius?

THOREAU is suddenly engaging, shrugging and smiling boyishly.

THOREAU: I won't know, will I?—until I write my heart out in the effort.

FULLER *(touched)*: How true, how true!—for all of us who aspire to literary fame! We must write our hearts out in the effort.

ALCOTT: Read us some of your work, dear Henry!

FULLER: Please do!

LOWELL *(a bit dryly)*: Indeed, *do.*

THOREAU *(frowning)*: My perfect book would be a foil whereon the waves of silence might break.

EMERSON *(impatiently)*: Henry, you're too young, and too inexperienced, for such attitudes. Read us your work, and have done with it.

THOREAU *(chastened)*: Yes, sir. *(Takes up manuscript, abruptly and awkwardly)* "W-Walking through the Lee farm swamp, a dozen or more rods from the river—"

FULLER: Is this a poem? an essay?

THOREAU pauses, staring at her.

EMERSON: Very likely, a passage from Henry's journal.

LOWELL: *I* would prefer poetry, or prose, with a fixed form.

ALCOTT: A journal possesses its own form—various and picaresque as a river.

EMERSON: Henry, please continue—

FULLER: Did I interrupt? Please continue!

As THOREAU reads his passage from his Journal, his delivery is weak and hesitant at first; then, despite asides and interruptions, which he seems not to hear, it becomes stronger and more assured. The last several lines are uttered passionately and beautifully.

THOREAU *(rising to his feet, as if unconsciously)*: "Walking through the Lee farm swamp, a dozen or more rods from the river, I found a large box trap closed. I opened it and found in it the remains of a gray rabbit—skin, bones, and mold—closely fitting the right-angled corner of one side..."

FULLER *(murmur, exaggerated compassion)*: Oh, poor *rabbit*!

THOREAU: "...It was so much vegetable mold, dead some years. None of the trap remained but the box itself, which had the appearance of having been floated off in an upright position by a freshet. It had been a..."

LOWELL stirs impatiently, sighs, pours himself more tea.

THOREAU: "...rabbit's living tomb. He had gradually starved to death in it. What a tragedy..."

ALCOTT *(aside to EMERSON)*: The Lee farm swamp! If I'd known, I would have rescued it!

THOREAU: "...to have occurred within a box in one of our quiet swamps! The trapper lost his box, the rabbit his life..."

FULLER *(aside, to EMERSON)*: A cruel equation!

THOREAU: "The box had not been gnawed. After days and nights of moaning and struggle..."

LOWELL has continued to make restless movements, sighs; glancing about as if inviting others to share his derision. But the others are listening intently.

THOREAU: "...heard for a few rods through the swamp, increasing weakness and emaciation and delirium, the rabbit breathes its last..."

FULLER: Ah!

EMERSON *(to FULLER)*: Margaret, please.

FULLER *(to EMERSON, childlike apology)*: Oh but I *am* listening!

THOREAU: "They tell you of opening the tomb and finding by the contortions of the body that it was buried alive. This was such a case. Let the trapper dream of the dead rabbit in its ark, as it sailed, like a small meeting-house with its rude spire, slowly, with a grand and solemn motion, far amid the alders."

A beat.

EMERSON *(puzzled)*: Thank you, Henry, but...it is not complete, is it?

ALCOTT is clapping his hands vigorously; cheeks damp with tears.

ALCOTT: Such sentiment! Worthy of Wordsworth!

FULLER: Very—"naturalistic." Most unusual. Rather too rough-hewn for *The Dial*, I'm afraid, but...

LOWELL *(sharply, to EMERSON)*: He *is* gifted, your young disciple. Gifted and limited. *(A chuckle)* Rousseau's Noble Savage, in Concord, Mass.!

FULLER *(giggling)*: "Savage"?—with a *Harvard degree*?

THOREAU has been unaware of his audience until this moment, and now turns to stare at them. He suddenly thrusts his manuscript into the fire, and strides out of the parlor. All look after him in astonishment.

ALCOTT and EMERSON react simultaneously.

ALCOTT *(distressed)*: Oh my, oh my!— *(He takes up a poker, tries without success to get the burning manuscript out of the fire.)*

EMERSON: What?—*Henry!*

THOREAU has retreated to his space at extreme stage right, in a fury, clenching and unclenching his fists. EMERSON hurries to the parlor door (but not beyond) to call after him, as the guests murmur and buzz among themselves. ("Did you ever—?" "What an outburst!" "He is a savage!" "Oh, look at it blaze!" etc.)

EMERSON *(angry, but a bit frightened):* Henry?—Henry Thoreau?—come back here. You are behaving most childishly. Under my roof!

THOREAU has thrown himself to the floor, hugging his knees in a childlike sullen posture.

Immediately after THOREAU's exit, LIDIAN has tossed down her handiwork to follow. She moves swiftly and purposefully, with dignity. THOREAU hears her approach but does not glance up. LIDIAN comes to stand close beside him. A beat. LIDIAN brushes THOREAU's hair from his damp forehead. THOREAU looks up at her. Freeze.

EMERSON, *at parlor door. (Not seeing THOREAU and LIDIAN.) Freeze.*

FULLER *(thrilled undertone):* A faun!—a wild, dangerous faun!

Lights out.

ACT II

Scene 9: Death by Lockjaw

In darkness, a sound of cheerful whistling. Lights up brightly. JOHN THOREAU, animated and vigorous, is preparing to shave, stropping a razor and whistling. Shaving soap on his face.

JOHN: It happened on New Year's Day.
   I was up early, and shaving, in my parents' house.
   I was happy at the prospect of a new year.
   I was happy at the sight of a fresh-fallen snow outside my
      window and a single bright red cardinal in a juniper tree.
   (JOHN imitates the cardinal's distinctive call.)
   I was happy for my dear brother Henry David.
   With whom I would be going ice-skating that morning.
   (Pause; considering)

Was I envious of his new life?
Living with Concord's first family—the Emersons.
A friend of the renowned Ralph Waldo!
Beginning to be published in Boston and New York journals!
Beginning to be KNOWN.
Henry Thoreau, *my* young brother.
(Pause, beginning to shave)
And Henry's improvements in Father's pencils
    were making the Thoreaus *prosperous!*—
    almost. *(Pause)*
(JOHN leans forward confidentially)
I guessed Henry's secret ambition, of all who knew him.
His passion to be a *great* writer—hidden like the side of the
    moon turned from us, even when the moon shines its
    brightest.

THOREAU *appears, extreme stage left, rear. Dim light. He wears his odd-shaped hat, outdoor clothes, boots. Listening.*

JOHN *(simply)*: I was closest to Henry of all the world.
    Yet I never plumbed his heart.
    I loved him.
    I believed he loved me...

THOREAU *(a cry of warning)*: John! Be careful—

JOHN: Ow! Damn! *(He has cut himself shaving; a thin trickle of blood on his cheek.)*

JOHN *wipes his face; puts a small bandage on his cut; sets aside his shaving things; brushes his unruly hair; dons a coat.*

JOHN: I thought nothing of the cut—of course.
    As boys, we'd cut, scratched, scraped ourselves a thousand
        times.
    As a boy, Henry had practically chopped off a toe. *(Laughs)*
    Him, the expert woodsman!
    So I thought nothing of the cut.
    And a day or two passed, and I began to notice pain—
    throbbing, swelling—
    (he removes the bandage, prods the tiny scratch)
    —the scratch *was* inflamed, not healing—
    I was running a fever—

our Concord doctor Bartlett examined it and
said it was nothing, it would heal.
But that night I began to have more pain—
sudden stabs of pain—
(touching his face, neck, arms)
—my joints—
(his legs)
—a terrible dizziness as if the earth opened before me.
So suddenly, I was NOT MYSELF—
I would never be MYSELF again. (Pause)
And in the morning—my jaws locked.
NO!

THOREAU (*overlapping*): NO!

THOREAU rushes to JOHN *who has sunk to the floor, writhing and convulsing, tearing at his clothes.* THOREAU *bends over him.*

Strobe lighting.

JOHN (*raving through "locked" jaws*): Where are you my brother help
me don't leave me Henry—

HENRY: John, I'm here! John—

JOHN'*s cries become inarticulate shrieks. A final convulsion, and stillness.*

THOREAU, *sobbing, lies over* JOHN'*s lifeless body.*

Lights out.

Scene 10: The Lovers

Lights up. Stage right, EMERSON'*s study, where* EMERSON *and* MARGARET
FULLER *are engaged in conversation. Some weeks later.* EMERSON *is seated
beside his desk, and* FULLER *is in a chair facing him.* FULLER *has brought
materials pertaining to* The Dial *for* EMERSON *to examine, and has also
given him a gift: a hefty, gilt-edged leatherbound volume.*

EMERSON: How generous of you, Margaret! A specially bound copy
of Kant's—

FULLER (*the syllables rolling off her tongue*): Kritik der reinen Vernunft!—

EMERSON *(leafing through the book, a wincing sort of smile)*: In the original German—of course.

FULLER: Well, Mr. Emerson!—didn't I promise I would instruct you in Kant's German, in exchange for your myriad kindnesses to me? Any time you wish...

EMERSON *(a bit evasively)*: If only my lecture tour in Ohio and Illinois were not imminent...

FULLER: Kant's *Undinge* can scarcely be grasped in our crude English translations; let alone *der Entfremdungsgefühl*.

EMERSON *(somewhat stymied)*: Indeed, yes. I mean—no.

FULLER *(dramatic gesture)*: *Entfremdungsgefühl*—"Perplexing unreality." Except in oases of spiritual enlightenment, like this very room, I sense it all about me.

EMERSON: Indeed?

Lights up on LIDIAN, stage left. In another part of the house. LIDIAN, hair in coils but not wrapped around her head, legs curled beneath her voluminous skirts, sits on the floor looking through the contents of the blue-painted trunk. (LIDIAN is barefoot, her feet hidden beneath the skirts.)

LIDIAN *(softly singing)*: "I saw a ship a-sailing
A-sailing on the sea...
And oh! it was a-laden
With pretty things for me..." *(Pause; she has lifted a child's toy or clothing out of the trunk)*
Why cannot I cry anymore? I'm not yet an old woman,
to have dried up.

THOREAU appears from stage left. LIDIAN is about to shut the child's item back into the trunk, but, seeing that it is THOREAU and not her husband, she does not.

THOREAU is carrying an oddly shaped, sculpted-looking object which we can't identify at first. (It is the lower jaw of a wild hog, bleached white, with big teeth and curving tusks.)

THOREAU and LIDIAN regard each other silently. During the following exchange between EMERSON and FULLER, THOREAU approaches LIDIAN, kneels on the floor close to her and offers her the oddly shaped object.

EMERSON and FULLER speak simultaneously. Each is rather keyed-up and excited; EMERSON of course is the more controlled.

EMERSON: Hmmm. And now, Margaret, these *Dial* galleys— *(He picks them up, frowns over them.)*

FULLER *(a bit breathless)*: Oh—Mr. Emerson?—I h-hope you are not offended?

EMERSON: With these?

FULLER: No, no!—You have not yet mentioned my letter of Thursday last. *(Squirming in agony, suspense, hope)* You *did* receive it?

EMERSON *(rubbing his nose)*: Hmmm.

FULLER: It may have been, I...argued too forcibly?

EMERSON: I scarcely recall.

FULLER *(nervous laugh)*: My clumsy little poem... *(Reciting, head at a tilt, both coy and pleading)* "Beam always thus,/ thou bright particular star—/ I would not have thee nearer./ Oh thou art blind/ With thy deep-seeing eyes." *(Blushing)*

EMERSON: Enigmatic verse.

FULLER: Rough, unhoned rhythms—

EMERSON: Such rhythms sometimes please.

FULLER: Yes?

EMERSON: And sometimes jar.

LIDIAN *(in a low voice)*: Henry, how did you find me *here*! *(Pause)* And what is this you've brought me? *(Pause; LIDIAN touches the jawbone, with a sudden wild little laugh)* Ugh!—it is the jawbone of a—hog?

THOREAU: The lower jaw of a wild hog. I found it at the base of Mt. Merrimack.

LIDIAN: Mt. Merrimack!—is that where you've been? *(Pause)* Such teeth! Tusks! *(Shudders)*

THOREAU: So beautiful.

LIDIAN: Beautiful?—yes... *(Holding the jawbone up, stroking it)*

EMERSON: Most of the persons I see in my own household I see across a gulf. I tried to explain this to poor Miss Fuller.

THOREAU: You should never have married. Damn you!

EMERSON : I *am* a bachelor in spirit. Yet women have loved me; I've never understood. *(Dryly)* Unless to credit it to Woman's appetite for hurt.

THOREAU: I believe Lidian loves me. I know Lidian needs me.

EMERSON: You will find, Henry, that Woman rarely knows her own mind.

THOREAU: Lidian is not "Woman"—she's herself. Ask her!

EMERSON *(pedantically)*: Woman knows what she is told. Her love, no less than her need.

THOREAU: Call her! Ask her!

EMERSON: You would have me embarrass my wife, to please a whim of yours?

THOREAU: Lidian is your "wife" in name only. All of Boston knows. *That* is embarrassing.

EMERSON: Indeed, all of Boston "knows"? "Knows" what?

THOREAU: About these "soul-mates" of yours—Margaret Fuller is only the most pathetic.

EMERSON: Margaret Fuller is an estimable individual. There is no one like her. As Poe observed, "There is Man, and there is Woman, and there is Margaret Fuller." *(Pause, chuckles)* I cherish her devoted friendship.

THOREAU: How do you think Lidian feels?—these sickly, dishonest Platonizing romances—in *her* house.

EMERSON: In strictest parlance, Henry, this is not Lidian's house, but mine. She lives here as my wife. At any time, as she well knows, she is free to leave, to visit her family in Plymouth, or to reside there permanently. As you, my young friend, are free to leave at any time.

THOREAU: Not without Lidian!

EMERSON: And where, Henry, would you go *with* Lidian? On one of your mountain-climbing expeditions?

THOREAU begins coughing, striking his chest with his fist.

EMERSON: *You* are the true bachelor, Henry Thoreau. Your passion is too pure for any woman.

THOREAU rushes at EMERSON with his fist upraised; EMERSON flinches, but stands his ground; several books fall from the edge of his desk.

THOREAU *(appalled at his own behavior)*:   My God!—I'm s-sorry.

A beat.

EMERSON *(goes to the door, calls)*:   Lidian? My dear—LIDIAN?

The men wait in silence for LIDIAN to appear. THOREAU paces anxiously; EMERSON is unmoving.

LIDIAN enters. Her hair is now perfectly groomed and her dress impeccable; she is no longer barefoot. Her expression betrays some initial anxiety, but she forces herself to be impassive; she does not look at THOREAU.

EMERSON *(holding out his hand to LIDIAN)*:   Lidian, Henry believes he has something to say.

THOREAU succumbs to another brief coughing fit.

THOREAU *(recovering, with an effort)*:   Lidian, I—l—love you. I want to—

LIDIAN, as if unhearing, goes hurriedly to pick up the books that have fallen from EMERSON's desk. She tidies up the desk as the men look on.

THOREAU: —want to m-make you happy— Lidian?—

LIDIAN stands beside EMERSON, her gaze downcast.

EMERSON *(a kind, condescending voice)*:   My dear? Do you have any response?

LIDIAN *(wetting her lips)*:   I love you, Henry, as an—elder sister.

THOREAU: That's a lie!

EMERSON: Henry. You forget yourself.

THOREAU: Lidian, look at me. Please—

LIDIAN *(not looking at him, in the identical voice)*:   I love you, Henry, as an—elder sister.

THOREAU (*hurt, pleading*): Lidian!

EMERSON: Mrs. Emerson has spoken, Henry. (*Pause*) And now I shall speak. (*His manner becomes imperial, devastating.*) I am most disappointed in you, Henry. To betray our kindness!—our charity in taking you in! But that is not the worst—the worst is that you have failed to live up to your promise *as a writer*.

THOREAU: Wr-writer...?

EMERSON: I had thought of you as one of that company who might snap the iron hoops that bind us. Yes, you have published— (*he lifts up, and lets fall, some journals on his desk, including* The Dial) —yes, your name is "known"—in our genteel quarters. But the American in you—the brute *gold*—does not yet flow. You lack ambition. You, a Damascus blade of a man, such as one may search through nature to parallel, laid up here, indoors with *us*, to rust and ruin!

This is a wholly unexpected assault which amazes THOREAU. *He is defensive, recognizing the truth here, but denying it.*

THOREAU: You don't kn-know my plans—

EMERSON: A fig for your plans! Every "promising" young poet out of Harvard has "plans"!

EMERSON, *grown fierce, advances upon* THOREAU, *who has been in retreat since* LIDIAN's *denial.* EMERSON *snatches up a sheet of paper from his desk and makes a waving gesture with it, as if to banish* THOREAU *out the door.*

EMERSON: Henry Thoreau, I see nothing for you now but that wilderness above Walden Pond—go out upon that, build yourself a hut, and there begin the grand process of devouring yourself alive. (*He thrusts the paper at* THOREAU.)

THOREAU: W-what is this?

EMERSON: A deed of purchase for that land—in my name. Take it!

THOREAU: Th-thank you very much! That's exactly what I'll do.

THOREAU *exits.*

EMERSON *turns back to* LIDIAN, *who turns quickly from him.*

Lights out.

Scene 12: Walden, 1845

Green-tinctured light. Again the sound of the Universal Lyre in its most ethereal tone. The atmosphere is dreamlike but suffused with joy. THOREAU *appears like a sleepwalker who comes awake, and grows vigorous, purposeful. He is unshaven and his hair disheveled. As he speaks, the light gradually shifts to the subtly golden radiance of indirect sunshine.*

THOREAU: To go to Walden. To return
  to Walden. The white-pine woods above the cove.
  Deep-emerald water. Floating clouds.
  Sky mirror. Shock of its cold.
  Transparency. Stillness. (Pause)
  To go to Walden at last.
  Earth's eye. You fall and fall forever.
  Geese flying like a tempest overhead.
  In the blaze of noon—a thrumming of bright dragonflies.
  To go to Walden where the blue iris grows in pure water.
  To go to Walden where red foxes run.
  To go to Walden where squirrels fly overhead in the scrub-
    oaks.
  To go to Walden where snakes glide invisible through the
    grass.
  To go to Walden to suck life's marrow from the bone.
  To go to Walden where the well for my drinking is already
    dug.
  It is no dream of mine but it may be that
  I, Henry David Thoreau, am a dream of Walden.

A beat. In another voice, more probing, at first skeptical; then rising to euphoria, determination.

THOREAU: To throw off "personal history"—
  to give birth to myself—
  to tear off the clock's damning hands—
  to obliterate Memory—
  to make myself the man I am not—
  to make myself HENRY DAVID THOREAU—
  no man's slave, and no woman's lover—
  no father's son, and no son's father—
  to go to Walden as a pilgrim, as a child—
  to worship God in each seed, each raindrop, each rock,

each heartbeat—
to begin again, in innocence—

A beat.

THOREAU: I SAY THAT IT IS POSSIBLE!

THOREAU constructs his cabin. Perhaps an ax floats, or flies, into his hand. By degrees a "cabin-shape" should emerge, ten feet wide by fifteen feet long, eight feet in height, with one door, one fireplace, two windows. Going through the motions of building the cabin, wielding the ax, perhaps a hammer, nails, saw, etc., in brisk rhythmic movements, THOREAU whistles intermittently: we recognize, if he does not, the whistling of his brother JOHN at the start of Scene 9.

THOREAU: Near the end of March 1845, I borrowed an ax and went
down to the woods by Walden Pond, and began to cut down
some tall arrowy pines for timber. I hewed the main timbers six
inches square, most of the studs on two sides only, and the rafters
and floor timbers on one side, leaving the bark on, so that they
were just as straight and much stronger than sawed ones. *(Pause)*
I dug my cellar in the side of a hill sloping to the south. It was
but two hours' work. *(Pause)* By April first, the ice of Walden
Pond began cracking. By May first, I set up the frame of my house.
By July fourth, Independence Day, it was boarded and roofed,
and ready for occupancy. By October first, the chimney was built,
the plastering and shingling were completed. *(Pause, proudly)*
My house, as fine as any in Concord I think it: ten feet wide by
fifteen long, and eight feet in height. The cost?—for such as
second-hand boards, bricks, windows, hinges, nails?—$28.12.

A beat.

THOREAU: If I seem to boast more than is becoming, my excuse is
that I brag for humanity rather than myself. *(Pause)*
I have heard no bad news. *(Pause)*
I am the first man of creation, the Adam of this shore.
And no rib torn from *my* side! *(Pause)*

THOREAU continues his brisk, matter-of-fact "construction."

THOREAU: My first year, I planted two and a half acres of beans,
potatoes, corn, peas and turnips. My second year, I planted even
less, for I'd found I needed less. *(Proudly)* My townspeople looked
upon me askance, as a wild eccentric, or hermit, but I was the

only free man of my acquaintance—for I was not anchored to any house or farm. No children's crying disturbed the peace of *my* woods. *(Pause)* For two years I lived in Walden woods, and for five years I maintained myself solely by the labor of my hands. I found that I could support myself by working but *six* weeks out of *fifty-two*—devoting the remainder of my time to living. And to writing.

THOREAU strides to his desk, takes up his ledger-journal and a pencil.

THOREAU: Very few books I carried into the woods. Very few I needed. For it was my own book I was writing—*Walden*. As I lived, I wrote of my experiment in living. As I wrote of my experiment in living, I lived. My words became me: HENRY DAVID THOREAU. I need no other epitaph.

A beat. THOREAU paces about. There is a tincture of mania in his euphoria which he manages, just barely, to control.

THOREAU *(gloating)*: I MADE MYSELF THE MAN I WAS NOT. AND, BEING SO MADE, I... *WAS.*

An echo as of thunder: "I WAS... I WAS... WAS..."

The radiant gold light has been steadily dimming; there is a corresponding sound of thunder. A sudden flash of lightning. THOREAU cringes in his cabin. A sound of pelting, drumming rain on the roof.

THOREAU: If the damned roof leaks, I shall not record *that.* *(Despondent laugh)* Am I...imprisoned here? *(Pause, looking out the window; as if reasoning with someone)* TO LIVE ONE LIFE, YOU MUST REJECT ALL OTHERS. *(Shivers; coughs; strikes chest with his fist)* Am I alone?—it is my CHOICE.

The storm continues. A discordant music. THOREAU loses confidence.

ELLEN SEWALL, as a girl of seventeen, appears at a distance, a taunting apparition. Her hair is loose and the front of her dress partly open.

ELLEN: Henry Thoreau...

THOREAU: No! I don't know you.

ELLEN *(seductive)*: Henry Thoreau. I did love you.

THOREAU: No.

ELLEN: Loved loved LOVED YOU. *(As she strokes her body)*

THOREAU: NO.

ELLEN: You were not MAN ENOUGH to take me.

THOREAU: NO!

ELLEN (*deliciously*): Animal. Crude. Henry Thoreau. You disgust me.

THOREAU kicks a chair across the room. ELLEN vanishes.

THOREAU: Leave me alone, you—*woman*! All Nature is my bride.

Rain continues drumming on the roof. THOREAU lights a candle at his desk and takes up his journal to write in it, but he's too excited to sit down.

THOREAU (*determined*): "I love to be alone. I never found the companion that was so companionable as SOLITUDE." Yes, good! "In my time at Walden, I never felt lonesome, or in the least oppressed by a sense of solitude, but once...when, for a dreadful hour, I came near to collapse." (*Pause*) No: strike that. "...when, for an hour, I doubted if the neighborhood of man was not essential to a serene and healthy life." (*Pause*) "...But I was at the same time conscious of a slight insanity in my mood, and seemed to foresee my recovery." Yes, exactly! "...In the midst of a gentle rain while these thoughts prevailed, I was suddenly sensible of such sweet and beneficent society in Nature..."

A lightning flash, and a peal of thunder so loud that THOREAU drops his journal.

JOHN THOREAU appears at a distance, as an apparition.

JOHN: Henry!—dear brother...

THOREAU: John!

JOHN: Come to me!

THOREAU (*shielding his face*): Am I dreaming? I *am* dreaming—

JOHN: I love you, Henry. I alone have plumbed the depths of your heart.

THOREAU (*frightened*): John, no—leave me alone.

JOHN: Brother, would you deny *me*? *My* suffering, *your* agony?

THOREAU (*guilty, despairing*): Am I to wallow in grief, forever?

JOHN: Better grief than nothing.

THOREAU *(picking up the journal)*: This that I have is NOT NOTHING!

JOHN *(tenderly, seductively, opening his arms to THOREAU)*: Brother! No one has loved us as we loved each other. Would you mock my suffering? Recall how I died.

THOREAU: Nature *is* sweet and beneficent. The world *is* good.

JOHN *(pleading, raving)*: BROTHER COME TO ME HELP ME BROTHER DON'T ABANDON ME BROTHER—

THOREAU: God help me!—

THOREAU drops the journal. He begins to have convulsions; his jaws lock in a grotesque parody of a grin. He tears at his hair and clothes, groaning in terror and anguish.

THOREAU: —help HELP ME—

A flash of lightning. A peal of thunder. THOREAU staggers toward his bed and collapses onto the floor. JOHN has vanished.

Lights out.

Light up. Next morning: a brilliant radiance, as at the start of the scene. The Universal Lyre in its ethereal mode. THOREAU, on the floor, wakes, and looks around in apprehension; manages to get up, unsteadily; washes his face in a basin. His clothes are torn and there is a bruise on the side of his face. He has a haggard, dazed look, but the terror is past.

Close outside the cabin, a cardinal sings.

THOREAU whistles in reply. A beat. The bird answers.

THOREAU *(in the doorway, sunshine on his face)*: That's it, then. I turn my face to—"the world."

Lights out.

Scene 13: "I Have Always Loved Her"

Lights up. Main Street, Concord. A summer day, 1854. ELLEN SEWALL OSGOOD and her friend RACHEL are walking together, carrying parcels.

Though, in scene 12, "ELLEN SEWALL" appeared as a beautiful young girl in THOREAU's imagination, the actual woman is much changed; we almost don't recognize her. She is thirty-four years old, still attractive, but decidedly matronly, and conspicuously pregnant. RACHEL has aged less well, with sagging jowls, dents beneath her eyes, a small mean downturned mouth.

The two women have sighted someone up ahead.

ELLEN *(gripping RACHEL's arm)*: Is it—him?

RACHEL *(peering nearsightedly)*: How fierce he looks!

ELLEN: They say he has grown strange.

RACHEL: I wonder he won't cross the street to avoid you.

ELLEN *(sadly)*: Oh, it's been so long…he sees me often in Concord, I'm sure.

THOREAU approaches ELLEN and RACHEL, oblivious of them. At thirty-seven, he is vigorous and robust; a striking figure, with a dark, handsome beard. He has a true woodsman's look and his skin is dark as if stained. No pretense of a townsman's clothes now. He wears a battered straw hat and carries a large bird's nest.

ELLEN: Henry Thoreau—!

THOREAU, following his own thoughts, pauses to blink at ELLEN. After an awkward moment, he smiles stiffly, tips his hat, and extends his hand to shake her gloved hand.

THOREAU: Mrs. Osgood.

ELLEN: I believe you know Mrs. —

THOREAU merely glances at RACHEL.

THOREAU *(coolly courteous)*: I'm sure we are acquainted. All of Concord knows one another rather too well.

RACHEL, insulted, draws in her breath sharply, and looks at ELLEN as if to say, Do you see what the man is like? But neither ELLEN nor THOREAU notices.

ELLEN *(shyly)*: I hope you are well, Henry?

THOREAU: And you, Mrs. Osgood.

ELLEN: And your family?

THOREAU (*bemused by social conventions*): So far as I keep up, all are well; or, in any case, not perceptibly worse. And—Reverend Osgood?

ELLEN: *Very* well.

THOREAU (*vaguely*): And, is it—your little girl?—

ELLEN: Oh, Becky is fifteen now! Linton is twelve. Elias is soon to turn seven. And— (*Breathless laugh, indicating her swollen belly*)

THOREAU (*a bit startled*): I see!

ELLEN (*gently chiding*): You've never once come to visit, as Joseph and I have asked you, Henry. All these years!

THOREAU: I'm afraid I am not one for socializing. I hope you will excuse me? (*A gesture as if about to walk on*)

ELLEN (*quickly*): Joseph and I are both great readers of yours, Henry. We subscribe to *The Dial* and *Putnam's*, and see your essays frequently. Joseph says you are to have a book published soon?— named for our own Walden Pond?

THOREAU (*genially*): I hope I don't bring notoriety upon it.

RACHEL: What *is* that smelly nest?

THOREAU (*exhibiting it, proudly*): A peregrine falcon's. A local rarity.

ELLEN (*examining it*): Oh! it's so finely woven! Are those the eggs?

THOREAU: Their remains.

ELLEN: Where did you find it?

THOREAU: On Mt. Merrimack, this morning.

ELLEN: Did you climb to get it?—isn't that dangerous?

THOREAU: I'm doing a study of falcons, hawks, and vultures, their breeding and migration habits.

RACHEL: Vultures—ugh! The nastiest things.

THOREAU: Yet Nature requires them, Mrs. —, even as Nature would seem to require you.

RACHEL (*sniffing*): Isn't it cruel of you, Mr. Thoreau, to steal the birds' nest from them?

THOREAU *(cuttingly)*: The falcons have finished with their nest, Mrs. — . The spring breeding season is over. The fledglings have made their debut, and flown away. Male and female peregrines are no longer quite so *passionate* and quite so *domestic*. *(Pause)* I fear the marital vows have been forgotten.

RACHEL is rebuffed. THOREAU again is about to continue on his way, but ELLEN nervously retains him.

ELLEN: Henry, I—I see the posters announcing your lecture at the Lyceum—is it next Monday? Joseph and I will certainly attend. Will you—

Socially ill at ease, not knowing how to extricate himself from this conversation, THOREAU simply turns away, mumbling a farewell. He tips his hat at the women and strides off. They stare after him.

RACHEL: It's *he* who smells!—I doubt he ever bathes.

ELLEN: Rachel!

RACHEL: D'you know what they call him in town?—"Dolittle." For his work is to *do little*—except tramp about in the woods, and write his—what d'you call them—"essays"—that nobody can comprehend; and that are blasphemous, if you could comprehend them. He is one of these wild-eyed Abolitionists, too: ready to free the Negro slaves, and invite them all up here.

ELLEN: But slavery is wrong, Rachel. Slavery is an evil thing.

RACHEL: That doesn't make the Negroes white like *us*, does it? *(A gesture at THOREAU's departing back)* What a shame it was, if God had to take one of the Thoreau brothers, it was John!

ELLEN: Rachel, that's a terrible thing to say. Henry Thoreau is a man of—distinction. *(Pause)* How proud I should be, if he were my husband.

RACHEL *(smirking)*: Henry Thoreau!—your husband! Don't you know— *(Whispering in ELLEN's ear)*

ELLEN *(offended)*: I don't believe it. Concord would pull a great man down to *its* level.

ELLEN walks off, toward stage right, with RACHEL, laughing, close behind her. THOREAU has almost exited, stage left.

Lights on THOREAU, who pauses.

THOREAU *(a rush of feeling)*: I have always loved her. *(Pause; he transforms this into prose for his journal, speaking in an altered voice.)* "Ellen Sewall. I have always loved her."

THOREAU *secures the nest in both arms and exits.*

Lights out.

Scene 14: The Arrest

In darkness, the distant sound of a village marching band. Lights up. Thoreau is addressing an audience. He stands on a platform, at a podium, manuscript in hand. Overhead is a scroll, gold letters on white: CONCORD LYCEUM. Stage left, an American flag. THOREAU is dressed slightly more formally than in the previous scene, without hat and boots. His eyes shine and his cheeks are flushed. His beard gives him a fierce Biblical-prophet look.

THOREAU: My townspeople—thank you for inviting me to speak on "Where I Lived, and What I Lived For." Many inquiries have been put to my family and me as to my motives for moving on Independence Day 1835 to Walden Pond; many rumors have been circulated. *(Begins to read, earnestly)* "I have seen young men, my townsmen, whose misfortune it is to have inherited houses, farms, 'property'... Who has made these luckless citizens serfs of the soil? Why should they begin digging their graves as soon as they are born? The mass of men lead lives of quiet desperation. It is a fool's life."

ANONYMOUS MAN *(shouts)*: Who's calling who a fool?

THOREAU *(speaking louder)*: "At Walden Pond, each morning was the first morning of creation. I rose early, and bathed in the pond, and it was a religious exercise..."

ANONYMOUS MAN *(laughing)*: Like a hog!

THOREAU *(throws down manuscript to confront audience)*: Be it life or death, we crave only reality. I am here to bring you—reality. God himself culminates in the present moment, and will never be more divine in the lapse of the ages. *(Strikes fist on podium)*

ANONYMOUS WOMAN: That's blasphemy!

THOREAU *(comes out from behind podium, excited, stammering)*: Blasphemy! Trade—capital—war-mongering—four million Negro slaves in the country—*that* is blasphemy!

The marching band music is getting louder. THOREAU tries to make himself heard over it.

ANONYMOUS MAN: Nigger-lover!

ANONYMOUS WOMAN: Abolitionist! Rabble-rouser!

THOREAU: Yes I am a "nigger-lover"!—yes I am an Abolitionist!

VOICES: Atheist! Rabble-rouser! Woods-burner! *(Chanting)* WOODS-BURNER! WOODS-BURNER!

THOREAU *(threatening, shaking fist)*: Who is it challenges me? I am no pacifist! I will fight you! I—

Marching band drowns him out.

THOREAU rolls up his manuscript and would leave, but the big, burly figure of Concord's constable SAM STAPLES blocks his way.

Music down.

THOREAU: Sam Staples?—let me by.

STAPLES: Henry Thoreau, as constable of Concord, under the authority invested in me by the Commonwealth of Massachusetts, I hereby place you under arrest.

THOREAU: Arrest? Me?

STAPLES: Come quietly, and there will be no trouble.

THOREAU: But *why*?

STAPLES cuffs THOREAU, who struggles with him; marches him briskly offstage.

THOREAU *(exiting)*: But—*why*?

Marching band continues as lights go out.

Scene 15: The Epiphany

Darkness. A man's rising, protracted laughter. Then silence. Lights up on a crude jail cell, with whitewashed walls, to which THOREAU, *still manacled, is being taken by* STAPLES. *The rear of the cell is in darkness. There are two cots in the cell, and on one of them, nearly hidden in the darkness, is the second* PRISONER. STAPLES *now has his billy club out and is using it, prodding* THOREAU.

THOREAU *(furious, frightened)*: And so!—I didn't pay my poll tax for six years!—what of it?—I scorn those who *have* paid!—I should think I would be rather more honored than— *(THOREAU cries out as STAPLES prods him hard with the billy club)* —S-Sam, my God—don't—

STAPLES *(blandly)*: Mr. Th'reau, you're resisting arrest.

THOREAU: Sam, you kn-know me—

STAPLES: Hell, if I didna, you'd be pukin your guts out by now.

THOREAU: But—

STAPLES: This is the Concord jail on the *inside*, pr'fessor. Where you and your highfalutin kind never been. C'mon!

THOREAU *(balking)*: I p-pay my highway tax—I pay my school tax— but I refuse to pay my poll tax! It's a matter of conscience. I refuse to support the U.S. Government in this filthy Mexican War to extend slave territory— *(THOREAU groans in pain as STAPLES strikes him in the knee with the billy club.)*

STAPLES *(cold, bland, unlocking the manacles)*: Make your speeches, Mr. Th'reau, pay your tax or rot in jail, *I* don't figure in it none. You'll find this ain't Walden Pond here.

STAPLES unlocks the cell door, shoves THOREAU *inside, slams the door and locks it.*

STAPLES: Here you stay, pr'fessor, till the tax is paid. *He* been here moren three months. *(Indicating the* PRISONER*)*

THOREAU *(wincing with pain, incredulous)*: Sam Staples, is this *you*? I taught your son Robert at the Concord School. You know me, you know my family… *(Pause, as STAPLES walks away)* Sam, I think my kneecap is cracked… Sam, have you no conscience? Don't you care that the U.S. Government is waging war against innocent men and women in the name of—

STAPLES *exits without glancing back, whistling. A beat.*

THOREAU *(grasping bars)*: Sam! SAM! *(Pause, to himself)* That brute isn't Sam. I *know* Sam.

PRISONER *behind* THOREAU *laughs.*

THOREAU *(turning, frightened)*: Who is—? Who are you? *(A beat)* Why are *you* in jail? Are you, too, wrongfully arrested? *(A beat)* I suppose you don't trust me? I, a penniless poet, one of the Concord "literati"... *(Ironic; pause)* I suppose I seem strange to you? *(Pause)* TELL ME THAT YOU KNOW ME, MAN! SPEAK!

A beat. PRISONER *shifts on his cot. A giant, hulking fellow. His mouth is slack; chin glistens with spittle.*

THOREAU *succumbs to a brief coughing attack, striking his chest with his fist.*

THOREAU *(breathless, momentary despair)*: My God, to be *jailed.* I never knew what it meant till now. To be mere *body.* Confined by bars, stone. *(Grasping bars)* All was fancy, till now. Words. *(A terrible thought)* If I should never be freed... But Emerson would not allow it...would he?

THOREAU *loses control; seizes bars and throws himself against them violently.*

THOREAU *(shouting)*: All jails razed! All jailers jailed! SAM STAPLES DO YOU HEAR ME! MY TOWNSPEOPLE DO YOU HEAR ME! I DEMAND THAT YOU RELEASE ME! All governments overthrown! All slaves freed! I refuse allegiance to the State! I deny the authority of the State over me! My conscience is inviolable! I follow a higher law! I will not submit! I will not pay a tax to support enslavement of the Negro! I will breathe after my own fashion! I SECEDE FROM THE UNITED STATES! *(Exhausted; a beat)*

PRISONER *laughs as if this is vastly entertaining. We understand that the man is retarded or mad.*

THOREAU, *on the floor, scrambles into a corner, pressing himself against the bars; presses his hands against his ears, appalled.*

Lights out.

Scene 16: "I Bring Not Peace But a Sword"

Darkness. In the background a crude, simple military-religious tune ("Onward Christian Soldiers") played by fife, harmonica and drum.

Lights up on THOREAU, *stage left. He enters with a cane, limping. There's a change in him—an angry, ironic intensity. His youth is gone.*

THOREAU *(to audience)*: In fact, that was the night I died—in Concord jail. Something in me turned outlaw. *(Pause)*

At stage right a VEILED WOMAN (LIDIAN EMERSON?) *is seen conferring anxiously with* SAM STAPLES. *She hands over several bills to him; he gives her a receipt and tips his hat to her.*

STAPLES *(unctuous)*: Ma'am, thank ye! I will release the poet at once.

VEILED WOMAN *and* SAM STAPLES *exit stage right.*

THOREAU *(angry, amused)*: Ha! I did not ask—whoever it was!—to pay my poll tax for me. *(Pause)* But it was too late. When I left the Concord jail that morning I saw you all with changed eyes. "You would betray me," I thought. "Who betray your own consciences hourly."

EMERSON, ALCOTT *appear stage right. Intense conversation.*

ALCOTT *(admiring)*: Ah, it was reckless of our Henry!—but, how courageous! The Boston papers have taken it up, I hear.

EMERSON: A mean and skulking act, and in bad taste.

ALCOTT: Waldo! Henry but follows his conscience, as we all must. *We* abhor slavery, do we not?

EMERSON *(sputtering)*: This has nothing to do with slavery, only with Henry Thoreau. "Concord's most illustrious figure"—the papers are calling him. *Conscience!*—Henry has played the buffoon to spite *me*.

ALCOTT: Surely not, Waldo—

EMERSON: To embarrass *me*. Daring Mr. Emerson not to pay *his* poll tax.

THOREAU *(interrupting, calling over as a boy might, in derision)*: *Blood* tax, you mean!

EMERSON *(ignoring him)*:   —*poll* tax—and be thrown into jail like a common criminal. But I will not rise to such cheap bait.

THOREAU *(approaching boldly, limping)*:   *Blood* tax it is, Mr. Emerson. Ask our Negro brethren to the south!

ALCOTT *(trying to intervene)*:   Friends! Friends!

THOREAU, EMERSON ignore him. EMERSON retains his dignity, barely, in the onslaught of THOREAU's withering scorn.

EMERSON: I was ashamed of you and for you, Henry Thoreau. A crude act of theatre to discredit the Abolitionist cause.

THOREAU: And where were *you* while I was jailed by the State, Mr. Emerson? Communing with your precious Over-Soul?

EMERSON: I warned you, Henry—*I* would not pay that poll tax for you.

THOREAU *(jeering)*:   —or with one of your sickly Platonic female sycophant soul-mates?

ALCOTT *(appalled)*:   Henry! This is not *you*—

EMERSON *(trying for a lofty tone but not wholly coherent)*:   The State— I have said—is a poor, good beast who means the best: it means friendly. I—abhor—violent men!—such radical acts of rebellion— treason—John Brown and his guerrillas—will lead to anarchy— to hideous civil war, bloodshed—

THOREAU *(an air of hurt, despite his anger)*:   Ralph Waldo Emerson who has taught us of the soul's freedom and nobility—"Whoso would be a man must be a nonconformist"—supporting the slavers!

EMERSON *(incensed)*:   Support the slavers!—*I*!—how dare you make such an accusation? I've given money to the Abolitionist cause; I preached against slavery when you were a careless boy setting fire to our neighbors' forest—

ALCOTT *(appalled)*:   Waldo! This is not *you*—

THOREAU *(excited, guilty)*:   That was an accident! I was but a boy! I'd built a fire to cook fish I'd caught on the Sudbury, and the wind came up unexpected, and—

ALCOTT: Now Henry, we know it was an accident. It is long past, and Concord has forgiven you.

EMERSON *(cruelly)*: *You* have forgiven Henry, and I have forgiven Henry, but Concord—not so easily.

THOREAU *(backing off, limping; hands to his ears)*: It is a nightmare. I will never wake from it. *(To* EMERSON, *emotionally)* You did not even visit me, Waldo. Not for a half-hour!

EMERSON: I could not. The prison is one step to suicide.

THOREAU: Not for ten minutes!

ALCOTT is leading EMERSON *away stage right.*

EMERSON *(calling back)*: I...did not know you were arrested, Henry...until you were released. There was no time.

THOREAU *(calling after, tauntingly)*: A new Abolitionist journal has asked me to write an essay on my experience, and so I will— "Civil Disobedience." I shall make it a document "for the ages."

EMERSON, ALCOTT exit. THOREAU *remains stage left, trembling.*

Lights up center-stage rear. "Onward Christian Soldiers" has grown louder. On a platform addressing an unruly crowd stands JOHN BROWN, *the radical Abolitionist leader. A fierce Old Testament prophet with flowing gray hair, a magnificent bristling beard, mad eyes; in old-fashioned formal attire like an evangelical preacher. A powerful orator who stirs the crowd to both fervent admiration and disapproval.*

BROWN: My friends!—my name is JOHN BROWN and I am called CAPTAIN by some—

A preponderance of cheers; some boos and dissension.

BROWN: —by slavers, the very Devil. I care not what ye call me, only that ye believe in my cause: the absolute abolition of that abomination in the Lord's eyes—the enslavement of mankind by man!

Interruptions of "God bless you, Captain!"—and other cheers; also "Traitor!"—"Rebel!"—"Nigger-lover!"

THOREAU *(to audience, in awe)*: At last—the great, doomed Captain John Brown! I knew our paths would cross someday.

BROWN: I have come in humility to beg you for help—to appeal to you, and you, and you—as Christian men and women—in our struggle to free the Negro from slavery in the United States—now and forever! I ask for funds not for myself but for my men; my army of brave guerrillas; we who have fought the Border Ruffians in Kansas who would make that state a slave state. *(Raising a chain)* What am I bid for this chain that bound my own son in Kansas?—it is blessed with the lad's very blood.

VOICES. *("Twenty dollars!"—"Thirty!"—"Forty!" etc.; at the same time cries of "Not a penny!"—"Traitor!"—"Nigger-lover!" etc.)*

BROWN *(shouting above the noise, as he stoops to hand the chain to a man)*: I thank you, sir, in the name of the Lord!

BROWN *next raises a bowie knife aloft which he waves in an hypnotic, seductive fashion as he speaks.*

BROWN: We—your soldiers in Christ—are not afraid to die in the sacred struggle, my friends. The Lord calls us to our destiny. Give us funds, to send us to our destiny—back into the field of struggle, and strife, and bloodshed, and VICTORY IN THE NAME OF THE LORD. *(Pause)* What am I bid for this, my own bowie knife—baptized in the Devil's blood at Pottawatomie!

VOICES *("Fifty dollars!"—"Eighty dollars!"; also, "Murderer!"— "Madman!"—"You are the Devil!" etc.)*

THOREAU *(shouting)*: One hundred dollars!

VOICES *(in shock, awe, disbelief, bemusement)*: One hundred dollars!

ANONYMOUS MAN: To—Henry Thoreau? Why, he has not a penny.

Lights down on the crowd; JOHN BROWN comes forward, limping; he greets THOREAU center-stage. The elder man and the younger bear some resemblance.

THOREAU *(hastily)*: A pledge, I mean, Captain Brown—a pledge of one hundred dollars. For I have not the actual—cash.

BROWN *clasps THOREAU's hand in such a grip that THOREAU winces.*

BROWN: No matter, no matter! You are Henry Thoreau, I am told?— the author of *Walden*. A beautiful book, for all that it is Godless. My son! *(BROWN hands THOREAU the bowie knife)* It is for you.

THOREAU: Captain Brown, I am—humbled. I am in the presence of—

BROWN *(matter-of-fact egotism)*: History. For I will prevail, even if my body is cast down. I do not fear to kill or be killed in the Lord's holy war. And so, I am invincible.

BROWN is walking off. Music rises. THOREAU limps after, tentatively.

THOREAU: But, Captain—you must not martyr yourself. You must take care, and live—

BROWN *(calling back)*: No. Mere life is for cowards. When I die— my rotting corpse will be raised above the living. The South will be devastated. I will prevail from above. VICTORY IN THE NAME OF THE LORD.

BROWN exits. THOREAU stares after him, then contemplates the knife.

THOREAU: It *is* stained with blood. Whose?

Lights out.

Scene 17: "...Sometimes It Has Rained Flesh and Blood!"

Lights up. MARGARET FULLER *and* JAMES RUSSELL LOWELL, *addressing the audience. Each is older than we've last seen them, but still youthful.* FULLER *is dressed in austere but rich dark blue garments with lace trim, and wears a handsome hat, as befits New England's most distinguished woman of letters, who is also a suffragist.* LOWELL *is dressed with more conspicuous fashion, and wears a stylish hat. Through the scene,* FULLER *raises a lorgnette to her eyes occasionally, and* LOWELL *a small pair of binoculars.*

FULLER *(awed, hushed, thrilled)*: And then—the faun became a roaring lion.

LOWELL *(with both distaste and awe)*: The author of *Walden*—an uneven but, on the whole, poetically written work—as I noted in my lengthy review in *The Atlantic*—rushing about to give speeches in Acton, in Medford, in Worcester, in Salem—even here in Boston at the Tremont Temple!—

Center-stage rear, THOREAU *stands elevated; we see that he is speaking passionately, but cannot hear his words. Lights on* THOREAU *are surreally tinted.*

FULLER: Adulation—and controversy!—in all the papers—the *Boston Traveler,* the *Journal,* the *Atlas & Daily Bee,* the *Liberator*—and my editorial in *The Dial*—"Henry Thoreau, Poet and Abolitionist"—

LOWELL *(overlapping, with disapproval):* Even in Boston where one expects more taste amid the citizenry, crowds came out to hear him.

FULLER *(peering through lorgnette into audience):* "A Plea for John Brown" was his masterpiece—yet also "Slavery in Massachusetts"—"Civil Disobedience"—

LOWELL *(overlapping irritably, peering through binoculars):* Such a raw, nasal, untrained voice—such awkward manners—has there ever been so *poorly groomed* a speaker at Tremont Temple?—and the man's linen, as *The Tatler* noted, none too fresh.

FULLER: Even Henry's stammer is most winning—

LOWELL: And he knows little of the dirt and treachery of politics—how his revered John Brown is but a murderer and fanatic—

FULLER: Henry's innocence!—knowing little of the dirt and treachery of politics. *(Giggling) The New York Tribune,* long an Abolitionist paper, advises "the Transcendentalist Henry Thoreau to limp on back to Walden Pond to cultivate beans and woodchucks"—

LOWELL *(with more concern):* And his health—he exhausts himself in such folly.

THOREAU *(a raw, strained, excitable voice):* Down with slavery!—down with the South!—pour your support, spiritual and financial, into the Abolitionist cause!—fear not strife, bloodshed!—in the name of Captain John Brown I beseech you!—for Nature is so rife with life that myriads can be afforded to be sacrificed and suffered to prey upon one another—tadpoles which herons gobble up, and tortoises and toads run over in the road; and sometimes it has rained flesh and blood!—

(This speech, partly from the conclusion of "Spring," Walden, may be delivered fiercely yet not quite coherently. THOREAU grows breathless with the effort, and begins coughing violently.)

FULLER *(stricken)*: Henry!

LOWELL: I warned him, and he would not listen.

THOREAU stumbles down from the platform. He would seem to be pushing aside people in his haste to exit; he walks with a cane, and has unknowingly dropped several pages of his lecture.

FULLER, LOWELL: Henry, here! We are your friends.

THOREAU, coughing, seems to recognize them; but continues pushing past.

FULLER *(hurt)*: Henry Thoreau! Of course you know *me*.

THOREAU: I am—history. I am—my destiny.

THOREAU stumbles; LOWELL and FULLER would catch him; but in a burst of surprising energy, THOREAU hurries away. Exits.

FULLER: He is ill. He is deranged.

LOWELL *(meanly)*: *You* are his adorer, Margaret. Chase after the faun if you will.

FULLER *(cuttingly)*: *You* are his adorer, James. Though too cowardly to speak your heart.

FULLER exits, leaving LOWELL shocked.

LOWELL stoops to pick up the papers THOREAU has dropped.

LOWELL: A madman's ravings...fevered, illegible handwriting. Still—he *is* history, I suppose. *(LOWELL folds up the papers with care, strides away.)*

Lights out.

Scene 18: The Prayer

Lights up on THOREAU, in an extraordinary posture for him—on his knees, in prayer. On the floor in front of him lies BROWN's bowie knife, the blade gleaming out of the darkness.

THOREAU *(with gritted teeth)*: God—in whom I do not believe!—save John Brown—who does believe. *(Anguished)* Do not let them hang him in Virginia, I beg You!

As THOREAU prays, center-stage behind him a screen is slowly illuminated with the front page of a newspaper reporting the execution of JOHN BROWN on December 2, 1859, and with a drawing or photograph of the hanging.

THOREAU turns to see this, and covers his face with his hands.

Lights out.

Scene 19: A Far Country

A jubilant sound of whistling. Lights up to suggest a blindingly bright spring day. THOREAU comes forward rather jauntily; it's he who is whistling. Though he walks a bit stiffly, he isn't using a cane. On his head is a wide-brimmed western-style hat; around his throat, a blood-red scarf. Otherwise his clothes are as usual and he is wearing boots. Over his shoulder a knapsack; in his hand the bowie knife.

THOREAU ceases whistling. Addresses the audience with dignity.

THOREAU: They said I was ill. I was never ill. I was burned clean of all illusion. *(Laughs)* What is man but thawing clay?—waked by the spring sun, excreted by the earth. And enduring. *(Pause)* Yes. Today. I think it will be today. I will kill my enemy and have done with this charade. *(He hides the bowie knife in his knapsack.)*

BRONSON ALCOTT appears, grown white-haired and grizzled, yet lively as ever. He and THOREAU are headed for Bush House.

ALCOTT greets THOREAU warmly, not just shaking his hand but embracing him. THOREAU responds stiffly.

ALCOTT: How long it's been, Henry, since you've come to Bush House! We've missed you, you know.

THOREAU *(with gritted teeth telling the truth though it pains him)*: I have missed you.

ALCOTT: Waldo will be so pleased to see you today, Henry! *(As they walk)* You're planning a new venture, I hear? To the West?

THOREAU: I go to Minnesota next month. For reasons of health.

ALCOTT *(concerned but tactful)*: Wouldn't a warmer, drier climate be more...beneficial? For one with your...

THOREAU: Weak lungs? No. We must make ourselves strong. I will travel by steamer three hundred miles up the Minnesota to the Sioux Agency near Redwood.

ALCOTT: And write another masterpiece. *(Pause)* How happy I am, Henry, you're returned to Nature. After the—unpleasantness of past years. I worried you had lost your love of Nature and had grown violent—like the enemy you abhor.

THOREAU: Is not Nature violent?—and violence, natural? I think so, Bronson.

ALCOTT *(not hearing; a radiant smile)*: Ah look: the apple trees you planted for the Emersons, how many years ago, are in the most wondrous bloom!

THOREAU squints as if blinded by the trees, shielding his eyes with his fingers.

ALCOTT catches THOREAU *as he sways almost imperceptibly. A subtle man, he makes no allusion to this.*

ALCOTT: Waldo is so proud of you, you know.

THOREAU *(surprised)*: He is?

ALCOTT: He gives everyone copies of *Walden;* took some to England on his lecture tour to give to Carlyle and George Eliot! Here, he has given copies to Nathaniel Hawthorne and this strange wondrous madman of a poet—Walt Whitman.

THOREAU *(stroking beard)*: I had a letter from Whitman.

ALCOTT *(lowering his voice)*: Margaret Fuller's death upset him terribly, you know. What a tragedy!

THOREAU *(dryly)*: Yes. In Margaret Fuller, Emerson lost his ideal audience.

ALCOTT *(sighing)*: *So* sad. To die young—only forty!

THOREAU: In a woman, forty is not young; in Margaret Fuller, forty was decidedly not young.

ALCOTT: Henry!—so cold-hearted. Is this you?

THOREAU: Perhaps I have misplaced my heart.

ALCOTT (*touching* THOREAU'*s arm*): Yet you were the one, I was told, who went to search for Margaret's body on the shore at Fire Island.

THOREAU (*sadly*): Yes. I was the one. But I found nothing amid the ship's wreckage—not even a manuscript.

Lights up on LIDIAN *at a window, unnoticed by the men. She wears a black dress and her hair is covered by a white cap.*

EMERSON *appears at the door. As he greets* ALCOTT *and* THOREAU, LIDIAN *quickly withdraws.*

EMERSON *is very gray; slightly stooped; yet still very distinguished, in his late fifties. An elegance of manner through which genuine emotion— or the wish for such—emerges.*

EMERSON (*warmly*): Henry!

THOREAU (*stiffly*): Mr. Emerson.

EMERSON: Don't be absurd: "Waldo"—please.

THOREAU: W-Waldo.

EMERSON *shakes hands vigorously with* THOREAU, *at whom he stares intently; and with* ALCOTT, *with whom he's on more familiar terms.*

EMERSON: Bronson, hello!

ALCOTT: Waldo, dear friend! We're just now admiring your apple trees—all in blossom.

EMERSON: They are?—yes, of course. But the air is chill, come inside.

ALCOTT (*brightly*): Where is Lidian, Waldo?

EMERSON: Lidian is—preoccupied with household matters.

EMERSON *ushers his guests into his study, where tea things and a bottle of sherry have been set out.* THOREAU'*s attention is immediately drawn to a volume on* EMERSON'*s desk which he opens and leafs through.*

EMERSON: James Lowell sends his regrets this Saturday. And— (*faltering*)

ALCOTT: Yes, yes. We will miss her—poor dear Margaret.

THOREAU, *frowning as he leafs through the book, says nothing.*

EMERSON: Tea, gentlemen?—Lidian has prepared some very nice things. And there is sherry. (EMERSON *pours himself a small glass of sherry.*)

ALCOTT *(surprised)*: Waldo!

EMERSON *(defensive)*: Well, it *is* an occasion. (To THOREAU) Our neighbor Nathaniel Hawthorne is quite a compelling writer, isn't he?—have you read this new *Marble Faun*?

THOREAU *rudely shuts the book and tosses it down onto the desk.*

THOREAU: I detest fiction. One world at a time.

EMERSON *(humorous, yet needling)*: *Our* work has nothing of the fictitious in it, Henry?

THOREAU *(flatly)*: Mine does not. I can't speak for yours.

ALCOTT *(trying to intervene)*: Concord has nurtured genius in differing types. I acknowledge fiction in my work, for truth is best expressed by ellipsis.

THOREAU: Truth is truth. It must be spoken bluntly.

EMERSON: Henry is unchanged over a quarter-century—he does not feel himself except in opposition. *(A bit aggressively)* He is a boy—and will be an old boy. *(Pause)* I fear for *Walden*, Henry—it is already an American classic; and you must be worthy of it, as a man.

THOREAU *(gripping his knapsack, too restless to be seated)*: What is this dissection of my character? Is that why I have been invited to Bush House today?

EMERSON: I had invited you many times; you spurned my hospitality. I would think, coming so belatedly, you might at least—

THOREAU: Apologize?

EMERSON: Explain yourself.

THOREAU: For being myself, Mr. Emerson, and not *you*?

EMERSON: The ugly truth came out last year, after Brown was hanged at Harpers Ferry—his massacre of unarmed men—and women—at Pottawatomie in Kansas. *You* have never acknowledged that butchery, Henry, in your martyred hero!

THOREAU *(agitated)*: I—do not believe all that I hear, or read. Hateful lies are told of Captain Brown—even now civil war *is* waging; and his prophecy is fulfilled.

EMERSON *(with cold fury)*: You know well that Brown was a fanatic, and a butcher. And—

THOREAU: And I am his heir? *(Pause)* I do not wish to kill or be killed but I can foresee the circumstances when—I must.

ALCOTT: Henry, what are you saying? We are pacifists here; we must forgive our enemies.

THOREAU moves behind EMERSON and ALCOTT, who confer earnestly yet inaudibly together. Lights alter surreally. THOREAU, agitated, takes the bowie knife out of the knapsack; stares at EMERSON.

EMERSON *(speaking as if THOREAU were deceased)*: I loved him, you know—as a son. He could not bear it, I think.

ALCOTT: Not bear love! A tragedy.

EMERSON: His pride.

ALCOTT: And not yours—?

THOREAU suddenly strikes EMERSON, or appears to strike him, with the knife: he grips its handle in both hands and brings it downward against the top of EMERSON's spine.

Lights shift to red. Lights out.

Lights up. The scene continues as previously. EMERSON, untouched, glances back at THOREAU, to urge him to join ALCOTT and himself.

EMERSON: Ever the hovering hawk, Henry! Please join us.

THOREAU has replaced the bowie knife in his knapsack. His face is drawn, intense.

THOREAU: No. Goodbye.

EMERSON: But—

THOREAU walks quickly to the front door, followed by EMERSON. *Lights down on* ALCOTT.

THOREAU: Your friendship is for summer weather only. Now I have tasted winter, I am not of your company.

EMERSON: Henry, you must not leave in anger.

THOREAU: Would you have me leave in sorrow? *(Sudden lyricism)* What a strange world we live in—with this incessant dream of friendship and love, where is any?

EMERSON: I...think of you as my closest friend, Henry. And yet—

THOREAU: What a gulf between us!

EMERSON: —this wildness of yours—

THOREAU: —this tameness of yours—

EMERSON: I thought of you as a woodgod, once: possessed of a higher knowledge—

THOREAU: I thought of you as a god, once: possessed of a higher knowledge—

EMERSON *(warning, emotional as if he's tasted this himself)*: Very seductive are the first steps from the town into the woods, but the end is want and madness.

THOREAU *(brash)*: Then that's my fate.

EMERSON *suddenly embraces* THOREAU. *It's an unplanned, desperate act for which* THOREAU *isn't prepared.* THOREAU *pushes him reflexively away, and hurries from the house.* EMERSON *stares after him in yearning.*

Lights out on EMERSON.

Lights up on THOREAU, LIDIAN *stage right.*

LIDIAN *has been waiting for* THOREAU *on the front walk. We should see her as* THOREAU *sees her, registering shock: Lidian is middle-aged, her once-lustrous hair streaked with gray and her features faded. She carries a single purple dwarf iris.*

LIDIAN *(breathless)*: Henry!—are you leaving so quickly?

THOREAU *(staring)*: Lidian...

LIDIAN *(self-consciously)*: I've...been ill. Jaundice...

THOREAU: I'm sorry to hear it.

LIDIAN: And you?

THOREAU (*striking his chest with his fist, smiling*): The Thoreau family curse—weak lungs. But I shall prevail.

LIDIAN: You were very brave—on the matter of John Brown.

THOREAU (*quickly, not wanting to speak of it*): Only compared to others not so brave. (*Pause*) I must leave, Lidian. Excuse me...

LIDIAN (*handing him the iris*): Henry—I picked this for you. Do you remember, long ago, you gave me irises for my little boy's grave.

THOREAU accepts the flower but will not look at LIDIAN.

THOREAU (*quickly*): No. I don't remember. But—thank you, Lidian.

THOREAU exits with LIDIAN looking after him.

Lights slowly down.

Lights out on LIDIAN. Lights up on THOREAU.

THOREAU has taken the bowie knife out of his knapsack; he places it on the stage before him.

THOREAU: My bowie knife I will leave here. (*Peering into the audience, in utter seriousness*) For you. Or—for you.

Lights out.

Epilogue: "When I Died..."

Darkness. A lurid red light flashing, as of fire. Distant alarms that become the melancholy call of an owl.

In this scene we don't see THOREAU, but hear only his amplified, enhanced voice; for he has become a voice now, a visionary of the American spirit. Yet there's emotion and passion in his language.

THOREAU: In winter nights at Walden I heard the forlorn note of a hooting owl...such a sound as the frozen earth might yield if struck with a sharp instrument.

Owl's call louder; then fading. The red light has shifted to darkness penetrated by flashing lights like lightning.

A sound of cracking ice.

THOREAU: By starlight I heard the whooping of the ice in the pond, as if it were restless in its bed; I was waked by the cracking of the ground by frost, as if it would penetrate my soul, and drive a spike through my heart at last.

Distant, and then louder, barking. A romantic, melodious sound at first; then manic, discomforting, recalling the demonic laughter of the prisoner in Concord jail.

THOREAU *(quickened voice):* …I heard the foxes as they ranged over the snow crust, in moonlit nights, in search of prey…barking raggedly and demonically as forest dogs…struggling for light…like rudimentary, burrowing men awaiting their transformation. Sometimes one came to my window, attracted by my light, barked a vulpine curse at me and then retreated…

(Pause; a cry of anguish and loss) Oh God, give me my world again!

Flashing lights down. Lights out.

Lights up.

The blinding-white light of the Prologue. We are in THOREAU's bedroom. THOREAU has been writing in his journal feverishly. The sound of the Universal Lyre comes up softly.

We hear the call of a cardinal. In the opened doorway is JOHN, who has whistled playfully to THOREAU. They might be boys again. JOHN makes a mischievous signal for THOREAU to join him.

THOREAU *(laughing):* John!—brother. Yes. It's time. I *have* had my world.

THOREAU sets the journal aside; rises from bed, moves unsteadily at first, then with more strength, to join JOHN.

Lights out.

THE END

Appendix

Author's Note

The Passion of Henry David Thoreau is a dream play, yet for the most part realistically portrayed. Scholars of Thoreau's life will note that scenes do not follow one another in strict chronology, nor are episodes dramatized "historical." They represent a dying yet fiercely independent man's reverie and are pierced by strangeness. Quotations from Thoreau's writings are taken out of context as are oral or written remarks by others. Wherever possible, the voices of these men and women have been used, woven into the fabric of a fictitious narrative. Where formal biography can accommodate the loosely structured, linear procession of events that constitute our lives, drama must be otherwise structured. And numerous people who figured intimately in Thoreau's life—his mother and his sister Sophia, to name but two—are not present. The family life of the Emersons has been simplified. My vision of Henry David Thoreau is that of the quintessential artist who creates a pure art out of the heterogeneous materials of his or her life—the "passion" of genius which is as mysterious as any phenomenon in nature.

In composing this play, I learned much from the Thoreau scholar William Howarth whose numerous writings on Thoreau—among them *The Book of Concord*, *Thoreau in the Mountains*, and *The Literary Manuscripts of Henry David Thoreau*—are exemplary. Other works consulted are *The Days of Henry Thoreau* by Walter Harding, *Ralph Waldo Emerson: Days of Encounter* by John McAleer, *The Best of Thoreau's Journals* edited by Carl Bode, and *Margaret Fuller: An American Romantic Life* by Charles Capper.

Prologue

The Universal Lyre. See *Walden*, "Sounds."

"Sometimes, on Sundays, I heard the bells, the Lincoln, Acton, Bedford, or Concord bell, when the wind was favorable, a faint, sweet, and, as it were, natural melody... At a sufficient distance over the woods this sound acquires a certain vibratory hum, as if the pine needles in the horizon were the strings of a harp which it swept. All sound heard at the greatest possible distance produces one and the same effect, a vibration of the universal lyre."

Scene 3

"The Fairy Ship"

I saw a ship a-sail-ing, A-sail-ing on the sea,···· And oh! it was a-

la-den with pret-ty things for me; There were com-fits in the ca-bin, And apples in the

hold; The sails were made of sa~tin, And the mast was made of gold.

The four-and-twenty sailors
  That stood between the decks,
Were four-and-twenty white mice
  With rings about their necks.

The captain was a duck, a duck,
  With a jacket on his back,
And when the fairy ship set sail,
  The captain he said, "Quack!"

II

Here I Am

Lights up. A park bench illuminated by a street lamp. An attractive but sullen WOMAN *in her late 20s or early 30s enters in such a way as to be glancing over her shoulder at the audience, both fearful and provocative. She wears a long skirt with deep pockets, dark-textured tights, an unbuttoned, loose-fitting jacket (perhaps suede or leather) with a snugly fitting low-cut sweater or blouse beneath; high-heeled shoes or boots. During the course of her monologue she frequently brushes her long hair back from her face, moves her shoulders restlessly, smiles, frowns, all very self-consciously, suppressing anger. An exhibitionist with a powerful need for revenge.*

WOMAN *(a glance at the audience)*: You're following me?—looking at me? *(Pause)* O.K.—here I am. I'm waiting. *(Unobtrusively touching an object hidden in her pocket)* Anybody makes a move on me, I'm waiting. *(Pause, walking about)* The first time—I'm not going to talk about it. *(Pause)* He was my…mother's brother. I never say his name. Nor think it, either. Took me ice skating, I was going to be "figure skating champion"—he said— *(glides gracefully through a skating routine) —he'd* be my coach. I was six years old. I believed him. *(She stumbles on the ice; now a rigid posture.)* I don't remember it too clear. *Don't you tell* he said *nothing happened* he said… *(Pause)* That long ago, you mostly don't remember. So I don't talk about it and anyway—he's dead. *(Pause, bitterly)* The first time I can really remember, yeah it's like yesterday, I was twelve years old in seventh grade and I was crossing through the park coming home from school, a dark cold day, a spring day but gloomy like the sky was pressing down low, I was alone and that's how you get selected but I didn't know it then. *(Mysteriously)* My mind was filled with—oh! such thoughts!— *(laughs)* —I was going to be a fashion model, or a, yeah a girl singer with a rock band— *(mimes singing into a microphone, exaggerated mannerisms)* —all kinds of crazy ideas, hopes. *(Pause)* So I was crossing through the park and I saw them up ahead but pretended I didn't, I mean I pretended to myself, too. That's what you do when you're scared to death. *(Pause)* They weren't black guys, they were *white* like me. Guys in the neighborhood sixteen, seventeen years old hanging around the old bandstand smoking reefer and here I came along, it was like an accident but it was fated. *(Pause)* No, they didn't *rape* me or anything, just chased after me hooting and yelling and grabbing me— *(she grips her breasts roughly)* —knocked me down in the wet grass. I was sobbing so scared, paralyzed-scared, and wetting my pants so they laughed at *that. (Pause; she goes to sit on the bench, arranging herself in an odd posture—her long legs spread, right foot curved inward so that the ankle rests flat on the floor, suggesting vulnerability; arms may be stretched along the back of the bench, head dropping back provocatively.)* Another time…a few years later…it *was* black guys…I'd gotten to talking with one of them…didn't know his name…in a video shop…hanging out after school…this boy says "Yo' pretty enough to be Miss America!" kind of jiving the way they do but I'm thinking "Yeah! yeah I guess I *am*" and we went out and there's his buddies in a car and I got in and… *(A beat, silence; then speaks with revulsion, wiping at mouth with the back of her hand, gagging)* Three hours they had me. Made me do things to them. Five of them, or six…behind the warehouse…by the river they terrorized me they told me they'd kill me for sure and dump my body in the river if I told, said they'd torch our building where M-Mommy—Momma— and I lived, just the two of us. So— *(shrugs, bitter resignation)* —I never told. Who'd I tell? Momma? She'd have died of shame. Our priest?—old pot-belly McGuire? *(Contemptuous laugh)* The cops in our precinct wouldn't have given a damn, you're asking for it going out with "niggers" they'd say, serves you right the guys in the neighborhood would say, nothing I could *prove* even if I'd gone to a doctor or the hospital which I didn't 'cause…I was too ashamed. *(Pause)*

WOMAN *gets suddenly to her feet; walks springily, sensuously about; lifting long hair and letting it fall; stretching.*

WOMAN: I was twenty years old when I fell in love for the first time. Oh, God!—"fell" is right!—like in quicksand! Doing temp work days, evenings I took courses at Monroe County Community College, where I met Ray Allis, my accounting prof, oh I was so admiring of him just looking at him in class shy like I was, I *am* shy, well one evening after class he asks would I like to have coffee with him at the student union and that was the...beginning. *(Laughs breathlessly, caresses hair)* He was separated from his wife he said, "irrevocably split" he said . . . so I believed him—I'm the kind of girl *always believes*. *(Mysteriously, nodding)* That's how you get selected, but I didn't know it then. *(Pause; dreamy-urgent voice)* I came to love Ray Allis so, lost fifteen pounds, couldn't sleep, Momma's worried asking me *what? what's happening to you?* and I'm saying *leave me alone what do you know?* I'd lie in the bath till the water got cold till my skin was all puckered like chicken skin! and white! half wanting to die there, y'know?...slash my arms with a razor, I was so...tensed up...hopeful...thinking oh he's going to marry me, Ray Allis loves me he says, loves loves loves me...kisses me all over my body when we're together...in his car, in a...motel room... Or I'm thinking, oh God what if he doesn't smile at me tomorrow in class, what if he doesn't call me again...Like my heart was all clenched tight— *(clenches her right fist, raises it high)* —with hope. *(Pause; sighs, bitter)* Well. Ray didn't leave his wife. And kid. I got a B– in the course. Which he said was a "gift." *(Pause)* I'd call him, sometimes. Hang up when his wife answered. Till he changed his number. *(Vague)* Used to drive by his house late at night...park out there...somebody called the police, once...maybe it was him. *(Pause. She draws pistol out of skirt pocket, sights along the barrel; strokes against the side of her face.)* This, I didn't have in my possession, then! *This*, just holding it, the weight of it, restores your pride. *(Smiles)*

WOMAN *returns to the bench, sits provocatively as before; studies the pistol reverently.*

WOMAN *(dreamy-angry)*: I'm not twenty years old anymore. I'm sure not. Lots of water over the dam since then. Momma died, I grew up, you better believe it. *Try* me. *(A rhapsodic aria)* You, mister— there's going to be a time, an hour, oh yessss you're going to press up against me all innocent-seeming, like in a bar, some singles Friday night, in a, a parking garage elevator, or—anywhere: grocery store, 7-Eleven. Mmmmm there's going to be that time—an accident—but fate—no way to avoid it—say I'm coming out of a women's restroom at a gas station on the interstate, me in shorts, T-shirt, sunglasses and you're headed for the men's room, the two of us collide, right?—you bumping into me accidentally-on-purpose, right? the way you do? *(Pause, smiling)* Or: say it's dusk, melancholy-wet like now, you're curious why this woman, this not-bad-looking woman, is sitting by herself in the park, the park deserted and she's sitting here— *(she arranges herself with legs spread, the outside of her right ankle flat against the ground; slips, sensuously, the pistol back into her skirt pocket)* —looking lonely, low and sad, there's these bruises under her eyes from not sleeping or maybe some guy's been beating up on her?—which excites you, right? Mister? Turns you on? So you follow her here? *(Laughs girlishly)* Sure. Try me. It's a date. Here I am.

Lights out.

THE END

Duet

A., a young man

B., a young woman

Lights up. A. and B. are speaking agitatedly together.

A.: Look, you know I love you but—

B.: I love *you*—

A.: —I told you and told you I'm not the kind of guy to—

B.: Please don't be angry with me!—

A.: —play games with—

B.: I just want to explain, why I haven't been home—

A.: —when I call you, and you don't answer—

B.: —I was at my sister's, I had to get to a place of—

A.: —what am I going to think? You want me to think—what?

B.: —quiet, where I could—

A.: I'm not the kind of guy who's going to be pushed around—

B.: —I just want to explain, please—I never meant—

A.: —so we better get this cleared up right now—

B.: —to make you think I was—I mean, I wasn't—

A.: You act like you're scared of me how's that make me feel for
   Christ's sake *I love you*—

B.: —I mean I didn't love you—I mean, I *do*—

A.: —it's just that I'm getting seriously pissed off the way—

B.: —it's just I'm scared of—

A.: —the way things are going, y'know?—

B.: —you—

A.: —like this game you're playing, like you're scared of *me*—that's an insult—

B.: If I could only have a, a little more—

A.: If I thought for one minute you were—

B.: —space to breathe in?—

A.: —betraying me—

B.: —I think we could, oh I know we could—like in the beginning—

A.: —Jesus Christ, I— *(Shakes head ominously)*

B.: —work things out—

A.: —I don't know—

B.: —I love you so—

A.: —sometimes I think—

B.: —it's just I get so scared, like last night—

A.: —we'd both be better off—

B.: —I almost wish I was—

A.: —dead.

B.: The way you look at me, your eyes—

A.: Jesus!—I'm crazy about you—

B.: That first time I—

A.: —first time I—

B.: —saw you—

A.: —saw you—

B.: —I knew.

A.: —I knew.

End on a rapturous note. A. *and* B. *in a prolonged kiss.*

Lights out.

THE END

Good To Know You
A Play in One Act

CHARACTERS:
CONSTANCE, late 30s
MARYANNE, late 30s
MURPHY, early 40s
TED, mid-30s, clearly the youngest of the four

SETTING: CONSTANCE's house.

CONSTANCE has prepared dinner for her lover MURPHY and their friends MARYANNE and TED. The couples are not married. It's the conclusion of the meal; CONSTANCE and MARYANNE have been clearing away plates, and MURPHY has been helping to some degree, pouring more wine and/or setting out coffee cups, etc. Candles are burning on the table.

Lights up as CONSTANCE, returning from the kitchen (offstage) to the dining room, continues recounting a story for her friends. She's an earthy, attractive, self-dramatizing woman.

During the exchange between CONSTANCE and MARYANNE, MURPHY and TED exchange glances. MURPHY has a good deal of nervous energy and may jump up once or twice from the table to pour wine or coffee.

CONSTANCE: —Yes, when I had Sharleen—*everyone* was into "natural" childbirth. Even men. My then-husband insisted on coming to my class with me, doing exercises with me, wanted to "share everything"—he said. *(Pause)* I'm telling you, pain was *in*. We were all eager to be *Mommy Cat*—to show we could do it.

229

Here I was all prepared for a "mystical" experience that never happened. What did happen was: 4 A.M. I got up to use the bathroom and my God the contractions started—fast—every three or four minutes—*not* every twenty minutes like we'd been told. The baby wasn't due for another week and oh God I was scared to death—

MARYANNE: Gosh, what happened?

CONSTANCE: My husband panicked.

MARYANNE: Oh, no. One of those.

CONSTANCE: Poor guy claimed he couldn't see—his eyes weren't working right—so *I* drove us to the hospital. *(Pause, smiling)* We both checked into the emergency room, like twins. Then I had thirty-six hours of labor—and no anesthetic—and in the end I was so worn out, couldn't push worth a damn and I was this howling animal and—I didn't know this till afterward—my husband had passed out twice. So they gave me a C-section—exactly what I swore I'd avoid. God, was I a mess!

MARYANNE: Yes, but you wind up with a baby.

CONSTANCE *(jubilant)*: You wind up with a baby. Yes!

MARYANNE: My first delivery—that was Ben—was pretty wild, too. The labor wasn't as long as yours but it was long—twenty hours. I'd have wanted to do natural childbirth too but it wasn't advised—I'd had a miscarriage before, and I was sort of sick and shaky through the pregnancy. Every time I went to see my obstetrician—we called him Dr. de Sade—he'd stroke his goatee and shake his head like my belly was a tragic mistake, but not *his* mistake. So when it came time, and I went to the hospital, I was totally doped up and out of it. *(Pause)* My then-husband wasn't even in town. *(Pause)* It was a forceps delivery—you know what that's like. Ugh!

CONSTANCE: Ugh! *(Sympathetically)* Did they tear you up pretty bad?

MURPHY and TED are listening to this with some discomfort. MURPHY is feeling faint; TED dips a napkin into a water glass and dabs his warm face with it. The women don't notice.

MARYANNE: Don't ask. *(Pause, lifting a plate)* Anybody want more spaghetti?—there's lots.

MURPHY, TED: No thanks.

CONSTANCE: What's wrong, Murphy?—you're looking a little pale.

MURPHY: Me? Oh no, oh no—I'm fine.

TED: *I'm* fine, I'm, uh, learning a lot.

MARYANNE: —Then, when I came to, in this dazed state, a nurse handed me this—baby—I thought was *myself*. My mind was sort of shattered and not-right—I'd gotten mixed up in time and thought the baby was *me*.

CONSTANCE: Oh, I know what you mean. With my daughter, it was the same way. Not seriously of course—just a fantasy.

MARYANNE *(lowered voice)*: You want to hear the weirdest?

CONSTANCE: What?

MARYANNE: I mixed up my husband with my father, too. I kept calling Carl "Daddy"—and he's *looking* at me, like he knows which "Daddy" it is.

MURPHY: That *will* give a man pause. A husband, I mean.

MURPHY drops to the floor to execute several brisk push-ups.

CONSTANCE *(shivery giggle)*: Those fantasies are *weird*.

MARYANNE: Well, they pass. You're so damned busy.

CONSTANCE: And learning to nurse. *That's* a trip.

CONSTANCE and MARYANNE laugh voluptuously. MURPHY is breathless from his push-ups, which no one seems to have noticed.

MURPHY *(rises, goes to the table to get his glass of wine)*: The crucial question is, Connie and Maryanne, would you do it all over again? Knowing there's so much pain?

CONSTANCE: So much *pain*? Murph, who's talking about *pain*?

MARYANNE: Admittedly there's pain. But pain isn't the point.

MURPHY *(to MARYANNE)*: *You'd* do it over again?

MARYANNE: Is that a serious question? Of course I'd do it again. I love my kids. Don't you love yours?

MURPHY *(to CONSTANCE)*: Connie, *you'd* go through it all again?

CONSTANCE *(annoyed)*: This is getting insulting. Of course.

MURPHY *(puzzled)*: Why's it insulting? I'm just asking. I mean it abstractly.

CONSTANCE: What's abstract about it? We're talking about my actual daughter and my actual son. Whom you know and I thought you liked—loved. Who *exist*.

MURPHY *(protesting)*: I know they exist. They're terrific kids. You know how I feel about them. But—

TED: —But to get them, what you had to endure physically, that's what Murph means. *Was the pain worth it?*

CONSTANCE: Look, of course—

MARYANNE: —that isn't the—

CONSTANCE: —there's pain, but—

MARYANNE: —you guys have it all wrong!—

CONSTANCE *(seizing control of the moment, impassioned and articulate)*: Of course you experience pain, it's like your entire body is being twisted in half, torn open, of course it's terrifying but when you're in it you're *in* it and you're not thinking. And each time is different so you can't ever be really prepared. But, in the end, as Maryanne says, you have a *baby*. Got it?

MARYANNE: You have a *baby*. Not a kidney stone.

CONSTANCE, MARYANNE, and TED laugh. MURPHY broods for a moment, then laughs, too.

MURPHY: Hey c'mon, I almost died with that kidney stone. That was sheer agony.

CONSTANCE: Right. So what'd you have when it was over?

MURPHY: What'd I have? A five thousand dollar hospital bill. My medical insurance rates went up.

MARYANNE: You had a *kidney stone*, not a *baby*.

MURPHY looks blankly at TED, shrugs.

CONSTANCE *(to MARYANNE)*: They don't get it, do they?

TED: *I'm* out of it, look—I've never had kids. Murph has, I haven't. *(Boyish smile)* I've never even had a kidney stone.

MURPHY *(behaving more as a host, on his feet offering to pour more wine into his friends' glasses)*: What we've been talking about tonight, it's a mystery to me. I mean—how do you women do it? I'd never have the guts.

TED *(affable shrug)*: I'd never have the guts, that's for damned sure. *(Shudders)* Brrrr! Just hearing you two talk about it gives me the shivers.

CONSTANCE *(ironically)*: Poor baby!

MURPHY: When I was in junior high, one of our teachers practically had a miscarriage in front of the class. Everybody joked about it afterward—guys, I mean—nervous joking—but I didn't laugh. I almost keeled over. I realized right then, *I* could never go through anything like that, what my own mother went through to have *me*.

CONSTANCE *and* MARYANNE *stare at* MURPHY *and* TED, *alert and startled.*

TED: Hell, to be truthful, if it was up to me to have a baby—the future of the human race would be very doubtful.

MURPHY: If it was up to *me*, Homo sapiens would be extinct already. *(Cheerful)* That fucking kidney stone was more than enough for me.

TED: It's a terrible admission to make, I guess, isn't it? I mean… *(Pause)* I love life. I think the world is a beautiful place, essentially.

MURPHY: *I* love my kids. And, well—lots of kids.

MURPHY *and* TED *begin laughing suddenly, loudly;* CONSTANCE *and* MARYANNE *look on in silence, stricken. The men now dominate the stage.*

As lights dim, the men's laughter subsides for a moment; then something sets them going again.

Lights out. Men's laughter continues into darkness.

THE END

Poor Bibi

A Play In One Act

CHARACTERS:

WIFE, a youngish woman

HUSBAND, a youngish man

BIBI, a creature of ambiguous species
(for this role it's suggested that
a petite, lithe young person with a
gymnast's background and a talent
for mime be cast)

VETERINARIAN

Darkness. We hear BIBI's *hoarse, strangulated breathing.*

Lights up. Stage right, WIFE *and* HUSBAND *mime being wakened from sleep. Extreme stage left,* BIBI *is sleeping on a pile of rags, breathing hoarsely.*

HUSBAND: What—what is it?

WIFE: Oh, dear!—

HUSBAND: Is it—?

WIFE *(sadly, severely)*: You know what it is. *(Pause, listening)* Tonight it's the worst it has ever been.

HUSBAND: Poor Bibi!

WIFE: Poor *us*!

WIFE *comes forward, to speak confidentially to the audience;* BIBI *continues as before, and* HUSBAND *goes, with some trepidation, to examine him.*

WIFE *(confrontational, defensive; yet with an air of anguish)*: Have you ever been wakened from sleep to such a sound? Night after night? In your own home, under your own roof? *(Shudders)* My nerves are in shreds!

HUSBAND *(kneeling by* BIBI*)*: Bibi! Bibi! Wake *up!* *(No response from* BIBI; HUSBAND *calls to* WIFE*)* Bibi won't wake up, dear. I'm afraid Bibi is...

WIFE *(hands over ears)*: —Don't say it!

HUSBAND: Bibi! *(Shakes* BIBI*)* Poor Bibi!

WIFE: Bibi is *dying!* Oh, don't say it!

HUSBAND *(calling to* WIFE, *an air of reproach, alarm)*: Bibi isn't in his cozy wicker basket by the stove, in the warmest snuggest corner of the cellar, he's dragged himself into the farthest darkest coldest corner... Bibi! *(Shaking* BIBI*)*

WIFE: Out of spite! After all we've done for him! *(Upset)* After loving him with all our heart...hearts...

HUSBAND *succeeds in rousing* BIBI *to a degree.* BIBI *is groggy, flailing about; snaps at* HUSBAND's *hand.*

HUSBAND: Bibi! Bad Bibi!

WIFE *(agitatedly beginning to dress)*: Oh, we'll have to go through with it—today. This morning. No more postponing...the inevitable.

HUSBAND *(more hurt than angry, calling to* WIFE*)*: Bibi bit me! On purpose!

WIFE *(briskly to audience)*: Oh, we'd known!—Bibi had been ailing for weeks. Months. The breed has a genetic weakness for respiratory infections, we'd been warned. *(Vexed, tearful)* Bibi himself was very much to blame. Oh, yes! We'd notice that Bibi was coughing, wheezing, and we'd try to take him to be examined, but—clever, cunning Bibi! He always knew; and managed somehow to improve for a few days. How many times that happened. And you can't force Bibi to do anything against his will, hardly!—I still have a scar from one such episode, last spring. *(Shows the back of her hand)* Of course, with Bibi, it's easy to be deceived. *That* had been one of the problems with Bibi from the start.

(Pause; nostalgia interlude)

In the beginning, though it was long ago, I can remember we were very happy. It had been promised to my bridegroom and me as we ascended to the altar that we would be very happy, perfectly happy, all the days of our lives. I believe this would have been so!—had we not weakened, and out of some emotion I still don't comprehend, brought Bibi home to live with us. *(Pause)*

HUSBAND *(to audience)*: We were *two*, my bride and me. And with the recklessness of youth thought we would expand our happiness to *three*.

WIFE *(abrupt change of mood, recollecting the past; vivacious, girlish)*: Oh, how we loved Bibi in those days! The happiest most energetic most innocent and delightful creature imaginable!

BIBI *erupts with energy. Scampers about the stage, as* WIFE *and* HUSBAND *look on in astonishment. He rolls over, somersaults, fetches a rubber ball tossed by the* HUSBAND; WIFE *gaily waves a scarf or a towel which* BIBI *grips with his teeth, etc.* BIBI *is the very image of joyousness.*

HUSBAND *(to audience)*: Our friends were frankly envious!

WIFE: They'd never seen anything like our Bibi!

HUSBAND: His pert little button nose—

WIFE *(squealing)*: —nuzzling against my bare legs! Ohhh!

HUSBAND: His ears pricking up so erect, his pelt crackling with static electricity when we brushed it— *(Mimes brushing* BIBI's *coat as* BIBI *rolls over in ecstasy)*

WIFE: Oh Bibi, you darling! Momma's little babyums *darling*!

HUSBAND: Bibi! Bibi! *(As* BIBI *scampers about)* Not up on the table, Bibi!—

A sound of breaking glass.

WIFE *(laughing, alarmed)*: Oh! Bibi!

HUSBAND: *Bad* Bibi—

WIFE: Not up the drapes, Bibi— Oh!— *(A sound as of tearing fabric)* Naughty!

HUSBAND *(alarmed but laughing, too; indulgent)*: Now that *was* naughty, Bibi! You know better, babyums!

WIFE *(clapping hands, laughing, in a kind of ecstasy)*: Bibi! Bibi!

HUSBAND: Bibi!

Bright sunshine. WIFE, HUSBAND *jog as* BIBI *scampers merrily ahead.*

WIFE *(breathless)*: Suddenly—there we all were! Running in the park!

HUSBAND *(breathless)*: —the three of us—

WIFE: Oh, what fun! How good this feels!

HUSBAND: So—healthy! So somehow normal!

As BIBI *vanishes stage left.*

WIFE: Oh, Bibi!—where are you going?

HUSBAND *(panting)*: Bibi, come *back*!

HUSBAND, WIFE *rush about agitated.*

WIFE/HUSBAND: Bibi! Bibi!

HUSBAND *(accusing to* WIFE*)*: It was your idea!—

WIFE *(tearful)*: It was *your* idea—

HUSBAND/WIFE: Bibi darling, come back!—

BIBI *reappears, stage right; scampers up behind* WIFE, HUSBAND.

WIFE: Oh! Bibi! Oh where have you been!

HUSBAND *(overlapping)*: Bibi, thank God!

BIBI *leaps up upon* WIFE, HUSBAND; *the three scamper along together in high spirits.*

Sunshine dims; abrupt alteration of mood.

WIFE *(as if stunned, baffled)*: Then, so suddenly, Bibi was no longer— young.

HUSBAND: No longer—Bibi.

WIFE: It seemed to happen overnight.

HUSBAND: *Not* what we'd been promised!

HUSBAND tries to pet BIBI, who snaps at him.

HUSBAND: Ow! Look!— *(Holds out bitten hand for WIFE to examine)*

WIFE *(shaken, tearful)*: *Not* what we'd been promised.

BIBI withdraws sulkily. WIFE, HUSBAND confer together.

WIFE *(to audience)*: If Bibi wasn't Bibi—exactly; if Bibi growled and snapped at us—the only people on earth who loved him dearly; if Bibi fell into the truly disgusting habit of gobbling his food and vomiting it in dribbles through the house—

BIBI mimes some of this behavior.

HUSBAND *(defensive, adamant)*: Are *we* to be blamed for relegating him more and more to the cellar, and out of our sight?

WIFE *(quickly)*: Not that our cellar is a dank, damp, unhealthy place. It is not. In fact, in the warm snug corner near the furnace, where Bibi's basket of rags was placed, it was really most cozy. It was really quite nice.

HUSBAND: We did not neglect Bibi, even so. He was always fed!— plenty of nutritional kibble in his dish. Plenty of water.

WIFE: Plenty of water!—

HUSBAND: Indeed it was impossible to ignore Bibi—with his whining, whimpering, clawing at the cellar door—

WIFE: And the loathsome messes he made which one of us (usually I) would have to clean up each morning!

HUSBAND: Yet it was impossible to be angry with Bibi for long—

WIFE: Oh yes!—when Bibi lay on his back, rolled over and showed his belly, which was his only trick really—

HUSBAND: —Bibi's only trick, but so winning—

BIBI rolls over, shows his belly, etc.

WIFE: —when he gazed up at us, his master and mistress, with eyes rimmed in mucus, with that look of mute animal sorrow—

HUSBAND: We saw that, yes, we loved him still.

WIFE: And how painful, such love!

HUSBAND: For it became increasingly obvious, poor Bibi's time had come.

WIFE: "We can't let him suffer!"—one of us said to the other.

HUSBAND: And the other, "We can't, God have mercy we *can't*."

WIFE, HUSBAND embrace each other. A beat. BIBI returns to his original position, extreme stage right, sleeping on rags; breathing hoarsely.

WIFE *(sighing, but resolved)*: Well. So be it. We made our decision.

HUSBAND leads the way, WIFE following. HUSBAND awkwardly snatches up BIBI, wraps him in a blanket; BIBI flails his limbs weakly.

WIFE: Oh don't hurt him!—poor Bibi!

HUSBAND: Bibi, it's *all right*. Nothing will happen to you.

WIFE *(continuing to audience)*: We carried Bibi out to the car—it was just past dawn of a cold November day—so cheerless! so stark!— I held Bibi on my lap—as we drove to the Family Pet Hospital & Emergency Service a few miles away. Oh!—I'll never forget! *(To BIBI)* Bibi, good Bibi, sweet Bibi, be calm. Trust us!

BIBI squirms in WIFE's arms but does not try to escape; whimpers, whines, groans.

HUSBAND: Yes, Bibi! Trust us! Everything will be all right, you'll see!

WIFE *(to audience, anxious and baffled)*: When we arrived at the hospital, we were amazed at how full the parking lot was—at seven A.M. And, inside—

HUSBAND: —the waiting room was packed.

WIFE *(to HUSBAND)*: My goodness, who are all these people!

WIFE, HUSBAND enter the waiting room, find seats. BIBI on WIFE's lap.

HUSBAND *(to audience)*: We were careful to keep Bibi wrapped up in his blanket.

WIFE: Not wanting prying eyes to see him.

HUSBAND *(glancing about)*: Such a crowd, so early in the morning—isn't it odd?

We hear yips, barks, whining, cries, groans, shrieks, etc. BIBI's hoarse strangulated breathing.

WIFE *(squinting into distance)*: Why, the waiting room is huge... seems to go on forever.

HUSBAND *(to WIFE)*: Shall I hold Bibi for a while, dear?

WIFE: Oh, no! We're fine, aren't we Bibi? *(Hugs BIBI)* We're all cozy and quiet, aren't we.

HUSBAND: Bibi is being very brave, isn't he!

WIFE *(passionately)*: We are all being very brave.

A beat, to indicate passage of time.

VETERINARIAN appears, stage right. A person in a blood-stained smock.

HUSBAND: At last!—

WIFE: —after waiting nearly three hours!—

HUSBAND *(to audience)*: —It was our turn.

HUSBAND, WIFE eagerly and with trepidation enter the VETERINARIAN's examining room. They lay BIBI on a table, still wrapped in his blanket.

WIFE *(tearful)*: Soon now, Bibi! Be brave...

HUSBAND: Everything will be all right, Bibi! We promise.

VET mimes washing his hands briskly; whistles through his teeth.

VET: What seems to be the problem here?

HUSBAND/WIFE *(anxiously)*: Oh doctor, our Bibi—

VET removes blanket from BIBI. Stares at BIBI.

VET *(after a beat)*: Is this... some sort of joke?

HUSBAND: Doctor, this is the way we found Bibi, this morning...

WIFE: ...he wouldn't eat for weeks, that's why he's so thin...

HUSBAND: ...a respiratory ailment...

WIFE: ...a genetic predisposition...

VET: My God.

HUSBAND: Doctor, you can help us…can't you?

WIFE *(a rush of words)*: If you could put a quick merciful end to Bibi's suffering… *(Hand to mouth)* Oh! What did I just say!

VET: I've asked you: is this some sort of joke?

WIFE/HUSBAND: J-Joke…?

VET *(furiously)*: What do you two mean, coming to me with—*this*?

WIFE/HUSBAND: Th-This…? This is Bibi…

HUSBAND: As my w-wife said, doctor, if you could put a quick merciful end to…

VET: How dare you! Are you mad?

WIFE *(rattled)*: "To sleep," doctor…if you could p-put him "to sleep"…out of his suffering…

VET: Out of here, both of you. Take "Bibi" with you, at once.

HUSBAND: Doctor, what on earth—? We're going to pay you, after all.

WIFE: Oh yes, yes—we have our checkbook—no, our Visa card—

VET is backing off in disgust, preparing to exit.

HUSBAND: You do this simple procedure for others all the time, doctor, don't you? *Why not for us?*

VET: Impossible! Unthinkable! Just take it—him—out of here, at once.

WIFE: Oh Doctor, please—*why not for us?*

VET: Before I call the authorities!

HUSBAND: But, Doctor—

VET: Appalling! Obscene! *(Hands over eyes)*

VET exits. HUSBAND, WIFE are left in a state of shock. BIBI flails about weakly on the table.

WIFE *(to audience)*: We…had never been so rudely treated before in our lives.

HUSBAND *(to audience)*: Simply unbelievable, such rudeness. I don't understand...

WIFE: *I* don't understand...

HUSBAND: As if such merciful procedures aren't done all the time, at the Family Pet Hospital as elsewhere...

WIFE: Oh, what a hypocrite, that doctor! Now what will we do!

HUSBAND *(an air of dread)*: Poor Bibi! What will we do!

Lights dim and lights up. Immediately following.

WIFE *(grimly, to audience)*: And so...I know you are preparing to judge us harshly...we did it ourselves.

HUSBAND *(defensively)*: Did what had to be done.

WIFE: Seeing that medical science failed us.

HUSBAND: Society failed us!

HUSBAND carries BIBI to rear of stage. WIFE comes forward.

As, in the background, HUSBAND mimes the drowning of BIBI, WIFE speaks in an elevated "tragic" mode.

WIFE *(to audience)*: A deep drainage ditch behind the hospital...filled with brackish, foul-smelling water. We had no choice! *(Pause)* Trembling, sick at heart, my husband...did what had to be done. *(Pause)* Bibi had to be put out of his misery. *(Pause)* Oh, horrible! God forgive us! We simply couldn't bring Bibi back home, to go through all that again. *(Pause)* For we too have grown, if not old, older. Our youth is past; our resilience, our early dreams. *(Pause, bitterly)* We to whom it was promised we would live happily forever. *(Pause)* And yet, not in our most terrible nightmares could we have imagined such an ending to our poor Bibi! Such a task for my poor husband! Forcing poor Bibi into that cold, foul water, pushing his head under! And how fiercely, how savagely Bibi fought! As if his life, even so wretched a life, was precious to him! *(Pause)* Our darling Bibi who had lived with us for so many years—transformed in an instant into a stranger, an enemy—a beast! Never had we truly known Bibi until then. *(Crying out as if stricken to the heart)* Bibi, no!

HUSBAND *(stricken)*: Bibi, *obey!*

WIFE: The struggle must have lasted ten minutes. Never will we forget! My poor, dear husband, the most gentle and civilized of men...provoked to desperation, rage...for *Bibi would not die* for the longest time. Hideous! And then, to die in such a place—a foul-smelling drainage ditch in a suburban field, beneath a November sky emptied of all sun. Imagine! *(Pause)*

BIBI is dead. HUSBAND staggers forward, stunned, hands trembling.

HUSBAND *(elevated diction)*: For we soon forget what we do, in the human desperation of doing it.

WIFE *(contemptuous, to audience)*: And you, you damned hypocrites—what will you do with yours?

Lights out.

THE END

Homesick
A Play in One Act

CHARACTERS:

"PINKTOES," a girl of about 20

"MR. AMERICA," Caucasian male, 37

SETTING: somewhere in rural Texas

TIME: the present

In the background, a red sky is illuminated.

Music. (Suggested: "End of the Night," The Doors)

Lights up. A young woman in a halter and jeans, provocatively dressed, enters, to sit on a bench; she's being watched, and eventually approached, by a husky, handsome man, in cheaply stylish but not new clothes; may be bearded; hair slickly oiled. PINKTOES flirts awkwardly with MR. AMERICA who smiles at her, notes with approval her pink socks; he seems to have convinced her to accompany him; as they walk off, he glances surreptitiously about, to make sure no one is watching. He may have left behind a crumpled cigarette package, which he returns to retrieve, thrusting it into his pocket.

PINKTOES and MR. AMERICA exit.

Music up. Lights out.

Lights up. PINKTOES, lying on a coroner's table, wrapped loosely in a coarse stained blanket, bare-legged, now wearing only bloodstained wool socks, addresses the audience. (At the foot of the table there is a clipboard with a medical report which she will later consult.)

PINKTOES *(childlike hurt, reproach)*: Momma—! *(Pause)* You see what's happened to me...it's your fault. *(Pause)* Wouldn't never of left home if...*you* know...you needed to love me better. *(Angrily wipes at eyes)* Now, nobody even knows what I am. Where I'm ending up. "Roscommon, Texas." Never heard of it before! Damn long way from home... *(Pause, accusing)* Jane Doe "Pinktoes" is my name here—that's all they know me by. 'Cause all I'm wearing, the Texas cops find me, is these old socks Grandma knitted for me. *(Indicates socks)* Ugh! How'd they get so...dirty? *(Stares at bloodstains; pause; shift in tone)* Hey: I remember opening my Christmas present from Grandma...how pretty the socks was. She'd been knitting them for me in secret not letting me know. *(Pause)* How long ago was that? I guess...a long time? *(Pause)* It's easy to forget, on the road...always moving...no place you *are*. *(Figures it out)* Yeah, O.K.: been gone from home four years. In December. It's Hallowe'en morning now, I ain't gonna get to December this year. *(Pause)* Momma, you listening? *(Stares into audience, hurt and accusing)* Naw, you ain't. I know.

Lights dim on PINKTOES.

Lights up on MR. AMERICA. *Manages to light a cigarette, though handcuffed.*

MR. AMERICA *(proudly, an air of reverence)*: First time, I was five years old. Ashland, West Virginia where I was born. My Momma run me out of the trailer 'cause she was...entertaining a guest...so I was down by the creek bank and it was dark and I looked and saw this...fire!...this Burning Bush...except it was going along the ground like a wheel. I was so scared almost pissed my pants! The Lord God giving me a sign! It came at me and I tried to catch it in my hand...rolling *whoosh!* along the ground. *(Demonstrates)* Oh! my fingers was burnt and blistered but I didn't feel no pain, I was struck down where I stood. And Momma next morning finds me sleeping under the trailer my hands so hurt like they was— *(he shows his scarred palms to the audience)* — *she* was repentant like a sinner called to judgment. *(Pause, dreamy)* Momma's hair like corn tassels and her face a shining light... *(Pause)*

(Self-condemning, repressed anger) There is a ministry of Love, and there is a ministry of Hurt. I know I was born to preach the Love not practice the Hurt and how—this—came to be— *(by "this" meaning his identity as a killer)* —before the Lord Jesus I don't comprehend.

(Defensive) "Pinktoes"?—*who?* When's this? *(Pause)* There's so many of them! And the pictures of them where they don't look nothing like who they were exactly but like others of them— females. *(Pause, muddled in his words)* I mean—*you* look at 'em, the pictures, and try to remember which one of 'em they're s'post to be...you'd be fucked, too. *(Pause)* Look, y'know who I blame? The police and the thr'pists always *letting me go. (Slicks back his hair, looking "innocent")* I'd tell 'em, "No sir, no ma'am, not me, I'm a good boy washed in the Blood of the Lamb, not me." *(Wide innocent mock-smile)* Union card in my wallet. *(Slaps pocket)* I look like anybody's boy cousin, eh? If I was a nigger, that'd be a different story! *(Laughs)*

(More somber, matter-of-fact) Well—maybe I remember. Yeah. This li'l girl all alone. Looking kind of sad, strung-out. My eye drawn to her by the will of the Lord—them *pink socks* she was wearing. I'm thinking, Is it a sign? O Lord, a sign from You? Truck-stop on I-35, Oklahoma. Headed south to Texas. *(Becoming more impassioned)* The sky all afire where the sun was going down, a long long time setting so my eyes was seared, I took that for a sign. *(In Biblical cadences) So he drove out the man; and he placed at the east of the garden of Eden Cherubims, and a flaming sword which turned every way, to keep the way of the tree of life. (Pause, shakes head as if to clear it)* She was alone at one of them picnic tables in the dusk...she'd been crying, her pretty face all puffy and eyes red so I was drawn to her as to a sister.

(MR. AMERICA and PINKTOES glance at each other, shyly.)

A poor lost soul needing help! Told her I'd buy us some Kentucky Fried Chicken, and a six-pack of Coor's, she looked like she was starving. And me, too. But not right here, I said, this ain't the place, I said. So I got her to my car and we drove off...how many hours, I don't know. She was asleep going into Texas, her head on my shoulder... *(Pause)* I accept my fate, it's no choice for a reasonable man. I know there is God but He is far away.

Lights dim on MR. AMERICA.

Lights up on PINKTOES.

PINKTOES (*voice rises to a faint scream*): I DON'T REMEMBER HIS
FACE, I COULDN'T IDENTIFY HIM! Just these tattoos up and
down his arms...mark of Satan. (*Pause, shakes head*) Yeah, I
believed him. There's been so many of 'em...mostly, they're O.K.
You got no choice, sometimes, you're that hungry...strung-out.
Damn ol' stomach growling, so hungry...I was embarrassed he'd
hear. Yeah and I'm so...dirty. Just don't know how I got so
dirty...it ain't my true self. Yeah I asked him could I take a
bath...wanted to wash my hair. He said sure! he'd rent us a motel
room...like brother and sister, he said. (*Shakes head, self-accusing*)
Shit! Did I believe him? Guess I did...

Funny how you're *in* your body so you understand it's just this
kind of...vehicle...God gave you to use. Right? Where the spirit
abides. (*Sings*) "This little light of mine, I'm gonna let it shine...
Let it shine all over God's moun-tain, I'm gonna let it shine..."
(*Voice trails off*) Grandma taught me that. (*Pause*) Once you're
dead, though, in folks' eyes, the body is all you *are*. And strangers
not even knowing your name.

(*Dreamy*) Grandma called me "honey." Picked me her favorite
to spite the rest of them. She'd say, "You're my girl, honey, ain't
you?" If Momma yelled at me, or slapped... 'Cause I was a little
slow through grammar school. Because I'd run off and hide. I
loved Grandma and she loved me. Because I was the one to help
Grandma wash her long hair, that she was *so proud* she never cut
all her life. Real pretty silvery hair—long, to here! (*Indicates her
waist*) "Your grandpa made me promise I'd never cut my hair,
so I never did. Isn't that something?—sixty years back. And him
dead since 1941."

(*Pause*) And I'd wash Grandma's feet for her where she was too
stout to bend. And clip her toenails, and bunions all grown over
like scabs. She had all these...whatdayacallem...geraniums, in
pots...I'd help her with. (*Pause*) Could be, Grandma's dead now.
I don't think about it. (*Pause*) Momma said I sure didn't take
after *her*. Yeah I hated my sisters—so *pretty-pretty*! You get your
way if you're *pretty-pretty* like on TV or in the movies so if you're
not, learn to make your own way. (*Belligerent*) Started in, age

thirteen, I wouldn't take none of their shit no longer. When I threw my plate on the floor, yeah I'd go hungry but they caught on to respect me. When I shouted, I sure didn't stammer.

Lights dim on PINKTOES.

Lights up on MR. AMERICA.

MR. AMERICA: Huh! It's these "court-appointed" thr'pists as they call themselves, and the l'wyers—nothing but a game with them, they don't give a shit. And the "doctors"—hoo, *that's* a laugh!—these jerk-offs at Plainfield couldn't speak English *nor* comprehend it. Dark enough to be niggers but *not*—one of 'em wearing a fucking turban. *(Indicating his own head with a winding motion; derisive)* Them saying I suffer from "temporal lobe trauma"—"lead and cadmium toxins"—from when I was a kid. Momma banged me around some, and Momma's men friends— O.K. But that's a long time ago. *(Pause, reminiscing)* This one time my mother was gone...went off with somebody...I hid out in the woods...getting stuff to eat out of garbage cans, dumpsters...one night, a guy took a shot at me with a .22, told me to get the hell out what'd I think I was, a fucking raccoon? *(Laughs, ironic)* Yes, and Jesus saying, "Light is come into the world—!"

(Urgent, matter-of-fact) There was this woman turned up in Blacksburg. Where we was then with one of Momma's man friends. She was slow-witted you could see. Said she would have sex with me then changed her mind seeing something in my face. She was a dirty whore. She was cross-eyed. She was the one I blame. *(Pause)* In a field beyond the old train yard there's oil drums, freight cars...she started fighting me, screaming so I got pissed— *(strangling motions with hands)* —shut her up good! Whore! Then I fucked her—good! Two, three times! Dragged some tarpaulin over her so nobody'd see then I went home to Mr. Cady's where Momma was "house-keeper"...I was fifteen years old. He was going to send me to Bible College, said he detected the fire of the Lord in my eye. *He* was in a wheelchair, poor old bastard. Momma'd get drunk and laugh saying all he had was a— *(gesturing at his crotch)* —old limp rubbery carrot. *(Laughs sadly)* They was going to get married but some folks of his fucked up the plans. *(Pause)* There was school there but I

didn't go. I'd make myself wait then go back to the train yard and every time I'd think there's nothing there, naw—and every time *she was still there* under the tarpaulin. And nobody knew! And nobody was going to know! *(Pause, breathing swiftly)* I'd get excited...I'd...yeah I'd screw her...couldn't stop myself. *(A moment's anguish; pause)* They don't judge you in that state. *(Pause)*

A beat. MR. AMERICA *hides his face, sways.*

(Approaches audience, abrupt anger, dropping his hands) Huh! I know you're thinking you are SUPERIOR to me. BETTER EDUCATED and BETTER BACKGROUND, huh! BETTER NOURISHED in your mother's womb and your mother wasn't no PROSTITUTE. *(Spitting gesture)* Well, fuck that! *(Evangelical voice)* "For unto every one that hath shall be given, and he shall have abundance: but from him that hath not shall be taken away *even that which he hath.*" *(Pause)* Think I don't know that? A man like me don't know that? God give me His sign, I am of the ministry of hurt. *(Rolls up his left sleeve to reveal a lewd crimson flame tattooed on his bicep)* Take heed: all through this United States of America there's those of us recognize each other by His sign. No matter how far from home we are—we are home.

Lights dim on MR. AMERICA.

Lights up on PINKTOES.

PINKTOES *(defensive)*: Naw, I never knew any of them other girls— s'post to be, what?—twenty-two!—that's been killed along I-35. If it was the same guy or some other bastard been killing 'em. *(Bitter satisfaction) Their* Mommas feeling like shit, too, eh? *(Strides about in the blanket, almost preening)* Why didn't I go to no shelter in Kansas City?—'cause I didn't want to. That's why. Assholes telling me what to do. *(Pause)* It's O.K. if you're sick, or feeble-minded, which ain't me. I like my independence. It's the open road, for me. *(Pause)* Yeah I should've sent some cards home— postcards. Fartherest west I was was the Grand Canyon once, and Salt Lake City, with some guy. Should've sent a Christmas card to Grandma, but I didn't. Now...it's too late.

(Pause) Just as well, Grandma probably ain't alive. She'd feel bad if she knew. *(Considers her body, inside the blanket)* Jesus! How'd I get all these scars—scabs—bruises—*bites*—and so damn skinny,

my ribs showing, collarbone—ninety pounds, about, at the end. You sure got no secrets from the coroner, eh? *(Wry laugh)* Some of the injuries fresh and some of 'em years old. Like this weird rip like a zipper, here— *(Indicates her left thigh)* Cut myself up running from a cop—behind a 7-Eleven store in Tulsa—ran into some barbed wire—bleeding like a stuck pig in the back of the squad car and the cops disgusted with me... *(Pause)*

Been pregnant one time, and lost it. The coroner picked up on that. Can't hide nothing from them...bastards.

V.D., too, it says on the record—"herpes." *(Mispronounces)*

The only jewelry on the "cadaver" is this little jade cross on a gold chain around my neck. *(Indicates necklace, on a thin chain)* Except it wasn't real jade some guy gave me, and it sure wasn't real gold. Anybody'd guess that, seeing me dumped there dead in the weeds like a tossed-away beer bottle. Dirty pink socks is all I'm wearing.

Yeah my stomach's empty. Just Coke he bought me at the rest-stop. Never did get that Kentucky Fried Chicken he promised, or the Coor's. Fucker!

Lights up on MR. AMERICA.

MR. AMERICA *(incensed)*: She was a Christian girl—I thought. Wearing a little cross around her neck. Poor sad child in the pink socks. So far from home, she said, she'd about forgot where was her home. I asked her was she lost and she said she ain't ever been lost. I asked her were her folks missing her at that very moment and she said No! nobody was missing her! ever! but she started crying...poor sad child. *(Pause; now reflective)* Oh God how she was hoping to get a bath, she said. Wash out some of her dirty clothes. Her pink socks—been wearing them so long. At first she seemed kind of scared of me, but interested like they are. Saying, Mister, I'm so tired, I'm by myself, I'm hungry—you got anything to eat? I sure took pity on her from the first sight. That's the tender kind can break your heart—if you let them.

(Sadly) I miss my home, too. My momma that was always moving around. But where she *was*, that *was* home. If I could get there...I could be washed in the Blood of the Lamb. Momma hoped to

make amends, her cousin was Reverend Willy Robbins baptized me and her together…we were happy, then. For how long I don't know but we were happy and nobody came between us… *(Pause, shakes head)* At Baton Rouge they said it was "delusions"—these things I told them they didn't want to believe. "Frontal lobe epilepsy"—so they give me these hot-stinging shots in the ass. Thorazine—that'll make you into a walking zombie. How I escaped?—I *walked right out*. Work-duty in the laundry and the laundry truck comes in, and the gates are open, and—*I walk right out*. Hoo! *(Throws off cuffs)*

(Continuing, matter-of-fact) I was driving down to Galveston where there was the promise of a job. Oil rig. I'm a good worker, I keep my nose clean I don't cause trouble. Any man knows he can trust me. Long as I'm not drinking. So any judge I come before, there's these "character references" and they're impressed. Never yet had a jury trial, nor wanted one. I told the police all I could remember but it was like a shadow—you can say, sure this is a "human being" but it don't *seem so*. There isn't the weight, or the—what you call it— *(rubs thumb and forefinger together)* —the thickness—*texture*. The actual killing, when it happens, it's like the shadow is there and a flame flies up over it and that is the flame of Death. *(Pause)* I have been a witness from, say, twenty feet away. This last time, they were in a drainage ditch, and I was up on a bridge. I saw—but if I blinked, or shut my eyes, it wasn't there. It ceased to exist.

(Contemplative) You learn to accept your fate. You bow your head. *(Sings, a tentative, flat, yet yearning voice)* "Jesus meek and Jesus mild, Jesus became a little child…" Amen! *(Pause)* Couple years ago in Blacksburg in the psych'ric hospital I visited momma at last. This fat bald bulldog-woman I wouldna known! Momma, I said, I was near to crying, oh Momma you used to be so pretty! and she said, So did you, and laughed. She said, Yeah, my yellow hair fell out one day I wasn't looking. *(Laughs)* Momma always had a sense of humor. These guys beating on her, and stealing from her and she could take it long as there was food to eat and clothes for me, I was her baby she nursed me at her breast. In the visitors' room right on that filthy floor we prayed together on our knees. I could see she would die soon, they had pumped her so full of poison she was like a waterlogged corpse, and one of

her eyes filmed over. She says, May God forgive me, son, that night I got drunk and burnt your hands, held your baby hands in the kerosene stove, and I was crying no matter who was watching me, I said, Oh Momma, that never happened, there's no need to be forgiven. She said, Son, that did happen, not once but many times, see these scars— *(He lifts his hands to contemplate the palms, turns them outward to the audience.)* I said NO MOMMA THESE ARE FROM GOD. These are a sign from God to me, and He has sent others. *(Pause, bitter)* Damn ol' senile woman! Bitch! WHORE!

(Regaining control, an air of regret) This girl last week, in the pink socks—that was the one I saw, I whispered, "Sweet Jesus, let me love her."
You want to offer your soul to somebody.
You want to do some fucking GOOD in the world.
We drove all night and the morning sky was like fire inside the clouds where there was God's face if you had eyes to see. *(Hiding his eyes)* A sheet of fire washed over the car, the hood all blinding... I was *hurt* all over my skin like...like lye...like a time I hoped to purify myself rubbing myself with lye...and there was a bridge we drove over exiting from the interstate, and a drainage ditch all dry...big cracks in the earth, and the earth so red...like Mars. That far away!

MR. AMERICA *and* PINKTOES *glance at each other, as before.*

Lights dim on MR. AMERICA. *Lights up on* PINKTOES.

PINKTOES: That far away! Everything's so far... *(Pause)* I saw his face but it was blasted in fire. I heard this hard voice out of the underside of the world...no human voice. *(Pause)* Help me, Jesus, help us who can't help ourselves!... *(Pause)* Naw. It ain't like that. It's just you. Nobody to help 'cause nobody to witness. *(Pause)* Raped me, and strangled me, and battered my head till blood leaked out my ears, nose and mouth like a burst tomato. Tore off all my clothes except my socks, he left. That's how the Texas cops find me Hallowe'en morning, driving out patrolling "Devil's Night" damage. This naked dead girl sprawled face down in the weeds in a drainage ditch. *(Pause)* Texas Interstate I-35 two miles east of Roscommon. Where I'd never been, had no connection with. I-35 runs from Salina, Kansas to Laredo,

Texas on the Mexican border—750 miles. Long stretches just empty, desolate like the moon. Where you find us, it's never where we're from—only where we're dumped. *(Pause)* "Caucasian female" the cops radioed in. "Caucasian"—*that's* what I am? *(Pause)* Said I'd been "good-looking," too. *(Laughs)* Maybe that's what the cops always say, out of pity? Like, y'know, they got their own sisters, daughters. They try to put the best light on it. *(Pause)*

Lights up on MR. AMERICA, *who may be addressing* PINKTOES.

MR. AMERICA *(appealing, initially almost boyish)*: Listen, Jesus as my witness, I never meant *harm*. I am born of the ministry of Love— not Hurt. I meant to get that fried chicken...that six-pack of Coor's.... Don't know what, what happened...

See: I never counted but they told me, of my thirty-seven years I have been in-car-cer-ated fifteen. Going back to Boys' Home when Momma had to give me up for a while. It's O.K. inside. It's what you know. Six A.M. the bell goes and you get up and wash. Six-fifteen a bell goes and you step out of your cell and march off to mess hall and eat and you're *hungry*—say it's cereal, it's toast, it's canned peaches or something—it tastes real good. And coffee! O.K. then you march out of mess hall dropping your spoon and fork in a bucket a guard's holding. You march to your work duty say it's custodian, or grounds, or tag shop where you dip license plates in paint. O.K., nine-thirty A.M. the bell goes and you can smoke. A bell goes and you get back to work. Eleven-thirty, bell goes again you stop work, wash up, march back to your cellhouse. Twelve noon, bell rings and you march to mess hall where you eat, and Jesus you're hungry—it might be meatloaf, fried potatoes, cornbread. *(Smacks lips)* Twelve-thirty a bell goes and you march out dropping your spoon, fork in a bucket a guard's holding. You return to work duty. At three P.M. a bell goes and you can smoke. A bell goes and you get back to work. Four-thirty a bell goes and you can wash and march back to your cellhouse. Five o'clock a bell goes and you march to supper. Five-thirty a bell goes and you march to your cellhouse for the night. *(Pause)* You can pray on your knees long hours. You can read if your eyes don't upset you. There's noise in the cellhouse like in the world but in your cell there's peace. In Boys' Home they beat me and fucked me up the ass, made me their slave, O.K. but that ain't now, now I am my own man, and nobody fucks with me. *(Pause)* You can make of your body a vessel of strength. *(He does several quick push-ups, then rises, flushed and triumphant, flexing biceps.)* You can prepare for your day of release hoping it won't come too soon. *(Pause, as he rolls up his other sleeve, to reveal a tattoo of an American eagle clutching a flag)* Which is why they call me "Mister America"—NOBODY FUCKS WITH ME.

A beat.

(Reflective, elegiac) Yeah—there was others. Never knew their names. Nor even faces. It's like the weather, the wind blowing the clouds across the Plains…never stops. *(Pause)*

PINKTOES *may be addressing* MR. AMERICA.

PINKTOES: Wasn't ever identified—wasn't a "missing person." Momma kicked me out, I'm *out*. Took some of her money with me so I'm not *missing*, I'm *out*. Washed her hands of me…can't say I blame her.

MR. AMERICA *(matter-of-factly)*: Yeah I confessed—I guess. Told the Texas cops everything I could remember, all my fucking life— said "yes" to anything they asked me. Nine hours of it. Hell-bent for the electric chair I guess…

PINKTOES: NO! I'M TOO YOUNG TO DIE! *(Hides her face; pause)* No. I accept my fate.

MR. AMERICA *(shrugs)*: Then the judge tossed it out—on account of I didn't have a lawyer. I told the cops I didn't want no fucking lawyer and I didn't—*don't*. O.K. but they talk so, they convince you. You need thr'py, he said. You're a casualty of our system. So, shit, O.K.—pleading guilty to "second-degree manslaughter" it was. *I* don't know. And all that past stuff I told the cops about the other girls—that's "delusion"—"con-fab-u-lation" they call it. *(Pause, bemused)* Yeah, there's a deal with the court—seven-to-thirty years. Up for parole in four years and I will be only forty-one then, not old. Not old, at all.

PINKTOES: They're thinking "Pinktoes" is from the Laredo stretch of I-35, or maybe east around Gainesville. Maybe one of the big cities—Houston, Dallas—where it's easy to get lost. Or maybe out of state. *(Pause, nodding)* Yeah—one of them sad little

shrinking towns in Kansas, Nebraska, Iowa nobody knows the
name of except the folks who live there, and, for a while, till they
forget, guys who pass through.

Lights down. PINKTOES *sprawls on the floor, face down; lies still. Music
comes up. (Suggested: "Push," Matchbox 20)* MR. AMERICA *stealthily
approaches her, fascinated by her in death. With one foot he subtly
rearranges her legs; stoops, rearranges an arm; strokes her hair; steps
over her, observing her with a perfectionist's eye; leans over to kiss the
back of her neck. He retreats with obvious reluctance, glancing about to
see if anyone is watching.*

Music down.

Lights out.

THE END

The Adoption
A Play in One Act

CHARACTERS:

MR., a Caucasian man in his late 30s or early 40s
MRS., a Caucasian woman of about the same age
X, male or female, of any mature age
NABBO, a child
NADBO, a "twin" of NABBO

SETTING: An adoption agency office. Sterile surroundings, merely functional furnishings. Prominent on the wall facing the audience is a large clock with a minute hand of the kind that visibly "jumps" from minute to minute. At the start, the clock measures real time; by subtle degrees, it begins to accelerate.

TIME: The present.

Lights up. We have been hearing bright, cheery music ("It's a Lovely Day Today") which now subsides. MR. and MRS. are seated side by side, gripping hands; they appear excited and apprehensive. They are conventionally well-dressed, as if for church, and do indeed exude a churchy aura. MR. has brought a briefcase, MRS. a "good" purse. A large bag (containing children's toys) close by.

To the left of MR. and MRS. is a door in the wall; to the right, behind them, is the clock. With lights up the clock begins its ticking, the time at 11:00.

MRS.: I'm so excited—*frightened*!

MR.: It's the day we've been waiting for—I'm sure.

MRS.: Oh, do you *think*—? I don't dare to hope.

MR.: They *were* encouraging, last time—

MRS.: Yes, they were!

MR.: They wouldn't send us away empty-handed again—would they?

MRS.: Well, they did last time, and the time before last—

MR.: But this *is* going to be different, I'm sure. They *hinted*—

MRS.: No, they all but *said*—*promised*—

MR.: —um, not a *promise* exactly, but—

MRS.: It was, it was a promise!—almost. In all but words.

MR.: Yes. They *hinted*—today is the day.

MRS. (*on her feet, too excited to remain seated*): The day we've been awaiting—for so long!

MR. (*on his feet*): *So* long!

MRS.: I feel like a, a bride again! A—virgin! (*Giggles*)

MR. (*touching or embracing her*): You *look* like a *madonna*.

MRS.: It's a, a—delivery—

MR. (*subtle correction*): A *deliverance*.

MRS. (*euphoric, intense*): We can't just live for ourselves alone. A woman, a man—

MR. (*emphatically*): That's selfish.

MRS.: That's—unnatural.

MR.: Lonely.

MRS. (*wistfully*): *So* lonely.

MR.: A home without—

MRS.: —children—

MR.: —is *empty*.

MRS.: Not what you'd call a "home"—

MR.: But we have means, we can afford to "extend our boundaries."

MRS.: Thank God! *(Eyes uplifted, sincerely)*

MR. *(glance upward)*: Yes, indeed—thank You, God. *(Pause)* Of course, um—we're not millionaires. Just, um—"comfortable."

MRS.: —"comfortable Americans"—

MR.: —of the "educated" class—"middle class"—

MRS.: Oh, dear—aren't we "upper-middle"? Your salary—

MR. *(finger to lips, stern)*: We are *not* millionaires.

MRS.: Well—we've "paid off our mortgage," we have a "tidy little nest egg," we've made "sensible, long-term investments"—

MR. *(cautioning)*: We are what you'd call *medium comfortable*. We can afford to extend our boundaries, and begin a—family.

MRS. *(almost tearful)*: A family! After twelve years of waiting!

MR. *(counting rapidly on fingers)*: Um—thirteen, darling.

MRS. *(belatedly realizing what she has said)*: I mean—twelve years of *marriage*. Not just *waiting*. *(Glances at MR.)* Oh—thirteen?

MR. *(defensive)*: We've been happy, of course. Our marriage hasn't been merely *waiting*—

MRS.: —for a, a baby—

MR.: —a family—

MRS. *(cradling gesture with her arms)*: —a darling little *baby*—

MR.: —strapping young *son*—

MRS. *(emphatically)*: We've done plenty of other things!

MR.: Certainly have! Hobbies, travel— *(a bit blank)* —paying off our mortgage—

MRS. *(grimly)*: We've been happy. We love each other, after all.

MR.: Sure do! Sweetest gal in the world! *(Kisses MRS.'s cheek)*

MRS. *(repeating in same tone)*: We've been happy.

MR.: Damned happy.

MRS.: We have snapshots to prove it—

MR.: Albums of snapshots to prove it!

A pause. MR. and MRS. glance nervously at the clock.

MRS. *(a soft voice)*: Of course, every now and then—

MR.: —in the interstices of happiness—

MRS.: —between one heartbeat and the next—

MR.: —in the early, insomniac hours of the morning, maybe—

MRS.: —in the bright-lit maze of the food store—

MR.: —like fissures of deep, sharp shadow at noon—

MRS.: —we have sometimes, for maybe just a—

MR.: —fleeting second—

MRS.: —teensy-weensy fleeting *second*—

MR.: —been a bit lonely.

Pause.

MRS. *(sad, clear voice)*: So lonely.

Pause.

The door opens, and X *appears.* X *is a bureaucrat, in conventional office attire; may wear rimless glasses; carries a clipboard containing numerous documents. He/She is impersonally "friendly."*

X *(bright smile, loud voice)*: Goooood morning! *(Consults clipboard)* You are—Mr. and Mrs.—?

MR., MRS. *(excited, hopeful)*: That's right! *(MRS. quickly straightens MR.'s necktie, which has become crooked.)*

X *(making a production of shaking hands)*: Mr.—! Mrs.—! Soooo glad to meet you!

MRS. *(flushed, hand to bosom)*: So g-glad to meet *you.*

MR.: Is this the— *(fearful of asking "is this the day")* —the right time?

X: No time like the present! That's agency policy.

MRS.: An—excellent policy.

MR. *(nodding)*: Very excellent.

X: And you're punctual, Mr. and Mrs.—, I see. A good sign.

MR.: Oh, we're very punctual.

MRS. *(breathless)*: Always have been!

MR.: We've been here since 7:45 A.M., actually. When the custodial staff unlocked the building.

MRS.: We came to the c-city last night. We're staying in a hotel.

MR.: —a medium-priced hotel!—

MRS.: We were terrified of missing our appointment—

MR. *(chiding MRS.)*: We were not *terrified*, we were—vigilant.

MRS.: Yes, vigilant—

X: It *is* wise to be punctual. Such details in perspective parents are meticulously noted. *(Mysteriously taps documents)*

MR. *(a deep breath)*: And   is   today   the   d-day?

MRS. *(a hand on MR.'s arm, faintly echoing)*: —the d-day?

X *(beaming)*: Yes. Today *is* your day, Mr. and Mrs.—. Your application to adopt one of our orphans has been fully processed by our board of directors, and approved. Congratulations!

MRS.: Oh—! Oh!

MR.: Oh my God!

MR. and MRS. clasp hands, thrilled. X strides to the door, opens it with a flourish, and leads in NABBO.

X: Here he is, Mr. and Mrs.—your baby.

MR., MRS. *(faintly)*: "Our baby!"

NABBO is perhaps eight years old. He wears a mask to suggest deformity or disfigurement, but the mask should be extremely lifelike and not exaggerated. His skin is an ambiguous tone—dusky or mottled, not "black." He may be partly bald as well, as if his scalp has been burnt. He has a mild twitch or tremor.

MR. and MRS. stare at NABBO, who stares impassively at them.

X *(rubbing hands together)*: So! Here we are! Here we have "Nabbo." *(Nudging him)* Say hello to your new mother and father, Nabbo.

NABBO *is silent.*

MR., MRS.: H-Hello!

X *(a bit coercive)*: Say "hello" to your new mother and father, Nabbo. "Hel-lo."

NABBO *is silent.*

MR. *(hesitantly)*: He isn't a, an actual—*baby*—is he?

X *(consulting document)*: Nabbo is eight months old. To the day.

MR.: Eight *months*—?

MRS.: Oh but he's—so sweet. So—

X: Our records are impeccable.

MRS.: —*childlike.* So—

MR. *(a bit doubtful, to X)*: What did you say his name is?

MRS.: —*trusting.* So—

X: "Nabbo." "NAB-BO." *(Equal stress on both syllables)*

MRS.: —needful of our love!

X *pushes* NABBO *toward* MR. *and* MRS. *He is weakly resistant.*

MR., MRS.: "Nab-bo"—?

X *(brightly urging* NABBO*)*: "Hel-lo!"

NABBO *remains silent. Visible tremor.*

MR.: Maybe he doesn't know—English?

MRS.: Of course he doesn't, that's the problem. *(Speaking loudly, brightly)* Hel-lo, Nab-bo! You've come a long distance to us, haven't you? Don't be frightened. We are your new Mommy and your Daddy— *(Points to herself and to* MR.*)* We'll teach you everything you need to know.

MR.: We sure will!

MR. *has taken a camera out of his briefcase and takes pictures of* MRS. *posing with* NABBO. NABBO *is rigid with terror of the flash.*

MR.: Beau-ti-ful! The first *minute* of our new life. *(Takes another picture)*

MRS.: This is a holy time. I feel God's presence here.

MR. *(to X, hesitantly)*: Excuse me, but is Nabbo a, um—little boy, or a little girl?

MRS. *(gently poking MR.)*: Dear, don't be crude!

MR.: I'm only curious.

X *(checking document, frowning)*: You didn't specify, did you? You checked "either sex."

MRS. *(eagerly)*: Oh yes, oh yes! "Either."

MR. *(protesting)*: Hey, I was just curious. I'm Daddy, after all.

MRS. *(fussing over NABBO, squatting beside him)*: He's "Daddy," dear; and I'm "Mommy." We've waited so long for you! Only for *you*, dear. Can you say "Daddy"—"Mommy"?

NABBO remains silent, twitching slightly.

MR. *(as if NABBO is deaf)*: "DAD-DY"—"MOM-MY"—

MRS. *(her ear to NABBO's mouth, but hears nothing)*: Of course, you're shy; you've come such a long distance.

MR. *(solemnly)*: From the "dark side of the Earth."

MRS. *(to MR., chiding)*: Don't be so—grim, dear. That isn't the right tone. *(To NABBO; singing)* "Little Baby Bunting! Daddy's gone a-hunting! Gone to get a new fur skin! To wrap the Baby Bunting in!"

MR. *(joining in)*: "—wrap the Baby Bunting in!" *(Laughs, rubs hands happily together)* I can't believe this is *real*.

MRS. *(to NABBO)*: Now, Naddo—

MR.: "Nab-bo"—

MRS.: That's what I said: "Nad-do."

MR.: Dear, it's "Nab-bo."

MRS.: "Nab-bo"? That's what I *said*. My goodness! *(She turns to the bag, removing a large doll from it.)* Look, Nabbo darling—just for *you.* Isn't she lovely? (*Urging* NABBO *to take the doll, but* NABBO *is motionless, not lifting his/her arms*)

MR. (*taking a shiny toy firetruck out of the bag; in a hearty "masculine" voice*): Nabbo, look what Daddy has for you. Cool, eh? (*Running the truck vigorously along the floor, making "engine" noises deep in his throat*) RRRRRRMMMMMMM! Cool, Nabbo, eh?

X (*holding out the clipboard and a pen*): Excuse me, "Mommy" and "Daddy": please sign on the dotted line, and Nabbo is yours forever.

MRS.: Oh, yes!

MR.: Of course!

As MR. *takes the pen to sign, however,* X *suddenly draws back. As if he/she has just remembered.*

X: Um—one further detail.

MR., MRS.: Yes? What?

X: It appears that—Nabbo has a twin.

MR., MRS. (*blankly*): A—twin?

X: From whom Nabbo is said to be inseparable.

MR., MRS.: "Inseparable"—?

X: They must be adopted together, you see.

MR., MRS. (*trying to comprehend*): Twin—?

(*The minute hand of the clock continues to accelerate.*)

X: Yes. An identical twin.

MR.: *Identical?* Like our *ch-child?*

X: Frequently, our adoptees are from large lit- (*about to say "litter," changes his/her mind*) —families. (*Pause*) The term "twin" is merely generic.

MRS.: I don't understand. Isn't our Nabbo one of a kind?

X: Nabbo is indeed one of a kind; we are all "one of a kind." But Nabbo also has a twin, from whom Nabbo is inseparable.

MR.: But—what does that mean?

MRS.: "Inseparable—"?

Pause. MR. amd MRS. stare at each other.

MR. *(suddenly, extravagant)*: Hell, I'm game! *(Throws arms wide)*

MRS. *(squeals with excitement, kneeling before NABBO)*: You have a twin, Nabbo? Another just like you?

MR. *(recklessly)*: Two for the price of one, eh?

MRS. *(faint, laughing, peering up at MR.)*: Oh, but—"Daddy"—are we prepared? We've never had *one*, and now—*two*?

MR.: Isn't that the way twins always come—in *twos*? Surprising Mommy and Daddy? *(Laughs)*

MRS. *(dazed, euphoric)*: Oh yes oh yes oh *yes*! *(Pause, voice drops)* I'm afraid.

Pause.

MR.: *I'm* afraid. Gosh.

X: I regret to say, Mr. and Mrs.—, that our agency requires, in such a situation, that adoptive parents take in both siblings. For, given the fact of "identical twins," there can be no justification in adopting one instead of the other.

MRS.: That's...so.

MR. *(wiping face with handkerchief)*: You got us there...yes!

X takes NABBO's arm as if to lead him back through the door.

X *(somber voice)*: There are so many deserving applicants registered with our agency, you see. Our waiting list is years long.

MRS. *(desperate)*: Oh—oh, wait—

MR.: Hey, wait—

MRS. *(hugging NABBO)*: We want them both—of course.

MR. *(wide, dazed grin)*: *I'm* game! —Did I say that?

X *(severely)*: You're certain, Mr. and Mrs.—?

MR., MRS.: Yes! Yes!

X *(goes to the door, opens it and leads in NADBO, with some ceremony)*: This, Mr. and Mrs.—, is "Nad-bo."

MR., MRS. *(a bit numbed)*: "NAD-BOO."

X: "NAD-BO."

MR., MRS.: "NAD-*BO*."

NABBO and NADBO, twins, stand side by side. They exhibit identical twitches and tremors, cowering together.

MRS. *(voice airy, strange)*: What a long long distance you have come to us—Nab-bo, Nad-bo! Yet we were fated.

MR.: From "the dark side of the Earth"—from "the beginning of Time."

MR. and MRS. behave like doting parents, fussing over the twins.

MRS.: We'll teach you the English language—

MR.: *American* English language—greatest language on Earth!

MRS.: We'll bring you to our home—

MR.: *Your* home, now—

MRS.: We'll love love love you so you forget whatever it is— *(pause, a look of distaste)* —you've escaped.

MR.: *That's* for sure! No looking back.

MRS.: No looking back, you'll be American children. *No* past!

MR.: We're your new Mommy and Daddy—know what that means?

MRS. *(pointing)*: He's "Daddy"—I'm "Mommy"—

MR. *(overlapping, hearty)*: I'm "Mommy"—he's "Daddy"—

MRS. *(lightly chiding)*: I'm "Mommy."

MR. *(quickly)*: I mean—I'm "Daddy." Of course!

MRS. *(taking out of the bag a cap with bells)*: I knitted this myself, for you! *(Pause)* Oh dear—there's only one. *(MRS. fits the cap awkwardly on NABBO's head; takes out a sweater.)* Thank goodness, I knitted this, too—

NADBO takes the sweater from her, puts it over his head.

MR.: You'll have to knit matching sets, dear. From now on everything must be in duplicate.

X (*smiling, but with authority*): Hmmm! I do need your signatures, Mr. and Mrs.—, before the adoption procedure can continue.

MR. *wheels in a tricycle. Both children snatch at it, push at each other. The child who gets it, however, has no idea what it is, and struggles with it, knocking it over, attacking the wheels.*

MR. *pulls in a wagon. Similar action.*

MRS.: Oh!—I nearly forgot. You must be starving—having come so far! (*Takes fudge out of bag*) I made this chocolate-walnut fudge just yesterday!

NABBO *and* NADBO *take pieces of proffered fudge; taste it hesitantly; begin to eat, ravenously; spit mouthfuls out.*

MRS.: Oh, dear! (*With a handkerchief, dabbing at their faces*) You mustn't be *greedy*, you know. There's plenty to eat here.

NABBO *and* NADBO *snatch at the rest of the fudge, shoving pieces into their mouths, though they are sickened by it, and soon spit it out again.* NADBO *has a minor choking fit.*

MR. (*with camera*): O.K., guys! Everybody smile! Say "MON KEE!"

MRS. *embraces the children, smiling radiantly at the camera. The children cringe at the flash.*

MRS.: This is the happiest day of my life. Thank you, God.

MR.: This is the happiest day of *my* life. (MR. *hands* X *the camera so that he/she can take a picture of the new family.* MR. *and* MRS. *smiling broadly,* NABBO *and* NADBO *cringing.* NADBO *tries to hide under the sweater, and* MRS. *gently removes it.*) Thanks!

X (*handing camera back to* MR.): Lovely. Now, we should complete our procedure. Your signatures, please—

MR., MRS.: Yes, yes of course...

Again, X *draws the clipboard back out of their reach, at the crucial moment.*

X: Ummm—just a moment. (*Peering at a document*) I'm afraid— Nabbo and Nadbo have a third sibling.

MR. *has taken the pen from* X's *hand, and now drops it.*

MRS. (*faint, hand to bosom*): A third...?

MR.: ...another *twin?*

X *(hesitant)*: Not "twin" exactly. With these high-fertility races, the precise clinical term is—too clinical. Let's say "identical sibling."

MR.: Tri-tri-triplets?

X: Not "triplets," exactly. *(Evasively)* "Identical sibling" is preferred.

MRS. *(vague, voice strange)*: Oooohhh another of you!—how, how—how *wonderful*. Your mother must be—must have been— *(draws a blank)* —if you had one, I mean. Nab-bo, Nab-do—I mean, Nad-do—?

NABBO and NADBO poke each other, but do not speak. Cap bells jingle. One shoves at the shiny firetruck, or the wagon. The other finds a piece of fudge and pops it into his mouth.

MR. *(awkward, dazed, to X)*: B-But I'm afraid—we really *can't*, you know. Not three. We'd only prepared for *one*.

MRS.: When we left home yesterday—to drive here—we'd only prepared—enough diapers, a single bassinet— *(Pause; a kind of wildness comes over her)* A third? A third *baby*? Is it possible? I *did* always want a large family...

MR.: But, darling, not in five minutes!

MRS.: We can buy a new house. More bedrooms! Bunkbeds! A bigger family room! *(Pause, breathing quickly)* I was so lonely in my parents' house—just the *one* of me. And everything done *for me*. Never a moment's want or deprivation... *(Pause)* My mother was from a large family—eight children. Dozens of grand-children.

MR.: But not in five minutes!

MRS. *(turning on him, cutting)*: What difference does that make? We've been infertile—*sterile*—for fourteen years. We've got a lot of catching up to do!

MR. *(wincing)*: Thirteen years...

MRS. *(laughing, trying to hug NABBO and NADBO)*: Here is our—deliverance! These "tragic orphans"—"from the dark side of the Earth." Human beings can't live for themselves alone...

MR. *(gripping MRS. by the shoulders)*: Darling, please! You're hysterical. You're not—yourself.

MRS. *(shrilly)*: Who am I, then? Who am I, then?

MR.: Darling!—

NABBO and NADBO have been cringing fearfully.

X *(with authority)*: Mr.—, Mrs.—? I'm afraid your allotted time has nearly transpired. Even as you dally— (X indicates the clock) —this past hour, 110,273 new "tragic orphans" have been, as it's said, "born."

MRS. *(hand to bosom)*: How many?—my goodness!

MR.: I think we've been cruelly misled here. I strongly object to being manipulated!

X: If you had troubled to read the agency's restrictions and guidelines handbook, Mr.—, more closely, you would not affect such surprise now.

MR.: I did read it! I've practically memorized it! We've been on your damned waiting list for a decade!

MRS. *(vague, intense, to X)*: There is a—a third sibling?—identical with our b-babies?

X: Identical DNA, chromosomes—identical faces and bodies. But, you know, not "identical" inwardly. In the soul.

MRS.: "The soul—!" *(A strange expression on her face as of radiance, pain)*

MR. *(awkward, flush-faced)*: Darling, it's just that we—can't. We don't have *room*—

MRS.: Of course we have room!

MR.: We don't have resources—

MRS.: Of course we have resources!

MR. *(tugging at his necktie, panting)*: We're practically in *debt*— paupers—

MRS. *(extravagantly, arms wide)*: We're wealthy!—we have infinite space—inwardly.

MR.: Inwardly?

MRS.: The soul is infinite, isn't it? *Mine* is, isn't *yours*?

MR. (*baffled*): My—*soul*? Where—?

MRS. (*tugging at X's arm*): *You* tell him! The soul is infinite, isn't it? "The Kingdom of God is within"—space that goes on forever!

MRS. has been working herself up into an emotional state; NABBO and NADBO are frightened of her. They cast off the cap, sweater, etc., shove away the tricycle; begin to make mournful keening sounds and rock back and forth, their small bodies hunched. X scolds them inaudibly; they make a break for the closed door, and X grabs their arms to stop them.

MRS.: What?—where are you going? Nab-bo—no, you're Nad-bo—I mean Nab-do—Nab-*boo*—come here! be good! you're ours, aren't you? Mommy loves you *so much*— (*Tries to embrace children, who resist her*)

MR. (*blank, dazed smile*): Daddy loves you so much! (*Pushes the tricycle back*) Since the beginning of Time!

MRS.: Since *before* the beginning of Time—

NABBO and NADBO cower, hiding behind X, who is annoyed at the turn of events, surreptitiously slapping at the children or gripping their shoulders forcibly. The mourning-keening sounds seem to be coming from all over.

MRS. (*hands to ears*): Oh, what is that sound! It hurts my ears—

MR.: Nab-boo! Nad-doo! Bad boys! *Stop that!*

X (*threatening children*): It's just some village dirge—nothing! Pay no attention!

MRS.: It's coming from here, too— (*Impulsively rushes to the door and opens it, steps through; X immediately pulls her back*)

X (*furious*): Mrs.—! This door can only be opened by authorized agency personnel! (*X shuts the door.*)

MRS. has recoiled back into the room. Hand over her mouth, she staggers forward as if about to collapse.

MR. (*rushing to help her*): Darling? What is it?

X: That door was *not* to be opened. I could call a security guard and have you arrested, Mrs.—! Taken out of here in handcuffs!

MRS. (*eyes shut, nauseated*): Oh...oh...

MR.: Darling, what did you see?

X *(loudly)*: Mrs.— saw *nothing*. There was *nothing* to be seen.

MR.: Darling—?

MRS. *(feeble whisper, leaning on MR.'s arm)*: Take them back. We don't want them.

MR.: What did you see, darling? What's behind that door?

MRS. *(trying to control rising hysteria)*: Take them back. We don't want them. Any of them. I want to go *home*.

X: Hmmm! I thought so. Poor risks for adoption.

MR.: Darling, are you certain? We've waited so long...*prayed* so long...

MRS. *(a small scream)*: Take them away! All of them! *(Hides eyes)* We're not strong enough—

X *(coldly)*: You're certain, Mr. and Mrs.—? You can never again apply with our agency, you know.

MRS.: Take them away!

MR. *(trying to speak in normal voice)*: We're sorry—*so* sorry—

X marches NABBO and NADBO out, and the door is shut behind them.

MR. *(weakly, belatedly calling after)*: Um—*so* sorry—

The mourning-keening sound grows louder. MR. and MRS. freeze; lights dim except on the clock face, where the minute hand continues its accelerated progress.

Lights out. Mourning sound ceases.

Lights up on MR. and MRS., who have come forward. Darkness elsewhere. (The clock is no longer visible.) MR. and MRS. speak in a duet of agitated rhythms, overlappings, a strange music that should suggest, though not too overtly mimic, the mourning-keening sound. This conclusion should be elegiac, a barely restrained hysteria; but it is restrained.

MRS. *(hands to her face)*: What have we done!—

MR.: It was a, a wise decision—

MRS.: —necessary—

MR.: —necessary decision—

MRS.: Waited all our lives— Oh, what have we done—

MR.: It was your decision—

MRS.: Our day of birth—delivery—

MR.: *Deliverance*—

MRS.: —weren't strong enough—

MR.: *You* weren't— *I* was— *(Pause)* —*wasn't*—

MRS.: What have we done!—not strong enough—

MR.: Who the hell *is* strong enough I'd like to know—

MRS.: God didn't make us strong enough—

MR.: —rational decision, necessary—

MRS.: —necessary— *(Clutching at her womb)* Oh! Oh what have we done! My babies—

MR. *(anguished, strikes chest with fist)*: I'm only human! What can I do! Who can forgive me? *(Pause, peers into audience)* Who *isn't* human? You cast the first stone!

MRS. *(hands framing face)*: That corridor!—that space!—to the horizon!—so many! And the *smell*. *(Nauseated)*

MR. *(reasoning)*: There isn't room in the heart—I mean the *home*— the *house*!—no matter how many bunkbeds. We're not paupers!— I mean, we're not millionaires. Who's been saying we *are*?

MRS. *(confused)*: Bunkbeds?—how many?

MR.: How many? *(Rapidly counting on fingers, confused)*

MRS. *(a soft cry)*: Our home—*house*!—empty!—

MR. *(protesting)*: Hey: there's *us*.

MRS.: So lonely!—

MR.: Rational, necessary decision—no choice.

MRS.: *So* lonely—

MR.: Look, I refuse to be manipulated, to be made *guilty*—

MRS.: So many years waiting, and so lonely—

MR. *(pleading)*: Who the hell *isn't* human? I ask you!

MRS. *(has found the knitted cap on the floor, picks it up lovingly, bells tinkle)*: God knows, God sees into the heart. Forgive us, God—

MR.: We had no choice.

MRS.: —no choice!

MR.: And we're *not* millionaires!

Lights begin to fade.

MRS. *(waving, tearful and smiling)*: Goodbye Nabbo!—Nadbo!—Nabdo?—dear, innocent babies! Mommy loved you so!

MR. *(waving, ghastly smile)*: Goodbye, boys! Sons! Your Daddy loved you so!

MRS.: Don't think ill of us, don't forget us! Goodbye!

MR.: Goodbye, sons! Be brave!

MRS. *(blowing kisses)*: Mommy loved you so! Goodbye!

MR., MRS.: Goodbye, goodbye, goodbye!

Lights out.

THE END

No Next of Kin

Lights up. A YOUNG MAN *wearing a denim jacket, jeans, baseball cap speaks.*

YOUNG MAN: This was last Christmas. *(Pause)*

I was hanging out at the house, lots of relatives dropping in and my mom's brothers came by bringing six-packs and got to drinking and bullshitting and my old man Ev'rett Tiggs's name comes up nobody's spoken in that house in twenty years. And my mom gets up and walks out of the room that way she has—makes you feel like shit, the hurt look in her face. *(Pause) He* left us, I was eight years old. Just disappeared so nobody knew was he alive or dead for a long time. Fucker! *(Pause)* So my uncle Duke is saying, Y'know I heard Ev'rett Tiggs is in a VA hospital in Pittsburgh, a bad case of lung cancer. And the others are saying the hell with Tiggs, that bastard is dead to all of us. Nobody's looking at me like they're ashamed and I, I'm...it's weird: I'm sitting there with a beer in my hand and my eyes open but I'm like—gone. My old man Ev'rett Tiggs I'd sort of been led to think was dead all these years... *(Pause)*

So next morning I'm on my way to Pittsburgh, thirty hours on the interstate. Told my mom I had to get away, decided to drive down to Ft. Lauderdale with some guys from work and she goes, I never can count on you, can I? *(Pause)*

What I'm figuring is I'll just take a look at the old man. Wouldn't give him the satisfaction of identifying myself. Walking out like he did, leaving us, my mom and two sisters and me, used to be he'd let me ride high up in the cement mixer cab with him, and the cement turning behind... It's gotta turn, if it don't turn it

275

goes solid and the goddamn truck goes *over*, my old man said laughing. He'd call me Kiddo. Out back of the school, in the playground, he'd pitch balls to me. They said I took after him, my hair and…face… *(Draws his fingers over his face)* Jesus! It makes you ashamed. You never get over it. People looking at me and seeing *him*. Soon as I turned sixteen, for sure I quit school. Moved out of the house but not too far away, I'm always looking out for my mom. *(Pause)* But not too close. *(Pause)*

Driving to Pittsburgh I was saying aloud, Look I don't hate you, I just want to ask *Why*? *Why* the fuck? That you would leave us like that and not say goodbye. And load the car like you did, your hunting stuff and power tools and other shit so it was premeditated, you knew, fucking *knew* you were never coming back. And mom waiting and getting scared, then crazy and wild screaming at us, blaming *us*. *(Pause)* Even at church there's people looking down on us where you'd expect better. Fuckers! *(Pause)* So driving to Pittsburgh I'm thinking I wouldn't say a word, I'd just stand where I could watch you, and maybe I could forgive you. I don't know—if maybe it was meant for me to forgive you. If God gave me a sign. *(Pause)*

So I'm kind of excited and scared and…I get there, Pittsburgh, and go to the VA hospital and tell them I'm looking for Ev'rett Tiggs; how he was my father I hadn't seen in twenty years. And they tell me he's gone.
I say, What? Gone?
They say, We're sorry, Mr. Tiggs, your father is dead. He died here December 3.
They're telling me more, how he was cremated at his own bequest, he'd said "No next of kin" and there was nobody to notify or give his things to. He was fifty-two years old. They asked did I wish a copy of the death certificate and I said, No thanks. *(Mimes walking away, shaking his head and laughing)* What the hell! *(Pause)*

Look, it ain't like I'm sad or anything—I'm not.
It ain't like I lost anything I ever had. *(Pause)*

All I was going to do was stand where I could look at my father. Just possibly I'd walk past him, by his bed or wherever, and see

would he look at me; maybe recognize *me*. Like maybe he'd go—
Son? Is that you? *(Old-man inflection)*
And maybe that would've been the sign God sent—that I could
forgive him. *(Pause)*

Maybe. I don't know.

YOUNG MAN *stares out into the audience, his eyes shimmering with tears.*

Lights out.

THE END

When I Was a Little Girl And My Mother Didn't Want Me

Lights up. An elderly woman speaks. Her voice alternates between urgency and bemusement; emotion and reflection.

My father was killed and I never knew why.
Then, I was given away. By my mother.
I was so little...six months.
There were too many of us, nine of us,
 my mother gave me away.
When I was old enough to know...I cried a lot.

My father was killed and I never knew why.
No one would tell me.
Now there's no one I can ask.
"Why? Why?"
It happened in a fight, in a tavern, he was only
 forty-four years old.
My father I never knew. Forty-four! Now, he could be
 my son.

I wasn't always an...old woman. Eighty-one.
I was a girl for so long.
I was a little girl for so long.
I was six months old when my father died.
And there were too many of us to feed, and my mother...
 gave me away.

WOMAN *hides her face very briefly in her hands; face composed.*

> There were nine children. I was the baby.
> I was born late, I was the baby.
> My mother gave me to her sister Lena who didn't have
>   children. This was in 1918.
> This was in the Black Rock section of Buffalo,
>   the waterfront on the Niagara River.
> Germans, Poles, Hungarians...immigrants.
> We were Hungarians. We were called "Hunkies."
> I don't know why people hated us...

WOMAN *pauses; decides not to explore this.*

> Uncle John and Aunt Lena were my "parents."
> We moved to a farm far away in the country.
> And my real mother and my brothers and sisters
>   moved to a farm a few miles away.

> Uncle John and Aunt Lena were good to me.
> I don't know if I loved them...I think I loved them.
> I think...I think they loved me.
> They wanted children but couldn't have them so it was
>   right, I think, that my mother gave me to them...
> it was a, a good thing, it was a...
> necessary thing.
> I would learn one day that it happened often.
> In immigrant families in those days.
> In poor immigrant families.

> My father was killed and I never knew why.
> They said he was a bad drinker, he got drunk
>   and was always in fights.
> The Hungarians were the worst, they said—
>   the drinking, and the fighting.
> They said he was so handsome, my father.
> My mother Elizabeth was so pretty.
> Curly hair like mine.
> They said he had a temper "like the devil."
> In the tavern there was a fight, and he died.
> A man took up a poker and beat my father to death.
> I never knew why, I never knew who it had been.
> Yet this was how my life was decided.

There is the moment of conception—you don't know.
There is the moment of birth—you don't know.
There is the moment your life is decided—you don't know.
Yet you say, "This is my life."
You say, "This is me."

WOMAN regards herself in wonder like a stroke victim regaining some of her awareness.

When I was a little girl and my mother didn't want me
I hid away to cry.
I felt so bad and I felt so ashamed.
My mother didn't want me.
When I was old enough I would walk to the other farm.
There was a bridge over the Tonawanda Creek a few
      miles away.
They didn't really want to see me I guess.
My name was Carolina, but they didn't call me that.
I don't remember if there was a name they called me.
They weren't very nice to me I guess.
They didn't want me, I guess I was a reminder of...
      something.

Elizabeth, my mother, never learned English.
She spoke Hungarian all her life.
She never learned to read. She never learned to drive
      a car.
My Aunt Lena never learned to drive, so the sisters
      didn't see much of each other.
They lived only a few miles apart, and were the only
      sisters of their family in America, but they didn't
      see much of each other.
That was how women were in the old days.

I loved my mother.
She was a short, plump woman.
Curly brown hair like mine.
People would say, "You look just like your momma!"
Then they would be surprised, I'd start to cry.
My mother was busy, she scolded me in Hungarian—
"Go away, go home where you belong. You have a home.
Your home is not here."

I loved my big brothers and sisters.
There was Leslie, he was the oldest.
He took over when my father died.
There was Mary, I didn't get to know real well.
They were born in Budapest.
There was Steve, who'd been kicked and trampled
    by a horse. His brain was injured, he would never
    leave home.
There was Elsie who was my "big sister."
There was Frank who was my "big brother."
There was Johnny...and Edith...
There was George, I wasn't too close with George.
There was Joseph, I wasn't too close with.

(Pause)

They are all dead now.
I loved them, but...
I am the only one remaining.
Sometimes I think: The soul is just a burning match!
It burns awhile and then...
And then that's all.

It's a long time ago now, but I remember hiding
    away to cry.
When I was a little girl and my mother didn't want me.

Lights out.

THE END

ACKNOWLEDGMENTS

Bad Girls was originally performed by the Georgia Repertory Theatre, Athens, Georgia, May 1995, and, in the altered version printed here, in the Contemporary American Play Festival, Shepherdstown, WV, July 1996.

Black Water was originally performed, with music by John Duffy, under the auspices of the American Music Theater Festival, Philadelphia, April–May 1997.

The Passion of Henry David Thoreau was originally presented in a reading performance at McCarter Theatre, Princeton, NJ, June 1996, and, in the altered version printed here, in a reading performance at New Dramatists, New York, March 1997.

Hear I Am was originally performed by the Philadelphia Festival Theatre of New American Plays, March 1995.

Duet was performed in the 1998 Featured Artist Series of the Turnip Theatre Company, New York.

Good To Know You, Poor Bibi, No Next of Kin and *When I Was a Little Girl and My Mother Didn't Want Me* were performed at the Ensemble Studio Theatre, October 1997.

Poor Bibi was originally performed at Northwestern University, Theatre Department, Evanston, IL, October 1995.

Homesick was commissioned by McCarter Theatre for a one-act festival, January 1995, and, in the altered version here, produced by 12 Miles West Theatre, Montclair, NJ, October 1997.

The Adoption was originally performed in Marathon '96, Ensemble Studio Theatre, New York, May 1996.

* * *

Bad Girls is an adaptation of a story of the same title originally published in *Boulevard*, Spring 1995.

Black Water is an adaptation of the novel of the same title (Dutton, 1992).

Here I Am and *No Next of Kin* were originally published in *Boulevard*, Fall 1997.

Good To Know You is an adaptation of a story of the same title, published in *Will You Always Love Me?* (Dutton, 1997).

Poor Bibi is an adaptation of a short story of the same title, published in *Haunted and Other Stories* (Dutton, 1994).

Homesick was originally published, in an earlier version, in *The Perfectionist and Other Plays* (Ecco Press, 1995).

The Adoption was originally published in *Conjunctions 25: The New American Theatre, 1995,* edited by John Guare.

Portions of the Afterword originally appeared under the title "Plays as Literature" in *Conjunctions 25: The New American Theatre,* 1995.

The Hand

A Philosophical Inquiry into Human Being

Raymond Tallis

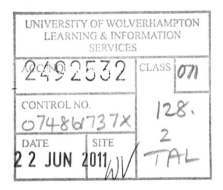

UNIVERSITY OF WOLVERHAMPTON
LEARNING & INFORMATION
SERVICES

AC/NO 2492532   CLASS 071

CONTROL NO.
0748673 7X   128.

DATE   SITE   2
2 2 JUN 2011 WV   TAL

Edinburgh University Press

For Terry, whose hands have borne me up

© Raymond Tallis, 2003

Edinburgh University Press Ltd
22 George Square, Edinburgh

Transferred to digital print 2006

Typeset in Sabon
by Koinonia, Manchester, and
printed and bound in Great Britain
by CPI Antony Rowe, Eastbourne

A CIP record for this book is available
from the British Library

ISBN-10 0 7486 1737 X (hardback)
ISBN-13 978 0 7486 1737 1 (hardback)
ISBN-10 0 7486 1738 8 (paperback)
ISBN-13 978 0 7486 1738 8 (paperback)

The right of Raymond Tallis
to be identified as author of this work
has been asserted in accordance with
the Copyright, Designs and Patents Act 1988

Contents

Part III Towards Chiro-Philosophy

Coda

Acknowledgements

This 'five-fingered salute to the hand' would be incomplete if I did not also salute the work of the many scholars upon whose work I have been unashamedly dependent. The observations of John Napier – a pre-eminent chirophile whose writings I have drawn upon at many places – in the Acknowledgement to one of his own books is particularly pertinent:

> Anyone who writes books about science or indeed about any subject that is rich in facts, figures and ideas is from the beginning up to his neck in debt. He must beg, borrow, steal, left, right and centre. His pilfering is usually made respectable by the inclusion of a bibliography, but formal citations do not tell more than a fraction of the story of an author's obligations to colleagues living and dead. (*Hands*, London: George Allen and Unwin, 1980, p. 7)

If this is true of an authentic scholar of the hand such as Professor Napier, it is even more true of an interloper such as the present author!

In the Introduction, where I describe the genesis of *The Hand: A Philosophical Inquiry into Human Being*, I particularly acknowledge the inspiration of conversations with Professor David Marsh, Dr Paulette van Vliet's thesis, which I had the pleasure to examine, and the work of scientists such as Professor Alan Wing. In all three cases, their benefactions were largely unconscious; from which it follows that they cannot be held responsible for any errors of fact and interpretation in this volume.

In the final three chapters I explore the role of the hand, and its tools, in human evolution. Here, I have strayed furthest from my own area of expertise and consequently my 'begging, borrowing, stealing' have been especially shameless. I have been heavily dependent upon a relatively small number of major texts, which are fully acknowledged, though the extent to which they have shaped, as well as informed, my thinking is perhaps not fully apparent. What will be apparent is that *The Hand: A Philosophical Inquiry into Human Being* is by no stretch of the imagination a primary work of factual scholarship. Any originality it has lies in the synthesis of material from widely disparate quarters – neurophysiology, palaeontology, etc. – and, above all, ordinary observations of daily life, in the service of a handful of philosophical (and, in the companion volumes, specifically ontological and epistemological) ideas about the fundamental nature of human beings and the origin of their profound differences from all other living creatures. Such scholarship as the book manifests has been requisitioned on behalf of philosophical arguments, whose implications will not be fully apparent until the trilogy, of which this is the first volume, is complete.

It is a special pleasure to acknowledge the work done on the typescript by Ruth Willats, who, in addition to her usual meticulous copyediting, saved me from quite a few factual blunders. She also made several fascinating observations, which I have been unable to resist stealing, thus making me further indebted to her.

This book would not have been published had it not been for the interest shown in my writing by Jackie Jones, Editorial Director of Edinburgh University Press, and her enthusiasm for and support of the overall philosophical project. The organisation of the proposed trilogy owes much to her. She has even suggested the definitive titles of the volumes. For all of this, I am enormously grateful.

My greatest debt is, as always, to my family: to Ben and Lawrence who have goodnaturedly tolerated my latest obsession expressed in, for example, a tendency to talk about pebble choppers at the breakfast table; and, above all, to my wife Terry, without whose love and support I could not have been a writer as well as a doctor.

The hand is the window on to the mind.

Immanuel Kant

Man's place in nature is largely writ upon the hand.

F. Wood Jones

I could worship my hand even, with its fan of bones laced by blue mysterious veins and its astonishing look of aptness, suppleness and ability to curl softly or suddenly crush – its infinite sensibility.

Virginia Woolf

> Proud man alone in wailing weakness born,
> No horns protect him and no plumes adorn;
> No finer powers of nostril, ear or eye,
> Teach the young Reasoner to pursue or fly. –
> Nerved with fine touch above the bestial throngs,
> The hand, first gift of Heaven! to man belongs;
> Untipt with claws the circling fingers close,
> With rival points the bending thumbs oppose,
> Trace the nice lines of form with sense refined
> And clear ideas charm the thinking mind.
> Whence the first organs of touch impart
> Ideal figures, source of every art;
> Time, motion, number, sunshine, or the storm
> But mark varieties in Nature's *form*.
>
> ...

The human species in some of their sensations are much inferior to animals, yet the accuracy of the sense of touch which they possess in so eminent a degree gives them a great superiority of understanding.

Erasmus Darwin

Introduction

ORIGINS

The origins of the volume you are (probably) holding in your hand are somewhat scattered and complex, and largely lost in the mists of Tallis. I can, however, remember the precise moment when I decided that, yes, this was the book I wanted to write next, though its gestation – or what I can remember of it – had begun at least a couple of years before.

As happens once or twice a year, I had agreed to act as external examiner for a doctoral thesis.[1] To my surprise, I found reading the thesis (an academic chore I usually dislike) an enjoyable experience. It was beautifully written – which made its 250 pages a change from the bad or mediocre prose I was used to. More importantly, its theme, not at first sight very promising, proved fascinating.

The thesis described a group of painstakingly executed studies of reaching and grasping movements in patients who had sustained a stroke affecting the arm. In passing, the candidate introduced her examiner to an entire literature about the control of upper limb movement of which he had previously had only the most rudimentary knowledge; in particular the work of experimenters such as Alan Wing and Pierre Jeanerod. This literature was a forcible reminder of the extraordinary achievements that are built into the most ordinary of our activities.

For her research, Dr van Vliet required her patients to reach out for, and pick up, a glass that was either empty or half-filled with water. This was an apparently simple task. The descriptions of her experiments and the literature to which she referred were, however, anything but simple; indeed, they proved a revelation of the obvious non-obvious. We shall visit this literature in due course (see especially section 2.2, 'The Genius of Reaching'), but it will become evident, as we examine them in some detail, that reaching, grasping and gripping cannot be something that we *do* because we could not manage to control all the relevant variables with the requisite precision. The action, in other words, cannot be entirely driven by conscious agency; it has to be predicated on (cerebral) mechanism(s) – more specifically on the availability of tailor-made motor programmes that can be requisitioned as required.

On the other hand, the action cannot be entirely downloaded to mechanisms because we would have no sense of doing it; nor could we relate it in a meaningful and flexible way to the flickering network of our evolving, highly specific and personal intentions and the unique world of meaning into which they are inserted; nor, finally, if the movement were created out of fixed and automatic mechanisms, could the action, or the strategy by which it is realised, be continuously modified in the light of rather complex unfolding aims, information and circumstances. This raises questions about the relationship between agency and mechanism in human actions.

It will be evident that the thoughts prompted by Ms (now, deservedly, Dr) van Vliet's rich thesis went far beyond those relevant to my role as external examiner. I had an inchoate sense of having come upon a different way of illuminating the kind of thing I am. At any rate, there was the feeling of something 'philosophical' in the background: something that might cast light on our own nature in the wider sense. This was not entirely appropriate because the kinds of actions that Dr van Vliet's work investigated are not unique to human beings: apes and other non-human animals reach out and grasp things. But human reaching opened up questions about other manual activities, some of which are unique to humans. I could not shake off the sense of something immensely interesting in the hinterland and worthy of exploration.

I tried to find an outlet for this feeling in a variety of ways. Most notably, I attributed Dr van Vliet's work to a fictional neurologist, a tragic, gifted character whose gathering unhappiness from a multiplicity of causes ends with his death – by his own hand. The complexity of Dr Langley's life has still to find its definitive formulation in *A Far Country*, which is at present, like so many of my fictions, a massive torso awaiting a full set of limbs. And then my preoccupation with the hand was displaced by an unexpected book on Martin Heidegger's *Being and Time – A Conversation with Martin Heidegger*[2] – which waylaid me in 1999. However, the hand still retained an important place, amongst reserve preoccupations, if only because of the number of times I typed out the word 'hand' in the course of writing the Heidegger book. For 'readiness-to-hand' (an English translation of the word *Zuhandenheit*) is a term Heidegger uses to denote one of the fundamental, indeed primordial, categories of Being in his ontology. According to Heidegger, the world is composed primarily of 'handy beings'; and 'handiness' is central to his so-called 'existential analytic'. The world, for the Heidegger of *Being and Time*, far from being the traditional collection of 'objective presences' that constitutes the physical universe of science, facing the equally traditional isolated subject, is a nexus of 'the ready-to-hand' disclosed in, by and to *Da-sein* or 'being-there'. It is not a rubble-heap of matter, or of discrete physical objects, but a network of meanings embodied in the ready-to-hand.

Without either of us knowing it, therefore, my long conversation with Heidegger in the spring, summer and autumn of 1999 was preparing me for a much shorter conversation I had on a late-night car journey in November 1999 from Londonderry to Belfast with Professor David Marsh, incumbent of the Chair in Orthopaedic Surgery at Queen's University, Belfast. Among other things, this conversation reminded me that my first encounter with the wonder of reaching and grasping with and the cleverness of the hand had not, after all, been Dr van Vliet's thesis. For it had been Dave Marsh who had first drawn my attention, several years earlier, to the extraordinary cunning built into the ordinary actions of the hand. He had become aware of this when he had been writing his thesis.

The circumstances of our conversation that November were propitious: we were being driven through the darkness by our genial host, Professor Bob Stout. I was mildly drunk and, moreover, much relieved at having discharged my duty as the first Desmond Whyte memorial lecturer. (My topic – The Future of Old Age – had bored my audience less than I feared it might have done.) We talked about this and we talked about that and we then fell to talking about the beautiful work Dave had carried out for many years before on the recovery of tactile sensation in the fingers following nerve injury. As we entered the outskirts of Belfast, travelling along a sodium-lit dock road that could have been anywhere, I realised that 'The Hand' was a theme that could bring together sufficient of my preoccupations to justify its being the subject of my next book. What I could not have then foreseen was the extent to which this theme would open and that it would lead the way into an entire trilogy, of which this is the first volume. It has become an instrument for helping me to get a handle on those things that, philosophically, seem to me to matter most: making sense of what it is to be a human being. This is a bold statement and most certainly requires explanation.

PURPOSE

According to Kant, getting clear about what it is to be a human being is philosophy's most essential preoccupation[3] – so that 'philosophical anthropology', far from being a rather soft and woolly subdivision of the discipline, may be its ultimate purpose, the point at which its different, more narrowly focused, enterprises – the philosophies of mind, of art, of ethics, ontology, epistemology, metaphysics, etc. – converge. Kant's is a view that I wholeheartedly endorse. Of course, for reasons that hardly need spelling out, we will never get entirely straight about ourselves, in the way that we may get straight about some of the things that lie outside of ourselves. We must always live our lives opaquely, acting out bodies, desires and thoughts that we find ourselves possessing and being possessed by. But it is not unreasonable to hope that, through a more compendious vision, founded on a tough sense of reality infused with the widest and most tingling sense of possibility, we might come to understand a little better our own nature; not our own individual nature – the nature of Raymond Tallis as opposed to that of A. N. Other – but our nature as examples of a universal (though not Platonic) type, as instances of humankind. Out of this may come not only a more precise definition of the limits, of the fixed 'given', within which all humans must live, but also and more importantly – since *l'homme surpasse infiniment l'homme* – an intenser understanding of how loose that 'given' is and how one might transcend the seemingly obdurate limitations it imposes upon one's life.

Interpreted in this way, doing philosophy may be seen as a means of coming upon oneself as from afar and alighting upon what one is, in the most usefully general sense. Out of this encounter may arise an enriched, more critical, less habit-prisoned, less parochial attitude to our life; a stronger feeling for its possibilities, its duties, its station in the wider scheme of things. We might even arrive at a better understanding of what is good for us; of what our ends truly are; and how better to order our affairs in our individual and collective pursuit of them. More probably – and, to be honest, more excitingly – we might arrive at a sharper awareness of the miraculous, complex, mysterious creatures we are. This is what, ultimately, philosophical anthropology may be about.

At the beginning of the twenty-first century, it may be felt that the history of the preceding hundred years has taught us more about human nature or human possibility than we actually want to know. Correspondingly, readers may feel sceptical of what may sound like a somewhat romantic expectation of the outcome of philosophical inquiry, particularly of an inquiry that takes its rise from a consideration of something as commonplace as the human hand. There is surely little room for human self-redefinition, and what little redefinition is possible is least likely to come from philosophical reflection.

After all, it will be argued, in the century that has just passed, humanity has utilised other ways of uncovering the essential characteristics – the greatness, the pettiness, the nobility and nastiness, the splendour and the nullity – of mankind. Some of the things that we have learned seem to suggest that there are severe limitations to human nature and that the given is not readily ripe for renegotiation. The nastiness of recent times, the argument will continue, differs from the immemorial nastiness of all times only in the vastness of its scale and the degree to which it has been organised.

To take an extreme example, the experience of the concentration camps – which demonstrated the ease with which an individual may be reduced to a crazed animal grubbing in the dirt and the readiness of others to take on the task of supervising that reduction, or to collude with it, or to ignore it – has, for some thinkers, provided an authoritative answer to the questions, 'What is man? What possibilities lie within us?'[4] The twentieth century taught us a practice of philosophical anthropology in which part of humankind may be redefined by the rest of humankind as trash and vermin. And it cruelly demonstrated that even distinctively human suffering is a reminder not, as Novalis claimed, of 'our high estate',[5] but of the profound ambiguity of our condition – as beasts, and worse than beasts, more beastly than beasts.

Beyond or beneath the devastating moral lessons of death camps, totalitarian states and total war, there is the additional daily evidence of the inescapability of our bodily condition and the defining limitations this imposes upon us. When, in *As You Like It*, the Duke says of 'the icy fang' and 'the churlish chiding of the winter's wind' that

> These are counsellors
> That feelingly persuade me what I am.[6]

he is articulating an important truth about us: whatever we may discover about ourselves, whatever human possibilities may be uncovered or postulated through reflection and exploration, we deceive ourselves if we forget how we remain fastened to our physical body and, through embodiment, are vulnerable to pain and suffering from within and without that body: we shall always be under the sway of its imperious needs. The very nature that nurtures us may also torture us, having no more care for a dying child than for the micro-organisms that kill her. And it is through our bodies that our enemies may seize hold of and possess us. Cold, starvation, illness, accident, bullies, persecutors, tyrants, bullets: these are reminders of our inextricated state. Through our bodies we are exposed to the anti-meanings of pain, nausea, shortness of breath. Sooner or later, we all die. And we usually die as animals die: panting like them; like them, vomiting, fighting for air, twitching, in pain. Such is the final common pathway imposed upon us all. These surely are counsellors that persuade us what we truly are. What price, therefore, human possibility? What new revelations about us are to be gained from philosophical anthropology? Surely there is nothing more to be learned.

I believe that there is much more to be learned, because we are distanced from our condition, and from our material, biological and ethical limitations, if only in virtue of our being aware of them, as Pascal proclaimed from the heart of his own suffering. The thinking reed is nobler than the universe because he, unlike the universe, knows that he is being crushed. And we may claim more than this Pascalian dignity: for our distance from nature is elaborated with extraordinary complexity. We have, for example, developed theories, myths, legends about our condition – as is demonstrated by the very lines just cited from *As You Like It* to express our limitations: we have the notion of our fallenness, of 'the penalty of Adam'. In the Duke's mouth, 'the icy fang / And churlish chiding of the winter's wind' become 'counsellors' that 'feelingly' persuade him what he is. He contrasts their counsel with that of the flatterers in the life of 'painted pomp' from which he has been exiled. The cold wind has become the antithesis of an (abstract) court counsellor and so, itself, is transformed into an abstract symbol. And the elaboration of our distance from our embodied state does not stop there. After all, the Duke's speech is itself an instrument of further, highly sophisticated, purpose: it is Shakespeare's means of representing the character of the Duke and of discovering the plot to us; and the play of which the speech is a part is in turn enacted, rehearsed, criticised, interpreted and – as in this Introduction – cited in support of an argument about the character of humankind.

Thus have we distanced ourselves from a state deemed to be natural, or the initial condition of the human animal – though it remains something to which so many are reduced – and in this respect we are not captured by the naturalistic viewpoint that understands us as a piece of nature. Whereas it is something of an exaggeration to say that (some of) humankind has 'spoken itself free of organic constraint',[7] it is no exaggeration to assert that we have, through a multitude of faculties, become insulated from this putative natural state, a state that we may observe even in our nearest relations among the higher primates. Granted that, at any moment, these distances, howsoever advanced our technologies, howsoever stable and beneficent our social and political and economic institutions, may be rescinded – and granted also that they will always implode when, in our dying, we become increasingly identical with our stricken bodies – the distances are real none the less and their scale and scope and complexity are easy to overlook.[8]

Even so, we are not entirely free from organic constraint and we are far from having left our animal state behind us; nor would we necessarily want to become purely and entirely human on any interpretation of the meaning of this term. We would not, for example, wish to be etherealised into words; or live in a world where all interactions are mediated through symbols or electronic or optotronic communication systems. The 'lightness' of our being would become 'unbearable'.[9]

These reflections open up wider questions about the limits and scope of our distinctively human nature. But we need to make that nature visible in order that those questions shall be addressed at the right level. And that is one, initial function of what might, with justification, be called 'philosophical anthropology'. The extent to which we have liberated ourselves from the condition of beasts and, indeed, from the condition of the rest of the natural world, is extraordinary; and placing this before ourselves is an essential step in the exploration of human possibility and extending the horizon of the meanings we may validly discover and create. This task is even more urgent when reductive neo-Darwinian thought and, in particular, sociobiology and evolutionary psychology, which have over the last few decades revived ideas that William MacDougall made popular in his *Introduction to Social Psychology* published nearly a century ago, have such a grip on the popular imagination. E. O. Wilson, Richard Dawkins, Steven Pinker, Daniel Dennett and many others have, like MacDougall, claimed to explain most aspects of human behaviour in terms of instincts built into the individual in the course of evolution. Such writers seem committed to persuading us to overlook the difference between ourselves and the animals.[10]

My aim, then, is precisely the opposite of that of much thinking that dominated the twentieth century and looks to remain dominant for a while in the present century. Many writers – anthropologists, psychologists, sociologists, biologists, even novelists – have argued that we have suppressed the truth about our animal nature and that we would understand ourselves better (and even learn better how to order our affairs) if we looked to our animal forebears for explanations of our behaviour and acknowledged the extent to which our human culture is rooted in our animal nature. Although it would be absurd to deny our animal roots, my view is that, far from being under-recognised, our proximity to other animals has been exaggerated. Our roots are not our leaves. More precisely, the distinctive mystery of human nature has been inadequately appreciated.[11]

The insistence upon our animality is only part of a wider tendency to belittle us, in the light of the events of the twentieth century which are, as Kenan Malik has pointed out, seen to be 'the consequence not of particular policies, or particular circumstances, but of the human condition itself ... the barbarism that [seemed] to lie within the human psyche itself'.[12] To some extent this pessimism about human nature has been a necessary corrective to the sometimes shallow optimism of articulate mankind's self-flattering accounts of itself, its actions and its motives – an account that denied the cruelty and hypocrisy of the best-heeled humanity; a corrective to conventional moral sentiments that were cruelly neglectful of the exploitation of the many by the few and to the rhetoric of spirituality, which concealed the manner in which religion was so often bound up with abusive power. As Albert Camus pointed out:

> That the demands of honesty were put to egoistic ends by the hypocrisy of a mediocre and grasping society was a misfortune that Marx, the incomparable eye-opener, denounced with a vehemence quite unknown before him.[13]

But just as sentimentality does not capture the whole truth, neither does denunciation. The routine pessimism which sees humans 'as soiled creatures who can only be understood in terms of pain, damage and degradation' (Malik 2000, p. 7) is too easy and, ultimately, shallow and hypocritical. Committed primary school teachers and nurses are as real as concentration camp guards or their tragic victims. As Camus warned, 'indignant denunciation' has 'brought other excesses in its train which require quite another denunciation' (Camus 1971, p. 168).

The cynical, unillusioned correctives to flattering accounts of humankind – of humans as 'manunkind', as e. e. cummings dubbed us – now themselves need correcting. To persuade those who argue that we are beasts – and worse than beasts – that, actually, we are utterly different from beasts, and are not only beastly, to advance a positive account of human exceptionalism – in short, to oppose most of what was said about humans in the century that has just passed – requires only that we remind them of what lies in front of their noses.[14]

Those who are able to see what is in front of their noses, and do not overlook the chasm that separates human beings from all other creatures, often identify language as the engine of the process by which humans have been progressively distanced from the natural world. Without wishing in any way to diminish the role of this complex, boundless miracle, I would suggest that human language is a manifestation of something more fundamental – the tendency of human beings to make things explicit[15] – and that language is part of a nexus of aptitudes deriving from this that distinguishes humanity. There are therefore other places than language to look at in the search for the drivers to the runaway cultural development of a creature that, uniquely, has a history divergent from evolution, other ways of illuminating this distance and the means by which it is achieved. One such place is the miraculous instrument called 'the human hand'; and one such way is to meditate on this wonderfully versatile organ.

It may be as justifiable to think of human beings as 'manukind' as to think of them as 'speaking animals' and to postulate the notion of Manu – that of the first man who laid down the law and formatted the disk of our collective human consciousness – as a displaced awareness of the centrality of our handedness to our nature and cultures.[16] A 'Hand Philosophy', therefore, may be a portal into thinking about our own nature: our greatness, our current limitations, our future potential. It is especially promising because the hand remains unarguably a bodily structure while, at the same time, it has played a crucial role in loosening the bonds that constrain us through our embodied state. The hand – by which we have manipulated, rather than talked, ourselves free of organic constraint – may point the way into the future of mankind. As a plausible biological starting point for our liberation from biology, it may have something to say about human possibility.

It is therefore as a contribution to philosophical anthropology – an essential preliminary to addressing questions such as, Who are we? Where have we come from? What are we? Where are we going to? – that this book on the hand is offered to the reader. The book is part of a wider project that has informed much of my writing: that of assisting myself, and perhaps thereby others, to know properly the most common-place truths about ourselves. In *Newton's Sleep*, I argued that the purpose of art was to help us round off the sense of the world, at least momentarily, by enabling us fully to experience our experiences.[17] This, I argued, was achieved through form – 'the moving unmoved' – which unites the more or less general ideas of experience with the contents of particular experiences. In the work of art, form is embodied and content is informed. Although *Newton's Sleep* envisaged art as answering to the fundamental metaphysical need of humankind to round off the sense of the world, I don't think its author ever fully believed Nietzsche's assertion that 'The making of art is the only metaphysical demand life

10   *Introduction*

now makes upon us'; for the rounding off of the sense of the world requires not only that we should fully experience our experiences, but also that we should truly know what we know. Philosophical anthropology, conceived as the pursuit of an immanent rather than a transcendental revelation, is one road to that knowledge. Reminding ourselves of the most obvious and indisputable facts about ourselves will not only bring us closer to truly knowing what we know, but will be an essential corrective to the despairing sense of nullity, physical vulnerability and moral emptiness that overtakes us when we dwell too exclusively on the large-scale, man-made catastrophes of the twentieth century. A corrective, too, to the sense of Wednesday afternoon obviousness that pervades our understanding of the world around us, the dim knowingness, the unsurprised taking for granted, that covers our consciousness with a thick layer of dust in our everyday transactions with the world. The hand – with all its complexity and the innumerable consequences of that complexity – seemed to offer a way of pointing towards, of reaching out for and grasping, the project of waking up out of ordinary wakefulness to the miracle of our worlded selves.

DISCLAIMER

After such an Introduction, the reader is entitled to expect much more than I can possibly give. Describing what this book is meant to be, however, is intended primarily as an indirect way of saying what it is not and implicitly excusing the absence of certain things. For example, although human neurophysiology is the science that lies closest to my clinical preoccupations, the reader will look in vain for an authoritative, or even connected, account of the mechanisms underpinning manipulative skills and other handly virtues. She will not encounter erudition worn lightly, but a work that is rather light on erudition. (Section 2.2, 'The Genius of Reaching', is a possible exception.) This warrants some justification.

There is, as Henry James once said, a fatal futility in facts. Nowhere is this more apparent than in a philosophical text: facts, other than the most elementary ones, are a distraction.[18] I spent nearly a decade talking electrically to the first dorsal interosseus muscle of the hand[19] but I have no wish to talk to, or of, this muscle here. It is of little philosophical interest whether the hand has ten, twenty or a hundred intrinsic muscles. The ulnar, radial and median nerves will scarcely warrant a walk-on part and the numerous and cleverly designed bones of the wrist will be lucky if they see their names in print.[20] For it would be hypocritical of me to try to excite you with information that does not excite me at all. I use this information in my daily work, but it is not intrinsically interesting enough to warrant attention in my free time.

The commitment to focusing on things that are philosophically relevant – howsoever intermittently adhered to (see below) – means that the book will not paint a complete portrait of its subject. This book is not, for example, a review of the recent literature on the neuroscience of the hand; nor does it aspire to be. If it did, I should be rightly criticised for the rather heavy concentration on certain sources and neglect of others. The lack of discussion of what medical science has uncovered about hand function and, more particularly, of neuropsychological studies of hand disorders (writer's cramp, the fascinating alien hand syndrome, apraxia, tactile agnosia) and recent work in brain imaging would also be culpable.[21]

I am not, however, concerned about the patchiness of the book's coverage. Indeed, I would be more uneasy if this book about the hand had turned out to be a handbook in the more usual sense and had pretended to encyclopaedic coverage. For it is easier to move over a wide surface than to keep in touch with the depths; to swim, as Wittgenstein said, along the bottom of the pool. The effort of thought is difficult to sustain: even when one is not voluntarily coming up for air, one tends to float up; to slacken from contemplation to exposition.

Not only is there no attempt to paint a comprehensive portrait of the subject of my loving attention, but there is a certain randomness in my choice of topics. There is simply too much to say about the hand: I realised, soon after deciding on my subject, that its scope was potentially boundless. Anyone who writes about the hand is condemned to be a butterfly. If, as I believe, what we humans are capable of doing with our hands lies close to the root of what sets us apart from (and, yes, above) the rest of creation, then tracing the ramifications of The Hand leads ineluctably into the boundless ocean of the human world. If 'the hardly achieved too little' were not 'to veer into the empty too much',[22] it was going to be necessary to place artificial, even arbitrary, constraints on the themes treated, and on the scale – the depth, extent – of their treatment.

Which is precisely what I have done. In addition to the unwilled limitations arising out of my ignorance of many of the disciplines into which I have dipped in my celebration of human handiness, I have imposed further limitations: I have, for the most part, restricted myself to those aspects which touch most closely on the essential purpose of this book; and my treatment of them has been shaped by similar considerations.[23] Even allowing for this, *The Hand: A Philosophical Inquiry into Human Being* remains a rather open-textured work.

Indeed, some readers, like the readers of anthologies of poetry, may be as upset by what it includes as by what it leaves out. As well as a philosophical inquiry, the book is a scientific inquiry, a sociological inquiry and (not unimportantly) a cultural romp.

In short, this is by no stretch of the imagination a systematic philosophical treatise. It is, as Wittgenstein said (in his case rather too modestly, in my case not) of his *Philosophical Investigations*, 'really only an album'.[24] A haptic analogy may be more appropriate: this book is itself like a hand groping in the dark – prodding, squeezing, etc., trying to determine the nature of its object. The central darkness, which we shall encounter again and again, is the mystery of our awakening to agency out of mechanism – and of the evolution of mechanism out of causation. This is closely connected with the uniquely sustained self-consciousness of humans, and with the emergence of first-person being and of knowledge out of sentience, which are the themes, respectively, of the second and third volumes of the trilogy – *I Am: A Philosphical Inquiry into First-Person Being* and *The Knowing Animal: A Philosophical Inquiry into Knowledge and Truth*.

In the pages that follow, the many-dimensional and almost limitless versatility of the human hand is offered as a key to the awakening of the cultured human being out of the natural pre-human animal, opening up the vast distances between human culture and the natural world. Through the hand, human culture waves away animal nature.

CONCLUDING COMMENTS

A couple of cautionary notes may be in order. First, my preoccupation with the near-miraculous capabilities of our hands must not be misunderstood. While I feel that this organ has 'had a hand' in driving the development of many aspects of our complex human nature, I do not believe that the special prowess of the hand can alone explain what is distinctive about that nature. (To do so would stray too close to a biologism that I deplore.) It is what is subsequently made possible by the hand – notably tool-use, signing and verbal language, and the positive feedback mechanisms they set in train vis-à-vis brain development – that finally accounts for human difference. Secondly, this book is at least as interested in using the hand to illustrate or to exhibit current human complexity as in using it to explain the origin of that complexity. Thirdly, while, as I have said, the book is light on facts and even lighter on erudition, I have not entirely eschewed factual exposition and I have always endeavoured to respect the objective knowledge that has been unearthed about the hand.

At the very least, I have tried to avoid making empirical assertions which are contrary to well-established facts or which would require factual support that I cannot provide. The claims I make in the latter chapters about the relationship between 'handiness' and number sense, and the role of the hand in driving, or leading, humans away from the natural world, may seem to exceed any evidence that I provide. At times, this is certainly true. The trouble is that the pre-historical, artefactual and fossil record is incomplete. There are huge gaps, most importantly when humans are supposed to have parted company from the pongids – approximately 4,000,000 years (between 4,000,000 and 8,000,000 years ago) – and with respect to the emergence of language. Spoken words leave no fossils and the absence of evidence of language is not the same as evidence of its absence.[25] How important these gaps are for the thesis that is advanced in this book I leave others to judge. A further difficulty is that human development has taken place only once, so that establishing causal connections is vulnerable to the justified charge of *post hoc* hypothesising. There is no way round this. Where speculations exceed possible empirical support, I offer them in the spirit of 'rational reconstruction', which is all that philosophical anthropology can aspire to be.

As will be evident from the quotations that form the epigraphs to this book, there is nothing original in my identifying the human hand as the key to the differences between mankind and the rest of animalkind. What is original about the thesis advanced in the present volume, and developed in greater detail in the subsequent two volumes, is the way I invoke the biology of the hand to explain, rather than to explain away, the profound differences between man and beasts and to defend the *reality of the ontological distinctness of humans.* In other words, I offer biology in support of the philosophical distinction between (comparatively) free humans and unfree beasts and not, as seems fashionable at present, as a way of eliminating it. To this extent the 'chiro-philosophy', which links biology and philosophy in the pages that follow, and which, I believe, reconciles Darwinism with an acknowledgement of the utterly exceptional nature of humans, is novel.

The biological importance of the wholly opposable thumb – its adaptive value – has been fully appreciated. The profound consequences for the animal's awareness and understanding, however, have not. The intuition at the heart of this book and its two successors is the conjecture that opposability, through its impact on the possibilities of the hand, utterly transforms the animal's relationship not only to external objects which it is manipulating, but also to its own body and this in turn feeds back on the relationship it has with those material objects, with profound consequences. These transformed relationships are the key to the central role played by 'handiness' in the transition from primate consciousness, which for all its complexity is not turned back on itself in any sustained way, to human self-consciousness and from animal behaviour to deliberate human activity. The hand, I want to suggest, took humans over the threshold dividing consciousness from self-consciousness, unreflective instinctive behaviour from true agency, and sentience, which is shared with other animals, from knowledge and feeling for truth, which is not.

Although I shall rove far and wide in developing my thesis, readers will find many facts set down here that are already known to them, which is exactly as it should be, and entirely in line with Wittgenstein's description of philosophy as 'assembling reminders [of what everyone knows] for a purpose'. Wittgenstein was preoccupied with the fact that thinkers are often unable to see what is in front of their noses. *The Hand: A Philosophical Inquiry into Human Being* is a contribution to the project of helping people to see what is in front of their noses. And that is why, despite my forays into pre-philosophical or para-philosophical anthropologies – evolutionary, social, physical – my expository energies have just as often been directed towards the obvious and well-known.

At any rate, I hope that most of what is in the pages that follow does serve my overriding aim of restoring our sense of human possibility. I hope also that it realises, at least in some small way, a subsidiary aim of achieving a mode of writing that unites the lyrical, the analytical, the argumentative and even the narrative modes. Or – if that is too ambitious – that the book moves easily between these modes. For this seems necessary if philosophy is going to realise what I believe to be its true function: that of helping us to wake up to, and out of, the wakefulness that lights up our days; to see what, in the widest sense, we are; to restore, in the face of various modes of reductionism and the cynicism that seem to dominate thinking about the nature of human-kind in this secular age, a sense of the fathomless depths upon which ordinary moments are built; and so to ignite an awareness of the infinite possibilities that lie open to human beings.[26] Even if this does not result in better ways of living our lives and of changing this world for the better, it may at least help to bring us closer to ourselves. The hand may be seen as the ultimate of those *bonnes à penser* (to use Lévi-Strauss's phrase) that help us to locate ourselves in nature and the wider scheme of things.

For me the goal of philosophy is at least in part about trying to obey the injunction *carpe diem!* – seize the day! But the day – the present moment – often eludes our grasp. One way to take hold of it is to get hold of ourselves; and one way, perhaps, of achieving this is to get a grip on ourselves by gripping grip itself: to vary Nietzsche's beautiful aphorism that 'spirit is the life that cuts into life', we might consider philosophy as the grip that tries to take hold of grips. The *carpe carpem!* of this book is, perhaps, preliminary to the *carpe diem!* of tradition.

In his diaries, Tolstoy wrote:

> The aim of an artist is not to solve a problem irrefutably but to make people love life in all its countless, inexhaustible manifestions.[27]

The same, I believe, could be said of philosophy. For these manuary meditations are, above all, an attempt to share my delight in our shared light, a celebration of a great and wonderful mystery. I trust this celebration will still glow in the mind even of those who do not fully accept the ideas it underpins.

The Hand: A Philosophical Inquiry into Human Being is a five-fingered salute to this miraculous organ, this 'tool of tools', that has shaped our very essence.

NOTES

1. Paulette van Vliet, 'Study of Reaching in Hemiparetic Stroke Patients', unpublished PhD Thesis (University of Nottingham, 1998).
2. Raymond Tallis, *A Conversation with Martin Heidegger* (Basingstoke: Palgrave, 2001). Heidegger's views about the hand will be discussed briefly in section 9.6.
3. This view is cited in Frederick A. Olafson, *What is a Human Being? A Heideggerian View* (Cambridge: Cambridge University Press, 1995), p. 1:
   > Kant argued that the domain of philosophy was defined by three questions – What can I know? What ought I to do?, and What may I hope? – and that these questions are facets of the more general question, What is man?
   A variation of this characterisation of the concerns of philosophy, without making explicit the fourth question about 'man', is to be found near the end of Kant's *The Critique of Pure Reason*.
4. Anyone who aims to think seriously about human nature should read Primo Levi's *Survival in Auschwitz: the Nazi Assault on Humanity*, translated by Stuart Woolf (New York: Touchstone, 1996) at least once a year. Nevertheless, we must not regard human nature as being defined by its worst manifestations. For an eloquent statement of this point (and many other correctives to current received libels about humanity), see Kenan Malik, *Man, Beast and Zombie. What Science Can and Cannot Tell Us About Human Nature* (London: Weidenfeld and Nicolson, 2000). My 'Against Dr Panglum', *Prospect*, February 2001, pp. 37–41 is a review essay on Malik's book.
5. Novalis, quoted in Herman Hesse's magic realist novel, *Steppenwolf*.
6. William Shakespeare, *As You Like It*, II.i.10–11.
7. George Steiner, *After Babel: Aspects of Language and Translation* (Oxford: Oxford University Press, 1974).

8. They are explored in Raymond Tallis, *The Explicit Animal: A Defence of Human Consciousness*, 2nd edn (London: Macmillan, 1999), in particular Chapter 6, 'Man, the explicit animal'.

9. Discussed brilliantly in Milan Kundera's *The Unbearable Lightness of Being*, trans. Henry Michael Heim (New York: Harper Perennial, 1999). I reflect on our increasing distance from the natural world, and its implications for our sense of ourselves, in 'The work of art in an age of electronic reproduction', in *Theorrhoea and After* (London: Macmillan, 1999).

10. Those who believe that the general patterns of human behaviour can be largely explained in terms of the adaptive tropisms of our primate ancestors should ask themselves why human beings are alone among the primates in appealing to complex notions – such as Darwinian thought – in explaining or excusing their behaviour. I am not, for example, aware of any male chimpanzee invoking the notion of 'the selfish gene' in defence of his sexual acquisitiveness.

    The profoundly misguided endeavour to 'biologise' human beings is extensively discussed in my *The Explicit Animal* and in *The Enemies of Hope: a Critique of Contemporary Pessimism*, 2nd edn (London: Macmillan, 1999) where I pay particular attention to the incorrect notion that civilisation is in some sense pathological because it suppresses, or denies expression to, our essential animal nature. Malik, *Man, Beast and Zombie*, is a superb critical account of biological reductionism – in particular of sociobiology and its kindred belief systems.

11. As I argue at length in *The Explicit Animal*. I shall spare the reader a repetition of those arguments here. I am not, of course, alone in this view. For example, two major scholars of human evolution (one, alas, a founding father of evolutionary psychology) write as follows:

    > Humans are so singular a species, with such zoologically unprecedented capacities, that it is a major biological mystery how evolutionary processes could have produced us out of our primate ancestors.

    John Tooby and Irven DeVore, 'The reconstruction of hominid behavioural evolution through strategic modelling', in *The Evolution of Human Behavior: Primate Models*, edited by Warren G. Kinzey (New York: State University of New York Press, 1987), p. 183.

12. Malik, *Man, Beast and Zombie*, p. 7.

13. Albert Camus, *The Rebel*, translated by Anthony Bower (London: Penguin Modern Classics, 1971), p. 168.

14. The wrong way to make visible the distinctive greatness of humanity is to appeal to the achievements of a handful of men and women of genius. Very few of us are geniuses, but we are all human. There is, moreover, a uniquely human genius in quite ordinary behaviour. Card-carrying 'geniuses' put out only a little from the mainland of humanity. Anyway, artistic and other forms of genius would not make sense without the setting of distinctly human needs and specifically human institutions, which express our collective, cumulative genius.

15. A notion expounded passim in *The Explicit Animal*.

16. It is pleasant coincidence, though it may be more than that, that manu is also connected etymologically with the Sanskrit verb man-, 'to think'. This is one of the many apparent connections that illuminate the fundamental thesis of this book – that prehension and apprehension are, deeply, one.

17. Raymond Tallis, *Newton's Sleep: Two Cultures and Two Kingdoms* (London: Macmillan, 1995). See especially 'The difficulty of arrival'.

18. This should not be taken to imply that philosophy thrives on error, only that philosophical discourses whose validity depends upon relatively recherché facts have probably taken a wrong turn. Philosophy should be, for the most part, a meditation – howsoever subtle and complex – on what everyone knows and no one is likely to dispute. The material of philosophy should 'lie to hand'.

19. See, for example, T. Petterson, G. P. Smith, J. A. Oldham, T. Howe and R. C. Tallis, 'The use of patterned neuromuscular stimulation to improve hand function following surgery for ulnar neuropathy', *Journal of Hand Surgery* 19(4), 1994, pp. 430–3.

20. Actually, they *will* see their names in print, but only because those names are so beautiful. Here they are: trapezium, trapezoid, scaphoid, capitate, lunate, triquetrum, pisiform, hamate. Such large names for such small bones! The smaller the bone, the larger the name – just as the tiniest English villages have the most barrelled names.

21. It does not reflect the author's ignorance in this area. I have spent the last twenty years researching in the field of neurological rehabilitation and, in particular, tactile neglect. Indeed, it is precisely because I am aware of the massive scale of the literature – and of many very good, even brilliant, popularisations in this area – that I have shied away from it.

22. R. M. Rilke, *Duino Elegies*, 'The Fifth Elegy':

> And then, in this wearisome nowhere, all of sudden,
> the ineffable spot where the pure too-little
> incomprehensibly changes, veering
> into that empty too-much?
> Where the many-digited sum
> solves into zero?

   Selected Works, Volume II, translated by J. B. Leishman (London: The Hogarth Press, 1967).

23. Actually, this is not strictly true. While I have tried to restrict myself as far as possible to information that is philosophically relevant – at any rate, to things that have provoked me into thought and which directly or indirectly serve my overriding purpose of illuminating the ordinary surface of things with light drawn from the extraordinary depths upon which the ordinary is founded – so that I should keep 'the big intuitions' alive and the fundamental ideas in view throughout writing this book – I have not always succeeded.

   The truth is, I have enjoyed myself too much in contemplating the hand to be entirely disciplined in the way that a philosopher should be. The many facets of the hand have such intrinsic charm and the pleasure of remembering and reflecting on them has been so great that things have sometimes got – well, out of hand, and the text has consequently incorporated material that is not entirely transilluminated by the philosophy. I won't, however, feel ashamed of my digressions, if my enjoyment is shared. At any rate, *The Hand: A Philosophical Inquiry into Human Being* has turned to be much less po-faced than the book I originally envisaged. And also less unified: in line with the fluctuation of intentions there is a multiplicity of styles and tones of voice. This does not, I trust, mean that I have totally lost my grip.

   Some digression, anyway, is necessary – to make visible how great is the surface area of the presence of the hand in human culture and so to make more credible the philosophical weight imputed to it in the later final chapters of the book.

24. Ludwig Wittgenstein, Preface to *Philosophical Investigations* translated by G. E. M. Anscombe (Oxford: Blackwell, 1953).

25. I am grateful to Mary Midgely for putting it this way to me in a characteristically generous and perceptive letter.
26. If this present book also contributes to restoring benign universalist conceptions of humanity – at a time when ethnocentricity has opposed this – then I shall not be unhappy. Ethnocentricity – which is an understandable reaction against narrow definitions of what it is to be a human being emanating from those who have economically derived power over the definitions – has its own malign potential: the oppression of the oppressed from within; the oppression of the oppressed by oppressors who are licensed not to recognise our common humanity. For a wonderfully rich, thoughtful and definitive account of the complex interrelationships between pluralist and universalist accounts of man on the one hand and racism on the other, see Malik, *Man, Beast and Zombie*.
27. Leo Tolstoy, *Diaries*, quoted in Henri Troyat, *Tolstoy*, translated by Nancy Amphoux (London: Penguin, 1970), p. 735.

OVERTURE

CHAPTER 1

Grasping the Hand

I.I PRELIMINARY GRAPPLINGS

Some natural tears they dropped, but wiped them soon;
The world was all before them, where to choose
Their place of rest, and providence their guide;
They hand in hand, with wandering steps and slow,
Through Eden took their solitary way.
Paradise Lost, Book XII: 645–9

It is tempting to say that, if Adam and Eve had been expelled from Paradise to fend for themselves on Earth without hands – or with paws instead of hands – the history of the human race would have been unimaginably different. In some respects it might have been happier; in most other respects, it would have been much worse. To think in this way, however, is already to miss the very point that it is the purpose of this book to labour; for, without the human hand, mankind would have had no history at all. The human past would have gone unrecorded and disappeared as completely as the past of other animals into the dark and backward abyss of time; and, deeper than this, humans would have had no history in the sense of a present life distinct from organic existence. There would not only have been no collective story of the human race; there would have been no cultural development separate from biological evolution. The burden of this book is that the special relationship we indubitably enjoy with respect to the material universe – which has for much of history been understood as a special relationship to God, or the gods, or the numinous powers that brought us into being – is to a very great extent the result of the special virtues of our hands. Whether or not we sit at the right hand of God in the order of things, our belief that we do so, and the evidence apparently justifying that belief, owes much to such seemingly unimportant facts as that the thumb has uniquely free movements. It is to such biological accidents that we owe our escape from biology; to such mechanisms our escape from mechanism.[1]

Getting to grips with something that has had such enormous consequences for the human race, and that is a ubiquitous presence in nearly every moment of every life, is not easy. This hand – this professor of grasping, seizing, pulling, plucking, picking, pinching, pressing, patting, poking, prodding, fumbling, squeezing, crushing, throttling, punching, rubbing, scratching, groping, stroking, caressing, fingering, drumming, shaping, lifting, flicking, catching, throwing and much else besides – is the master tool of human life. The brain's most versatile and intelligent lieutenant, the master grasper, it is simply ungraspable. We may, however, try to bring its multifarious, multi-talented, multi-skilled faculties to some sort of order by describing the functions of the hand as, variously: manipulative, exploratory and communicative. In the hand are combined an organ of manipulation, an organ of knowledge and an organ of communication: a three-in-one, it acts, knows and speaks.

These different kinds of function are, of course, interactive, indeed integrated: the hand acquires knowledge through action; its knowledge guides its actions; and it acts and acquires more knowledge through communication. In this respect, the hand is perfectly suited to its special relationship with the brain. The increasing versatility of the hand speaks to a growing brain, perhaps (as I shall argue) is the main driver of its growth, and the links between prehension and apprehension, between grasping the material things of the world and grasping the sense of things, grow thicker and more numerous. The master instrument of the Masters of the Universe is also the ur-tool which has given birth to a bewildering variety of tools serving human needs with ever greater effectiveness and indirectness. Out of the intelligence nurtured through the interaction between fingers grappling with the obdurate materials of the world and the brain to which they speak, ultimately come the tools that aid in devising the principles according to which other tools will be designed. It is probable that, with the use of tools – the hand's great gift to humanity – came even greater gifts. Tools, embodying mediated interaction with the world, opened windows of consciousness through which a new kind of understanding entered: the intuition of general principles underpinning the interaction between the needing body and the environment that might supply its needs.

1.2 THE MANIPULATIVE HAND

Fine manipulative skills and dependence on tools to exploit resources are a hallmark of the human species ... The human hand lies at the centre of [manipulative] skills, and its ability to assume a variety of positions and to resist high levels of mechanical force allows it to perform a great variety of tasks.[2]

We are not, of course, unique in our grasping hold of the world, or parts of it, with our upper limbs. All sorts of animals scoop, swipe, sweep, grasp the things they want to eat or want to kill. Non-human primates have quite an impressive portfolio of grips, ranging from the brute power grip that enables them to swing through the trees to the finger movements necessary to extract a nut from a shell or a peg from a board. But they fall far short of the multi-dimensional dexterity of *Homo sapiens*. The cleverest manipulative activity a chimpanzee indulges in is using a stone to crack open a nut.

There are many reasons for this unique capability of the human hand, which although it did not come all at once, many consequences of which date from 100,000 years ago or less – a brief minute in evolutionary time.[3] There is the crucial fact that humans, unlike other primates, are upright; bipedal locomotion frees our hands for manipulation. This is, of course, merely permissive rather than enabling. Human manipulative pre-eminence is also due – in part – to the anatomical features of the hand.

In common with those of other higher primates, human hands are, in a very precise and literal sense, highly flexible: the entire hand can flex at the wrist; the fingers can flex at the carpophalangeal joints which connect them with the back and palm of the hand; and the fingers exhibit internal flexion at the so-called interphalangeal joints. In addition, in humans, the fingers can rotate; in particular, the thumb and little finger are able to move across to the palm. The thumb is particularly versatile in this regard, being able to touch, to interact with, to cooperate with, every other finger in a variety of ways. It is able to touch not only pulp to pulp with the other fingers but also with the thumb sides of the fingers. This is in part due to the fact that the thumb is long enough compared with the other fingers to be able to reach their tips.

The versatility of the hand is further extended by several other features:

1. We are able to rotate the palmar side of the index finger towards the thumb.
2. The joint at the base of the middle finger is obliquely oriented to resist forces generated by the thumb pressing objects against the other

fingers. In apes, the joint is transverse because the finger is required to resist the forces produced during locomotion. The resistance of the fingers to pressure in humans is increased by the expansion of the fingertips.

The most important free gift the human hand enjoys, the key to its distinctive handiness, is the comparatively free movement of the thumb. The thumb is related to the wrist via a joint – the trapezio-metacarpal joint – which connects the first metacarpal bone (the bone in its first section) with the trapezoid, one of nine small, short bones in the wrist. This is where most of the movements of the thumb take place. The anatomy of this joint is therefore very important in determining the range of thumb movements.

As in chimpanzees, the joint is composed of interlocking concave and convex surfaces which form a saddle. The difference between ourselves and chimpanzees is that the saddle interlocks more in chimpanzees, and this restricts movement; in particular, it prevents opposition of the thumb to the other fingers. This has huge implications, as we shall see, for our grip on the world around us, for our prehension, and ultimately apprehension and comprehension, of the universe.

It is too easy to give the hand sole credit for the multifaceted genius of human manipulation. But what else would one expect of the master manipulator than that it should take all the glory for itself? Other parts of the body, however, have a hand in dexterity. And so, too, does the brain that is hand in glove with the hand and that both teaches and learns from it, as each ratchets the other to new heights. Of this more presently. For the moment, we note that the role of the arm in positioning the entire hand, so that it can pull off its daily feats of brilliance, is particularly apt to be understated. Any tendency in that direction will be pre-empted by the next chapter – a piece of affirmative action that will ensure that the arm enjoys the credit that is due to it – and that we do not allow ourselves the 'biologistic' (cf. scientistic) idea that the whole of civilisation is built upon the properties of a joint between the trapezium and the first metacarpal bones. (See section 1.5 for a further discussion of this.) For in the end, it is not so much the slight anatomical difference between ourselves and chimpanzees but a something else – a something that enables us to make something extra-ordinary, an entirely unprecedented world and mode of being in the world, on the basis of this slight anatomical difference – that we should, ultimately, be trying to grasp. The opposable thumb, crucial to human development, would not have been such a launching pad had it not been for what was already in place.

Leaving this aside for the present, what are the immediate consequences of these special features of the human hand? The human hand has many more degrees of freedom than the primate hand. The range of available grips and the modes of manipulation these grips make possible are almost limitless. Capturing the immediate consequences of the opposable thumb and all the other developments that come together in humans is therefore almost impossible. One can, however, impose some kind of order by classifying the grips that are available to the human being.

Napier[4] looked at the function of the hand as a whole and suggested that there are two broad types of prehension movements – power and precision grips:

> The object may be held in a clamp formed by the partly flexed fingers and the palm, counter-pressure being applied by the thumb lying more or less in the plane of the palm. This is referred to as the power grip. The object may be pinched between the flexor aspects of the fingers and the opposing thumb. This is called the precision grip.

This is not a complete account of the matter. As the illustration shows, a comprehensive manual of grips would have to break down the precision grip into different kinds; for example, the scissors grip, where the fingers act in isolation from the thumb, and the hook grip, which may be quite powerful, though the thumb and palm are scarcely involved. Moreover, Napier's classification does not capture the multiple, non-standard, perhaps non-repeatable sequences of not-quite-standard grips that are involved in the ordinary complex tasks of everyday life, such as tying shoelaces, buttoning and unbuttoning clothes, or trying to get hold of a slippery object with protuberant ur-handles. Or the combination, in a continuum of movement, of prehension and exploration, when one is trying to get at an object, or adjust it, or fix it when it is broken. Every hour of every day, I seem to catch myself using a new grip.

Nevertheless, this is an inspired start. It grasps the two fundamental dimensions of prehension and manipulation: power and precision. We can allocate the more stereotyped grips to one or other of these categories. The precision grips include polydactylic bravura performances such as the five-jaw chuck, useful for turning the larger knobs on a machine; the three-jaw chuck for holding a pen or turning a smaller knob; the two-jaw chuck (pad-to-pad) for threading a needle; and the two-jaw chuck (pad-to-side) for turning a key in the door. The power grips include: the squeeze grip for holding sticks and hammers and rackets; the disc grip for twisting off jar lids; and the spherical grip for squashing fruit and squeezing testes and holding tennis balls.

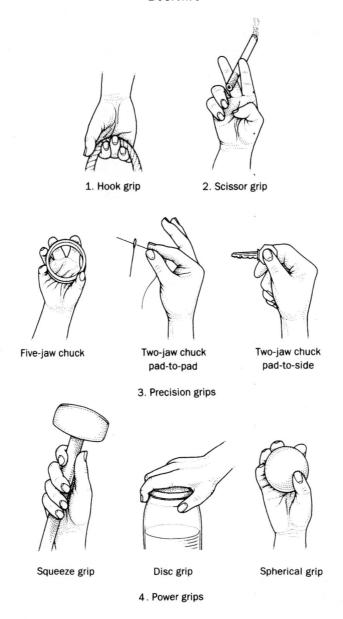

1. Hook grip   2. Scissor grip

Five-jaw chuck   Two-jaw chuck
pad-to-pad   Two-jaw chuck
pad-to-side

3. Precision grips

Squeeze grip   Disc grip   Spherical grip

4. Power grips

Some human hand grips. While the special properties of the human hand permit a boundless range of grips, the ones illustrated above are the most common. Grips in the ape are mainly limited to those in which the fingers flex, or fold, over objects and the thumb prehends small items between its palmar surface and the side of the index finger.

(Reprinted from *An Introduction to Human Evolutionary Anatomy*, Leslie Aiello and Christopher Dean, p. 372, © 1990, with permission from Elsevier Science.)

The grip is, of course, only a means to manipulation, not manipulation itself. It is the floor upon which the dance of manipulation takes place. The squeeze-gripped hammer has then to be swung; the disc-gripped jar lid has to be turned; the bi-digitally trapped thread has to be advanced through the needle's eye. But without the grip, the hand movement would not be manipulation at all; it would be pointless twitching, flailing, jittering, fidgeting.

Manipulation is not, of course, a function solely of the isolated hand. Directly or indirectly, it engages the arm and the body as a whole. My legs steady my body, which stabilises my arms as I throw my weight into unscrewing that resistant jar lid or put all my force into swinging the hammer on to the stone. As the emphasis moves from power to precision, so less and less of the body is engaged: there is successively a brachialisation, a chiralisation and (numinously) a digitalisation of manipulation. The battle against Adam's curse will move from the ordeal of the effort of power to the ordeal of the effort of precision and the aching muscle will be replaced by the aching mind.

1.3 THE KNOWING HAND

The motor activity of the hand – reaching, gripping and manipulation – cannot function in the absence of what is usually called 'sensory information'.[5] This information takes two forms: knowledge of the hand and knowledge acquired by the hand; the hand as known and the hand as knower. This separation is somewhat artificial, as we shall see: there is close and continuing integration between different modes of sensory information; morever, the two forms of information merge in proprioception: the hand's self-knowledge, in which it is both the means to, and the object of, knowledge; that which makes knowledge possible and that which is known.[6]

The information the hand needs to support its manipulative function is most clearly evident in the first stage – where the information is also most sharply distinct from the hand itself – namely in *reaching out* prior to grasping, shaping, etc. Here the hand is under predominantly visual control: the target is located, the relationship to the body determined, the motion initiated to home in on the target – these are all regulated by sight, which measures what needs to be done and the progress of the doing. (This account hardly begins to do justice to 'the genius of reaching', which we shall address in Chapter 2, section 2.2.) Even when the target object is reached, manipulation is still usually assisted, if not regulated, by sight. Although it is possible to carry out many habitual actions in the dark – even complex ones such as tying one's shoelaces –

they are easier if there is visual assistance. And if, for some reason, the target object proves not to have standard properties or the expected spatial location or disposition, then visual guidance is even more important and may be an essential precondition of success.

There is, however, much self-guidance by the hand. Nothing could be wider of the mark than the image of the hand as 'a dim groper' when it is deprived of visual support. It has exquisite knowledge of the size, shape, surface, texture, density, pliability, etc. of the object it manipulates. The blind person reading Braille at a rate of hundreds of characters per minute is but an extreme example of the ability we all have to utilise tactile awareness. And although tactile knowledge is acquired serially – as when, for example, the fingers move over a large object – unlike the all-at-once of knowledge gathered through sight – it is not a mere vapour trail of transient revelation, but a cumulative understanding of the properties of individual objects, of their relations and of the general behaviour of material things.

The non-dimness of the groping hand becomes even more apparent when it is appreciated how it has simultaneously to acquire 1) knowledge of the object it is feeling or manipulating and 2) continuously updated awareness of its own location and disposition. The two have to be integrated without being merged or confused: toucher and touched have to be known separately and in relation to one another – separately *and* together – so that the former can reveal the latter. This is of immense importance for the distinctive relationship of humans to their bodies and, via this, to the world in which they live: we shall connect it, eventually, with the birth of science and the digitisation of nature. (See Chapter 8.)

Not all tactile awareness is subordinated to the sensorimotor control of the movements of the hand produced by the arm or of the movements of individual fingers in manipulation. The hand is an organ of exploration and cognition in its own right: it interrogates objects not merely as a preliminary to acting upon them; it interrogates them to determine what they are and whether it is worth acting upon them. The human hand is, as Napier has it, 'the chief organ of the fifth sense' – touch:

> The hand has advantages over the eye because it is a motor and sensory organ in one. It can observe the environment by means of touch and, having observed it, it can immediately proceed to do something about it.[7]

It can also, as Napier points out, 'see' in the dark and, because it is at the end of a long, highly flexible limb, it can 'see' round corners. Thus the hand sorts, assigns, classifies. Interestingly, there are different visual pathways in the nervous system for supporting the hand in its different functions of acting upon objects and of extracting information from them.[8]

The sensory system of the hands is, unsurprisingly, complex and exquisitely finely tuned. From the huge literature on this topic, I choose at random one or two snippets of information. First, there is the obvious fact that there are many modes of tactile sensation: light touch, pressure, temperature, pain are the most obvious. These conscious sensations are supplemented by less conscious modalities that support the control of manipulations – for example, the joint position sense, which tells me where my hand is in relation to my body, where my fingers are in relation to one another and what position they are in. And these in turn are supported by even less conscious feedback from joints and muscles which provide on-line control of evolving activities – and our hands are always more or less engaged in evolving activities.

These senses are themselves regulated – made more or less sensitive according to circumstances. For example, pressure receptors are set to detect not absolute pressures, but changes in pressure and rate of change of pressure and proportionate changes in pressure. The skin may be displaced by the same amount, with similar consequent warping of the underlying sense endings, and yet this may produce a strong sensation or a weak sensation, depending upon the background pressure, or what has happened before. The sense endings, here as elsewhere, are more sensitive to change – and to the rate of change and proportionate change – than to standing conditions. This is true at the level of unconscious feedback, which informs motor control mechanisms, giving information about limb, hand and finger movement and position and posture. The sensitivity of the spindles in the muscles, which record muscle tension and changes in tension, may be up-regulated or down-regulated as required, thereby decreasing or increasing proprioceptive acuity.

The acuity of touch is greatly enhanced by the dilatation of the fingertips and by the ridges on our palms and fingertips – the unique prints – which amplify small changes. The neural support for tactile, as well as manipulative, activity is reflected not only in the extraordinary density and sensitivity of nerve endings, but also in the enlargement of the spinal cord in the neck and, more strikingly, in the disproportionate representation of the fingers (and in particular the thumb) in the sensory part of the cerebral cortex. The homunculus represented on the sensory (and indeed the motor) cortex, indicating which parts of the cortex are dedicated to servicing which parts of the body, has grossly – indeed grotesquely – swollen fingers.

In the cerebral cortex, different components of touch are integrated into more complex tactile awareness. The movement of the fingers over a surface creates a sensation of texture. The overall pressure detected by a large number of displaced sensory endings gives an idea of weight and size. Active manipulation gives a sense of the malleability of the object. The combination of weight and size (and, inferred from that, density), of the texture, gives a notion of the material of which the item is made and, indeed, its general identity. This, to repeat, is far from 'dim' groping: it is a highly cerebral matter, as is demonstrated by the huge expansion of the cortical representation of the relevant fingers in individuals who use their hands for skilled tasks – violinists, Braille readers.[9]

Any more facts – however wonderful – at this early stage, will result in our losing sight of – or losing touch with – the fundamental nature of touch. I shall import them as required from time to time, but I want to avoid the danger of our knowing too much and wondering too little. For touch would be just as astonishing if the hand were more dim than it in fact is. In accordance with this, let us examine the fact that 'knowing touch' or 'knowledgeable-knowledge-acquiring touch' is less obvious than may seem at first sight – or indeed at first contact.

Haptic[10] knowledge seems at first sight – or at first contact – more straightforward than, say, vision because it seems to be unmediated. The toucher and the touched, the knower and the known, are directly applied to one another. This is in contrast to sight or hearing, where experience is mediated by a third party – by light (usually called 'light energy' to make the underlying materialism more plausible), or sound ('sound energy'), or whatever. Touch is direct; or, at any rate, its mediations are hidden, being inside the body of the toucher. How can we avoid knowing what we actually bump into?

The answer is, of course, quite easily – just as every object other than a conscious living organism manages to avoid knowing the objects it bumps into. The laptop and the surface on which it sits are unaware of each other; the laptop keys are unaware of the fingers that are utilising them to type this sentence. Mutual pressure between objects is therefore not a sufficient cause – or explanation – of the awareness that is tactile sensation; even less is it a sufficient cause – or explanation – of the special kind of overall awareness that is called 'knowledge'. Less again is it a sufficient cause – or explanation – of the active knowledge acquisition that comes from exploratory behaviour, from interrogative manipulation, that seeks information and selects the information it wants.

In short, physical objects, with the exception of conscious, living bodies, do not really touch, nor are they really touched by, other physical objects. That is why the physiology of touch – which is ultimately about the transfer of energy from one body to another and within one part of one body to another part of that body – does not give us an account of anything truly corresponding to touch. The physiology of touch boils down to the physics of touch and so boils out touch because physical objects do not touch. To touch is to awaken to awareness; it is to be awoken to awareness; it is to touch and be touched in the multiple senses of being affected:[11] that which touches us in the physical sense actually or potentially touches us in those other senses. To be touched, for example, is to be prompted to possible action. The metaphysics of the fingers' ability to touch cannot therefore be reduced to, or derived from, the physics of touching objects.

The seeming straightforwardness and immediacy of touch, therefore, is an illusion. It appears even less straightforward when we reflect, as we did just now, that the touching hand knows itself as both touched and touching at the same time as it knows what it is that it touches and that it is touched by. Nor is it immediate: to lose itself in the object of touch is to lose the object of touch; touch must keep its distance from the touched. Only in this way will it acquire the knowledge of the touched and through touch enjoy virtual possession of the touched. (The distance is not, of course, a physical distance.) We shall return to this when we reflect on The Playful Hand – in particular The Carnal Hand – and the Abstract Digits of the Counting Hand. And it will emerge as a major theme of Volume 3, *The Knowing Animal: A Philosophical Inquiry into Knowledge and Truth*.

For the present, let us settle for the reflection that the hand, as an organ of cognition, shares in the mystery of all cognition: it recognises, assigns, sorts, classifies something which is other than itself. And this is not the end of the matter: the close or paradoxical distances built into touch – distances physically crossed and cognitively opened up – lie at the heart of the hand's ultimate emergence as the master toolmaker – a step that speeded up the interaction between prehension and comprehension – and opened up a crack of wakefulness into the full light of our ordinary days. Of this, much more in this and subsequent volumes.

I.4 THE COMMUNICATIVE HAND

The hand manipulates, the hand knows and the hand communicates. Different hand shapes are assumed for manipulation, environmental exploration and communicative gestures. The postures assumed for manipulation – grasping objects of all sorts of shapes, applying and directing forces for working upon, moulding or stabilising hand-held objects with widely varying properties such as hardness and weight – are often stereotyped because they depend upon maintaining certain relationships between the elements of the hand, between the hand and the arm (as in the oblique angle assumed at the wrist when a hammer is held in readiness for use) and between the arm and the rest of the body. They are doubly constrained by the physical relationship between the body and the object and by the demands of the object. The postures assumed for exploration are less constrained. There are limits imposed by the physical relationship between the object and the body, but the object itself may be explored and manipulated at random: there is no fixed order or path of haptic inquiry. The postures assumed for communication, however, are at once less constrained and more stereo-typed. They bear little relationship to any external objects; indeed, they are often entirely arbitrary; or if originally 'motivated' (in the linguist's sense of a non-arbitrary relationship between a sign and its meaning, as in a pictorial or iconic sign, where the sign looks like what it means), their original motivation is lost in the mists of time; or if still motivated, somewhat formalised – for they are, in the final analysis, not the real thing but gestures; if actions, only indirectly so. The very word 'gesture' connects with the notion of a merely symbolic or token action.

The hand waves, salutes, applauds, greets, insults, indicates help-lessness or surrender or despair, threatens, interrogates, informs. These are its telecommunications. Between the telecommunication and the proximate communications of intimate contact is the formal touch of the handshake and the complex ambiguities of hand-in-hand, of manucaption. And then there are the close, indeed intimate, communi-cations of the hand. The hand touches, pats, strokes, caresses, gropes, penetrates; and so comforts, demonstrates affection or desire, or exhibits one of many kinds of love, arouses, violates, hurts. Communication here moves more closely into direct manipulation: waving is quite different from pinching as a means of attracting and securing someone's attention. There is fathomlessness in these proximate communications: in the caress where the object touched by the fingers is itself aware of being touched and is itself a creature that touches. There is a rich sensual, social and metaphysical territory to explore here. If the subject is to be handled with the right touch, much tact will be required.

1.5 FROM PREHENSION TO APPREHENSION: PRELIMINARY SPECULATIONS

The guiding intuition of this work is that there is a deep connection, or there are deep connections, between the special properties – powers, capabilities – of the human hand, in particular its manipulative prowess and self-awareness, and our distinctive human nature. This intuition is less reductionist and more complex than may appear at first sight.

To deal with reductionism first. *The Hand* ... would fail in its purpose – indeed, it would achieve precisely the opposite of what it aimed to achieve – if it were seen as a contribution to what may be designated, by analogy with scientism, as 'biologism'; the practice of the belief that the distinctive nature of human beings can be explained in biological terms; that, for example, the huge differences between us and our nearest animal kin resides solely in certain anatomical or physiological differences. The suggestion, for example, that the specific properties of the human, as opposed to the non-human primate, hand are all that there is to the difference between culture and history on the one hand, and nature and evolution on the other, would be an example of such biologism. The crucially important differences between human and non-human hands do not alone account for the infinitely complex phenomenon, unique in the order of the universe, of human culture. It is not so much the differences – which are very important – but the ability to make much of the differences. We may think of the emergence of the distinctive capabilities of the human hand as lighting a fuse on a long process that entrained many other parts of the human body and many other faculties as it unfolded.

So much for reductionism. What about the complexity of the intuition? It is partly intrinsic and partly due to my own vacillating uncertainty about what, fundamentally, it is trying to tell me or I am trying to do with it. The intuition is about how a small difference could be the basis of a larger difference and how this, in turn, could be the basis of an even larger difference. Linguists often quote Humboldt's wonderful insight that language – or more precisely, language-speaking communities – make infinite use of finite resources.[12] I would suggest that this is one of the most enduring and distinctive characteristics of humanity. It is not, therefore, simply the anatomical difference that accounts for our extraordinary nature, but what further differences are progressively created out of that difference. Any explanation of our difference in terms of minor biological difference simply highlights this ability to make unlimited differences out of finite one. Explaining this cannot be simply a matter of biology, though it cannot be independent of biology – just as the riches of poetic language cannot be explained entirely by the versatility of the human larynx, though without the speech that is made possible by the special properties of the larynx the riches of poetic language would not have arisen.[13]

We shall return to the role of biology presently. First, let us stay a little with the complexity of the intuition. The sense in which contemplation of the astonishing versatility of the human hand will contribute to a philosophical anthropology is not entirely determinate or stable. The simplest notion is that examining the unique properties of the human hand will explain the origin of our differences and hence help us to achieve a definitive account of our nature and place in the larger scheme of things. This belongs with the biologism I have already rejected. The less simple notion that it is what we do with given or 'factical' differences, specifically our ability to build big differences on small ones, that explains our distinctive nature is a little nearer the mark. But this must be supplemented by the notion that the human hand is a rather auspicious place to be the site of crucial differences, as we shall explore in due course: it is just the place where a small difference may be amplified into a big one.

The point of the present work is not confined simply to accounting for our origins; indeed, this is only a small part of its purpose, and is arguably subordinate to another purpose: that of getting a handle on ourselves. It is driven by the belief that, through contemplating the boundless versatility of our hands, what we do with and achieve through them, and our relationship to them, we can make visible our huge differences from other forms of animal life. Which is why we shall always, in the pages that follow, be wobbling between something that looks like description and something that looks like explanation and spend much time in redescriptions that will seem like explanations. And why, too, we shall stray so far afield, contemplating not only grips but also gestures, not only handshakes but also gloves, not only gloves but also fashions in gloves.

I hope this will prove sufficient to distance what follows now, and subsequently throughout this book, from crude biologism. Let us now return to biology and its wider ramifications – for the hand is not isolated from the brain, nor manipulation from discourse, nor manual activity from the evolving global frameworks of emergent human consciousness – in order to examine the fundamental fact that humans are (seemingly) more awake to the world than are animals.

The biological record notes the distinctive anatomical structures of the bones and muscles of the hand; of the neural systems in the sensorimotor pathways; and of the integrative and cordinative structures of the brain and spinal cord. This is the given. Also given is the palae-ontological record, which suggests that the development of manual dexterity and increase in brain size are dependent processes in human evolution. Indeed, according to Steven Pinker,

> Precision tools and precision intelligence co-evolved in the human lineage and the fossil record showed that the hand led the way.[14]

How robust that claim is, given the absence of direct observation and the scarcity and indirectness of fossil and archaeological evidence, is not clear. It is, however, an attractive idea[15] and one that is worth reflecting on.

What is it about human manual activity that makes it particularly apt to drive the growth of intelligence? If we could understand this, then it would become easier to imagine an unstoppable upward spiral: manipulative activity enhances intelligence; intelligence permits more complex manipulative activity; this in turn enhances intelligence. This way of understanding would be even more attractive because it would allow us to subscribe to the dialectical relationship between manipulative activity and intelligence without necessarily buying into a materialist or neural account of the mind whereby the enhancement of intelligence was identical with the increased representation of certain functions in the brain, in turn due to the altered connectivity and reorganisation of mass activity in the brain – such as can be revealed by brain scans.[16]

There seems to be at least two aspects of human manual activity that make it particularly apt to be the driver for increased individual and collective intelligence. The first relates to its manipulative function; the second to its cognitive or exploratory function.

To examine how the distinctive manipulative functions of the hand might drive intelligence, let us revisit certain features that seem to be of crucial importance for our manipulative prowess. The first is the freedom of the thumb to rotate at the carpo-metacarpal joint, which makes it opposable to the fingers and capable of being used in combination with them to pick up small objects. This, however, is a feature shared with the great apes and cannot, therefore, alone account for the evolution of a distinctively human intelligence. The versatility of the hand arising from the opposability of the thumb is, however, massively augmented by the increased mobility of the human thumb at the wrist compared with other primates and, more importantly, by the increased length of the thumb which allows it to cooperate in different ways with the other fingers – with pulp-to-pulp contact or thumb pulp to finger side. The benefits of this are further enhanced by the ability to rotate the palmar side of the second finger towards the thumb and by the special properties of the joint at the base of the middle finger which enables it to resist forces generated by the thumb pressing objects against the other fingers.[17] What might be the special significance of this?

Its significance lies in its permitting not merely a wider range of grips, of modes of prehension, but a limitlessly varied range of grips, each of which can be customised for the needs of the moment. Such grips do not merely happen in response to the stimulus of the moment: they are

adopted, fashioned, created, *chosen*. The hominid, that is to say, *uses* his
hands in a way that other animals do not use their hands or, indeed, any
other parts of their bodies. Even in the 'absorbed coping' (to use
Dreyfus's phrase[18]) of daily existence there is a potential distance
between the human animal and a bodily part that serves its needs. This
is captured by F. Wood Jones's observation that

> the difference between the hand of a man and that of a monkey lies not so
> much in the movements which the arrangements of the muscles, bones
> and joints makes it possible for either animal to perform, but in the
> purposive volitional movements which under ordinary circumstances the
> animal habitually exercises.[19]

The body becomes a more explicit servant of those needs: it sticks out in
a more than physical sense. A new distance opens up between the
(needing) organism and its (need-relevant) environment, a distance
implicit in deliberation and crossed by it. Between the non-stereotyped
prehensions of the hominid hand and the stereotyped graspings of the
animal paw there is opened a gap which requires, and so creates the
possibility of, *ap*prehension to cross it. The object of its prehension is
more clearly an object: it is not seized absentmindedly, even less manipulated absentmindedly; it is not assimilated, dissolved into the entirety
of the world of the activity. And, correspondingly, the prehending subject
is more clearly served by an organ of prehension. The relationship to the
latter becomes more explicitly instrumental. As we shall discuss, the
hand under such circumstances becomes an inchoate tool, an ur-tool, en
route to its becoming the master-tool, or Tool of Tools.

The limitless variety of grip permitted by the independent movements
of the fingers – so-called fractionated finger movements which both
human and non-human primates can carry out[20] – in relation to the
versatile thumb makes non-standard grips the standard. It is because the
grips are customised, chosen or used that the manipulated world is not
only prehended but apprehended as it is in itself; or, rather, it is not
totally absorbed into the relations of the moment. The grip is tailored to
the object, respecting its singularity, its *haeceitas*, which means that
objects do not dissolve into general, instinct-addressed, unreformable
implicit categories. Manipulative knowledge – which perceives the
object, reaches for it, grasps it, lifts or holds it, shapes it or uses it to act
on something else in the world, or place, replaces it – is the distance
between the genius of prehension reaches (shared with other animals)
and the different mysteries of apprehension and comprehension, unique
to humans.

So much for the interaction between the manipulative function of the hand and the growth of intelligence. What of the cognitive function of the hand? Sensation guides exploration and manipulation (prehension, shaping, control) and also gives knowledge arising out of exploration and manipulation. (Manipulation and exploration are also not clearly separated, as lovers well know.) This double function is apparent in all pawed creatures: there is nothing distinctively human about it. In the context, however, of the deliberateness of human manipulation, the cognitive hand becomes a co-servant with the manipulative hand of the new form of wakefulness. The hand as tool is more sharply set off from the world it is operating on. The proprioceptive information about the hand itself – the guided manipulator, the directed explorer – becomes more explicit. There is a duality – developed to a lesser or greater degree – in any interaction between hand and world: between the hand as known object and the hand as knowing subject. It is possible to see this duality prefiguring – as we shall discuss in section 10.2, and in more detail in *The Knowing Animal* – the duality of the knowing, known self; or the human identity as the known knower.

This account of things also touches on the puzzling fact that intelligence develops in parallel with manipulative precision and not, say, with increasing visual acuity and more complex visual awareness. One would expect the subject–object duality to develop most readily in response to the emergence and increasing sophistication of a telereceptor such as the eye, which is clearly separate from the things it makes available to consciousness. Moreover, the eye is richer in information: it is estimated that 90 per cent of the sensory information that reaches us comes from vision.[21] The eye, however, is literally a transparent organ of cognition: it has no separate presence, except when it has been injured and in the minor events of gaze redirection and blinking. The eyes are not active, even less interactive, in the way the hand is; the gaze has no retroactive presence to itself, unlike the grope of the active – manipulative, exploratory – hand. Proprioception from the eye is largely unconscious and takes the form of reafferentation to counter any illusion of instability of the world that might come from the movement of the head and eye.[22] If the eye has come to be seen as the quintessential appurtenance of the subject, and the gaze has come to be seen as the subject's archetypal power, this has, I shall argue, been established on the back of the subject–object divide opened up by the cognitive hand.

These, then, are some of the reasons to echo Pinker's observation that, 'precision tools and precision intelligence co-evolved' and 'the hand led the way': the evolution of precision intelligence has been driven by the precision grip of the human hand. The manipulative hand, in which grips and modes of manipulation are chosen, awakens the twin notion of the independent object 'over there' and the subject 'in here', the basis for the human animal's sense of coming at the world from outside of it, in turn the basis of the inquiring and ultimately the scientific standpoint – the intuition that drives the search for objective knowledge.

There is, however, another important element in the linkage between prehension, apprehension and comprehension: the progessive develop- ment of increasingly complex tools. The role of tools in the boot- strapping of intelligence – and 'the co-evolution of precision tools and precision intelligence' (Pinker 1997) – seems self-evident. The use of tools taxes the intelligence; a taxed intelligence becomes more highly intelligent; and a higher intelligence can devise more precise tools further to tax the intelligence. But this common-sense account of the matter misses out what is philosophically interesting about tools.

Tool-use is not unique to humans. (We shall return to tool-use in section 9.3.) What is unique to humans is the way tools are used and the cognitive, indeed epistemological, context of tool-use, and what this leads to in terms of tool development. Chimpanzees[23] and humans both use hammers of sorts; but only humans use computers. Why? Because the fundamental insight behind human tool-use does not inform animal tool-use. This is why the repertoire of animal tool-use remains severely limited – seizing a cane to poke at something, using unshaped rocks to crack open nuts – and evolution of animal tool-use over time is negli- gible, so that the discovery of a new form of tool-using behaviour, however trivial and unimpressive, causes huge excitement among ethologists. Indeed, I will argue that the animal use of tools, far from being an early or primitive form of human tool-use, is not tool-use at all – except in a metaphorical, anthropomorphising, sense.

The missing insight in animal pseudo-tool-use is the one already alluded to: the notion of *instrumentality*, which is rooted in the notion of the hand itself, and subsequently the body, as an instrument and ourselves as operating on the world. The relationship to the world mediated through tools is possible only against the background of a relationship to our own bodies grasped as tools; more specifically of the body as the support for the hand grasped as a tool. The ability to exert a deliberate choice between manipulative strategies is the necessary pre- condition of, and provides the fundamental insights behind, the expro- priation of materials outside the body as tools. The extricated hand is the precondition of the extricated tool; the distance between the hand and the world it is manipulating is replicated and elaborated in the distance between the tool and the use to which it is put.

The insight that lies behind tools is uncovered or elaborated or exfoliated in: the storage or retention of tools for future purposes; their manufacture, as opposed to the mere discovery of 'natural' tools; the development of tools to manufactured tools. That chimpanzees lack the fundamental toolmaking sense is evident from these facts: they do not store tools; they do not manufacture tools with which to make tools; they do not re-form tools.

In the tool thus fully understood is embodied the understanding of general principles; indeed, the grasping of the principle of 'The Principle'; of the occasion as the instance of a general type of occasion; of an individual action as an example of a general type of action; of the context of general possibility instantiated in actuality. At first the tool embodying the principle precedes the principle: levers were used before the mathematics linking mechanical advantage to the ratio of distances to the fulcrum was conceived. Later, the principles anticipated the tools – as in the case of computers.

This process was very protracted and it had a very slow start: the penny was a long time dropping.[24] Stone tool technology – the outcome of a single basic idea, that one can produce a sharp edge by knocking a flake off a cobble – appeared about 2.8 million years ago. There was little change in tool-use over the next 1.5 million years until the first hand-axes were made in Africa. Although sharp flakes were often produced as a spin-off from the manufacture of pebble choppers and hand-axes, a 'flake industry', in which the production of flakes was the primary purpose, did not develop until about 400,000 years ago. Progress remained agonisingly slow: even the Neanderthals – 'the ice-beleaguered side branch of the human race', as Napier (1971, p. 104) describes them – who refined flake-based tools, shaping the flakes with soft hammers to produce evenly curved, notched or saw-tooth-edged implements, did not make tools with handles. There was no long-term planning and task-specificity associated with toolkits. The primitive tools they had were compensated for by their powerful arms and hands. Only 100,000 years ago, with the emergence of *Homo sapiens sapiens*, ourselves, were the tools more customised to tasks and had built-in leverage to increase their power: hafts of wood and polished bone permitted the development of compound tools. This has enabled manipulation to become, within the last 40,000 years, as Trinkaus (1992) says, 'one of the dominant aspects of our biological and cultural adaptation'. The fuse that was lit several million years ago has now turned into an explosion and, indeed, an exploding explosion. This is wonderfully captured by John Maynard Smith:

About 400 million years ago the first aquatic vertebrates evolved; at least two million years ago man's ancestors first chipped stones to make simple tools; less than ten thousand years ago, in the Neolithic revolution, animals and plants were first domesticated. If a film, greatly speeded up, were to be made of vertebrate evolution, to run for a total of two hours, tool-making man would appear only in the last minute. If another two-hour film were made of the history of tool-making man, the domestication of animals and plants would be shown only during the last half minute, and the period between the invention of the steam engine and the discovery of atomic energy would be only one second.[25]

The link between prehension and apprehension and comprehension may be expressed in a preliminary way as follows. The almost infinite variety of grips awakens the notion of choice and makes agency more aware of itself. It also awakens the sense of the body – or at least the hand, supported by the body – as an instrument. The hand's communication with itself as well as with the objects that it manipulates enhances this sense of the hand as an instrument: the thousand grips with their customised solutions to problems – for example, walking along holding a book and a cup in a single hand – mixing precision and power grips, requisitioning spare fingers, etc. makes of the hand an implement, a thing of use at a distance from the body I am, and so the master-tool, the father of the possibility of tools. The early tools made this sense of agency both more explicit and more effective. The human agent worked on the manipulated world via mediators. These mediators were effective because they embodied general principles. Deliberate, mediated, generality-directed or principled action is intelligent. The visibility of the principle in the tool opens it up to critical examination and so to gradual reform: tools are embodied abstractions and generalisations, existing between, and so outside of, the situations in which they are used. The first thing to be reformed was how the tool was used, and the understanding of the world implicit in, and arising out of, the better use of stereotyped tools. The next (and much more recent) step was to reform the tools. The final steps were to create tools in accordance with pre-existent explicit principles. This included manufacturing tools to make tools. By this means, experience woke to increasing knowledge; and procedural know-how woke to a knowing-that that would better inform know-how. The longer the chain of mediations, the greater was the awareness of what was being done and why and how. Many-step mediations are steeped in more complex apprehensions of wider and more general truths about the world.

This, then, is a first sketch of the upwardly spiralling interaction between the evolving ability of humans to manipulate the world and their increasing intelligence understood in the most general sense as a wakefulness to the possibilities of the world around them inasmuch as they are relevant to immediate, mediated and remote needs. Tools, abstracted from individual occasions and yet important to them, point the way to further abstraction and the development of an abstract intelligence – or an intelligence that works with and through abstractions. Thus the link between the specificity of manipulation and the generality of intelligence; between prehension, apprehension and comprehension.

We shall return to these ideas – fundamental to our philosophical inquiry – in the penultimate chapter of this book and speculate in the final chapter as to what they may have to say about our nature.

NOTES

1. I am talking here about necessary not sufficient conditions. I should emphasise at the outset that I do not believe that the hand entirely explains our distinctive nature as human beings – any more than I believe that the structure and the function of the human brain (or at least as it is currently understood) does. To suggest this would be to go back on all that I have argued in *The Explicit Animal*, 2nd edn (London: Macmillan, 1999) and *On the Edge of Certainty* (London: Macmillan, 1999) and elsewhere.

   Not that I am entirely happy with the position that I have argued in those two books, as I have discussed in 'The troubles of antineurophilosophy' (*The Knowing Animal: A Philosophical Inquiry into Knowledge and Truth* (forthcoming)). For the present, I am happy to begin with the belief that the special properties of the hand played an important role in permitting us to become what we are and to use the functions of the hand as a way of taking hold of our distinctive and extraordinary nature – a nature that does not fit into nature as currently understood. I shall revisit the question of the interaction between the hand and the brain and the hand and the mind in the penultimate chapter of this book, although I will briefly examine the relationship between prehension and apprehension in the present chapter.

2. This section is heavily dependent upon Eric Trinkaus's beautifully written and beautifully illustrated little essay on 'Evolution of human manipulation', in S. Jones, R. Martin and D. Pilbeam (eds), *The Cambridge Encyclopaedia of Human Evolution* (Cambridge: Cambridge University Press, 1992).

3. John Maynard Smith, *The Theory of Evolution* (London: Penguin, 1975), p. 311.

4. J. R. Napier, 'The prehensile movements of the human hand', *Journal of Bone and Joint Surgery*, British Volume 38B, 1956, pp. 902–13.

5. This is not an entirely satisfactory term, as it leads to all sorts of confusions. To describe sensations as 'information' is to import into lower-level awareness connotations that strictly belong to higher-level awareness (awareness that is the result of someone being informed by someone of something) and to succumb to what I have described as 'the fallacy of misplaced explicitness'. The term 'sensory information' is even more unsatisfactory when it is extended to include unconscious feedback, as arises from muscle and joint receptors during ordinary controlled movement.

   The metaphorical, or extended, use of the word 'information' may seem innocent but, as I have discussed elsewhere, it lies at the top of a slippery slope, at the bottom of which lies a good deal of the nonsense that props up neurophilosophy and materialist theories of the mind. (See, for example, the entry on 'Information' in 'A critical dictionary of neuromythology', in Tallis, *On The Edge of Certainty*.) So long as 'sensory information' is used in full knowledge of the potential fallacies it may give birth to, it remains a useful portmanteau phrase.

6. The exact sense in which this is not precisely true is important, as we shall see.
7. John Napier, *The Roots of Mankind* (London: George Allen and Unwin, 1971), pp. 176–7.
8. See M. A. Goodale, L. S. Jakobsob and P. Servos, 'Visual pathways mediating perception and prehension', in A. M. Wing, P. Haggard and J. R. Flanagan (eds), *Hand and Brain* (London: Academic Press, 1996), Chapter 2.
9. The relevant literature is referenced in V. Pomeroy and R. C. Tallis, 'Neurological rehabilitation: a science struggling to come of age', *Physiotherapy Research International* 7, 2002, pp. 76–89.
10. 'Haptic' means 'related to or based on the sense of touch' (*Webster*) and is derived from the Greek *haptein* to fasten, or *aptein* to touch. My excuse for using this somewhat obscure word here – it is listed in the Supplement of my edition of the *Oxford English Dictionary* – is that it is the only exact correpondent I can find to 'visual' and because it sounds so lovely.
11. I owe this way of putting it to Hubert L. Dreyfus. See *Being-in-the-World. Commentary on Heidegger's Being and Time Division* I (Cambridge, MA: MIT Press, 1991).
12. Wilhelm von Humboldt, 'Language makes infinite use of finite resources'. Quoted in Noel Minnis (ed.), *Linguistics at Large* (London: Paladin, 1971), p. 31.
13. The relationship between the origin of uniquely human communication and the anatomy and function of the larynx is discussed in E. S. Savage-Rambaugh and D. M. Rambaugh, 'The emergence of language', in *Tools, Language and Cognition in Human Evolution*, edited by Katherine R. Gibson and Tim Ingold (Cambridge, Cambridge University Press, 1994).
14. Steven Pinker, *How the Mind Works* (London: Penguin, 1997), pp. 194–5.
15. Especially, perhaps, to those of a Marxist or cultural materialist persuasion, for whom the evolution of consciousness passively reflects the evolution of the means of production. We shall allude to Marx's early, penetrating ideas on the relationship between human tool-use and the development of human culture and individual human societies in the Appendix to Chapter 9.
16. The plasticity of the nervous system and, in particular, the shaping of the organisation of the brain by the very activity it drives is a fundamental notion of modern neurobiology. See, for example, D. V. Buonomo and M. M. Merzenich, 'Cortical plasticity: from synapses to maps', *Annual Reviews of Neuroscience* 21, 1998, pp. 149–86. For an account of this, with its relevance to the rehabilitation of individuals with neurological damage, see, for example, Pomeroy and Tallis, 'Neurological rehabilitation'.
17. Here, as previously, I have been helped by Trinkaus, 'Evolution of human manipulation'.
18. Dreyfus, *Being-in-the-World*.
19. Quoted by Roger Lemon, 'Control of the monkey's hand by the motor cortex', in *The Use of Tools by Human and Non-human Primates*, edited by A. Berthelet and J. Chavaillon, A Fyssen Foundation Symposium (Oxford: Clarendon Press, 1993), p. 51.

20. This is associated with a huge expansion of the corticospinal tract in primates and the unique feature of direct connections between the cortex and the motorneurons in the spinal cord. These pathways are preferentially active during precision rather than power grip and are effective here because they make restricted projections to a limited number of hand muscles which are co-activated for gripping movements. (Lemon, ibid.). The key experiment which identified the role of the corticospinal tract was that of Kuypers and Lawrence, which showed that monkeys in whom this tract was transected recovered power, but were unable to deploy the fractionated finger movement necessary to extract a nut from a container.

21. This is the standard claim, universally repeated. How meaningful it is is uncertain. See Tallis, 'Information'.

22. For a discussion of reafferentation and its significance, or lack of significance, for the sense of self, see Raymond Tallis, 'A critique of the Aleksander and Dunmall's extension of the Zeki-Bartels hypothesis of a mechanism underlying the unity of sensation', in *The Knowing Animal: A Philosophical Inquiry into Knowledge and Truth*, Volume 3 of this trilogy.

23. For a review of tool-use among chimpanzees, see Nancy M. Tanner, 'The chimpanzee model revisited', in *The Evolution of Human Behavior: Primate Models*, edited by Warren G. Kinzey (New York: State University of New York Press, 1987).

24. See Trinkaus, 'Evolution of human manipulation'.

25. Maynard Smith, *The Theory of Evolution*, p. 311.

CHAPTER 2

The Armed Hand

2.1 TWO FINGERS TO OVER-DIGITISATION

The majority of the tasks we perform with our hands require differential movements of the fingers. The emphasis on dexterity moves ever more distally, from our trunk, to our arms, to our hands, to our fingertips. The relative importance of various bodily structures supporting the tasks of daily living is reflected in the motor and sensory cortex, where the homunculus representing the different parts of the body is grotesquely distorted: the space allocated to the thumb is hugely greater than that allocated to the trunk; and each finger is regulated by almost as large an area of cortex as the entirety of the arm.

As life evolves towards *Homo sapiens* – the deliberate animal – and as *Homo sapiens* comes into his own, it seems that brachiation gives place to chiralisation and chiralisation gives way to digitalisation. It is important, however, not to exaggerate the extent to which the actions mediated by the fingers are liberated from the rest of the body. Just as the more refined classes tend to forget the manual labour upon which their refinement depends; or, more fundamentally, we all somehow overlook the bodily functions necessary for us to be able to write poetry; so we tend to give too much credit to the visible, surface events – the exquisite end-product – and too little credit to the humbler processes that underlie them and make them possible. The drawing room forgets the furrow, the boudoir the coal face.

There is a general propensity, therefore, to underplay the essential enablers. We must resist the tendency to forget that even a highly digitised activity such as typing out this sentence depends upon the appropriate chiral adjustments: my wrists have to hold my hands in the correct position and orientation; the function of my hands as a whole depends upon the supportive and transportive activity of my arms; and this activity, finally, requires the maintenance, and continuous adjustment, of the posture of my trunk, itself requisitioning forces from my legs and head and elsewhere. In addition, I have had to walk to this seat and adopt an appropriate position next to the laptop. In short, almost every part of my body is implicated in an action for which my fingers take the lion's share of credit.

The tendency to over-digitise our account of manual activity is understandable in a world where bodily power has been replaced by precision and where precision has been liberated, by the abstract digitisation of measurement that permitted science-based technology, from the body; where, in short, energy-consuming activity has been supplanted for much of the time by information transfer and we have the world at our fingertips. Work for most people is less brachial and more digital. This is true, even of what used to be called manual labour.

By beginning with the function of the hand – seen largely working as a whole – I hope to guard against attributing too much of our human behaviour to the activity of digits. The hand – which is warm as well as dexterous, lecherous as well as intelligent, powerful as well as precise – needs to be given its due.

If the hand is badly done by in a digito-centric account of human dexterity, the arm is even more so. Which is why this Part of the book, dealing with the hand acting as whole, begins with the arm; for an unarmed hand would be helpless. In subhuman primates, arm and hand (or paw) are of equal status; indeed, earlier in the evolutionary tree, in pre-mammalian species, they are hardly differentiated anatomically. Uniquely in humans, there are many functions for which the activity of the arm is largely subservient to the manipulative and exploratory functions of the hand. It is important, however, to remember that the differences between humans and all other animals are built upon capacities that we have in common with non-human creatures. Most importantly, the freedoms we uniquely enjoy grow out of the mechanisms that reach their most complex expression in monkeys. The manipulative ability of humans is predicated upon the brachial skills of other primates: opposability put the final coping stone in place that enabled humans to enter sustained self-consciousness and to embark upon a path of increasing collective and individual freedom (as we shall discuss in Chapter 10, and at greater length in *I Am: A Philosophical Inquiry into First-Person Being*). These skills, most importantly, include certain functions in which hand and arm seem to play a more equal role. Nowhere is this equality more apparent than in reaching, whose genius it is now our pleasant task to explore and celebrate.

2.2 THE GENIUS OF REACHING

Voltaire said of Sir Isaac Newton that with all his science he knew not how his hand moved.[1]

To reach out for an object is to make contact with a world that, at the same time, one remains distanced from. Prehension in this respect lies at the root of apprehension and comprehension. Less fancifully, it is the motor equivalent of telereception. Consider, by contrast, encounter through smell. The snuffling animal, even one following the trail of an object to its source, assimilates the object to itself. The mouth–nose–tongue is not distinct from the animal. Reaching also has a clearer element of choice, of selection, of deliberation: it consequently makes the body parts involved look much more like an implement. The mouth is rarely, if ever, an instrument in this sense, even in humans for whom the entire controllable body is potentially or actually instrumentalised. The interaction between myself and the world implicit in reaching is tripartite: first, the object; secondly, the engaged bodily part; and finally, myself – my wishes, the rest of my body as background, etc. – whose needs or wishes are to be met. In reaching, we are served by a body part, or body parts, that acquire pre-instrumentality.

Reaching is likely to get overlooked because it is preliminary to the real business – to grasping or gripping and to the manipulation that this then permits. And yet it is extraordinarily complex. In order successfully to reach out for an object, I have to do all sorts of things – or all sorts of things have to be done. (Whereby hangs a tale that lies at the centre of this book. See section 2.3 below for a first glance at this.) One (admittedly artificial) way of breaking down this task is into: 1) transportation of the hand to the object that is to be grasped; and 2) forming a particular posture for the fingers in anticipation of what is required for grasping the object.[2] This is more difficult than might appear at first sight. As recent investigators have shown, the appropriate finger posture is adopted while the hand is being transported to the object before it reaches its target and tactile information from the object is available. For example, my hand assumes a remarkably accurate glass-shaped aperture well before I enclose a glass. Moreover, there are many elements to each component of reaching, all of which have to be planned in advance and controlled – and if necessary modified – during execution.

Here is one way of breaking down the task of reaching out for an object and grasping it:

1. The object has to be located. It has to be related to me, to my body, to

my arm. Behind the sense of the object 'over there' has to be the sense
of 'me here'.

2. The relative locations of the object and myself have to be translated
into more or less precise measures of distance and direction. The
object has to be sensed as being within reach and as requiring a
certain size and direction and speed of reach. Its size must also be
assessed and, on the basis of its general appearance, its nature (apple,
fly, brick) and its likely characteristics (heavy or light, firm or
squidgy, rough or smooth) has also to be guessed at.

3. Once the trajectory between hand and the object to which it is being
transported is determined, the arm has to be set in motion, assume a
reasonable speed and then – so that it does not fly past it or knock it
over – slow as it approaches the target. This is described by movement physiologists as the 'bell-shaped velocity curve'.

4. All of this must be achieved irrespective of whether there are objects
intervening between hand and object (which will have to be circum-
vented) and irrespective of whether unexpected events occur (for
example, the object is moved or the arm is jogged) which will require
on-board adjustments to the original trajectory.

5. In the meantime, the hand position – the degree of cocking at the
wrist, for example – and posture have to be coordinated with the arm
as the reaching movement gets under way. The aperture of the
grasping hand has to be wide enough to accommodate the object
snugly, but not so wide as to allow it to slip. The aperture has to be set
in good time, but not so early that it is likely to be inaccurate because
it is based on inadequate or inferior information.

Let us examine one or two aspects of these elements. The account
that follows is by no means exhaustive or even systematic. I simply want
to alight, butterfly fashion, on some matters of special interest; to gather
a bouquet of amazements and wonders.

Localising the Object

It is self-evident that successful reaching depends upon locating the
object one is reaching out for. Like so many other aspects of hand
function that prove to be not at all straightforward, this at first seems
very straightforward: the object is over there and I reach over there. To
put it at its simplest, where I see it, I reach for it; or, in those instances
where reaching is not guided by vision, I reach for the object where I
remember it as being. In either case, reaching is guided by knowledge of
the location of the object. Unfortunately, this does not explain how it is

that I successfully localise the object I am reaching out for. It immediately opens up innumerable questions. For example: 1) What precisely does this knowledge of location actually know? 2) How is this knowledge made available to me? 3) How is it used by me?

From the point of view of reaching, the location of the object is its location *with respect to me*, where 'me' is understood to be some location on my body. Locating the object in this way is a necessary precondition of defining the journey the hand must take in order to get to the object. It is not enough, however, to settle for 'I am here and the object is there. The trajectory is from here to there.' This would not translate into a specific action. 'There' has to be specified more precisely in relation to here. This specification has at least two components: distance and direction. It is conventional among experts to think of direction as being specified with respect to the frontal plane. This is an imaginary plane, like a sheet, in front of the body, which underpins coordinates in two directions: vertical and from side-to-side. Distance, in the context of this model, comes to seem like depth – the third dimension. If we think of the location of the object as a set of values in a coordinate frame of reference, then the question of specifying 'there' or the 'there–here' relationship becomes at once clearer and more puzzling.

The coordinate values of the object define the distance from 'here' to 'there'; those values, however, are determinate only if their origin, and the location of the 0,0,0, are predefined. An implicit or explicit frame of reference is needed to determine spatial relations. There seem to be several candidates for the 0,0,0 position: the body; the centre of the body; the arm itself; a key point in the arm; and, quite differently, the perceived location of the reaching self or of the intending self or of the intention. Several of these candidates seem to be problematic, but we shall come back to them in due course. First, let us examine the relevant scientific literature.

The scientists remind us, first of all, what has to be achieved in reaching. When I reach out for an object, I extend my arm in order to transport my hand. The extension of the arm is multi-joint affair: I extend my arm at the elbow and at the shoulder joint. At each joint, there may be a combination of movements: for example, both extension and rotation at the elbow joint. We shall examine this in more detail when we consider transporting the hand. For the present, it is sufficient to note that there are three connected problems faced by the individual in trying to get the hand to the target.[3]

1. Representing[4] the 'target position in space preparatory to goal-directed movements' and translating this representation 'into an

appropriate set of joint angles for shoulder, elbow and wrist' (the so-called 'sensorimotor transformation problem').

2. Choosing a specific trajectory to the target posture that will ensure that the object is reached 'from the many that are possible (the motion planning problem)'.
3. Determining 'the joint torques (or muscle forces) that will achieve the desired trajectory ... (the inverse dynamics problem)'.

It will be evident that, with respect to Problem 1 – that of representing the target position in space and translating this into a set of joint angles – the frame of reference which will define these positions is best anchored in the very structures that have to do the work. One such frame of reference for the forearm would be affixed to the upper arm, while the frame of reference for the upper arm would be affixed to the shoulder. In fact, the evidence suggests that the posture of the arm is represented in a frame of reference whose axes are vertical and horizontal – though the latter, in turn, may be defined by the posture of the trunk (and so refer back to the subject's body) – with vertical being co-axial with the trunk and horizontal being at right angles to that.

The evidence at present is still a little patchy and the translation of the sense of starting position and of the target position and of the relationship between them into specific trajectories and the plotting of those trajectories in terms of altered joint positions at the shoulder, elbow and wrist, remains wonderfully obscure. What is certainly true is that the frames of reference will not be very stable. Indeed, it is possible that two frames of reference may be in play at the same time – as when I make a complex reaching movement that involves constant shifting of the trunk, either as part of the reaching or as an accidental accompaniment of reaching. Far from being reserved for rare virtuoso performances, this complexity is probably present in most reaching movements. We do our reaching, after all, while we are busy with other things: walking, adjusting our sitting position, etc. Reaching is always inserted into a dynamic situation, rather than being the isolated action performed against stable background that is usually examined in the laboratory. Even in this context, there is some evidence that subjects may use a frame of reference that is intermediate between one fixed in space and one fixed to the forearm.[5]

Despite the incompleteness of the scientific account of our ability to locate the target of our reaching and translate that location into terms that are relevant to the act of reaching – often unhelpfully described as 'telling the arm/brain what has to be done' – there is much food for philosophical thought here. For example, the last point about the if we assume that the frame of reference of movement that so puzzled us just now is supplied *gratis*.

In the simplest act of stationary, unwobbling individual reaching for a non-moving, rigid object clearly visible in broad daylight – when, in other words, world and objects are behaving as well as possible – a set of complex transformations will be required in order to translate what the reacher can see into guidance as to what she has to do. This is not merely a matter of mapping from, say, a visual frame of reference or a coordinate system appropriate for the retina of the eye to another sensory system, for example, the sensations from the arm or hand. On the contrary, it is a sensorimotor transformation, from sensations to a motor frame of reference in which movements are specified. Just how complex this is becomes clear when we think of the movements that have to be specified and of the specification of the means by which they are to be achieved. These are problems 2 and 3 – 'the motion planning problem' and 'the inverse dynamics problem' – of those listed at the beginning of this section. The motion planning problem itself breaks up into a multitude of constituent problems. Let us start by examining these a little more closely.

Of the many challenges to be overcome in the planning of a reaching movement, one that has attracted considerable recent attention, is that of the excess of 'degrees of freedom'.[9] The position and posture of an object may be defined according to six characteristics. First, the centre of mass of the object (roughly the location of its physical centre) may be specified as a set of values in three spatial dimensions: up/down, left/right, backwards/forwards. The posture of the object is defined according to three descriptors: pitch, roll and yaw. These six variables define the final position (location and posture) of the hand grasping the object. In reaching and grasping, there are two other elements to be considered: the path to be followed as the hand is transported to the object; and the type of grip, for example, the amount of force, with which the object is to be gripped. Even if we set aside the limitless possibility for variation in the trajectory taken towards the target object and in the grip assumed on arrival at the target, the number of possible postures I (my body) may assume to hold the object is limitless; for I can make the appropriate contact with the object by any number of combinations of flexing, etc. at the hips, abducting, etc. at the shoulder, extending, etc. at the elbow, flexing, etc. at the wrist; and so on. The number of descriptors needed to characterise the reacher's position in space is identical to the minimal number of mechanical degrees of freedom that characterise the human body. It has been estimated that, even if one confines one's counting to the joints, with their different directions of movement, there are about one hundred such mechanical degrees of freedom. The arm, excluding the fingers, has seven mechanical degrees of freedom: three at the shoulder, two at the elbow, and two at the wrist. The fingers add a large number of degrees of freedom; but, even if we forget about the fingers, and if we make things even simpler by assuming that the arm is isolated from the rest of the body (or the rest of the body is not mobilised in reaching), it is evident that more degrees of freedom (seven) define the positions that the arm may adopt in grasping a particular object than define the position that the object may adopt (six). This means that there are countless arm postures that can be utilised to take hold of the object. If we then consider the trajectory to the target as a series of hand positions, each of which could be instantiated as one of a limitless number of hand positions, then the ways of reaching for the object are seen to exceed the modes of describing the object position and posture by even more orders of magnitude. The reacher, in other words, is spoiled for choice.

All right, you might say, there are many ways of skinning a cat. Surely this makes cat-skinning easier, not more difficult. It would do, were it not for the fact that, as we have noted, the path to the target has to be highly programmed: the path is automatically set to be the shortest, and the velocity curve is bell-shaped and scaled to the distance to be traversed. (There is the additional requirement of pre-programming the hand aperture, of which we shall speak presently.) The programming either has to be such that it can remain invariant under the limitless possible trajectories and hand positions that any reaching can utilise; or there must be some mechanism for solving the degrees of freedom problem so that only a small subset of the possible pathways and final positions are utilised.

Models have been suggested for ways in which reachers overcome the degrees of freedom problem. These include: coupling or mandatory linkages between joint movements or positions, thereby reducing the degrees of freedom; biomechanical constraints arising out of the material and kinematic properties of bodily structures, so that events in one part of the limbs mechanically determine events happening in other parts; and cost-containment strategies, limiting the choice of programmes, whereby the motor system adopts those trajectories and postures that consume minimal energy. So far, none of these models fully accounts for the ability of the reacher to choose one strategy out of the many thousands that are possible or to exercise choice while still respecting the pre-programming requirements we have specified. The precise details of these models and their failure adequately to solve the problem is less important than what it tells us about reaching; that it is are made up of, things we could not do or even will to do. 'The Genius of Reaching' lies beyond the deliberative scope of the greatest genius in the world.

As I sit here now, at this word processor, I am about as free an agent as it is given to humans to be. I am pain-free, even worry-free, in no overt way disabled. I have no immediate obligations. The country I live in is at peace and reasonably prosperous. The agenda I am following is one that I have chosen rather than had thrust upon me. I am doing something that I want to do, and what I am doing – consciously thinking – is as reflective, as deliberate, an activity as it is possible for humans to engage in. And yet ...

I note, first of all, that it is supported by things I am not (actively) *doing* – albeit I am intermittently aware of them – such as breathing and maintaining my posture. Granted, these are mere background; part of an enabling context. They do not disturb my sense of choosing myself and expressing that choice through actions I have chosen. But what about those chosen actions themselves? They are not merely supported by, but are riddled through with, mechanisms I have not willed and could not will even if I wanted to. Leaving aside the various incidental fidgetings that fall between things that I do and things that merely happen, as part of the continuity between my official activities, there are three things that I seem most importantly to be up to.

1. *I am drinking coffee.* This involves, among other things, reaching out for the mug, grasping it, bringing it to my lips, tipping it so that its contents fall into my mouth and returning it to the desk top, ensuring as I do so that the hand that has it in its grip slaloms between the clutter of my immediate environment so that the mug has an unbumpy flight through the air and has a soft landing.
2. *I am typing.* This is more manifestly skilled and complex. I am required to: locate the right keys on a keyboard; transport my hand over the keyboard in order to bring the fingertips to the correct locations; keep those same fingertips in such relative positions that several keys may be pressed in rapid succession; use this action to inscribe the words – which, in the time-honoured way, I am inclined to say are 'in my head', which have already been mentally transcribed into their written representation and the latter analysed into their component letters – on to the screen; and to check at the same time that I have made no errors, breaking my flow where necessary to correct those errors, while continuing to think.
3. *I am thinking.* This, very roughly, means translating what I am trying to recall, wonder at, make visible to myself, into a linear or capillary

stream of realisations, and this in turn into a jet of words put together into sentences, themselves organised into larger linguistic units such as paragraphs and the chapters to which they relate. Linguists and neuropsychologists typically identify at least dozen or more steps in this process, all of which seem to be real to them, rather than mere artefacts of description, because they seem to be separately interferable with by, for example, brain damage. The steps must, of course, be to some extent concurrent rather than serial: the search for one word will take place as I am mentally transcribing its predecessor and correcting an error that has occurred in the typing of another, slightly more remote, predecessor.

I am doing these three things and yet I am not doing them. It will be evident from the previous section that, although my drinking coffee is most certainly a voluntary act – I want to do it, I have the sense of doing it rather than its merely happening to or in or near me, I choose when to do it, nobody else is forcing me to do it, it corresponds to an appetite I have and a habit I am fond of, etc. – I could not have brought it about by my own volition. Even its simplest component, namely reaching out for the handle by which to lift the mug, contains many things I simply could not plan, regulate, control or implement; for example, getting my hand in motion in such way as to approach the mug at a reasonable rate and yet controlling the trajectory so that I don't overshoot the mug or knock it over; or shaping my hand in anticipation of the grip that it will assume round the handle. Likewise, my typing is proceeding far too fast for 'conscious willing', 'deliberate doing', to keep up with it. Again and again, I see that it is done; that I have hit the right keys in the right order. Typing has become as automatic, though not of course as reliable, as reaching for a mug and the posture of my fingers, adjusted as required depending upon what letters have to follow what letters, is as unchosen as the anticipatory grip posture my hand adopts when I reach for a mug, or the trajectory it assumes, and the bell-shaped velocity curve (scaled for distance) that characterises its trajectory. This is a learnt skill and it has become automatic – in contrast to the deliberate 'doing typing' that was the hallmark of my 'hunt-and-peck' days when I was learning to type in the 1970s.

What is surely not automatic, one might think, is the process of thinking whose products the typing records. If anything is voluntary, thinking surely is: there is an effort of thought (though it is most usually experienced when thinking has come to a halt and there is a struggle between the would-be thinker and the distractions from thought – or between rival lines of thought); and there is reflection in both the process and its product. It also seems to engage the minimum of external material, so it seems least caught up in mechanisms. But, of course, there is a passivity that reaches to the heart even of thought.

It would be conventional at this stage to allude to great thinkers who report that their great thoughts often come to them unbidden, not infrequently when they have abandoned the struggle to think those great thoughts and they are thinking of something else, or daydreaming or full-blown nightdreaming. But to do so would be to miss the general applicability of the point that is being made. *All* thoughts come either unbidden or only partly bidden. The words that compose the thoughts, their precise organisation into sentences, their connections are not manufactured by ourselves. They are given to us. The difference between the passivity of daydreaming (or the more profound passivity of nightdreaming or delirium) and active thought is not much more than that, in the latter case, one holds oneself in readiness, one retains one's position in the 'vicinity' of the place where the solutions to the problems seems to lie, and rejects alternative themes as distractions. But, of course, even this most intimately personal and seemingly self-charged and most voluntary element of deliberate thought is still the plaything not only of chance – anything may come up in that 'vicinity', even if there are no external (bodily or environmental) distractions, the vicinity only roughly specifies its contents or products – but also of the mechanisms that enable the thinker to specify, arrive at and remain in it. For example, the semantic field of which we need mastery to keep ourselves in the vicinity can be requisitioned only by memories and other cognitive processes over which we have only partial control.

I am not suggesting that we should replace 'I drink coffee' with 'Coffee gets drunk', 'I type' with 'Typing occurs' and 'I think' with 'Thinking happens'. There is an indubitable difference between voluntary and involuntary actions and between any kind of action and a material event. Walking downstairs for a purpose is not the same as accidentally falling downstairs. Reaching out for cup of coffee in order to satisfy one's desire for it is quite different from an involuntary movement such as hemiballismus, when the arm, flung out, may make contact with the mug. Or, to use Wittgenstein's example, there is a difference between 'I lift my arm' and 'My arm goes up'. The difficulty is characterising that difference and, even more, developing an idea of how one might account for it.

There is, let us repeat, such a thing as voluntary activity. And the first-person agent that informs that activity is real: 'I think' does not boil down to 'It thinks' or 'There is thinking'. But everything we do is riddled with mechanisms: the doing is not merely built on the happening;

happening is the very material out of which it is built. In the case of voluntary activity, the happening is typically described as being composed of a specific subset of mechanisms most commonly called 'motor programmes'. The concept of a motor programme is not entirely clear but it has several aspects to it.

The first is that it is a chunk of activity, which brings together a succession of individual movements or a multiplicity of controls. Both of these aspects are captured in the following definition of a programme: 'A set of commands to muscles required for coordinated action.'[14] The main function of the 'programme' is to embody linked sequences of muscle activity to bring about an action that an individual commanding individual muscle groups could not possibly bring about, having neither the necessary knowledge nor the skill. At its minimum, the notion of a motor programme carries with it the idea of a pre-packaged sequence, or sequence of sequences, which once switched on works fast and mandatorily and completely.

A seemingly straightforward example would be the programme or programmes said to be built into the controls for the act of walking. Here, the set of commands to muscles will ensure the alternating movement of the legs and the coordination of, for example, the swing phase of the gait in one leg with the stance phase in the other leg: this will ensure that while one leg is moving through the air, the other leg is firmly on the ground, giving the body support. This is enormously more complex than it sounds. For example, the distribution of activity in the flexors and extensors of a given leg must be carefully controlled, to ensure a smooth passage through the air in the swing phase and careful control of the ballistic elements. All of this will need to be adjusted to take account of the posture of the rest of the body, the kind of ground that the walker is negotiating (micro- and macro-texture, incline, obstacles to be avoided), and the speed with which the individual wishes to walk. It is, in fact, yet more complicated: work on the initiation of gait in both normal subjects and subjects with higher-level gait disorders[15] has shown what needs to be achieved in taking the first step, in order to ensure that the centre of pressure of the ground reaction forces and the centre of mass of the body are related so that pressure can be taken off one foot prior to the swing phase and transferred to the other without overdoing it and causing the body to topple over.

Notwithstanding this complexity, walking, which has at least some highly stereotyped features, such as the monotonously regular alternation of the two limbs, seemed a promising candidate for motor behaviour explicable in terms of motor programming. And yet its complexity seems to put it out of reach of automatic control. An even greater complexity is to be found in the control of reaching, as we have seen. What chance is there, then, that it could be accounted for by automated motor programmes? It seems equally evident, however, that no one could voluntarily regulate all the things that have to be regulated in order to achieve reliable and functionally effective contact with the target object. From which it follows that reaching has, at least in part, to be automated, to be built up out of standardised motor programmes.

While it is perfectly obvious that voluntary activity must be built up out of involuntary mechanisms, there are profound problems in understanding this. There are particular problems with the standard physiological understanding, encapsulated in the notion of the motor programme. These become evident when we consider the standard ploy invoked by movement physiologists: proposing that the automation incorporates 'calculations' that the brain (or part of it) 'does', which permit customisation of the programmes to the singularities of the individual action. According to other descriptions, motor programmes include not only 'commands' and 'calculations', but also 'if–then' and other logical operations. This shows how it seems impossible to make sense of cerebral control – requisition and modification – of motor programmes, to describe them in such a way that they deliver what is needed, while avoiding anthropomorphisms. 'Commands', 'calculations', 'instructions', 'logical operations' reflect the misplaced explicitness that I have mentioned earlier (see note 4) and I do not want to repeat those criticisms here. Suffice it to say that attributing to the brain, or parts of the brain, or neural circuits, the ability to *do* things that we, whole human beings, most certainly cannot do seems unlikely to solve the puzzle posed by the complexity and ingenuity of the mechanisms upon which, supposedly, agency is built.

The attractiveness of doing so is, however, entirely understandable: 'The brain does X' lies half-way between 'I do something' and 'Something happens'. It is as if the brain, which is somehow me-and-not-me, an ownerless piece of living tissue and 'mine', is able to straddle the gap between 'I do something' and 'Something happens', between someone performing an act and an event happening. The master metaphor – describing the brain as a computer – enables its activity to assume that mid-position even more plausibly because the notion of computation makes available a whole field of anthropomorphic terms – 'commands', 'codes', 'information handling', 'calculations' – that have gained respectability during their years of use by engineers in their descriptions of the functions of machines and their components.

Even if we overlook this 'semantic laundering' and somehow manage to avoid using anthropomorphic terms, the notion of motor programmes remains unclear and consequently is still unsatisfactory as a way of mediating between the seemingly simple voluntary actions we 'just do' and the extraordinarily complex mechanisms out of which they are woven. We have already noted that the problem is that very few actions are absolutely specifiable. Consider seemingly highly stereotyped action such as walking: left–right–left–right, etc. At first sight, as we have noted, nothing could be more amenable to 'encoding' in a motor programme put out by central pattern generators in the spinal cord or stored in the supplementary motor area of the cerebral cortex.[16] And yet, it is true to say that no two steps are exactly alike; or, more helpfully (as motor programmes are not about cloning identical physical events), there is a huge and continuous variation in the kinds of steps that I might take – depending on the ground I am walking on, the context of each step (as, for example, when I am recovering from a stumble or cruelly mocking someone else's gait). It may be argued, against this, that motor programmes specify the content of my activities only in a very general sense.

This 'rough specification' could work in two ways. The programme might consist of very small 'action-atoms', which could be combined in any number of ways, allowing almost limitless variation and custom-isation of the action to the goal towards which it is directed and taking account of the unique context – initial conditions such as bodily posture and previous actions, and physical circumstances – in which it is mobilised. The trouble with this way of ensuring action-customisation while still relying on motor programmes is that choosing very small elements creates a new problem: that of having voluntarily to put very large numbers of such elements together. This challenge seems to be no less daunting than if the action is conceived of as a whole. Alternatively, the programme could specify the action in very general terms; not in the sense of 'stand roughly here', as this would not capture the precision which characterises so much of what we do, above all of what we do with our hands; but in the sense of indicating the general principles that inform, and so limit, it. In other words, the content of the action would not be closely scripted, or indeed filled in, at all; only its form or boundaries would be. This would correspond to the widely used notion of a 'schema', a concept that has been used in a variety of ways in the writings of psychologists such as Piaget and Bartlett, and neurologists such as Head and many others. Here, it has a minimalist sense: that of the general form of a behaviour, or behavioural element, which could have a wide variety of instantiations, customised to the occasion. For example, the 'job specification' for 'reaching' might include certain automatic constraints (and a general form may be best understood negatively as a constraint or a boundary in this sense) such as that the aperture of the hand should not deviate more than a certain amount from the true size of the object; that the velocity of the hand moving towards the target object should be bell-shaped; and so on. These broad constraints would still leave considerable scope for customising actions. (And all actions are, to a greater or lesser extent, customised.)

This still does not provide anything really answering to our ability to customise – and in the deepest sense to choose – our actions: choose that we act, when we should act, how we should act. For I can reach for a cup in any way I like at any time I like. I can deliberately move my hand slowly towards the cup in defiance of the bell-shaped velocity curve; I can voluntarily make my hand aperture narrower than the target object until I have made contact with it and still grasp the cup successfully. It is possible, in other words, for me to overcome these programmes, to set them aside, and still execute an act which is believed typically to incorporate such programmes. Reaching while flouting the programmes is not all that much more difficult than reaching *tout court*, which suggests that some of the programmes at least – the higher-level programmes, such as those that define the velocity curve, at any rate – are not central to the act. The lower-level programmes are mandatory – for example, those that ensure relaxation of the biceps muscle (which flexes the elbow) when I am extending my elbow in a normal reach; or those that ensure that large numbers of component motor units in a muscle fire together and are recruited in a certain order. But I can overcome the higher-level programmes – as when I parody another person's reaching or grasping technique or cruelly mock the tremulous reach and grasp of an alcoholic. This suggests not only that 'doing reaching' is different from automatic 'reaching' or reaching while I am busy doing – and thinking about – other things.

In the end, we have to concede that there are very few actions that can be pre-programmed. Most of the things that we do are unique, even though they may have stereotyped components. Examples of actions such as reaching – for all that they are wonderfully complex, as we have seen – are atypical in more than one sense. First, reachings are usually only one part of more complex sequences of actions and their coordination and organisation extend over several perceived components: to use a linguistic analogy, we act sentences not individual words or morphemes and those action-sentences are enacted with reference to a wider context that is composed of my immediate circumstances, my medium-term aims and my larger-scale or longer-term goals – action-paragraphs and action-stories. A typical, trivial action is bending down to tie up our shoelaces, an act in which at any given time several things are going on (maintaining the bent posture, reaching out for the lace, stabilising it, moving one lace over another, solving the complex practical topology of knotting, etc.) and which extends over very many moves. Moreover, that act itself is embedded in a unique context – I may be bending from an unusual angle, while in hurry and talking at the same time.

In summary, it seems as if actions are far too difficult for us to be able fully to enact them. We are tempted to suggest that the bit that we do is founded upon a much greater component that merely happens or composed out of programmed elements. We are further tempted to think of this programmable bit as the background while the voluntary, unprogrammed (and unprogrammable) part is the foreground, the action. The sense of what one is doing and the sense that one is doing comes from the unprogrammed bit. Maybe so; but it remains difficult to see how one can voluntarily requisition involuntary programmes to support one's voluntary activity. And it is difficult, moreover, to identify a non-programmed component. Even the unprogrammed bit has to be composed of lower-level programmed components.

There are, in short, insuperable obstacles, if one accepts that we are not clever enough to 'do' all the components of our voluntary actions (even simple ones such as reaching) to understand how voluntary action can dovetail with, or build upon (never mind be 'built out of'), involuntary components. Or, to put this another way, we have no means of understanding how we might requisition mechanisms to enable our voluntary actions; by what mechanisms such mechanisms are requisitioned; how our agency is carved out of pre-programmed components; how freedom enacts itself through automaticity.

Why, it might be asked, have all these rather general problems preventing us from understanding motor activity been raised in the context of a discussion of the rather particular action of reaching? It is because reaching, which we share with many other animals – elephants and squirrels as well as other primates – in those animals falls short of what I would describe as fully voluntary activity. In Chapter 10, I shall bring together various arguments adumbrated at intervals in the chapters to come, and make a case for the seemingly daft idea that the origin of true agency lies on the far side of the wrist crease; that the manipulations of the full-blown hand, unique to humans, transform our relationship to our own body, to the world with which we interact in pursuit of our needs, appetites and desires; that true 'chirality' ignites an inchoate and ultimately self-fuelling awakening out of the automatism which is the very fabric of animal behaviour and still necessarily supports the heights of human activity. Reaching, which we share with many other species, and is a necessary basis for their prehensions, with us becomes a step towards apprehension and comprehension because of the special relationship of the hand to itself, and to the rest of the human body. Although other reaching animals engage in manipulations, they do not do so in the way that we do; which is why they do not, or not in any sustained way, cross the threshold separating consciousness from self-consciousness. Building on the fractionated finger movements developed to a unique degree in primates, full opposability of the thumb and fingers, and the liberation of the forelimb from the demands of locomotion, were the final steps that enabled humans to pass into the realm of agency and the unprecedented pilgrimage of humanity through a nature human beings have transformed. While reaching in animals is largely 'happening', human fingering and manipulation are 'doing'. Much of what is proximal to the wrist is shared with animals; distal to the wrist we have no peers. *And it is what happens distal to the wrist that, in the first instance, imports true 'doing' into the world.* Agency (and the agentive self) grows from the tips of our 'meta-fingering' fingers. This, then, retroacts upon what is proximal to the wrist, importing doing into more and more of the body, and, via tools, into what happens beyond the wrist, making the world increasingly the product of doing rather than happening.

Before we come to discuss this, however, there will be a long digression aimed at making the infinitely versatile hand visible.

NOTES

1. John Napier, *The Roots of Mankind* (London: George Allen and Unwin, 1971), p. 176.
2. Here I am dependent on the collective genius of the scientists contributing to *Hand and Brain. The Neurophysiology and Psychology of Hand Movements*, edited by Alan M. Wing, Patrick Haggard and J. Randall Flanagan (London: Academic Press, 1996).
3. These are as set out in ibid., pp. 147–8.
4. I have been trying, with incomplete success, to avoid the standard terms – 'represented', 'encoded', etc. – because they express a 'misplaced explicitness' which lies at the heart of what I have called 'the language of neuromythology' (see Raymond Tallis, *On the Edge of Certainty*, London: Macmillan, 1999, especially the entries under 'Language (code)', 'Misplaced explicitness' and 'Representation (model)'. But I knew my resistance would crumble in the end.
5. J. F. Soechting, D. C. Tong and M. Flanders, 'Frames of reference in sensorimotor integration: position sense of the arm and hand', in *Hand and Brain*.
6. The notion of 'egocentric' coordinates and 'egocentric' space is an ambiguous one. I wish to use it in the Husserlian sense, captured by David Bell as follows:

> The living body, that is, functions as the absolute point about which all spatial relations are experienced as orientated. Phenomenologically, the space I inhabit and move about in, the space which characterises my perceptions and experiences, does not present itself to me as unorientated, uncentred, abstract

Euclidean space; rather spatiality is experienced in ways which call for description in egocentric terms: things are near me or far away, above me or below, facing me or facing away, to the right or to the left, moving with respect to me, receding perspectivally towards the horizon, and so forth. But regardless of how much objects may change their spatial positions, and regardless, too, of how much I might change mine, 'a firm zero of orientation persists, so to speak, as an absolute *Here*'. The living body is always 'the middle point of a surrounding world', it is necessarily the geometrical centre, the *Nullpunkt* of orientated, egocentric space. (David Bell, *Husserl*, London: Routledge, 1990)

The notion is used differently by some physiologists. M. A. Goodale and colleagues ('Vision for perception and prehension', in *Hand and Brain*) speak of an egocentric space that is 'viewer-centred' – which roughly corresponds to the Husserlian notion; but also of 'egocentric coordinates' which may be variously 'retinocentric, head-centred, or shoulder-centred'. This locates the zero point not in the self, or the conscious I, but in a part of the body. This ambiguity is important because it suggests that the *de facto* position of certain bodily parts – retina, head, shoulder – at or near the centre of the sensory or sensorimotor field automatically translates into 'zero of orientation'. Fascinatingly, however, is that the objective centre does not provide the underpinning for, or legitimise, the subjective centre; rather that it – the eye, the head, the shoulder – gets stipulated as centre at the same time as it is utilised as such. This kind of mysterious 'bootstrapping' seems to be the heart of agency, which conjures as well as utilises egocentric coordinates.

7. In order to avoid complicating the discussion too much, I have omitted another element essential to the sense of the position of the object in relation to the reaching hand/arm/body/person; namely the sense of the position of my hand or arm in themselves. I return to the hand's self-awareness in section 4.3. Suffice it to mention here that I cannot know where my hand lies in relation to the object, and hence determine the reaching task to be executed, without having immediate knowledge of where my hand is: the hand must continually mutter its presence to itself through all sorts of intrinsic talk (muscle proprioceptors) and extrinsic experience – the warmth and pressure of surfaces upon which it sits, etc. Patients who have severe loss of proprioception without actual weakness, may have extreme difficulty initiating actions, even pseudo-paralysis, for this reason. (There are, of course, visual cues; but I do not have continually to keep my arm and hand in view in order for them to be ready for deployment in reaching, etc.)

8. My main source here is C. Ghez, S. Cooper and J. Martin, 'Kinematic and dynamic factors in the coordination of prehension movements', in *Hand and Brain*.

9. This and the next few paragraphs are effectively indeed are a paraphrase of David A. Rosenbaum, G. J. Ruud Meulenbroek and Jonathan Vaughan, 'Three approaches to the degrees of freedom problem', in ibid.

10. Paulette van Vliet, 'An Investigation of Reaching Movements following Stroke' unpublished PhD thesis, University of Nottingham, 1998.

11. Goodale et al. put the different challenges facing the two systems rather elegantly:

Action systems do most of their work on-line; perceptual systems do most of their work off-line ... while similar (but not identical) visual information about object size, shape, local orientation, and location is available to both systems, the transformational algorithms that apply to these inputs are uniquely tailored to the function of each system. (*Hand and Brain*, p. 26)

The existence of two separate visual pathways for perception and prehension become more fascinating the more one thinks about it. It is difficult to know how firmly established the two pathways with their different functions are. (Mapping these kinds of distinctions onto anatomically discrete parts of the brain is always a little vulnerable to semantic fashion.) That there is a ventral stream permitting the formation of ideas about the enduring characteristics of objects and their spatial relations to one another and a dorsal stream utilising instantaneous object features organised within egocentric frames of reference, mediating goal-directed activity; that the ventral stream presents objects as they are in themselves – and draws on an understanding acquired over time – while the dorsal stream presents objects as they are in relation to me and my immediate needs. The coexistence of these two streams of information enables one simultaneously to relate the world of objects to oneself and one's needs and, at the same time, to acknowledge the objective reality of objects. By having these two streams, it is possible to bring the object within the sphere of oneself and one's needs while, by not subordinating them in this way, avoiding the danger of magic thinking or even a kind of egocentric philosophical idealism. It allows the ready-to-hand to coexist with the present-at-hand, the object-in-relation-to-me and the object as independent material presence, to coexist in the same object. The dissociation, seen in some patients with highly localised lesions, between recognising objects (agnosia) – seeing them as they are in themselves and thus their possible use – and difficulty in reaching out for them (optic ataxia) – seeing them as they relate to me – suggests that this twin 'take' on objects is a reality. Patients with this problem can direct their eyes; so it is not global spatial problem; rather a more specific problem of utilising spatial knowledge to support spatially dependent goal-directed behaviour.

12. This experiment is reported in Neil Smith, *Chomsky: Ideas and Ideals* (Cambridge: Cambridge University Press, 1999), p. 19.

13. I would not wish it to be thought that I believe that the role of the arm is always subordinate to that of the hand; that it exists only to 'serve up' the hand, as a chauffeur to transport it to the places where the hand gets on with the serious and difficult business. There are actions where the arm is the protagonist and the hand a (relatively) dumb terminal – as in fending off, throwing and punching. But just as, even here, the hand is not entirely dumb; so, even in fine manipulative – fingertip – actions, the arm retains a central role. Without exquisite postural control of, and emanating from, the arm, threading a needle, for example, would be impossible. And although it is natural to postulate a hierarchy – the body stabilises the arm; the arm transports and stabilises the hand; the hand working as whole hand directs and stabilises the fingers; the unengaged fingers stabilise engaged ones – this example in a sense makes the opposite point. Namely, that every action engages the whole body: stability of truncal posture, the location of the arm, the angle of the hand, etc. – all of these constitute the enabling setting that makes fine manipulations possible.

14. *Hand and Brain*, p. 504.

15. R. Liston, J. Mickleborough, B. Faragher and R. C. Tallis, 'A pilot study supporting a new classification of higher-level gait disorders in patients with cerebral multi-infarct states', *Age and Ageing* (in press).

16. See, for example, R. Liston and R. C. Tallis, 'Higher-level gait disorders in cerebral multi-infarct states', in *Parkinson's Disease and Parkinsonism in the Elderly*, edited by Jolyon Meara and William C. Koller (Cambridge: Cambridge University Press, 2000), pp. 99–110.

CHAPTER 3

The Talking Hand

Let us for moment direct our attention to the seemingly insignificant parts, the arm and the hand, and their capacity for language and signifying ... What rich movements, what expressiveness there is in the hand. The hand over the forehead shows ... pain and worry, deliberation and reflection; it shades the shyness of the eyes; brought to the mouth it signifies silence, to the bosom protestation, proud self-esteem, heartfelt affection. Pleasure and malicious delight clap their hands, desperation wrings them, reverence folds them.

Hence, as a famous writer says about the pantomimic expressions of the hands, that by them we can desire, promise, summon, reject, threaten, pray, plead, refuse, ask, admire, confess, fear; by them display shyness, doubt, indignation, flattery, agreement, delight, empathy, wrath, desperation and admiration; in short, all the emotions that spring up in our bosom.

Johan Ludvig Runeberg[1]

3.1 INTRODUCTION: THE SIGN-MAKING ANIMAL

The hand manipulates and so shapes the physical world; the hand explores and thereby comes to know the world – for its own sake, sometimes, but usually to manipulate it better; and, finally, the hand communicates and by this means discovers another sphere – that of fellow humans – and another mode of manipulation – by means of signs.

The human hand is free to talk, to act as an agent of friendly and hostile, of intimate and formal, sociability, because for bipedal man, uniquely among the vertebrates, the upper limb is not otherwise engaged in locomotion.[2] The emancipated hand is often idle and available to serve new purposes: bipedal man can walk and wave at the same time. Because bipedal man is upright and walks tall, his hand is also more visible: if its signals carry further than those of other species, it is because it can stand on the shoulders – well not of giants, but of the erect human body. Moreover, the fellow creatures to which handspeak is addressed have, because of their upright posture, an increased range of vision – another reason why gestures speak so loud.

Bipedalism alone is not sufficient to explain the complex communicative function of the hand. Something more is required: the ability we have already noted to make larger differences out of smaller differences. In this, as in other respects, the making much of differences is the distinctive human faculty. We shall begin by examining this faculty – which itself may or may not be one of the multifarious consequences of handiness – before looking at the complex, multiple, communicative functions of the hand.

At the heart of the matter is another important and deeply mysterious ability, unique to *Homo sapiens*: namely, the capacity to turn happenings and actions into signs – and into signs of signs. We use our bodies and parts of them, and the things they do, as signs not only of those bodies, or of bodily parts or actions, but as metonyms or icons of other actions or of actions and events related causally to them. Precisely because we shall in due course be exposed to a profusion of manual examples, let me illustrate these processes with few non-manual examples.

The special feature of the human gait is not merely that it is bipedal, or that it is continuously as opposed to intermittently bipedal, but also that it takes the form of striding. At each stride, the arm opposite to the forward leg, the swing leg, swings forward to compensate for the twist of the trunk. The twist of the pelvis is more marked in women than in men. Since women also have broader hips and more bodily fat over the buttocks and hips, the difference in twist is augmented. As Napier observes,[3] 'this sexual difference has been exploited in our culture so that the undulating swing of the female hips and buttocks has become a potent visual signal in many civilizations'. It metonymically signals the female body, and, by further extension, femaleness, or the female body taken in its sexuality. That is just the beginning: by standing for femaleness, it can also be used by a female to signify sexual availability; by a male to mock, through stereotyping, femininity, in shared jokes with male friends. In this context, it is used to signify the putative mindlessness of the female who can be identified with her bodily characteristics; to signify not merely femaleness but effeminacy; and, through the gait seen as 'mincing', men, construed as effeminate, such as homosexuals and transvestites; and, finally, adopted as a means by which gay men may signal to, and make fun of, each other and themselves. A long pilgrimage for a small difference in gait.

Another example is coughing. This involuntary action is triggered by the need to clear the airways. The threshold for coughing, however, is lower when one is anxious. Coughing therefore comes to be secondarily associated with nervousness. For this reason, it can be used to signify anxiety or nervousness in situations – such as in the theatre – where this state of mind is to be portrayed. Because it is an involuntary action, and a noisy one, it may also betray the cougher's presence when she wishes to remain concealed. Equally, it may be used deliberately to draw attention to oneself and to 'say' 'Here I am!' – in short, to indicate one's presence. This deliberate or artificial cough is an iconic sign (a sign that, like a picture, physically resembles that which it signifies) of a true cough which is itself an indexical sign or metonym of 'one who coughs' or of 'the presence of one who coughs'. The story does not end here: artificial coughs may be used to signify the umbrage of someone who feels overlooked – 'I am here. Have you forgotten me?' – both in reality or in the theatre, where it may indicate, metonymically, someone who is always overlooked or whose views are overlooked or whose feelings are being trampled. As an added layer of complexity, the sign may in turn be used to signify a poor actor who resorts to stereotyped ways of indicating a certain sort of character: the theatrical cough may be intended to signal a thespian cliché and hence 'amateur dramatics'. A long and twisted tale.

There are many other ways in which we can use bodily parts or functions to signal themselves or more than themselves or something other than themselves. The exposed buttock, the flashed penis, the patted belly, the protruded tongue, the shrugged shoulders – the list is endless. The bodily surface most densely populated with signs and gestures is, of course, the face, where the piercing stare, the pouted lip, the bared teeth, the wrinkled nose, the smiling lips and many other expressions of emotions felt, and emotions and other responses signalled, are subject to a thousand modulations. The hand, however, is special; it combines the exquisite control that the face commands with the distance from the sensed locus of the person of more distal parts of the body: my face is inseparable from myself (though I may deliberately utilise it, as when I adopt a facial expression to give a certain impression, or when, like Mr Verhovensky in *The Devils*, I practise my smiles in the mirror) whereas my hand is at a slight distance from myself. The face most naturally expresses emotion and only secondarily is used to signal emotion (or some other reaction); the hand, which is visible, as the face usually is not, to the person making the facial gestures, is therefore especially suited to make deliberate signals and meta-signals. It also, of course, has greater visibility and, as in the waving hand, can draw attention to itself.

The hand's expressiveness may be less subtle and varied than that of the face, but its expressiveness is more explicit: hand gestures more clearly use a bodily part deliberately to signal something.

The gestural capabilities of the hand reflect the very special relationship we have to that organ; in particular those characteristics, which we shall discuss later, that have made of it the tool of tools, and our relationship with it instrumental. In the hand we have woken up out of and to our own bodies to be able to use them deliberately – and this includes our expropriation of them deliberately to signify. The range of gestures is limitless and I will choose only a handful – such as waving and insults. I will subject clapping to a more sustained examination, as it is a rather strange activity and used for a curious combination of quite different purposes. The hand may also communicate through its appearance. I will therefore consider, without going too deeply into the matter, what makes a hand beautiful or ugly, and stumble into the complex world of manicure and Nailomania.

Throughout this random walk, I want to keep in view the peculiar and fundamental facts: that we humans turn activities into signs and turn those signs into signs of signs – almost *ad infinitum*; that we use our bodies and parts of them as active signs; and that we indulge in the activity of deliberate meta-signification, so that we not only make what happens – and, more importantly, what we do – signify but also make it meta-signify.[4]

The many-layeredness of the complexity of the deliberate employment of our own bodies to signify is eloquently illustrated in the evolution of the meaning of the word 'gesture'.[5] Gesture orginally meant 'the manner of carrying the body, bearing, carriage, deportment (more fully, gesture of the body)'. The notion of carriage is crucial: gesture is connected with gestation, the carrying of an unborn infant. We not only live our bodies but we also carry them, as a mother carries a child – just as, uniquely among living creatures, we not only live our lives but also lead them. This is interwoven with the remarkable idea that one's external appearance, far from being a mere consequence of the body-engaged-in-action, can be used to signify itself – the body, the action, the body-in-action – and then something more than itself. I bend down to tie my shoelaces. Thinking that someone may wonder what I am doing, I italicise or caricature the action to dispel ambiguity. Or: I tie my shoelaces, and the action symbolises my tidiness or my taking trouble to be tidy. Gesture then came to signify 'the employment of bodily movements, attitudes, expression of countence, as a means of giving effect to oratory'. Finally, it settled on its present meaning, which has a wider reference but is more bodily localised: 'A movement expressive of thought or feeling'. The transition from bodily carriage – unconscious and/or mandatory and involving the entire body – to signifying gesture – deliberate and essentially, as opposed to accidentally, signifying and mobilising only a portion of the body – is an extraordinary leap, and one whose completion is reflected in the passage from gesture as noun to gesture as verb.

For reasons that we shall examine in due course, the hand had more than a hand in this.

3.2 GESTURING

The range of gestures is limitless; they are as innumerable as the hairs on the back of a werewolf's hand and, although there is some standard-isation, there is huge variation in the ways in which a particular gesture may be realised: there are (famously) national preferences, dialects, stylistic variations adopted by groups (sometimes to indicate group membership) and idiolects. Since I shall examine only a few out of many thousands of gestures and my choice is arbitrary, I would like to be able to say that the few gestures I have chosen have been singled out because they illustrate some fundamental principles, and therefore stand for an entire class of gestures, but this would not be true. For I am unaware of any such underlying principles and I suspect that there is none. When bipedalism liberated the hand from the endless business of locomotion, the work the Devil found for these newly idle organs was characterised by free creativity. If there is an enduring principle informing the creation of gestures, it is anarchy.

According to C. S. Peirce's much adopted classification, signs may be: iconic, signifying through their resemblance to the significate (as in a picture); indexical, signifying through causal relationship with the signi-ficate (as when clouds signify rain); and symbolic, signifying not by virtue of their properties but through a rule or convention (as in the case of 'arbitrary' signs of natural language such as English). Gestures do not have to be iconic (though they may be), nor indexical (though they may be) and, even where they are symbolic, like linguistic signs, they do not have to interact in a systematic way with other gestures in the way that linguistic signs do with other linguistic signs. Language, said Hughlings Jackson, is not just a 'heap' of separate words; it is at least in part systematic and many words have sense only as part of the system (for example, 'the', 'or', etc.). By contrast, the language of manual gestures is a sign heap!

Here, then, are a few entries snatched at random from the Manual of Manualese that is currently written only on the air – a few handfuls of gestures, mere gesture towards gestures.[6] The message I wish to convey is not about underlying principles but about richness. A richness that stems from the anti-principle of 'anything goes'. While there may be short runs of what linguists call 'motivation', in which the signs are transparently what they mean and they spawn transparent derivatives, the equivalent of grammatical or systematic motivation, amenable to anything like an '-emic' (see below), is not to be found. The lack of any intrinsic organising principle to be captured in a classificatory system, along with the need to impose some kind of order on what follows, has dictated the initially arbitrary but now naturalised principle of alphabetical order, borrowed from the second-order sign system of written language.[7]

Air-punching

Many gestures are a business of the whole arm rather than the hand alone – air-punching gestures above all. Air-punching seeks maximum visibility: it is designed to speak to wide-open, densely populated spaces. It asserts the simplest form of solidarity, which may be shallow and provisional or tap into the deepest strata of communal feeling: membership of a crowd. The air-punching delight of the home crowd is directed at the abjection of the away crowd whose team has conceded a goal, the match, the trophy: kiss my arse, eat my shorts.

It invites others to join in – rejoice with me – and acceptance is not entirely optional; for arms end in fists. The arm wants to become part of a forest of arms, so that each arm-holder is enlarged to a crowd, each partakes of the collective power. It coerces a response: if you are not rejoicing with me, like me concussing the air with a powered fist, then you are against me. My triumph is your defeat; our victory is your nemesis. Meanwhile, our raised arms show that we shall go upwards and onwards. In the air-punching delight of the drunken football crowd, the political party taking to the streets, in the air-slicing salutes of the Fascist rally – where political parties are militarised and the military politicised – the hand is fully armed.

Beckoning

Beckoning may be written in Ulverscoft Large or in lower-case micrographia: the entire arm reaches out and pulls itself inward to the body; or the elbow extends and flexes; or the fingers curl and uncurl; or (in the finest print) the index wiggles its distal phalanx. Throughout the differences in scale, some things remain unchanged: nothing is reached, nothing is touched, but something is gathered in, something less than, and more than, the empty air that beckoning does not even try to harvest: namely, the distances between me-here and you-there, which are crossed and folded up. Come here, pay attention to me, do not stray mentally or physically, be with me, be part of me.

There are so many tones of beckoning. The impatient: 'Come on! Where have you been? Can't you see me, you idiot? Hurry up!' – expressed in rapid, high-frequency, whole-arm movements. The friendly: 'Do join in. You are welcome. Think of yourself as one of us' – captured in the relatively smaller-scale movements, perhaps only of the distal part of the arm and the hands. The seductive: 'Come here, my darlink' – with the little finger, moving perhaps a little more sinuously than it is accustomed to – disambiguated, if ambiguities remain, by the nodding head.

Since we are not engaged in establishing a science or pseudo-science of paralinguistic phenomena, it is worth admitting that the correlation between tones of beckoning and scale of the movements deployed is a rather loose one. Think of the schoolmaster beckoning the erring student to the front of the class. How much controlled anger, or sadistic delight, or power lust or simple fed-upness can be packed into that index finger oscillating with sinister deliberation at a relatively leisurely frequency, supported by the fixed stare at the target and a slow head-nodding that answers by pre-emptive strike the 'Who? Me, sir? Out to the front of the class? Why? Why me?' questions implicit in the target's protesting surprise as he walks towards the reckoning at the proximal end, the originary source, of the beckoning.

Blessing

In order to bless people, at least two conditions have to be fulfilled: you have to make the right movements with your hands; and you have to be the right person – someone who has been ordained to act on God's behalf. (Whether the blessees are then actually blessed depends upon their state of mind, their life history, etc. The felicity conditions for the performative of blessing are, in other words, very complex.) One such person is the Pope and I once saw him on television being driven in his bullet-proof Popemobile (a necessary precaution because his blessings are not always received with gratitude) blessing a huge crowd lining the streets of a poverty-sticken African township. The crowd looked largely malnourished and had clearly been standing in the hot sun for some while.[8] The disconnection between his blessing and any actual blessings likely to flow from it made the physical character of the act rather visible. He looked like a mad conductor conducting the cheers.

We shall return to conducting presently. For the present, let us remind ourselves what blessing is and what it involves. The road from its origins to the Pope's gesturing is long and winding: its history is one with many cunning passages. In its initial meaning, to bless was 'to make "sacred" or "holy" with blood; to consecrate by some sacrificial rite which was held to render a thing inviolable from the profane use of men and the evil influence of men or demons' (*Oxford English Dictionary*). This cluster of notions antedates by far the Pope and his religion; if we are to believe the anthropologists, it reaches through many layers of the collective human consciousness to the blood sacrifices associated with hunting.[9] At any rate, the purpose of blessing was to make something sacred, consecrated or 'hallow'. Fortunately, the association between smearing with blood and blessing was broken: the Pope might have found it messy, not to say dangerous, to pour buckets of blood over the crowd that lined his route, and a Popemobile equipped with water cannon charged with blood might not have conveyed the right impression of dignity. Blessing could be enacted less bloodily by 'the utterance of a formula or charm'. By a series of further steps, the effect of the formula or charm could be achieved by making what is called 'the Sign of the Cross'. We need to examine these steps in order to understand how humanity arrives at being blessed by a celestial conductor in a Popemobile.

The act of blessing takes the form of making the Sign of the Cross in the air. This sign, by a happy coincidence, is isomorphous with the membership of the Top Table in heaven: the cross has three visible points and these correspond to the number of the members of the Trinity. At the top (or the Top) is God the Father, on the right hand of God is God the Son, and on the left hand is the Holy Ghost. By writing the Cross – or the sign of it – in the air above the crowd, it is apparently possible to shower them with the beneficence and holiness that emanates from the Trinity. (And it doesn't matter how crudely the cross is signed.) This is wonderful: one can bless on an epidemiological scale and so do for the general spiritual health of the nation what public health measures aim to do for their physical health.

But how complex the gesture is! It is rooted, first of all, in the fathomless concept of the sacred and in the notion of Special Entities in whom, because they are imbued with this sacredness, the Truth and Ultimate Meaning of the world lie. (Truth and Ultimate Meaning are identical with presence, where the presence is a Real Presence.[10]) Secondly, it relies on the notion of an individual – the Pope – specially qualified to disseminate this sacredness: His Holiness can broadcast Their Holiness.

Thirdly, there is the notion that that Holiness may take up residence in the Cross upon which one of these Special Entities was supposed to have been crucified. Next, there is the lucky – or slightly contrived – coincidence by which the points of the Cross may be seen to stand for these Special Entities. Then there is the belief that pointing to these points, or iconically signifying the Cross by tracing a path between its points in the air, will invoke the Cross, and hence the Special Entities and their powers, regarded (in the teeth of much evidence to the contrary) on these occasions as overwhelmingly beneficent. There is the final notion that, as a result of a Special Someone making this sign, those who fall within the ill-defined sector of the space it gathers up, within its catchment area, the space towards which the gesture is directed, will be blessed.

From blood to ritual sign, from holiness in general to holiness embodied in the Cross, from Powers in the Sky to deities skewered on the tips of a cross, from the iconic sign of the Cross to the Cross – this is indeed a long journey.

The Speaking Hand draws meaning from the depths of the collective human consciousness.

Conducting

The conductor of the orchestra, seen through incomprehending eyes, would look like a madman, blessing all he sees: Nietzsche in Turin self-pinioned on euphoria above the awaiting abyss. Seen through comprehending eyes, his gestures seem comparatively straightforward. Above all, the conductor beats time: he puts the passage of time in italics and by this means tightens the connection between the passage of notes and something even more elusive than they – the passage of the moments. The upward and downward movement of his bare hand or baton-wielding hand creates a visible equivalent of the clock's tick-tock. He synchronises the inner watches of the members of the orchestra, so that those notes that should sound together do sound together and those that should sound in sequence do sound in sequence.

Now, the representation of time in rhythmic hand movements seems motivated in the semiologist's sense of a sign that is naturally connected with its significate. The conductor does with his hands what the rest of us, following rather than driving the orchestra, do with our feet and heads or, if we are mindful of annoying our neighbours, inwardly. His brachial oscillations are like the tos and fros of a pendulum and similar to many other repeated, rhythmic movements, representations of time series whose inter-event intervals are equal: the bobbing of things on the waves, for example; and the movements associated with the very instruments producing the notes. So we are insufficiently impressed by the transformation of time into space, by the representation of time by back-and-forth, up-and-down, side-to-side.

We should be more impressed, of course. What other creature takes hold of the fundamental rhythmicity of the universe (which encompasses its own body) and 1) makes it visible in gestures such as rhythmically waving hands; 2) uses that rhythmicity to give itself collective pleasure; and 3) perfects the expression of that rhythmicity by means of an iconic expression of the required rhythm? One could go on …

The conductor does more than beat time, of course. He also regulates loudness. He places his finger to his lips when he wants piano rather than forte, or pushes his flattened hand further and further down, as if he were stuffing the sound back into a suitcase. Or he assumes his full height in a terrifying constrained inner leap, raising his baton like a weapon, as he commands the orchestra to (as the saying goes) 'release all its forces' and permits the held-back cataclysm to burst through the walls of silence. He gestures to sections of the orchestra, requisitioning them one by one, as if he were pulling levers. He points to soloists, as if he were pressing buttons. He caresses the music, he cups it between his hands, as if it were a delicate flower he was about to smell, a glass of wine whose bouquet he is drawing through his Roman nose, or the breasts of the mistress we know that he must have awaiting him back-stage. His eyes, his hair, his stance, his flying coat-tails all place his gestures, his signals, in upper-case bold. At the climax of the climax, he swoops from the height of his height, like a hawk at stoop, and the music that was borne under his hands falls on its sword, skewered by the rapier of his baton.

And now it is the audience's turn to use their hands. They must show their appreciation 'in the usual way'. The conductor's hands, however, have not yet finished their work. He makes one final gesture: as if he were lifting them up, he brings the orchestra to its collective feet where it collectively basks in a new rhythm, bathing in the downpour of sound that signals their success.

Fist-shaking

The arm is self-armed, for it has powers within itself to destroy as well as to create: it has coiled-up strength and it ends in a hand that in its dimmest, angriest, stubbornest, blindest mode forms a fist. Arm-powered, the fist is strong enough to smash the ribs, to crush the face, to put out the mind forever. The tightly curled, compressed hand – self-dusted with congenital knuckles, whitened as the skin stretched over them is exsanguinated, the fingers bunched in a laager of self-protection – is stone-hard. A punch is no mere gesture. It is the cash value of a thousand other gestures, gold ingots to the paper currency of a thousand menaces.

So it must be used sparingly. The punch must be threatened more often than it is used. Hence even the closed fist – the dimmest posture of the hand – may ascend to the higher-level gestural mode and a quite high level of self-consciousness. We shake our fists at those we threaten and at those whom we would like to threaten, using the image of the action, or of the organ that would enact the action, to instil fear. The raised fist is a warning, a standing performative whose perlocutionary force is to frighten or frighten off: 'Keep your distance', 'Stop looking at my woman', 'Pay up', 'Don't cross me ever again'. And so on.

The hand cannot help being intelligent, even in its least intelligent mode. The raised fist, which is initially the iconic sign of the act of punching – a virtual punch at right angles to the line joining the puncher to the punchee, threatening a real one along the axis between the one body and the other – can in turn become a sign of itself and so be quite formalised. I, who have never punched anyone in anger since early childhood, may imagine myself using a standard issue fist-shake to indicate my displeasure with someone suitably non-aggressive whom I perceive as beyond the reach of intelligent persuasive speech and out of whose range I am. The fist as icon was used by at least one political party threatening to bring down the old order and a closed-fist, airborne salute – synchronised, orchestrated air-punching at rallies – was the time-honoured signal of political and other crowds.

It gets even more complicated. We may cite the closed fist as a sign of other things – abstract notions such as that of aggressive proletarians, for example. Some writers have famously shaken their fists at the sky and hence at the god who is supposed to be inhabiting it. Did not Edmund Gosse once ask the fatalistic Thomas Hardy why he thought it right to raise his hand from the pleasant Wessex lands and shake his fist at God?

Hand-gun

Since we are talking about the hand as an instrument of violence, and, more particularly, its symbolic representations, we may as well talk about other weapons.

Between the ages of six and twelve, I rarely left the house, or indeed my bed, without being armed to the teeth.[11] When I found myself without hardware, I was still not entirely naked: I could mobilise the zero degree or ur-gun: my hand. My index and middle finger formed the barrel; the rest of my hand, with my thumb crossed over my half-flexed ring and little fingers formed the remainder. I was then at liberty to shoot to my heart's content, puffs of air through the saliva in my mouth creating the sound of gunfire. Equipped in this minimalist fashion – without even a cowboy hat or a waistcoat or a sheriff's badge – I felt no less the 'Cisco Kid than when I had the full regalia, a heavy Colt 45 and ten boxes of 100 caps and each shot – the bursting of a little papule of explosive that looked like a vaculitic lesion – was accompanied by the wonderful scent of detonated gunpowder.

Most relevant, perhaps, to our main purpose is the fact that the hand-gun served me so well, despite having little visual resemblance to the real thing. There were, however, some abstract correspondences. For example, there was a tendentious isomorphism between, on the one hand, the butt and main of the gun and the barrel, and, on the other, the main of my hands and my two fingers. This was, however, far from a replica. The barrel was nearest to realism, though even here there were serious deviations. While the hand-gun, like a real gun, was plausibly twin-barrelled, the two barrels in the case of the gun were side-by-side and in the case of the hand-gun, one on top of the other.

I labour this small point because it opens on to a larger principle, one that Erich Gombrich explored in his *Meditations on a Hobby Horse*: that our artefacts, particularly those used in play (and possibly in art), stand proxy for objects in the real world not because they look like them, in the literal sense of replicating their putative visual appearance, but in virtue of evoking them by means of crucial but scattered points of similarity – such as are seen between a hobby horse and a horse.[12] That was why I could live out the life of the 'Cisco Kid with such little supporting material; without even knowing (and I don't know even now) what ''Cisco' meant. More widely, our gestures, although they seem more analogue than digital, have only a distant iconic relationship, if any, to the things they signify, though, in the wonderful unravelling of the complex surfaces of human manuality, they may acquire all sorts of secondary iconicities (and indexicalities) as they pile layer upon accreted layer of signification.

Just a brief adult coda to my childish hand-gun experiences. I was talking to someone in my office once and my secretary unexpectedly pointed an imaginary gun at me. It appeared that I had put my foot in it and to quite some depth as she was normally highly respectful. I was shocked and angry at being charged, convicted and sentenced to being chided in the same moment; it pulled me down to earth. This was the first time the imaginary gun had dealt real wounds.

Hand-wringing

Medical students are taught not only to pick up subtle, technical signs of illness, but also to look for more obvious, 'lay' signs – things that a concerned mother or attentive husband would notice and comment on. Such obvious signs of illness include the outward marks of inward distress. Among these is hand-wringing.[13] Video tutorials on the diagnosis of depression will pan away from the patient's tormented face with its tale of sleeplessness, loss of enjoyment, sense of unworthiness, delusions of incompetence, to the hands, which are seen to clasp one another tightly and rub against one another.

I begin with this extreme example of the despair associated with hand-wringing because it shows how this gesture, unlike many, is psychologically motivated as an action before it becomes formalised as a sign. The motivation seems to be as follows. When you are depressed, bereaved, intensely worried, the world seems a comfortless place. The only place of refuge is your own body and its living warmth. You want to hug yourself. People in an extremity of fear do precisely this: they cross their arms across their chest. In more chronic states, as in continuing anxiety or in depression, the self-hugging migrates distally, to the hands. Hand-wringing, then, is muted or displaced self-hugging: the body seeks comfort in itself through the solace each hand finds in the warmth and understanding and responsive companionship of the other.

Hand-wringing makes sense, therefore; so much so that it reinforces itself and becomes a highly stereotyped sign of anguish, sorrow, etc. As an effect of these emotions, it becomes an indexical sign of them, and, as we have noted, a diagnostic sign of chronic or abnormally pronounced and dysfunctional emotions. It is then available for representation as a gesture, to be used by actors enacting grief. It can also modulate into other, cognate gestures, as when the mutually wrung hands are raised in prayer, and mercy is begged from God, a secular superior, or from an adversary or assailant. Finally, it can be used metonymically to stand for much more abstract and remote kinds of upset, concern, worry: 'There was much hand-wringing in Government circles today over the failure to reach the target for reducing hospital waiting lists.' This hand-wringing is a long way from the lukewarm comfort of one hand hugging another in the extremity of anguish.[14]

High Five, The

'Give me five,' he says. And naturally you obey, for even middle-class white women and grandees in the shires now know what it means. This is a gesture that began in the underclass, and was a sign of solidarity among the disaffected, the marginalised, ethnic minorities. In a very few years, it has moved from the streets of Brixton to the drawing rooms of leafy Surrey.

Lest there is still a drawing room where its meaning has not yet penetrated, this is what a High Five is. The flattened hand – usually the right hand – of one person smacks the flat of the raised hand – also usually the right hand – of another. It may be a greeting, but it is usually a sign of shared delight when co-presence has already been established. This double aspect is reflected in its physical form which combines the manual contact of the hand-shake with the raised hand of the brachial shout of joy. The High Five shows that you are on the same side, because you delight in the same things, and because you want to share that delight. The forest of hands, which goes up when the wicket falls or the goal is scored, may pair off as A and B and B and C and C and A turn to smack with the flat of their raised hands (held in the coronal plane, by the way) the flat of the other's raised hands: this is our triumph, mate.

The natural habitat of the High Five is in the sporting field where triumphs are immediate and clear cut as they are in few other places in life. It is most at home on the field in big, preferably televised, sporting events. Its truest home is on the cricket pitch, with the West Indies Test side: the mighty Curtly Ambrose co-smites with the mighty Courtney Walsh. High Fives are here affected by rampant inflation: both hands are deployed and four hands collide. The High Five gives place to the High Ten and the High Ten is repeated several times: High Twenty, High Thirty, and so on.

Although the High Five has made it to the drawing room, it is not entirely at home there. Here, it is not so much a sign of delight as a sign of a sign of delight; it is a sign that you are one with those who signify their delight in this way. It shows that you, too, are one of the lads.

National Variation

We speak with our vocal organs, but we converse with our entire bodies.[15]

If foreigners are funny, their gestures are even funnier. The funniness of foreigners' speech comes primarily from the fact that we cannot understand them; the funniness of their gestures comes from the fact that we can half-understand them. For although it would be quite wrong to claim that there is a universal language of gestures, their gestures are often the same as ours; what is different is the quantity, the style and the context. Gestures, in short, provide us with rich material for national stereotyping and useful fodder for nationalism – 'an inflamed state of national consciousness' (Isaiah Berlin).[16]

The Latin races – the French, the Italians – are, we North Europeans believe, gesticulacious. Their numerous, loud gestures contribute little to the sense of what they are saying, adding only emphasis; empty and uncontrolled, the gestures are just what one would expect of a nation that does not queue in crisis but panics; does not fight but runs to safety. And they suit the warm climate, a world where windows are open on to the street for much of the year and communal life is a spectacle. The gestural poverty of the Northern races, of the Anglo-Saxons and the Scandinavians, is equally fitting: their reined-in habitus corresponds to their secretive nature, to the stiffness that freezes their upper lips, to the impenetrable world of the buttock-clenched (or, to use Freudian technicality, tight-arsed, or purse-sphinctered) people of the cold and darkness. Fitting, too, for those who pass their lives in sealed-off rooms and venture out into the streets only on set-piece excursions. Life lived – or half-lived – in rooms does not require extravagant gestures: the mere flicker of a mouth surmounts the threshold of visibility.

None of the above is rooted in epidemiologically sound, demographically robust, population-based studies. Confirmatory bias can, therefore, reign unopposed: I see an Italian waving his arms, confirming that Italians wave their arms; I see an Italian not waving his arms and that will be one Italian I do not remember. Or, if I remember him, the stillness of his arms will not be part of the memory. Even if an epidemiological study of national variation in gesture were worth doing (it is not), the results would be soon out of date. Increasingly, I notice my friends and colleagues and chance acquaintances in the street using more and more paralinguistic support. I notice it in myself: more gestures as I lecture on the podium, for example. It is part of becoming a good European: gestural harmonisation.

Neapolitan Gesture (Unnamed)

Since we have crossed the Channel, let us stay there and reflect on a gesture that is said to have changed the history of philosophy. According to the legend, it was mobilised during a train conversation between the great philosopher Ludwig Wittgenstein and his favourite intellectual sparring partner, Piero Sraffa.[17] The story was told to Norman Malcolm by Wittgenstein himself and is reported in Malcolm's *Memoir*.[18]

The central idea of Wittgenstein's *Tractatus Logico-Philosophicus* was that propositions were in some sense pictures of the states of affairs they described. They were obviously not pictures in any straightforward sense: even a simple proposition describing a simple state of affairs – 'The cat is on the mat' – is not literally a picture. What Wittgenstein argued was that there was an identity of logical form between the proposition and the state of affairs. The proposition described the state of affairs in virtue of being a model of it, with a one-to-one correspondence between the elements of the described reality and the elements of the proposition.

This was a rather abstract, not to say vague, idea, but Wittgenstein adhered to it for over a decade – until his train journey with Sraffa:

> One day ... when Wittgenstein was insisting that a proposition and that which it describes must have the same 'logical form', the same 'logical multiplicity', Sraffa made a gesture, familiar to Neapolitans as meaning something like disgust or contempt, of brushing the underneath of his chin with an outward sweep of the fingertips of one hand. And he asked: 'What is the logical form of *that*?' Sraffa's example produced in Wittgenstein the feeling that there was an absurdity in the insistence that a proposition and what it describes must have the same "form"'. This broke the hold on him of the conception that a proposition must literally be a 'picture' of the reality it describes. (Malcolm, *Memoir*, p. 69)

If the legend is true – and we have only the chief actor's word for it – then this was a portentous gesture; for the collapse of the picture theory and of the representational theory of language opened the way to many of the most important notions in *Philosophical Investigations*, including the disastrous – and disastrously influential – notion of 'language games'.

Especially interesting for our present inquiry is the lack of correspondence between the physical form of the gesture and its meaning or, more broadly, its significance. Doubtless, the sweep under the chin is meant to indicate something disparaging about the maturity or masculinity of the insulted interlocuter; that, for example, he is beardless youth but, as is the case with the saluting we shall come to presently, this is not uppermost in the mind of those who use the sign, for whom it is purely conventional. The sign signifies without in any way looking like the thing it signifies; or being structurally related to it; or sharing a logical form with it. In this regard, it is similar to a linguistic sign. In another respect it most certainly is not.

As we have already noted, manual gestures are not components of systems. Attempts to systematise gestures – to develop kinesics[19] or an '-emic' analysis analogous to that of phonemes and morphemes – are doomed from the start. The meaning of linguistic signs is mediated through their value; their value – like that of the currency (to use

Saussure's analogy) – is derived from their position in the language system, from their oppositional relationship to one another. The meaning of individual gestures is established independently of any system. Gestures, by contrast, are anarchic. Very Neapolitan, in short.

'Only a Gesture'

Gestures carry the stigma of being not quite, well – not quite. They fall short in some unspecified but quite fundamental respect. As a result, describing something as 'a gesture' is not exactly to give it full endorsement. We may praise 'a nice gesture' (a surprise farewell party for retiree), 'a statesman-like gesture' (as in unlocking negotiations that have stalled on a vacuous matter of principle), 'a gesture of sympathy', but still think to ourselves, 'this is only a gesture'. And the word 'gesture' gets linked far too often with the word 'empty' for it to remain untainted with its associate's hollowness.

I won't dwell on this for fear of being judged obsessive. Suffice it to say that gestures can be fully paid-up actions, too. Riots triggered by hate speech and laws prohibiting certain kinds of 'free speech' demonstrate how speech is not just a stream of tokens: speaking is acting, speaking acts on the world, speaking changes things. If speech is an act, then so is gesture: it is a flesh act.

Prattle

Which is not to say that gestures are never empty, pointless, vacuous, superfluous, and so on. Far from supporting speech, they may distract from it. They may be irritating, particularly when the speech they accompany is the product of a rather slow-moving and not very disciplined mind or, even worse, is mended to the slow mind the recipient is assumed to have. Gestural prattle is a particular vice of painstaking and emphatic explainers: teachers, doctors, social workers, cultural critics, etc. There seem to be more gestural prattlers about since people learned to talk about 'communication' and the importance of it.

I shall never forget – or not anyway until I am either demented or dead – the spectacle on television of one such explainer. He was a Marxist art critic who came out with one clumping banality after another. He spoke these banalities slowly because, it seemed to me, he believed that they had depth, the true depth that only simplicity can fathom, and he felt that it would take time for his listeners to sink to the bottom of his aperçus: they had to be savoured, contemplated. This critic had also spent much time in Europe, so he was (to hark back for a second to national variation) very favourably disposed to gesticulation. At times, he shaped with his hands the air above the table at which he was sitting, as if he were giving his thoughts a last polish before putting them on display. Sometimes he moved his hands downwards in time with his own verbal emphases, to emphasise his emphasis. At other times, he raised, and slightly wagged, his index finger as his exposition struck moral, or moralistic, gold.[20] And so on and so forth. Throughout the half-hour long talk, his hands were never still: he was enjoying their eloquence, he could see the beauty in their communicative balletics. A pity he had nothing to communicate.

Precision

Let us return a little closer to the home key.[21] It will be recalled that the special properties of the opposable thumb had momentous consequences (which we have hardly begun to explore) for the evolution of humanity. Some degree of opposability of the thumb and the other fingers is found in non-human primates; what is unique in mankind is the degree of completeness with which the thumb can oppose the other fingers, especially the index finger, ensuring that the two fingers make maximum contact.

This opposition of thumb and index finger, which has huge significance for the development of human beings, is, as John Napier says, also a universal sign. It says: Bravo! Magic! Spot on! Success! How many of those who use it are unaware of its underlying significance and of how much of human culture rests on it. The sign is a kind of reverse metonymy – in which the whole, or something that stands at the source of the whole, is made to stand for a minute part.

Salute

This book is a long salute to the hand and to our nature as human beings. It would therefore be remiss not to say something about saluting.

There are many kinds of salutes and the notion of 'saluting' frays at the edges (as we reach back in linguistic time) into the broader notions of greeting and wishing good health and all sorts of signals of welcome, recognition and courtesy. Saluting, what's more, may have almost any kind of person, thing or notion as its intentional object. Awakening Christians, for example, are enjoined to salute the happy morn. To gain control over this huge topic, I want to focus on the most formally developed salute – the military salute.

We have already visited the more brutal military salutes – the air-

punching and air-slicing Fascist and other military-political salutes –
where the emphasis is hardly on courtesy or the sentiments of health.
We shall confine ourselves here to the conventional salute favoured in
countries where the army and the government have sufficient distance
for the notion that the army acts on behalf of the people and the nation
– even on behalf of The Greater World Good – rather than the government, to seem plausible.

Everybody knows what this salute looks like and has probably enacted
or playacted it themselves. It therefore probably requires no description,
except that describing it makes it, and its strangeness, visible. The right
arm is abducted at the shoulder and moves sideways in line with the
coronal plane of the body until it reaches the horizontal. It is at once
flexed at the elbow, so that the hand then approaches the temple – roughly
where my hand-gun (see above) would point when I playacted suicide.
The fingers and thumb are extended to the maximum and the hand,
whose palm and fingers are parallel to the coronal plane of the body, is
as flat as possible. The temple is touched briefly and then the hand is
brought straight down, by the shortest route, back to the initial position: the extended arm close to the body, all the digits flexed, with the
exception of the thumb, which points down by the seam of the trousers.

The entire sequence has to be performed with 'military precision' – in
accordance with a kind of magic thinking that thinks that the chaos and
unpredictability and vertiginous horror of battle can be fended off by
controlled deportment. The salute has therefore to seem geometrical
and rigid, machine-like rather than human, inorganic rather than flesh-
driven. And that is why, though simple, it has to be practised and
continuously angry regimental sergeant-majors can be driven to greater
heights of fury by poor quality salutes. The opportunities for error are
increased as saluters are grouped together and have to act in synchrony.
The command 'Saaaa...lute!' has therefore two differently designed
components: an initial warning syllable that is sufficiently prolonged to
capture the attention of the most dilatory soldier and gives him time to
ready himself for response; and a second syllable that triggers the action,
which is sufficiently short to ensure synchronicity of response within the
perceptual resolution of the most keen-eyed and critical observer.
Nothing is more dispiriting or bodes more depressingly than a scattered
shower of arms raised like a broken Mexican wave and followed by a
succession of asynchronous thigh slaps. Gestures may be arbitrary signs
in the sense that linguists mean when they use the term; but they are also
conventional; so arbitrariness does not mean 'anyhow' is OK; and the
convention has to be adhered to.

The salute salutes the institution, recognises the authority that underpins it and affirms the authority of those within it. When a junior passes a senior, the junior salutes first, confirming his junior rank and the senior replies in kind, confirming his seniority. Mutual saluting is an enactment of the asymmetry: I am beholden to you and you are not beholden to me, though we are both beholden to the institution that underwrites the relative junior rank I suffer and the relative seniority you enjoy. In accordance with this asymmetry, a junior's salute has to be smart and attentive; the senior's can be more relaxed, rounder at the edges, slangy, more personal, dimmed with preoccupation with other things.

By this means a massive, complex hierarchy is reinforced: salutes are little tacks helping to keep it all in place. And even these little tacks have to be used sparingly. A soldier cannot salute every time he encounters a senior; for if, as is often the case, he is with seniors all the time, he could find himself permanently saluting and consequently disabled by a form of partial motor status epilepticus: *status salutandis*. So saluting has to be confined to first and last encounters, or to exits and entrances – when the senior person enters and leaves the junior's presence. The necessary definitions in a crowded barracks where all ranks are mixed together are complex but soon learnt.

So much for the extraordinary significance of this extraordinary act. Where did it get its form from? I can remember when I first learned this, and discovered in passing that seemingly natural signs had conventional and rather vulnerable origins. According to the etymological legend, the salute was derived from the habit of knights who acknowledged their ladies by shading their eyes against the radiance of their female beauty, as if they were protecting their eyes from the sun. How complex this is! There is first of all the metaphor of beauty as a form of radiant light and the conceit that this light – emitted rather than merely reflected – might dazzle the eye. Once the metaphors are established, it is possible to be literal-minded or to exhibit the concrete thinking of the schizophrenic. This permits the use of the natural action of protecting the eyes from the sun as a sign of protecting the eyes from the metaphorical radiance. The next step is to extract and abstract from this sign of adoration and desire the objective respect implicit in it, so that it could then be generalised to superior beings of all sorts. The final step is to narrow the range of superior beings whom it would be appropriate to salute: one's military superiors.[22]

The exact route by which saluting (which seems to have international currency) journeyed from Camelot to Aldershot is uncertain. For all I know, the supposed starting point may be apocryphal – and the story mere folk etymology.[23] If it is true, however, it should make Americo-

phobic characters (such as my schoolboy self) pause when judging the
US army version of the salute. This American salute tends to have lower
definition, its flight path is closer to the body and the plane of the flat of
the hand nearer to the horizontal. The return also has a less disciplined
trajectory. The whole affair seems more casual, less geometrical. To my
1950s self it was one with the gum-chewing sloppiness that characterised a nation that, as our English teacher said, used 'will' where 'shall'
would have been grammatically correct and where everyone was on
first-name terms with everyone else. It was far too democratic: the
sloppy salute, insufficiently differentiated from civilian greetings, seemed
to fulfil all De Tocqueville's gloomy prognostications about the long-
term outcome of democracy in America. By approximating the round-
edness of the officer's more casual response to his non-commissioned
subordinate's salute, the American salute reflected a flattening of
hierarchical gradients. At best it was a workmanlike salute that forgot
that it was supposed to be a tack helping to hold together the mighty
pyramid of social relations.

Against this hostile interpretation, the folk etymology may suggest
that the US version, far from being a corruption of the original and so a
sign of decay, is closer to the origins – to the eye-shading that a flattened
palm aligned with the coronal plane of the body, with its middle finger
touching the temples, could not have possibly given. The 'sloppy',
'democratic' American salute is in fact more authentic, like music played
on period instruments.

Spoken Gestures

'I was tearing my hair out in lumps' I am often insufficiently surprised to
hear myself say. It is not just that I am almost bald so I have no hair to
tear out, least of all in such generous portions. It is also because this is a
gesture, like not a few others, that is frequently spoken of but rarely if
ever enacted. Presumably there have been instances of individuals
whose rage was so intolerable that they would turn to self-destruction,
perhaps as a counter-irritation (as when one rubs a painful leg) or
perhaps symbolically to bruise themselves an exit from the world. Their
example was then so compelling that they became a paradigm of the
manner of expressing the emotion in question. Most of us are a little
more self-controlled and prudent: we no more tear out our hair in lumps
than we bite the carpet;[24] but even for us, the gesture has a use: it can
symbolise extreme emotion and signify its extremity. Allusion to the
action, along with the suggestion that one was minded to perform it,
would be sufficient.

All of that makes sense. So why am I surprised to hear myself using the expression? My baldness is not an issue because the purely verbal status of the action – a verbal gesture towards a manual one – is established. Perhaps it is because one might expect that, without refreshment at the fount of the first order – the occasional, first-hand example, of someone in an acute depilatory rage – the verbal gesture would lose its symbolic force.

Not necessarily. After all, we don't take seriously everything we say. And too easy reference to gestures doesn't destroy them completely. Spoken gestures remind us how often we exaggerate in our everyday talk. And why shouldn't we? It is fun; language is a tool not only for communication but also for self-expression and play. And so is the talking hand.

V (Outspoken Gestures)

As every schoolboy (and girl) truly knows, there are two kinds of V sign: the one is a signal of victory and the other is loved and abhorred as a 'filthy' sign. They are both of immense interest.

The V for Victory sign is, in Britain, inescapably associated with the end of the Second World War in Europe, with the famous, emblematic celebrations on 6 May 1945, in particular in London, and with the person of Sir Winston Churchill. Even if we confine the scope of our reflections to that occasion, the sign remains a complex one. The Victory V sign is an iconic sign of the written form of the initial letter of a non-iconic, indeed, arbitrary, linguistic sign. It is thus four steps away from the abstract concept that it signifies:

$$\text{Victory} \longrightarrow \underset{\text{(spoken word)}}{\text{'Victory'}} \longrightarrow \underset{\substack{\text{(written representation} \\ \text{of spoken word)}}}{\text{VICTORY}} \longrightarrow \text{V} \longrightarrow \text{V sign}$$

This long and winding path enjoyed secondary reinforcements. The BBC call-sign used throughout the war to cheer everyone up was made up of the opening four notes of Beethoven's Fifth Symphony. These, fortuitously, corresponded to the morse code for the letter V: three short notes and one long one were translated into three dots and a dash. Beethoven's Fifth was also his Vth. It all hung together, so long as one assumed that Beethoven was more of a decent chap than a patriotic German, a citizen of the world on the side of humanity rather than a rabid Hun, and that he would be rooting for an Allied rather than an Axis victory. (The evidence – his hostility to the self-emperorisation of

Napoleon, the impeccable sentiments in *Fidelio* – is reassuring on this count.)

The association of the Victory V sign with Churchill carries additional resonance, drawing on that special moment at the end of the war in Europe. The smiling, rather mischievous, slightly dishevelled, 'indomitable' figure with a cigar and an alcoholic flush, was a mighty metonym of the spirit of the nation he had led. This was true dignity, a dignity that allows itself a little deshabillé, as opposed to the iron pomp of the humourless Boche. That, at least, is the story.

I note, as a small afterthought, that the V hand could have created a shadowgraph of a long-eared rabbit. This is only to delay the next agenda item: 'filthy V'. The connection between the two V's is reinforced by a scurrilous claim made by a schoolmate – he was the form clown and spent most of his time joking and had therefore to have two goes to get into medical school – in the late 1950s. According to J. F. (I shall withhold his full name as he is now a well-established doctor of considerable means), Churchill was so drunk that he confused his V's and instead of celebrating Victory went round inadvertently telling the crowd – and through the newsreels that filmed his victory salute – the world to fuck off. J. F. spent an hour or more making me laugh at his 'Confused Churchill' sketch in which the portly, grey-haired, overcoated, bowler-hatted, leader staggered around the classroom, shouting 'V for Victory' while he made the 'filthy V' sign. The last two minutes of this performance were observed by the form master who at last invited J. F. to come to the front of the class (see 'Beckoning' above). It is a remarkable thought that the similarity between the two signs should have exercised so many schoolboys in the 1950s. Perhaps it was the harbinger of the rebellions to come.

Of course, they are not as similar as J. F.'s ectopic cabaret required. The abusive hand often lies on its back rather than standing upright – except when the abuse is particularly vehement. Secondly, filthy V tends to be more mobile than V for Victory. Its motion can vary from long, languid, sinuous, jeering V, to vicious V that rapidly stabs the air, with all stations in between; and the angle between the fingers can vary from 30 degrees to, as in the stabbing V, nothing at all. There are also 'whispered' or 'murmured' V signs that consist of the signer simply rubbing his parted fingers against his face; or, while furtively looking around for authority figures, wiggling a low-held pair of fingers, pointed in the direction of the recipient.

Still, the confusion was a good story and it kept many a schoolboy going. So, too, was the claim that the V stood for vagina, which, when I first learned of this as a twelve-year-old, was about as filthy a word as you could get. The origin of filthy V is, if one believes the standard story, however, comparatively innocent – if, that is, one accepts that violent death is a rather more acceptable ancestor than the female genital tract.

The story goes as follows. In the Hundred Years' War, the longbowmen were particularly feared: their arrows went faster, further and were more likely to be on target; the massed bowmen created a terrifying shower of Hell from the sky. Drawing back the string and keeping the arrow's flight snugly against the drawn string, required a special grip – a three-jaw chuck (see section 7.3) in which the thumb was opposed to the index and middle fingers. An efficient way of putting a bowman out of action once he was captured – and certainly cheaper than holding him prisoner and having to feed and keep guard on him – was to chop off either the index finger or the middle finger, or preferably both. The captive could then be safely returned to his own side, for his career as a bowman was at an end. This prompted the tradition by which undamaged bowmen, who could continue to send Hell raining from the sky, used to mock their enemies by exhibiting their intact index and middle fingers. It then became a general sign of mockery and contempt: the filthy V sign, the letterless V sign created by the unlettered yeoman of England, who were England's best hope for – Victory.

The V sign has certainly outgrown the innocence – or at least the sexlessness – of its origin. It is certainly very rude now and the translation into 'fuck off' seems precise. It is good for a laugh and creates a *frisson* of delight in certain settings. These settings are becoming fewer and have now to be quite high up on the Vicarage Tea Party scale. A few years ago – before even mothers collecting children from school would V sign lorry drivers and other men who would ogle or patronise them, or cut them up or steal their parking space – the catchment area of shock was much wider. Tony Harrison, an excessively self-conscious and not very talented poet who prides himself on his outspoken Northern bluntness and his proletarian roots, published a volume called *V*. Although *V* has justly been described as 'a poetry of painful simplifications of history, culture and politics',[25] it brings this entry nicely to a close; for, being a child like myself for whom Churchill's V was the great icon, he links the two V's by tracing the journey from that V for Victory to Margaret Thatcher's 'Fuck off'.[26]

Waving

It is appropriate that we should end this section with waving. Waving, however, has many meanings. Yes, we wave goodbye. But we also wave hello. And we wave to draw attention to ourselves – 'Here I am!' – with its implicit beckoning. (I refrain from beckoning because I believe that identifying my presence will be enough to draw the other to me – such is the natural attractiveness that I have or, more likely, such are the conventions.) And we wave people to go 'over there' – though this waving modulates into pointing (of which more in section 6.2).

It would be nice to end on a note of transparency, with a natural sign that is self-evidently what it means. But even here, we shall encounter complexity on which we have already supped full. The fact that waving means so many different things – hello, goodbye, here I am, over there – indicates quite clearly that its relationship to any one of its meanings must be conventional, rather than iconically or causally motivated. This is reinforced by the fact that its manifestations show a good deal of variation, between countries, regions, genders, personality types, situations. Italian girls, for example, are typically shown waving farewell by synchronous flexing of the five fingers of the half-elevated hand. (The number of data, n, upon which I base this observation = 1.)[27] This is entirely different from my own whole-hand, broad sweep, window-cleaning wave (least self-conscious when I am waving off a child). Even the same person, waving in the same circumstance, may show gross variation in her style of waving; as when, for example, the waved-at recedes; then the waving changes frequency and amplitude and the interval between on and off periods gets longer, seeming itself to symbolise the increasing intermittence of the communications – phone calls, letters, e-mails – in the separation to come.[28]

Even granting that waves cannot be an entirely natural, transparent sign – since waving may be used to express many meanings and there are wide variations in the way it is performed – surely (it will be argued) there are some invariants, some natural elements, that will be universally present. The one invariant that is conserved is the elevation of the arm and the engagement of the hand (or at least part of it – remember the 'ciaou-ing' Italian girl) in rhythmic movement. Both the elevation and the rhythmic movement increase the visibility of the body: the person uses a part of the body to draw attention to the body as a whole. We may dance up and down to attract the attention of someone whom we are meeting, when they are far away or we or they or both of us are in crowd. The energy of our delight (or anguish) may be harnessed to making the hand-writing (or arm-writing) larger. The natural invariant, or inner essence, of waving is revealed when it is used in a life-threatening situation. The waver who is drowning or is drawing another's attention to great danger strips the waving of 'ciaou' boutiquery and concentrates on visibility: maximum movement and maximum altitude.

The wave may be rendered more potent as an attention-attractor with attachments: the handkerchief, the pullover, the stick add to altitude and movement. The implement adds an extra joint to the wrist and so an additional degree of freedom, more novelty and consequently greater penetration of the recipient's consciousness. The traditional association between the handkerchief and waves of farewell prior to prolonged separation arises because the handkerchief can serve two functions: amplifying the size of the wave (so that it may be visible for longer and from further); and dealing with the flow of tears and even mucus that the recession of the loved one from personal presence to the impersonal world may prompt.

Other invariants in waving, conserved across many local dialects and idiolects, prompt reflection on the interplay between nature and convention in the development of gestures. Hands have to be moved in waving to draw attention to the organism, because moving stimuli are more likely to attract attention; the sensory system all the way to the cerebral cortex responds more to changing stimuli, and movement is, of course, the primordial manifestation of change.

This gesture, whose characteristics are motivated by (sensory) physiology, is then available for being transformed and conventionalised: a physiologically natural signs evolves into a semiotically arbitrary one. So we get a new direction opening up: the birth of arbitrariness and all that follows from that. Gestures, unlike linguistic signs, still have one foot in indexicality or iconicity and have a toehold in physiologically defined naturalness. This gives them a doubleness: a gesture that is motivated with respect to one frame of reference becomes arbitrary with respect to another. This, perhaps, may sharpen the kind of bodily self-consciousness and wider wakefulness that we have already connected with the function of the hand and which we shall explore in due course.

The wave – both hail and farewell – takes us to the end of our random walk around a few arbitrarily chosen exhibits in the world of The Talking Hand and back to our founding intuition – the special role of the hand in the awakening of the human animal, in the creation of the possibility of culture and history lifted out of the evolution of the animal kingdom. We should be waving flags.

3.3 CLAPPING AND OTHER HAND SHOUTING

Sometimes The Talking Hand shouts. The commonest form of hand-shouting is called clapping. In accordance with one of the fundamental principles of hand-speak – that of making a little go a long way by using the same action for different purposes – clapping may be used to transmit many different meanings.

Single or arrhythmic claps may serve variety of functions; for example, to draw attention to oneself: 'Here I am!' This in turn may have any of a variety of consequential functions; for example, to warn off or frighten away some other sentient creature: 'Here I am. Watch out [you crows/foxes, etc.]. Lay off [my crops/chickens, etc.].' Or to capture the attention of another or other(s): 'Quiet now, please'; 'Listen up you people'; 'I think we ought to start. It is my great pleasure to introduce.' Clapping, at the least, is not an empty gesture: as linguistic philosophers (after J. L. Austin) would say, it has perlocutionary as well as illocutionary and locutionary forces. At any rate, as a pre-propositional signal of a presence (and even misleading, indexical sign of an even greater presence, or the presence of something greater or more frightening than oneself), it is a primitive utterance.

Clapping is one of the many ways in which the left hand engages in dialogue with the right hand. This one is a little different from those we shall examine in section 4.2 for it is not private: it is a dialogue that exists to be heard or overheard. The other dialogues are largely silent and they are about self-presence, not presence to others. The public nature of clapping is underlined in collective clapping as in musical, ritualistic or applausive clapping.

Clapping is primitive music; as in the clapping that accompanies the dance, the wooden clappers that have been manufactured to make sound, since ancient times, and even the clapping that breaks out when revivalist meetings are struck by lightnings of hope and delight and delusion. It is a rhythmic, non-referential utterance, a minimally organised sound created for delight and self-transformation.

The communal nature of clapping is asserted in its rhythmicality, through which crowds aspire to synchronicity. In the religious rite this binds the celebrants together[29] as each, through the separate actions that are assimilated into the collective sound, is himself or herself taken up into the collective. Outside of religious ritual, the collective sound may be enjoyed for itself, as a primitive form of music, supporting the dance, combing the tangled souls of the participants into the perfections of rhythmic succession, with all their foregone conclusions, with a form that binds what has just happened to what will happen next, entraining the consciousness of the dancers into a delicious, active–passive daze, in which each willingly succumbs to a collective rhythm that belongs to everyone and to no one in particular. In this daze, the dancers lose themselves and the limitations that constrain them: as the everyone/no one, each is immortal.

This is the very opposite of individual *Da-sein*'s authentic being before death, where each faces the terminus that is his or hers alone.[30]

Which may be why some feel queasy at the notion of religious services that involve much clapping, especially when the clapping is located not in a sunbaked desert town but in a suburban, redbrick church. The injunction to children to sing 'If you're happy and you know it clap your hands' links happiness and clappiness in a form of religious participation that is then described as 'happy-clappy' where demotic speech routs the cadences of the King James' Version of the Bible and cheering oneself up in dark times has priority over apprehensions of the Inscrutable Greatness of God.

Even so, it is sobering (even to the undrunk) to reflect how potent is the voice of the Talking Hand when, in this way, it unites in chorus with other talking hands! Primitive music, primitive utterance, primitive prayer: more reminders of how the genius of our hands lies near, or at, the source of our distinctive human nature. Even in polite society, far from those places where bare feet kick up dust in the unmetalled villages of the world, the ritual of clapping can still inspire, as when we pool our manual shouting to 'to show our appreciation in the usual way'.

Take the big classical concert. After the perfect sounds, there is the thinnest wafer of silence. It takes courage and confidence to be the one to break it. But somebody does. And the applause breaks, controlled catastrophe. After the supreme expression of human virtuosity – 'That wonderful violinist. And he looks so young, too!' – the shortest of pauses is followed by the crudest of all manualisations; after the most brilliant of discourses, the simplest of all utterances. The noise of clapping – a fat-dropped downpour on a thin roof – in our ears is an acoustic violation; a phenol gargle after the finest claret.

Why do we choose this way of expressing our delight – so violently at odds with the music? Does it not have to be brutally simple precisely because – just as in the ritual dance – we wish to assert our collectivity and thus our collective approval? Clapping is a dance of the upper limbs and has to be easy, so we can all say the same thing in chorus: clapping in unison, we clap in step. When we break step, the clapping starts to fade and the outliers sound like the after-splashes falling from the gutters and the trees after the downpour has ceased. Not for the present: we are in full collective hand-cry. In the chorus of hands, we become one and can say: 'We approve!' Not 'I approve!' or 'I+I+I+I, etc. approve!' The approval is intersubjective and, therefore, nearly objective. The approval is official. Even the separate 'Bravos' and the footstamping are predicated on the ground bass of the collective clap.

We signal our approbation, our admiration to ourselves (and thereby we say we are part of this collective, this collective event) but we also signal it to the others, who wish also to signal their approval to

ourselves. The audience's clapping, addressed forwards to the per-
formers, is also addressed sideways to itself. 'We' are placed in italics,
fellow communicants at the great occasion, whose less organised buzz
of excitement afterwards confirms that we were *there, then*. And the
duration and intensity of the applause calibrate the greatness of the
occasion. And so – we owe it to the occasion and to ourselves who want
reassurance that those expensive tickets were justified – the applause
continues and we continue it; and, though we pace ourselves, our palms
sting and our arms ache.

Not everyone, of course, is so naively enthusiastic. There are those
who contribute to the applause without, as it were, pitching into it. And
this is reflected in clapping style. The naive clapper will adopt a clapping
style where both hands contribute equally to the percussive sound that
is produced – amplified by the air trapped between the palms – and their
equally hard-worked hands will collide in the mid-point. The more
reflective applauder, however, will hold one hand steady and pat it with
the other. Beyond naive and reflective clapping, there is, of course, ironic
clapping, where the action is signified – often by light patting of one
hand on the other – rather than performed and the sound produced is
minimal. 'I suppose one ought to applaud. After all the pets expect it
and they did their best.' Or distracted clapping, as one talks to one's
partner, with a slight, fixed smile on one's face, 'Let's get moving and be
at the front of the queue in the bar/cloakroom/car park.' Clapping may
be muted and distorted because one hand is holding the programme, or
the clapper wants to preserve her delicate hands.

In short, this simple act of applausive clapping may express a
staggering range of human social awareness from a putative primitive,
collective consciousness, to the most atomised of individuality, from
aboriginal to Augustan *mentalités*.

And that is not the end of the matter. Clapping that passes judgement
on what has been seen or heard may not always be favourable. Ironic
clapping may degenerate into sarcastic clapping. The most incompetent
performance may be disportionately praised, the disproportion intending to highlight the incompetence. Clapping itself may be modulated to
show displeasure: the applause is thin[31] and short-lived. The audience
rummages for coats under seats just when they should be devoted to
showing their appreciation 'in the usual way'.

Most hurtful of all is the slow hand-clap. This is a motivated sign, in
the technical semiotic sense already noted. What motivates it is the
assumption that the more pleased and excited people are, the faster the
rhythm of their clapping: four beats per second is twice as pleased as
two beats per second. Slow hand-clapping – perhaps as slow as 0.5 bps

– is very clearly not excited or pleased. The clapping, sinister like the slowed beat of a dying heart, shouts dispraise.

Our clapping hands, however, usually praise: they express our delight in nature, in our own bodies, in the talents of our fellow men. Clapping is in some respects secular prayer. But, as in the ritual dance, clapping may be addressed to God; and not only collectively. The clapped hands have only to pause and we have the posture of stilled pleasure, and stilled awe and arrested fear. If they unfold from mutual clasping to long-fingered elegance, we have prayer: 'Two hands fold into one, a gesture meant to carry man into the great oneness.'[32] Or the arrested moment of entranced delight as we press our hands together, paused on the systole of clapping, and with shining Hollywood eyes, look upwards at the object of our adoration or the spectacle that amazes us.

Clapping characteristically involves two hands. Hence the force of the irritating question: 'What is the sound of one hand clapping?' The question – which brings to mind complacent spiritual teachers, asymmetrical acolyte–initiate relationships, and all the occidentalist flapdoodle of wisdom hailing from one point of the compass and the bores who profess or regurgitate it – is not as wise as it sounds. If clapping encompasses using the hand to generate sounds of praise, then the sound of one hand clapping is the sound of a hand rhythmically thumping a handy percussive surface: the electively or involuntarily one-handed are able to bang on the table. If this is to extend the definition too widely, then the question is stupid – though not as stupid as those who recite it as evidence of their own enigmatic wisdom.

This uncomfortable digression is, however, a reminder that the hands can produce other sounds than clapping. The entire hand may drum and thus overcome communication problems in the jungle where intervisibility is limited by the luxuriant growth of exotic plants. Separate fingers may also drum. This may amount to mere digital wittering or it may involuntarily signify, or be used deliberately to signify, the impatience with which the drumming is traditionally associated – innocently, ironically or mimetically. Finger-drumming may also produce satisfying sound effects, such as the galloping of horses, where a triple rhythm is executed by the combined activity of the index, middle and ring fingers while the thumb and the little finger look on in admiration. Two hands drumming in this way may invoke an entire dust-cloud-raising herd fleeing before bush fires or rustlers. The single hand may in turn be used to tap out the 'gallop' rhythm heard when a stethoscope is applied to the chest of a patient in the early stages of heart failure for the instruction of medical students.

A different kind of drumming is heard in poetic metre. The name of one kind of metre, the dactyl, is inspired by digital anatomy. The dactyl is a metrical foot composed of one long and two short syllables – for example 'swimmingly' or 'Longfellow' – a waltz-sequence that seems to be analogous with that of the phalanges of the fingers. Apart from the notion of finger-like (metrical) foot, the comparison between the duration of the sounds (or the intensity of their stress) of words and the distances between interphalangeal joints is wonderfully fanciful and cross-modal. Dactylomancy perhaps.

There is also a two-digit call – finger-snapping – which serves a variety of communicative functions. Characteristically, it is used to summon flunkeys and others whom one wants to put in their place by underlining their flunkeyness. It is not always calculatedly discourteous: it may be innocently egocentric, ignorant and autocratic. In less hierarchical times, and in more democratic societies, individuals working in service industries do not see themselves as servants and they are consequently liable to respond to the two snapped fingers with (literally or metaphorically) two other fingers, silent but no less eloquent, of their own (see section 3.2).

I can still recall the pleasure I felt as a ten-year-old at acquiring the art of moving my thumb over my middle finger in such way as to produce an audible and decisive snap – a sound quite different from the feeble whisperings of one finger moving over the other. Since I could already ride a bicycle and swim, I felt justified in considering my portfolio of talents to be complete. Finger-snapping was a desirable skill in the late 1950s because it was associated with pop music. The lead singer's snapping kept the rhythm, and signalled the start of the piece. Snapping, in consequence, signified the snapper as one who was both confidently in charge on the stage and, at the same time, so inward with the rhythm that he could achieve a specially desirable state called being 'sent'. Closed-eyed finger-snapping was an established metonym of the kind of individual most young people fantasised themselves as being: a pop singer. Closing the eyes served the double purpose of excluding sensory information that might be counter to one's fantasy and of indicating one's 'sent' state. (Being 'sent' was the 1950s' relatively innocent predecessor to the 1960s' being 'stoned'.)

Not long after I learnt to finger-snap, I found another way of making my hands talk. By gripping them palm to palm and squeezing out the trapped air, I was able to produce farting sound. This carried none of the immemorial resonance of clapping, nor even the up-to-the-minute glamour of finger-snapping, but it gave me a certain amount of pleasure. Now, forty years later, it reminds me how many ways the hand has of speaking, how many complex routes there are from the hand's movements to the final, often multi-layered, meaning it intends. I think this deserves a round of applause. Perhaps you would like to join with me and show your appreciation in the usual way.[33]

3.4 HANDSOME

The hand may be at rest and silent and yet still eloquent, speaking through the beauty of its structure. All hands are beautiful, but some are more beautiful than others.

Saying what it is that makes a hand beautiful is no easier than saying what it is that makes a face beautiful. Or what makes a cat beautiful. Or a sky beautiful. In all cases, while beauty may seem to lie on the surface, that surface is beautiful because it signifies something other than itself. Consider an obviously structural feature: why are long-fingered hands beautiful? One could imagine that they appeal because they could caress more effectively (see section 5.1); but that is not the case: caressing takes place at the fingertips and these have the same surface area, irrespective of the length of the fingers they terminate; and the amplitude of the caress depends on the movement of the arm, not the length of the fingers. Perhaps it is because long fingers are analogous to long legs and these are attractive for all sorts of reasons. This seems, to say the least, tendentious. As well as being long, beautiful fingers taper and have oval rather than square endings. Why? Is it because this makes them look longer? Beautiful fingers have manicured nails: these are long and sharply parabolic. The fingers they adorn are made to look longer and more tapered ... We are going round in circles.

Perhaps we shall make better progress if we look past the structure to something that it signifies – the person, the life, the world. Beautiful hands are often idle hands. The delicate, smooth skin on the dorsum, the long, unbroken nails, the soft palms, are markers of social position. The sons (and daughters) of toil are horny-handed – the friction of the heavy material world with which they grapple prompting proliferation of the protective stratum corneum; their fingers are scarred with the accidents of manual labour; their nails are broken, or pre-emptively cut short. Their gnarled[34] digits may – if their owners inhabit the pages of novel – lead one to anticipate a regional dialect; one that, in a rural setting such as Wessex, will make a tangled hedgerow out of speech, and a dialogue burdened with a spindrift of apostrophes signifying all the ways in which accent falls short of Received Pronunciation, which is the non-regional norm to which the awakened once aspired. All of this is true; but the perfect hand is a less reliable marker of a consumer who does not produce, of membership of the leisured classes, now that production is less of an ordeal of power or even of manual precision and work is less liable to leave scars and cause hypertrophy of the stratum corneum, since working hands more often manipulate information than manipulate matter and energy. The beautiful hand is no longer reliable as a sign of leisured wealth.

We may look past the surface not to what people don't do, or elect not to do, or are spared from doing, because of, say, the privilege of wealth, to what they do do. Can one not fancy that a hand is beautiful because of what is done with it, because of the skills coiled up in it? Look, say, at a surgeon's hands and find them beautiful because of the courage, the compassion, the dexterity and manual nous exercised through them. Look at a mother's hands and see the soothing, the kindness, the care in them. (All that stroking of fevered or fretted or frightened foreheads!) I think not. I cannot help noticing that the surgeon's hands are not beautiful. That the mother's hands are red from all that washing and washing up. Two of my favourite pianists have hands that I have described to myself as 'podgy'. Their hands looked neither wondrously skilful nor tuneful – simply podgy. There is a total dissociation between the physical appearance of the hand and the soul of the hand-owner.[35]

And yet we do believe, somehow, that the appearance of the hand reveals something about the life. Kant's assertion – one of the central premises of this book – that 'the hand is the window on to the mind', referred to the general faculties of human hands and what they tell us about the general capabilities of the human race, not to the specific characteristics of individuals. Even so, the hand seems to stand for the life, for the world, for the inner person, of its owner. Even the temperature of the hand has been taken to signify the man or woman within: cold hands, warm heart. This may be physiologically true – blood being diverted from the skin in cold environments to reduce heat loss and so maintain core and *coeur* temperature – but it carries little empirical weight when applied to the psychological heart. Nevertheless, a hand may stand for a world – the more so the less beautiful it is, the more marked it is by the accidents of a life of caring, toiling, striving. Like Van Gogh's painting of a peasant woman's shoes, as discussed by Heidegger,[36] they may, if contemplated in the right spirit, reveal a world; this master tool, the hand that makes the ready-to-hand handy, may be an index of the nexus of things and preoccupations that fill the life, an accumulated record of lived time.

Heidegger certainly believed in the significance of the appearance of hands. When Karl Jaspers, whose wife was Jewish, challenged Heidegger – at their disastrous last meeting before the war – about his support for

Hitler and asked him how 'a man as coarse as Hitler could govern Germany', Heidegger replied ('in all seriousness'), 'Culture is of no importance. Just look at his marvellous hands.'[37] A glance at the numerous pictures in Ian Kershaw's biography[38] shows nothing remarkable about Hitler's hands at rest, though they may have been more impressive when gesticulating during his public and private harangues or when saluting himself as the personification of the glorious future of his nation. I note only that he had quite swollen dorsal veins which would have made them easy to access for intravenous infusions and may suggest something about the temperature of the heart.

There is a double dissociation between the beauty of the hands and the beauty of the person within. Not only may the euchiral be vile but the kakachiral may be inwardly quite beautiful. In support of this, I provide another datum. One of the most sweet-natured people I know is a woman who has rheumatoid arthritis. Her hands are horribly mangled. The aphorism 'handsome' (and the connection between this term and hands is multiple and close) 'is as handsome does' applies, it seems, even more to hands than it does to faces.

I cannot end on sober note. Beauty in hands is not to be trusted as a guide to inner beauty, but it remains beautiful. So let us return to think about an aspect of chiral beauty that no one mistakes for an index of inner grace: the beauty of the fingernails. Anyone can grow, shape and paint their nails: beautiful nails lie within the grasp of all. Only women, however, tend to reach out for them. Long, manicured nails signify aspects of womanliness that feminists have subjected to a merciless critique. They are seen as pathognomonic of a woman who is inactive (only idle hands can keep such nails pretty and unbroken); who is the object of male desire, rather than a subject in her own right; who is decorative, frivolous, disempowered, a plaything or playmate rather than a serious player in the world. She is a mysterious creature occupying a zone triangulated by various archetypes: 1) the occupant of the harem, whiling away her days eating sherbet, taking warm baths and prettifying herself in anticipation of her number coming up to occupy the sultan's bed; 2) the bloodsucking vamp, the destructive enchantress, who lures men, caught by their desires, to self-destruction; 3) and the prophetess/witch/crystal ball gazer occupying a temple, cave or in secular societies a fairground tent surrounded by duckboards on mud. Archetype 3 – the prophetess, etc. – may have uncut rather than manicured nails – she is busy with the occult and the things that seers see – and her nails may have collected grubbiness. But all of these types – whose characteristic mark on the male body is the scratch inflicted sometimes during intercourse – are, of course, remote from the

'Bugger! I've just broken my nail' typist fresh from her latest manicure.

But then Nailomania – which seems to have grown, rather than shrunk, with the rise of feminism, suggesting that nail-care is such fun that its political incorrectness should be ignored – is anyway wonderfully remote from the essence of nails and a tribute to the transforming power of human consciousness, especially when collectivised into human societies. Nails covering the dorsal surface of the fingertips are common to humans and primates. This additional feature improves manipulation; makes scratching more satisfying than it would be without nails and safer than it would be with claws; and, most importantly, protects those precious fingers as they explore and manipulate a world full of hostile encounters.

The nail corresponds to the claw, hoof or talon of other animals: nail is a little plate of modified horn. It grows upwards from the nail base, which is attached to, and gains nutrients from, the richly vascularised nail bed. The cells die as they lose touch with the nail bed and in the first phase of their death, they form the lunula, or little moon, near the nail base. Then they gradually migrate upwards as they are pushed on by the press of newcoming cells, living and freshly dead. The anaesthesia of the nails, like that of the hair, makes them especially amenable to being subordinated to aesthetic ends: to being pared, filed and painted and then inspected with satisfaction or despair.

We leave the hand at the nail, at the very tip of the fingertips, waving it farewell for the present, conscious that the nails will not miss us. After all, they fail to notice our death, and continue to grow for a while. The message from the sacked capital takes time to reach the furthest-flung provinces and the news of the death of the emperor whose welfare they have done their little bit to support is still travelling towards them as they busily extend from the tip of the dead hand.[39]

NOTES

1. Johan Ludvig Runeberg, 'On the plastic arts of the Greek'. Runeberg (1804–77) was Finland's national poet. I am enormously grateful to Professor Bo Pettersson of the University of Helsinki who drew my attention to this passage and translated it for me. The speech was first published in *Efterlamnade skriter* I (*Posthumous Works* I) and is here quoted from the manuscript of the critical edition of the collected works, whose volume of Runeberg's non-fiction prose is currently being edited by Ms Pia Forssell.

2. It might be objected that bipedalism is not unique to man. This is absolutely correct. What is unique about man is that he is continuously bipedal as opposed to having occasional bipedal episodes. (We shall return to this in the final chapter.) This is why it is so funny to think of dogs boxing and, as the phrase goes, 'trading punches'.

3. See John Napier, *The Roots of Mankind* (London: George Allen & Unwin, 1971), p. 163.

4. One of the few enduring legacies of French structuralism is to have made us aware how anything can be made into a sign and, in particular, how actions that are not originally signs can come to signify themselves. This was brought home to me the other day by something that I caught myself doing. (It is bit embarrassing, which is why I relegate it to a footnote.) I was urinating and I heard someone coming towards the toilet, which had a door that would not lock properly. I redirected the jet of urine away from the porcelain, where it was silent, to the water in the bowl, where it would make a noise, as a way of signifying to the oncomer that the toilet was occupied. Here, as so often, the incidental noises associated with the action are made to serve as an indexical sign of the action. Again and again, the structuralists – most notably Barthes in his structuralist phase – emphasised how actions may be turned in this way into signs. We open our umbrellas to protect us from the rain and so umbrellas come to signify rain – or, more abstractly, prudence and foresight.

   The strengths and weaknesses, the insights and the blindness, of the structuralist reduction of the human world to a nexus of signs are illustrated by Barthes' semi-popular *Mythologies* (selected and translated from the French by Annette Lavers, London: Paladin, 1973). The individual essays on the signs embedded in aspects of everyday life are often witty and perceptive; but Barthes' attempt, especially in his final essay, 'to analyse semiologically' the language of mass culture results in the kind of absurd, evidence-lean global generalisations and omniscient posturing to which he was prone throughout his writing career which made much of what he, and his fellow structuralists, difficult to take seriously. (See my 'Evidence-based and evidence-free generalisations', reprinted in *A Raymond Tallis Reader*, Basingstoke: Palgrave, 2000). There was also the problem of his tendency to give form (and the system of signs) priority over content and individual acts of signification. But that is a much bigger story, which I have discussed in many places, perhaps most usefully in Raymond Tallis, *Not Saussure* 2nd edn (London: Macmillan, 1995).

5. The definitions that follow are from *The Oxford English Dictionary*. According to David Levin, 'to gesture' also means 'to bear', 'to bring forth', 'to give birth' and 'to make appear'. 'Mudra as thinking: Developing our wisdom-of-being in gesture and movement', in *Heidegger and Asian Thought*, edited by G. Parted (Honolulu: University of Hawaii Press, 1987).

6. There will be one or two more gestures to come; for example, pointing.

7. The use of the alphabetical order for the entries, which do not have any intrinsic order, was prompted by re-reading of Barthes' part-wonderful, part-daft *A Lover's Discourse: Fragments*, translated by Richard Howard (New York: Hill and Wang, 1978).

8. For the full story, see 'Suffer, little children', in Raymond Tallis, *Fathers and Sons* (Newcastle: Iron Press, 1993).

9. See, for example, Dudley Young, *Origins of the Sacred: the Ecstasies of Love and War* (London: Little, Brown, 1992). This is discussed at some length in Raymond Tallis, *Enemies of Hope: a Critique of Contemporary Pessimism*, 2nd edn (London: Macmillan, 1999), especially 'The pathologisation of culture', passim.

10. See George Steiner, *Real Presences* (London: Faber, 1989).

11. Contrary to the teaching of psychologists, this has not made a violent psychopath of me; I remain the prudent physical coward I always was, though, since my adult life

has been pretty unphysical, my cowardice has not yet been put to the test. Psychologists should take note of the complex ways in which things are connected – and disconnected – in our lives and our individual and social consciousnesses, as these account of our 'simple' gestures perhaps illustrate.

12. Ernst Gombrich, *Meditations on a Hobby Horse* (London: Weidenfeld and Nicolson, 1963).

13. See also section 4 for a discussion of hand-rubbing.

14. A cousin of tormented hand-wringing is the hand-wringing of the obsequious. This combines the anguish of deference, of the desire at all costs to please, and a corresponding terror of displeasing, with the obeisance of the supplicant, whose hand is not quite raised in prayer. It is less closely connected with hand-rubbing, which we shall visit in section 4.2 when we consider the exquisite, subtle and wonderfully private dialogue of the left hand with the right.

15. D. Abercrombie, 'Paralanguage', *British Journal of Disorders of Communication* 3, 1968, pp. 55–9.

16. Isaiah Berlin 'The bent twig', in *The Crooked Timber of Humanity*, edited by Henry Harvey (London: Fontana, 1991), p. 245.

17. In the Preface to *Philosophical Investigations*, translated by G. E. M. Anscombe (Oxford: Blackwell, 1953), he pays tribute to the criticism 'which a teacher of this university, Mr. P. Sraffa, for many years practised on my thoughts', adding 'I am indebted to *this* stimulus for the most consequential ideas of this book', p. viii.

18. Norman Malcolm, *Ludwig Wittgenstein. A Memoir* (Oxford: Oxford University Press, 1958).

19. R. L. Birdwhistell, *Kinesics and Context* (London: Penguin, 1970).

20. See section 6.2 for the full loathing.

21. I owe this entry to the pregnant observations of John Napier in *The Roots of Man*. See p. 181.

22. Of course, there are all sorts of salute-like gestures used in civilian life to show respect: the raising or tipping of the hat; the tugging of the forelock as a substitute used (when hatlessness was relatively novel) by the hatless; and many other bodily gestures of deference, from standing up, head-bowing, to curtseying and, via salaaming, to total prostration.

23. It does seem to be the kind of thing that a pedantic uncle would tell a bored nephew. Now I may be that boring uncle except that there's nobody about – we are all too scattered and I am too preoccupied to teach my siblings' children anything. Fortunate generation of nephews whose uncles are too busy to bore them.

24. Hitler allegedly used literally to lie on the floor chewing the carpet when he was in a pet, which earned him the nickname 'Teppichfresser'. I owe this information to Ruth Willats (personal communication).

25. Michael Schmidt, *Lives of the Poets* (London: Weidenfeld and Nicolson, 1998), p. 894.

26. I cannot resist mentioning two other rude gestures I encountered when I was a doctor in Nigeria. The one consisted of exhibiting the five fingers of the hand by placing them as they would look after ball had been thrown. It came to signify 'you bastard' by the following path. In the Muslim area where I worked, men were allowed up to four wives. The five fingers represented five wives and the gesture translated as 'son of fifth wife'. (Fingers standing for wives is an interesting abstraction, which should cause Freudians some concern.) The other Nigerian gesture involved almost the opposite movement: the fingers were brought together

in a not quite closed five-jaw chuck, as they made sinuous palpating movements. This represented an exploratory procedure (see section 5.2) of very special kind and, by this means, was made to signify: 'I feel your mother's breasts!' The language of manual insults seems almost as rich and is certainly as complex and indirect as the language of verbal insults.

27. Ruth Willats (personal communication) also has an interesting and plausible theory about the special wave of the Italian girl. Psychological studies show that men find 'babyish' girls more attractive, presumably because they are less threatening and more likely to be compliant. Most babies when they first learn to wave do so by flexing their fingers. The finger-flexed wave, which Mrs Willats has seen in other Barbie Doll females, and is not peculiar to Italian females, is an attempt to enhance their attractiveness.

28. For full account of this, see Raymond Tallis, 'Customary infidelity subsequent to departure', in *Fathers and Sons*.

29. And what, after all, does religion mean other than '*religio*' or binding – with the participants in the ritual being bound together through together being bound back to the common source of their separate lives, the deity?

30. See Raymond Tallis, *A Conversation with Martin Heidegger* (Basingstoke: Palgrave, 2001).

31. We talk about 'thin' applause when it is reluctant, but not about 'fat' applause when it is rapturous. Correspondingly, we describe an event as being 'thinly' but not as being 'fatly' attended. Presumably the thin applause at a fatly attended occasion reflects the fact that the attendees attended only thinly.

32. Martin Heidegger, *What is Called Thinking?* Lecture I, translated by Fred D. Wieck and J. Glenn Gray (New York: Harper & Row, 1968), p. 16.

33. Although it has nothing to do with the theme of this book, I cannot leave the present topic without pointing out that 'clapping' is quite unconnected with those illnesses one has 'dose' of. 'Clap', meaning gonorrhoea and friends, is probably derived from the Old Provençal term *clapier*, rabbit warren, which was used to refer to a house of prostitution. The history of words has 'many cunning passages'. I don't, however, think that there is any connection between *clapier* and bunny girls.

34. A gnarl is 'a knotty protuberance on a tree' (*OED*), but it has close cousinage with 'snarl' and 'gnaw'. Poverty and over-work do that to you.

35. The dissociation between physical appearance and character, personality, true nature, etc. has often been commented on with respect to other parts of the body, in particular the face. Here is one example chosen at random – from Patrick Hamilton's *Hangover Square* (London: Penguin, 1974):

> Netta Longdon thought of everything in a curiously dull, brutish way, and for the most part acted upon instinct. She was completely, indeed sinisterly, devoid of all those qualities which her face and body externally proclaimed her to have – pensiveness, grace, warmth, agility, beauty. (p. 124)

A rather vulgar exploration of the theme is to be found in Raymond Tallis's poem, 'The mind's construction', in *Fathers and Sons*.

36. See Martin Heidegger, 'The origins of the work of art', in *Basic Writings*, edited and translated by David Farell Krell (London: Routledge & Kegan Paul, 1978).

37. This exchange is reported in Elzbiet Ettinger, *Hannah Arendt. Martin Heidegger* (New Haven and London: Yale University Press, 1995), p. 48.

38. Ian Kershaw, *Hitler. Volume I 1889–1936 Hubris* (London: Viking, 1999).

39. As a doctor, I cannot resist pointing out that the hand is enormously informative,

laden with signs of disease. There are vast numbers of diagnostic signs crammed into the nails alone: clubbing – indicating diseases of the lung, the heart, the liver, the bowel, etc.; pitting of the nails in psoriasis; leuchonychia or white nails in protein malnutrition; splinter haemorrhages under the nails as in infective endocarditis; spoon-shaped nails of iron-deficiency anaemia. And that's just for starters.

CHAPTER 4

Hand Talking to Hand

4.1 MANUCAPTION

And brother clasps the hand of brother
Marching to the Promised Land.

The gesticulating hand talks to any- and everyone. It is an inescapable consequence of its reliance on visibility that it should be visible to one and all. My wave may be directed to you and you only, but everybody can see me waving. Indeed, I feel a little self-conscious as I wave you off; consequently, my waving becomes a bit of a performance. But the hand has other, more private, ways of communicating, mediated not by vision in a visible world common to all, but by touch. Since only what is touched experiences the touch, the hand may speak through touch directly, and exclusively, to hand. What speech, what new meanings, may emerge in silence, when hand meets hand, when this master manipulator, this explorer supreme, this peerless communicator, meets another like itself! The nearest you may come to holding the world in the palm of your hand is to hold the palm of another's hand in the palm of your own.

One person takes another's hand. The dictionary that grasps everything has a word even for this: manucaption. This single action – a distal, fractional hug; a part-embracing part-embrace – encompasses a multitude of sins and good deeds, a thousand silent speeches, dozens of different modes of togetherness: the first step towards violation, the small change of companionship, the last comfort as the abyss opens.

Manucaption begins with the child holding its parent's hand: for safety, for comfort, for guidance, for nothing at all – other than for being unselfconsciously together with an adult who has not yet been compared or judged. (They are not types those adults, but archetypes.)

The little hand lies in the large one; the sky-rise parent beams down on the low-rise, skipping child and all's right with the world. For a while, at any rate. Until the child wants to wander, to stray out of range, longs to be unseen. 'Take my hand!' – and the skipping and dancing drag on the parent's arm. Now, the hand is a tether: 'Do as you are told! Take my hand!'

Soon, the parental hand is an embarrassment, a social as well as a physical encumbrance. The once innocent child, innocent of its innocence, becomes aware of its childish state and finds it to be cringingly infantile, like crying and wet pants. The hand will still be grasped instinctively, for comfort, in moments of sorrow and terror. At the school gate, for example. Or at least for the first few years; though not in the years to come – not there, above all, where the manucaptive fears the jeer: 'Mummy's child.'

And then the hands unclasp and do not return. The parent, who sometimes felt tethered by the child she tethered – the child who went at her own pace and had an altitude problem, dragging down its sky-rise manucaptive to its own low-rise world – suddenly discovers herself to be free and, in her freedom, somewhat abandoned. The parent's emptied hand signifies a wider emptiness, a greater loss. The transparent, always visible child has become increasingly opaque and ever more intermittent in her visibility. The first age of manucaption ends, like the others, with letting go.

Several years barren of manucaption follow, until the beloved child metamorphoses into a lover daring to take or to receive the hand of an object of love – a hand that resists, or consents, or responds in an uninterpretable way that defeats palmistry. The return to manucaption is charged with carnal awareness. The hand, it is discovered, has a texture – a wonderful firmness, an unbelievable softness, a haptic lucency – that narrowcasts how different each is from the other. The imprisoned hand is a metonym for the other's body; the imprisoning hand a metonym for the other's self. And vice versa. She is a miracle, he is a mystery. Or vice versa. Manucaption discovers, or acts upon, the unexpected finding that some others are as deep as oneself. That they, too, are worlds rather than the litter of ordinary hours – except that, their depths being unknown, they are mysterious, miraculous, achingly desirable. The other's body, with its hidden places – behind the eyes, inside the clothes – signifies those depths. Unlike one's own body, or the generic body of the anatomy book or of the ordinary clothed passerby, it is thrillingly familiar–unfamiliar.

Manucaption, which sips that body by taking hold of its outrider, is also a declaration – with all the risks this carries. Fortunately, the act is ambiguous enough for tracks to be covered if necessary. The screwed-up resolve of the manucaptor may be gloved in casualness: the hand is taken as if distractedly, it is played with. Even if the game involves tracing the inner surfaces of the fingers to the pudendal web between a digital fork, this may just plausibly be construed as the extension of companionship rather than as an advance into a quite different territory.

A wide repertoire of responses is available to the recipient of this chiroromantic advance – usually, at first, a she – depending on whether manucaption is welcome or whether, on the contrary, it provokes terror and loathing, such that the pressure and warmth of the other's hand, its fleshly presence, is experienced as pre-invasion and the knowledge the manucaptor enjoys through her hand of her fleshly, different being is suffered as theft. The hand may be snatched away – 'I don't want you touching me!' – or quietly removed, a response that says 'I don't want you, but neither do I want to hurt you'. Or it is allowed to lie there inertly, the significance of the contact being denied by the hand's being disowned. The outrider is vacated and the owner retreats into Fortress Self, leaving the would-be prison-hand without a prisoner. Manuduction as the forerunner of seduction – *la ci darem la mano* – fails.[1] Under such circumstances, the manuductor finds those wonderful textures and warmths, which meant so much, reduced to mere physical properties, vacated like the Russian steppes before the Napoleonic advance. The warmth that mingles with his now means nothing because it is not addressed to anyone, specifically not to him.

Warmth, after all, is entirely impersonal and the transfer of heat from one body to another can take place without any significance at all, as when one person is accidentally pressed against another in a packed underground train. (This impersonality of bodily warmth was immensely reassuring to the fastidious Marcel Grossman, the great mathematician who collaborated with Einstein in a crucial phase of his ten-year journey towards the General Theory of Relativity. Grossman once confessed to Einstein that he could never sit down on a toilet seat warm from a 'pre-sitter' without a shudder. When Einstein pointed out that the heat was entirely impersonal so that to receive it in this way was not to be subject to an unwanted intimacy, Grossman found that he was able in future to withstand, without a shudder, the exposure of his bare buttocks to the heat left over from the bare buttocks of a pre-sitter.)[2]

The conversation between the lover and his would-be object continues while the stalled dialogue between the hands is denied: she turns a numb ear to its plea for closeness. Or maybe not: perhaps she proves manuductile after all: there is the famous 'answering squeeze' that novelists of all sorts can take off the linguistic peg to secure the transition from friendship to love. This is the squeeze that says 'Yes' to him-become-you-become-thou; or to the idea of 'us' and all that that may mean. It opens the way to the bespoke happiness and unhappiness of 'The Couple' – whose stereotypically linked hands belie the uniqueness of the manner in which their lives are shared.

And so to the third age of manucaption –

> He married a girl to stop her getting away
> And now she's there everyday

– and the long companionship of marriage. The many hours and days of the hand-in-hand signify the cross-bridges between, the interwovenness of, two journeys through life. Out of their conjunction will sooner or later come a third journey, and perhaps a fourth, or even a fifth: the journeys of the children in whom they are joined; children who also come between them and so disjoin them a little. Between their two hands are inserted the two hands of another, one hand holding on to Daddy and one hand holding on to Mummy. Their manucaption is henceforth mediated, as each holds the hands of a third party. Until the children leave their parents, as they themselves once did, to live their separate lives, to seek other hands to hold. Our lovers' hands are re-joined.[3]

This, then, is the third age of manucaption: so many hours of warmth, of quiet togetherness, the ground bass under the long conversation that is their marriage, the quiet hum of direct knowledge and directly being known: co-presence, beyond need and carnality, but which encompasses, and can modulate into, either. This is what we shall remember, afterwards, of our years of togetherness, perhaps: 'Dear as remembered hand-warmth after death'. This is what Fanny Brawne denied John Keats and denied herself: 'This living hand, now warm and capable of earnest grasping …'

Pause for a digression: the formal hand in hand, otherwise known as The Hand-Shake. This does not, of course, have a time of life specific to itself, notwithstanding that there is an age at which it comes of age and handshaking is natural rather than forced. Although it is the quintessentially adult greeting, it is deployed even by children: such is its versatility. At its most adult, it is the sign of 'the done deal'. My favourite example is the famous, much-photographed handshake between the chief executives of Guinness and Argyle Foods after their bloody takeover battle. The handshakers are drinking, respectively, Guinness out of a whisky glass and whisky out of a Guinness glass, demonstrating the happy merger of the two firms. It was the picture most often used in the lavish press coverage of the fraud case that dragged on for so long afterwards, and became an iconic sign of the greedy, deregulated 1980s.[4]

Let us not be glibly cynical. The handshake remains, for the most part, an underwritten earnest of sincerity, of authenticity, commitment and probity. Regular guys have regular handshakes: they, and their handshakes, are firm rather than limp, and dry rather than damp. Their shaking is sustained, what is more, for the correct duration: not so brief that the clasp seems furtive and not so long that it becomes intimate – 'inappropriate' as Mr Clinton might say. Irregular guys – conmen, fraudsters, etc. – of course, have even more regular handshakes. They have that extra dazzle of authenticity, like the special whiteness of false teeth.

The handshake is ubiquitous in the world of business and the wider world of businessmen. It is a mark of fraternalism, actual or potential. More importantly, it signifies equality between the participants – hence its potent contractual symbolism: each is equal in the eyes of the economy and of the law. Although, like the pin-striped suit, the handshake is most at home in the world of business and is happiest in a sociality built on contracts, like the pinstripe, it goes much beyond this. It may be a token of conciliation or reconciliation – and so is famously given or withheld in private and public differences. The handshake between Itzak Rabin and Yasser Arafat and the refused handshake between Bill Clinton and Fidel Castro were headline news world-wide. They sent out opposite signals: Let us forget the past sufficiently to do sufficient business to our mutual benefit. Let us remember and respect the past and signal that doing business is not the ultimate value.

Deal conclusion, greeting, ungreeting (farewell), reconciliation, congratulation: how adaptable the handshake is! From the conclusion of a treaty to the small change of hello and goodbye, from the reconciliation between two superpowers to the reconciliation between two small children – its scope is astounding. The handshake's declaration of friendship, forgiveness, greeting, congratulation and trustworthiness is not, of course, always to be taken at face value. We warmly greet those whom we do not wish to meet; we congratulate rivals whose success nauseates us; we manually bury our differences with those against whom we still feel ill-will and against whom we still plot revenge.

So perhaps we should not be glibly cynical. We should be profoundly cynical. For the duplicity of the handshake arises not simply from the fact that it belongs to the formal ballet of public endearments, or that it is rooted in the cold world of legally enforceable contracts. No, it goes deeper: the handshake is born of distrust. To grip another's hand is to engage in a preliminary exploration; originally it was a way of determining that the other was unarmed or of demonstrating that one was oneself disarmed. This accounts for one of the fundamental differences between handshakes and other forms of manucaption: both parties engage the same – the right – hand. Other forms of manucaption are about his left hand and her right – or vice versa.

The other difference relates to duration. The phasic handshake shows how far away it is from, say, the tonic hand-in-hand of true friendship and companionship, the loving hand-holding of marriage. It is sad to reflect, therefore, how under the influence of venal lawyers, and of angry claimants in a secular world, this distance is shrinking. The increasing ease and frequency of divorce, the anticipation of this in prenuptial agreements, the extension of alimony to palimony, the displacement of the priest by the attorney as the key official overseeing the sacred union between two lovers – all of these point to an erosion of the ideals of the lover or the modulation of these ideals, via the cooler notion of companionship, into the wary sense that the emerging relationship is between two partners to a deal, equal in the sight of the lawyers. It suggests, perhaps, that the explicit contract of marriage and the implicit contract of other 'stable unions' is becoming more of a contract than anything else – a deal that has to be continually shaken on.[5]

This is not a cheerful thought but perhaps a suitable preparation for the final phase of manucaption: when hand-in-hand brings comfort – to the ill, the frail, the bereaved and the dying. This is the hand of compassion, of love, and asserts our fundamental solidarity as human beings,[6] marking the final phases of a marriage towards involuntary divorce, the long journey of illness from healthy being to afflicted being and from afflicted being to unbeing.

Man and wife go together to the doctor. They hold hands as they prepare for the diagnosis: the pronouncement that sentences one of them, sentences them both. At that moment the disease – its name, its being pinned to one of them – is a mere fact. They continue hand-in-hand as the illness unfolds and the fact swells into an anti-world large enough to occlude their shared world. Until, at last, their two lives are disjoined by fear, by pain, by nausea, by incontinence, by bodily disintegration, by mental confusion. Those gestures she loved or loathed warp into a delirious carphology that reaches out not to her, but to the creatures that decorate the opaque sphere of his solitude.

Towards the end, only the occasional squeeze, faintly answered, keeps contact alive. Inexorably – though their hands are still joined – he floats beyond her help: she watches from the shore as he drowns in the sea of his stricken body. His hand cools, betraying that he is now ebbing even from the unjoined world where he is alone to the worldless non-place where he is not. His cold hand's unawareness of the warmth of hers speaks the absoluteness of their parting. The strange, even wonderful, accident of their meeting, which acquired through their staying together a false *post-hoc* inevitability, betrays its true nature: a frail chain of coincidence underpinning an accident of cohabitation. Their world-lines came together; for a while, ran on close, parallel tracks, linked by manucaption; and then diverged.

And this is how it must always be: manucaption yields to manumission – the letting go, the setting free. Dying is involuntary liberation from the bondage of the flesh and from all the secondary bondages that human flesh acquires, reversing that moment, portrayed in Michaelangelo's emblematic painting, when the act of creation sent mankind forth from the hand of God. Death cancels the initial manumission from nothingness; and the hand that has lain in another created being's hand for so long is taken back into the invisible nothingness whence it came. It cannot even wave its hand-mate goodbye.

The last squeeze is unanswered.

4.2 THE DIALOGUE OF THE LEFT HAND WITH THE RIGHT

The human body is an ark filled with pairs. They may work together – as in the case of the two eyes supporting a shared visual field and cooperating in the perception of depth and distance or the two legs achieving walking; or they may ignore one another, as in the case of the two nipples or the two pinnae; or they may compensate for each other where one fails, as in the case of the two kidneys; or they may do all of these things – as in the case of the hands. The hands may work separately for some tasks and in cooperation for others. In addition to cooperating, however, they are available to each other in a further sense, unique among paired structures: they communicate with one another. The communication between either of the hands and other parts of the body – as in rubbbing, scratching, poking, picking, etc. (see section 5.1) – creates a rather special bodily self-awareness; it is possible that the communication between the left hand and the right hand of the same person brings a yet more developed 'awakefulness' that is distinctively human. It is within the framework of this possibility that the point of the following observations is best understood.

Let's begin with the simplest of their dialogues: hand clasping. The hands can join with pleasing symmetry as each lies in the other's palm and their union is secured by the fingers flexed over the side of the hands and the two are hasped together by the thumbs, one on top of the other.[7] There is a choice as to which hand's thumb is on top – and consequently as to which hand is manucaptor and which manucaptive. (In my own case, the right or dominant hand is usually the manucaptor.) Palms are crossed not with silver but with palm-flesh. This snug position gives comfort: it brews a cupful of warmth and shelter. Through the clasped hands, the body silently asserts: 'I am we and we are safer in each other's hands.' When the air is cold, other resources may be mobilised: the palms may be parted and hot air blown through the operculum between the separated thumbs and the hands are rubbed together (of which more presently) to add the heat of friction to the air-fuel. Other threats to well-being or safety may be answered with a firmer self-clasp which says: I am hanging on to myself and I am not going to let myself go easily. As the temperature falls or threats increase, the arms work with the hands in a self-hug and the self-hugged trunk curls, crouches and bends to minimise the surface of exposure.

In less fraught circumstances, hand may clasp hand in more elegant and complex embraces. For example, the fingers may interlace, with digits from alternate hands slotting into the very webs between the bases of their opposite numbers. In this position, the fingers can curl comfortably and satisfyingly over the dorsum of its opposite number while the thumbs are free either to interdigitate or to separate sufficiently to circle round one another in that ultimate symbol of empty activity, twiddling.[8] Even more elegantly, the hands may touch and greet each other solely at the fingertips, a position that is most comfortably sustained when the elbows are supported on a desk. This is a good posture for the hands when they want to engage in salon talk with one another. It permits their owners to exhibit long, well-manicured fingers, a certain quantity of well-bred at ease and a considerable amount of reflectiveness. The fingertips are available for inspection (often described as 'minute') while the right word is sought to deliver a headmasterly rebuke or formulate a critical appraisal of stereotactic precision.

This is the dialogue of the hands of someone whose emotions are restrained and refined and whose circumstances are remote from natural or man-made brutalities. The clasp, by contrast, is about apprehension; and also about hope and even delight: hand-clasping is future-directed. There is a special form of still dialogue between hands that, like hand-clasping, points to the hopes and fear for the future, but it reaches beyond secular expectation and envisages a future that lies outside human time. This is prayer which, in its canonical form, has the fingers elegantly superposed on one another, but all pointing upwards, in the rough direction of the half-imagined recipient who, for lack of local habitation, is located in the locationlessness beyond the sky. Anguished prayers, in which the emotive element dominates over the cognitive and personal need over theological concerns, may be less elegant: the fingers collapse into a clasp which is raised beseechingly to the higher being – the foreman or God – from whom the worst is feared and the best is sought.[9]

The hands may talk audibly to one another, as in hand-rubbing. This may be very loud indeed: the occupant of the room next to mine in my Oxford college used to keep me awake as he rubbed his hands together. Perhaps I was particularly sensitive to this sound as my father spent many hours when he was embodied rubbing his hands together. This was part of a complex ritual that involve irregular bending of the knee and clenching his teeth, so that the masseter and temporalis muscles stood out. His children are aware of being potential hand-rubbers and I have avoided this vice only through constant vigilance. Over the years of observing it close to, I have had much opportunity to reflect on the function it serves. Generating warmth is an obvious one and my father, having only the thinnest buttering of flesh on his bones, lived on a very cold planet – a planet made colder by his frugal habits: heating rooms created bills and bills were proof of waste. Hand-rubbing also greeted, and applauded, warmth: the abovementioned ritual was most often triggered by his arrival at a warm fire after the ordeal of getting up and dressed in a cold house or working in a cold garden.

Self-warming sometimes modulated into frank glee and this gives me the cue to wonder why hand-rubbing should be so characteristic an expression of glee at a current pleasure or an imminent one (hands being rubbed as a dish is set down before the rubber) or excitement at an expected pleasure or favourable event.[10] Perhaps it works as follows. Hand-rubbing raises the hands' awareness of themselves. While it is a little too much to suggest that each hand is giving the other a hand job, in the more technical sense, there is clearly an overlap here. However, the pleasure is not sexual or even sensual; rather it is sensuous. Each hand puts the other in pleasurable italics and that is a way of the body realising itself, of its being-here. This may intensify the realisation of self that enables one to grasp the thing that is giving, or is about to give, one pleasure. (I offer this with a good deal of tentativeness.)

The opposite of gleeful hand-rubbing is hand-wringing, which we have already spoken of (in section 3.2) as a sign addressed to the outside world rather than part of the conversation between one hand and the other. Even so, the sign is motivated; as we suggested, the wrung hands provide shelter for each other, each hugs the other. The difference between hand-wringing and hand-rubbing is partly a matter of tempo and, correlative to this, of expansiveness: hand-wringing is slow and clotted compared with the *allegro con brio* of gleeful hand-rubbing, as if the happiness were tuned in to a higher frequency than sadness. The shelter offered by hand-wringing is, of course, psychological and symbolic rather than physical as in warming hand-rubbing.

All animals groom themselves or get groomed. Human grooming, however, is a little different. It involves other agents than the body itself, some of them manufactured: water drawn from the well rather than secreted by the salivary glands; and in recent centuries soap, a luxury that came into general use only in the nineteenth century. The water itself is held in an appropriate, usually purpose-built, container and ensuring its continuous availability is a major logistical exercise. When it fails, the suffering of the unwashed – from mutual and self-disgust – is very great. Grooming is also rather formalised and typically occurs at set times or on set types of occasion. There is bath-night, of course; and the wash at the beginning and end of the day. There is a rational preference for washing the hands before lunch or after voiding or before certain procedures such as cooking or performing surgical operations. All of this is quite unlike the grooming of animals, which occurs without ceremony; indeed, anyone who has been exposed to the spectacle of a dog grooming its insufficiently private parts will say with too little ceremony. In many cases, washing in humans enjoys the same privacy as urination and defaecation and the words 'washroom', 'bathroom', etc. encompass facilities to serve both voiding and grooming functions.

The point of this rather long digression is to draw attention to a highly elaborated set of behaviours in which the hand has a key role aimed at keeping ourselves clean – that is to say, to keep our surfaces free of accumulated bodily secretions and accidental excretions and of the material that may stick to our bodies during our passage through the material world of which we are, and are not, a part. We do not use our tongue to clean ourselves – it lacks reach; nor do we use our feet – they lack the necessary manipulative skills. No, we use our hands.

The hands tend the rest of the body and perform a crucial role in dividing the single body into a multiplicity of agents and patients: when I wash myself, one part of my body operates upon another part that is relatively passive. This division into agent and patient, this operating upon our body with part of our body, helps to underline something we shall return to: our transcendence of our own body, made possible by the hand's explicit assumption of its role as instrument. In such actions, we are not exclusively on one side or the other: we are both the actor and the acted upon. This is reflected in the interesting Greek verb which occasioned the one joke in Liddell and Scott's massive lexicon of Greek: "'Louomai: I wash" (but this is very rare)'. For the Greeks, the verb to wash is neither entirely active nor entirely passive but is in the middle voice.[11] Nor, in English, is it either transitive or intransitive. It can take or leave an object: when we ask 'Are you going to wash?' we don't have to specify the object: it is assumed to be oneself. But we can, equally grammatically, ask 'Are you going to wash yourself?', as if one's self were in this respect like someone else, or even an object, such as a car.

In view of the central role of the hand in actions on the body, such as washing, there is a particular interest in the washing of the hands, the most frequently performed ablution as the hands have to be kept meticulously clean, if only because they are on show and grubby hands bespeak other bodily and even spiritual[12] grubbiness. (You could have an anus hung with more dingleberries than Oxford Street with Christmas lights, and no one would know.) Besides, as the prime manipulators, with their hands into everything, they have the potential to spread their (possibly infected or otherwise contaminated) dirt to others. And so they wash each other more than anything else. This washing is a remarkable dialogue, as the left hand washes the right hand washing the left hand washing the right hand. The medium used – soapy water – enables the seeming impossibility whereby the rubbing by the left hand that cleans the right hand is identical (because the movement is relative) to a rubbing by the right hand that cleans the left hand. At any rate this is a fascinating example of a symmetry between agent (the washing hand) and patient (the washed hand) and involves a continuous reversal of roles.[13]

Not all humans beings participate in handwashing with equal enthu-siasm. Small human beings are especially averse to the act of separating dirty hands from handy dirt. Washing occurs only to instruction, or threat, and both may require repetition. It is difficult to see why this is so, except that it is an action that takes time and gives no pleasure – for little ones haven't reached the age at which warm, soapy water and amphibious self-caresses give pleasure and the bathroom is a place of refuge. It is, however, possible to cheat and the most ingenious and memorable cheat was recorded in that most metaphysical of all comics, *The Beano*. The two characters in the cartoon (whose names escape me) eluded the bimanual imperative of handwashing, by working together: they clasped each other's right hands and shook hands beneath the water. In this means they contrived not only one-handed washing but also, by the very same action, to congratulate themselves on successfully evading the parental edict – a breathtaking economy of effort![14]

4.3 THE INTERLOCUTORS

The interlocuters[15] in the dialogue between the left hand and the right are enantiomorphs; that is to say, they are similar but not identical, 'the same and not the same'; rather, each is related to the other as an object is related to its image in a mirror. They are not superposable. (Try it and see.) The left hand and the right hand are two halves of a whole, but not identical halves. The doubleness of the hand, of hand talking to hand, which impacts so fundamentally on our relationship to our own bodies and has a finger in our being able to wake up out of said bodies, so that we may use them as if they were instruments, is augmented by this fundamental difference between our two hands.

There are at least two – quite profound and entirely different – consequences of enantiomorphy. The first is that the treatment of the two hands is not, how shall we put it, even-handed. The hands are not equal in the sight of the agent: right and left hands tend to take on roles of protagonist and assistant, lead and support: in right-handed people, for example, the left hand simply gives the right hand a hand: it is the right hand's right-hand man. One hand, in short, is dominant, the other non-dominant; one primarily manipulative, the other ancillary.[16] This asymmetry of our symmetrical hands, their being an unequal couple, emphasises their doubleness and the transcendent role of the actor in relation to them: the non-superposable hands are both servants of some transcendental agent: the Trinity – left hand, right hand and Boss – is established. The instrumentality of the hands, and the altered relationship to our bodies that arises retroactively from this, is by this asymmetry underlined. The non-superposability of our hands, I would like to suggest (with fluctuating levels of confidence), is an important aspect of our wakening out of our bodies and their mechanisms to ourselves as agents using our bodies for definite purposes. The separate working of the hands, which makes them both tools of an agent which we ourselves are, is italicised by their differentiated roles and so, consequently, is our sense of agency. It is as if the symmetry of our hands – in virtue of which they are the same but (being mirror images) not superimposable and so not the same – awakens a bodily awareness, which is in turn italicised by their non-equivalence, which arises out of laterality or handedness.

A second consequence of handedness relates to the formatting of egocentric space – the space by which we feel ourselves surrounded and whose centre we, as individuals, occupy. Of course we are born and live at the centre of the experienced world: the sense that 'I am here', 'I am at the centre of the world', is implicit in experience itself. My experiencing body defines what counts as 'here' and what is 'there' in virtue of importing into the physical world the deictic coordinates of 'here', 'there', 'near', 'far', etc. But these are, of course, volatile – they change as I move bodily and as my attention fluctuates. The difference between left and right, however, is at once subjective – it is established with respect to 'me' – and objective – it is established with respect to a particular, enduring side of my body. The non-superposability and differential function of the hands thus links the vagaries of deictic space with something objective and enduring. This validates the division of the universe 'out there' into the left-hand side and the right-hand side. The asymmetrical body, spelt out in the hands that are at a distance from the perceived centre of self, underwrites both the lateralised universe and its own localisation in the middle of everything. It stands out from the world and is (as we shall discuss in the subsequent volumes) uncoupled from the material world that absorbs the organism so that it is able to engage with it on different, more favourable, terms.

Handedness evolves after birth, though some have claimed that the foetus demonstrates handedness in the womb: by fifteen weeks' gestation, most babies show a preference for sucking the right thumb.[17] As it emerges, all sorts of secondary lateralisations follow. Foot dominance, eye dominance, and so on, however, are probably not consequences of hand dominance; rather they are different expressions of a common underlying cause. But there is no doubt that the outcome of this asymmetry alters our entire stance to the world: we lead with the dominant hand, whether hand-shaking, writing, defending ourselves or playing sport. And while not everyone is right-hand dominant, right-hand dominance dominates even those who are left-handed. Even the left-handed are obliged to shake right hands with their right hand; and most instruments are designed for the right-handed. Right-handedness is unmarked and invisible, left-handedness marked, visible and even deviant. When a batsman is left-handed this is noted, but not when he is right-handed. And we describe an unexpected move as coming from 'left field'. To see a left-handed person writing is to marvel at the dexterity of writing: we are astonished not at what they write, but that they can write at all. Right-handedness is assumed to be dexterous, while the left hand is sinister. Sinistrality arouses supicion. 'Bend sinister' marks the coat of arms of the bastard child whose entitlement is questionable, but whose ambitions will be proportionately inflamed. Left-handed is half-way to being cack-handed – which implies incompetence – and in right-handed people, the left hand is often delegated to demeaning tasks such as that of absturging the podex – hence the 'cack' in 'cack-handed'. There are, in sum, huge secondary reinforcements of the asymmetry between the two hands and hence of the lateralisation of the world, so that left and right are not merely different halves: they are made explicit by being both equal and different; equal and not equal.[18]

Handedness is a concept of central importance in organic chemistry: some molecules exist in distinct mirror-image forms, related to each other as the right hand is to the left. These enantiomers have, for the most part, identical chemical properties but some may differ crucially, in particular in the way they interact with other-handed molecules, including some that we have in our bodies. In other words, they may have profoundly different biological properties. A dramatic and terrible example of this may have been the drug thalidomide, which has cast its twisted shadow across the pharmaceutical industry for nearly half a century.[19] Thalidomide is chiral: it has left- and right-handed forms. There is some suggestion that the enantiomers differ vastly in their propensity to cause birth defects, though the matter is complicated by the fact that the 'harmless' enantiomer converts to the 'harmful' one under physiological conditions. This adds an additional bitter irony to an avoidable catastrophe which led to the birth of so many children with a syndrome whose most strikingly terrible feature is 'phocomelia' or 'seal limbs'. An appreciation of the lethal difference between the left- and the right-handed forms of the drug may, in the end, have saved the limbs of the children: this handed drug took away the hands of so many children.

The division into right and left is not confined to the material universe. It is also used to allocate or divide possibilities: 'on the one hand', 'on the other hand'. The thesis is on the right, the antithesis on the left. And it may come to signify the relations between persons: sitting on the right hand of God or a person or a body is not precisely equivalent to sitting on the left hand; the right-hand man is superior to the left-hand man and is less likely than the left-hand man to be a woman. And so on.

The two hands are materially equal but not identical. They have physical symmetry either side of a plane, but even this symmetry is undermined by the functional dominance of one hand over the other. There is an important additional asymmetry: the usually dominant right hand is directed from the hemisphere where the so-called speech and language centres are located. This licenses the fanciful notion that the right hand has privileged communication with the other great engine of cultural development and evolving human consciousness: the word. Whether or not it is helpful to think in this way, it is an inescapable fact that the left hand is and is not the Other to the right hand, it is and is not its equal. And it is true that there is more than a maximum of a few feet of space between them. They therefore have something to say to each other and their conversation can be genuinely consciousness-raising. They are sufficiently different to feel each other's warmth as the warmth of another – or an almost-another; they warm each other as a kind of gift that passes between them and this contributes in an important way to the handed one's sense of being here.

It is perhaps an overstatement to suggest that they have knowledge of one another, or that what passes between them is knowledge, rather than experience.[20] But in their interaction, a distance is implanted at the heart of the seeming immediacy of a touch: we have a touched toucher touching a touched toucher – and vice versa. And so it is possible that something not too far from knowledge comes out of the encounter and a division – of the kind necessary to raise self-consciousness – or a bodily awareness that generates bodily self-consciousness, emerges.

Let me develop this a little before leaving it alone for the present. Somewhere (it may be in *Philosophical Investigations*), Wittgenstein comments that the left hand cannot give the right hand a gift. I want to say that perhaps, in a limited sense, gifts can flow freely between the two hands: the left hand can warm up the right hand, giving it the gift of comfort. More importantly, the left hand can give the right hand something like knowledge of itself. (This is the strange thing when one looks at a body that has been laid out, and one hand is folded in another: the hands no longer know – or indeed have anything to do with – one another.) The transaction that is both external, between parts of the body, and internal – within the body and within the person – is possibly the forerunner of another crucial internal gift: that of thinking (to oneself), which begins with entertaining possibilities and ends with silent soliloquy. It might be too much to suggest that thinking to oneself and discovering through thought, and 'coming to oneself' through thought, grew out the of the internal–external relationship between the left and the right hand, but perhaps it might not.[21]

4.4 THE HAND TALKING TO ITS SELF OR THE SELF

It is perhaps more than a little overstatement, even a case of The Fallacy of Misplaced Explicitness, to think of the hand in communion with itself, of a transcarpal (or carping) monologue. But I use the term metaphorically, to try to capture the quite explicit sense that the hand has of itself: a bodily self-awareness localised in the hand; an inchoate selfness that is ambiguously both *in* and *of* the hand. This self-awareness, we shall later argue, lies at the root of more general bodily self-awareness and, indeed, the self-consciousness, or more precisely the selfness, that characterises human, as opposed to animal, being.

The hand communicates with itself in various ways. In manipulation, especially precision manipulation, it has continually to report to itself in order to initiate actions and to keep those actions on track. The conversation may be virtual or subconscious, as in the feedback from muscles and joints that is said to enable the cerebellum to 'calculate' (and re-calculate) trajectories during manipulative movements; or just above the threshold of consciousness, as when the hand adopts and maintains a certain posture. This mixture of unconscious and sub-conscious feedback is essential for the sensorimotor integration that underpins coordinated exploratory or manipulative activity. It may be fully conscious, as in the experience the hand has in exploring and shaping the world it deliberately encounters. In summary, the hand has to know itself in order to initiate an action, in order to execute an action effectively and in order to know that it has completed an action.

The concept of proprioception – awareness of parts of the body itself as opposed to awareness of the external world – spans all these kinds of 'knowledge' or 'self-communion', from the barely conscious sense of being upright to the exquisite embarrassment of knowing that one's relaxed upright posture is being judged sloppy and insolent. Propriocep-tion is essential not only to control actions, but to initiate them. If actions are, at the very least, movements of bodily parts from A to B, A has to be defined; or rather it has to be existentially established: it is where my hand (or whatever) is now. The *de facto* location that any object has is not sufficient to establish 'here', even less 'here as starting point'.

This is not merely theoretical speculation. As we have already noted, patients with very severe proprioceptive loss (so bad that they are unaware of the own limbs) have great difficult initiating movements, and may indeed be effectively paralysed, even though the muscles and the motor pathways of the nervous system are intact. The need for manual self-communion is even more profound than this. O'Shaughnessy has argued plausibly that tactile perception requires proprioception.[22] More profoundly still, Cassam[23] has suggested that spatial awareness, and the sense of being located in the (spatial, physical) world, depends upon proprioception. His argument goes as follows:

> Suppose, for example, that S is aware of her right arm as moving forward in relation to her own body until it meets an obstruction which prevents it going any further despite the fact that it is not yet fully outstretched. It would be natural to describe this as a case in which S is aware of some-thing solid at the point of obstruction, and is thereby also aware of her own solidity, or, at any rate, the solidity of her arm. The important point here is that this awareness of solidity depends upon S's proprioceptive awareness of the position and movement of her arm in relation to the rest of her. (Cassam 1997, p. 62)

The particular role of the hand (as opposed to, say, the bottom or even the feet) in this regard is that it is active tactile perception associated with exploration and manipulation that presents us with the most pronounced sense of our own solidity. Yes, we are rendered bodily self-aware, and are given an account of our own solidity, as we experience the counter-thrust of a chair against our bottom; but the activity in manipulation and exploration links that sense of solidity with our effort and deliberation. Moreover, the arm, and even more the fingers, protrude from the mass of our body: they are more explicitly *there*. The material reaction of the world gives us a sense of our action, a sense that is mediated by the reports that the hand gives of itself. To put this provocatively: we truly touch the world only if the hands that touch are self-touching.

Many aspects of proprioception are seen in other parts of the human body and, indeed, are not unique to human bodily being. What is unique to human proprioception, and derived from manual proprioception, is self-touching, which is linked to the special role of the hand in exploration and manipulation. The latter is also associated with what I shall describe (in Chapter 10) as 'manipulative indeterminacy'. The sensorimotor uniqueness of the hand – the result of a combination of self-touching and manipulative indeterminacy – is, it will be argued, the key to its unique role in transforming our relationship to our bodies and permitting the human organism to acquire true agency.

Of this, more in due course. For the present, we note that the hand's self-touching is highlighted further by other sensations arising from within it, some of them continuous, such as warmth, and others, such as pain, intermittent. The multiplicity of the self-sensations creates the possibility of further internal distances within the hand's awareness of itself or our awareness of our hands: the flickering envelope of ordinary proprioception forms a background against which warmth and pain may be located, making the hand's self-awareness layered.

The hand's warmth is of particular interest. We have already touched on it with respect to manucaption and in the context of the dialogue between the two hands. I want to explore it further here. The exploration will take us beyond what is metaphysically illuminating but simply irresistible. For I want to talk about gloves.

Gloves, like all articles of clothing, are devices that allow the body to draw comfort from its own metabolic fires. The hand warms itself by enclosure in gloves which capture its own heat and feed it back to it. Clothes in general and gloves in particular remind us of our extraordinary relationship to our own body, whereby we see it as an object that has to be tended, not only episodically, as in feeding or grooming, but continuously to ward off potential as well as actual hazards, as in protective clothing and shelter.[24] (The instruction to 'wrap up warm' says so much about the nature of human being! It reminds us that what is distinctive about us is not the small detail that we are *naked* apes, but the hugely elaborated fact that we are self-clothed animals.) The gloved hand harvests its own heat, warms itself with its spilt warmth: the hand warms the glove so that the glove can warm the hand. This utilisation of one's own metabolism – and the transformation of what is directly experienced and suffered in the first person into something that is used by a quasi-first person – becomes startlingly apparent when one comes upon one's own warmth in a reassumed glove.[25] Actually, or at least objectively, this is less a case of the hand warming itself than of the glove slowing down the heat lost from the hand, although the warmed glove is a mini-depot of the warmth we squander in a cold planet.

All of which seems straightforward, and that should be the end of the story. But with human beings no story ever ends. The brilliant notion that one might make a pelt as protection from a hostile environment rather than relying on the mediocre pelt secreted by one's body is just the beginning. The notion can be inflected to meet different threats. Gloves have many dialects: boxing gloves and gauntlets and oven gloves and plastic gloves and rubber gloves and so on to protect against cold and heat and water and corrosive materials and enemies and contestants and nettles and infections and bats and balls and so on. The generic glove is adapted to numerous different functions.

Some modifications aim to overcome the problem that gloves make the hand metaphorically as well as literally thicker. The numbing fabric intervenes between the exquisitely sensitive fingertips and the objects being manipulated or explored, muffling the signals picked up from the surfaces of the world so that they speak more quietly to the inquiring hand. And tight sheaths make the fingers less nimble. The solution to this problem is the fingerless glove, which has holes through which the naked fingers and thumb may protrude. In other cases, dumbness is of less concern and warmth more important: the mitten, where there are no separate stalls, is the answer here, although the thumb has its own accommodation. Mittens can trap more warm air and so are favoured where cold is the major concern. Little children, who find it difficult to perform the extraordinarly complex act of inserting fingers into gloves, may also prefer mittens and, because they are famously feckless, their mittens are attached to a piece of elastic threaded through both sleeves, so that they cannot be parted from them by carelessness.[26]

By another interesting inversion, the glove may be made to stand for the hand, as when someone is asked to keep their dirty 'mitts' out of something. And the opposite of manucaption – as when a lover is jilted – may be signified by 'giving the mitten'. Whether or not this Victorian phrase has any connection with its seemingly literal roots, there is no doubt that manucaption is very unsatisfactory if the captive's hand is sheathed in leather or cloth. Numbness meets numbness and carnal co-presence is muffled.

The habit we have already discussed that humans have of turning things into signs of other things – in particular of the world they come from – and into signs of signs adds new twists to the tale of gloves. For gloves, which provide some protection from predatory nature, may be used to signify a distance from the messy, uncouth world. White gloves place the dirt of the world at an enhanced arm's length. Gloves, that is to say, are not only useful devices to separate our hands from the brutality of the natural world; they may also be fashion accessories helping us to define our position in the social world. Gauntlets signify both the upper-class origin (who else could afford such luxuries?) and the bravery (for they are worn by the doughty, who participate in wars, tilting and falconry) of the wearer. They also inspire a gesture once real and now only spoken of: throwing down the gauntlet and picking it up. On the radio just now, I heard that The Leader of Her Majesty's Loyal Opposition had thrown down the gauntlet to the Prime Minister. How far we have travelled from the tool of the self-warming hand!

The special genius of gloves is reflected in the complexity of their shape. No other item of clothing is so essentially, as opposed to accidentally, complex. The donning and doffing of gloves involves transformations of shapes, including several steps such as the reverse intussusception of the cloth fingers as the glove is put on, having previously been unpeeled from the hand. No wonder little children have to train for so long, even to assume mittens! No wonder, also, that the challenge of putting on gloves is beyond many neurologically damaged patients:

'A continuous surface' he announced at last, 'infolded on itself. It appears to have' – he hesitated – 'five outpouchings, if this is the word'. Later, by accident, he got it on, and exclaimed, 'My God, it's a glove!'[27]

We have been talking about the hand talking to itself and about the hand's self-presence and its presence to the body. This is in turn an element – and a very important one – of the body's presence to itself. The notion of self-presence clearly incorporates the notion of the presence of something that has a distinct identity. The kind of self-presence we are talking about is a standing intuition which might be expressed in propositional forms: 'This is me'. The most intimate, basic and enduring mode of self-presence has been described by Kant as 'The "I think" that accompanies all my perceptions'. This 'I think' is, as has often been pointed out, almost empty of specific content: any content imputed to it has the habit of becoming something the self is aware of and so outside of the self. Kant's 'I think' is an empty ideal or logical subject; almost the presupposition in perceptions rather than an accompaniment of them. There is a need to find some way of attaching it to something other than itself so that this I moves on from being a bare subject, a mere logical form, to something which genuinely has identity.[28]

At any rate, the sense that anything as solid as a bodily part is me is always contaminated with the feeling that the part is merely owned by, attached to, or in some other sense distant, or separable, from me. This distance disappears only when the bodily part is engaged in an action, is totally given over to it. In short, there is a tension between the reflective sense of selfness and the explicit sense of (bodily) presence. What gives the hand, supremely amongst parts of the body, the ability to awaken the sense that 'I am this thing' while at the same time allowing 'I can use this thing' is that it is present at several levels: the self-warming hand as subject-and-object, as agent and patient, is underlined not only by the infinite number of degrees of freedom of the grips it has at its disposal – and we shall revisit this fact in due course – but also by the background–foreground, the layeredness built into the experience of the hand. Although the back of our hand is supposed to be something we know so well that it is stitched into our sense of identity, in fact it is quite possible that we might fail correctly to identify the back of our own hands out of a line-up of similar hands.[29] What makes our hands so familiar to us and so close to our identity is the interactions that we have described. It is through our hands that we expropriate our own bodies, get a first-person grip on the organism that we live, and, through this, get a grip on the world. The self-warming hand is the crucial link in the circuit of selfness – in virtue of which I am that which I am – as is the manipulative hand which integrates this feeling with that of ourselves as (responsible) agents. Selfness takes its rise out of the self-communion of the manipulative hand.[30]

NOTES

1. This is one of the examples of 'bad faith' that Sartre gives in *Being and Nothingness*:
   But then suppose he takes her hand. This act of her companion risks changing the situation by calling for an immediate decision. To leave the hand there is to consent in herself to flirt, to engage herself. To withdraw it is to break the troubled and unstable harmony which gives the hour its charm. The aim is to postpone the moment of decision as long as possible. We know what happens next; the young

woman leaves the hand there, but she *does not notice* that she is leaving it. She does not notice it because it happens by chance that she is at this moment all intellect ... And during this time the divorce of the body from the soul is accomplished; the hand rests between the warm hands of her companion – neither consenting or resisting – a thing. (*Being and Nothingness*, translated by Hazel Barnes, London: Methuen, 1957, pp. 55–6)

2. The story is told in Banesh Hoffman, *Einstein: Creator and Rebel* (New York: Viking, 1972).

3. I don't know how epidemiologically sound this is, but it seems that older married couples are less self-conscious than they used to be about walking hand-in-hand, and they are less likely to graduate with advancing years to walking arm in arm. It is as if this is no longer seen as gesticular mutton dressed as lamb. In more tactile nations, of course, it is not unusual for girls and even boys to walk hand in hand.

4. My favourite private handshake is that between my two children – aged at the time eight and four – after a long and harrowing row provoked (like a world war) by some trivium, with tears on both sides. The four-year-old silently held out his still dimpled hand to the eight-year-old: 'Shake on it, Ben?' The little hand was slightly cocked: he was not yet an expert in the gesture.

5. The horrible mixture of calculation with intimacy – combining care for oneself with indifference for the welfare of the other – that may be present in sexual relationships is, of course, taken to its extreme in prostitution. I am reminded of 'the sailor's handshake', which the sailor, out for a bit of R&R, uses before he settles on the woman whose services he is about to purchase. This is not an old-fashioned, if slightly out of place, act of courtesy, as is made clear by the somewhat unusual nature of the action. It is more of an arm-shake: the sailor takes hold of the forearm, so that he can palpate the elbow of his intended to check for swollen lymph glands, a sign of syphilis. He doesn't mind infecting her with a serious disease, but he is certainly not going risk contracting such a disease from her; after all, he is paying.

6. But professional carers here are still not free of contracts; and lawyers who, noting the asymmetry between the manucaptor and the manucaptive, do not hesitate to point out that touching patients without their permission is an assault in law.

7. This is the position adopted for hand farting – see section 3.3.

8. Etymologically, this was a word created with the intention of combining twirling or twisting and fiddling (with trifles). Quite so.

9. It is perhaps worth reminding ourselves that hand clasps are also a means of dealing with the peculiarly human discomfort arising from not knowing what to do with one's hands. Such clasps are often quite closely prescribed; for example, what the Prince of Wales does with his hands while his walking is highly standardised, and there has been little change over the last thirty years. The formal clasp, in his case behind his back, is a way of keeping idle hands in play just in case they should forget themselves and start picking their owner's nose or servicing an itchy bottom or pleasuring HRH's genitals as alertness fades and drowsiness liberates more automatic, instinctive behaviours.

10. So much so that it is one of those spoken gestures discussed in section 3.2: 'When the others/our enemies/Her Majesty's Royal Opposition hear about this, they will be rubbing their hands with glee.'

11. This joke is not present in all editions of Liddell and Scott. In their lengthy entry on the verb to wash, the middle voice is instanced in Homer, with a few quotations to illustrate washing oneself. The active voice is used when someone else is doing the

washing, usually female slaves, taken in war and employed in the bath-house to wash the guests. (I am indebted to Mr Donald McCleod for this information.)

12. The assimilation of the notions of physical and spiritual, of outer and inner, dirtiness and cleanness, is, of course, formalised in many religious rites which involve washing and even immersion in water.

13. If I were a Marxist, I would talk about the dialectics of handwashing and the contradictions built into it. But I am not, so I won't. Of course, handwashing is not irrelevant to Marxism: the heirs of Marx have many crimes to wash their hands of.

14. I have not said anything about the action of drying the hands. This is a very large topic and there is space for only one observation. Traditionally, the hands work together with some kind of manutergium to accelerate the process of drying which, if it were entirely dependent upon evaporation, would not only take an unconscionable time but would also leave a filmy deposit from the dirty, soapy water. My father relished this form of hand-rubbing and would prolong the action beyond what was strictly necessary. Towards the end of his life, however, public toilets increasingly preferred hot air driers. You still had to rub your hands together – or the hands still had to rub themselves together (an ambivalence that lies at the heart of my argument throughout this section) – in order to spread the water over the surface and hasten the process of drying. My father once said to me, 'I hate this Scrooge-like hand-rubbing'. It was not the Scrooge-like hand-wringing he hated so much as the lack of satisfying friction.

15. A literary critic's take on some of the themes in this section is explored in a wonderfully rich paper by Ralf Norrman, 'Creating the world in our image. A new theory of love of symmetry and iconicist desire', in Max Nanny and Olga Fischer (eds), *Form, Miming, Meaning. Iconicity in Language and Literature* (Amsterdam and Philadelphia: John Benjamins Publishing Company, 1999).

16. I am aware that the literature about handedness – neurophysiological, neuroanatomical, neuropsychological, demographic, pathological, sociological, pedogogic, anthropological, historical, etc. aspects – is massive. It would be arrogant to say that most of it is irrelevant to my purposes. To be more honest: it is an ocean which I must skirt with circumspection in order to avoid drowning. My treatment of the topic must, of necessity, be unpardonably superficial and brief.

17. P. G. Hepper et al., 'Handedness in the human foetus', *Neuropsychologia* 29(11), 1991, pp. 1107–11.

18. Doubtless a postmodernist or two has somewhere expatiated upon the left hand as Other to the right hand; of the alterity of sinistrality. Doubtless, too, in a fever of association, this will have been connected with postcolonialism, feminism, Lacanianism, etc. The Professors of Ismism will have had a field day. Even so, it is true that sinistrals have been badly treated. Ruth Carter reminds us (in *Mapping the Brain*, London: Weidenfeld and Nicolson, 1998) that the French word 'gauche' is used in English to mean 'awkward', that 'amancino' in Italian means deceitful as well as left, and that, in St Matthew's vision of the Last Judgement, God will set the sheep on the right and they will be despatched to life eternal, while the goats will be placed on the left and will be given a one-way ticket to hell-fire.

19. The terrible story is recounted with wisdom and understanding by the Nobel prize-winning chemist Roald Hoffmann's aptly named *The Same and Not the Same* (New York: Columbia University Press, 1995). Like Primo Levi (whom Hoffmann cites in his chapter on thalidomide, 'When something is wrong'), Hoffmann combines the dispassionate ethos of the scientist with a profound moral sense.

20. Or usually, anyway. There are, of course, times when one hand does deliberately acquire knowledge of the other hand – as when I check a finger to see whether it is tender, pressing it with the finger of the other hand.

21. I often wonder how the more enduring spatial relationships between family members, in particular siblings, influence how they think of, remember, even react to, each other. For nearly ten years, when they accompanied us together on innumerable car journeys, our two boys occupied the same seats in the back of the car; Ben, the older, was always on the left of Lawrence, the younger. From his earliest consciousness of an outside world, Lawrence was therefore exposed to Ben as a body, a person, a force, an interlocutor, an antagonist, etc., to his right. I cannot help feeling this may have done something to structure his awareness of his older brother – in addition to the fact that the latter preceded him, making him 'and Lawrence' – shaping his sense of where he fits into his world.

22. See B. O'Shaughnessy, 'The mind–body problem', in R. Warner and T. Szubka (eds), *The Mind–Body Problem* (Oxford: Blackwell, 1994).

23. Quassim Cassam, *Self and World* (Oxford: Clarendon Press, 1997). This book should be read by every self, whatever world he/she lives in. Incidentally, it is interesting to compare Cassam's and O'Shaughnessy's observation with this from Sartre, discussing sexual caresses:

> If my body is no longer felt as the instrument which cannot be utilized by any instrument – i.e, as the synthetic organization of my acts in the world – if it is lived as flesh, then it is as a reference to my flesh that I apprehend the objects in the world. This means that I make myself passive in relation to them and that they are revealed to me from the point of view of this passivity, in it and through it … Objects then become the transcendent ensemble which reveals my incarnation to me. A contact with them is a *caress*; that is, my perception is not the *utilization* of the object and the surpassing of the present in view of an end, but to perceive an object when I am in the desiring attitude is to caress myself with it. (*Being and Nothingness*, p. 392)

The overlap here supports something that I have believed for some time: that, at the deepest level, the so-called Anglo-Saxon and Continental philosophical traditions are striving for the same kind of understanding and with comparable rigour and imagination and that their preoccupations cross and re-cross. See Raymond Tallis, 'Philosophies of consciousness and philosophies of the concept. Or: Is there any point in studying the headache I have now?', in *Enemies of Hope: A Critique of Contemporary Pessimism*, 2nd edn (London: Palgrave, 1999).

24. The Saxon word for body – bone-house – is a striking inversion. The house that shelters the body becomes a metaphor for the body that shelters the bones.

25. The heat is, of course, impersonal, just like the heat from the buttocks of Grossman's pre-sitter.

26. Even cruder are oven gloves where the hand is not engaged in precision grips but in simple power lifting.

27. I think I owe this to Oliver Sacks, but I have lost the reference.

28. This issue is discussed with wonderful subtlety by Cassam, *Self and World*. See also 'That I am this thing', in Raymond Tallis, *On the Edge of Certainty* (London: Macmillan, 1999). It is the central theme of volume 2 of this trilogy, *I Am: A Philosphical Inquiry into First-Person Being*.

29. The appearance of the back of our hand is no more identified with our identity than are the palmar creases which are supposed to signify our unique trajectory through

life or the fingerprints which improve our tactile sensitivity and grip and are unique to us. Knowing things 'like the back of my hand' is no great knowledge. We could not pick our hands out of an identity parade. And, as John Napier points out, many of us could not even say, without looking, whether our ring finger was longer than our index finger, or vice versa.

30. It is no accident that thumb-sucking is one of the most characteristic behaviours of infancy and early childhood and thumb-sucking prolonged beyond this a feature of immaturity and of profound lack of confidence. To suck one's thumb is to encounter one's 'embodied selfness' through its deepest root. It is the timidest form of self-assertion, italicising oneself through a sheltering circuit of selfness.

CHAPTER 5

The Playful Hand

5.1 INTRODUCTION

If everything goes according to plan, this will be the shortest chapter of the book. While it is entirely appropriate that we should remember how much of the hand's busyness is given over to play rather than serious matters relevant to one's own survival and that of others, it is important not to spend too much time with The Playful Hand. Sex and sport, the preoccupations of the next two sections, are, along with politics, the most over-talked and over-written about themes in contemporary life. I shall address both of them with a brevity that, in the case of sport, may raise the suspicion of contempt.[1] Moreover, my approach will be somewhat oblique and my reflections may not be able to withstand the charge of being random.

5.2 THE CARNAL HAND

Once animality woke up out of simple mechanisms and the life of the organism became increasingly a matter of actions rather than of metabolic events, reflexes and reactions, then it was important for survival that useful actions – such as eating and copulating – should be associated with pleasure, and that failure to perform them should be associated with pain.[2] The animal body became a source of pleasure. In the case of humans, who have woken out of instincts and tropisms, pleasure and pain are important shapers of behaviour. The pleasures of the human body range from the very primitive, shared with animals, such as the enjoyment of the taste of food and the filling of the stomach, or warmth after cold, or the opening of the bowels, to very complex indeed. Although some of the more complex pleasures may be solitary – for example, the enjoyment of the sensation of warmth on one's arms as

one lies in the sun – most are shared. They are woven in with companionship of others and, in particular, with the sense of a privileged
relationship with others, or with another. As Hegel famously observed,
the difference between man and other animals is that humans have an
appetite for recognition by others, an appetite that is derived from our
unique sense of being selves.[3]

This distinctive need is self-evident in the case of the sexual impulse.
At the heart of human sexual pleasure is delight in being acknowledged
and accepted by another. This is as true of perverted sexuality as it is of
sexual relations between people for whom sexuality is an expression of
love. Pornography works because its customers imagine they are
addressed personally by the beautiful bodies that figure in it and that, by
witnessing the things they are permitted to see, they have the kind of
privileged access to another's privacy that normally would be afforded
only to a lover. And the same is true of prostitution: at its most benign
interpretation, prostitution permits the client access to a more realistic
inflatable doll. Malign sexuality – rape, child abuse, other forms of
sexual domination – demands or tries to extort the acknowledgement
that love and adoration would give freely, by forcing the object of its
desire to give the assailant her entire attention. Violation, pain, terror,
invade the other person, so that the acknowledgement that is freely
given in love is stolen from the person.

The complexity of human pleasures, and their capacity for modulating into uniquely human vices, for being transformed from simple
delights to elaborate perversions, reaches deep, therefore, into our
'species being'. To descend from this high-level observation of the glory
of human love and the tragedy of its perversions, to the hand – and even
to hand jobs, those paramount solitary vices where imaginary partners
are, unknown to themselves, press-ganged into service – may seem more
than a little bathetic. The hand, however, is a window even here.

Sexuality is a powerful reminder of the extent to which our sense of
ourself is inextricably interwoven with our awareness of others; and the
extent to which our existence for ourself is inseparable from our
existence for others. The means to sexual delight, however, should be
equally powerful reminders of how the sense of the other, of the other's
otherness, is built on a sense of otherness in oneself and of one's complex
relationship to one's own body. The 'shuddersome delight' of sexual
experience with others is rooted in the strange delight of certain bodily
sensations. And in this, the hand has – well, a hand. While the essence of
sexuality is not simply a glorified hand job, fully developed sexuality
owes much to the hand.

I shall not stray far into the endlessly fascinating details of physical lovemaking. Nothing that follows need be kept from children. For the role of the hand in sexuality may be best understood in relation to something a little less emotive – namely scratching – though we shall stray into the more questionable territory of tickling and caressing.

'"Where ah itchez, ah scratchez". Comment.' This was the first question that confronted me in my finals paper in Animal Physiology at Oxford. The answer that I gave to this seemingly straightforward observation – that I scratch where I itch – was not entirely satisfactory and it played its part in my failure to get the expected First. It was posed as a question about localisation of sensations, and the guiding of actions by those sensations, to which a purely physiological answer was expected. (The answer I gave was purely physiological but inadequate.) It will be evident from what has been said so far during the course of this book, and in particular in the last chapter, that the issues are not purely physiological; that is to say, they cannot be satisfactorily addressed by talk that confines itself to the behaviour of neurones, acting singly or in concert. To understand what is at issue, we need to start not from scratch but from itch. We need to think a little more deeply about the experience of itch, its localisation and the action it prompts.

It is my body, or a part of it, that is itching; equally, it is me that is itching: because *it* is itchy, *I* am itchy. When I locate an itch, I distance myself from it – it is 'over there', on my toe, or just out of reach at my back. And yet I am not distanced from it, as is evidenced from the fact that there could never be any question as to whose itch it is. The itch is so unquestionably mine that it seems rather perverse to assert that I have mere ownership of it. The itch, in another sense, therefore is not over there. There is and there is not a distance between myself and my itch. What makes this distance real – a real but inner distance – is the act of scratching; for, in order to scratch, I have to make a movement with my hand. Inside the action is the schema of the distance to be traversed from one place to another – from its rest position to the site of the itch – by my hand. It is the job that the hand does that places the itch – which I experience and which is consequently part of me – 'over there'. It ratifies the divide within myself that has to be crossed.

This divide, and the external location of the itch (as opposed to its direct experience), are even more evident in the case of certain itches where the site of irritation cannot be quite located, where one has to experiment to find it. This is particularly likely in relatively unvisited areas of one's body that are relatively poorly supplied with sensory endings – such as the back – when scratching may take the form of trial and error, or one arrives at the site of the itch by successive approximations. The hand has to guide itself to the target and to be guided to the target.

The relationship between the scratching human being and the itching human being, when both are the same person, incorporates several different kinds of distances, both explicit and inchoate.

At this stage a hand goes up in class. Surely, it will be objected, there is nothing especially human about scratching and no analysis of the scratched itch, however minute, will throw light on a distinctively human essence and the remarkable nature of human sexuality and the hand the human hand has in it. What about the horse rubbing its innocent behind on a tree? I would argue that horse's localisation of the itch is not explicit: nor is it a question of one part of the body localising the itch on another. It is the involvement of the hand that makes explicit the distance we have alluded to, and the doubleness that is implicit in it.

A hand goes up again: What of other animals that scratch themselves using paws – dogs, monkeys, etc.? Surely the distance is present here? Doesn't the paw, like the hand, have to locate the itch, or has to be guided to the spot that is located, just as in human scratching? Possibly; but there are still two sources of difference between human and non-human scratching. The first is that getting at the itch may be more difficult: clothes often intervene and they, unlike fur, have to be displaced for a satisfactory resolution. Secondly, scratching is the result of a decision – or frequently is. I scratch deliberately, at the appropriate time. I have to have permission to scratch. This will depend a little bit on a ranking of parts of my body. I will have no compunction in scratching my arm in public, more compunction about scratching my nose (lest it be misread as nose-picking), even more compunction about scratching my perineum or genitals. Scratching may be carried out stealthily – as when the genitalia are scratched through the trouser pockets – or furtively, as when an itchy perineum is scratched when one is out of view. The distances between oneself and oneself are thus typically subject to a massive cultural elaboration and even non-calculating, spontaneous scratching is carried out with deliberation. The pleasure built into scratching thus becomes a very private pleasure; or a contributor to the unfolding territory called one's privacy. This private pleasure is quite different from the private pleasure of, say, opening one's bowels because it has to be performed as opposed to being let happen.

All of these considerations confirm the justice of separating animal itch-scratching from human itch-scratching. The hand crosses the distance from 'I am itching' and the 'itch over there'. This distance is built upon a subject–object relationship within the human's own body that is not present in the itching animal for which there is simply a 'there is itching' or (for the propositional form says, indeed concedes, too much) 'itching!'

I might be tempted further to justify my beginning my exploration of sexuality from itch by noting that sexual sensations are co-located physiologically in the spinothalamic tract. I desist, however, because I am aware that that tract also carries impulses associated with pain. (Itch seems to have a middle place between sexuality and pain: uncomfortable in itself, like pain, and delicious, like sexual sensations, in its relief.) Nor am I sufficiently a reductionist to see the itched scratch as the paradigm of a satisfied desire. (Indeed, if one was favourable to reductionism, a quenched thirst or a sated hunger would be a better analogy, because neither is localised like an itch.)

The real reason for starting from itch is to suggest that the foundation of the relationship between bodies in sexual experience is rooted in the internal relationships of each of the bodies with themselves – in sensations and experiences such as itch that are mediated by the circuit of the hand where one acts upon oneself. The hand-job is the primitive sexual act. Before another hand goes up, I would emphasise that sex is not simply about sensations: it is about symbols, and power, and permission, and privilege and even love, and the world that love and affection refer to. But at the heart of human sexuality is something called love-making – unknown to animals – which crucially utilises sensations, and in this the hand has more than a mechanical role. Lovemaking is what separates human recreational sexuality – characterised except in its most brutish forms by play, by foreplay and afterplay, as well as coitus – from animal copulation. The hand is an essential part of this play.

Before we move in close to our topic, let us pause at a mezzanine position: tickling. Tickling is pleasurable and it is sometimes a preliminary to sexual contact. Sexuality can be in deadly earnest – *Venus toute a sa proie attachée* – but it can also be light, funny, Mozartian, when lust and affection may contend for the upper hand. Tickling may be innocent or not so innocent; under the guise of this ambiguity, the difficult transition from the non-sexual to the sexual may be secured. The hands-on of the tickler and the yielding helplessness of the tickled may modulate into caressing or even groping (depending on how it is taken) by the tickler and a more profound yielding of the tickled. Tickle, in short, may be a component of slap and tickle. But it is interesting in its own right because it is half way between caressing and scratching.

Unlike scratching, tickling has neither pretext nor prompt. It creates any itches that it scratches and they can be relieved only by the cessation of tickling. It has often been asked why one cannot tickle oneself. It has equally often been suggested that this is because tickling is quasi-aggressive, or a dummy assault that is withdrawn even as it is enacted: the other person lays hands on one but does not hurt or cause damage.

Tickling induces laughter because of the relief of this continually asserted-and-withdrawn threat: we cannot threaten ourselves. This would not, however, explain how tickling has such a sustained response: the threat should not be felt after the first time and tickling should lose its impact.

A more plausible explanation is that tickling induces intense uninvited sensations that one cannot escape and that, since these sensations emanate from the action of another person, there is a feeling of helplessness and invasion that eventually modulates into an agonised desire to wriggle free which is only partly resolved by the laughter one emits to tell onself that this is 'not serious'. This is supported by the fact that the most ticklish sensations originate from vulnerable areas of the body – such as the underside of the foot and the belly and other soft, unprotected flexor surfaces – and are themselves slightly uncomfortable. Under some circumstances, the sense of helplessness is exacerbated by the possibility that the assault may modulate into a more literal invasion of one's private parts, so the sense of threat may not be entirely absent or the feeling entirely unfounded. If this sense of inescapable invasion and the associated sense of helplessness underpins the feeling of being tickled, then it is obvious why one cannot tickle onself: it is not a matter of sensation but of the potential significance of the sensation. The significance of the sensation lies in its signalling that another is in control.

The tickling hand is a bearer of significant sensations.[4] Their significance is not under the control of the recipient: there is a new distance between toucher and touched because the tickled body and the tickling hand have different owners; a new opacity emerges. And yet there is the deep familiarity: it is as if the other awakens the self and brings it to the surface and makes one *be* that surface awareness. And this brings us to the caress, and not before time: we have remained too long at the threshold of foreplay and the carnal hand is almost crazy with frustration.

Our digression into tickling must not allow us to lose sight of the fundamental fact that the communication between either of the hands – as in scratching, rubbing, picking, poking – and other parts of the body has already created a distinctive, higher level bodily self-awareness and it is this that is at the root of the special relationship that may be established to the other's body in lovemaking. The caress is infused with an awareness or at least an intuition that the other person, too, has this special relationship to his or her own body. That is why it may be a means of taking hold not only of a body but of a self through the body – or through the interaction between the other's body and mine. It seems to bring back the other from his or her world, so that he or she comes to be at one place. This seems to be the chiromantic basis for Sartre's romantic idea that we may possess the world through another, who yields to our seductive advances. (Though there is a tension between the generality of the desirable body that one caresses, and the almost impersonal generality of the appetites that energise sexual desire and light up certain parts of the body as 'erogenous zones', and the irreplaceable particularity of the person whom one endeavours to access through their body.)[5]

The carnal hand is a subdivision of the cognitive hand. Hand function depends upon sensation – in other words, sensation will guide its activities (manipulation and exploration) – while at the same time the hand is a device for acquiring knowledge of the world through exploration. (Just as in human relationships, we manipulate in order to know as well as knowing in order to manipulate.) The palpable world is at one's fingertips. The palp of the fingers in an organ of revelation. The especially intimate association in humans between chiral sensation and chiral exploration opens up non-utilitarian possibilities: the hand gets to enjoy its own sensations for their own sake. And they are rather special sensations in an additional sense which it is worth examining for a moment.

In order that I should touch something so that I can know it, I have to be touched by it. The other senses do not entrain this requirement for reciprocity. The seeing eye does not have to be seen, nor the hearing ear heard, nor the smelling nose smelt. In the case of seeing, hearing and smelling the sensation does not have a location separate from the thing that is seen, heard, smelt. The sensations are referred to their sources in the case of sight and sound and, at the very least, to the extracorporeal air in the case of smell. (The lack of clear external referent makes smell more invasive than sight or sound.)[6] Touching is different. The touching itself has a clear location on the body: when I palpate an object, the palpation is clearly located on my fingers. The location of, say, seeing in my eyes is only inferential and indirect and depends upon the discovery that if I move my head or close my eyes, my visual experience changes. Touching breeds touches in the toucher: the touch of the touched. And being touched, which is located in a part of one's body, draws attention, awareness, to that part of the body. To touch someone is to make them both a touchee and a toucher whose touches focus them on the touched place.

This is what lies in the hinterland of the caress. Its strokes induce tactile sensation in the stroked and, at the same time, give knowledge of the body of the stroked. The knowing touch potentially brings the touched to the place that is known, so that it is the self-of-that-moment, as well as the body, that is touched. The summons to be where the toucher touches your body does not, of course, have to be obeyed. You may be more aware of the pressure of the seat under your bottom, or of the likelihood of being caught, or of the bus timetable which is stacked against you. But there are certain places which are more likely to command that you should become them. Everyone knows where and what they are: they are the so-called erogenous zones. It is worth pointing out that to some extent it is the social and symbolic significance, as well as the richness of sensory innervation, that determines which parts of the body command that you rush towards, or become, them when they are touched. The greater authority of strokes on the plantar surface of the foot as compared with the dorsum may be attributable to the richer sensory innervation of the former, necessary for protection of the bare-footed. But, while it is true that the genitalia are more richly innervated than the shin, the greater attention that caresses addressed to the former command over the latter manifestly has other reasons. The scrotum, for example, is rich in both sensory endings and social prohibitions.

This aside, the principle of the caress is that we are touched by that which we touch and our touchings and being touched are localised on our bodies and draw ourselves down to the places where we are localised. Touches (or at least 'touches with intent') therefore touch not only bodies but also, under certain circumstances, persons who become those touched parts. The caress localises, or aims to localise, the other's self in the part of the body that is touched and thereby endeavours to take hold of the other's self. The caress that delights in the texture of the other's body does so because in so doing, it enjoys the other's enjoyment of her body, and hence of the caress which signifies that he or she is present (or consents to be present) at the point where the caresser touches and is touched.

This is as appropriate a place as any to reiterate what it is that is special about the hand and that makes it quite different from the prehensile organs that grace the distal ends of the upper limbs of other primates: full pad-to-pad contact between the thumb and the other fingers – full opposability. While some other primates show a degree of opposability, because their thumbs have limited powers of rotation and are relatively short, opposability is incomplete. Only in humans is there a large surface of very intimate contact between the pulps of opposing fingers. Opposability, combined with the ability (which is not unique to humans but is seen in some other primates) to move the fingers independently, made it possible for the hand to become a stunningly versatile organ for interacting with the world. There is no other organ like it in the animal kingdom. The hand, moreover, is richly supplied with sensory endings, so that the multitude of grips it can draw upon may be perfectly adapted to the objects it is exploring and manipulating and be exquisitely regulated during manipulation by very subtle feedback processes. In this respect, there is, of course, much overlap with other higher mammals. However, the human hand, through the complete opposability of the thumb, has another feature: in the touching tips of the fingers, the body communicates with itself as well as with the extramanual world with unprecedented intensity. We shall discuss, in Chapter 10, how this starts a process that will result in the emergence of a self within the body and of a human world of selves within the natural one available in some degree to all sentient creatures. This is the instrument that is mobilised in the caresses of *Homo amoris*.

To speak in this grey manner does little or no justice to the warmth, passion and, above all, the tenderness of chiral (or carpal) knowledge. To get a little closer to our object, it may help to remind ourselves of the many strategies the hand deploys in pursuit of knowledge of the material world.[7] Here are a few:

Properties Investigated	*Exploratory Procedure*
Texture	Lateral motion
Temperature	Static contact
Global shape/Volume	Enclosure
Hardness	Pressure
Weight	Unsupported holding
Global shape/exact shape	Contour following

In lovemaking, all these exploratory procedures are deployed in an infinite variety of combinations and sequences. Lateral motion reveals the smoothness of the thigh. Static contact savours the warmth of the arm. The D-cupping hands, combining Enclosure and Unsupported holding, discover the wondrous shape and volume and weight of the breasts, while their fluctuant softness is uncovered by the slight fluctuations of the Pressure of the hands enclosing them. The lover's Contour following index finger traces the sulcus between the full lips that she has found so fascinating. And so on.

In touching the other's body, one seems directly to touch the other's inner difference to which the outer difference provides access. Touch seems to uncover the difference, and make it available, as one gets to know the special and private texture of that different person; to know this strange body that is not at all strange to the person whose body it is. The welcome caress gives the caresser the sense – perhaps the illusion – that one is getting closer to knowing what the body is like for the other; how it seems to him or her from within. Touching the body, one seems to lay a hand on lived time.

As we have already noted on several occasions, touch is far from simple. Its complexity reaches new heights (and depths) in lovemaking. When what the touching hand touches is the body of another person, who may or may not want to be touched, and the touch is purely for the sake of touching, the resulting haptic consciousness is many-layered. The toucher will be aware of the touched; but the touched will be also aware of the toucher; and the toucher will be aware of the touched's awareness of being touched. The toucher will look for signs indicating how the touch is being received. The touched will be aware of the toucher's awareness and may shape the signs accordingly: sighs of pleasure may be made to seem more spontaneous or at least more audible. The toucher will be equally aware of this second-order awareness of the touched and will read, and appreciate, not only the signs but the intention imparted in making the signs. (*Homo sapiens* is not only alone in transforming coitus into lovemaking. Man is the only animal that fakes orgasm.)

The account so far may suggest a clear and stable differentiation of the roles of patient and agent; but in lovemaking (as opposed to groping and touching-up, which we shall address shortly) there is not only an alternation of roles but, within a single caress, it may not be clearly who is predominantly the touched and who the toucher. (This ambiguity is even more evident when manual touch is succeeded by other, more intimate, kinds of touch.)

This, then, is the vertigo of the true caress: knowing the knowing knower who knows the knowing known, etc. It stands on the threshold of many impulses: to know, to be known by, to seize, to possess, to pleasure, to delight, to give comfort. Touch sits on the cusp between giving and taking: between giving oneself, giving pleasure, promising one's future, and taking the other, uncovering, asserting ownership; between saying 'Thou' and saying 'Mine'; between 'I am yours' and 'You are mine'; between 'I will take you' and 'I will give myself'; between 'I will free you' and 'I will possess and imprison you'. The special magic of touch in lovemaking comes from this originary fact that the haptic gaze of the hand has always to be reciprocated: while I may look at you, you may not return my gaze or even be aware of it, but if I touch you, you are obliged to be aware of it. Your awareness may be slight, as when two heterosexual, middle-aged men are pressed up against one another in a packed tube train, but not if the touch is clearly intentional and addressed.

To take our investigation of sexual touching further, we need to think back to itching and scratching. The deliberate act of scratching an itch when it is appropriate to do so incorporates, as we noted, a rather complex awareness of one's own body, in which inner distances – between the itch which I locate over there and the same itch as I experience it directly – are established and crossed – not to speak of a highly elaborated awareness of the rules which govern human grooming behaviour, arising out of a transformed relationship to our body that makes us aware both of the appearance of the body and of the appearance of its behaviour. This higher bodily self-awareness is accessed when one person touches another: the touch is imbued with a sense of the other's bodily self-awareness. More specifically, a true caress, which wants to touch not just the body but the person and his or her world, sees the caress as a way of bringing that person to a touchable surface: he is to be found at that place where he is touched and feels delight. This helps to overcome the invisibility of the person who remains hidden even within the nakedness of the unclothed body.

Or seems to: we do not know whether the sighing touchee is really there at all or whether, like Mrs Shandy at the moment of Tristam's conception, she will be preoccupied with the fact that the clocks have not been wound up, or whether the touched is suffering from savage indigestion and only pretending to be interested in what is happening. To know the person, one must learn their life, their needs, their joys and their hopes. There is, in the end, no shortcut through the body to another person's world; indeed, the intercourse of bodies can be totally disconnected from the world. And it is at this point that touching may turn nasty and caresses take a murderous turn. Those who cannot relate to others' worlds – terminally egocentric psychopaths who are desperately needful of the unconditional love of others but have none to give themselves – may still try to seize the other through her body. The psychopath cannot tolerate the notion that there is a person beyond what he can see and touch and bring to the surface through his touch. The straying attention that betrays the hidden person, the world beyond his world and this moment where he dominates hers, is called back through pinches, slaps, blows and, if this fails, strangulation. Touch is used as an instrument of pain, terror and violation. The other is seized through the forced absoluteness of her attention – in the moment of pain she is reduced to the part of her body that he is hurting. This reduction, this imprisonment, is reinforced by terror which says that there is no world outside of this place of pain. And he retains possession beyond the moments of his invasive touch through a lingering sense of violation. In such circumstances, the exploring hand is both degrading and degraded: the agent of revelation, uncovering each to the other, becomes an instrument of manipulation through defilement.

I mention this, only to ensure that the metaphysics of sexual touch does not become too sentimental. At a lesser extreme, it is to be noted that there is a difference between being touched and being touched up; between an exploration that is a mutual discovery – each to the other and each to him- or herself – and unreciprocated groping, where the lascivious groper moves not a hand but a paw over a gropee sitting out the experience in paralysis and distaste. Even when the touch is welcome, the incompetent lovemaker may be unable to rise above the grope.

The perfectly judged caress requires exquisite awareness of the other person, at the very point when one might be most self-absorbed. Caressing at its best is feminine – as if care-ess were the female mood of care. The lover who knows how to caress makes dynamic touch – which combines manipulation, exploration and communication – the means of creating a safe place for the other's self-disclosure. At the heart of the caress is the acknowledgement of what we humans are more than anything else: creatures who crave recognition and who want to be loved for what are in ourselves.[8]

This is why, above everything, the carnal hand requires – tact.[9]

5.3 HAND GAMES

The hand manipulates the world. This is essential for physical survival in the wilds of nature and economic and social survival in the human wilderness. Manipulation is work, but work can be enjoyable: there is satisfaction in the exercise of a skill. The skill may be exercised for its own sake, just as the sensations necessary to direct exploration and manipulation of the world may also be cultivated for their own sake. Hunting may turn from a necessity to a sport; running from a means of getting urgently from A to B (or urgently from A to Anywhere Else, when there is a predator or an enemy at A) to athletics. Since the hand is of pre-eminent importance in so much serious human business, it is not surprising that it figures pre-eminently in fun.

The variety of hand games – or games that involve the hand – seems limitless. The unadorned hand is involved in throwing. This has many modes: simple throwing, baseball chucking, the exquisite intricacies of spin bowling, and the power of discuss hurling and shot putting and hammer throwing. Anything and everything may be thrown under formal regulations: balls, tree trunks, frisbees, cowpats. The hand deploys its power in grappling (wrestling), in lifting (weights), in pulling (carts) and tugging (of war). The sporting hand may be supported by special gloves – as in boxing, cricket, baseball, goalkeeping, etc. It may be armed with bats, rackets, clubs, cues, lariats, firearms ... I pause at this point for fear that I might turn to *Roget* and my promise to be short on sport will be broken. Let me instead focus pretty well at random on just two aspects of sport: catching and numbers.

When we catch things we often astonish ourselves. Not infrequently catching has happened before we have decided to do it. This is as true outside as it is inside sporting contests: many a time I have caught, say, a cup before I have fully announced to myself that it is falling and in danger of being broken. The set-piece catches are, of course, those that we most admire. I mention the informal, unsung ones because catching is best seen as the genius of reaching writ large plus the genius of grasping.

In order to catch a ball that is sent in your direction without any warning – apart from the standing general afternoon-long warning that says you are playing a game of cricket and there is a batsman at large – you have to move smartly to a place where the ball is within reach of your hand. The whole body has to be transported to the right place at the right time and there to assume an appropriate posture. This may be a relatively 'simple' matter of positioning yourself so that the ball falls into your hands. Even this is not quite as simple as might appear. How do you know where to go in order to intercept the ball? Experiments that involve simulation of catching on 'trained' neural networks, suggest that when you catch a ball, you run so that as you watch the ball your angle of gaze above the horizontal increases continuously but at a decreasing rate.[10] It is remarkable, however, that this is not how we believe that we succeed in arriving at the right place at the right time. According to the experimental psychologist Peter McLeod, if you ask people

> to describe what happens to their angle of gaze as they run to catch a ball, they say that they look up as the ball rises through the air, and then down as it falls. While this is a good description of what happens if you look at a ball in flight from the side, it is completely incorrect if the ball is coming towards you.

McLeod's observation on this discrepancy is of particular interest:

> It's almost as if the subconscious self knows it can solve the problem and doesn't want to have interference from the conscious self ... The conscious is allowed to have some theory to keep it quiet, but the subconscious just gets on with solving the problem.

The enigma of mechanisms mobilised, or requisitioned, by agency gets more knotted!

The knot is drawn even more tightly when we consider the routine virtuosity of the slip fielder whose diving catches require the body to be flung across the field and whose intercepting hand is unfolded from a moving reference point. Interception may be achieved by any one of several end-postures of the arm. (The problem of too many degrees of freedom again – see section 2.2.) So there has to be an instantaneous selection of the end-posture in order that the flying body's target position, and its trajectory to that position, may be determined and the arm undergo the right amount of unfolding. Unless, moreover, the flying body's journey and the brachial unfolding are correctly paced, the desired intersection with the anticipated position of the ball will not occur. Modelling will have to take account not only of the ball's flight, but also of the current position and speed and direction of movement of the arm.

This is just for starters. For there is a good deal to sort out in advance about what should take place – happen or be enacted – when the hand makes contact with the ball. Mere collision is not enough: that would result only in a sore hand, a dropped catch and an angry bowler. The posture of the hand needs to be predetermined. Too small an aperture will mean that the ball never gets bedded in and bounces off (leaving a sore fist in its wake). Too large an aperture will means that it slips out (resulting in a frustrated fielder with a stinging palm). Assumption of the right aperture and posture of the hand is not enough: the open door of welcome has, at the very moment of contact, to turn into a barricade or cage of fingers, with fingers and thumb moving in precise formation to make the arrival into a captive. The work of the snatch squad has to be simplified by arranging that the stiffness or impedance of the arm measured at the hand is precisely matched to the ball at the time of the impact. If the impedance were too high – and the ball ran into a brick hand – it would bounce out again before the fingers had a chance to hug it; and if the impedance were too low, it would knock the hand out of the way. (There is evidence that reflex pathways are switched on and off, thereby continuously modulating the impedance just before and just after the impact.) Well held, Sir Hand! A round of applause is in order.[11]

The applause may be withheld on the grounds that the fielder is merely the site where certain mechanisms are released; that he hosted the events rather than enacted them. That the genius of catching is merely a variant on the genius of reaching, an activity which, we have already noted, is riddled with passivity: when we reach out for an object, we are dependent upon a host of mechanisms – for example, those that regulate the movement of the arm in the ballistic phases of its trajectory – of which we have little understanding. Given that the studies referred to just now suggest that catchers are in the grip of wrong ideas about

catching even as they catch, we might feel even more justified in with-
holding our support. It is important, however, not to draw the wrong
conclusion from the fact that catching incorporates many layers of
automatism; to suggest that the cricketer is merely the 'site' of the
catching and to replace 'Jones catches the ball' with 'It – Jones's body –
catches the ball'. We shall not make this error, and incorrectly conclude
that cricketing stars are automata, if we recall the full context of the
spectacular catch. This will include the game of cricket which Jones
took the trouble to attend; the many hours that Jones spent practising
catching; the special arrangements he made to ensure that he could
attend nets; and so on. Remembering this will ensure that we reinsert
the self – Jones – into the moment that seems quite void of Jones'
consciousness.[12] A round of applause is most definitely in order: for the
moment of dazzling virtuosity is the product of hours, days, weeks and
months of dedication.

Sport is full of these virtuoso versions of the manifold dexterities of
daily life. And a sporting career will clock up many thousands of documented and undocumented acts of bodily genius. Which bring us to our
second theme. Sooner or later numbers will start entering the scene: the
personal best time, the number of first-class centuries, the lifetime's total
of home runs, the furthest distance hurled, the total PGA earnings, and
so on. The shouting dies away and sweat and toil and delight and
disappointment and precision and grunt all fade into the spaceless,
odourless, silent pages of the almanac. The obsession with numbers and
units – runs, weights, times, distances – prefigures the digital world we
shall explore in due course.[13]

5.4 POSTSCRIPT: HANDY (LIKE)

What follows is both deadly serious and semi-serious.

Before the hand breaks up into its fingers and brachio-chiral gives
place to chiro-digital, I'd like to take a last look at the notion of the
'Handy' or, as my fellow Liverpudlians used to say, ''Andy' or ''Andy,
like'. I want to revisit something that I didn't quite get to the bottom of
when we were talking about 'The Genius of Reaching'; namely, the very
nature of 'The Handy' and the connected notion of 'over there', 'within
reach'; and, after this, glance briefly at the notion of 'The 'andy (like)'.[14]

The ready-to-hand is a fundamental category in Heidegger's ontology. In *Being and Time* Heidegger argues, against scientism, and the
objectivising and instrumentalising ontology of a vision dominated by
technology, that the world does not consist primarily of material objects
– the neutral objective presences of scientific investigation – or of

isolated subjects somehow encountering or constructing those presences. So far as humans are concerned, the world – the world that is truly lived in – consists of beings that are 'ready-to-hand'. The 'ready-to-hand' includes things such as tools (though is by no means confined to tools) which are linked in a nexus of signification that is the world of *Da-sein* – or being-there – which is the human world. Being in the world of the ready-to-hand is not something that *Da-sein* achieves; being-in-the-world is constitutive of *Da-sein*. While the world of material objects – the world envisaged in physics and, indeed, in objective science – is composed of separate pieces, material items, which can never truly touch or be in touch with one another. Though nevertheless the world of *Da-sein* consists of separable items, they are in communion with one another inasmuch as they support each other's meaning. No materialist account of the interaction between hammers and nails or between human bodies and other material bodies could generate the connection between the hammer and the nail or my awareness of the world in which the hammer and the nail make functional sense and that sense implies and incorporates the sense of rooves, dwellings, human need for warmth and shelter, and so on. The world of the ready-to-hand really is a world in which everything belongs to and with everything else; the world of the present-at-hand, of the physics that deals with 'objective presences', is a heap of separate things.

In trying to clarify the notion of the ready-to-hand, Heidegger examines in great detail the relationship between objective physical distances and the subjective notion of 'over there'; between the idea of objects set out and separated in physical space and the notion of handy beings in *Da-sein*'s world. According to Heidegger,

> the aroundness of the surrounding world, the specific spatiality of the beings encountered in the surrounding world is grounded in the world-liness of the world, and not the other way round, that is, we cannot say that the world is in turn objectively present in space.[15]

The world of *Da-sein* is not something that is put together by, is a result of, an aggregation of inert material objects. Nearness and farness do not come into being like this. 'The structured nearness of useful things,' he argues, 'means that they do not simply have a place in space, objectively present somewhere' (ibid., p. 95). The place of the useful thing is to be understood 'in terms of a totality of the interconnected places of the context of useful things at hand in the surrounding world' (ibid.). The spatiality of *Da-sein*'s being-in-the-world is therefore rather special: it shows the character of what he calls de-distancing and directionality.

These are the dimensions of 'over there': they are not objective physical dimensions but existential dimensions.

It is de-distancing that is of particular interest to us:

> De-distancing means making distance disappear, making the being at a distance of something disappear, bringing it near. *Da-sein* is essentially de-distancing. As the being that it is, it lets beings be encountered in nearness. (ibid., p. 97)

What more primordial example could there be of 'making distances disappear' than reaching out and grasping an object? Behind the genius of reaching is a deeper genius: the sense that things are there to be reached, the intuition of reachables. Human reaching, as a preliminary to grasping and manipulating, is, like the ready-to-hand and being-in-the-world, written into the constitution of *Da-sein* – of the sense of who, what and where we are. To borrow one of Heidegger's favourite terms, the concept of de-distancing confers 'equiprimordial' status to the intuition of the ready-to-hand and the possibility of reaching out for it. At the heart of our grasp of the world is the sense that the world is 'there' to be grasped. Reaching and grasping are based upon an intuition that the object which is over there is not irredeemably over there: it is potentially here. It is available.

The links being made here may cause some discomfort. First of all, reaching must reach out for something real. The handiness of the ready-to-hand must be rooted in its really being physically near: it cannot be grasped if, objectively, it is many arm lengths away. To give readiness-to-hand priority over 'objective' spatial proximity raises the question about the reality of what is reached for: reaching arms are, above all, realists. Illusory apples cannot solve real needs and the belief that apples are handy in the sense of being literally within reach cannot be illusory.[16] Reaching, touching and grasping are the touchstones of reality.

Another concern arises from the fact that reaching and grasping are not unique to humankind. *Da-sein*, however, is identical with human being.[17] What is it about human reaching and grasping that has such portentous consequences? – consequences that inform the entirety of this enquiry into the hand and also underpin Heidegger's ontology. It would not be quite accurate to defend the uniqueness of human being-in-the-world by arguing that de-distancing is not part of the animal's ontology, that it simply bumps into what it takes hold of, that its grasp is not driven by an inspired sense of the availability of the object, by the sense that the distance from it can be cancelled because object and animal belong to the same world. This is not where the difference lies.

The difference lies in the clarity with which this 'handiness' is appreciated by humans and the extent to which it is explicit and elaborated. The handy object – ready-to-hand – is a focus for a sense of possibility in the way that 'pawiness' is not – the 'pawy' is hardly developed. This sense of possibility is constitutive of *Da-sein*. *Da-sein*, according to Heidegger, projects possibilities for itself. It is possibility (in relation to explicit need) and not (just) spatial proximity that makes the object handy.

The pre-eminent manipulative skills of *Homo sapiens* greatly extend the range of possibility: objects can be manipulated to make them of use in ways that are not prefigured in their intrinsic nature. That is why the human world is a nexus of signifying things, almost a store-shed of actual and possible tools. (This was true before the world became filled with artefacts and the landscape became a toolscape.) De-distancing is intensified by manipulation which links the object more precisely into interest and need. Toolmaking man extends the range of handiness in every sense – more kinds of things, further things. Even the stars become in a sense ready-to-hand. It is the successive interactions between the reaching hand (or the collective reaching of hands) and the reached for world that increasingly makes the human world uniquely a nexus of the ready-to-hand.[18]

All of which is at once exciting and complex. We shall return to de-distancing when we consider another of its modes – the virtual reaching of pointing. For the present let us seek a little light relief and switch our attention briefly from the 'handy' world of Heidegger to the ''andy (like)' world of my Liverpool childhood. Liverpool may stand for the world, or the world picture, or the lack of world picture, that all philosophers and those who would wish to adopt a philosophical viewpoint have to escape. ''Andy (like)' is a dephilosophised 'handy'. Everything that is ''andy (like)' is obvious; most obvious of all is its 'andiness. Everything is foreknown, obvious, and anything that is not foreknown is treated with suspicion. The jeering Professors of Piss-taking – of which Liverpool has not a few – will deflate astonishment and not allow complexity. 'Yer talk nice, lad, but your clothes are shabby.'

To deal with this anti-philosophical view, I need only to borrow two of the fingers we shall discuss in the next Part of this book and ask them to cooperate in a gesture which we have already explored – and signal victory for wonder and something else for 'idle talk' which is 'the possibility of understanding everything without any previous appropriation of the matter.[19]

NOTES

1. For confirmation of this suspicion, see Raymond Tallis, 'Serious fun', in *Theorrheoa and After* (London: Macmillan, 1999).

2. It is important that this should not be misunderstood. I am not suggesting that the emergence of consciousness, and of agency out of causation and mechanism, can itself be explained in evolutionary terms; only that if an animal has to act consciously to survive, then it is a good idea that the right (survival-promoting) actions are rewarded with pleasure and the wrong (life-threatening) ones are associated with pain. This distinction is elaborated in Raymond Tallis, *The Explicit Animal*, 2nd edn (London: Macmillan, 1999). See especially 'Biologising consciousness: I evolutionary theories'. We shall return to the relationship between biology, behaviour and agency in volume 2 of this trilogy.

3. For an additional discussion of the relevance of this insight to human sexuality, see Raymond Tallis, 'Carpal knowledge: a natural philosophy of the caress', *Philosophy Now*, September/October 2001, pp. 24–7. It is also discussed in Raymond Tallis, *Enemies of Hope*, 2nd edn (London: Macmillan, 1999).

4. Identical hand movements may induce an unbearable sense of tickle or a delicious feeling of being caressed, depending upon the context and the significance of the touching.

5. This thought has been influenced by Christopher Hamilton's illuminating chapter on 'Sex' in his marvellous *Living Philosophy: Reflections on Life, Meaning and Morality* (Edinburgh: Edinburgh University Press, 2001).

6. The case of taste is more complex: the taste is located within the body – in the mouth – but it is not *of* the body. The tongue doesn't taste itself – even when, as in illness, we have a nasty taste in the mouth that appears to be unrelated to anything put into it. Taste differs from touch, because the sensation is still of the (tasted) object and not of the body. Taste is also peculiar because it depends upon touching the tasted object, which has to be placed in the mouth; in some respects, it may be regarded as a subdivision of touch, which becomes distracted by the taste that is the sign of something other than the touched part of the body. The tasting mouth, moreover, is not an exploratory organ in the way that the hand is: it loses itself in the object that loses itself in the mouth. Except, perhaps, in early childhood, where the mouth is a much more important organ of cognition. The toddler puts the object in the mouth in order to get at its true nature.

7. What follows is deeply indebted to the fascinating chapter on 'Manual exploration and haptic processing', by Susan Lederman and Roberta Klatzky, in Alan Wing, Patrick Haggard and J. Randall Flanagan (eds), *Hand and Brain: The Neurophysiology and Psychology of Hand Movements* (San Diego: Academic Press, 1996).

8. In *The Knowing Animal*, we shall examine the idea that lovemaking brings human knowledge back to its roots in the special relationship of the human body to itself; and that the caress aims to bring the self unpacked from that special relationship back to the body and make it literally tangible.

9. There are many variations of each exploratory mode. For example, the series of horizontal dashes as in stroking may be replaced by a series of vertical dots as in patting. And I have dipped into only a small part of the spectrum of caresses, which spans many different ways of being together – from the mother soothing the forehead of a sleeping, fevered child to the pre-grope of the clumsy lover.

10. I owe this information to a chance reading of an article by Georgina Ferry about the work of the experimental psychologist Peter McLeod. 'The cricketer's eye', *Oxford Today*, Trinity Issue, 2001, p. 30.
11. I have simplified the fielder's task a little by assuming that the catch is one-handed. If both hands are involved, they will have to communicate with one another so that coordinated activity, rather than a three-way crash between two hands and their prey, results.
12. The relationship between agency and mechanism, between reason-informed behaviour and its automatic components, is visited at many points in this trilogy. The most sustained examination of the issue is in volume 2: *I Am: A Philosophical Inquiry into First-Person Being*, though it will also be discussed in Chapter 10.
13. This paragraph is haunted by Philip Larkin's wonderful poem, 'At Grass', about racehorses in their retirement:

> Almanacked, their names live; they
> Have slipped their names and stand at ease.

14. The exposition that follows is very brief. I hope it is not so brief as to be incomprehensible. There are many brilliant short accounts of Heidegger's ontology, notably Richard Polt's *Heidegger: An Introduction* (London: UCL Press, 1999) and David E. Cooper's *Heidegger* (London: Claridge Press, 1996). My own views about the strengths and limitations of Heidegger's ontology are given in *A Conversation with Martin Heidegger* (Basingstoke: Palgrave, 2002) and will be further developed in volume 3 of this trilogy.
15. Martin Heidegger, *Being and Time*, a translation of *Sein und Zeit* by Joan Stambaugh (New York: State University of New York Press, 1996), p. 94.
16. Illusory apples cannot solve real needs. While it may be argued (as I will discuss in Volume 3 of this trilogy) that needs are not the real properties of things – of the material organisms we are – they are real in another sense. Needs have an objective aspect – for example, biochemical evidence of dehydration or protein-calorie deficit. All that is 'unreal' is the experience of need. And we are given experience of needs in order to deal with them, so that we survive. (If objective dehydration were not associated with subjective thirst, then, in the absence of instinctive mechanisms that link the former with the latter, we would not behave appropriately.)
17. Heidegger was sometimes ambivalent about whether animals were, or had, *Da-sein*. However, he is fairly unequivocal in some places and his analyis makes sense only as a description of (uniquely) human being-in-the-world. In a footnote on p. 53 of *Being and Time* he specifically equates human being with *Da-sein*.
18. The alert reader will notice a bit of fancy footwork here. I am not suggesting for a moment that the special properties of the human hand underpin the 'worldliness', the 'enworlding, enworlded', capacity of *Da-sein*. This would be rather to put the cart before the horse. Ontology is prior to anatomy – even to functional anatomy. However, I am suggesting that the hand has had a hand in the elaboration of the world as the ready-to-hand. Where I am fudging the issue is over the question of the level at which, and the extent to which, the hand has had a hand in this extraordinary development which it is one of the tasks of this book and its two successors to make visible in order that it may be celebrated.
19. Heidegger, *Being and Time*, p. 158.

PART TWO

CHIRO-DIGITAL

CHAPTER 6

One-Finger Exercises

6.1 INTRODUCTION

Although it would be absurd to imagine the fingers acting in isolation from the body of the hand, or the arm, the majority of the tasks that people perform with the hand require differentiated movements of the fingers. It is this fractionation of the movements of the fingers which are able to achieve full opposition with the thumb, that makes possible the characteristic genius of human manipulations and establishes the great distances between human manipulation and the most sophisticated animal pawing. Opposability superimposed on top of fractionated finger movements opens up the possibility of the infinitely varied grips of the human hand.

Even though the digits work separately, they are also great team players and, while different sub-sets of digits are prominent in different activities, there are very few manual actions that do not place demands on all the fingers. For example, when I hold a pen, this seems to involve only the thumb, index and middle fingers; indeed, I classify penmanship as 'a three-fingered exercise'. The stabilising role of the fourth and little fingers, however, is not negligible. Even pointing – a one-finger exercise if ever there was one – requires the other digits to flex and so clear the field to give the index finger the necessary prominence.

We shall examine this teamwork in the next chapter when we look at a few 'polydactylic exercises'. The purpose of the present chapter is simply to introduce the members of the team and to celebrate a few of their idiosyncrasies. The thumbnail portraits that I offer are by no means complete: I have simply described things that I have found of interest and used the facts that happen already to be at my fingertips or available in the books that are ready-to-hand in my study.

6.2 THUMB

If I went in for catchy titles, then this book would be called 'Thumbs up for the Thumb' or 'The Rule of the Thumb'; for, as already noted, it is the special properties of this digit that have enabled us to manipulate the world in the remarkable way that we humans do and bring so much of nature under our collective thumb so that the earth bears the human thumb-print and sometimes looks rather too well thumbed.

The thumb – otherwise known as 'pollex' – is not, of course, unique to mankind or even to higher mammals. The term strictly refers not only to the first digit of the human hand but to 'the innermost digit of the forelimb in air-breathing vertebrates'. The insignificant appearance of the thumb makes it difficult to believe what difference it – or the difference in the behaviour of human as opposed to non-human thumbs – makes to every aspect of our lives. This ugly dwarf among the fingers lies at the root of manipulation; it is he – the opposable thumb – who has made us human beings lords of creation. If the other digits could form judgements, he would doubtless be despised by them, be the butt of their jokes.[1] After all, unlike the others, he has only two bones or phalanges, hence his name which means 'stout' or 'thick'. 'Thick' is far from the mark: he is the brightest boy on the block. Of course, he looks like a serviceable dwarf: Tom Thumb, the resourceful thumbling. Or Alberich the ugly one, who gave up love for power. And power he certainly has: in any cooperative enterprise, he is the team leader, the foreman, the bosun, the captain, the lynch-pin. And like all good leaders he never tries to go it alone. He knows what the result would be: all thumbs is the opposite of dexterous.

He enjoys this authority because, as we have already observed in section 1.2, he differs from the other digits in a supremely important respect: freedom of movement. The thumb can be moved in many more directions than the other fingers, so that he can speak to them all, and they can all speak to him, but they cannot speak to each other. If, then, the thumb is the ring-master, it is because he is the only digit able to relate to all the others and, what is more, in an asymmetrical fashion. Tip-to-tip contact with the other digits seems reciprocal; but when it is a question of side-to-side, the thumb seems be the toucher, controlling the pressure, and the other finger the touched. And this has incalculable consequences.

Let us revisit this seemingly minor difference and tease it out in a bit more detail. The thumb is essential for both power and precision grips. (There are one or two 'primitive' grips – such as the scissors grip and the hook grip, both of which we shall discuss in the next chapter – in which the thumb has a minor part to play, but they are the exception.) It is not the fact of opposition but its degree that is uniquely developed in humans. As John Napier puts it:

> The mass of muscle at the base of the thumb, known as the mound of Venus or more prosaically the ball of the thumb, is composed of a series of small muscles that acting together produce a rotatory movement by which the thumb swings towards the palm. This movement is known as *opposability*. For the movement to be of functional significance the thumb must oppose something. In man, the most precise function that the hand is capable of is to place the tip of the thumb in *opposition* to the tip of the index finger so that the pulp of the two digits make maximum contact. In this position, small objects can be manipulated with an unlimited potential for fine pressure adjustments or minute directional corrections. Opposition to this degree is the hallmark of mankind. No nonhuman primate can replicate it. Although most people are unaware of the evolutionary significance of this finger–thumb opposition they cannot be unaware of its implications in international sign language; it is the universal gesture of human success.[2]

The precision exhibited in this gesture of precision lies precisely at the heart of the book's concerns.

Full opposition is necessary for precision grip. In prosimians, such as lemurs, opposition is comparable to that of a pair of pliers: it is described as 'pseudo-opposition'. Woolly monkeys use the adjacent sides of the the thumb and index finger and middle fingers, 'just as one might pick up an object with a pair of blunt scissors, using them in the manner of forceps' (Napier 1971, p. 183), though there is an increased use and increased sensitivity of the fingertips. In catarrhine monkeys, in whom power and precision grips are fully differentiated, the anatomy of the thumb is similar to that in humans: the thumb is opposable and the index finger is capable of a good deal of independent movement. There are two important differences from humans. First, there are still heavy demands made on the monkey's forelimb from locomotion and, in addition, but not unconnected, the environment does not demand of the monkey the high degree of manipulative skill that is required of man. Catarrhine hands are still, in essence, feet. Secondly, the opposition between the thumb and the index finger is nowhere near as functionally effective as it is in man. The length of the thumb compared with that of the index finger (the so-called opposability index) is less in non-human primates compared with humans. The difference between the opposability indices of man and, say, a baboon – respectively 65 per cent and 57 per cent – is slight; and yet out of that slight difference so much has come. It is the greater comparability of the lengths of the thumb and index finger that enables the pulp surfaces of the thumb and the index finger to be approximated in a way that is crucial for the distinctively human precision grip and for the manipulation of the planet.

Apes missed out on this development because they invested in adaptation to a mode of locomotion called brachiation – swinging from one hold to another by means of the arms. This led to a conflict between the demands of locomotion and of manipulation. Locomotion won and brachiation made the fingers the servants of the hands. A long thumb would get in the way of the hook grip of the ape swinging through the trees: the thumb was therefore kept short. Apes may have been swinging up the right trees but, from the longer-term point of view of eventually gaining power over nature, they were barking up the wrong one. Napier quotes a study which found that, whereas in apes the muscles controlling the thumb constituted 24 per cent of the total hand musculature, in man they constituted 39 per cent. This is why the earth is not the planet of the apes.

It is probably stretching the analogy too far to suggest that, like Alberich to whom we compared him just now, the thumb has traded love for power. He is, however, the father of technology. In precisely what way, we shall examine in Chapters 9 and 10. For the present we note that many different modes of gripping that the opposable thumb, superimposed on fractionated finger movement, makes possible open the way to the multitude of tools that enable us to grasp, shape and transform the world, so that ultimately our lives are passed in a uniquely human world at so many distances from the natural world that encloses us. From these numerous modes of gripping arise the infinitely various and subtle modes of human prehension, apprehension and comprehension. With his grip, the thumb has enabled us to wriggle a little out of the grip of the world. We know how to subordinate the natural order of things to our needs: we are able to thumb a ride on the energies of the natural world whose laws we have uncovered.

'He'! Yes, he – for all the reasons given so far. And also because his name is derived from 'tum', which means 'to swell', as in 'tumescence'. Cocked, he shows his essence. And much more besides: the cocked thumb says many things; for, even when free of the burden of direct manipulation, he still manipulates the world. Think of all those things the upwardly cocked thumb can mean: 'Let the gladiator live'; 'That's just right'; 'Don't back any further'; 'Quality performance'; 'Yes, I agree'; 'YES!'; 'All the best': 'You're my mate'. 'We've won/done it/ pulled it off!' The thumb may even hitch a ride from the entirety of language as when it is used to communicate with a speech-impaired person who may respond by thumbs up for 'Yes' and thumbs down for 'No'. Even this potent secondary binarisation of the boundless semantic field created through human communication can be played with. The thumb may be made to vacillate between the 'up' and the 'down' positions in order to symbolise uncertainty. Intermediate elevations and declivations may be assumed to represent intermediate degrees of enthusiasm, agreement, approval: one, two or two and a half cheers.

One could go on forever. To bring a potentially interminable meditation to an end, let us declare 'thumbs up', ladies and gentlemen, for the thumbness that has liberated us from the dumbness of mental numbness.

6.3 INDEX

Mr Bucket and his fat forefinger are much in consultation together under existing circumstances. When Mr Bucket has a matter of this pressing interest under his consideration, the fat forefinger seems to rise to the dignity of a familiar demon. He puts it to his ears, and it whispers information; he puts it to his lips, and it enjoins him to secrecy; he rubs it over his nose, and it sharpens his scent; he shakes it before a guilty man, and it charms him to destruction. The Augurs of the Detective Temple invariably predict, that when Mr Bucket and his finger are much in conference, a terrible avenger will be heard of before long.

... [Mr Bucket] is in the friendliest condition towards his species, and will drink with most of them. He is free with his money, affable in his manners, innocent in his conversation – but, through the placid stream of his life, there glides an under-current of forefinger.[3]

Pointing

The index finger indicates; and though this may seem self-evident, the action is not as transparent as may appear at first sight, a fact to which the frustrated owners of stupid dogs will testify.

You throw a stick, the dog doesn't see where it has landed and you end up fetching it yourself. Pointing in the direction of the stick does not help at all. The dog does not understand the import of pointing, failing to grasp not only what it is that the pointing is pointing at, but also that it is pointing at anything at all. It doesn't get the point of pointing. This is especially irritating because pointing seems like a natural language that should be comprehensible not only to any human being but also to any creature that has a certain level of intelligence: it should be able to *see* what you mean. Even a dog as stupid as yours, you feel, should be able to grasp that you are pointing at that stick over there and showing him where the stick is.

And yet, the more you think about pointing, the more remarkable and complex it appears. It is easy to miss the complexity and to imagine that pointing is a self-explaining means of communication, especially as it is one of the earliest modes of communication used by infants. We have all had the initially delightful and ultimately wearying experience of being in the company of an infant passing through the pointing stage. The little finger, still looking soapy as if reflecting the child's incompletely woken consciousness, is used to pick out objects of interest and thereby to interrogate the world: 'Wazzat? Wazzat?' the child asks, again and again, pointing in turn to the many objects the world contains: 'Doggy', 'Moon', 'Mummy'. The enumeration of these objects is not only a naming ceremony, a low-budget christening, but also a primitive kind of celebration, constructing a poetry of nouns and objects, discovering and establishing and reinforcing and revelling in the connection between them, signalling the emergence of another voice housing Being in language, another human assuming her privileged status as 'a shepherd of Being'. And the adult in turn points to things and says: 'Doggy', 'Moon', 'Mummy', reinforcing those links between the wondrous world of things and the strange world of those sounds that will come to mean things.

Because pointing seems so transparent as a means of communication, some philosophers, most famously St Augustine, have regarded so-called 'ostensive' definition as the obvious means by which a child acquires the vocabulary of its native language:

> When they (my elders) named some object, and accordingly moved towards something, I saw this and grasped that the thing was called by the sound they uttered when they meant to point it out.[4]

Equally famously, Wittgenstein, in the opening sections of his *Philosophical Investigations*, criticised this story about language acquisition.[5] It did not, he argued, take account of the fact that language is not merely (to vary Hughlings Jackson) a noun heap: there are many words that have quite different functions from those served by nominal nouns – for example, conjunctions, articles, prepositions, etc. Even those words apparently labelling concrete objects do not function in isolation, though they may seem to do so in the telegraphic speech of small children waking out of their *infans* state. Words, Wittgenstein argued, operate through being integrated into expressions; expressions, moreover, have meaning 'only in the stream of life'. A noun or name heap would *say* – indicate, express, represent, indeed *name* – nothing.

Moreover, ostensive definitions – definitions that are 'enacted' by pointing to an example of the object defined – would not help the infant to tie the knot between a word and a referent. For how, Wittgenstein argues, without a good deal of pre-existing understanding, would it know *what* was being pointed at? An adult pointing to a cat and saying 'Cat!' could be pointing to one of many different things: the whole cat, or its fur, or its naughtiness, or the fact that it is surprising that it is there at all when it should be in its basket. And is it not true, also, that the language that is acquired is infinitely richer and more subtly organised than the language that is taught? No quantity of successful pointings could begin to help the child grasp how language works and how we can use it to mean things to others.[6]

These questions, however profound, are still too superficial, too detailed, to uncover the truly remarkable nature of pointing which is hinted at by the dog's frustrating inability to see what I am pointing at and that I am pointing at it. After the passage quoted above, St Augustine goes on to say this:

> Their intention was shewn by their bodily movements, as it were the natural language of all peoples: the expression of the face, the play of the eyes, the movement of other parts of the body, and the tone of voice which expresses our state of mind in seeking, having, rejecting, or avoiding something. (*Confessions*)

Pointing is central to this putative 'natural language' – literal 'indication' using the index finger. It is the finger, protruding from several sorts of background – the pointer's body, the complex noise of her material presence and self-presence, and so on – that is supposed to pick out the intended referent. According to this account, the pointing finger is a kind of referring expression and the object, the pointee, is the referent. Thus the natural language of 'Pointish' is supposed to connect the world divided up according to physical or geometrical space with the world apportioned according to semantic space.

Actually, pointing is not as 'natural', in the sense of requiring no further interpretation, as we may think. The fact that the pointee is to be located along a line extrapolated from the long axis of the arm or index finger is not self-evident. Nor is the rule that the projection should be in the direction leading from the shoulder to the finger, and not vice versa. Admittedly, protending and grasping – where reaching is along that axis and along that direction – which literally pick out objects, by picking them up, would argue for these rules but only indirectly; and, as constraints on possible interpretations, they would not stand up to counter-instances. The fact that no other animal points, or understands pointing, testifies to the unnatural nature of pointing.

Even if one acknowledges this, it is difficult to resist the notion that Pointish is a half-way stage between the world of dumb animals, like our dog, or dumb humans, human beings like an infant, and the world of less dumb human beings like me. And in one sense it is. Seeing the point of pointing, to the point of pointing things out oneself, is at least half way to the explicit communication systems of the human being. And that is why the dog cannot, while an infant can, make that half-way stage. There is an awe-inspiring world of understanding built into the literal indications of the primordial pointer.

My pointing something out to you, using a part of my own body as a pointer, is predicated on something rather extraordinary in my relationship to my body and, through my body, to the extracorporeal space around it and in my sense of the relationship between my body and extracorporeal space. Pointing uncovers profound, foundational intuitions that I have about what it is to be myself in the world. I use my finger to divide up the space around me into sectors; I select a region of 'over there' but do not merge with over there: it is as if my body partly wakes out of its surroundedness to know that it is surrounded and that that surrounding can be partitioned and dissected. In pointing, we see an early step from the experiential space we share with beasts to geometric space which only humans occupy; from implicit 'thereness' to the abstract space of mathematical and linguistic discourses.

The communicative act of pointing something out, or of understanding that someone is pointing something out, is also inseparably linked with a wider sense of other people as sharing a world in common with oneself, a common space, but accessing it from different viewpoints, so that they may not have the knowledge that one has oneself. While the pointing-supported cry 'Doggy!' may be seeking attention and praise – for cleverly using a word – it also implies a recognition that another person has different noticings from oneself. Pointing points to where the other person should attend – or ad-tend – in order to share one's noticings, to participate in a positional advantage one has.

Successful pointing, in short, requires many of the underpinnings necessary for language as humans understand it: the abstraction from the perceptual space that surrounds one; a sense of one's body as an object that is located as are other objects, in this half-abstracted space; a sense of others as being located in a world that is both shared with oneself and importantly different from one's own world, so that they may be ignorant of what one knows, but at the same time capable of being cured of that ignorance – in this instance by means of indication; a world of knowledge and ignorance.[7]

While the kind of pointing we have been talking about may be primitive, it is also rich and complicated and, I'm sorry to say, specifically human, so that, however hard you point the stick out to the dog, you will have to fetch it yourself.[8]

Wagging

The forefinger singles out objects by pointing. Sometimes that object is another human being. This finger, which says 'You!', picks you out of the crowd. It volunteers you. It chooses you. It highlights you. You are the [lucky, unlucky, right, in-the-wrong, etc.] one. You are, anyway, the One and, curdled thus to sweating solidity in the blinding light of indication, are made to be your visible self, skewered on the axis extending from another's forefinger. The index finger is, above all, the finger of blame. It locates blame and then, with that sinuous beckoning we have already dwelt upon (in section 3.2), draws in the culpable one to its interrogation and punishment.

The index sometimes underlines its anger by wagging up and down. The wagging forefinger, however, by no means confines itself to blame. On this very complex matter, however, I will be brief not only because I have already gone on too long about pointing, but also because wagging is very irritating and the less we dwell on it the better. For wagging the index finger is not just a way of emphasising what is being said, like articulating with special clarity in order to be helpful. On the contrary, it is a means of asserting oneself, of dominating one's interlocutor.

The wagger talks *at* – not with or even to; the wagger towers as well as talks. 'Listen up,' wagging says. 'You mark my words.' 'Clean out your ears.' 'I shall say this only once and I shall say it clearly, so that even someone as stupid as you can understand.' And, by the way, 'Don't you dare contradict, doubt, disobey'. 'I am [factually; conceptually; morally] right and you are [factually; conceptually; morally] wrong.' 'I know more than you; I understand more than you; I matter more than you.' 'The meanings are mine, they are in my keeping.'

The wagger canes the air, prods the space between the two of you, and so whacks and rams the message home. The wagger points to his or her own meanings and pre-empts yours or pushes them to the margin: there is room for only one set of meanings; though there are two of us, there is only one valid viewpoint and this, validly, brushes aside, erases, the other. At best the other's observations are tolerated briefly as interruptions. You, the wagged-at, exist, of course, but only in the wagger's world, as a part of it, to be made to understand it. The wagger, on the other hand, does not exist in the wagged-at's world as a mere part of it, obliged to swallow your meanings.

The severest form of wagging beats in time to the words, so that each one is a suasive slap: 'Do not' (wag) 'do' (wag) 'that' (wag) 'ever' (wag) 'again' (wag). 'Und-er-stand?' (wag, wag, wag). The wagger does not merely tell you: he tells you off and puts the error of your ways in italics.

There is only one reply to his wagging finger. Return the digits with exactly 100 per cent interest. (See section 3.2.)

Other

It would be a pity to end our celebration of this remarkable character on a sour note. The index finger would have grounds for complaint if it were portrayed simply as a pointer and wagger. Although it already has had more than its share of column inches – disproportionate, at any rate to its own column inches – some of the other roles of the index finger at least deserve a mention. Where would nose-picking and other even less acceptable modes of grooming be without the index finger? It is so handy for entering small orifices and so intelligent when it is inside them. It presses buttons and (with a little help from colleagues) pulls triggers. It is the supreme prodder, able to hit the target with stereotactic precision and to regulate the pressure of the prod with extraordinary accuracy and tact. Even more admirably, it helps us to count – pointing to each object in turn and reciting the numbers in ascending order of magnitude (more of this in Chapter 8) – and, when we are tyros, to keep our place as we read.[9]

There is more, much more, to be said about his remarkable digit, but the index finger is not the only one that counts in the great scheme of things.

6.4 MIDDLE

But why *impudicus* for the middle finger. Possibly because it was used as a gesture of derision in Latin and some Arab countries ... perhaps because being the longest digit it is ideally disposed to carry out the sexual caresses of the female genitals or indelicate scratching operations.[10]

The middle finger has little in the way of distinctive identity and terri-tory of its own. It is the supreme team player: although it is the tallest and strongest member of the group, it submerges itself in the collective effort. It comes into its own in the power grip, especially in those extreme instances where the hand agglutinates to a fist. This grip – used in pulling, tugging, dragging, etc., in all the real work that flows from the penalty of Adam, and so in the saving of lives and the making of the makings of dinner and other essential actions – owes much of its power to the unobtrusive efforts of this Stakhanovite, this selfless dray horse.

On the very rare occasion when it is given its own moment of separate glory, the gesture that results is not of the politest. This fact must not be interpreted as betraying the accumulated resentment of a pathologically polite and compliant giant who one day goes berserk and butchers a crowd of people with his bare hands. Though the logic of this very rude gesture does derive from the finger's size and its particular ability to fill a certain cylindrical cavity in the female body and one can therefore understand why the structure into which it is, by implication, inserted may have a preference for this finger over the others – thus giving a lie to the popular myth that size doesn't matter – this should not prompt a prolonged reflection on the nature of rude gestures. We have already reverted too often to the significance of the cooperative efforts of two divergent fingers.

6.5 RING

This digit evolved long before rings, of course, long before the institution of marriage and the linkage between betrothal and marriage and rings, a convention that dates back only a couple of thousand years to the Romans. To call this digit the ring finger is therefore something of a *hysteron proteron* – putting the cart, or the Cartier, before the horse. Even a kind of category error. And yet it is a respectable error, for the fourth finger is nominated thus even in anatomy books which, one would have thought, would deal in cultural – geographical, historical – invariants, because biology digs beneath culture. Nevertheless, such books routinely inform us that (for example) damage to the ulnar nerve affects the sensation of the medial side of the *ring* finger. Out of consistency, one ought to call the fourth finger on an ape the ring finger!

With that little bit of pedantry out of our system, we are free to think about the curious institution of placing rings on the ring finger. The connection is marriage and the vow of fidelity is something that the Professors of Obviousness will relish: it is a symbol of the exclusive sexual relationship between the man and the wife: the finger is the penis and the ring the orifice that will accept it. The fact that both parties may have fingers and both may have rings – so that they are exchanged – is but a detail, given that the analogy is so compelling: you can't get a second finger into the ring.

There are poignant overtones. The nobility of gold that makes it resistant to all the corruptions that degrade base metals permits it to underwrite the enduringness of the relationship. Hence an 'eternity ring'.

Marriage may be the nearest we approximate to eternity in human relations: to embark on marriage in one's youth is to have a sense of the permanent impermanence of one's life; to lay down one of the major features of one's old age.[11] This is the adornment that nurses and mortuary attendants are most likely to have to remove from our bodies. Look at this and meditate on how your body is only on loan. Look at the ring on your finger and consider how your corruptible finger will one day be as unowned by you as the ring, sold on, encircling the finger of a stranger.

There are less poignant overtones. The ring speaks of other, less morally demanding, things than enduring commitments: it broadcasts current wealth; it stands metonymically for the submerged pile of Mammon which is to be shared between the troth-bound pair; and it places the best possible interpretation on the social location to which the couple will accede by their chosen bond. The cost of the ring makes a complex statement murmured in the twilit borderland between value and price: it says how much she is cherished and how much she has or will cost.

As time passes, the unchanging ring will enclose a changing finger. As the bearer engrosses, for example, or her fingers are swollen with arthritis or oedema, the ring will dig itself a little trench from which it cannot be extricated when the time comes for the ring to be separated from the body as the body has become separated from the person. The mortuary attendant seeks permission to apply the wire cutters and we are reminded that the eternity of the eternity ring is only relative; and that there is a truth that lies deeper even than troth.

Our inquiry, our thoughts, have still not cut deep enough into the institution. Why should a heavy metal deposit on the fingers be a symbol of fidelity, of social standing, or even (as in the case, for example, of the signet ring) of authority? To adorn oneself in this way, or to permit oneself to be adorned, or stamped, connects the immediate appearance of the body with the station one has in life. The living body is used as a mount to exhibit the standing features of the curriculum vitae. This is what I am – beyond this body you see before you, that occupies space, casts a certain kind of shadow and exerts pressure on the seat on which it is sitting.

So much for the fourth finger: the site where the body is used to talk about the life. The beringed ring finger may be the index of a world.

6.6 LITTLE

About the little finger, there is little or nothing to be said. This is the little or nothing. End of portrait.

No. Just wait one moment. The little finger has its fifteen minutes of fame, indeed notoriety. For example, when I was a boy, there was much talk of 'the U' and 'the non-U'. It was U or upper class to use the word 'napkin'; non-U or beyond the pale to use the word 'serviette' to refer to the same type of object. Same referent, but different sense, different tone, different connotation. There were also U and non-U ways of comporting oneself and even of manipulating objects, especially the objects that played a central role in important social rituals. One such ritual was the taking of tea. Now, the manner in which one held the teacup was a crucial marker of social position – either the position one occupied or the position to which one aspired. The 'U' way of holding the teacup – and the utter antipodes to the mug-enclosing fist – required that all but the little finger of the dominant, cup-holding hand should be recruited to the task of gripping the handle. The little finger, however, should be disengaged and, moreover, its disengagement should be clearly advertised by the tea drinker, who should ensure that it was well free of the other fingers, waving in a space beyond the angle between cup and handle.

The origin of this convention is obscure. It is easy to speculate how what seems to be a purely arbitrary sign might be natural or motivated. The freeing of the finger demonstrates the lightness of the cup, thereby broadcasting 'bone china' rather than 'earthenware'. The grip itself is rather awkward: it is therefore anti-utilitarian and proclaims conspicuous waste (a conspicuous waste of physical effort and dexterity) – and the very opposite of the utilitarian bimanual power grip which is designed to support a large mug of soup handed out by the Salvation Army and, at the same time, permit the hands to be warmed, so meeting two basic needs in an economical way: nutrition (or hydration) and warmth. The U grip, with its free-floating little finger, is a grip remote from physiological need and the malodorous world of mere survival – of sweat, of labour, of trade – which is characterised by the domination of power over precision, of coarse agglutinated grips over exquisite fractionated movement. The freely waving little finger is conspicuous – and gratituitous – fractionation.

The hermeneutic examination of this exquisite mode of prehending exquisite crockery in exquisite circumstances could be extended indefinitely. But this would be to dwell for too long on the surface of this extraordinary phenomenon at the cost of exploring (very briefly) one or two of its depths.

When I think of that little finger waving in the breeze I think of my childhood, I think of my brother and I think of the many hours we spent mocking posh people and the would-be posh. Accents, expensive tastes, servants – they all figured in our jokey mockery. We didn't really believe that there were individuals who held teacups in that way; it was sufficient that there was enough belief around for us to use it in our private contribution to the class war. The stereotype within – and between – our minds of the social aspirant was fed on whatever nutrition that lay to hand – including suburban myths. I mention all this for one purpose and one purpose only: to draw attention to the complexity of human consciousness – even of the human consciousness of two youngsters growing up in the 1950s. Teasing out that complexity would be a very long business and might be tedious. So I shall content myself with a few pointers.

We begin with a mechanical solution to an elementary task – transporting fluid to one's mouth – and this mechanical solution is transformed into a sign. Style, fashion, etiquette become markers of social alignment, social position. These markers are aped (no word could be less appropriate for this uniquely human act)[12] by those who wish to achieve, or hint at, a particular social position by means of one or two of its (very trivial) markers. The word then gets round that such aping takes place. Two young boys – my brother and myself – who have a standard understanding of the nature of snobbery incorporate mockery of it into the constant jokiness that helped to keep quarrelling at bay. Several decades later, they recall their piss-taking on this particular matter of the 'U' way to hold a teacup as a means of reasserting their solidarity after a period of estrangement.

Such long steps take! Such distances travelled! So many complexities assimilated! So many dimensions created in the mind! And each step, distance, complexity, dimension, properly treated, would be the theme of an essay longer than this entire book.

This, then, the little, rather than the nothing.

NOTES

1. This is a corrective to the rather masculinist interpretation of the thumb. But see the final part of this entry.
2. John Napier, *The Roots of Mankind* (London: George Allen and Unwin, 1971), p. 181. The brief account of the evolution of opposability that follows has drawn on Napier's engaging pages on the hand, as is the preliminary discussion of grips in the next chapter.
3. Charles Dickens, *Bleak House*, Chapter 53.
4. St Augustine, *Confessions*, First Book, paragraph 13.

5. Ludwig Wittgenstein, *Philosophical Investigations*, translated by G. E. M. Anscombe (Oxford: Blackwell, 1953), paragraph 1 onwards.
6. These last two examples underline how reference does not occur as an isolated act; that it is an integral part of verbal communication in the wider sense and can be understood and achieved only in relation to a communicative intent.
7. A poignant consequence of this connection between pointing and the notion of other people needing to know things that one knows oneself – needing to have things literally pointed out to them – is that one of the earliest signs of autism is the failure of the child to enter the pointing stage. Autism is characterised by limited imagination, a tendency to repetitive activity and narrow interests and, above all, by abnormal social development and a failure of the impulse to communicate with other people. Increasingly, this catastrophic failure to become a fully developed human being, with the empathy that is at the heart of humanity, is being interpreted as a failure to develop the notion that other people have minds, that they have different viewpoints, needs, knowledge, etc. (There are other interpretations – for example, that autism is the result of an inability to divide one's attention between an object out there and a person out there to whom one might point out an object.)
8. That pointing points to something very deep and utterly distinctive in us human beings cannot be over-emphasised. Another way of highlighting this would be to take a Heideggerian stance on this matter and develop some of the points made earlier, in section 5.4.

   Let us for the sake of argument treat pointing as a primitive mode of reference. Reference, at any rate, is a means of making explicit and it involves the 'de-distancing' and directionality that is the character of the spatiality that is possible – as we discussed in section 5.4 – only on the basis of the 'being-in' or 'being-in-the-world' of *Da-sein*.

   > De-distancing means making distance disappear, making the being at a distance of something disappear, bringing it near. *Da-sein* is essentially de-distancing. As the being that it is, it lets beings be encountered in nearness. De-distancing discovers remoteness. (Martin Heidegger, *Being and Time*, a translation of *Sein und Zeit* by Joan Stambaugh, New York: State University of New York Press, 1996, p. 97).

   > Only because beings in general are discovered by *Da-sein* in their remoteness, do 'distances' and intervals among innerworldly beings become accessible in relation to other things. (ibid., p. 97)

   > What is at hand in the surrounding world is, after all, not objectively present for an eternal spectator exempt from *Da-sein*, but is encountered in the circumspect, heedful everydayness of *Da-sein* (ibid., p. 98)

   > Circumspect heedfulness decides about the nearness and farness of what is initially at hand in the surrounding world. Whatever this heedfulness dwells in from the beginning is what is nearest, and regulates our de-distancing. (ibid., p. 99)

   > To be near means to be in the range of what is initially at hand for circum-spection. Bringing near is not oriented toward the I-thing encumbered with a body, but rather toward heedful being-in-the-world, that is, what that being-in-the-world initially encounters. (ibid., p. 100)

   > *Da-sein* understands its here in terms of the over there of the surrounding world. The here does not mean the where of something objectively present, but the where of the de-distancing being with ... together with this de-distancing. In

accordance with its spatiality, *Da-sein* is initially never here but over there. From this over there it comes back to its here, and it does this only by interpreting its heedful being towards something in terms of what is at hand over there. (ibid., p. 100)

Circumspect heedfulness is directional de-distancing. (ibid., p. 100)

The pointing index finger indicates the de-distancing nature of *Da-sein* and (perhaps) the *Da-sein*-lessness of beasts.

It has been pointed out to me (Ruth Willats, personal communication) that dogs do seem to point at things. Pointers most obviously do. As Mrs Willats notes, however, this is an entirely different business from human pointing. The pointer aligns his body in the direction of the object of interest. This is quite different from a human using a part of the body as a pointer: in the case of the dog, the pointer (that is used) is not distinct from the dog that points; the dog is not *utilising* a part of its body to point something out. Moreover, the objects that are pointed out are linked to the dog by a rather narrow range of instinctively shaped interests. The dog would not point, for example, to single out a feature in the landscape. This is linked in turn with the dog's failure to develop the notion of independent objects, of objective space, and of notions such as 'over there'.

9. It was said of one of my surgical colleagues that, after he had cut his index finger during an operation, he was unable to read for several weeks.

10. John Napier, *Hands* (New York: Pantheon, 1980), p. 38.

11. It is entirely out of place here to recall George Bernard Shaw's observation that it was because the English are not a very spiritual people that they invented cricket to give them an image of eternity.

12. The original apes were, of course, animals that 'imitated human form and gesture'. The derivative apes were humans who imitated their betters, as in the aping by commoners of the manners of the court. Common to both is the aspiration to be, or to become by looking like, a 'better'. The notion of a 'better' is an extraordinary example of the naturalisation of social roles as eternal kinds.

CHAPTER 7

Polydactylic Exercises

7.1 INTRODUCTION: THE ORDEAL OF PRECISION

According to the theological myth, we fell from an original state of grace and the best we can hope for is to be returned to this state, or something like it, after we have shed our bodies like a husk – if, and only if, those bodies have behaved as well as bodies might reasonably be expected to behave. According to biologists, however, our original trajectory is in the opposite direction: we have risen.[1] The biological rise does not, however, mirror-match the theological descent. Although, according to evolutionary theorists, we have advanced from an original state indistinguishable from that of the beasts to a condition quite extraordinarily distant from that of the beasts, it is one that is unprecedented in the universe. We don't quite know how to judge it (as we shall discuss in Chapter 11). The theological fall was, of course, much faster than the biological ascent. Things, however, are speeding up. Collectively, for all, even the privileged few, humanity has put more distance between itself and the beasts in the last 500 years than it did in the previous 6,000,000. We have no idea where it is all going to end; not, at least, whether it is going to end in tears or laughter; in cataclysmic slaughter or general well-being and even grace. In either case, the digits, acting in concert with one another, will have had a crucial hand in what has happened. For our domination of the natural world is the result not only of the (tool-amplified) power of the hand, but also of the (tool-enhanced) precision of the fingers. The progress we have made in trying to deal with the consequences of being expelled from paradise, or in trying to deal with the consequences of our awakening from the animal condition, have been rooted in precision rather than in power; or in precision that has greatly magnified our power.

The two dimensions of power and precision are reflected in the different prehensile actions that the fingers are capable of. John Napier, who first classified the grips in this way, emphasised the different role of the thumb in both types of grip. In the power grip, the object is held between the undersurface of the fingers and the palm of the hand. The role of the thumb is merely to maintain stability: it is not opposed to the other fingers. Indeed, the thumb has no special role: it is simply one of the team, a finger among fingers. Examples of power grips are: enclosing a pebble prior to chucking it, holding the haft of a hammer, gripping the top of a jar in order to twist it off, or encircling the neck of an assailant whom one is trying to strangle. In precision grips, on the other hand, the object is held between the tips of the fingers and the opposed thumb – as when one holds a thread as it is inserted through the eye of a needle or a key to be inserted into a door.

The thumb is never entirely dumb. Although it does not exhibit its special opposability in power grips, it brings to those grips some of the intelligence that it mobilises in precision grips. The way the thumb is deployed in holding the haft of a hammer or the top of a jar or a ball about to be thrown is carefully gauged to get the correct counter-pressure. Moreover, the kind of grip that is used is dictated not by the shape or character of the object, but by the way in which it is to be manipulated. Napier illustrates this with the example of unscrewing a tightly closed lid, where the power grip phase of unscrewing the lid is followed by a precision grip phase of lifting it off the jar. In neither case is the thumb directly opposed to the finger; but the lessons learnt – or the control acquired – in precision grips utilising the opposed thumb enable this digit to be deployed intelligently in each phase of the action and to adjust its behaviour in an optimal way in order successfully to negotiate the transition from a power to a precision phase.

This freedom to adjust the grip as the situation requires – and the discretion to refrain from using the opposability of the thumb – lies at the heart of the manipulative genius of the hand. In real life, all grips are modified according to the precise nature of the object, the angle from which one is coming at it, what one wants to do with it and the circumstances under which it is carried out. While there are standard grips, they are all deployed in slightly non-standard ways, being custom-ised to the occasion. Underpinning this are the so-called fractionated finger movements upon which, as we have observed, opposability is built: the ability to move the fingers independently of one another. Experi-ments on monkeys (most famously those of Lawrence and Kuypers) have shown that this ability depends upon the intactness of a particular pathway in the nervous system unique to higher primates: the cortico-spinal tract which descends directly from the primary motor area of the cerebral cortex to those motor neurons which connect the spinal cord with the muscles. If its corticospinal tract is transected, a monkey recovers both the power of the arm and the ballistic control of the hand, but not the ability to move the fingers independently (necessary, for example, to get a nut out of a hole).

The connections between the cerebral cortex and the relevant muscles are complex: many neurons connect with several different muscles and many muscles are connected with several different neurones; there are no simple labelled lines between cortical neurones and muscles. This is believed to be the mechanism by which the complex synergies – different hand muscles working together – necessary for the patterned movements that underlie manipulation are achieved. And they are complex: to move one finger while keeping another still requires specific mobilisation of antagonist muscles, damping down co-activation of other fingers or preventing passive movements of those fingers. The development of increasing capacity in the postnatal child to demonstrate fractionation of finger movement seems to depend upon pruning of an initial excess of connections between neurones and muscles. There are, that is to say, some pre-formed patterns and synergies, but these are then shaped and reshaped in accordance with the experience and demands of postnatal life. The patterns, that is to say, are plastic.

Herein lies the true genius of the hand: out of fractionated finger movements comes an infinite variety of grips and their combinations. And from this variety in turn comes choice – not only in what we do (this may be need-driven or even instinctive) but in how we do it, which cannot be instinct-driven. With choice comes consciousness of acting: the arbitrariness of choice between two equally sensible ways of achieving the same goal awakens the sense of agency.[2]

But we are getting ahead of ourselves. (These matters will be discussed in Chapter 10 and in more detail in Volume 2.) Suffice it, for the present, to note that the degrees of freedom permitted by formidable combination of fractionated finger movement and the opposable thumb opens up the possibility of an infinite variation in how we grip and in the way we pass from grip to grip in manipulation. Most actions, even relatively simple ones like tying one's shoelaces, require numerous transitions between grips and so create unprecedented combinations of grips. Indeed, one could think of grips as being in many ways analogous to the units of language – perhaps syllables rather than full words – out of which unique actions are fashioned. Developing this linguistic analogy further, we might note that while there is much variation in individual grips, there may be 'token' grips that realise certain abstract standard kinds. In the end, however, the analogy does not fully hold up because the duration and the composition of grips can vary much more widely than that of words, whose variation, after all, has to be *oppositional* – that is, systematic. Or, more precisely, the variation exhibited by grips is continuous, whereas that exhibited by syllables and words, by phonemes and morphemes, is discontinuous: there is a flip from one type to another without intermediate positions.

As Napier himself admits, some grips elude classification into power and precision grips. He gives two unclassifiable exceptions. These are grips that do not involve the thumb at all: the scissors grip (see section 7.3) and the hook grip (see section 7.4). The distinction between power and precision, however, remains useful, for it enables us to see human history at a glance.

Initially, the life of hominids – after their expulsion from paradise, or when they took a separate path from the pongids – was an ordeal of power. Slowly but surely, this became an ordeal of precision. One form of effort gave way to another: the unpleasant experience of hauling, heaving, crushing, ripping, grubbing, striking, tearing, grappling, and so on gave way to the less unpleasant, but still not altogether pleasant, experience of executing precise movements in aiming, fabricating, planning, and so on. More accurately, the power to inflict, to expropriate, to control, in the service of needs was invested less in strength and force and more in precisely guided activities that indirectly augmented strength and force. Grasping became increasingly indirect.

The precise hand was able not only to fashion tools, but also to liberate tools from particular circumstances. Tools made explicit the general principles implicit in particular types of effortful action. Stored tools and shaped tools lifted manual interactions from concrete interactions to the general possibility of interaction. The tool, embodying a general principle, could be liberated from the body that used it: tools were no longer mere prosthetic extensions of a body taken as an invariant background, a given, of any situation. The precision of the precise hand could be invested outside the hand – supremely exemplified in the wheel, which was a means to locomotion but looked nothing like a leg. Needles not only did not look like human fingers but were several steps away from the function of the finger. The notion of a thread to hold things together is a very abstract notion – that of a non-intermittent or standing pinch. Armed with such abstract notions, the precision of the hand that made tools possible could be reinvested in the tools themselves. Precision tools and precision tooling of tools emerged out of the originary precision of the hand with its opposable thumb added to fractionated finger movement.

We shall revisit this theme in section 9.3; but for the present we note only that the ordeal of precision that succeeded the ordeal of power was increasingly supplanted by the ordeal of mental labour. The aching muscle gave way to the aching, cramped controlled limb, which gave way to the aching mind-brain. The consequence was that the human being acquired powers that no one looking at the human body could have dreamt of. The thinking reed could manipulate the earth. We lucky latecomers – denizens of the twenty-first century – have inherited a world created on the back of these million-year ordeals of power and thousand-year ordeals of precision.

Although the ordeal of precision is now in many cases downloaded to tools which also carry the ordeal of power on our behalf, we still have to live, work and deport ourselves in the interstices between the tool-borne automated nexus of our lives. The car largely runs itself and the steering is powered, but we are still required to grip the steering wheel and manipulate it directly in order that the car shall follow the route to our destination. We have to button our clothes and tie our shoelaces. Our days, in short, make huge demands on us for precision. The craftsman's and the tradesman's work is still steeped in the ordeal of precision which many of us experience only at weekends in pursuing our hobbies and doing DIY.[3] In these activities, as we move from grip to grip, different fingers come to the fore. Although the sections that follow pick out grips that utilise subsets of fingers, there is hardly a grip that does not in some way involve all five fingers or the entire hand.

As we rejoice in the fact that we, the precision animals, have conquered the earth, we should spare a thought not only for those that are still immersed in the misery of effortful, repetitive physical labour, but also for those species that have just missed the boat. Those whose paws just failed to achieve the status of hands and whose grip, howsoever powerful, had the wrong opposability index, so that the world slipped out of their grasp and they remained a part of nature instead of rising, at least temporarily, above it.

7.2 TWO FINGERS

Of this particular sub-set it may be felt that enough – perhaps more than enough – has already been said. Digits, however, may be paired for other reasons than signalling victory or insulting one's conspecifics. The combination of index finger and thumb is of unparalleled importance in our lives: it is the most important immediate expression of the possibilities opened up by the opposability of the thumb which is the cornerstone of human culture and the civilisations that have grown from it.

Using the thumb and forefinger to create a two-jaw chuck gives rise to at least two families of precision grips: the pad-to-pad two-jaw chuck, as is used when we hold a thread we are trying to pass through the eye of a needle; and the pad-to-side two-jaw chuck as when we are holding a key being inserted into or turned in a lock. Even the combination of the index and large finger is not exhausted by its role in making rude and/or victorious signals. Together they form the basis of the so-called 'scissors grip' used in holding a cigarette.

The scissors grip is actually quite primitive, so we shall deal with it first. Along with the hook grip, it is one that we share with non-human, non-smoking primates; indeed, they use it more than we do. According to Napier (1971, p.180), this grip is employed by New World monkeys, which have a non-opposable thumb, to pick up small objects. Old World monkeys, which have an opposable thumb, use it less often. Apes such as the orang-utan, which have such small thumbs that they are almost useless in opposition, very often mobilise the scissors grip to grasp small objects. In humans, it is used almost exclusively for smoking and is employed as a secondary sign of this habit.

When we were children, we used to bring up these two fingers to our mouths, to signify the adult and sophisticated act of exposing ourselves to forbidden stimulants and carcinogens. The cigarette grip has a wide variety of dialects. At one extreme is the fully exposed, straight-fingered posture of the cocktail party goer, whose scissors seemed incomplete without a cigarette holder. At the other is the furtive quick-smokie-behind-the-stack-of-palettes-before-the-boss-comes grip, in which the hand is held behind the back between puffs and the fingers are curled over to provide further cover for a cigarette cupped in the palm. Since the latter posture sometimes requires extra care and control, in order that the fag (and it is a 'fag' rather than a cigarette) should be concealed but the hand not burned, a more precise grip – between forefinger and thumb – is sometimes used. At any rate, the style of scissors grip is an excellent resource for actors capturing and signifying stereotypes through metonyms: on the one hand, the chattering aesthete with much free disposable resource; and on the other, the furtive workman with rather less. So although the scissors grip is primitive in the sense of being shared with non-human primates, it is far from primitive in the way that we choose to use it and the complex layers of meaning we may build on it.[4] Nothing about human beings is as simple as evolutionary psychologists and others with an 'animalomorphic' agenda would have us believe.

We have already noted that the opposition of the thumb and index finger – not unique to mankind, but uniquely developed in mankind – is 'the universal gesture of success' and the keystone of human dexterity. Although it lies at the heart of the manipulative function of the hand, there are relatively few grips that are composed of it alone. It is used to pick up small objects and to extract small things from inaccessible places, when there is not room for more than two fingers. It has a particular function in plucking – fluff off the floor, feathers off chickens, illusions off the bedsheets in a fever, and so on. And the two fingers work as an isolated team in comparative exotica, such as pellet-flicking and pinching the bodies of one's conspecifics, which have the common intention of inflicting pain for aggressive, sexual or aggresso-sexual reasons.

The important functions of index finger–thumb combinations in the two-jaw chuck are almost always supported by other fingers, even though the latter do not attract much credit. While threading a needle probably involves almost pure use of the two fingers – both on the threading and the needle holding side – turning a key in a lock involves counter-pressure from the middle and possibly the other two fingers in order to stabilise the thumb–index pair. Indeed, as we have already noted (see section 1.1), the joint at the base of the middle finger is obliquely oriented to resist forces generated by the thumb pressing objects against the other fingers. This said, the index and thumb could achieve most of what they do do, if clumsily, without the other fingers, but the latter could not take over the functions of the thumb–index upon which hands-on dexterity, toolmaking and tool-using, and civilisation itself depend. The precision function of these two opponents – in an opposition that illustrates William Blake's aphorism about true friendship – has shaped our world. What more can one say?[5]

7.3 THREE FINGERS

The triplet seems a relatively rare combination, which may explain why 'the three-jaw chuck' does not warrant a place of its own in Eric Trinkaus' delightful little portrait gallery of grips.[6] This is an illusion. For, while the combination of three fingers is rare, the combination of two fingers and a thumb is actually much commoner than appreciated. This oversight arises because the role of the third digit – usually the middle finger – is predominantly 'merely' supportive. It doesn't have a named part and at times seems almost an optional extra. You can, for example, stir your tea with the spoon held in two fingers or three. It is, however, more natural to use three fingers, in order to stabilise the index–thumb combination. This will confer an extra charge of rotatory power and permit more precise control of the spoon, which has to be held at a mechanical disadvantage if the fingers are not to be dipped in hot liquid, thus avoiding an excess of tinkling. Likewise, when the cup is lifted to the lips, the handle may be held between two fingers. This, however, is either awkward or graceless. If the thumb and index are used alone, it is impossible to hold a full cup safely unless the thumb is placed on top of the handle and the index finger is curled underneath in a distinctively primitive fashion, reminiscent less of the tea party with its orchestrated exquisiteness than of the Typhoo chimps. The three-fingered approach, with the thumb and middle finger pressing the outer surface of the handle and the index finger gripping the inner surface, permits both grace and stability.[7]

The three-digit combination is not, therefore, as rare as it may seem when the thumb and index finger are allowed to take all the credit. There will, however, have been many occasions in the remote past upon which the present is built when getting that nut out of the shell or that juicy morsel out of its lair will have required three digits working in unison, cooperating with an exquisite sense of teamwork. Each feels the other's pressure either directly or indirectly through the desired object. They talk, murmur, hint and nod to one another. Each adjusts accordingly and the morsel is secured for presentation to the mouth. These are the kinds of actions which, endlessly repeated, supported the emerging hominids until they were ready to become the kind of creature that eventually created nuclear power stations and the great symphonies of Ludwig van Beethoven.

Teamwork requires that one, or at most two, digits should be identified as the key worker, the foreman, the convenor. This role is typically taken by the thumb and/or the index finger, leaving the middle finger to assume a lesser role. The three-fingered team is a combination of two chiefs and one Indian. A little bit of affirmative action, of celebration of the marginalised, on behalf of the middle finger, may therefore seem to be indicated.

There is an important sign – not a grip but a genuine three-finger exercise – in which all three digits participate as individuals and as equals. This is the representation of the so-called Thumb-and-Finger rule, which encapsulates two fundamental principles in electromagnetism and captures something that underpins pretty near everything that differentiates life 150 years ago from life now. A brief digression into electromagnetism is called for.

A varying magnetic field can induce electicity to flow in a conductor such as a metal wire. An effect equivalent to a magnetic field varying over time can be created by the movement of a conductor with respect to a magnetic field: the wire breaks through so-called lines of magnetic force. Conversely, a wire through which a current is flowing is surrounded by a magnetic field: the current creates a magnetic field centred on the wire. The dramatic revolution that we have witnessed in human affairs over the last 150 years has been driven by devices that exploit these two kinds of relationships between motion, magnetic fields and current flow. The relationship can be used to turn the motion of a wire through a magnetic field into electricity, as in hydroelectric power where the falling water rotates a coil of wire. Conversely, the relationships can be used to turn electricity, via the magnetism induced by its flow, into motion, as in an electric motor. It is no exaggeration to state that Faraday's discovery in 1831 of the induction of electrical flow in a circuit situated in a variable magnetic field is one of the greatest events in the story of mankind's ever-increasing ability to understand and control nature.

It is time now to return to our three fingers which together are used to represent the three dimensions of space and, through this, the relationship between the direction of the movement of the conductor through the magnetic field, the direction of the flow of current and the direction of the resulting force. There are two rules. The left hand rule is as follows:

> If the thumb and first two fingers of the left hand are arranged at right angles to one another on a conductor and the hand oriented so that the first finger points in the direction of the magnetic field and the middle finger in the direction of the electric current then the thumb will point in the direction of the force on the conductor.[8]

The right hand rule goes like this:

> If the thumb, the forefinger, and the middle finger of the right hand are bent at right angles to one another with the thumb pointed in the direction of motion of a conductor relative to a magnetic field and the forefinger in the direction of the field, then the middle finger will point in the direction of the induced electromotive force.[9]

Thousands of physicists, engineers and technicians, the true unacknowledged legislators of the world, have relied on these fundamental principles to bring warmth, light and comfort to the cold, dark, comfortless places of the earth upon which we have been cast. These rules of thumb (and two fingers), then, lie at the heart of the technological revolution that transformed the human world in the period between Faraday's great work on electromagnetism and the ascendancy of information technology. The three digits are at right angles to one another and so their positions satisfyingly echo the three dimensions of space.

With such power at the tips of three fingers, no wonder I almost forgot the most important of all three-fingered exercises; the one that, more than any other, has changed the face of the universe and man's place in nature. It lies at the heart of cultural evolution, and those innumerable processes that have permitted humans and their lives to be transformed independently of changes in the human genome or even the human body. I am, of course, referring to the act of writing from which arise the treaties, letters, invoices, ledgers, journals, petitions, poems, passenger lists, monographs, graffiti, reports, edicts, novels, notes, contracts, histories, recipes, sentences of death, geographies, scientific articles, and so on that have shaped and transmitted our collective consciousness, our collective powers and our growing wisdom and foolishness. Even the mighty right and left hand rules are only distant children of the pen-driving hand.

Before the concept of moveable type and that of handwriting merged in the notion of typewriting and the word processing that descended from the typewriter,[10] writing was a matter of penning or at least quill-ing. Penmanship requires the cooperation of three fingers. The barrel of the pen near to the nib lies snugly between the two pads of the thumb and index finger and the side of the middle finger. While it is, again, possible (just) to write with the thumb and index alone, the middle finger ensures that the tail of the barrel at the opposite end to the nib is lodged comfortably between the base of thumb and index, cushioned on the little belly of first dorsal interosseus muscle. This helps to relate the movement of the fingers to the movement of the pen tip distally and the movement of the hand as a whole at the wrist proximally and so control the passage of the pen over the page. A beautiful example of teamwork and the very embodiment of precisely the coherent behaviour that, for good or ill, writing makes possible. The pen sits just as snugly in the hand when it is moved across the page to sign the death sentence as when it completes the scientific paper that describes the newly discovered cure for a fatal disease.

The penholder grip has massively extended our grip on the world. For writing embodies the notion that signs can be manufactured and stored, and that knowledge (or the possibility of it)[11] can be laid down outside our bodies. Our ability to communicate our collective experience by writing to later generations has, more than anything else, contributed to the extraordinary acceleration of the evolution of human life; for there is no longer any need 'to wait for genetic assimilation of a new adaptive advance made by an individual'.[12] Writing has made evolutionary theory

– itself a piece of writing – largely irrelevant to understanding what we humans currently are. Of which more presently, though we make a preliminary note of the fact (to be discussed in Chapter 9) that the hand lies behind language and so behind the writing that still requires the hand to inscribe.

There is so much to say about writing – and its million derivatives, including the manifold institutions it makes possible – that it may be best simply to confine ourselves to a few remarks about manipulations of meaning traced out in wiggly lines – about the mystery of manuscription. Here, at any rate, are a few thoughts, set out (courtesy of writing) in space:

A Drop of Ink[13]

The white page milks the pen,
the nib's arrhythmic dance
unravels the ductile darkness of the ink
to a quinkled, esoteric shade of light:
mind-light that the sun
(now drying characters it does not comprehend)
remotely lit.

A drop of midnight, thus unwound to light,
embodies Meaning – the dark heart of the light,
its being known, the inmost gleam of light.[14]

7.4 FOUR FINGERS

Of this ensemble there is less to be said. What do four fingers do together? Drumming on the table impatiently, musically or just annoyingly; tapping out the gallop rhythm of a horse or a failing heart; mocking the primitive sound effects of early radio or echoing the mockery of those sound effects by the less early radio of my childhood (see section 3.3). The four fingers may be associated, also, with those dreadful last moments before the fall into the abyss. As strength fails, the curled fingers can remain flexed no longer, the hand yields to fingers and fingers yield to fingertips and fingertips to scraunching nails, and the terminally exhausted hand lets go of the branch or the sill or the overhanging rock and its owner succumbs to acute gravitational poisoning.

We seem to have moved from precision back to power. The four fingers unite in the kind of grip favoured by our brachiating ancestors. But here, as with the scissors grip, indeed as always, things are not so simple; you can't go back. Let me take an example. I associate the four-finger hook grip with the beginning and end of term at university and the walk from Oxford station to the digs or from the digs to the station. The cases were heavy and there were many pauses. The distance between the pauses, however, could be extended by mobilising a reserve tank of manual endurance. This involved instituting a rota – between a full handle grip to a hook grip that involved only the fingers and gave the thumb and certain muscles controlling the other fingers a rest, as which a change is as good. My recollection of those journeys is not of dim, primeval, inchoate tropisms, of a brain poorly lit by the light filtered through the luxuriant vegetation, but of very precise and sometimes angry thoughts: calculations of distance gone and distance to be gone; anticipations of the term to which I was making my sweaty progress; rueful recollections of Nietzsche's observation that we are possessed by our possessions (and imagining my quoting it to my impressed or inattentive fellows); and fury at the paternal parsimony that forbade the use of a taxi.

The important thing is that, in choosing this primitive grip (suitable, as Napier points out, for strap-hanging in the tube and for lifting sash windows), I was exercising a choice, utilising constrained manipulative indeterminacy. This is very deep territory – and one to which we are again and again drawn – but the definitive treatment will be postponed until the final chapter. Instead, because tetradactyly has relatively little territory of its own,[15] I shall use its slot to repair an early omission. In characterising the functions of the hand, I spoke of its role in manipulation, exploration and communication. This does not quite cover a further, crucial, function: portage.

The hand that is freed from the demands of locomotion to shape things, to find things out and to signal to other hand-holders, is also free to carry things. It can, therefore, devote many of its hand-hours to gathering, accumulating, hiding, storing, transporting everything – clobber, comestibles, cases, weapons and kids. The hand was on the scene before the handbag, the sack, the suitcase, the cart, the lorry, the container vessel. Like these, but on a vastly reduced scale, it can hold things in store ready for use – for example, a weapon taken on a hunting trip, or a handful of nuts, a packed lunch. Storing things in the body in this way, a holding-in-readiness, keeps the objects that are needed next to the very place – the potentially hungry body – where they are needed. In this way need and its internal accusative are both kept apart – the needful is retained before the need has arisen – and held together. Need itself is by this means visibly objectified and so raised to a higher level of awareness, preparatory to its being generalised, as it is in agriculture and subsequently in barter and exchange.[16]

The carrying hand awakens another long, intense flash of light.

7.5 FIVE FINGERS

There is something called a five-finger exercise – 'a piece of music written for the purpose of affording practice in the movement of the fingers in pianoforte playing' (*Oxford English Dictionary*). The rationale behind the exercise is 1) that practice makes (relatively) perfect; and 2) that acquiring perfection at one task (doing the five-finger exercises) will improve one's performance of others (perfected 'Chopsticks' will take playing closer to the Heaven where the Ideal Original lies) – the principle of so-called generalisability. This is how we come to astonish ourselves and perform without effort things that previously lay beyond our most effortful endeavours. I want to talk about practice and generalisability.

First of all practice. It lies at the heart of motor learning and its essence is repetition. You do things again and again and eventually you do them fluently – easily and accurately. Indeed, in one sense you stop doing them at all: they happen with your permission, collusion, etc. Take standing upright. At first there is a lot of wobbling and correction and grabbing for support: standing upright is something you do; and you are not able to do anything else at the same time. A distracted toddler is likely to fall over. Subsequently, standing up does not count as an activity at all; it is merely the background, the context, the necessary condition, for particular activities. Standing becomes 'doing standing' only under very difficult circumstances – as when, for example, you try to remain standing on a wobbly platform or on a bus going so rapidly round the corner that you think the driver is attempting to centrifuge your bodily parts and set out for work that morning with the sole aim of separating mitochondria from nuclei. A less extreme example is walking: at first you *do walking*; subsequently you walk – and this encompasses everything from deliberately putting one foot in front of another (as when one is picking one's way carefully over difficult terrain); through voluntary ambulation round a course; through being a place where walking occurs while one gets on with spontaneous activity.

The outcome of practice, in short, is that the activity becomes less voluntary: more and more of it is downloaded to mechanism. This is reflected in what is seen in the brain using methods of imaging cerebral activity during the activation of a task.[17] While you are learning a complicated movement with your fingers, functional brain imaging techniques show that a greater part of the cerebral cortex lights up during execution; moreover the representation of the individual fingers in the cortex, as shown by mapping techniques, is expanded. As the task becomes learned to the point of becoming automatic, so that it is no longer effortful, and indeed it is no longer 'done' but, as it were, 'happens', the area of cortical representation becomes less. One way of interpreting this is to see the activity, having become routine and commonplace, being downloaded to structures lower down in the hierarchy of the nervous system: to the servants.

Practice makes perfect. Practice hands over our actions to automata within us. Neuroscientists like to call these automata 'motor programmes', a concept we have already interrogated. Implicit in the notion of the 'motor programme' is that voluntary movements, actions, are made up of stereotyped elements which can be put together in more or less stereotyped sequences, to create the whole movement, action or even behaviour. Because, it is argued, they may be combined in so many different ways, the bespoke requirements of the moment (every action, after all, begins in a different context, has a different starting point, is initiated at a different distance from the goal) can be fulfilled with 'off-the-shelf' components. This is how we astonish and delight ourselves with our fluency, as I do now, typing while I think (and hardly *doing* what I did so painfully for so many years, in the 1970s, when I spent hours and hours and hours hovering indecisively over the keyboard) so that there is only a wafer-thin gap between the voice in my head and the words on the screen, between the privacy of my cortex and the publicity of the text.

It's a good story, but it makes little or no sense. It certainly explains nothing, as a few, not terribly searching, questions will demonstrate. In what form are the programmes stored? Are they reverberating circuits – the form which memories are supposed to take in the brain? And what do the programmes specify? Generic or ur-actions? In either case, in what manner are the relevant movement units specified? Abstractly in the form of parameters such as velocity, force, acceleration, distance? Hardly: every action is different in all these respects. Even walking over smooth, predictable ground has infinite variation. And every stumble – as every pavement – is unique. Is the programme a second-order abstract schema? In which case, what are the abstractions? For example, it may be argued that, while every act of walking is different, there are certain relationships between its elements that have to be maintained and these are the invariants that are inscribed in the motor programme: for example, a certain relationship between the centre of pressure and the position of the leg in initiating gait. The question then arises as to how these abstractions are merged when the units are stitched together to make a whole; and how the realisation of abstract programmes is varied from moment to moment, as happens in walking over rough ground. (Most of the world.)

Even if we knew how to clarify these puzzles and to think of ways of investigating them, there would still be fundamental, unanswered questions. For example: By what means are the programmes taken off the shelf? What voluntary action could requisition these mechanisms and weave them together into the bespoke motor performance that is required? And if the process of requisitioning and blending were itself automatic, based upon involuntary mechanisms, at what point does the action become voluntary? In what sense is it a deliberate deed? We have, in short, no notion of the interaction between the reflex and pre-programmed, on the one hand, and the deliberate, on the other; or between the voluntary customised and the mechanical prefabricated. Least of all in the case of the hand where, more than anywhere else in the body, the customised dominates over the prefabricated.

And so, while we accept that practice makes perfect, we have no idea how. The neuromythologists think they know how: they see that recurrent activity of a particular neuronal circuit causes both microscopic and macroscopic changes. Microscopically, the synapses that link neurones swell and increase in numbers, so that the passage of electro-chemical energy down certain pathways is eased, or facilitated: it is more easily triggered off. Programmes are built up into virtual machines because neurones that 'fire together wire together'.[18] But this phenomenon is also seen in the case of 'kindling' in the brain – whereby abnormal (and undesirable) activity eventually, by a process of positive feedback, predisposes to spontaneous firing of the nervous system such as is seen in epileptic fits. Hardly a model for the exquisite triumphs of learned activity. To play the piano, or to type the verb phrase 'to play the piano', is not the same as having a fit. Macroscopically, as we have already noted, there are changes, with repetition, in the amount of brain activity associated with the task. But size isn't everything and, as already noted, the cortical representation of an action, which grows during learning, may actually shrink when automaticity is achieved. Which brings us back to where we were when we noted the apparent down-loading of voluntary activities, or parts thereof, to automata, as if the 'highest' centres of the brain were a great artist who is able to leave the casting of his sculpture to the artisans in the foundry.

With so little explained, we have no chance of making sense of the generalisability of our acquired skills. How the hours spent reporting the trajectory of the quick brown fox over the lazy dog help us to type with such consummate ease phrases such as 'the generalisability of our acquired skills'. How hours of making an involuntary audience of neighbours curse God at being forced to endure an insupportable number of repetitions of Five-Finger Exercises is the necessary precursor to enchanting a voluntary audience of thousands with the Busoni transcription of the Bach 'Chaconne'. Of course, there are important commonalities between the skills that make noise and those that induce rapture but since, as will be clear from the foregoing, we don't know how, or in what form, the skills are stored once acquired, we cannot begin to conjecture what form those commonalities take. (A pianistic space constructed out of stumbled-over scales? A keyboard space erected in the uncombed tangle of undisciplined consciousness out of repeated typings of banalities?)

The question becomes even more pressing when what we have to do is an exercise that benefits from practice and looks like a set-piece but is also totally unstandardised. I am thinking of something like tying one's shoelaces in a variety of hurries. The grips that are required will vary from time to time because we shall be approaching the laces from different angles and with different lengths to tug on, different tugging forces required and different coefficients of friction between our fingers and the fabric of the laces. The sequence of grips – which seem more like syllables than full words in the action-sentence – will also be open to an infinite variety of possiblities. The same applies to all the buttoning and unbuttoning that mark the beginning and end of the day. Every action is, as the linguists would say, a nonce-word, so it is inappropriate to think of it as being built up out of a series of prefabricated elements.

We astonish ourselves and each other with our learned skills. And while we seem to explain it by practice and we imagine we know what practice does and how it does it, we of course don't. We go to a concert and marvel at the deliciously organised sound created by the stunning choreography of the musician's dancing fingers. And yet we overlook the extraordinary achievements that our own arrival at the concert hall requires of us. The many maps we have utilised in finding our way round and out of our house, in threading our way through a city many hundreds of thousands of times larger than our bodies to a building which would be a mere pinpoint if viewed from our starting place, and in locating the right seat. The many conventions we have understood and acted upon in getting to our rightful place in the auditorium: the theory of tickets (underpinned by many complex conventions, such as those that give the symbol its specificity, and those underlying the exchange of services for cash); the thousand systems that have made it safe for us to propel ourselves in metal-hulled vessels to the concert; and so on. But even these large-scale actions should be overshadowed, as they are underwritten, by the millions of different digital skills we have deployed in enacting our rather abstract intention to do something called 'going to a concert'. I think of the many different grips I have employed in getting washed and dressed; in preparing the meal; in making the house safe before setting out; in opening up and driving and stowing the car; in getting out our tickets which were stuck in the corner of a rather small wallet, etc. Against the background of all those skills that the audience shares with one another and the pianist, the latter's additional virtuosity – and the point of our pilgrimage – seems to put out only slightly from the mainland of the collective genius of human beings.

All of this becomes visible when we encounter patients who have so-called apraxias. These are unfortunate people who, due to brain damage following a stroke or some other cerebral insult, have lost the ability to execute learned movements, despite having normal power, and no numbness and no problem with coordination and intact motivation. Apraxias illustrate by default the mystery of the emergence of human agency in a world of causes and mechanisms, of exquisitely shaped deliberate action in an organism largely running on reflexes.

Through our hands, above all, we have woken out of the world of reflex activity into the universe of agency, of accountable deliberation. To this fundamental point we shall yet again return in the final chapter.[19]

7.9 TEN FINGERS

In talking of five-finger exercises, I have given examples such as piano playing, typing, tying one's shoelaces, buttoning and unbuttoning, etc. These, however, are ten-finger exercises. Once we go beyond grips to actions, from prehension and exploration to actual manipulation, both hands are required and the issue of bimanual coordination comes to the fore. In some cases, bimanuality can be bypassed, inasmuch as one can carry out half of the action at a time; in others, it most certainly cannot. One can play the piano single-handedly and there have been a series of single-handed piano concertos – many of them composed for a decidedly ungrateful Paul Wittgenstein who had his right arm blown off in the First World War – but no single-handed violin concertos. The bowing and the fingering must work in concert if the instrument is to bring off its daily miracle of stroking silence until it weeps a world.

There are many different ways in which the two hands may cooperate in different tasks.[20] The necessary teamwork is quite different in swimming, catching a ball, playing the piano, typing, and holding an orange while peeling it. In the first case, the two hands have to move symmetrically during the cycle. In the second, they have to create between them a varying aperture that is at first wide enough to admit and then tight enough to retain the ball. In the third, there has to be both independent use of the fingers but synchronisation of, or a controlled temporal relationship between, the activity of the two hands. In the fourth, the action of the fingers of the two hands has to be independent, but the hands will have had to divide the keyboard between them and the sequence of pressed keys shared between the two hands has to be strictly controlled. In the last example – the orange – the two hands carry out entirely different but interdependent task: the one stabilises it while the other manipulates it.

All of these suggest that, while there must be independent control of both hands, there has to be overriding control of their joint activity. For essentially bilateral activities, such as breast-stroke swimming, in which the hand movements have to be initiated at the same time and to some extent remain in rhythm, it has been suggested that the coupling of the two limbs takes place at a fairly low level, possibly through pattern generators in the spinal cord, similar to those that regulate the reciprocal movments of the legs in walking. When we are talking about more complex cooperative activity – 'purposeful and goal-oriented bimanual synergies' – correspondingly complex inter-hand coordination is required. There is a division of labour between the two hands: in right-handers, the left hand is usually the postural hand, being responsible for the relatively lowly task of stabilising the object; while the right hand is used for fine manipulation. The left hand also provides the spatial reference for the right hand. This is believed to reflect hemisphere specialisation, with the left hemisphere – the one that looks after the right hand – being rather superior in right-handers to the right hemisphere. Under such circumstances, it seems that the left hemisphere not only controls the more difficult task but also assigns the roles of the two hands. Where there is damage to this hemisphere, role assignment does not take place and there is conflict between the hand as to which is to do what.[21]

In a task in which a spring-loaded drawer has to be pulled open and a tasty morsel extracted when the draw is fully open, the synchronisation between the two endpoints – the full opening of the drawer by the left hand and the arrival of the right hand at the exposed morsel – is very close indeed and not altered even if there is a delay in initiating one or other of the components. This indicates that there is 'end-point control' combining the two elements of the action – the left-handed contribution and the right-handed contribution, securing the necessary dead heat.

It would be something of an understatement to say that we are not certain how this is achieved. It has been suggested that it is neither visual guidance nor tactile and related signals generated by one of the limbs that ensure the synchronicity between the end-points of the actions of the two hands, but a memorised plan. This suggestion raises the question – cousin to the question about supposed storage of motor programmes – as to the form this supposed memory takes, since the individual hands may take many different paths to the endpoint; in short, that invariant inter-manual result is achieved by widely varying means. This so-called 'motor equivalence' is dramatically demonstrated in experiments in which the task just referred to is performed in the dark, or the drawer-pulling left hand is loaded, or the hand anaesthetised. These changes sometimes alter the performance of the left hand – often slowing it down enormously – but do not interfere with synchronicity. Moreover, subjects are quite unaware of having adjusted the action of the unimpaired hand to mend its trajectory to that of the impaired hand.

How this very precise and robust end-point control of bimanual activity is achieved therefore remains mysterious. If this is true of highly artificial simplified behaviour in the laboratory, with carefully controlled, stereotyped actions being initiated in a standardised, stable context, how much more difficult it must be to explain the achievement when, for example, we are running along and clap our hands together to catch a fly, or reach for a falling ball when we are flying sideways, or angrily buttoning a shirt as we walk downstairs, or stabilising a cup while we stir its contents en route to pointing something out to someone with the index finger of our non-stirring hand. The attempt to explain this by postulating a system that imposes a coordination of parts, so that the overall ensemble of actions has a lesser variance than the sum of the variance of its constituent parts, seems to fall foul of the fact that every action is a unique part of an unfolding network of actions and the net is constantly billowing in the wind of external contingency and internal attention-driven whim. One is very tempted to conclude that we are able to accomplish most of the ordinary manual and bimanual things we do only because *we know what we are doing and are not stupid or in coma.* But this would not help us to understand the means by which we achieve the deliberate goals we set ourselves.[22]

We have reached the tip of our fingers. Our next move is into the virtual digits of the mathematised world the hand-awoken human animals create in order that they may discover and control the universe in which they find themselves and distance themselves yet further from the animal body that is not a fate but a springboard from which they can leap.

NOTES

1. Here, as in the previous chapter, I have drawn on John Napier's *The Roots of Mankind* (London: George Allen and Unwin, 1971).
2. Since we are on the topic of the limitless variety of grips, I cannot resist reporting something that I have begun to notice since I started this book: how I seem to invent a new grip every day. Just now, for example, I ascended the stairs carrying in my right hand a tray laden with a coffee pot, etc. and in my left hand a plate bearing a couple of muffins and my glasses. My right-hand grip had two main elements: my thumb curled over the rim of the upper surface of the tray; and my fully extended fingers forming a flat plate supporting the undersurface of the tray. The exquisite, and continually adjusted, balance between the pressures applied by the hooked thumb and the flat fingers ensured that the tray remained horizontal and, indeed, scarcely wobbled, as I walked up the stairs. It is possible that I may have employed a grip roughly similar to this one before, though I do not recall doing so.

   My left-hand grip was also a composite. My index and middle finger supported the undersurface of the plate and my thumb was curled loosely over my spectacles sufficiently to restrain them from slipping over the plate as I walked up the stairs but not so tightly as to crush their rather delicate stems. The two fingers under the plate were attended by the ring and index finger, curled up but in readiness in case of a sudden displacement – possible since the ceramic surface of the plate had low friction – that would require rapid and decisive corrective action. I feel even more confident that this composite grip was unprecedented.

   The combination of the two hands – working quite independently and yet ready to act together to save the situation if a catastrophe had to be averted – was certainly a *hapax legomenon*.

   The new grips and non-canonical versions of standard ones deployed with seemingly limitless inventiveness are necessary because the objects we have to deal with are non-standard, are approached from non-standard angles and in invariably non-standard situations. Ordinary living is, from the point of view of dexterity and manipulation, effectively a matter of tying one's shoelaces – which present themselves in a variety of different ways – when one is trying to steady oneself on the deck of a ship in a heaving sea.
3. World-wide, of course, many people are crushed still by the ordeal of precision and as many by the unrelieved ordeal of physically effortful labour.
4. 'Fag' and 'cigarette' belong to different worlds. More precisely, 'fag' belongs to a particular world and 'cigarette' is relatively neutral as to worlds. The latter is shaggy with connotation, while the former has relatively clean-shaven denotation. It is staggering to think how coherent, close-knit the worlds of meaning and signification are: that the downtrodden, plebeian world of 'fag' – a world in which smoking has declined from a sophisticated act to a furtive habit and 'from a pleasure we do not need to a necessity that gives us no pleasure', from the gesture to the chronic bronchitis that follows from its repetition – should be signified in a grip so different from that which signifies 'cigarette'.
5. The thumb only rarely forms duets with other than the index finger. The only example I can think of is the interaction with the middle finger in finger-snapping. The middle finger is ideal because its length and its power give the maximum pressure and and the greatest velocity of impact on the thenar eminence.
6. See Erik Trinkaus, in Leslie Aiello and Christopher Dean, *An Introduction to*

Human Evolutionary Anatomy, p. 372, and reproduced on p. 26 of this volume.

7. There are, of course, many primitive ways of gripping a drinking vessel. The primitiveness may be anticipated in the very structure of the vessel – as in the primitive mug (or, worse, the beaker) as opposed to the refined bone china teacup. A mug is typically gripped with both hands curled round the body of the container. Such a degraded mode of prehension suits adverse conditions – war-time, life at sea, pauses in endurance sports. The curled fingers provide extra stability under destabilising conditions, and they are rewarded, moreover, with a quota of heat from the beverage-heated container – a conspicuousness of parsimony that lies at the antipodes of the conspicuous waste of High Society. The ideal uniform for mug-drinking occasions is military – if possible, naval, with a cap, duffle coat and binoculars – which emphasises that the beverage-drinking ceremony is not the main business that is going on. The appropriate beverage is cocoa laced with rum.

8. *Webster's Third New International Dictionary of the English Language* (Chicago: Encyclopaedia Britannica, Inc., 1961).

9. Ibid.

10. Developed commercially as the result of a collaboration between an inventor of genius – Christopher Latham Scholes – and the gunsmiths E. Remington and Sons. This was proof not that the pen was mightier than the sword, but that the typewriter was mightier than the hand-gun, although the same pistol-shot precision was required for both. (The first author to submit a typescript rather than a manuscript – Mark Twain – was also damaged financially by investing in moveable type.)

11. This pedantic distinction is essential. See 'Information' in 'A critical dictionary of neuromythology', in Raymond Tallis, *On the Edge of Certainty* (London: Macmillan, 1999). As William Worthington put it, the invention of writing was the most wonderful of human discoveries, making us 'Masters of other Men's labours and studies, as well as of our own' (*An Essay on the Scheme and Conduct, Procedure and Extent of Man's Redemption*, quoted in Roy Porter, *Enlightenment. Britain and the Creation of the Modern World*, London: Penguin, 2000, p. 74).

12. John Maynard Smith, *The Theory of Evolution* (Cambridge: Cambridge University Press, Canto Edition 1993), p. 329.

13. From Raymond Tallis, *Fathers and Sons* (Newcastle: Iron Press, 1993).

14. I have not revisited here one of the most exquisite and deadly uses of the three-finger grip – its employment in bowmanship, as in the legendary skill and courage of the English longbowmen. But I didn't want to be dragged into yet another discussion of V signs.

15. Actually, not as little as might at first sight appear. I have just caught myself eating a pear, using an interesting variant of the four-jaw chuck. The thumb is kept out of the way in order to make sure that the flesh to be avoided and the pear to be bitten are kept separate. After each bite, by means of a movement I cannot explain, the four jaws manage to rotate the pear so that it is evenly eroded. Shortly afterwards, I found myself carrying out four empty milk bottles, with one digit inserted in each of the bottles. The little finger was free. The thumb maintained a counter-pressure from within its bottle to pack the four more closely together and so ensure that none defected from the quartet.

16. For a more detailed account of the collectivisation of the individual needs of organisms into scarcity and of related matters, see Raymond Tallis, *The Explicit Animal*, 2nd edn (London: Palgrave, 1999) and the third volume of this trilogy *The Knowing Animal: An Inquiry into Knowledge and Truth*.

17. For a review of the rather complicated relationships between cortical representation of a function, the process of learning and the learned programmes, see Richard Frackowiack, 'Plasticity and the human brain: Insights from functional imaging', *Neuroscientist* 2(6) 1996, pp. 353–62.
18. D. V. Buonomano and M. Merzenich, 'Cortical plasticity: from synapses to maps', *Annual Review of Neuroscience* 8, 1998, pp. 149–86.
19. I have avoided another five-finger exercise as I wanted to end this section on a happy note. The exercise I have avoided is one, anyway, that we have already alluded to in section 3.2 – the delivery of a knuckle sandwich from a curled fist. This is a disheartening regression from precision to power and from a higher to lower form of communication and suasion. Damn.
20. What follows owes much to the excellent chapter 'Two hands – one action: the problem of bimanual coordination', by Mario Wiesdanger, Loeg Kazennikov, Stephen Perrig and Pawel Kaluzny in A. M. Wing , P. Haggard and J. R. Flanagan (eds), *Hand and Brain* (London: Academic Press, 1996).
21. The evidence for this hierarchical control is less certain than the evidence for specialisation of role, as Wiesendanger et al. point out (ibid.).
22. A recent fascinating study (F. Mechsner, D. Kerzel, G. Knoblich and W. Prinz, 'Perceptual basis of bimanual coordination', *Nature* 414, 2001, pp. 69–73) has investigated the respective roles of motor programmes and perceptual guidance in two relatively simple but voluntary tasks – bimanual finger oscillation and bimanual four-finger tapping. The authors argue on the basis of their findings that the coordination of the two hands is on the basis of visual perception and not on the basis of a 'motoric' representation of the pattern of actions. They speculate that 'voluntary movements are, in general, organized by way of a simple representation of perceptual goals, whereas the corresponding motor activity of, sometimes extreme, formal complexity is spontaneously tuned in. It may be that this kind of movement organization that makes the richness and complexity of human voluntary movements possible, be it in sports and dance, skilful tool use, or language'. In short, that deliberate voluntary activity, however simple, depends upon seeing (in the widest sense) what needs to be done, seeing that it is being done, and seeing that it has been done. The requisition of motor programmes requires knowing what one is about. Although how this translates into action when no one knows how to mobilise motor programmes to order remains a mystery.

CHAPTER 8

Abstract Digits

8.1 INTRODUCTION AND DISCLAIMER

The overarching theme of this book is to examine the extent to which the hand has had a hand in the ascent of the species *Homo sapiens* to its present domination of the Earth and to try to understand why this might be the case. Beyond the particular consequences of our extraordinary dexterity – which in themselves might have been enough to make us rather superior chimps, but not the totally different kinds of being that we are – the special properties of the hand have woken us up, or contributed to waking us up, in more general ways. And making this – our very special wakefulness – more visible is the ultimate aim of the book. As we shall discuss in Chapters 9 and 10, we not only do more things with our hands than other primates do with their paws, but we do them differently: dexterity not only delivers an increased range of skills, but also truly deliberate activity and, consequently, a whole new range of skills no other primate could conceive.

What lies behind this power of the hand to wake us up from animality? The first is something we have already alluded to and will examine in due course: the extraordinary versatility of our hands, and the limitless degrees of freedom available to us in the manner in which we can grip and manipulate things, has helped to make us animals that *choose*. When we seize hold of things, we select the grips that we deploy. Although there are constraints on the range from which we choose, these are not so narrow that the grips can be regarded as entirely pre-programmed and/or instinctual; nor so wide that random movements would suffice. In our uniquely human manipulations of the world outside of our bodies, we are truly agents and our hands are the instruments of our agency. This argument lies at the heart of the present book. Suffice it to say, for the moment, that the possibility of choice opens up two master-intuitions: the intuition of the hand as a tool, which makes explicit the notion of a *tool*, that serves a general purpose. This, in turn, opens on to, or opens up, the *notion of general purposes*. The latter notion entrains several notions: of the generalisation of need; and, as a correlative of this, of *general properties in the world* answering to, or failing to answer to, or being made to answer to, those needs. The second – which is distinct but closely connected – is the role of the hand in the development of 'the number sense', the theme of the present chapter.

Before proceeding, it is perhaps worth mentioning something that I should have spelled out before, though it is of particular relevance here. Much of what I have had to say about the hand and most of what I shall say in this chapter is speculative or intuitive. This will be evident to many readers, but I want it to be known that I am aware of this. I shall not, of course, ignore or go against the facts that are known in this area – in so far as they are known to me. But facts that bear directly on the overarching ideas of this book about the role of the hand in awakening us to the possibility of agency and to entirely new ways of acting upon the world are so few and far between that this is a very loose constraint. (I shall visit some of the relevant evidence in the final chapter.) This does not, I trust, mean that what follows is entirely baseless. It does not, however, pretend to be a definitive or authoritative account of the relationship between the special properties of the human hand and the unique character of human beings as enumerating animals, as quantifying creatures. I offer the story that I tell as a heuristic device which may help to generate more precisely formulated and clearly testable hypotheses; but, more plausibly and more interestingly, as a way of making visible something of what lies in the background of our number sense. If this lies closer to celebration (and amazement) than analysis and proof, I shall not, as readers who recall the Introduction will know, be too dismayed.

8.2 THE NUMBER SENSE: FROM MAGNITUDES TO DIGITS

Our ability to count contributes more than any other faculty to explaining why, over the last few centuries, we have come to count more than any other species on earth. Counting, in its various forms, lies at the root of the science that, at least since the Renaissance, has established the domination of our species over the Earth – to such an extent that, by the end of the twentieth century, our collective concern for our well-being had to take into account the well-being of the planet whose particular life-supporting properties seem to be threatened by the consequences of our technological conquest of the Earth. Science, and more precisely science-based technology, has made us the first species to be concerned for its environment as a whole and as anything other than a source of the means to life. We feel that we are a threat to the very Earth that has, since time immemorial, called the shots and threatened us.

The number sense[1] that lies at the heart of science and the miraculous technological revolution that relies upon it, as well as underpinning many aspects of social life, most notably the economic exchanges that bind it together and make us able to work cooperatively in a sustained way, are many-layered. Before we examine the putative role of the hand in the development of this sense in ourselves – and in ourselves alone – it will be useful to examine the different layers of the number sense. The contrast between adult humans and animals and as yet incompletely developed humans is a useful way of making this complex sense visible.

There is evidence that many animals have a (very limited) sense of the magnitude of things and, beyond this, of their numerousness. A crow will notice when one man out of a group of three has disappeared out of its sight and, alerted, will consequently fly away. This suggests that it can tell the difference between two things and three things. It would be quite reasonable to dismiss this as a mere pre-numerate sense of magnitude, remote from the abstract notion of quantity that is the essence of genuine numeracy and genuine counting. If the crow's observation could be expressed in propositional form, it will merely be that 'Something has gone' rather than that 'two objects are now present, while three were present before, so that one object has gone'. Even so, while it is obvious that the crow is not comparing two abstract quantities – 'two' (humans) and 'three' (humans) – and concluding that one abstract quantity – 'one' (human) – has been subtracted, there are experiments that apparently suggest that some animals may be able to perceive something that corresponds roughly to an inchoate notion of abstract quantity.

Rats, for example, seem to be able to identify quantitative equalities across sensory modalities. If a rat is trained to press a left lever in response to four flashes and a right lever in response to two flashes, it will preferentially press a left lever if two flashes and two audible tones are presented simultaneously. Some writers have interpreted this as implying that the quantity two has been abstracted from each of two flashes and two tones and these abstracted quantities have been added up to make four; or that, at the very least, the rats are aware of the equi-numerousness of two pairs of stimuli addressed to different senses. There is, however, another interpretation: that the rats are merely responding to equal total quantities of stimuli and are able to abstract these quantities from stimuli, irrespective of their kind. This more cautious interpretation seems more plausible and does not suggest anything corresponding to a developed number sense in the animal.

A more compelling or challenging example is the apparent ability of primates to do simple sums. For example, chimpanzees will preferentially select a tray that has a heap of three biscuits with a heap of four biscuits next to it (seven in all) rather than one with 5 + 1 biscuits on it, even though the five-biscuit heap is the biggest single heap. One interpretation of this is that the animal does two sums – 3 + 4 and 5 + 1 – and concludes that the former generates a larger number than the latter. Again, however, there is a more conservative, and more plausible, interpretation; namely that the chimpanzee simply compares two gestalts or wholes – the group total of biscuits on the first plate with the group total of biscuits on the second plate – and determines the one to be bigger (in a quantitative but not a fully numerate sense) than the other.

There are, however, even more impressive observations on chimpanzees which have been interpreted as demonstrating that they are able not only to add whole numbers, but that they can also do fractions. For example, they will choose half an apple in preference to three-quarters of an apple when they have been trained, by a system of rewards, to choose a half-filled glass in preference to a full one. It is as if they can recognise the abstract numerical equivalence of half an apple and half a glass. Even more abstractly, they will match a three-quarter-size disc rather than a full disc when they have been trained to select a quarter apple plus a half glass.

The notion that this corresponds to genuine counting rooted in a full-blown numerical sense is, however, undermined by a consistent observation, in animals and in human infants, that, as the quantities to be discriminated get bigger, so the ability to match correctly gets poorer. To put this another way, the minimal distance between two quantities which can be successfully discriminated, where one of them is to be preferentially chosen, increases as the magnitude of the quantities increases. For example, the ability to discriminate between four and five is worse than between two and three. Only the discrimination between four and six is a good as between two and three. This would seem to suggest that it is not numbers of objects, but magnitudes as a whole, that are being compared.[2]

This rather more conservative reading of the abilities of apparently numerate animals is supported by the observation that in extremely young children, and in adults exposed very briefly to different numbers of objects, the same laws of magnitude (the numbers of objects in the groups being compared) and distance (the difference between the numbers of objects in the groups) apply. This is consistent with the interpretation that the seeming counting is actually direct perception of comparative magnitude and not a mediated enumeration of counted objects; a matter of feelings of perceived bigness and smallness and not actual numbers being derived and compared. This explains the otherwise odd fact that only the first few quantities – 1, 2, 3 – can be discriminated with high accuracy.

The point of this digression into animal and developmental psychology is not only to demonstrate that, as Stanislaus Dehaene says, 'animals do not possess digital or discrete representations of numbers' (p. 27), but also to remind ourselves of the profound difference between quantity understood as absolute or relative bigness (and smallness) and quantity understood as lesser and greater numbers or understood as mediated through larger and smaller (abstract) numbers. When numbers really are employed, the otherwise implacable laws of magnitude and distance – in accordance with which there is increasing inaccuracy for larger and larger numbers – observed in animals and innumerate humans can be evaded. Once we are numerically competent, we can substract 100,000 from 100,001 with the same accuracy as we subtract 1 from 2. For animals, Dehaene says, 'numbers are approximate magnitudes' (p. 30); which amounts to saying that they are not numbers at all – they are approximate magnitudes, where approximateness is a matter not of abstract numerical but of perceptual similarity.

Notwithstanding the rather surprising experimental results noted above, it looks as if animals do not have a developed number sense in the way that adult human beings do. Human numeracy has many levels. On the first level is recognition of a single object (of a certain kind) as '1 [x]'. A sheep, for example, counts as '1' and so does a goat and a leaf. The next step (only a small one and, indeed, implicit in the first) is to count two objects of a single kind as '2 [x]'. The next step is to count two objects of different kinds as '2 [y]', where y corresponds to a superordinate kind under which both objects fall. For example 'one sheep and one goat would count as 'two animals' and 'one sheep and one stone' would count as 'two objects'. Now it might be argued that the animal experiments already referred to demonstrate that non-human animals, such as rats and chimps, are able to perform this abstraction and count across categories, and that we are therefore entitled to conclude that they count in a real sense. However, the magnitude and distance effect shows that this is not the case. Indeed, there is plenty of evidence to show that, in the case of single integer separation, they cannot get beyond three. Their sense of magnitude is merely '1, 2, 3, many' and scaled-up versions of this. This failure to get beyond '1, 2, 3, many' should prompt one to view with suspicion any assumption that animals can really count up to three. The failure beyond three indicates that what is happening 'up to three' is not counting in the real sense; that the abstract notions of 1, 2, 3, etc. have not emerged; for if they had emerged, there would be no reason why the abstract notions of 4, 5, 6, etc. should not also have emerged. A true number sense would not credibly end at 3; for there is built into a true understanding of 1, 2 or 3 an appreciation of the fact that they belong to a series that can be extended forever. You cannot have a fully developed notion of a number that does not extend beyond 2 or 3. Moreover, exactness would have extended undiminished beyond 1, 2, 3 and the magnitude and distance effect would not have been observed. 1, 2, 3 as appreciated by animals are not precise magnitudes.

There are even reasons, Dehaene suggests, for regarding concrete instances – singletons, duplets, triplets – as being perceived as qualitative magnitudes and directly – like red, yellow and blue. At any rate, they would not correspond to anything like numbers: 'the class of all equinumerous classes'.

The *naming of numbers* is the next clear-cut step towards a fully-fledged number sense and is a decisive break with the limitations of the animal quasi-numerical sense of magnitude. This is also, of course, the last preliminary step before numbers can be isolated and given an existence of their own through being lodged in symbols, in spoken or written numerals. This step itself can be broken up into several sub-steps. One can imagine a first stage in which objects such as seeds were used as tokens to signify numerical magnitudes. 'Six' would be symbolised by six seeds set out in a row. Here the notion of number is not entirely emancipated from that of perceived magnitudes – a long line of seeds versus a shorter one – although the fact that the preciseness of one-to-one correspondence was unaffected by the size of the line would already suggest partial emancipation. The next step is to use spoken words to name and symbolise these abstract magnitudes. Finally, there is the development of discrete, non-representational, written symbols for numbers. This completes the process by which numbers are separated from perceived magnitudes and the uniquely digital world of a uniquely human culture emerges fully from the analogue world of perception that humans share with other animals. The act of counting items by pointing to them in turn and reciting the numbers corresponding to their abstract magnitudes is self-evidently a complex outcome of this long process of dawning numeracy.

The representation of magnitudes as numbers does not, of course, end with the enumeration of self-defining or self-delimited objects –

such as seeds and pebbles and sheep – each of which counts as '1'. The quantification, and ultimately the mathematisation, of nature that underpins – and drives and is expressed in – science and science-based technology, requires several further steps, most crucially the creation of units of measurement. We shall return to units in section 8.4.

8.3 DIGITS AND DIGITS

We have identified some of the crucial ways in which the number sense of human beings differs from what Dehaene calls the 'numerosity' of animals. Which is not to say that the two are entirely unconnected. As Dehaene says (p. 40), 'the number sense we inherit from our evolutionary history plays the role of a germ favouring the emergence of more advanced mathematical abilities'. In other words, our number sense and animal numerosity share common roots. It is important, however, not to exaggerate the degree of overlap between our current number sense and what animals actually apprehend, otherwise we shall miss important things about ourselves. While there may be a common root, the animal side of the root remains a root while the human side of the root grows into a huge, million-leaved tree.

This warning is not entirely superfluous, as Dehaene shows:

> That our apprehension of numerosity does not differ much from that of other animals may seem unremarkable. After all, mammals show a fundamentally similar visual and auditory perceptual apparatus. In some domains, such as olfaction, human perceptual abilities even turn out to be quite inferior to those of other species. But when it comes to language one might think that our performances should set us apart from the rest of mankind. Obviously, what distinguishes us from other animals is our ability to use arbitrary symbols for numbers, such as Arabic digits. (ibid., p. 73)

The distinction to which Dehaene quite rightly draws attention is, however, more profound than is suggested by this passage and, in particular, by the claim that 'our apprehension of numerosity does not differ much from that of other animals'. The ability to use arbitrary symbols for numbers goes to the very heart of the profound difference between the human and the animal sense of quantity; between the animal sense of (comparative) magnitude and the human awareness of abstract 'howmuchness'. The fact that the introduction of numerals enables humans to escape the law by which noticeable difference has to be corrected for size (so that for animals and undeveloped humans the difference between 80 and 90 is as difficult to detect as the difference between 8 and 9) suggests that the human number sense was radically different from the very beginning and that it has escaped its origin in any faculty of comparative perception shared with animals. Indeed, it may indicate that the later developments reach back into the early inchoate sense of number and change its character: our number sense is different from animal number sense root and branch – and the branches and leaves change the roots; so that even when we are counting only up to three, this is entirely different from experience of magnitude enjoyed by animals. Our 'three' is utterly different from a chimpanzee's 'three': the latter is a comparative magnitude and the former an abstract quantity.

To return to a point that has already been made: that animals and infants do not really count even up to three is evident from the fact that they do not count beyond three. Their sense of comparative magnitude does not go beyond '1' v. '2' v. '3' v. 'many' or even '1' v. '2' v. 'many'. A sense of a numerical series that does not reach beyond three does not qualify as a sense of a number series at all. If you truly grasp numbers up to three, then your understanding will not stop at three. Likewise, the suggestion that non-human primates can handle fractions – based on the experiments reported in the last section – is also to be taken with a pinch of salt. The notion that half an apple is equal to $\frac{1}{2}$ an apple and that the latter embodies the abstract quantity of $\frac{1}{2}$ is belied by the very limitations that identical experiments show. If animals really understood the notion of $\frac{1}{2}$ (as opposed to that of a split apple) then animals should also understand the notion of $\frac{1}{8}$ or of $\frac{1}{2} \times \frac{1}{2} \times \frac{1}{2}$. Describing 'half an apple' as '$\frac{1}{2}$ apple' or 'apple/2' is already to infuse into our interpretation of what the animal is doing our own numerical sense for which there is no independent evidence in beasts. (This is an example of what I have elsewhere described as The (ubiquitous) Fallacy of Misplaced Explicitness, by which we import into animal, or machine behaviour, an explicit sense of what is going on that strictly belongs to the observer and to the consciousness of human beings like the observer.)[3]

It is evident, then, that a fundamental change in the sense of magnitude is necessary in order to get beyond '1, 2, 3, many' to an appreciation of an infinite series of numerals; so fundamental that it is misleading to think of the animal that can discriminate only between '1, 2, 3 and many' as having grasped the first three or four terms of the infinite series. The law by which discernible distance has to be corrected for size and the fact that the number sense does not reach beyond three, demonstrate that the animal does not possess even the first element of a numeral sense, only a perception of relative magnitudes, understood in a quasi-analogue rather than a digital sense. Unlike percepts such as red, yellow and blue, numbers have an intrinsic order. That animal '1', '2' and '3' are not fully developed cardinal numbers is revealed in the fact that they are not ordinals. While there is a natural ordering of 1, 2 and 3 – with 2 always being between 1 and 3 – there is no natural order between 'larger' and 'smaller'. Without ordinality, the numbers are insufficiently set off from mere magnitude to be ready-to-be-named and counted off.

So what is it that makes possible this transition from the analogue world of animals to the digital world of economic, technological and scientific man? How does it come about that the sapience of *Homo sapiens* has been so extraordinary enhanced by digitisation of the world in which this unique animal lives? I want to suggest that the hand has a hand in it; more particularly that the complex fractionation of the hand in independently moving fingers and in fingers that can themselves be fractionated in interphalangeal flexion, are crucial to the breakthrough from the animal sense of magnitude to a true number sense.

Several features seem to make the hand, and in particular the fingers, apt to act as midwife to this breakthrough:

1. the special relationship that we have to our hands;
2. the fractionation of finger movement and connected with this, the sense of agency and choice;
3. the rough equivalence of the fingers;
4. and the intrinsic order of the fingers.

Let us examine each in turn. (They will be re-examined in greater depth in Chapter 10.)

My Special Relationship to My Hand

This is something we have touched on many times. I want to revisit it here not only in order to cast light on the number sense, but in order that the number sense should cast light on this special relationship.[4] Let me approach it from a new angle and illustrate and explore it through the example of an ordinary touching of one's own body.

I am lying in bed. Most of my body is warm, apart from my shoulder, which is exposed above the sheets. If I touch my cold shoulder with my warm hand, I am sensorily aware in the same moment of several things: the coldness of my shoulder; the cold touch of my shoulder on my fingers; the warm touch of my fingers on my shoulder; and my shoulder's being warmed by my hand. In other words, I have a complex experience that has many layers, which are simultaneously and yet separately subjective and objective. The hand experiences (subjectively) its being cooled by the shoulder and objectively that the shoulder is cold; the shoulder experiences both (subjectively) that the hand is warming it (giving comfort) and (objectively) that the hand is warm. The distance between the object and subject is, of course, only partial: it is not the same as the distance between a subjective experience of an objectively cold material object that is not one's own body. But there is still a distance. And this distance is real because active exploratory behaviour makes the explored surface of the body (the shoulder) and the exploring surfaces of the body (the hands) respectively active agent and passive patient, and so mirrors, or at least hints at, the asymmetry between a known object and a knowing subject. The distinctive status of the hand as an organ of cognition, passively receiving information and actively seeking out knowledge of the world, helps to sustain this asymmetry. This underpins a very special relationship to one's hand – which may, of course, subsequently be taken up elsewhere (for example, the mouth and the foot) – and breaks the spell of our immersion in the body, in its experiences, and the world revealed through those experiences.

The Sense of Agency and Choice: the Hand as a Tool

As we have already noted, the ability to use the fingers separately in exploiting the special manipulative prowess of the hand arising out of the opposability of the thumb and other characteristics described in section 1.2, creates choice. Although there is a relatively small number of standard grips, there are limitless non-standard grips which we use in everyday life and there is infinite potential variation, in the case of the standard grips, in the precise way in which they are deployed. There is choice and, more importantly, an element of arbitrariness in the final choice. This arbitrariness, however, is constrained. The grip, unlike other motor activity, is always customised to a unique occasion; so variation is both necessary and, at the same time, limited in its range. I can grip a cricket ball in many different ways, but the range of comfortable and secure grips is fairly narrow.

This constrained arbitrariness is a supreme awakener, awakening the sense of the body as a tool and hence of agency. Of all bodily doings prior to the emergence of speech, those involving the hand are most developed as voluntary actions[5] and are the key to the ultimate development of the sense – that we enjoy, uniquely in the animal kingdom – of our bodies being instruments. This, in turn, enhances our inchoate sense of our hand – and its fingers – as standing out from our body, as something attached to, as well as part of, and even assimilated into, ourself.[6] The multiplicity of our fingers is thus a visible fact; their multitude in consequence makes of them a potential instrument for enumeration. These fingers, which are objectively there as mine, 'them' as well as 'me', are lined up to be an abacus.

This is a complex role, reflecting the complexity of our relationship to our digits. Our hands retain a finger in the mathematical pie in different ways: the fingers may be used for counting – either in one's head (a kind of abstract inner pointing); or externally, using the index finger to point at each of the objects to be counted in turn; or, indeed, as a very preliminary exercise when we count our fingers, not in order to determine their numbers – this is given to us rather directly – but in order to practise enumeration, and the use of the names of numbers. This, however, is only a springboard to a true digitisation of the world. The carnal digits are a bridge to the abstract ones; from the material world with its magnitudes to the ethereal world of numbers.

There is a further aspect of hand function that makes the human hand particularly suitable to act as midwife to the mathematised world of *Homo faber*, *Homo economicus* and, above all, of *Homo scientificus*. When we choose our grips in order to manipulate the world, this grip is at once utterly particular and yet satisfies a general principle, expresses a general strategy. Through our customised grips, we enact and – courtesy of our complex subject–object relationship with our hand – also experience the fusion and separation of the general and particular. This fusion also lies at the very root of the intuition of number; of an object as an instance of a number; of the reduction of one sheep to 'one'. The hands are thus particularly apt to be the site of the birth of a particular kind of abstraction: bodyless or disembodied quantity – which is the essence of number.

There is one another aspect of digital function that is worthy of note and seems to forge another link between the embodied creature that is the human being and the abstract world of numerical quantities. We are able to touch our fingers with our fingers: this is the essence of opposability. In primitive, everyday counting, we often 'count off' what is before us on our fingers. Fingering our fingers, we meta-finger the world: through this higher-order touch, we grasp what is there by counting it. Counting, an abstract grasp, is an essential step in the passage from prehension to apprehension and comprehension.

The Rough Equivalence of the Digits

With the exception of the toes, to which we do not have the same special relationship as we have to our fingers (not the least because we cannot 'toe' our unopposable toes in the way that we finger our opposable fingers) – or not primarily at any rate[7] – there is no other structure that is replicated so lavishly as the digits. We have two of many things but ten of no other, apart from our toes. Once the special relationship to the hand is established – on the basis of the differentiation of subjectivity and objectivity and the awakening to the body as instrument that we have already noted – then this unique numerousness is there to be exploited as a means of enumeration. The fingers are particularly apt for this because they are roughly equal; or at least their inequalities are not sufficiently large as to prevent their being taken as equivalent. (The manipulative indeterminacy to which we have already referred has implicit in it a – limited – substitutability of fingers.) Each finger counts the same as every other finger and so each counts as one. This stipulated equality, which sets aside a degree of difference, lies at the heart of the intuition of digitisation: it is this that enables carnal digits to become the basis of numerical digits. They each count as one and so can be added and subtracted: they can literally be added in and taken away by flexion and extension at the carpo-phalangeal and inter-phalangeal joints.

Cardinals and Ordinals

The fingers establish cardinality by their equivalance: each counts as '1'. But, as we have already noted, numbers are distinguished not only by cardinality but also by ordinality: individual numbers belong to a system and have a fixed place in that system defined by the determinate relations between them. Unlike red, yellow and blue they have an intrinsic order. That the '1', '2' and '3' of animals are not fully developed cardinal numbers is demonstrated, if further demonstration were needed, in the fact that they are not ordinals. While there is a natural ordering of 1, 2 and 3 – with 2 always being between 1 and 3 – there is no natural order governing the relations between 'larger' and 'smaller'. The chimp that can distinguish 1, 2 or 3 items has no sense of the ordering of 1, 2 and 3. There is, after all, no reason why the smaller magnitude should be 'before' the greater magnitude or the intermediate magnitude lie between the two. There is an ordering of numbers such that 3 has a relationship to 4 that is equivalent to the relationship that 5 has to 6 but not the relationship that 6 has to 5 or 5 has to 3. Without ordinality, the numbers are insufficiently offset from mere magnitude to be ready-to-be-named and counted off. The notion of ordinality – which is typically connected with that of relative magnitude, but may be linked to a fixed or canonical order of temporal occurrence (as in dates) or order of spatial occurrence (as in house numbers in a street) – is unknown to small children or non-human animals. The differences of magnitude remain resolutely scalar and, indeed, are incompletely quantitised.

The fingers inspire not only the cardinal aspect of digitisation but also the ordinal aspect. While counting could theoretically begin at any point in a row of fingers, the special relationship between one finger and another is fixed and there is a natural order among the fingers, which consists in moving from one end of the row – with the thumb as a reference point – to the other. Counting on the fingers, which provides a sense of cumulative, quantitative magnitude, also tethers those magnitudes to fixed relations in space and so underpins a sense of objective or intrinsic ordinality. Counting on the fingers, which may include counting the fingers *with* the fingers – counting one finger using another to pick it out[8] – which naturally goes from one end of the row to the other, may (because of the right hand dominance of most of the human race) tend to go from the left to the right, with the fingers on the left hand being counted (by being touched) by fingers on the right hand followed by fingers on the right hand being counted by the fingers belonging to the left hand.

It seems possible, therefore, that the special relationship between the fleshly digits of the hand and counting using virtual or abstract digits can be rationally reconstructed and the unique number sense of human beings accounted for. Once the fingers have established the abstract notion of numerical quantity, numbering may develop in many different directions: giving numbers names; creating symbols for those names; using those symbolised names to manipulate abstract quantities in the operations of addition, subtraction; and so on. And these steps are, of course, only the beginning: once the numbers themselves are given names of their own, the fingers may be used to count objects external to the body, by pointing to things in turn and reciting the number corresponding to the cumulative quantity. The fingers may be used to keep count – an almost literal use of them as an abacus. And they may be used to do simple sums, with fingers being added and taken away.

All of this builds on naming numbers – a crucial step in abstracting quantity from quantities of objects – and then creating (written) symbols for those names – for abstract quantities, so that they can be handled separately and have a life and presence of their own. The jump from the sense of number, derived from our special relationship to our fingers, to using names for numbers that can then be stored and manipulated, seems rather abrupt. It is not, however, entirely inexplicable because, I want to argue, even the simplest counting unmediated by names and symbols is shot through with meta-counting, or awareness of counting, that makes the necessary step to names and symbols for names a little easier to understand. When we count our fingers using our fingers, we are counting the counter, or enumerating the enumerator. The 'second order' is thus built into the 'first order' precisely because of the special relationship to body parts that is necessary for digits to serve their enumerating purpose. When we count our fingers, we count with our fingers because we use our fingers to do the counting, to count them off. We finger our fingers and this 'meta-fingering' provides an implicit model for the 'hands-off' prehension that is the essence of counting and dealing with the quantities that emerge from counting. Even in silent counting, the fingers are (implicitly) 'standing' symbols for numbers as well as being the body parts that engage in episodic acts of enumeration. When they are numerically disengaged (as they are for the most part) they still count as corporeal symbols for what they are.

It is hardly surprising, therefore, that early extracorporeal symbols for numbers are visually close to the natural symbols that the fingers themselves form; for example, tallies look like rows of fingers, which can be added to or struck out. The first numeral – '1' – looks like a finger. The second numeral, usually taking the form of two uprights, looks like two raised fingers. And so on. Fingers, as well as being that with which we count, may also come to be a primitive embodiment of the numeral by which we count and the product of counting. The Romans had a special reverence for the number 10, according to Ovid, 'because it is the number of the fingers by which we are wont to count'. This was reflected, according to David Ewing Duncan, in Romulus' repeated use of the number 10 in organising his new kingdom, 'dividing both the 100 senators and his military units of spearmen, infantry and javelin throwers into groups of 10'.[9] Bearing more directly on our present concern is Duncan's suggestion that

> Latin numerals themselves – I, II, III, IV, V, VI, VII, VIII, IX, X – are probably meant to represent fingers counting up to 10, with the V perhaps equating to an upraised thumb and index finger and the X to an upraised palm.[10]

The central role of the fingers in counting is reflected in the ubiquity of the base 10 in numerical systems. As Dehaene puts it, 'The preponderance of base 10 is due the contingent fact that we have ten fingers' (1997, p. 117).

> How did human languages ever move beyond the limit of 3!? The transition to more advanced numeration systems seems to have involved the counting of body parts. All children spontaneously discover that their

fingers can be put into one-to-one correspondence with any set of items. One merely has to raise one finger for the first item, two for the second, and so on. By this mechanism, the gesture of raising three fingers comes to serve as a symbol for the quantity three. An obvious advantage of this is that the required symbols are always 'handy' – in this numeration system, the digits are literally the speaker's digits! (ibid., p. 93)

This is beautifully expressed and true as far as it goes; but it has to be supplemented by the more fundamental point that the hands lie at the origin of counting – at the root of the fact that there is such a thing as counting, that there is a keeping count – because we have a very special relationship to our hands, and to the rest of our body made plain in our hands. This, and not merely the fact that nothing could be handier for our counting fingers than our counted fingers, is why we count 'to the base finger' rather than 'to the base forearm' or 'to the base toes'. And why the numbering system was, ultimately, liberated from the body entirely and its digits became entirely abstract.[11]

8.4 UNITS: FROM COUNTING TO MEASUREMENT

It is counting that has made us the Lords of Creation.[12] The digitisation of the material world in which we live has permitted us to predict, shape and control it to an extraordinary degree. Counting lies at the root of pre-scientific technology and, to a much greater extent, the science-based technology upon which civilisation and our more or less civilised lives depend. The digitisation of nature does not, however, consist merely of enumeration of existing, self-delimited objects. There is another important step before we can get from fleshly digits to the digital world in which we live: *measurement*.

Measurements may apply to concrete pre-existing objects or to relatively abstract quantities, such as distance or duration or temperature. The transition from enumeration (of pre-existent, or self-delimited) objects to measurement requires the creation of units. Units are second-order abstract quantities and are clearly social institutions as well as being reflections of what is 'out there'. The number of instances of a natural kind such as sheep is a constant: a flock of three sheep is composed of three sheep and that is the end of it. By contrast, the number built into a size – distance, size, duration, etc. – will depend upon which unit is used. The distance from A to B may be 3 (miles) or 5,000+ (yards) or 15,000+ feet or just under 5 kilometres or an hour's walk.

The key to the transition from enumeration to measurement is the unit and a unit is a ratio. It is possible to see the origin of units in fractions. A single sheep may be measured in sheep units: it is $2 \times \frac{1}{2}$ sheep (units) or $4 \times \frac{1}{4}$ sheep (units). In this case, the object is compared with itself and is presented as ratios of itself. The bold step is to decree a standard example and make that the basis of the unit. In the case of sheep, this might be to take a standard sheep based upon some particular sheep and then to see other sheep as being proportions of that standard sheep. In this way, any given sheep can be presented as an abstract quantity – for example as '1.5' (of the standard sheep). This is clearly inconvenient because the standard sheep cannot be carried around and, without the standard sheep to hand, and with memory being fallible, there would be calibration drift. There is a need for a portable standard. This next bold step is to see that the standard does not have to be of the same kind as the thing it is measuring. We don't need to use sheep units to size sheep. By this means, 'How many?' can be translated into 'How much?'

One rich source of constant, portable and fairly standard standards is the body itself. And so the early units were based upon lengths of bodily parts: the 'cubit' (the distance from the elbow to the end of the middle finger), the 'ell' (derived from ulna – the forearm), the 'fathom' (the span of the embracing outstretched arms), the 'foot', the 'inch' (the size of the royal thumb), the (finger) 'span' and, of course, the 'hand'. The house was six cubits high, the horse was 16 hands, the glass of water was one finger, etc. This was an advance, even though there were problems arising out of the manifest variability of the size of body parts. Measurement is the one thing in which size indubitably does matter. Even so, the process of using one's bodily parts to measure objects out there has as a prerequisite a degree of objectivity in the relations to one's own body: to use one's forearm to measure the size of something testifies to an extraordinary inner distance from that bodily part, a highly elaborated instrumental relationship to it. This relationship has been developed as we have emphasised on the basis of the distances established through the special relationships humans develop to their hands. The same, of course, applies to using the hand itself as a measure and the foot is no less dependent on this than the hand.

On top of objectification – of one's own body and of the relationship between one's own body and a thing out there – there is generalisation of my body: my forearm becomes an instance of a general forearm. Only in this way could it act as an abstract quantity – as a 'cubit'. Your forearm and my forearm are in this respect identical: there is nothing privileged about my forearm just because it is mine. Or, rather, I forgo the naturally privileged status that my forearm enjoys simply because it is my forearm. It is this abstraction from individuals, even where the individual in question is a part of my own body, that allows humans to use the quantity of one thing to characterise the quantity of another; or to reduce both of these things to quantities, to ratios. Out of the cubit based upon a generalised forearm, and the foot based upon a generalised foot, comes a more radical notion: bodily parts objectified and generalised as mere instances of abstract quantities pave the way for non-bodily parts to quantify other objects and extract from them abstract quantities such as length. The use of a third party, such as a stick that has no special relationship to any individual, seems an inevitable next step and a solution to the problem that not everyone has bodily parts of the same size. The 'inevitability' of the next step is deceptive: the idea that several pebbles may be used to weigh one pebble, that one might use the weight of the several pebbles actively to characterise the weight of the single pebble, is not only daring but manifestly complex. Weighing the weight of an object takes the wakefulness originating from the second-order awareness of 'fingering fingers' to new heights.[13]

The use of generalised body parts is but a first step in the long evolution of the collective human genius that underpins digitisation of the world from the natural abacus of the fingers to the abstractions of counting, barter (exchange) and measurement – from rations via ratios to abstract units. Quantified distances and masses and times are all embedded in collective agreement, where personal impressions and perceptions are subordinated to an agreed objective measure.[14] This objectivity is related in part to the emptying of content: the unit is a ratio – and the quantity measured in units is a collection of instances of the ratio – in which personal impressions, particularity are cancelled out. A distance, for example, is merely a ratio between one abstracted length and another abstracted length.

The idea that a *single* distance can be *several* miles is really rather extraordinary, not simply because there is a reduction of 'surroundingness' to an abstraction – distance. The truly extraordinary aspect of the notion is that it rests upon a seemingly contradictory notion – that, say, a *single* goat can be *so many* kilograms (of meat). Where does this notion come from? How can something be one continuous thing and, at the same time, several discrete things? The hand here also provides the necessary inspiration, for it too is one and many. As a closed fist it is a unity. When it is opened, it divides into five fingers, able through fractionated finger movements to act independently. The fingers themselves, being equivalent, have the property of units. The fingers can count as one – and equal – or as equal fifths. The fact that the hand is both one hand and five fingers allows us to develop a way of seeing that counts an object as one object and X units: one goat *and* 100 lb of meat.[15] (This would not be apparent to any other primate, even those that have quite advanced fractionated finger movements, because their relationship to their paws is not such as to awaken the second-order carnal awareness which is the necessary precondition of numerate fingering.)

The reduction of size, shape, weight, duration, etc. – in short, the characteristics of the material world around us – to abstract, unitised quantities leads the way to the reduction of change over time to unitised quantities and, what is more, of patterns of change to relationships between the general forms of quantities. Thus arises the *equation*, with all its power to predict and direct the fabrication of artefacts intended to shape the world or order things according to human need.

There is a long story to be told here: it is the history of science from pre-scientific technology to the present science-driven, increasingly globalised world of the twenty-first century. It is not the place even to hint at it here. Suffice it to note that the primary driver to measurement and unitisation was economic. The need to move on from counting objects and reporting 'How many?' to measuring 'How much?' arose out of trade and the necessity for the appearance of objective fairness in barter. One sheep does not translate into the same number of dinners as another sheep: there are big sheep and small sheep. Certain commodities – flour, fabric, etc. – do not take the form of self-defining objects: the nouns that name them are 'mass' rather than 'count' nouns. Direct enumeration, therefore, was insufficient to ensure fairness. If trade is the interaction between strangers which required that they treat each other as equals – or at least seem to do so – we may think of measurement as an instrument of democracy, and a primordial mode of human communication (with commodities, like words, having shared and agreed values), as well as the most powerful instrument for the 'scientification' of human consciousness. Counting is central to trade, of course; but trade was the key driver to the evolution of (objective) measurement and the growth of objective quantitative knowledge and the emergence of science.[16]

8.5 THE UNREASONABLE POWER OF THE PRECISION OF ABSTRACT DIGITS

Quantification empowers. The animal that does the most counting counts most. To count objects is an extraordinary thing to do to them; even more extraordinary is, as we have seen, to quantify a single object, to count its size, by enumerating the units in it, performing this enumeration against a fixed enumerator consisting of a standard number of units – a ruler, for example. (Quantification is the mobilisation of prefixed ratios.) Yet more extraordinary is to distil out of the notion of abstract quantification that of certain abstractions to be quantified – and yet these are the very basic parameters of science. By these means – enumeration, abstraction, unitisation – the virtual fingers of our mathematical digits have enabled us to grasp the world more firmly and, temporarily, to loosen the world's grasp on us. A comparatively recent consequence of this is the transformation of the work the world requires of us: as we reply with precision to the power of the forces ranged against us, and precision ascends ladders built out of quantitative abstraction, mathematisation, from handiwork to brainwork, so the nature of human life and labour changes. The manualisation of our interactions with the world paved the way for liberation from manual labour. The world of work progresses from manual to digital activity and from carnal to virtual digital activity, as prehension becomes ever more complexly mediated and the requisite touches ever lighter. The hands of the sons and daughters of toil become ever less horny as the requirement is less for direct power than for indirect precision.[17] Numbers are the most potent instruments of precision prehension. From the tips of our fingers, we reach out into the furthest reaches of the universe; and the supposedly cold science that has grown out of our fingertips expands the pocket of warmth that we wrap round ourselves in the boundless, bitterly cold universe.

All of this is quite inexplicable. Einstein famously commented that the greatest mystery was the partial intelligibility of the world. One of the darkest and most wonderful aspects of this mystery is that intelligibility has been so greatly increased by our ability to transform the analogue world of our perceptions into the digital world of mathematics. Why does digitisation – enumeration, unitisation, the transformation into equations abstractly mirroring the unfolding order of things – so enhance our power? The effectiveness of mathematics seems, as the physicist Eugene Wigner expressed it, 'unreasonable' – a wonderful and mysterious gift. After all, mathematics has its own internal history: once it grew out of its roots in trade it developed without regard to any application to the physical world. Tensor calculus, which proved to be the ideal mathematical instrument to enable Einstein to develop the General Theory of Relativity, is only a comparatively recent and rather spectacular case in point. It was created by playful mathematicians as a purely abstract way of capturing the non-Euclidean geometry created in the spirit of – well, mathematical creativity. Even so, the General Law of Relativity has proved to be the second most succesful theory of all time, exceeded only by quantum electrodynamics, itself founded upon highly abstract mathematics, also developed without regard to the physical world. The effectiveness of mathematics seems even less reasonable if you believe, as many (including Stanislaus Dehaene) do, that the human mind *creates* mathematics – that even the elementary number sense, not merely the higher reaches of abstract algebra, are products of the human mind. Or if you consider that, as Max Born points out,[18] units, the basis of all objective scientific measurement, are 'to a high degree arbitrary, and are chosen for reasons of their being easily reproduced, easily transported, durable, and so forth'. Nietzsche's joking fable,[19] that 'in some remote corner of the universe, poured out and glittering in innumerable solar systems, there once was a star on which clever animals invented knowledge', begins to seem more than a joke.

Dehaene solves this puzzle by pointing out that, although mathematics is a creation of the human mind, this does not make it a merely human institution, a social construct. It can reach out to the universe because the human mind, too, is a creation: it is a natural product of the same evolutionary processes that gave rise to the human body and subject to the same selective processes that gave rise to the body. The mathematics created by the human mind is of survival value because the mind, and its various cognitive organs, have been shaped by the forces of evolution. Mathematics, mental creation or not, is constrained to be true.

This is ingenious but not, in the end, convincing. I have discussed elsewhere why I believe that evolutionary theories of explicit human consciousness and of the truths afforded to that consciousness are utterly misconceived and I shall not repeat the arguments here, as they are not strictly relevant to the matter at hand.[20] It is, however, worth noting that those organs of the mind that are supposed, according to orthodox evolutionary psychology, to have helped us to deal with the problems faced by our Stone Age ancestors are unlikely to have been so shaped as to make it possible for us to create the kind of mathematics – tensor calculus, etc. – that would be required for future theories of the universe, or indeed, to inform the science-based technology that has utterly transformed our lives. Science, after all, has delivered added survival on a large scale only over the last few hundred years.

The mystery of how it is that the development of the unique human wakefulness made possible by our special relationship to our hands into digitisation of the analogue world presented to our active and suffering sensorimotor bodies should in turn have enabled us to control that world, and to an incredible extent, remains intact.[21]

NOTES

1. I have borrowed this phrase from the title of a delightful and fascinating book of this name by Stanislas Dehaene, *The Number Sense: How the Mind Creates Mathematics* (Oxford: Oxford University Press, 1997). Much of the factual evidence about the number sense in non-human animals and developing humans is derived from this book, as will become evident.

2. To remind the reader, as Dehaene puts it:

   > the parameter that governs the ease with which we distinguish two numbers is not so much their absolute numerical difference but their distance relative to their size. (ibid., p. 76)

   We shall discuss the implications of this presently.

3. See the entry 'Misplaced explicitness', in Raymond Tallis *On the Edge of Certainty* (London: Macmillan, 1999).

4. Other bodily parts have been suggested as having a crucial role in the generation of our conception of number. It is a commonplace of radical feminist thought that the numerals 0 and 1 stand respectively for the vagina and the phallus and the equation of women with emptiness and and nullity and men with fullness and integrity is symptomatic of the misogyny and phallocentricity of our digitised world. I think this is implausible. The 1 is clearly derived from the finger and the 0 entered the scene much later than 1. 1 has been observed inscribed on bones between 20,000 and 30,000 years old. Zero, on the other hand, was not invented until at least 200 BC, and even then it was only a placeholder and not a fully developed number in its own right. 1 and 0 did not, in other words, emerge as a pair of binarily opposed elements.

   If the zero and the vagina (seen in an implausibly idealised cross-section) look alike it is because they serve the analogous functions of being an empty space, or a placeholder. Just as the finger and the phallus have some similarities because they have, among their functions, that of poking into holes. This is not, however, their only, or even their chief, functions.

   Moreover, the radical feminist theory of numbers – which is intended to draw attention to the subordinate status of women by showing how this is inscribed even in the abstract language of computational mathematics, which seemingly places zero (woman) below 1 (man) – could be turned on its head. Zero could be seen as a cross-section of a phallus and 1 as the unoccupied vagina viewed as a slit.

   Perhaps one shouldn't take such post-Freudian arguments seriously – even to the extent of bothering to disagree with them.

5. Speech may seem to be yet more deliberate. However, although the choice of words is a highly conscious activity and voluntary to a unique degree, the motor activity underpinning speech production is automatic. If I had to 'do' talking, I would have great difficulty finding enough cognitive resources to think about what I am saying.

6. There is striking evidence of the comparative distance we have from our hands – and the fact that it is opened up early on – in the sure-fire strategy adopted by paediatricians when they need to examine an anxious child. They begin by saying 'Show me your hands' and this accustoms the child to being examined. If the doctor had begun with, for example, the chest or the mouth or the abdomen, all cooperation would have been lost. The hand, however, is a kind of anteroom – me and not-me – which enables the invasion implicit in examination to be phased in. (I owe this information to the paediatric neurologist Dr Chris Verity.)

7. There are immensely courageous and talented individuals such as thalidomide victims who, lacking properly developed upper limbs, use their feet (and mouths) to execute actions that are usually the sole preserve of the hands – and with extraordinary success, as exemplified by foot-and-mouth artists. This does not, however, disprove the role of the hand as the primary driver to the development of a distinctively human world; for such individuals live in a world that has been largely created by the handed. It was only when the hand was liberated from the demands of locomotion that it was able to develop as it has and was free to fashion a world in which there is such a thing as art or, indeed, tools such as paintbrushes.

    There is an analogy here with blind individuals. The fact that they are able to function extraordinarily well does not alter the fact that vision is the chief source of information and the world as we know it is a world that has been made possible and fashioned by the sighted.

    This deals in passing with the concern that some may have that I might be suggesting that the handless are in some sense sub-, pre- or inhuman. The distinctively human world was created by handed humanity but the handless are not thereby prevented from full participation in it. (Though it does underline the distinctive brutality of chopping off the hands of thieves. 'Be-handing' is close to beheading.)

8. Is there no end to the layeredness of our relationship to our own body!

9. David Ewing Duncan, *The Calendar* (London: Fourth Estate, 1998), p. 41.

10. Ibid.

11. Liberation of number from the body is, however, gradual. Dehaene, *The Number Sense*, has much to say of interest on the topic of counting on one's fingers. He points out that young children have great difficulty calculating without using their fingers, because 'words vanish as soon as they have been uttered but fingers can be kept constantly in sight'. He reminds us how complex even this primitive form of counting is, how much understanding it entails: that counting is an abstract procedure that applies to all kinds of objects; that while the order in which the numbers are recited is crucial, the order in which one points to the objects being counted is irrelevant; and that words have to be recited in precise one-to-one correspondence with the objects to be counted.

12. What follows is a very superficial account of the mystery of measurement and there is no discussion of the key issue of the *validity* of the digitisation of the universe and whether it brings us nearer to the objective truth of how things really are. This will, however, be discussed in volume 3 of this trilogy, *The Knowing Animal: An Inquiry into Knowledge and Truth*.

13. The connection between numbering and the instrumentalisation of the body that begins with the hand is strikingly illustrated in the use of one's foot to measure a distance; and of walking a distance simply in order to quantify it.

14 As W. H. Auden put it so beautifully:
    'And strangers were hailed as brothers by his clocks'
                        'Sonnets from China' VIII

15. Whether the ability of the fingers to divide into parts (by flexing) is the inspiration of fractions – halves and thirds – is a matter for speculation even more dubious than the reader has had to tolerate in the body of this chapter.

16. A couple of further comments about merchants as midwives of mathematics. First, the transformation of needs into objective requirements acknowledged in the collective consciousness of humans, and the objects of need into exchangeable commodities,

was well advanced by the time the first 'tallies' were introduced. (The earliest evidence is of notched bone harpoons in Africa dating from about 6,500 BC.) Secondly, the earliest advances in abstract mathematics had other drivers than the requirement to regulate trade; notably the need to regulate the world through prediction – hence the earliest mathematics was connected with the creation of calendars and to predict seasonal variations such as the ebb and flow of large rivers. Understanding the heavens – a project connected with theological approaches to regulating the world and dealing with well-founded anxieties – also occasioned mathematical advance. There were many paths to the extension of the hand's reach, via virtual digits, to the far corners of the universe.

17. This progressive liberation is traced in Raymond Tallis, 'The work of art in an age of electronic reproduction', in *Theorrhoea and After* (London: Macmillan, 1999), and discussed again in Chapter 9.

18. Max Born, *Einstein's Theory of Relativity* (New York: Dover Editions, 1962), pp. 4–5.

19. Friedrich Nietzsche, 'On truth and lie in an extra-moral sense', a posthumously published fragment. I discuss this in some detail in 'Explicitness and truth (and falsehood)', in *On the Edge of Certainty*. I will return to it in volume 3 of this trilogy.

20. See, for example, Raymond Tallis, *The Explicit Animal: A Defence of Human Consciousness* (London: Macmillan, 1991) and *On the Edge of Certainty*. The misconceptions underpinning both evolutionary psychology and evolutionary epistemology are of such fundamental importance – and, by accident, throw light on so many other things – that I revisit them yet again in Volume 3.

21. Which is not to suggest that mathematics gives us a definitive account of the world. *Pace The Hitchhiker's Guide to the Galaxy*, the answer is not 42, nor indeed, any other number, or constellation of numbers, or patterns of mathematical symbols. Russell pointed out that our scientific account of the world is cast in mathematical form not because we know so much about the world, but because we know so little. To take an analogy perhaps a little too far: the numbers that grew out of the digits can grasp the world but cannot grasp 'right through' the world. Numbers give us the general form of things, but not their specific content. It is an unfounded Platonic prejudice that general form is closer to reality than specific content. We shall return to these matters in Volume 3.

CHAPTER 9

The Tool of Tools

According to Aristotle ... human intelligence is directly related to the possession of hands, in so far as hands are the organs that enable us to use tools: 'We should expect the most intelligent animal to be able to employ the greatest number of organs or instruments; now the hand would appear to be not one single instrument but many, as it were an instrument that represents many instruments' (*De partibus animalium*, IV, X, 687a). Aristotle, then, looked at the human hand as the tool of tools.

François Jouffroy[1]

9.1 PROLOGUE: THE SELF-SHAPING HAND

After our sojourn in the airless, grey-lit realm of abstract digits, it may be a relief to return to the open, sunlit analogue world again. Our enquiry in the present chapter[2] will focus on the tools that assist the hand in shaping the world in which manukind lives. We shall round off our reflections on tool-using humanity with a brief allusion to the infinite variety of its handicraft. Let us, however, begin our meditation on this miraculous 'tool of tools' with something in which it could hardly have had a hand at all: its own genesis. The hand, the great shaper of the world, is of necessity, itself shaped. It is – notwithstanding the title of this section – not truly self-shaping; for this great agent, the agent of agents, is passively brought into being – a crux that places the darkness of unresolved mystery at the heart of this book, and at the heart of our lives.

In the ill-lit, silent aquarium of the womb, the hand grows into itself. The process begins very early on in foetal development. Arm buds are recognisable as small swellings by 26–27 days of embryonic life, not long after the mother has missed her period, and when the future doctor, docker, artist, boxer, saint or mass murderer is about 2–3 mm in length.

By day 32, by which time perhaps the mother has confided in her best friend, the bud has grown into a paddle-like forelimb. By the following weekend, when the partner has been informed, slight depressions are apparent at the end of the growing bud. These 'finger rays' are the first hint of the digits to come. During the next ten days, while the embryo is growing from 13 mm to 30 mm and the story of the mother's condition is propagating via telephone calls and corridor conversations over a widening circle of friends and relatives, the forelimb evolves rapidly. Finger rays develop into distinct notches at the end of the limb bud. These in turn evolve into pre-digits linked by webs. The webbed fingers separate. The Famous Five are in place. A couple of weeks later, by which time even the father's parents know of the expected event, the fingers sport tiny fingernails. Meanwhile the bones and the muscles and fat and skin of the arm, hands and fingers have started to differentiate: an 8-week old, 30 mm-long embryo already has distinctive muscles in the upper arm, the forearm and the back of the hand. The apparatus of reaching, grasping, manipulating and tactile knowing is in place.

This amazingly rapid self-formation of the tool, by which humans, directly or indirectly, individually or collectively, manipulate the world for their 70 or 80 years of life, raises all sorts of questions. These are usually described by embryologists as being the problems of regional specification, pattern formation and spatial organisation. Put more simply, these problems boil down to two sorts of question: how there is differentiation into specific types of cell; and how those specific types come to lie in the correct positions with respect to one another. More simply still, how cells acquire the right properties and end up in the right place. This last is particularly intriguing: how do nail-bed cells find their way to the fingertips while the cells that are destined to become the fibroblasts from which the shoulder muscles develop stay close to the trunk?

Early development – in fact, the first four weeks – is the most crucial. During this time an apparently homogeneous group of cells is transformed into a miniature animal consisting of:

1. the central nervous system;
2. the notochord – a midline axis around which the vertebral bodies are organised, the basis for the skeleton;
3. the lateral mesoderm – between the inner (endoderm) and outer (ectoderm) layers of the embryo – from which arises the connective tissues;
4. the somites, which father, among other things, the skeletal muscles;
5. the branchial arches, from which are formed a multitude of structures

at the head end of the foetus, ranging from the exquisitely shaped bones of the middle ear to the muscles for facial expression and the bones of the larynx;

6. the integument, which is the forerunner of the skin, with its incredibly complex structures serving a variety of functions, including protection, temperature regulation and tactile sensation; and, finally,

7. the gut – which is, well, the gut.

Although in the next 7 or 8 months, there is, according to Slack,[3] 'a good deal of growth, of histological differentiation of the organs, and the specifically human, rather than the general vertebrate, characteristics of the organism become established ... all this takes place on the framework of the basis body plan which was laid down in early development.' As Lewis Wolpert has pointed out, it is not birth, marriage or death, but gastrulation – the step by which the third embryonic layer (between the ectoderm and the endoderm) is formed – that is truly the most important time in your life. It is this that creates the concentric arrangement of highly differentiated structures around a central axis.

How does all this happen? How is it that growth does not simply generate a larger and larger blob of cells? How do we have such exquisitely differentiated tissues that are so wonderfully adapted to their different functions? How do all the cells that belong to a particular structure come together? How do the cells supporting cooperative stuctures adopt the correct relationship to one another? How, for example, do the different nerve endings that support our exquisitely sensitive and intelligently active fingertips find themselves next to the dermal ridges that enhance their sensitivity, and near to the blood vessels that keep them supplied with oxygen and nutrition and close up against the muscles whose contractions they must regulate – which latter in turn must be appropriately connected with tendons, bones, skin, etc.? I ask these questions – made even more challenging by our gene-based understanding, which suggests that nearly all the instructions required for building a new organism are contained in the genes that come together during fertilisation – knowing that we have no clear answer to them.

There have been many theories as to how different parts of the developing bodily systems of the embryo are posted to the right address. At the beginning of the twentieth century, German scientists postulated the existence of 'morphogenetic fields' analogous to physical fields, such as the electromagnetic fields: positional information would be available to the cell from these fields, because the field would have different characteristics at different locations defined with respect to some notional reference point. In the absence of any clear idea as to what the fields, or the reference point, were composed of, this, however, looked more like a re-description of the problem than a step towards a resolution of it.

In an attempt to give the hypothesis greater explanatory value, it was suggested that the reference point was a region described as 'dominant', around which the field was organised – rather like the pole of a magnet. The gradient in the field could indicate both where the cell was and its distance from where it should be. The next problem was that of determining how the gradient was established; of specifying the variables – metabolic or otherwise – that were distributed in a graded way in order to create the gradient that would encode positional information.

More recently, it has been suggested that regular fluctuations in cellular activity may result in localities where there are oscillations of greater amplitude and frequency. These areas act as centres from which trains of waves radiate in all directions. Positional information can then be specified in terms of the phase differences between two or more trains of such oscillations. Initially random oscillations in near-equilibrium conditions may, by a feedforward process, create patterns of high-amplitude oscillations which label differentiated areas, guiding the movement of cells.

These ideas have inspired a huge amount of admirable and ingenious experimental work and some very sophisticated mathematical modelling. Additional mechanisms – for example, self-assembly at a multi-cellular level (analogous to the self-assembly of complex molecules) and different kinds of adhesive interactions between different types of cells (cells that glued together, grew together) – have also been thrown into the equation. Even so, theories of differentiation and regional specialisation and spatial organisation within the embryo – beginning with the inaugural miracle by which the basic body plan is laid down – remain hopelessly inadequate. No one can tell me how these warm hands of mine, with their exquisitely sensitive, wonderfully agile fingers tapping out these very words, grew into themselves in the silent, ill-lit aquarium of Mrs Mary Tallis's womb in the spring, summer and autumn of 1946.

This is a particularly pressing and even poignant mystery for the author of a book devoted to (amongst many other things) demonstrating the central role of the hand in the genesis of distinctively human agency. It reminds us of the inescapable fact that our freedom must itself always be the child of processes we have not chosen; that our ability to act is rooted in events for which we can take no credit or blame; that

agency has to grow out of causation. We have to accept that the hand –
which has assembled so much, and in conjunction with other hands has
helped to transform nearly the entire planet – was itself once helped into
being by handless and handleless forces common to the physical and
natural worlds over which it rules as lord and master. The tool of tools
was created without any of its tools, as it was a prerequisite of all of
them.

9.2 TOOL-USING, TOOLMAKING AND THE TOOL OF TOOLS

And we must confess that it is in the human hand that we have the
consummation of all perfection as an instrument.[4]

It is a nice conceit to conceive of the human hand as the supreme tool,
the master-tool, the tools of tools. Things, however, are a little complicated. It is both true and untrue, or appropriate and inappropriate, to
think in this way. It is certainly the case that, without hands, we would
not have been tool-users in the way that human beings are: we owe to
the special dexterity of our hands our extraordinary history as makers
of instruments to manipulate the world in which we find ourselves, a
history which has seen us emerge as both 'the most constructive and the
most destructive life form on the planet'.[5] The hand, however, is both
less than a tool, being more of a precursor or precondition of distinctively human tool-use (and toolmaking), than a tool in its own right;
and more than a tool, for there is no tool yet devised (or likely to be
devised) by man that will come anywhere near the prodigious versatility
of the human hand.

We shall revisit the general question of the relationship of mankind as
handkind in the genesis of mankind as toolkind towards the end of this
chapter, for it opens on to wider, even metaphysical questions, which are
the theme of the next chapter and the underlying preoccupation of this
book and its two successor volumes. For the present, however, we shall
focus more narrowly on the relationship between man and tools.

The use of tools has been identified as one of the hallmarks of
mankind. Benjamin Franklin famously defined man as 'the toolmaking
animal'[6] – an assertion that can be assented to only after considerable
clarification. We need to have a more precise idea of what a tool is and
of what is distinctively human about the way in which we humans use
tools.

According to the *Oxford English Dictionary*, a tool (derived from the
Old Teutonic word for 'to prepare' or 'to make') is 'any instrument of
manual operation'. Less narrowly, it is defined as 'a mechanical imple-

ment for working upon something by cutting, striking, rubbing, or other process directly operated on by the hand'. The range of forms of such tools is enormous: hammers, brushes, clothes, needles, levers, to name but a few simple examples. The tool is not necessarily hand-held, of course; indeed, as we shall discuss presently, the history, or recent history, of tools has been one of progressive emancipation of tools from the hand of the tool-user: the tool has given way to the gadget and the machine. A wider definition captures this: 'A tool is an independent physical intermediary for acting upon the environment.'[7] More generally still, it is an object other than a part of one's own body used as a means to achieve a particular end: it is 'an object that extends the capacity of an agent to operate within a given environment' (Ingold, in Gibson and Ingold 1993, p. 283). Leroi-Gourhan[8] points out the obvious fact that a tool is not just a material object: it exists only through a movement that makes it effective; an object becomes a tool when it is linked to a *technique*; its toolness is not inherent in its material composition. (Just as any event may be a sign or not a sign depending upon its being used or interpreted as sign.) That is why a tool may be used for a variety of purposes, including some that were not envisaged when it was factored. Consider, for example, the uses to which bricks are put.

Tool-use has three components: the purpose of the tool (to a greater or less extent embedded in the material upon which the tool acts); the material of the tool; and the capability of the tool-user. The shape and composition of elementary tools have to conform not only to the material they have to work on, but also to the sort of grips we can manage. The design of the first tools had to fit a power or precision grip: there was a reciprocity between hand mechanisms and tool design. The intermediary role of the tool is spelt out in its membership of two pairs: hand-tool; and hand-material. As Paillard points out, 'The most primitive tools were probably inspired by the diverse uses of the hand e.g. a scooper instead of the "cupped" palm to transport hot liquids.'[9] Quite early on, the body ceased to inspire the shape of tools; and it ceased to be necessary to take account of the kind of grips of which the human hand was capable. The hand was required only in a minor capacity – in the extreme case simply in the use of its index finger to push a button. As tools gave way to gadgets and to machines that required tending rather than manipulation, the double pair – hand-tool plus tool-material – was to a greater or lesser degree collapsed into a single pair: hand-material. This took a long time, but it casts a retrospective light on the question we need now to address: in what sense is even very early tool-using unique to man, given that animals, too, avail themselves of objects used as tools?

The nature of animal tool-use has attracted considerable interest and provoked intense controversy. Those who are determined to elide or erode the differences between man and other animals – at present in the ascendant, certainly among scientists – emphasise the similarity between human and animal tool-use; the standard-bearers for human exceptionalism (amongst them the author of this book) emphasise the differences. That animals do use tools is not in doubt. What is at issue is how different is their use of tools compared with ours and the significance of this difference. To be clear about this difference one needs first to get clear what humans and animals, respectively, achieve through tools.

Tool-use arguably reaches quite far down the notional hierarchy of beasts in the animal kingdom. (Though it is important not to extend the notion of tool-use too widely; otherwise, we shall be forced to accept that what a thrush does with a snail to get it out of its shell amounts to tool-use). For example, the woodpecker finch on the Galapagos uses cactus spines or twigs to poke into the cracks of trees and then drops them to free up its beak to catch any insect that comes out. This, however, is highly stereotyped and does not vary from finch to finch or from year to year. It is the one shot the finch has in its locker and can be attributed to instinct. And the same view can be taken of tool-use in all other animals up to primates, in particular monkeys. The latter, however, exhibit a wide variety of tool-using behaviours which are worth examining and reflecting upon in a little more detail.

Chimps, in particular, provide a challenge to the notion that there are aspects of tool-using unique to man.[10] For a start, the repertoire is a little more impressive than that possessed by non-primates. Some thirteen kinds of tool-using behaviour have been documented. Chimps may use sticks as levers to open bees' nests, and sticks and stones as weapons in defence – for example, to kill snakes – or to chase other animals away from their food. This may be less impressive than it at first appears: aimed throwing is relatively rare even in chimpanzees and the tools are hardly customised to the occasion: it is usually just a question of what lies most readily to hand and is consistent with Berthelet's observation that tool-use in animals is 'fleeting and haphazard'.[11] More strikingly, they use stones as percussion hammers to break open the shells of nuts. This is particularly noteworthy because, as Bresard points out, it requires complementary activities of the two hands, with one hand stabilising the nut while the other wields the percussion hammer.[12] The cracking of nuts, which can also be accomplished with sticks, requires foresight as well as coordination of actions: choosing the nut and the anvil and the successive positions of the nut and the precise blow to be aimed at the nut. Foresight is yet more evident where objects are gathered together and even stored and kept for future use. In captivity, some chimpanzees may hold a container in one hand while putting objects (e.g. nuts) into it with the other hand.

Most impressive of all is the use chimpanzees make of sticks for termite fishing. They poke long, slender twigs into the heart of the heap, through the exits; these become covered with termites which are then licked off. Termite fishing is of particular interest because chimps will go to considerable lengths to get the right kind of fishing rods. They will travel as much as fifteen yards away to look for suitable twigs and they will prune the leaves and side branches so they can slip into the nest more easily.

Finally, chimps not only exhibit tool-use but also tool re-use, though, while tools may transported up to a few hundred yards, they are usually left at the place of use and this leads to the problem of finding the tool again. There is even an inchoate sense of ownership: the chance of a tool being taken is proportionate to the distance between the owner and the would-be owner.

It is easy to get overexcited about these examples of tool-use in chimpanzees[13] and over-interpret these very modest achievements: the highest level of technical prowess of chimpanzees – the supreme tool-users in the non-human animal kingdom – is breaking open nuts with a stone used as a percussion hammer! The overestimation of the sophistication of animal tool-use is usually the result of reading too much into what is actually taking place. It is easy to weave a pretty story of foresight, planning, cunning, shrewdness and abstract thought into the use of a seized stick to drive off a snake or a denuded twig to fish for termites. Whether this is grounded in observation or simply the result of projection of human faculties into animals may be argued at length. What settles the argument for me, however, is the fact that animal tool-use even in chimps does not progress beyond its rather low ceiling. Chimps are chumps. If there really were so much intelligence, foresight, cunning, etc. in the use of a percussion hammer to crack a nut, then that same intelligence, foresight, cunning, etc. would have been expressed elsewhere and had more impressive manifestations. (Nor would nut-cracking using a hammer be so rare; nor would it take so long – five years – for a young chimp to learn how to do it.) There would have been more impressive tool-using behaviours than termite fishing; not perhaps the erection of a nuclear power station but at least something a bit more compelling than a stick thrown at a snake. The argument here is comparable to the one that we deployed in section 8 highlighting the difference between animal and human number sense: an animal that can count only up to three cannot really count. Likewise, an animal that does not take tool-using beyond the employment of a percussion hammer is not really using tools in the full sense of the word, in the way that humans do.

We shall return to this when we examine what I believe to be the fundamental insight – present in humans, absent in animals – that underpins human (genuine) tool-use. For the present, let us note one absolutely pivotal difference between human and animal tool-use: the nature of the tools that are used. In the case of humans, these are made; whereas in the case of animals they are found and, at best, modified. Granted, chimpanzees, as we have noted, may shape tools to particular ends; for example, cutting sticks and grass to the right length, and removing leaves and bark. This is modification not manufacture. The tool is not created *de novo* as a result of a prolonged process of manufacture, as is seen in the case even of the most primitive tools – such as pebble choppers (of which more presently) used in earliest palaeolithic times. At the most, animals make minor modifications of existing objects.

Morever (and this is conceptually crucial), animals use only their bodies to modify tools: breaking them with the hands and cutting them with their teeth. In contrast, human tool-use, from the earliest time, is associated with what Jean Kitahara-Frisch has called 'secondary tool use':[14] using a tool to make a tool. There is, he points out, a fundamental difference between using a stone hammer to break up nuts and employing a stone hammer to shape another tool by detachment of fragments or flakes. While the use of hammers, as opposed to other tools such as sticks, may reveal a certain amount of cognitive distance between the animal and its environment, this distance is a mere crack compared with the distance that is implicit in, say, a hand-axe or a pebble chopper. There is no immediate reward for making a hand-axe; there are many steps to the reward; there is a complex chain of intermediaries. Biologists might point out that making a hand-axe is not as complex as in nest-building, but the latter, unlike toolmaking, is programmed and stereotyped. All the birds of the relevant species do it, and at certain predetermined times. Nest-building is 'switched on'. Toolmaking is discretionary and is often delegated to particularly skilled individuals: it is an individual, not a species behaviour.

Secondary toolmaking, what is more, underlines the status of tools as tools; and, as a precondition and consequence of this, the implicit principles – the abstract sense of need, or possible need, the general properties of the material the tool is envisaged to work on – start to crystallise out of the experience of being in a general environment. The traffic, what is more, is not just one-way: the tool is made because of an inchoate sense of the principle (of possibility, etc.) and the finished tool then makes that principle (of possibility) more clearly evident. A feedforward mechanism is at work, though, for reasons we shall examine presently, this was at first painfully slow.

The uniqueness of human beings, then, lies not so much in tool-using as in toolmaking. This, Napier points out, 'involves a shift in cerebral activity from percept to concept'. 'Imagination,' he emphasises, 'is basic to tool-making', adding that

> Abstract thinking is not a talent of non-human primates which live on a strictly 'here and now' basis and for whom the past and future have very little meaning. Some inkling of the power of planning ahead seems to be possessed by chimpanzees, whose tool-modifying activities suggest that they lie in the grey area within the spectrum of tool-using to tool-making – a stage of dawning comprehension.[15]

Which does not, in animals, dawn.

Even in humans, the day was a long time dawning. It took millions of years for toolmaking fully to grow beyond tool-using and for the principles implicit in toolmaking to become explicit. Human tool-making goes back at least 2.5 million years with the development of the pebble chopper, 'made out of cobbles from which a number of flakes have been struck off from both faces to form a cutting edge where the flake scars meet' (Napier 1980). The pebble chopper has two important features: the butt of the implement, which is not actively shaped – it is smooth and rounded and has a design specification that fits the hand that grips it; and its appearance, which is highly standardised.[16] The first feature emphasises the relationship between the hand and the tool, making the status of the tool as an auxiliary to the hand, the primary agent, explicit. The second feature underlines the nature of the tool as an artefact, as something made in accordance with a prior, highly visible, specification. Standardisation is not seen in the tools used by animals. This points to something to which we shall return: the cultural or societal dimension of tool-use.[17]

Familiar as we are with a dizzying rate of change in the tools we use, it is arresting to think that the pebble chopper had no rival for over a million years – until about 1.5 million years ago, when the hand-axe, whose primary function (cleaver, pick, frisbee-like projectile?) remains uncertain, appeared on the scene. Another million years were to pass until, about 400,000 years ago, flakes came into use; or, at least, a flake industry evolved, in which the flakes were the primary purpose of the toolmaker, rather than being a discarded or opportunistically used consequence of the manufacture of pebble choppers or hand-axes. The flakes were used as scrapers for cleaning hides and knives and, ultimately, for shaping wooden spears.

Only with the emergence of a flake industry could it be said that tool-making was fully liberated from tool-using and man had escaped Napier's pre-dawn zone of tool-modifying. To throw away the core and hang on to the product, so that the tool is less than 50 per cent like the material object from which it was derived, is to invert the process that produces pebble choppers and hand-axes. The distinction between shaping (where the goal is the pebble-tool itself) and debitage (in which the detached flakes are the goal) is profound, and underlines the notion of a tool made explicitly to be a tool, a tool conceptually liberated from the material world of interaction in which it is embedded. The tool, like a truly linguistic sign (a connection we shall explore presently), wears its nature on its sleeve: its intention permeates it. The flake industry stands at the end of a long journey of consciousness that began with the use of eoliths – wind- and water-carved stones that can be employed as tools – and Mary Leakey's manuports – natural objects that had been transported from elsewhere and stored for use. And the journey has hardly started.

It is worthwhile reflecting on some of the subsequent steps in this journey. The first is the invention of the haft or handle. Among other things, this exploits one feature of the hand that makes it particularly suited for tool-using: it has a much wider range of movement at the wrist. (Using a hammer requires both a very powerful handgrip and great skill in the control of wrist movements.) The handle amplifies both the precision and the power the hand can deliver through tools. Even more importantly, for the present argument, the haft or handle is an explicit link between the tool and the hand. Put another way, this highlights the two pairs – tool–hand and tool–material – by both separating and linking them. This amounts to an explicit acknowledgement of the fact that what makes the tool easy to manipulate and generally chiro-philic is not the same as what it is that makes it effective in working the material addresses.

It is extraordinary to think that at no time in the 2.4 million years spanned by pebble choppers and hand-axes did the notion of the handle, or the more general notion of the composite tool, dawn on humans. The emergence of the handle illuminated both the notion of the tool as an instrument to operate on an external world and of the hand as an instrument wielding it. We may suppose that this literal articulation of the triadic relationship between tool handle and material world – and the separation of the 'business' end of the tool from a 'support' or 'auxiliary' end – itself transformed the relationship between humans and the material world. Moreover, once the notion of the handle was made explicit, it could itself become the subject of improvement: for example, lengthening to increase the range of access of the tool, to reduce required bodily movement or (as in a pick-axe) to increase its motive force.

The handle is the first step towards uniquely human composite tools, dubbed by Reynolds 'polyliths': instruments made of portable, enduring elements – liths – held together by fasteners – interliths.[18] The development of binding material and of knots was another major phase in tool development: composites could work as one despite their elements being drawn from different sources. The 'chimera' of a stone knife with a wooden handle – a fabulous beast unforeseen in nature – or a metal knife with a bone handle was a huge advance on the handled tool carved out of the single piece of material. The interaction between hand and tool was set to become even more complex.

Correspondingly, tool manufacture became more elaborate. Some elements were unique to anatomically modern man, who emerged 50,000–100,000 years ago: prismatic blades produced by indirect percussion; well-developed bone/antler/ivory technology; heat treatment of raw materials to increase their flaking properties. The latter was an extraordinary step because (as Toth and Schick point out)[19] it depends upon observing an external phenomenon lost in the noise of natural events, discovering the principle that lay behind it, and designing a means of controlling and harnessing the process.

Another critical step was the formalisation of interliths and giving them existence as distinct objects or materials: stitches, knots, glue, hasps, etc. The needle represented a huge conceptual advance. Here was a tool that had no function in itself: it had a purely subsidiary function or third-order function – as a guide to the thread that would hold together other artefacts, some of which (e.g. purses, sacks) could be conceivably described as tools. (Whether it is appropriate to call 'clothes' tools is not clear. It is self-evidently not idiomatic to do so.[20]) Needle-and-thread is an example of a second-order composite tool: one used to make (or to repair or modify) tools that are themselves composite. Stitching humankind has travelled far beyond the universe of even the most versatile tool-using chimpanzee. Fundamentally, the development was one in which the 'inter' in interliths was given independent existence or aseity. To borrow a term from linguistics, interliths were liberated from their syncategorematic state. The emergence of thread and of other explicit links between components of composite tools was not only a major step forward in toolmaking but, I shall argue, in the 'humanising' of consciousness as ever higher orders of self-consciousness.

Let us step back for a moment or two and reflect on the significance of the distances that have opened up between human and animal tool-use. The key notion is the difference between tool-modification and toolmaking. Man is not limited to minor tinkering with a material object in order that it should serve some purpose (as when a chimpanzee strips the leaves off a twig to make it a more efficient fishing rod), but uses tools to make tools that will be some time in the making. While it is important to avoid over-intellectualising the toolmaking process,[21] it should not be forgotten that the production of even the simplest tool involves many steps in a chain of operations. Flint knapping to produce a hand-axe requires many hours of concentrated activity and a dialogue with the material that is being shaped and with the product that is emerging. It is necessary to maintain attention over a period of time and to have a sustained sense of what is possible with the material, a clear idea of the end-product informing control over execution. The profound intellectual distinction between tool-modifying and toolmaking is even more evident in flake industries as opposed to flint-knapping. While some may argue that the production of a hand-axe is simply the extreme end of tool-modification rather than pure toolmaking, chipping away at the pebble in order to release a flake is pure toolmaking. The flake is a brand-new object and beyond argument an object *made in order to be* a tool rather than an object used or modified opportunistically as a tool.

9.3 TOOLS AND THE ORIGIN OF HUMAN CULTURE

A tool[22] that has been made 'through and through' – as opposed to being the result of a modification of an existing natural object or even such an object used 'on the hoof' – is more than just a tool, in the sense of something that can be absorbed into daily activity. It 'sticks out'. It is also a sign. What it signifies is very complex: it is both a sign of itself – recognisably a tool – and it is a sign of a world beyond itself, or a world to which it belongs. If a pebble chopper or a hand-axe is a stone that speaks a human purpose, a hafted hammer or a more complex polylith speaks those purposes more loudly. The tool casts an oblique light on the profoundly different relationship that humans have to the natural world in which they find themselves, compared with even the most highly developed beasts.

Most importantly the tool, therefore, signifies itself. The more sophisticated the tool, the more explicitly it is a self-referential sign. It stands out from the natural world. A French archaeologist talking about eoliths once remarked: 'Man made one, God made ten thousand – God help the man who tries to see the one in ten thousand'.[23] The same problem would not trouble the archaeologist faced with a hafted axe or a piece of cloth. The explicit tool is manifestly connected with its human use, indeed its particular function; and, as tools become more special-ised and more complex, so the functions and the relationship between tools and their functions become more explicit. Although progress was at first almost unbelievably slow, the development of this explicit relationship eventually drove a process of continuous improvement in the power and precision of tools. (What may have held this back for a couple of million years we shall see shortly.) As Berthelot says, 'If a tool is the offspring of gesture and thought, it implies that a man passes a critical judgement on his own technique.'[24] And this critical judgement reaches far back and has far forward-reaching consequences:

> Once man had managed to hold the first rock in his hand, and started to examine it by handling it between the thumb, the index and the middle finger, he thus inaugurated the era of experiments, and of observations, and consequently, hypotheses.[25]

The manufactured tool manifests human intentions in space and stabilises them in time: it is human purpose made visible, offset from the natural world.

Human purposes are interlocked: an individual's purposes interact and interlink with one another; and they interlink with the purposes of other humans belonging to the same community or culture. The purposes made visible in the tool are not those only of the individual toolmaker but of the community to which he belongs. A tool is a sign, therefore, not only of the means and ends of a particular individual but of a world, a form of life, a community of individuals who share that form of life. That is why, for an archaeologist, a tool may be a window onto a world. The tool reaches into, and lights up, a world in different ways.

While an object becomes a tool only when it is linked to an agent, to a subjectivity, and is therefore a sign of a person, this is not the whole story. As Ingold[26] points out, the tool must not be thought of in isolation: it is linked to a technique: a technique for tool manufacture and the techniques in which it is employed: a flake is only a tool when it is being used for scraping hides, sharpening weapons, etc. This means that the tool points beyond itself to a world of tools and a world in which that world of tools is embedded.[27] Tool-using involves cooperation, imita-tion, teaching – even kinship relations – and so is inextricably connected with personhood and sociality. Tool-manufacture requires the growth of collective knowledge and collective ownership of the product. Mastering a technique integrates a human into a group. As Ingold puts it, a tool 'is not only a physical conductor of the users' activity but also a vehicle for the social appropriation of nature'.[28] The tool is 'a material extension of a person' and 'the acquisition of technique part and parcel of the acquisition of personhood in the process of socialisation' (ibid., p. 285).

In summary, therefore, the tool's social status and its endurance over time make it an external representation of, an underwriting of, the individual's social existence and his endurance over time. One could imagine the tool requiring a modicum of higher order – self- and collective consciousness – and then fostering the further growth of it. The power of the tool to signify the society to which it, and the individual tool-maker, tool-user, belong is dramatically illustrated by tool ritualisation and the role of tools in religious rituals. For example, sacred axes may be used by the Awigobi for such purposes.[29] They are rubbed with grease and are kept in sacred cupboards at the back of the men's house and can be seen only by a select group of men during ritual ceremonies of war, ancestor cult and fertility.

Toolmaking, as well as tool-using, reach into – and deepen and firm up – the complex structure of shared meanings that is a society or culture. Since toolmaking is a skilled, not an instinctive, activity, it is hardly surprising that the ability to make tools, unlike the ability to make nests, is not one that is uniformly distributed. Even stone knapping necessary to produce a pebble chopper is difficult. There is therefore the basis for differentiation of labour and for a hierarchy orthogonal to animal hierarchies based upon the size of the beast and the strength of the brute. In some Stone Age settlements, it appears that the most skilled flint-knappers had quarters nearest the hearth.[30] The rise of know-how (a precursor to the rise of know-that) as a key to social success had begun. The most skilled flint-knappers would have a status that could not be mapped on to the kind of status enjoyed by dominant individuals in animal communities. The craftsman and subsequently the professional, the scholar, whose wares are cognitive – first, procedural knowledge embedded in practical activity, and then, declarative knowledge of facts and principles – are forms of human life that mark huge distances between animal and human societies.[31]

9.4 EOLITH TO SUPERCRAY

The tool – through which the idea of intention, of agency itself, could be extricated from action, and manual skill is profoundly socialised[32] – lies at the heart of social development and the emergence of distinctively human complex societies. The tool, moreover, in virtue of making agency visible, thereby makes agency aware of itself and able to reform its instinctive or inherited or received procedures. More fundamentally, it assists the process by which planning may be more externalised and behaviour moves from an implicit procedural mode to a more explicit, sign-mediated, declarative mode. We may see the tool – or, more generally, the artefact – as key to the transition from biological evolution to cultural evolution, massively amplifying the hand's role in this regard. It embodies new possibility in a permanent way: it is frozen possibility and intelligence or at least understanding of the modes of efficacious prehension. And so it permits a quasi-Lamarckian transmission of acquired characteristics. These cultural characteristics are not genotypically driven nor phenotypically embodied, but outside the body and inside the collective or social mind. By this means an initial continuity between the earliest hominids and animals gives way to the sharp discontinuity that we now observe between ourselves and our nearest primate cousins.

The emergence and evolution of tools and of the surrounding technology are not only at the centre of culture, but lie next to the hand, at its very origin. When tools were artefacts rather than mere naturefacts – 'found tools' – the appropriation of a material object for linking a means to an end made both the end to be achieved and the means employed to achieve it more explicit. Because the artefact was explicitly what it was, it, too, was not only perceptually but *conceptually* visible. In consequence the tool – incidentally but very importantly – could operate as a *bonnes à penser* in the Lévi-Straussian sense of 'an object to think with'. This was a crucial advance towards individual and collective self-consciousness; or, more precisely, for reasons that will be clear from what has been said above, promoted the linked progress of individual and social or collective human self-consciousness.

The unique sociality of human consciousness[33] is captured in the relationship between the tool, the technology of which it is a part, the tool-user and the community to which he belongs. This relationship may account for the paradoxical fact that, although (according to what we have just been saying) toolmaking made both tools and the means and ends they served explicit, tools themselves at first developed extraordinarily slowly. The interval of approximately 1.5 million years between the pebble chopper and the hand-axe and the further interval of 1,000,000 years between the hand-axe and the flake industry suggest a slowness of uptake that requires one to modify the observation made in the passage quoted earlier (Napier 1980, p. 126):

Once man had managed to hold the first rock in his hand, and started to examine it by handling it between the thumb, the index and the middle finger, he thus inaugurated the era of experiments, and of observations, and consequently, hypotheses.

Why did this journey from the eolith to the SuperCray computer have such a slow start? I would like to suggest that it was held back precisely because of the way the tool embedded individual employments of techniques and skills in a technology that is collective. Given that critical insights can come only to individuals, the inertia of the collective would act to nullify an individual's potential innovative contribution.

The extraordinary stability of tools such as hand-axes over time (1.5 million years) and over space (Europe, Africa, Asia) could not have been an accident, nor due solely to inertia. Variation must have been actively suppressed and progress held back. There must have been deliberate standardisation, whereby the tool was required to conform to the standard pattern, irrespective of whether there were purely 'spandrel' elements in that pattern. Conformity in toolmaking would be part and parcel of a wider conformity that ensured the individual's integration, even incorporation, into a particular culture. When manufacturing tools, the toolmaker would be making a sign as well as an instrument, and he would want his sign to say the same things as had the tools made by his predecessors.

This wish would be reinforced by the ritualistic role of tools, to which we earlier referred, mandating stability in the physical characteristics of the tool irrespective of any consideration of its primary function. The ritualistic tool is no more amenable to being reformed than is the ritualistic Cross: to modify a hand-axe might be an act of impiety. If the tool were an instrument of communication between people – and across generations – between the living and their dead ancestors – it would have to be standardised, just as words have to be standardised. In short, the social essence that reaches to the heart of tool-use makes the heart of the toolmaker conservative. The tool is shaped not merely by the material upon which it works and the ends to which it is a means, but by the inchoate sense of the society to which it belongs, with its habits, customs, traditions, laws and institutions. The forces of conservatism prevailed until (anthropologically speaking) very recent times. The inventor was until only a few centuries ago a mad loner; only since the Renaissance has technology been driven by permanent self-criticism, with a consequent accelerating rate of revolution in the range and power of the tools mankind has placed at their own disposal. The time when toolmakers were craftsmen whose period of apprenticeship was intended only to enable them to imitate the unimprovable skills of the master is not so distant. Setting quality standards meant blocking any innovation that could not be judged by those quality standards.

Once the tool had been liberated from the uncritical weight of tradition, the scene was set for a permanent revolution in toolmaking and tool-using. The principles made visible in the tool could be revisited again and again and the tool itself endlessly re-examined, rethought, and refashioned in the light of them. Visible purposes and visible means could interact in an ever-upward spiral. A cardinal result of this has been the increasing liberation of the tool from the hand, and indeed from the body.

This, it could be argued, began early: the wheel, for example, was neither modelled on the body nor did it have to take account of the capacities of the body in order for it to be used effectively. Wheels, however, were in a sense a free gift: the rolling stone, the rolling log, served up the notion of the wheel to the mind once it was prepared: it was a natural event before it was an embodiment of an abstract principle; conceptually, the wheel is a naturefact. The true liberation of the tool from the example and limitations of the human body began with simple machines.[34] Levers partly freed tool-use from the limitations of the body: the power of the hand was magnified. Pulleys, catapults, springs, etc. were the offspring of this general principle. The real break-through was the development of complex devices that did not merely magnify the power of the hand, but started simulating some elements of its dexterity, carrying out chains of operation. The use of tools to mitigate the ordeal of power was followed by the use of tools to mitigate the ordeal of precision.

This – the gradual replacement of the tool by the machine – is, of course, very recent. Its real development depended upon the harnessing of natural forces in a new way. Mechanical forces such as those directly encountered and exploited by the human body could be controlled only by more and more complex mechanical devices, with pulleys, cogs and levers required to do more impossible things with consequential unreliability. (That is why from the perspective of the present, hydro-dynamic devices, for example, seem ludicrous Heath Robinsons.) The development of steampower (a wonderfully ductile force), electricity (an even more ductile force and one that could be stored and released as required) and electronically encoded information (most wonderfully ductile of all) enabled machines to be imbued with ever-greater levels of dexterity. The gap between the one-way water valve and the electronic switch is about 200 years; in terms of precision and precision-controlled power it is many times greater than the gap between the pebble chopper and the flake, which came 2.5 million years later.

The supplanting of the tool by the ultimate in composite tools, the machine, reduced the direct role of the individual human agent in shaping the material universe. The machinist is not a craftsman, working with material and expressing his skills: he merely switches on the machine and tends it, with almost as little control over or comprehension of the functioning of the machine as the herdsman tending his cattle has of the metabolic processes by which grass is turned into meat. The skill has moved into the collective brain of the inventors and entrepreneurs – in thinking up machines, drawing up invoices, making investment decisions. The tool itself is now purely objective, an objectification of abstracted human intentions corresponding to abstracted human needs. The labourer is a mere operative, a tool to serve the machine, to ensure that it functions effectively, a hired hand whose hands are mainly 'in attendance', invigilating, ready to intervene if something goes wrong; or, if continually active, merely as an as yet irreplaceable component in a concert of machinery. The manual activity and the engagement of the person are pushed to the margins. In the machine, the tool is liberated from the limitations of the tool-user's body: pressing a switch, pushing a button, which release both power and precision, require neither power nor precision. The power resides in the machine and the precision resides not in the skill of the person tending it but in a collective genius distributed over many thousands of technicians and scientists and their hundreds of fundamental ideas, and their ten thousand patentable improvements.

Demanualisation of tool-use is associated with depersonalisation: personal expression though tool-use – even if it is only the expression of an individual struggle to achieve the immemorial, impersonal skills of the crafter of standardised products – has gone. The 'hands-on' contribution is derisory. The craft lies not in the user but in the machine itself, with its high specification. Even agency seems to lie not with the operative, who merely initiates a process over which he has no control, but with the machine and the institutions – the factory, its owners, the state – of which it is a part. It is this that makes technology – in truth, the most distinctive expression of personhood and humanity – seem impersonal, even inhuman.[35] Modern technology places the human agent at odds with the machine: the moments of his own life, his own flickering cognitive skills, face the accumulated genius in the machine, centuries of embedded cognitive activity: his role is neither hands-on or even thoughts-on – for the thoughts he is enacting (or that are being enacted through the machine he is tending) are the collective thoughts of anonymous others. There is a division between knowledge – which is embedded in the machine and often hidden from the operator – and practice. Practice has become detached from the hands of the practitioner and from his subjectivity.

The emphasis of our discussion so far has been somewhat 'internalist': we have looked at the evolution of tools as something driven (and held back by) the character of tools as signs – in particular as explicit, visible, manifestations of human intentions. This is at odds with our fundamental sense of the tools as being part of something that goes beyond the tool: the culture of the tool-users and (more importantly) the toolmakers. This social dimension makes the significance of even primitive tools rather complex: the tool expresses not just the individual who makes it, and tool-using is an expression not just of the person who uses it, but also of the community to which the tool belongs as part of the individual's heritage. It is interesting to reflect how, with the development of tools into complex machines, in particular those that are involved with mass production, the agency of the individual has been increasingly displaced by the agency of the collective such that the individual's moment of intention is peripheralised compared with the congealed, collective intention embodied in the machine which itself is part of a greater complex of machines and contracts and institutions and suppliers and consumers that makes up modern society.

Although we can unpack a good deal of society, and of the drivers to the evolution of tools and tool-users, from the tool considered in isolation, there are two other self-evident drivers (leaving aside accidents of history and geography): language and brain development. A few words on each are in order before we re-examine the reasons why human beings are the unique tool-users they are and prepare the way for the final chapter, which will take our argument towards its appointed philosophical destination.

9.5 TOOLS AND LANGUAGE

There are many ways of linking tool-use and the peculiar linguistic skills of human beings without committing oneself to a definite position on any putative causal interactions between the one and the other.[36] One thing is certain: distinctively human tool-use antedates the emergence of human language by at least two million years. Since vocalisation leaves no fossil-echoes, the ability to use langage has to be inferred from things that do leave fossils: skulls from which the evolution of the vocal apparatus can be reconstructed; and artefacts and other less direct pointers to ways of life that may or may not have involved or required communicating things that only human language can communicate. Moreover, determining when human language came on the scene depends upon a prior definition as to what will count as language. (Jaynes, for example, identifies several stages in the journey towards true language: bringing vocalisation under voluntary, cortical control; modifying cries by differentiation of their intensity and the manner in which the final phoneme was uttered, which corresponed to 'near', 'far', 'behind the hill', etc.; the separation of commands; and the emergence, successively of life nouns, thing nouns and proper names.)[37] Even allowing for these sources of uncertainty, it would seem likely that language, understood as 'a symbolic structure for regulating joint action and joint attention',[38] did not emerge much before 50,000–100,000 years ago.

The original difference between what chimpanzees can achieve with tools and what early humans achieved with them cannot therefore be attributed to language. Even though it is possible to exaggerate the complexity of early hominid stone-tool production,[39] there is no doubt that there are crucial differences between the former and chimpanzee tool-use, as has already I hope been made plain. It is obvious, however, that in the forty or fifty millennia since the full emergence of language, the latter has had a central role in driving the accelerating development of human tool-use, resulting in the extraordinary fact that progress in the last hundred years has been greater than progress between 2.8 and 0.4 million years ago or, indeed, between 400,000 and 3,000 years before the present.

But it is equally arguable that, prior to this relatively recent time, the relationship between tool-use and language was the other way round: tool-use was itself a crucial precursor to the development of language. While language (and more recently written language) was important for tool-use transmission and facilitating the passing on of the mysteries of the craft – and prior to language, and the collective memory it stores, toolmaking was improvised with much discovery, loss and rediscovery – it is arguable that the experience of, and interaction with, tools held in collective ownership created the context in which language could emerge. A tool, after all, is, as we have discussed, a sign; and there are several important features tools share with truly linguistic signs.

Tools, like linguistic signs, are expressions of possibility. The pebble chopper stands for an entire repertoire of potential actions, corresponding to a range of needs expressed in a range of possible situations. The possibilities in question point in two directions: to the individual agent for whom the tool is available; and to the society or culture of which the technology is a part. Like linguistic signs, tools have both a private, individual, subjective face and a public, collective, objective face. Tools as signs have another important feature in common with linguistic signs: they are signs that wear their status as signs on their sleeves; *they are signs that signify their status as signs.*

I have argued elsewhere that this explicit character of being signs is what distinguishes human (and in particular human linguistic) signs from the natural signs that operate on, or are used by (and the lack of precise difference is itself important), non-human animals.[40] It is because they are explicitly signs that human signs can be, and are, actively used to mean the meanings they have. Understanding the meaning of what someone says depends upon interpreting what it is they are deliberately meaning. The signs are not mere effects of a cause or symptoms of some underlying state; they are produced in order to induce a particular understanding in another. For them to be effective in this way, signs have to stand out from the background of the flow of natural events – including natural vocalisations, such as grunts and cries. Not only do they have to be produced rather than merely occurring; they have to be seen to be produced; or self-evidently to have occurred only as a result of being produced. This is assured by their being otherwise unoccasioned – or, to borrow the linguist's term, unmotivated – by the situation in which they take place. This absence of extra-linguistic motivation of signs is broadcast by their having no necessary connection with what they signify or indeed the signifying context: they are not part of a causal chain; nor, like mirrors and other natural iconic signs, are they part of the natural world. This is the deep meaning of the famed arbitrariness of the linguistic sign to which Saussure drew attention and which was so lavishly and disastrously misinterpreted by the so-called 'post-Saussurean' thinkers.[41]

The relevance of the arbitrariness of the linguistic sign to supporting claims for the role of the tool as precursor of the emergence of distinctively human language is that tools-as-signs are explicitly signs because they are, in a sense, arbitrary. It may be argued that the hand-axe is a motivated non-arbitrary sign, inasmuch as its form is constrained by two sorts of considerations: the shape and capabilities of the human hand; and the material upon which it has to work. Those two motivations, which embed the tool in a distinctively human culture, or community of human agents, however, make it *un*motivated with respect to its natural setting: the tool is set off from the natural world in which the human agents and their tools are situated. The hours spent shaping the tool are hours in which it journeys away from the natural world from which it was taken; its journey from naturefact to artefact, and the presence of human intention, the labour, implicit in its altered form, lift it out of the natural world of which it is a part and make it an explicit sign of the world which it serves, a sign that signifies its status as a sign. The very lack of evolution of early tools – their amazing standardisation over hundreds of thousands of years – may have been connected with their status as (pre-linguistic) signs. The form of the tool, initially motivated by the shape of the hand and the properties of the material upon which it is to work, acquires a secondary arbitrariness (the equivalent of a correct pronunciation) by the replicative and imitative element in the transmission of tool culture and the passing on of the mysteries. Standardisation beyond that dictated by function lifted the tool yet further above the ruck of nature and more clearly separated the socialised human agent from the world of natural causes.

This latter explains why tools, being signs of themselves, wearing their status as tools on their sleeves, should not have been thereby exposed to critique and constant reform – or not at least until about 50,000 years ago, when a rival system of arbitrary signs emerged – in the form of spoken and (much more powerfully) written language.

It would be an exaggeration to describe the tools of early hominids as themselves amounting to a 'language' or even a 'proto-language'. They do not, for example, belong explicitly to a system. But there are very important overlaps between human tools and linguistic signs. It is, as Reynolds has argued, the social structure of manual skill that differentiates human tool-use from that of non-human primates, 'which remains highly individualistic despite the highly social nature of these species'.[42] Human tools – even the most primitive stone tools – are cooperatively produced and cooperatively used, and held in common ownership. It is not difficult, therefore, to think of tool-using and social behaviour co-evolving and creating fertile ground for the emergence of linguistic communication which latter, in turn, joined the process of co-evolution, with all three elements driving each other forward.

Tools also prefigure the kind of classification that is characteristic of human language. Man has been described as 'The Classifying Animal'; it would be more accurate to describe him as 'The Reclassifying Animal'. This would also avoid the danger of assimilating the classification embodied in human language to the general behaviour-directing discriminations that are seen widely in the animal kingdom.[43] The arbitrary linguistic sign under which the designated object is classified is distinct from it – hence the endless arguments between nominalists and essentialists – and for this reason, the object is not utterly identified with its class: it is available for explicit reclassification. The tool is also a classifying device in this very complex sense: it classifies the various substrates upon which it operates along with each other. They are, however, seen to be separate from each other: 'axe-ables' both do and do not belong to the same class. This volatility corresponds to the axe itself which is one object with many specific functions and a single, less well-defined, overriding type of function. It is also reflected in the transformative effect of the tool: the latter changes something (relatively stable) into something else (relatively stable). Unlike the transformations wrought by animals (as when a prey is killed and eaten) both the substrate and the product are relatively stable. They survive to haunt one another. The object is thus both inside one class and outside another and inside the second class and outside the first. The tool is thus arguably at the root of the reclassifying skills of speaking mankind.[44]

There is another important point of similarity between tools and uniquely human language: tools are at least tacitly composite. The simplest tools have a proximal end, which is held and adapted to the user's grip, and a distal end, which is adapted to the material that is to be worked upon. This differentiation is made explicit in hafted tools which combine two parts which alone would be of little use. There is a kind of 'syntax' of tools. As Reynolds points out, 'the artifacts manufactured by humans are typically made of distinct parts, often useless in themselves, which fit together to form a functional whole'.[45] This is more than a little reminiscent of a sentence of speech whose elements – 'the', 'sat', etc. – do not deliver anything alone but do so when working in a coordinated fashion. One could even see analogies in the grammatical exclusion principle, whereby a noun cannot have two articles, with the fact that a knife cannot have two blades. Likewise, in the mutual definition of haft and blade, and in the fact that neither has any value in isolation, one can see the germs of the differential nature of linguistic signs which derive their value from their opposition to one another.

9.6 BRAIN, TOOLS AND LANGUAGE

It is important not to press too far the analogy between distinctively human tools and distinctively human linguistic signs, as it is not clear whether composite – as opposed to simple – tools preceded the emergence of language: whether hafting, never mind the use of interliths, really did antedate speech as we know it. (It is certainly more than somewhat speculative to think of the handle as the precursor of the definite article, tempted though I am to do so!) What is beyond doubt is that tool construction and tool-use involve complex chains of actions. We could express this less contentiously – especially in view of Ingold's warning about over-interpeting the sustainedness of the intention required for tool manufacture – by suggesting not so much that there is a 'grammar' of tools as that both linguistic production and tool production involve complex motor sequences. So, of course, does walking or pursuing a rabbit. What makes the tool-related sequences significantly close to language is that tools are concerned with possibility – and standing as opposed to evanescent possibility – as words are; and, connected with this, that tool production is about the future and tool-use is implicitly classifying. Naturally, there will be a huge overlap between tool-use, language-use and other complex, sequential activities – such as finding one's way home using visual recognition of particulars rather than smell. But there seems to be a special relationship between language and tool-use: the key may be a common neural substrate.

In the light of this, it is therefore of particular interest that Tobias has found that the brain of *Homo habilis*, whose fossil remains are often found associated with stone artefacts, and who emerged 1.75 million years ago, shows the first sign of the Broca and Wernicke areas of the brain, which are the parts of the cortex active in language production and reception respectively.[46] This suggests either that tool-use drove the development of the neural substratum of language (though it took over 1.5 million years for the brain-owner to speak up) or that there was a significant overlap between the neural substratum for tool-use and that for language-use. In addition, it is possible that, as tools further reduced the modest role of the mouth for grasp and manipulation, so the skull was freed to support the changes necessary for language and speech.

The sequencing of neural structures to underpin both language- and tool-use may be best explored, Kitahara-Frisch suggests,[47] 'not by seeing analogies between tools and language but by seeing common require-ments'. Tool behaviour employs several cognitive layers: the biomech-anical layer (for example, the relationship between precision grip and stone-tool manufacture); a layer that constructs most of the action sequences; and the problem-solving layer in which all of the elements appropriate to the task are brought together. Unfortunately, unlike language, tool-use and toolmaking do not seem to have domain-specific cognitive requirements. Kitahara-Frisch's account of the common require-ments for toolmaking and language would, however, fit with the notion that tool-using behaviour sets the scene neurally for the emergence of language by helping to foster the emergence of the appropriate neural substrate.

This substrate is to be found in a greatly expanded frontal lobes (supported and informed, it has to be said, by greatly expanded temporal lobes – concerned with memory and time – and greatly expanded parietal lobes – concerned with vision and space). According to the standard account, the frontal lobes have two major components: the associative area; and the premotor area. In the premotor area are stored the commands that drive the motor keyboard of the primary motor area – 'set' and 'task' neurons. In the primary motor area, speed, amplitude and force are set. Kinetic formulae or motor programmes are said to be located in specific areas – for throwing, guiding the hand to the mouth, and so on. Importantly, there are two ways of steering motor activities: reactive, in which the activity is driven by sensory input; and projective, which is driven by information stored in the memory by imagery or internal representations of desired goals. (These are described as respectively 'data-driven' and 'memory-driven' control of motor activities.) The prefrontal cortex damps down reactivity and reduces interference from sensory inputs: the agent doesn't get blown off course as a result of being solicited by every object within reach. This permits sustained plans and objectives, and connecting activity with overarching intentions.

We could summarise this standard account by saying that the frontal lobes are (speaking very crudely) responsible for storing complex motor sequences and regulating their implementation. This is connected with the ability – not unique to humans but developed to a unique degree in them – to defer actions on both a micro- and macro-scale and a closely connected ability to generate and handle abstract categories. The micro-postponement of actions is essential in motor sequencing: action 10 in a sequence should not take place before action 5. The macro-postponement of actions is essential for the constraints necessary to successful socialisation, which will often depend upon inhibition of immediate impulses. The resistance to being solicited by every object and event is connected with the ability to detach onself from the actual experiences of them – and the very local, specific sense they make – in order to classify and (more importantly) *reclassify* them.[48] This, as we have already suggested, is an overlapping feature of language- and tool-use. Separating complex manipulations from immediate reactions is what permits the prehensile hand to emerge as a toolmaker. The small difference of anatomy thereby opens up the huge difference between culture and history. The hand is apt to become 'the servant of a planning and creative brain'. And its tool-use, a precursor of language, trains up the brain for specifically linguistic activities, or drives the development of the brain in that direction.

A further fact of note is the close proximity of the cortical representation of the hand (and in particular the thumb) to that of the mouth – linking dexterity and speech. A final neurological clue is the relationship between handedness, language function and tool-use. The right-handed bias of human beings – in contrast to the left-handed bias of non-human primates – is evident from analysis of tool design at least as far back as

200,000 years ago, but the overwhelming preference for the right hand did not emerge until much later.[49] This shift, Napier argues, 'did not fully manifest itself until the life-style of early man started to include activities which require a high degree of delicacy and precision': in short, there appears to be an interdependency of lateralisation of hand function – handedness – and handiness. This, in turn, appears to have a close connection with language: in the overwhelming majority of human beings, the cerebral hemisphere that serves the dominant hand is also the one that houses the centres for most linguistic functions.

The notion implicit in this discussion is that the activity that is permitted by brain development to a certain level will of itself drive the brain to higher levels of development. There will be, as so many authors have suggested, a 'feedforward' mechanism whereby co-evolving processes promote each other: tool-use will select for brain development and increased sociality; sociality will drive forward tool development and select for brain development; and brain development will permit more complex tool-use and social awareness. The mechanisms that drive this circuit will be a complex mixture of conventional Darwinian genetic selection of the most adapted individuals; of Lamarckian transmission of collective or community (procedural and declarative) knowledge; and of Darwinian-Lamarckian selection of those individuals most able (practically, cognitive, emotionally) able to take most advantage of the collective knowledge.[50] Darwinian evolution will, of course, have made a relatively small contribution in the time-frame of recorded human history.

9.7 BEYOND BIOLOGY AND BIOLOGISM

In our discussion of the role of tool-use in the emergence of the speaking, socialising, thinking human animal, and in the emphasis on a brain whose progress towards increasing size and complexity is driven by tool-use, etc., we are courting the danger of giving way to biologism. In order to avoid this, it may be worthwhile looking at how far 'pure biology' can take us and see what remains to be explained.

The story so far seems to be as follows. The special dexterity of the human hand, and the effect it has upon the human being's relationship to her own body and to the surrounding world, underpins the unique capacity of hominids for tool-using, itself based upon a distinctive ability to make the tools they use. Once this is given, then tool-use may start a process that leads directly and indirectly to the increasing sophistication of implements and to an emerging technology that lies at the heart of the culture which sets us off from our natural state and makes us lords and masters of the universe. Within this overall story, it is possible to identify a nexus of sub-plots. For example:

1. The increased demands made upon the hand by the tools the individual has inherited from the community drive plastic reorganisation and growth of those parts of the cerebral cortex that control the hand. These demands would also favour the bearers of larger, more plastic brains.

2. The larger, more plastic brains would lead to the development of more complex tools or the more complex and inventive use of tools.

3. The mediated interaction between the tool-user and material world would make available new kinds of experiences of the world. This, again, would drive brain growth and reorganisation and enable new understanding of the properties of the material approached from a variety of mediated as well as unmediated angles.

4. There would be further neural developments arising out of the broader and deeper sociality driven by the experience of (mute) cooperation in tool-manufacture, tool-ownership and tool-use. Selective survival of those able to respond neuroplastically to these drivers would ensure that individual gains in sociality would be transmitted down the generations: they would be selected for progressively more complex tool-use and its linked sociality. Socialising humans would be more likely to live longer than autistic ones.

5. The neural circuitry that favours sociality and underpins enhanced tool-use and tool-mediated understanding of the world could, on the principle that old things may be put to new uses, lend itself to other purposes. The tool-controlling sequencer might be used to regulate other favourable sequential actions.

6. The example of tools inspires the more general notion of a general sign that is both arbitrary and has a social dimension – the prototype of a linguistic sign. The all-purpose neural sequencer could lend itself to the development of language production and analysis.

7. Language, a relative latecomer, permits the direct transmission of accumulated knowledge and expertise about tools and the world in which they operate. Tools can therefore be imagined out loud, worked on collectively in public shared understanding. There would be the beginning of Manhattan-sized projects.

8. With the emergence of writing and then of the distinctively human number sense taking understanding ever further beyond the scope of the individual's experience and permitting more and more precise prediction, the design of tools would be more cognitively driven, with both the tools and the worlds they are working on made

manifest in their general, abstract form. Technology would drive the science that would inform advances in technology.

9. As a consequence, the rate of development of tools would gradually accelerate until it reached its present vertiginous speed. Procedural understanding is made visible – and criticisable and improvable – in declarative knowledge. Written knowledge is liberated from body-base memory (even collective memory) to be located in the extra-corporeal store of potential memories.

10. Humans are increasingly able to make tools and develop machines that can take over direct motor behaviours – or parts of them – or support them: first, added power and then added precision.

11. And so continues the merry-go-round with the tool-using hand, the evolving community of toolmaking and tool-using humans, linguistic behaviour and an increasingly powerful brain driving each other onward and upward to enable *Homo sapiens* to achieve ever greater heights of social and individual sophistication and increasing mastery of the material world.

So much for the pretty story and its sub-plots. There is an opposite account of the relationship between hands and intelligence advanced by Aristotle in contradiction to Anaxagoras. Aristotle fully accepts, as we saw in the epigraph to this chapter, the key role of the hand in the evolution of human culture. Against Anaxagoras, however, who asserted that it is because he has hands that man became the most intelligent among animals, Aristotle argues that, to the contrary, it is because of his intelligence he has hands. This view corresponds to Heidegger's. In *What is Called Thinking?*, he argues as follows:

> The hand is infinitely different from all grasping organs – paws, claws, or fangs – different by an abyss of essence. Only a being who can speak, that is, *think*, can have hands and be handy in achieving works of handicraft ...
> Every motion of the hand in every one of its works carries itself through the element of thinking, every bearing of the hand bears itself in that element. All the work of the hand is rooted in thinking.[51]

There is an important truth in what Heidegger has to say here, especially as he does not mean to use the word thinking in a narrow, cognitive sense: much of our handiwork is guided by thought, or by intelligence in the wider sense – by procedural, if not by declarative, knowledge. But this is only half the truth, because what Heidegger fails to do is to ask the fundamental question: How did the hand become such as to be thought-guided? How, more importantly, did humankind become 'the thinking animal' able to guide action with explicit, complex and often abstract thought? How, in short, did the hand get to be so different? The answer that we have offered here, and will further elaborate in the next chapter, is that it is because of its intrinsic properties which transformed the relationship of humans to their own bodies. As a result, the hand could then become thought-guided; and the hand became the tool of tools that inspired other tools and also transformed our relationship to our other bodily parts. (We may use any part of our bodies 'thought-fully'.) In short, I agree with Anaxagoras that we became uniquely thoughtful animals because we had hands (which are importantly different from paws) and disagree with Aristotle's and Heidegger's claim that it was thoughtfulness which made our hands so different from paws. Once we have been established as thoughtful, intelligent, agentive, etc. creatures, then the interaction between hand, brain, language, intelligence, thought, etc. becomes more a dialectic (or quintalectic!) of equals.

The account I have given of the hand, and its role in making humans collectively and individually so smart, may seem to come dangerously near to pure biologism, with the drivers to increasing human consciousness being organic processes, including the selection of those individuals who are most adapted to the rigours of the natural and the early social worlds. Biologism is unsatisfactory for many reasons; but the most important is that, denying the operation of exceptional events and forces in human origins, it cannot account for the exceptional nature of humans. To resist the inexorable pull of biologism, which tends to terminate in an explanation of the special nature of humans in terms of the special characteristics of their brains – neural sequencers and the like – we need to go back to the first step: the origin of human tool-using; and to do that we need to go back to the hand and consider again what it is about the hand that makes humans able and inclined to use tools in the utterly distinctive way that they do. To do this, we need to look beyond and beneath the ontogenesis of tool-using man to the metaphysics of the human hand – and to examine 'the abyss of essence' (to borrow Heidegger's phrase) by which the hand differs from all other prehensile organs seen in the animal kingdom.

In trying to explain how mankind became toolkind through handkind, we shall not leave biology altogether – to do so would be sheer folly – but we shall endeavour to understand how the biology of the human organism made possible something that goes beyond biology and the organic body to something that lies beyond the body construed organically. How the small discontinuity between ourselves and our nearest primate kin set off a train of events resulting in the massive discontinuities we now see.

To take account of the biology – and of our undubitably biological nature – while not succumbing to biologism, we need to see certain features of human biology (the characteristics of the human hand, emerging in the context of other unique features such as bipedality and also characteristics shared with other higher primates, such as fractionated finger movements) not as determinative but as permissive. Human difference resides not in the anatomical differences of the hand *per se*, nor even in the consequent differences in cerebral control; rather, it is what these differences permit; the paths of development they enable us to take. When the hand is liberated from locomotion, this does not necessarily result in toolmaking – just as when the mouth is liberated from the duties of prehension and power grip by the developing prehensile powers of the hand, it does not follow that it will inevitably start talking. The permission is not a sufficient reason; so there will still be a gap left unclosed by our strenuous onto-chirology, but the gap will be smaller and the mystery that it marks better defined. Thus we enter the final phases of our hand philosophy.

9.8 EPILOGUE: HANDICRAFT

Before re-entering the world of abstraction, let us pause for a celebration of the extraordinarily rich world of tools and artefacts that humans have created, that second nature they have planted, for good or ill, in the heart of nature. I will be brief, for the topic has no natural bounds and our recitation could go on forever.

Pause, first, to glance at – and delight in – the sheer multiplicity and variety of the tools and other artefacts – 'the gear and tackle and trim' – with which we have surrounded ourselves. (The temptation to consult *Roget's Thesaurus* will be resisted.)

Let us start with tools that help the hand in a function that has received only a mention: the hand as a carrier. The hands of bipedal man are freed to carry things: young, food, weapons, tools, etc. And he has tools to help him with the job: sacks, bags, rucksacks, handcarts, prams. And tools to help him to carry himself, to give himself up to translation: carts, coaches, buses, trains, planes, container vessels. Handyman collects and distributes commodities over the face of the earth. A multitude of different things – naturefacts and artefacts, materials raw, cooked and synthesised – may converge in a single dwelling, a single item, which may embody the labour of many, built on and shaped by the ingenuity of many more.[52] And so we devise a multitude of containers to help us to transport small and large objects, ourselves, armies on the march ...

Since we have spoken of armies, we may as well mention weapons –

spears, axes, guns (pistols in silk-lined boxes and guns on mighty emplacements), bows and arrows, quivers, magazines, tanks, warships, war-planes – and note that there are so many ways of hurting other living creatures in order to subdue, eat, revenge oneself upon, convert, terrify, etc. them. Let us move on hastily and think of agricultural implements – spades, ploughs, spades, hoes, rakes, combine harvesters – and of the instruments that are used to support the arts of peace: sporting kit, surgical instruments, musical instruments, the gear of the painter or sculpture.

Works of art speak to us, and so do telephones, handwritten, typed, printed, xeroxed pages, televisions, semaphore flags, dictaphones, phonographs. As do instruments that record, measure, investigate, explore, probe. Pulling items at random out of this basket, we find: magnifying glasses, optical fibres, telescopes (light and radio-), Geiger counters, ultrasound probes, ear trumpets ...

Suddenly the earth comes to seem like a huge heap of tools and other artefacts to assist us in our individual and collective daily activities. Drills, steamrollers, earth movers; bottles, cans, vases, bowls, boxes, wrapping paper, envelopes; cutlery and crockery; instruments of torture; tools to make tools; tools to support tools – plugs, switches, buttons, dials; traps, springs, bait; windmills, grindstones; keys, locks, alarms (house-worn, body-worn); brooches, pins, buttons; brushes, dusters, vacuum cleaners; glass, slates, bricks; wheels, cogs, ball bearings; loaves, pre-cooked meals, portions of this, that and the other; gas faucets, hot water taps, electricity meters; light bulbs, candles, rush flares, torches; perfumes, make-up, masks, fancy dress; monstrances, fonts, altars, bejewelled crosses; washing machines, microwave ovens; umbrellas, sunglasses, parkas; ladders, glue.

The list is endless. There are tools to assist us in all our doings – from making bridges to making love, from conducting war to growing food: tools that shape things, that move things, that keep things warm, that hold, injure, catch, things that conceal things, that communicate things, that polish and wipe things, that break or break open things. Tools multiply, gather in dwellings where they support the complexities of our ordinary days, linked – wired, piped, welded – together in the massive tool-nexuses of factories, until the entire world seems a boundless tool-chest.

As we look about us at the endless tool-scape of the world, it is difficult to believe that they sprang ultimately out of the tool of tools, the ur-tool, with its four small fingers and an even smaller thumb. Tools break all the bounds of possibility: tools make humans able to go absurdly fast, to reach places so far above the earth, they hardly seem heights, to be acquainted with the nanoscopic, to know round corners, beneath layers of darkness, across huge spaces, to be warm where it is cold, to feed off tropical fruits in Arctic climates.

There is one tool, however, that the tool-of-tools has not yet managed to create: itself. This attempt to cancel out our initial helplessness, when we simply grew into being and our hands were shaped without help from any agent, least of all ourselves, has failed dismally. In many ways, creating an artificial hand would be the final step in our instrumentalisation of the world, which is reduced to manipulation and the knowledge that informs manipulation.

The reader who recalls 'The Genius of Reaching' (section 2.2) will have no difficulty understanding the failure to create a fully functioning prosthetic hand. If reaching is well-nigh impossible, what of grasping and, even more difficult, manipulating, objects? Most artificial hands can receive any one of six commands – manoeuvre, grip, squeeze, hold steady and a couple of others I have forgotten – and these must define the task that has to be performed. The trouble is the plan is formulated as an abstract idea and there are many different ways of carrying it out. Moreover, given the uniqueness of every task, and of the objects upon which the task has to be performed, these abstract schemata will usually be too approximate to be of any real use. Abstract plans do not have a specific spatial realisation – or even a defined range of spatial realisations. Only God would be equal to the fabrication of such a tool.

Which prompts this thought: that the notion of the Hand of God as the shaper of the universe and of mankind within it – so beautifully captured in Michaelangelo's masterpiece (referred to in section 4.1) – is a displaced sense of the wonder we should feel at our collective human genius at fabrication. We do not, that is for sure, admire this collective genius sufficiently. We take the most complex network of interacting tools for granted. Sneering at technology is almost routine, though writing down the ingenuity, and the practical and theoretical knowledge embedded in even the simplest item, such as the much despised polystyrene cup, would take a lifetime. Doing full justice to the ideas, the visions, the manual and wider practical skills that are implicit in all the steps that led to the mass manufacture of such objects would fill a book of many thousands of pages.

We tend to become most acutely aware of our tools when they break down; when, that is, as Heidegger puts in his inimitable fashion, '*Conspicuousness* presents the thing at hand in a certain unhandiness' (*Being and Time*, p. 68). Under such circumstances, they may be contemplated in themselves rather than being lost in what Herbert Dreyfus describes as 'absorbed coping'. Artefacts may, sometimes, however be contemplated in a state far from irritation. There is the fetish of commodities, delighting in the labour that went into the making of the object. But there is also a supposedly more disinterested delight in the object for its beauty: the aesthetic contemplation which, for Schopenhauer, was detached from the will – the will to possess, the will to act, the will to use.

And so our toolmaking skills may be lent to creating objects that are not primarily tools, that are enjoyed for their own sake. We noted how even the earliest tools acquired a significance that exceeded their practical utility, instancing the hand-axes that had a religious resonance and were treated as sacred objects. As, indeed, they should be granted this significance, embodying, as they do, a mode of consciousness, a way of being, that was unique in the universe. In displacing the collective genius of *Homo faber* on to an imaginary transcendental being, the early users of artefacts were simply doing what Durkheim and Feuerbach said that all religious believers do: projecting the distinctive greatness of humanity on to the heavens. Aesthetic delight in artefacts stands at the midpoint of making a fetish-commodity out of the tool and making of it an object of veneration. The 'aura' that Walter Benjamin spoke of in relation to the 'original' of a work of art combines delight of possession and awe at the artist, whose handiwork the (original) work of art represented. The special status granted to the craftsman (his position nearest the hearth) was not due simply to his usefulness but to the respect his abilities invoked.

The work of art keeps the artefact close to the skill of the hand. Handicraft – carving, cutting, stitching, joining – keeps the artefact in the forefront: it does not dissolve into its functions. The artefact is not merely there to assist manipulation: it is there to be contemplated and to celebrate man's unique nature as artificer and the world remade to a greater or lesser degree in accordance with human need. Eventually the object of use, with its incidental beauty, gives rise to the object of beauty which is not subordinated to use: the painting on the cave wall, the jar that is not used to contain anything, but is made to be its beautiful self: the weaver, the potter, the painter, making things to be contemplated rather than used. Until the object liberated from use finds another function: as a commodity that can be bought and sold, a piece of real estate.

At the centre of the artificer's genius is sureness of touch, a tact that is transferred to the objects he makes. It is in the spirit of such tact that I end, certain that a hint is better than an encyclopaedia, that a glimpse of the endless toolscape of mankind, the boundless realm of artefact, through the oriel of a narrow preoccupation, may say more than saying everything.

NOTES

1. François Jouffroy, in *The Use of Tools by Human and Non-Human Primates*, A Symposium of the Fyssen Foundation, edited by Arlette Berthelet and Jean Chavaillon (Oxford Science Publications: Clarendon Press, 1993). Aristotle in his turn attributes the notion that the hand is at the root of humanity to Anaxagoras: 'Anaxagoras says that because of having hands, man grew the most intelligent among animals.' Interestingly, Aristotle dissents from this view and says (I think), 'it is because of his intelligence he has hands'. (I am grateful to Professor Alan Wing for drawing this to my attention.) We shall revisit the relationship between humanity, hands and intelligence in section 9.7.

2. I have been dependent in this section, whose topic lies well outside my area of specialist knowledge, upon the standard texts, some of which I ungratefully groaned over as a medical student. However, I am thankful to J. M. W. Slack's *From Egg to Embryo. Determinative Events in Early Development*, Developmental and Cell Biology monographs (Cambridge: Cambridge University Press, 1983) for an inspiring account of the fundamental mystery of the self-organising foetus. I have also consulted – as always with benefit – the *Encyclopaedia Britannica*. The essay on 'Growth and development' (15th edition, update, 1993) is a masterpiece of lucidity and compression.

3. Slack, *From Egg to Embryo*, p. 3.

4. Charles Bell, quoted in John Napier, *Hands* (New York: Pantheon, 1980), p. 59.

5. Kathleen Gibson, in Kathleen R. Gibson and Tim Ingold (eds), *Tools, Language and Cognition in Human Evolution* (Cambridge: Cambridge University Press, 1993), p. 131.

6. For more discussion of the connection between Franklin's 'Man the toolmaking animals', and the fundamental human faculty of making things explicit, see Raymond Tallis, *The Explicit Animal*, 2nd edn (London: Macmillan, 1999).

7. Bressard, in Berthelet and Chavaillon, *The Use of Tools by Human and Non-Human Primates*, p. 78

8. Leroi-Gourhan, in ibid., p. 398.

9. Paillard, in ibid. As Mircea Eliade has pointed out:

> The most ancient stones that we know of were worked with an aim that did not prefigure in the human body. This is specifically the case in cutting (an action which is different from tearing with the teeth or scratching with nails).

Quoted in ibid., p. 406.

10. Tool-use is seen in monkeys phylogenetically remote from chimps – at least in captivity. These are the Capuchin monkeys. Their surprising skill may be due to their eating a wide variety of foods that have only a seasonal availability. However, unlike chimps, they do not store tool-based solutions to tasks: they continue a trial-and-error approach even after they have found a solution. And they cannot transfer solutions to other tasks: it seems as if they do not acquire or apply a common, abstract operational schema when confronted with a variety of tasks. Moreover, when they watch their fellows successfully carrying out an operation, they do not repeat the movements in order to copy the success, as humans would. Nor, unlike chimpanzees, do they show any aptitude for choosing tools – for example. selecting between a short stick and a solid chopper.

11. Aimed throwing isn't a particularly elevated achievement. Indeed most primates are poorer at it than some other more primitive animals. As Ruth Willats (personal

communication) points out, squirrels are especially impressive marksmen, when they want to discourage those who stray too near their drays. Hence the practice of seasoned commuters alighting at Barnes Common Station to walk down the centre of the road rather than the oak tree-lined pavement to protect themselves from acorn bombardment!

12. The interaction between the hands and the establishment of hierarchical relation-ships between the hands – which we identified in section 7.6 as a driver to instrumentalisation of the body – is vastly less developed in chimps than in humans. Laterality is not seen in non-humans and the hierarchies between fingers fall far short of those seen humans. This is another aspect of the failure of the non-human animal body to become instrumentalised by its owner.

13. There has even been the suggestion that, because there is considerable variation in tool-use from chimp colony to chimp colony and this is not always clearly related to external constraints imposed by the environment, chimpanzees even exhibit something close to cultural relativity. However, the variation seems more to be a variation in *in*competence. Chimps that major on termite fishing often don't use a percussion hammer for breaking open nuts. At any rate, chimps do not seem to learn about tool-use from humans and gorillas don't learn about it from chimps. There is little cross-species imitation.

14. J. Kitahara-Frisch, in Berthelet and Chavaillon, *The Use of Tools in Human and Non-Human Primates*.

15. The difference between tool-modifying and tool-using is explained very clearly by Napier in *Hands*. Tool-using is 'an act of improvisation in which a naturally occurring object is utilised for an immediate purpose, and discarded'. Tool-modifying 'consists of adapting a naturally occurring object by simple means to improve its performance: once used it may be discarded or retained'. Toolmaking 'is an activity by which a naturally occurring object is transformed in a set and regular manner into an appropriate tool for a definite purpose' (p. 115).

16. To an extraordinary degree. Hand-axes, their successors, were stable for more than 1,000,000 years and over several continents (Africa, Europe, Asia). We shall discuss the possible meaning of this astonishing stability presently.

17. It has been argued that the rate of progress was slow because humans were too busy hunting to survive to reflect on their tools. The more compelling explanation – namely, that tools were deliberately standardised – is one that we discuss presently: that it was not a failure of innovation but suppression of it which accounted for the astonishing conservatism of tool design over so many hundreds of thousands of years.

18. Peter Reynolds ('The complementation theory of language and tool use', in Gibson and Ingold, *Tools, Language and Cognition in Human Evolution*) contrasts polyliths with the nearest that animals get to composite tools: polypods. The latter simply hold together through gravity and have limited survival in different positions. Man is unique in making polyliths.

The composite nature of human tools means that the interaction between tools and society is extremely complex and the sociality implicit in human tool-use even more so. Tools may be made not only of different components but of different materials which have disparate provenances. The gathering, mining, working, transporting, buying and selling of the raw materials out of which tools are to be made adds many additional layers of complexity. The number of steps in the manufacture of a Bronze Age hasp (and the number of people directly or indirectly involved in its production) must be enormous.

19. Nicholas Toth and Kathy Schick, 'Early stone industries and inferences regarding language and cognition', in Gibson and Ingold, ibid., p. 356.

20. The notion of a tool becomes increasingly complex and its boundaries more misty. Ingold (ibid., p. 433) has suggested the following definitions: 1) A tool is an object that extends the capacity of an agent to operate within a given environment. 2) An artefact is an object shaped to some pre-existent conception of form. Not all artefacts are tools and not all tools are artefacts – cake is an artefact and not a tool, a stone pebble used as a paperweight is a tool and not an artefact.

21. Some writers – notably Ingold (in Gibson and Ingold, ibid., pp. 337, 355, 356) – have warned against overstating the extent to which the intention of the toolmaker was operative in the making of tools and the extent to which the finished product was in his mind throughout the process. Some have suggested that the elaborate and beautiful hand-axes were merely the standard products of a process of producing flakes. The highly stereotyped appearance upon which we have already commented then becomes merely a consequence of the constraints of the material. Ingold has argued, what is more, that the product is arrived at when the flaking process comes to an end (and you have only to plan flake by flake) and/or the core breaks. In other words, it is finished when it is abandoned, not when it has reached a pre-ordained standard form and finish.

    Ingold's argument is particularly interesting because it is linked to his wider views about the tendency in modern anthropology, and indeed in many areas of thought, to 'over-cognitivisation' in our accounts of human behaviour and culture. 'People,' he argues, 'use material tools as well as words as aids to thinking ... both speech and tool-making are not only ways of acting in the world, they are also ways of getting to know it' (ibid., p. 432). (We grapple with the world as a way of thinking about, with, and against it.) Ingold rejects

    > the cognitivist account of technical action as the mechanical execution of plans or schemata already arrived at by an intellectual process of reason ... [To] understand the activities of tool-use and speaking, they must be seen not as behavioural products of the operation of higher intellectual faculties, internal to their possessors, but rather integral to the functioning of an entire system of perception and action constituted by the nexus of relationships set up by virtue of the immersion of the agent in his or her environment. (ibid., p. 433)

    Ingold here is at one with Dewey's arguments against 'intellectualism':

    > By 'intellectualism' as an indictment is meant the theory that all experiencing is a mode of knowing, and that all subject-matter, all nature, is in principle, to be reduced and transformed till it is defined in terms identical with the characteristics presented by refined objects of science. The assumption of 'intellectualism' goes contrary to the fact of what is primarily experienced. For things are objects to be treated, used, acted upon and with, enjoyed and endured, than things to be known. (quoted in Richard Polt, *Heidegger: An Introduction*, London: UCL Press, 1999)

    I have called the same tendency 'The fallacy of misplaced explicitness' (see Raymond Tallis, 'A critical dictionary of neuromythology', in *The Explicit Animal*, London: Macmillan, 1999). Heidegger's emphasis on the primacy of the ready-to-hand over 'objective presences' in *Being and Time* (translated by Joan Stambaugh, New York: State University of New York Press, 1996), makes a similar point.

22. The early Marx was deeply aware of the central role of tools in separating humanity from nature. See Appendix to this chapter.

23. Napier, *Hands*, p. 126.

24. Berthelet and Chavaillon, *The Use of Tools by Human and Non-Human Primates*, p. xiv.

25. Ibid., p. xv.

26. Ingold, in Gibson and Ingold, *Tools, Language and Cognition in Human Evolution*, p. 440.

27. As Heidegger said, the tool belongs with 'the referential totality of signification' that is 'the worldliness of Da-sein' and is part of a web of signification, a nexus of implements serving needs and belonging to institutions.

> Strictly speaking, there 'is' no such thing as *a* useful thing. There always belongs to the being of a useful thing a totality of useful things in which this useful thing can be what it is ... A totality of useful things is always already discovered *before* the individual useful thing. (*Being and Time*, p. 64)

For a discussion of this, see Raymond Tallis, *A Conversation with Martin Heidegger* (Basingstoke: Palgrave, 2002).

28. Ingold, *Tools, Language and Cognition in Human Evolution*, p. 440.

29. Berthelet and Chavaillon, *The Use of Tools by Human and Non-Human Primates*, p. 373.

30. Karlin et al., in ibid.

31. Trade guilds – the collective memory of traditional technical processes – go back to the time of King Solomon. They are not only the means by which knowledge and expertise are transmitted, but also a way of maintaining high-quality workmanship and of keeping the shop closed to all but those who have gone through the period of training.

32. The way we hold tools has two sorts of constraints: the anatomy and physiology of the hand (which, though standardised, is solitary); and the gestural tradition to which the tool-user belongs (which is highly socialised). The tool is both a discrete object and an element in a technological system; a singular material object and the realisation of a symbolic form.

33. Illuminatingly discussed in Kenan Malik's *Man, Beast and Zombie: What Science Can and Cannot Tell Us about Human Nature* (London: Weidenfeld and Nicolson, 2000). It was Hegel who captured this most tellingly when he pointed out that the difference between man and animals was the fundamental human need, not experienced by animals, for recognition by other humans.

34. This may seem to be at odds with the passage quoted earlier fom Mircea Eliade (see note 9). Perhaps one ought to say that until the invention of the lever – prefiguring the autonomous tools that are machines – tools were only partly liberated from the human body: not detached from it though not precisely modelled on it, either. This 'mezzanine' position is appropriate for the early stages of tool-use which has driven our awakening from our bodies, sense experience and reactivity to self-consciousness, knowledge and genuine agency-driven activity. (More on this in Chapter 10 and in the subsequent volumes of the trilogy.)

35. According to Ingold ('Tool-use, sociality and intelligence', in Gibson and Ingold, *Tools, Language and Cognition in Human Evolution*), when manual tool-use gave way to machine-use, the necessary technical relations were removed from the human subject as the agent and the repository of experience. It is this that creates the modern opposition between technology and society. This is the antipodes of the state of affairs in hunter-gatherer society where social and the technical are inseparable because techniques are embedded in individual skills. Hunter-gatherers,

Ingold says, are at odds with one of the most basic premisses of Western thought –
'that the mission of man is to achieve mastery over nature' (p. 441) and to try to
maximise the distance between society and nature, to pre-empt being assimilated
into it.

Perhaps art, which helps to mediate between man and nature, is an attempt to
correct the errors of this mission. At any rate, the opposition, Ingold claims, is
misconceived. Specifically, it should not be taken for granted when we try to make
sense of human evolution, in particular the the evolution of the human mind. The
'Machiavellian' story advanced by Nicholas Humphrey to explain the origin of
human intelligence, and which assumes that the manipulation of others is a
primordial social aim, reflects this misunderstanding of the way we are connected
with nature. Manipulation is coercive, but the fundamental relationship between
man and nature is revelatory or cooperative; and technology and society are not
opposed. The reduction of the environment to an adversarial nature only occurs
'when people cease to participate, adopting a stance of contemplative detachment'
and 'nature' becomes 'a physical world of objects confronting the isolated human
subject' (ibid., p. 443).

36. Gibson and Ingold, *Tools, Language and Cognition in Human Evolution*, from
which I have already quoted extensively, offers a wonderfully comprehensive,
thoughtful and thought-provoking exploration of the relationsip between the
development of technology and the emergence of language.

37. See Graham Richards, *Human Evolution: An Introduction to the Behavioural
Sciences* (London: Routledge & Kegan Paul, 1987), pp. 269–70.

38. S. T. Parker and K. R. Gibson, 'The importance of theory for reconstructing the
evolution of language and intelligence in hominids', in B. Chiarelli and R.
Corruccini (eds), *Advanced Views in Primatology* (Berlin and New York: Springer-
Verlag, 1982), pp. 42–64. Quoted in Richards, *Human Evolution*, p. 259. Two
events in prehistory that are thought unquestionably to entail the existence of
language are the colonisation of Australia 40,000 years ago and the appearance of
sculptures and bas reliefs in different parts of Europe before 32,000 years ago. (Iain
Davidson and William Noble, 'Tools and language in human evolution', in Gibson
and Ingold, *Tools, Language and Cognition in Human Evolution*, pp. 363–88.)

Many writers have put the origin of language as far back as 100,000 years ago, in
the last Ice Age, on the basis of the (relatively) sudden increase in the diversity and
complexity of tools round about this period. According to the Australian
archaeologist V. Gordon Childe, the sudden change in tempo of technological
progress 'might reasonably be attributed to the increasing use of a more flexible
system of symbols with which 'to operate in the head' as a substitute for physical-
trial-and-error processes'. Claire and W. M. S. Russell, who quote this remark, also
suggest that the increased mobility of humans, and the increasing likelihood of
encountering people of different cultures, necessitated ways of making explicit things
that could go without saying within a culture – and hence necessitated language.
('Language and animal signals', in *Linguistics at Large*, London: Paladin, 1973). To
this one might add that the greater complexity of tools may also have necessitated
communication in order to ensure continuing production and appropriate use.

While this seems entirely reasonable, this does not alter the fact that tools, and
before that, the hand, got there first. Moreover, the necessity for language could not
be met if there had not been much prior preparation – which brings us back to brain-
shaping by tool-use and by more direct modes of manipulation.

39. As Ingold points out, the final product (e.g. a hand-axe) may not be an aimed-at or goal product. The flakes may have been removed from the cores adventitiously, at different times and in different places. The events leading up to the discovered artefact are linked in a long chain only because of modern-day analysis, leading to the fallacious assumption that the end product was prefigured in the prior plan. This is part of Ingold's argument against over-intellectualising the process of tool-making. See note 19.

40. See Raymond Tallis, *The Explicit Animal*, 2nd edn (London: Macmillan, 1999), especially 'Language and consciousness', pp. 230–6; and Raymond Tallis, *On the Edge of Certainty* (London: Macmillan, 1999), especially pp. 47–9.

41. See Raymond Tallis, *Not Saussure*, 2nd edn (London: Macmillan, 1995).

42. See Gibson and Ingold, *Tools, Language and Cognition in Human Evolution*, p. 341.

43. For a full discussion of this, see *The Explicit Animal*, especially pp. 184–8.

44. The fact that the possible significance or range of possible meanings of the object is not exhausted by the first or even the subsequent category into which it is put leads to the intuition that there is, in the object, a residuum that is not captured by any classification at all; an intrinsic essence that lies beyond language, beyond sense, beyond even the sum total of its appearance to humans. This lies at the root of the philosophical notion of 'substance' or the scientific notion of 'matter' and to that of a world of 'objective presences' that lies beyond and beneath and is more fundamental than the human world; to use Heidegger's terms a world of 'the present-at-hand' that underpins the world of 'the ready-to-hand'. (See Tallis, *A Conversation with Martin Heidegger*; and Volume 3 of this trilogy.)

45. Peter Reynolds, in Gibson and Ingold, *Tools, Language and Cognition in Human Evolution*, p. 407.

46. Berthelet and Chavaillon, *The Uses of Tools by Human and Non-Human Primates*, p. 241.

47. Ibid.

48. See Tallis, *Not Saussure*, 'Reference restored' – in particular sections 4.2, 'Theories of universals', and 4.3, 'Words, senses, objects'.

49. Napier, *Hands*, p. 138.

50. There have been many other stories of the interaction between the hand and language. Among them is Hewes' theory (G. Hewes, 'An explicit formulation of the relationship between tool-using, tool-making, and the emergence of language', *Visible Language* 7(2), 1973, pp. 101–27), which places tool-use and toolmaking at the centre of language development, but also emphasises the role of gestures as intermediaries between the implicit communication of tool-using and the explicit communication of vocal speech.

William Calvin has proposed 'The unitary hypothesis: a common neural circuitry for novel manipulations, language, plan-ahead and throwing?', in Gibson and Ingold, *Tools, Language and Cognition in Human Evolution*. He suggests that language, tool-using and abstract thought develop in the wake of a skill – aimed throwing – which has several characteristics that make it rather promising as a driver to the requisite kinds of brain development: it is important for survival (both in defence and attack); prowess in it, and the associated survival value, have no obvious ceiling – throws can get better and better; it mobilises, indeed requisitions, a huge amount of neural activity, involving as it does visual understanding, predictive ability (where will the running target go next?), ballistic control, etc., so that a fourfold increase in neural tissue permits only a 26 per cent increase in throwing accuracy; and it involves a neural sequencer which, once developed, could be lent to other functions, such as planning forward a sentence, selecting its elements and stringing them together.

The transfer to the mouth of a skill acquired by the hand in throwing (as is needed in speech) is made more plausible because of the previous transfer (in the other direction) of a skill from mouth to hand: in bipedal man, the hand liberates the mouth as the chief instrument of grasp and as a power grip organ. This in turn permits reshaping of the skull and expansion of the brain and the liberation of the mouth as an organ of speech and other expressions. (Other animals have their mouth too full to speak.)

The eventual co-emergence of increasing dexterity and of language enables the further development of the hand both as a toolmaker and as a means of communication. 'The evolution of cerebral structures embodies the tight interaction of manual activity and the symbolic activity of language' (p. 43). It is no coincidence, therefore, that both language function and hand dominance are most marked in man: the hemisphere that speaks is also the one, typically, that controls the dominant hand. Gestures, toolmaking, sequential ordering of symbols (verbal and non-verbal), sequential utterances and programmes of manipulation are stored in the same hemisphere.

51. Martin Heidegger, *What is Called Thinking?* translated by Fred D. Wieck and J. Glenn Gray (New York: Harper & Row, 1972), p. 16. I am very grateful to Bill Radcliffe for drawing this passage to my attention and also to a paper by David M. Levin, 'Mudra as thinking: Developing our wisdom-of-being in gesture and movement', in *Heidegger and Asian Thought*, edited by G. Parted (Honolulu: University of Hawaii Press, 1987).

52. Martin Heidegger, *Being and Time*, p. 68. Levin, 'Mudra as thinking', has beautifully re-expressed Heidegger's view on the essential tact of the craftsman:

> There is a *tactful* way of handling things, a way of manipulating, which is mindful of their dimensionality, and which maintains them *in the dimensions of their Being*, that is, in the tangibly open dimension of ontological difference. The hands give to Being our gift of thought *whenever* they handle things with a skill that *cares* for the richness, the inexhaustible depth, of their being. (p. 249)

APPENDIX:

KARL MARX AND THE COLLECTIVISATION OF HUMAN CONSCIOUSNESS IN TOOLS

Isaiah Berlin ('The Philosophy of Karl Marx', in *The Power of Ideas*, edited by Henry Hardy [London: Chatto and Windus, 2000]) has brilliantly summarised Marx's understanding of the central role of tools in human development, and in explaining the difference between man and beasts, as follows:

For Marx, men differed from objects in nature principally because they were able to invent tools. Man was endowed with a unique capacity not only for using but for creating instruments to provide for his basic needs – for food, shelter, clothing, procreation, security and the like. These inventions then altered man's relations to external nature and transformed him and his societies, thereby stimulating him to make futher inventions to satisfy the new needs and tastes brought about by the changes which, alone among the animals, he brought about in his own nature and the world. For Marx technological capacities are man's fundamental nature: they are responsible for that awareness of the processes of living and conscious direction of them which is called history. Men are made what they are and differ from each other, not through some fixed inner principles of their nature ... but by means of the work they cannot avoid doing if they are to satisfy their needs. Their social organisation is determined by the ways in which they labour and create in order to preserve and improve their lives ....

So far, so good. Then things start to go awry:

[Marx] held that any technological advance in human development carried with it its own intellectual and moral horizons ... Man-made technology determines ideas and forms of life, and not the other way about: needs determine ideas, not ideas needs ... The windmill, for Marx, creates a certain type of social organisation, and this in turn gives rise to opinions and attitudes and ways of life likely to promote, maintain and resist attack upon that particular society – that is to say, that particular distribution of power and authority among men – whether the men in question realise it or not. (pp. 116–17)

The first passage captures the centrality of tool-use to human evolution but the second overlooks what lies behind tool-use: the intuition of the agentive-self through the instrumental relationship we humans, of all living creatures, have to our bodies due to the properties of the hand. It is this intuition that drives development and not only liberates us from material determinism. It also prevents our ideas from being totally absorbed into the unconsciousness embedded in the historical, social and economic order – in other words, from jumping from the frying pan of physical determinism into the fire of psychosocial determinism. Marx, in other words, got us half-right, but he missed the centrality of the conscious human agent because he did not see that the development of tools was not a natural, inevitable, unconscious process. The evolution from the windmill to the spinning jenny and the social order that followed therefrom was driven by the fundamental human intuition 'That I *am*', 'That I *do*'. He took technology for granted: he did not go far back or deep enough in his thinking. Technology for me is one of the bases of human self-consciousness and the drivers to the ever-increasing power of humans to be agents; for Marx, it is merely a means by which one form of unconscious passivity, expressed in instinctive behaviour, is replaced by another – the historical unconscious which enters the unknowing soul of each of us.

If Marx had seen what lay behind tool-use and realised that it was an expression, of a most intimate kind, of the agentive self, then he would not have given technology and the organisation of the means of production priority over the conscious agent, and made ideas secondary to material circumstances. He would not have asserted that 'it is not the consciousness of men that determines their existence, but their social existence that determines their consciousness'. He would have seen that social existence is permeated with complex and sophisticated conscious- ness; that men, unlike animals which merely live, lead their lives; and that there is no paradox in the idea-led changes.

If he had appreciated this fundamental point, the Marx-pocked history of the twentieth century might have been so different. The denial of the conscious human agent, and the tendency to judge people's argu- ments by their proponents' provenance rather than on their intrinsic merits, which has justified so much terror, might have been less influential.

PART III

TOWARDS CHIRO-
PHILOSOPHY

CHAPTER 10

Getting a Grip on the Conscious Human Agent

10.1 RECAPITULATION

Humans are so singular a species, with such zoologically unprecedented capacities, that it is a major biological mystery how evolutionary processes could have produced us out of our primate ancestors.[1]

Despite, however, the continuing accumulation of evidence for the capacities of apes, many ... remain convinced that the differences between non-human species and human beings are vast ... Other animals possess elements that are common to human behaviours but none reaches the human level of accomplishment in any domain – vocal, gestural, imitative, technical or social. Nor do other species combine social, technical and linguistic behaviours into a rich, interactive, and self-propelling cognitive complex.[2]

In the previous chapter, we left much business unfinished. Our examination of Man the Toolmaker brought us – and by no accident – to the border between biology and philosophical anthropology. In this chapter, we shall cross that border. Before we do so, a certain amount of recapitulation is in order: we shall rehearse those conditions that predispose the human hand to develop its unique properties; remind ourselves of some of those properties; and glance again at some of the biological and cultural consequences of those unique properties. This will provide an entrée into a consideration of philosophical implications of these biological and cultural consequences. The story we shall piece together is one that will attempt to reconcile two apparently irreconcilable facts about us: that we are biologically closely akin to other animals; and that we are like no other animals in some absolutely fundamental respects. I shall try, in short, to give an account of how it is that from our initial continuity with other animals, we became profoundly discontinuous with them, so that we now look at them across a great (and real) gulf.

Chiro-genesis

The story as to why we have such marvellous hands goes back a long way. For many, perhaps most, palaeontologists the story begins with a change in the weather – in the eastern and southern region of Africa about 4 to 8 million years ago. There was a drop in global temperature resulting in cooler, drier conditions, and marked seasonality. The earth, in short, became less hospitable and at times frankly parky. A consequence of this was a loss of tree cover and the expulsion of our pongid ancestors to the plains.[3] Life in the treeless plains favoured the upright position and the development of telereceptors (such as vision) over proximate receptors (such as smell) as an adaptation to a foraging lifestyle in the savannas. Bipedalism – which brought advantages in hunting and the use of weapons and in food gathering and carrying – was especially suited to open ground. The combination of bipedalism and the predominance of vision (which bipedalism also helped by elevating the eyes) made the upright primate a formidable hunter-gatherer.[4]

Bipedalism also released the forelimbs from locomotor duties. Although other animals assume the upright position from time to time, only humans are overwhelmingly bipedal and are alone capable (as we noted in section 3.1) of *striding*. Their forelimbs were consequently able to develop in ways that did not have to take account of the needs of weight-bearing. More precisely, the distal end of the forelimb was freed to become a true 'hand', as opposed to a paw or foot-hand.

The perfection of the hand did not merely result in, say, firmer prehension: this is not a distinctive faculty of man. Other primates can grasp things. What is specific to man is the *range* of grasps and manipulations: of grasp as the ground of manipulation. Bipedalism made it possible to build on the prehensile skills already available to tree-living pongids, who relied on prehension of a sort to travel by brachiation, and to seize hold of leaves, branches, food, enemies and conspecifics. (Tree life had increased the value of manipulation.) In the apes, whose 'hand' is nearest to our true hand, the hand is busy, when the beast is arboreal, with climbing, maintaining balance and food-collecting and, when the beast is on the ground, with locomotion (knuckle-walking).

The sustained liberation of the hand in the upright position, then, freed it to develop its dexterity and the augmented dexterity that was made possible through tool-using, tool-modifying and toolmaking. A further modification of the simple notion that bipedalism is a necessary condition of fully developed manual prehension is, however, required. First, the early hominids were not consistently bipedal and yet had some tool-using skills. *Homo habilis* (who exhibits significant brain expansion compared with earlier hominids) and who appeared hundreds of thousands of years before the permanently bipedal *Homo erectus*, was capable of some toolmaking.[5] Moreover, it is possible to use tools without being upright – for example, in the squatting, kneeling or sitting position. However, toolmaking, as we understand it in humans, is predicated upon a predominant liberation of the hand from locomotion and a hybrid foot–hand role with a consequent freedom to manipulate and carry things, to explore the world and to gesture, and this permits it to develop as a primordial instrument.

The upright position and the open plains which favoured vision over smell in turn stimulated inquisitiveness.[6] Even touch, that most proximate of senses, opened up: the hand was free to explore the environment – to be promoted from (in Sir Charles Sherrington's words) 'a simple locomotor prop to a delicate explorer of space'. Being nearer to the head and its sense organs than any foot or other hind-limb could be, this manual exploration, working in conjunction with that of the eye, could reach higher levels of sophistication; correspondingly, hand–eye co-ordination – in which the hand was under the control of the eye as well as being controlled by proprioception – created new possibilities of control.

These possibilities were driven towards ever-greater realisation and elaboration, by another consequence of the move into the open plains, where food was less plentiful and not simply there for the taking. In contrast with the state of affairs in the well-stocked larder of the Edenic forest, food in the plain had to be gathered, foraged for and, if all else failed, hunted down. Hunting demands that strategy should substitute for blind instinct, and motivates the supplanting of natural weapons by better, hand-made weapons.[7] As many palaeoanthropologists have pointed out, even if there were such a thing as an 'instinct to hunt', there could not be an instinct as to how to hunt: every chase is different. There was, consequently, an additional drive to the growth of intelligence. Being able to read the battle, to anticipate the behaviour of one's prey and even of one's fellow hunters, and to act on this, would have survival value. The same would apply to self-protection against animals and enemies in the open plains.[8]

A process was thus started whereby the hand, liberated to specialise in purely manipulative duties, and progressively adapted to this purpose, would be one of the key drivers to a network of recursive or iterative processes that would lead to the unique and complex cultures of humanity. The more dexterous use of the hand, along with tool-use, would result in the growth of intelligence and of the underlying neural substrates for programmed activity (along the lines suggested in sections 9.5 and 9.6) permitting the hand to be used in a yet more complex fashion. The dexterity that permitted the direct use of the hand, along with the awakened sense of the hand as instrument, would also permit tool-use; the intelligence that came out of that dexterity permitted tool-making. These in turn would make greater demands on the hand–brain and, through the sociality of tools, the hand–brain–mind would tap into a collective culture. The deposition of culture outside the body in a variety of artefacts, ultimately and most notably writing, would ensure an ever-more rapid evolution of culture and, in view of the hybrid status of tools, a co-evolution of collective culture and individual mind. One consequence would be a further, yet more rapid development of tools, which would finally be liberated from the constraints from human dexterity.

The Unique Properties of the Human Hand

Thus the six-million-year trajectory of expelled pongid from the forest to the *salon*. We have identified the pre-eminent versatility of the hand as the engine driving the human species on this unprecedented journey whose final destination remains obscure. Before we consider more precisely why this biological fact should enable us to escape the constraints of biology – collectively, as a species, for an indefinite time and individually in the small space between our biological maturity and our biological death – let us remind ourselves of the particular characteristics that make up the unique handiness of the human hand.

Many elements come together in the human hand. We have focused earlier on the opposability of the thumb but this, of course, is only part of a constellation of chiral virtues, albeit the one that most obviously distinguishes humans from the other primates. There is also the replacement of claws by nails, adding to the prehensile capacity of the long digits and the mobile thumb. Nailed digits can flex closely and grip, albeit in some cases in a rather primitive fashion. Tarsiers, for example, have a single prehensile pattern 'which is neither a precision grip nor a power grip; for want of a better word, and at the same time to illustrate the catch-as-catch-can nature of the movement, we can call it a grab'.[9] When the hand was freed from the requirements of locomotion, the characteristics of the 'foot-hand' – for example, palmar pads and 'heel' – were gradually eliminated and replaced with extended fingertips, a well-developed thumb and a broad palm. In humans, the last element of 'footness', the palmar heel, is eradicated. The ape, however, is otherwise constrained by its evolutionary past: its hand is highly specialised for brachiating, which requires an extremely powerful hook grip and has relatively little in the way of precision grip.

The human hand is also unlike the ape hand in being relatively unspecialised: it is totipotential and so can develop in whatever direction will be of benefit. More particularly, it can participate in the progressive spiralling interaction between hand and brain – and subsequently between hand, tool and brain; hand, tool, culture/society and brain; hand, tool, culture/society (spoken) language and brain; and, finally, hand, tool, culture/society, written and spoken language and brain – with relatively little impediment.

Among the assets the hand brings to the interaction are properties that are common to other primates, for example, fractionated or independent finger movements. One card – its ace – is its alone: full opposability of the thumb. Opposition between finger and thumb – perfect true opposition – is a complex matter and two things are necessary for it to be achieved, in addition to the ability of the thumb to move towards the fingers. The first is rotation of the thumb towards the finger to which it is opposed. It requires a saddle joint at the base of the thumb. This is possessed by Old World monkeys and apes, but not by New World monkeys and prosimians. True opposers, therefore, form a rather exclusive club. The second is an appropriate relative length of thumb and index finger, so that fingertip can meet fingertip. Unfortunately, the Old World monkeys and apes are rather unimpressive in this respect; for example, the orang-utans have the shortest thumbs and the longest index fingers. Only humans have an opposability index which permits tip-to-tip contact. The ape hand is, as we have noted, adapted for brachiating – a development that took place after the separation of pongids and hominids – where a long thumb would get in the way. (This evolutionary inheritance remains even though modern apes rarely leave the ground and travel by knuckle-walking.)[10] The club of true, perfect opposers is thus very exclusive indeed: only we humans are in it.

So we have a hand that has three adaptations that make it particularly adapted to precise movements: flexible fingers that can be moved independently; nails instead of claws; and a thumb of the correct relative length with a saddle joint at the base to permit rotation, allowing full opposition. There are two further design characteristics. First, the muscles at the base of the thumb are especially well developed, being proportionately more powerful than those in any other primate. Precision can be backed up by precise power. Secondly, the tips at which the fingers touch each other or an object being manipulated between them, which full opposability allows to make full contact, are richly innervated with exquisitely tuned nerve endings, so that they form sensitive touch pads which can provide the information to regulate touch, grip and manipulation and this humans inherit.

So there we have it: the human hand, the tool of tools. But does this provide us with an explanation of the huge gulf that has opened up between ourselves and the other animals? Does it begin to account for the origin of human culture – which, uniquely, stores accumulated knowledge and ever more efficient means of interacting with the world, outside of the human body – and permits the transmission of acquired know-how, and rapid development of our collective lives quite independently of any change in the human genome? Do we understand the role of the human hand in the transformation of one – out of all the beasts – into a creature that builds cities, writes books and reflects on its place in a universe that it knows and understands more deeply than any of the beasts?

The story of how the human hand utterly transformed our relationship to the world we live in (and to everything in it, including our conspecifics) is far from complete. We need to explain not only how we do more things with our hands but how we come to do them so differently; how true handedness and dexterity deliver not only an increased range of skills, but also truly deliberate activity.

'Ontoological' (*sic*) Anthropology

Human manipulative prowess, as reflected in both our anatomy and our technology, emerged slowly during human evolution. However, within the past 40,000 years it has become one of the dominant aspects of our biology and cultural adaptation.[11]

The first hominid to use tools is *Homo habilis* – 'handyman'. It was he who first augmented the anatomical advantage of the tool of tools by giving it some tools to work with. With him began the series of feed-forward processes that have led to our present extraordinarily complex civilisations. These processes could be represented in several ways, but here are a few:

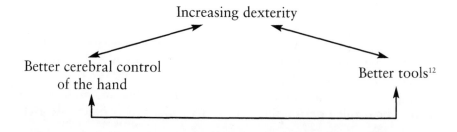

Increasing dexterity

Better cerebral control of the hand

Better tools[12]

Or:

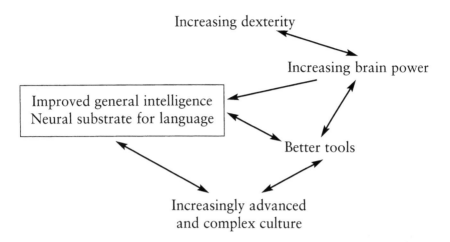

Or:

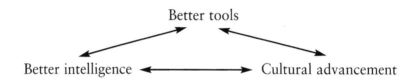

There is much work to be done in unpicking each of the connections in more detail, as we did in the previous chapter with respect to the relationship between tools and sociality, tools and language, and tools and brain power. Additionally, we could examine some of the reasons why humans might be particularly driven to acquire toolmaking skills; for example, early man's need to get at underground roots for which he would need sharpened sticks and, in order to sharpen the sticks, the need to develop a flake industry. This lies outside both the scope of this book and the author's competence. We note only that the interaction between dexterity, general intelligence and cultural development could reach the point where culture starts to evolve autonomously, so that, for example, ever more complex tools may be developed with a correspond-ing increase in intelligence: the biological fact of dexterity would be decreasingly important and biologically determined limits on dexterity cease to be a constraint.

The observation by John Tooby and Irven De Vore that 'organisms are systems of co-evolved adaptations; a change in one feature resonates through the system, changing other features in the adaptive constellation'[13] is highly pertinent. It is of particular relevance when one is trying to allocate credit for the singularity of *Homo sapiens* between various biological features. I have taken humans by the hand and it might be thought that I could just as well, perhaps, have taken them by other things and invoked increasing brain size as the primary driver behind the great discontinuity that has opened up between ourselves and the beasts from which we once differed relatively little. Why, then, have I argued that hands are the primary drivers: that they make the difference that lies at the root of all our differences?

Why not, after all, fall in with the current fashion for making the brain the explain-all and gather up the entire process into developing brain function. Without necessarily succumbing to the heresy of ortho-genesis, according to which there was a preordained direction in evolution towards increasing brain size and intelligence, we could put together any number of orthodox Darwinian stories about selection for increased brain size and intelligence.[14] It is certainly true that the brain, as the final common pathway for the self-perpetuating improvement arising out of the initial lead that hominids had over other primates, is now the favoured story. 'The hand is the tools of tools,' Jouffroy asserts in a typical formulation, 'because the human brain never stops devising increasingly sophisticated tools and instruments to be manipulated by it.'[15] The recent convergence of neuroscience, cognitive psychology, evolutionary theory, computer science, anthropology and one or two other disciplines, makes a brain-led account – and a computerised version of the mind as the software of the brain – almost inescapable.

Notwithstanding, I do not believe that the brain provides a satis-factory explanation of our special status as the bearers of culture and history into a world of ahistorical organic nature. There are some very general reasons why we should not be satisfied with the brain as any kind of explanation of us as conscious, civilised (and uncivilised) animals. I have set these out at length elsewhere, but it is sufficient to note that the brain isolated as it is in neurophilosophy does not explain any aspect of our consciousness and the special properties of the human brain (greater overall size, expansion of certain areas, distinctive patterns of connectivity) does not add to our understanding of the distinctively human aspects of our consciousness.[16] Cerebral explanations seem plausible only because of the anthropomorphic language in which they are expressed, such that the brainly mind and the mindly brain seem one and the brain has all the properties of a fully paid-up self and citizen – as is evident in the passage just quoted, which has the brain 'devising increasingly sophisticated tools and instruments' to be manipulated by the hand. But there are more specific concerns about brain-based or cerebro-centric explanations of human evolution and the way in which the small anatomical differences of the human hand open up such an ocean of difference between us and the beasts, to make a usually safer, sometimes more dangerous, usually gentler, sometimes more brutal, an ever richer, ever deeper and ever more complex human universe in the natural world.[17]

First of all, tool-use is not closely linked with increasing brain size. For example, the gorilla has a comparatively enormous brain and yet has little or no tool-using skills – in contrast with Capuchin monkeys, primates phylogenetically distant from both man and apes, and with comparatively small brains, which show comparatively versatile tool-use.[18] Indeed, gorillas show no interest in objects placed purposefully in their path. Chimpanzees, by contrast, which have approximately the same size brain as gorillas, exhibit at least thirteen different examples of tool-using behaviour.

Of greater relevance is the fact, already discussed in the previous chapter, that chimpanzees did not take tool-use and toolmaking further than they did. It seems to have arrested at the rather unimpressive stage of the percussion nut hammer. This, I shall argue, is because tool-use is not just a matter of special dexterity. Although the chimpanzee is by far the best tool-user in the animal kingdom, it has neither the anatomical basis of dexterity – nor indeed actual dexterity – of inferior tool-users such as the gorilla, which shows that chimpanzee's superior tool-use is not mediated through dexterity; nor – and this is the deeper point which we shall elaborate presently – is its superior tool-use *mediated through a different kind of bodily self-awareness*. This may account for its failure to break through a low, fixed ceiling of achievement in tool-use.[19]

This low ceiling itself should give us pause for thought. While chimpanzees seem set to undermine all the sharp dichotomies between man and beasts, they still fall far short of human technological achievement. To put this a little less diplomatically, the harder we try to show how clever superior animals such as chimpanzees are, the clearer it becomes to us how unimaginably clever humans are.[20] When we try to account for this difference – the failure of even the most intelligent animals to go beyond the first step in toolmaking – the following observation may provide a clue: the inconsistent relationship between tool-use and the ability of species to recognise themselves in a mirror. Capuchins, who are tool-users, do not display self-recognition when viewing a mirror image of themselves and this is not a manifestation of a wider failure of spatial recognition and representation.[21] On the other hand, tool-using chimps and orang-utans do, and non-tool-using gorillas and gibbons do not, recognise their mirror image.[22] No animal, moreover, is aware of its own appearance to the point of adorning its own body – with the dramatic exception, of course, of *Homo sapiens*. In other words, there is a lower level of bodily self-awareness in even the most intelligent animals compared with humans. This would fit with the notion, to be developed in due course, that tool-using in humans – unlike that in animals – is an offshoot of a different, unprecedented kind of bodily self-awareness – in particular the sense of one's body as an instrument (and of oneself as an agent) – derived not simply from the unique dexterity of the human hand, but from the means by which that dexterity is achieved. At any rate, it suggests that human tool-use is rooted in something that even the highest non-human primates do not possess.

This difference is captured by Paillard, who suggests that tool-use in higher (non-human) primates is not distinct from a more general ability to incorporate tools into a body schema. Instead,

> We are dealing with a primitive sensorimotor process of a general nature; it accounts for the continuous adaptation that is required for motor commands to match the dimensional changes of the growing skeleton and also for the many kinds of sensorimotor recalibration that are needed in daily life.[23]

The limited (unimpressive) tool-use by non-human primates is a manifestation of a more primitive adaptation to a growing body. In contrast, as Kohler points out, human tool-use

> is a *social* activity based on *complementary* relations between the hands, whereas chimpanzee tool use is the incorporation of the objects into whole-body locomotive skills.[24]

There is, in short, a profound, *qualitative* difference between how humans and how even the highest non-human primates use tools.

Now, while the development of tools is, indeed, 'the single most important force behind human evolution',[25] this is not the end of our inquiry into the root of human culture: we have to explain why tool-using in even the most intelligent non-human primates remains so primitive; why, with only trivial exceptions (and the use of a percussion hammer to crack open a nut, it should not be necessary to point out, is trivial compared with a steam engine or nuclear power station, or even with the manufacture of a hand-axe), non-human animals remained forever on the threshold of true toolmaking; why dawn never dawned for creatures other than man.

Why should the difference between the paw and the hand lie at the root of the widening gap between animal nature and human culture, between evolution and history? Why should the hand, for all that is a uniquely prehensile extremity, enable us so to get such a grip on the world that, almost wherever we look, we see not the Hand of Chance, or even the Hand of God, but the Hand of Man? In addressing this question, we must always bear in mind that the human escape from biology cannot be entirely explained in biological terms or in terms that biology can capture. The seeming paradox we have to face is that, while the jump from higher primates to humans may be a product of nature, it cannot itself be part of nature: when, as has happened, our organic bodies have to some degree – and between the boundaries of our organic birth (and subsequent organic growth and development) and our organic death – become liberated from organic constraint, this cannot be analysed as a purely organic process. More generally, to confine ourselves to the biology of organisms – even if that organism contains a magic organ such as 'the brain' – when we are trying to answer an essentially philosophical question is to move beyond biology into biologism.

The discussion that follows attempts to respect the fact that humans are both organisms that have come into being through processes that are seen throughout evolutionary history and at the same time agents, persons, selves, who cannot be explained satisfactorily in biological, or indeed physical, terms. It places the hand behind the tool – or the hand as ur-tool – at the origin of humanity and of a distinctively human evolution. What the hand brought to the table was not simply increased dexterity but an utterly different sense of self. This is how the hand comes to be the key to awakening of the 'cultured' human being out of the natural pre-cultural animal by virtue of transforming the relationship of human organisms to their own bodies.

10.2 THE DAWN OF THE CONSCIOUS HUMAN AGENT

That evolution, over all-but-infinite time, could change one physical organ into another, a leg into a wing, a swim bladder into a lung, even a nerve net into a brain with billions of neurons, seems remarkable, indeed, but natural enough. That evolution, over a period of a few million years, should have turned physical matter into what has seemed, in the most literal sense of the term, to be some kind of metaphysical entity is altogether another matter.[26]

What is the nature of the human mind and how did it arise? Does the evolution of the human intellect represent an expansion of capacities already present in our animal predecessors as postulated by Charles Darwin? Or are there major discontinuities between animal and human minds – gaps so vast as to demand spiritual or other dramatic explanations of the origin of human powers ...? These basic evolutionary questions remain unanswered more than a century after the publication of *The Descent of Man*.[27]

Introduction

The problem we have set ourselves, highlighted by our comparison of the limitless ability of humans to use tools they have themselves made with the severely limited capacity of animals for tool-use with nature-facts, is how humans have come to be so different, even from their nearest relatives in the animal kingdom. In trying to determine our place in the scheme of things, we humans are, as has been said, 'in the awkward position of having to acknowledge that the known physical basis of dissimilarity between themselves and apes does not justify the perceived degree of behavioural dissimilarity'.[28] It is appropriate to ask, therefore, how it is that, out of relatively small differences between ourselves and our nearest animal kin, such huge differences arise.

One way of dealing with the question – indeed, the most popular approach over the twentieth century – has been to deny that the differences between us and other creatures are actually so great. We are apes, it is asserted, even if we have lost our hair and so are fairly described, as Desmond Morris described us in his bestseller of the 1960s, as 'naked apes'. The massed ranks of ethologists, cognitive psychologists, neuro-scientists, molecular biologists, evolutionary theorists and many others have made what Daniel Dennett called 'Darwin's daring idea' that we are essentially animals into the most wearisome commonplace of the thought of the last hundred years. Sociobiology and evolutionary psych-ology are two flourishing, comparatively new, disciplines committed to understanding, respectively, social behaviour and the individual mind in terms of evolutionary theory and assimilating sociology and psychology to evolutionary biology. At their heart lies a denial of the scope and profundity of the difference between man and animals[29] – a denial wittily encapsulated in W. S. Gilbert's couplet: 'Man, however well-behaved, / At best is only a monkey shaved.'

The denial of the special status of humans once seemed liberating, if only because it was connected with the rejection of a theological world picture which justified much iniquity and the self-interested exploitation of piety by the powerful. Now that liberation from the shackles of theologically underpinned oppression is less of an issue, at least in the

West, overlooking the exceptional character of humans is simply boring. We humans, it should be unnecessary to say, are utterly different. But anyone who refuses to ignore what is in front of her nose – that one thing a human most certainly is not is merely a shaved monkey (and the fact that monkeys do not shave, even less buy shaving tackle, gathers up a mass of differences that evolutionary biologists are inclined to overlook) – has to explain how, out of small differences of anatomy and even smaller differences of physiology and metabolism, such huge differences in ways of life and ways of being have resulted. We have to explain how out of a small story such a big story grew and how out of a small biological difference there came huge differences that cannot be understood (though they can be misrepresented in a transiently plausible way) in biological terms: how, starting with biology, humans were led out of their biology into a culture of selves and societies upon which biology can cast no light.

The story of a big difference growing out of small ones is importantly one of 'a light dawning over the whole'.[30] This light is brightening and at an accelerating pace, and is one that we need to make sense of if we are to advance our understanding of what it is to be a human being and what future possibilities are open to us. We shall not further our understanding by trying to assimilate the light of human consciousness to the unilluminated darkness of pre-human life.

The Passage from the Animal Organism to the Human Agent

I shall set out the steps in this story in the form of a series of linked theses which bring together some of the things that have been said before and connect them with the deeper questions concerning human nature: in short try to move smoothly from biology to philosophical anthropology. The essence of the argument that follows is that our handedness, and our special relation to our hands, transform our relationship to our own body and, through this, to the world. It is important to emphasise that many aspects of this thesis will be touched on only superficially and they will be revisited in subsequent volumes of the trilogy. In Volume 2, *I Am: A Philosophical Inquiry into First-Person Being*, I shall examine the origin of agency and identity in much greater detail. In Volume 3, *The Knowing Animal: A Philosophical Inquiry into Knowledge and Truth*, I shall investigate the more remote and subtle consequences of the transformation of our relationship to the universe that have eventually resulted from the unique properties of our hands; in particular, the birth of objective knowledge.

1 *Human beings are uniquely agents in a way that no other animal, or living or non-living matter, is*

Conscious agency is the difference that lies at the heart of our differences. To a degree not seen anywhere else in the animal kingdom, human beings act rather than react. This is reflected in the fact that our behaviour is very often explicable only by appealing to (general, abstract, immaterial) reasons rather than to (material) causes; and that we are uniquely distanced from any putative instincts we are supposed to have inherited from our animal or hominid forebears. Even behaviour that we seem to share with animals – feeding, aggression, sexual behaviour – is mediated through a million layers of often quite abstract discourse, which frequently takes the form of reasons that justify actions, remote from instincts or tropisms that drive human actions.[31]

Many writers try to deny these differences. If 'animalist' accounts of humans seem plausible – and they must do because so many people seem to take them seriously – it may be because they tendentiously redescribe what goes on in ordinary human life in such a way as to make it sound like what goes on in ordinary animal life. Suppose, for example, you invite me out for a meal. Having learnt that you have just taken on a new mortgage, I choose the cheapest items on the menu and declare that I am full after the main course, so as to spare you the expense of a pudding. A chimpanzee reaches out for a banana and consumes it. Both the chimp and I may be correctly described as exhibiting 'feeding behaviour', but this obscures huge differences between her behaviour and mine. Here's another example. I decide to improve my career prospects by signing up for a degree course which begins next year. I have a small child. I therefore do more babysitting this year in order to stockpile some tokens. A cow bumps into an electric wire and henceforth avoids that place. Both of us have been exhibiting learning behaviour. Again, the difference between the two forms of behaviour is greater than the similarities. This will be evident to anyone who is not bewitched by some kind of theoretical assumption such as E. O. Wilson's creed that 'behaviour and social structure' are biological phenomena, indeed '"organs", extensions of the genes that exist because of their superior adaptive value'.[32]

How did we, uniquely among living creatures, get to be so different in our behaviour? More specifically, how did we become true agents?

2 If we take seriously the fact that we are biological entities, then we need to start by looking at the things that most clearly differentiate us from our nearest animal kin, who are not agents in the way that we are

In other words, we look for 'hallmarks of mankind'. There is a small number of these which we have discussed in part in the preceding chapters. They include: language (with its very special characteristics in humans);[33] a pronounced sociability; bipedalism; tool-using; and dexterity. An additional feature is a large brain but (as we have already remarked) brain size doesn't really explain anything. Besides, it is likely to be a consequence, rather than a cause, of the other two. (Ortho-genetic accounts of intrinsic evolutionary trends to, say, ever larger brains are, as discussed earlier, now discredited.) It is more plausible, as I have discussed in the previous chapter, to imagine a positive feedback mechanism by which increased hand-use and linguistic activity drive brain growth, and this in turn leads to increased versatility and more complex linguistic behaviour. Bipedalism – walking on two legs all the time, except, perhaps, on Saturday night – is merely an enabling factor that permits the development of the hand. Tool-using is a consequence of the advanced status of the hand and brain. The hand is a key element.

What makes this versatility possible?

3 Humans are unique in having a fully opposable thumb

Other primates are able to oppose their thumbs to the side of one or other of the fingers (usually the index finger) but cannot make a full touch-pad-to-touch-pad opposition. The special human capacity is due to two things: a saddle joint at the base of the thumb which enables it to rotate as it opposes; and the relative similarity of the length of the thumb to that of the index finger. The opposability of the thumb is crucial to the exquisite control of the hand in precision grips. The latter also depend upon the ability to move individual fingers independently (fractionated finger movements), which is shared with one or two other primates, although we possess it to an unparalleled degree because of the massive expansion of a special pathway in the nervous system, the direct corticospinal tract. This, then, is the basis for our incomparable dexterity.

Why is this dexterity so important? How does it connect with the question of the uniqueness of human beings as agents?

4 The dexterous hand prehends the world

In order to grasp the world in the way that it does, the hand has to customise its grips to meet the very special requirements of widely different situations, materials, contexts. It can do this. This continuous variation in the characteristics of available precision grips – many of which are 'soft grasps' that conform very precisely and without distortion to the singularity of the object and respect its properties – means that, at any given time, there are many grips to choose from. Successful prehension of the object cannot, therefore, be achieved by automatically mobilising, or downloading, a predetermined pattern of finger movements or postures. The necessary movements and postures, even within a single act of gripping, and certainly during the course of manipulating a gripped object – for example, a pear while eating it – will require frequent changes of grip. The tailored prehension of the object incorporates, perhaps awakens, certainly reinforces and makes less fleeting a more explicit sense of the otherness of the object, its intrinsic character, its difference. The object revealed to the human grasp is more itself than the object grasped by a non-human primate: the object is more objectified and the gap with the emergent subject widens.

The correlative of the infinite variety of grips necessary to prehend the material world with precision is a wide range of choice of grips available at any given time to the gripper: although the grip has to be tailored to the object, the precise grip I deploy will be the result of choice. The dexterous hand is thus a *choosing* hand; the dexterous human inescapably chooses the grip, within a quite precisely determined range of possibility.[34] With dexterity comes a (non-quantum) indeterminacy[35] and, out of that awareness of choice, the sense of agency. It is important to appreciate that the diversity of manipulations, of modes of prehension, is possible because of the relative non-specialisation of the human hand. The great apes, by contrast, have hands that are specialised for brachiation and arboreal prehension. Human hands are associated with (constrained) 'manipulative indeterminacy'.

The awareness of agency, unique to humans, will gradually awaken during the development of individual humans: the margin of discretion will widen and the prehensive strategies will become more complex and lead to ever more complex and deliberate choices. For the individual, this will be the result of experimentation during development; for the culture as a whole, upon which the individual draws, this will be the result of progressive elaboration of tools.

Now it might be argued that customisation of grip and constrained manipulative indeterminacy are not unique features of humans; that the difference is only a matter of degree, rather than of kind. After all, we noted that dexterity alone does not determine tool-use: chimps are much better tool-users than the more dexterous gorillas. Something else beyond dexterity and wider choice of groups, is required.

What else will drive this gradual awakening to and of agency?

5 The human hand is not only an organ of manipulation, it is also an organ of exploration and of cognition: it is the chief organ of the fifth sense

When we touch something, the situation, as we noted in section 1.3 and elsewhere, is rather complex: we get to know the object through the interaction between our material hands and the material of the object. Our knowledge of what the object is – the kind of thing it is, the kind of material of which it is composed – is *relative* knowledge, calibrated against our own bodies: the object is large, hard, rough, cold, etc. relative to the physical properties of my fingers. Fingers, unlike eyes, 'level' with the objects they sense: there is a reciprocity; the object that is touched touches the object that is doing the touching, etc.

When the object in question is our own body, additional, crucially important, layers of complexity result. Let us return to an example we used earlier. I am lying in bed. The sheets have slipped off and the upper half of my body is cold. My warm hand touches my cold shoulder. The hand feels the cold shoulder and, in doing so, feels its own warmth. At the same time, my cold shoulder feels my warm hand and, by this means, feels its own coolness. The hand can thus feel its warmth directly (as a warm feeling in the hand) and indirectly (as a warm feeling of the hand in contrast to that of the shoulder). Likewise the cold shoulder.

There are other ways of capturing this multiplicity which seems to open up inner distances within the individual. In touching ourselves, we are divisible into at least two subjects and two objects. (That's leaving aside all the background bodily awareness and awareness of the things around the body.) The hand (subject) is aware of the coolness of the shoulder (object). The shoulder (subject) is aware of the warmth of the hand (object). There is, therefore, a double distance within the individual as an embodied person.

One may anticipate several objections to this argument for the key role of the hand in opening up inner distances within the body, distances which, we shall presently suggest, *reinforce an instrumental relationship to one's one body* (in addition to its being directly experienced as that which one is) and in which, more specifically, as a result of the emergent status of the hand as a tool, agency is established. The two objections that seem to lie most readily to hand are: 1) that non-human animals touch and explore their own bodies; and 2) that the situation I have described would seem to make the shoulder, as much as the hand, the bearer of the subject–object pairing. I need to deal with these objections before getting on to the really interesting issues.

In response to objection 1): Yes animals do touch themselves in all sorts of ways. But the thing they touch with – paw, foot-hand, tongue – is not the same as the kind of thing we touch with. For reasons set out above, the hand, with its history of choosing grips, is already half way to being an agent – or, more accurately, the agent of an agent, or that agent's tool. The cat's mouth, more specifically its tongue, does not have this status as an agent; it is, moreover, not distanced from the implicit viewpoint of its consciousness. The mouth is not something that the cat 'has', or 'uses'. Nor is an ape's hand – even the hand of a chimpanzee – such an inchoate agent. The difference is in part due to the unique sensitivity of the hand (its sensory apparatus, amplified by those beautiful papillary ridges that make up our fingerprints) and the unique interaction of its sensitivity and its dexterity in manipulative exploration. These two things underline its status in humans as the active subject to its object's passivity, thus emphasising the differentiation between subject (the hand, and to a lesser extent the shoulder) and object (the shoulder and to a lesser extent the hand).

What about objection 2)? Surely my shoulder or other non-manual parts of the body could be the bearer of a subject–object pairing. But why, particularly, the hand as the source of our sense of choice? I have discretion as to how other parts of my body are employed – as, for example, when I determine the precise way in which I take a step. What is special about the hand is that this discretion affects a part of the body to which we already have a special relationship – as I have discussed in relation to itching and scratching.[36] It is also – in contrast with gait – choice within constraint and not on the background of stereotypy – in contrast with gait. So we have a limited choice, made more real by its limitation and not against the background of stereotypy. Moreover, when it comes to touching ourselves, the relationship between the hand and the part it touches is not symmetrical: the hand has, well, the upper hand: it is manifestly the exploratory agent and the shoulder manifestly the explored surface. Although touch is reciprocated – the toucher in each case is also a touchee – there is this hierarchy of roles because the hand has come to the shoulder, and not vice versa. The hand (subject)–shoulder (object) pairing is not cancelled out by the shoulder (subject)–hand (object) pairing as they might be if they were equal as well as opposite. (This differentiation of roles is, what is more, almost at the same spot, unlike the characteristic differentiation in looking. The gaze is usually unreciprocated: the objects I look at do not usually look back at me and where viewer and seen are at a distance from one another.)

We need at this point to notice another basis for the asymmetry between the hand and the rest of the body which underpins the initial establishment of subject–object distances within the body: the full pad-to-pad contact between the thumb and the other fingers that results in a comparatively large surface of very intimate contact between the pulps of opposing fingers. These pulps are intensively supplied with sensory endings, so that the multitude of grips it can draw upon may be perfectly adapted to the objects it is exploring and manipulating and be exquisitely regulated during manipulation by constant, direct and subtle feedback processes. As a consequence, *in the touching tips of the fingers, the body communicates with itself as well as with the extra-manual world with unprecedented intensity*. This underlines the very special relationship to our hands that, in the first instance at least, we do not have to any other structure in our body.

The in-house murmur that accompanies and directs manipulations raises our awareness of our hands to a higher level. Through opposability we finger our fingers and so, through 'meta-chiral being', achieve meta-carnal awareness. There are many ways in which the fingering fingers of the human hand differ from, say, the self-addressing of an animal licking its paw. The most important is that in the former, 1) the touching parts are similar (finger-to-finger); 2) there is wide range of possible 'meta-fingerings' which can be selected at will; and 3) the self-addressing is located, by the rest of the forelimb, at a distance from the emergent centre of consciousness, localised around the head, perhaps at the putative origin of the visual field. A cat's tongue licking its paw exhibits neither of these characteritics; nor does the monkey's paw scratching its back – because the back is not readily located 'at a distance' and the touching parts are dissimilar. The self-fingering hand is at once more intensely self-addressed and more localised, and at a remove – it has to be transported at the end of the upper limb to the place where it does its business – and from the putative centre of consciousness of the animal.

The carnal self-consciousness achieved in the hand is of a different order from the awareness achieved in any other bodily part or (one might speculate) achieved through the interaction of bodily parts in the animal organism. It is this that places the hand in a 'superior' position in its interactions with other bodily parts – at least in the first phase or in the evolution of the human race or in the development of an individual human being. This layered awareness in the human hand is underlined by the evanescent hierarchies that are created during manipulative activity – between foreground and stabilising fingers and between lead and assistive hands. This is why self-exploration by humans using their hands is fundamentally different from the self-exploration of the animal licking its paw or scratching its ear.

The differentiation of roles, so that one part of the body – the exploring hand – is superior to another – the explored part – maintains the inner distances: the subject–object distance awoken within your body is not cancelled by an equal and opposite object–subject distance. Opposite, yes; equal no.[37] When the exploring hand opens up these inner distances, the transition from consciousness – widely present in the animal kingdom – to self-consciousness is secured. That the shoulder is there and that the hand is knowing it lies at the heart of the distinctively human mode of consciousness, in which the subject of awareness is at once distanced from herself and comes to herself (in the same place, in a kind of not-quite-coincidence). (We shall revisit this in Volume 3, when we consider our advance from sense experience to knowledge, from sentience to sentences; how, in short, when we wake out of our animal bodies the world is presented to us as an objective reality with (only) partially scrutable properties of its own.)

The hand's role as an exploratory tool confirms and underlines its status as an agent – but only once the intuition of agency has been already ignited. In the exploratory and manipulatory hand, prehension and comprehension are integrated, indeed fused. What is envisaged is a process of awakening, driven by or rooted in a very special – unique – relationship to our body opened up by our very special relationship to our hand, with its unique genius. This special relationship has two aspects: the motor side and the choice of grip; and a sensory side and the complexity of self-touching. The two come together in sensorimotor integration.[38] This integrated sense of our hand, of ourselves as manipulators and of our relationship to our manipulating cognitive hand, enhances our sense of our body as our own and as ourself.

But how, precisely, does this relate to a sense of agency?

6 At the heart of agency must lie the sense that certain events are actions and that they are my actions

This sense is the necessary condition for some *happenings* of my body to become *explicitly* my doings. The feeling that this (biological) body is mine – or the haunting of this body by an intuition of identity or (at best) ownership – is a necessary precursor of the sense of agency. It is opened up through the special relationship we have to our hands and, through our hands, to our body at large. The sensorimotor set of inner distances arising out of the hands creates the sensorimotor awareness of self; the sense of an 'I' that is to some degree identical with this body or, at any given time, with a subsection of it. Linked to the sense of self is the sense of agency which, in turn, rests upon and then italicises and rests more firmly upon, the sense of self. (It seems reasonable to envisage this as an iterative process that takes place during the individual's early development, rehearsing the gradual evolution of human self-consciousness over several million years.) The (sensory) distances and the (motor) efficacy turn the fact of our animal body into the ground floor of the sense of the human self; it makes the tautology – 'This body is this body' – available as 'I am this thing'. The thus-made-available (sensorimotor) quasi-tautology becomes the agentive self which is both presupposed by and italicises the available tautology.[39]

This lies at the root of the difference between animals that merely use tools made out of things that lie immediately to hand and humans, who not only use tools but also make them; or between the human toolkit whose range and richness we only hinted at in the previous chapter and the impoverished toolkit of even the brightest non-human primates. Toolmaking in humans is driven by a fundamental intuition of agency, in turn arising out of an instrumental relationship to the body; or of one part of the body to the other; in particular of the body to the hand or hands it uses. Without the developed sense of agency and the body-as-instrument, there could not be a fully developed sense of the tool or the toolmaking that flows from this. The separation within the body of the agent and its instrument – as when I use my hand – is the foundation for the explicit use of tools and of the distinctly human history of growing manipulative skills – namely, the history of the development of tools that massively extend the hand's versatility. The increasing use of tools also retroacts upon the hands that use them, underlines the hand's status as a master-tool, and, by making new demands upon the hand, pro-motes its ever-increasing dabness. So the tool makes the hand more handy in several senses and in many ways.

This instrumental relationship to one's body opened by the instrumental relationship to the hand will also spread to other parts of the body: the leg (as in deliberate kicking), the shoulder (as in battering something down or in being put to a wheel), and even the mouth[40] may be put into an instrumental relationship to oneself as agent. I *use* my leg to kick something. I *put* my shoulder to the door. I *head* the ball. (What a remarkable verb 'to head'! What an extraordinary elective use of a head heading is!) And so on.[41]

An interesting light is cast on the pervasive agency of the human body by the difference between animal self-grooming and the human toilet.

When I wash myself using soap and water or dry myself using a towel, I am operating upon myself in a way that the animal is not. The use of mediating instruments – soap, towel – in this activity underlines the separation within the individual of the body as object or substrate and the body as operator. Washing, as we have already noted (section 4.2, The Dialogue of the Left and the Right Hand), does not quite arrive at the active mood: it belongs to a middle mood in which the body is *both* active and passive. An animal licking itself is neither active nor passive, neither an agent nor a patient.

Where humans use tools to operate on the extracorporeal world, the instrumental status of (at least part of) the body is even more clearly established. Here the division within the body – between the part that is the tool and the remainder that is either the tool support or the tool-user – has enormously complex and wide-ranging effects beyond its being the necessary precursor of true tool-use. It in part explains the early liberation of tool design from analogy with the body we remarked upon in the previous chapter. The fact that either the hand or the shoulder can be used to push over an obstacle means that certain instrumental uses of the body are liberated from proscribed design features: the underlying (mechanical) principle utilised by the tool is made explicit in the shared purpose of the two body-part tools. In other words, the tool itself is not lost in, or merged with, or dissolved into, a body-tool complex. This creates the cognitive framework for tools that are not only not mere extensions of the human body but also are not modelled on the body: for example, the wheel.[42]

Chimpanzees could not have invented the wheel because – for this reason, and the connected reasons set out in section 10.1 – they do not conceive of tools *per se* as separate from their own bodies. The fully developed extracorporeal notion of a tool had to await the awakening of the special agentive relationship of the embodied creature to its body; the sense of the body as agent; or as the instrument of one's agency, mediating between a need – or a wish, or a desire – and its fulfilment.

Further consequences flow from the manner in which the tool-using body becomes itself more firmly embedded in its role as an instrument. When the levering power of the arm is enhanced by the use of a literal lever, the arm acquires the status of a lever. Beyond the retroactive transformation of the body into a kind of toolkit, the instrumental relationship to one's own body extends to include care of the body (as in hygiene or, more complexly and abstractly, medicine),[43] and the deliberate acquisition of skills (practice, appenticeship in manual skills) and physical grace and fitness (dance, sport). Making one's body more proficient and less clumsy, by training over a long period of time, teaching oneself by practice and repetition so that one can surprise oneself with grace, is an impressively sustained, elaborate, complex consequence of this.[44]

And this, of course, is just for starters. The tools we use, and which are not assimilated into the body schema (though in the moment of most competent use they may need to be), themselves cast light on our relationship to the world outside of the body. The successful instrument throws incidental and useful illumination on the character of the material world in which it is employed. Through tools we more explicitly operate on the (material) world, at a distance (physical and cognitive) from it. In tool-mediated manipulation, we are awoken more sharply to the general properties of that world (in 'feedback' as we struggle from the slight distance of mediated contiguity) as substrate, and to our (embodied) selves.

Tool-mediated interaction with the world may become increasingly indirect: there is a progressive dialectic between stored, purpose-built tools and the abstract general principles they embody. We are consequently further distanced from mere immediate reactions, and from instincts and tropisms. The tool promotes the progressive growth of the reason-driven or reasoning agent out of the instinct-driven or material-cause-shaped organism. The tool, eventually, brings in its wake a growing sense of a world that has a legible order, that is (at least partially) intelligible. The ordering of nature as the 'ready-to-hand' – as the untooled hand orders it – evolves into a world that is the nexus of the 'ready-to-be-manipulated' – a distinctively human mode of being in the world and being enworlded, as Heidegger first pointed out. Tools themselves gradually develop autonomy as they are shaped by abstract principles into automotive machines operating upon a world that is increasingly reduced to the digital skeleton of itself. Although this is a long way on from the pebble chopper, the fundamental insight – or at least the ontological framework – was already inchoate in the relation to the world implicit in the pebble chopper.

In summary, the dexterous hand is a choosing organ and, in consequence, contains the seeds of agency: manual choice, in the context of the especially intimate interaction with the object, underscored by constant direct feedback – about the position of our hands, their relationship to the object of interest and the progress of whatever operation is being performed – through skin sensation, limb proprioception and vision, generates a very special relationship to our hand when it is engaged in manipulative activity. (To repeat: in the touching tips of the fingers, the body communicates with itself and the extra-manual world with unprecedented intensity.) This relationship, in turn, fosters a relationship with our own bodies that is not seen elsewhere in the animal kingdom. The hand becomes a tool; the body becomes an instrument; and we emerge as true agents. Deliberate action begins to replace instinctive behaviour, tropisms, and so on (even though such actions must still be fashioned out of, or built upon, biological mechanisms).

The development of the sense of oneself as an agent, acting directly or indirectly through the instrument of one's body, lies at the root of the emergence of human self-consciousness and the sense of self. 'I act (deliberately) therefore I am' has always seemed to me to pin down the basis of the sense of the self better than 'I think therefore I am', which can seem merely a bare, almost tautological connection between two empty forms. The hand opens up the body to itself as an instrument, awakens the sense of self and of the (cultural) world to which the self relates – the world Heidegger described as that of the ready-to-hand.

These linked roles of the hand as an incomparable exploratory organ and peerless manipulative tool together create the sense of oneself as a subject haunting (using, suffering, enjoying living and being) one's body and, inseparable from this, the sense of agency:

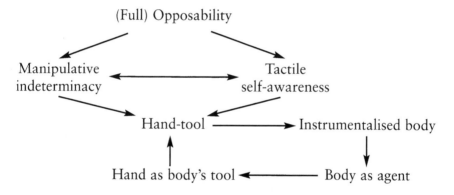

The hand, in short, awakens the intuition of the agentive self.

The various tributaries feeding into the sense of self – or the sense that 'this body is mine' and my 'instrument' – may be set out in different ways. For example:

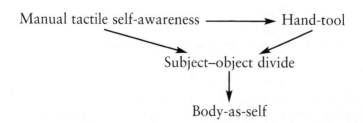

The hand-tool places the world at one's fingertips: it becomes a nexus of the ready-to-hand, of tools, in the Heideggerian sense. The tips of the palpating fingers are organs of revelation of an objective world to a subject: they are the ancestors of the organs of object-cognition that developed within the human mind. The knowable world begins as a palpable one.

The subject–object, agent–patient relationship within the body is many-layered, even within the hand: manipulation has a hierarchical structure, such that a part (for example, the palm and unmoving fingers) acts as a stabilising background and the rest is active foreground. In bimanual activity, one hand may lead and the other follow, one stabilises while the other manipulates, and so on. While in much non-human animal activity, one part of the body may also act as a stabilising background for foreground activity, this is developed to an unparalleled degree in humans, in whom secondary bodily hierarchies are established and dissolved at will. Humans are layered subjects within, acting through, instrumentalised bodies to an extent that other animals are not. The agent–patient or subject–object differentiation that begins with the hand infects the rest of the organism: the foot (as when I take a deliberate kick at a ball), the shoulder (as when I charge a door), the mouth (as when I break a thread between my teeth) may become explicit carnal tools.

It may seem implausible that the hand should carry such a huge metaphysical burden. It seems less so if, as is reasonable, we conjecture that other beasts, particularly other higher primates, come very close to the threshold that separates engaged awareness from self-conscious agency. We have already alluded to the evidence for self-consciousness in non-human primates; but there is no sustained self-awareness – analogous to a rocket that does not achieve escape velocity enabling it to remain aloft in orbit. The hand, moreover, is required only to start off the process (though it remains intimately involved in many other developments that keep up it going). Ultimately, the hand will seem to have a relatively minor role in maintaining and sustaining human distance from the animal life as instrumentalisation is diffused throughout the body and beyond into a world of naturefacts and artefacts, of objects-as-tools.

The notion of a *threshold* is intended to indicate how small a distance had to be crossed to start the journey that led away from animality. We may imagine that non-human primates – unlike, say, elephants – have almost everything in place necessary to achieve bodily self-consciousness and the sense of agency; all that is needed is an extra margin of manipulative indeterminacy and of manual self-addressing, coming from full opposability, to lift the organism from bodily consciousness to bodily self-consciousness, with a consequent differentiation of agent and tool within the body.

Talk of thresholds being crossed, may, however, mislead by suggesting sudden, complete change. The process must be envisaged as gradual – taking several millions of years. Transition from the intuition of the agent-self to a fully developed complex human self confronting the kind of world we now inhabit was anything but sudden. We may envisage a feedforward mechanism, by which the consequences of self-awareness, and the intuition of agency, themselves enhance self-awareness and sharpen and extend actual agency. Things that are fleeting in non-human primates – the use of the body as a tool, the use of tools to extend the body's tool-power – become increasingly securely established and have an ever-extended efficacy in humans.

When the hand makes this possible by transforming our relationship to our own bodies, making us true agents and true selves, the self is *assumed* in both the sense of being presupposed (in actions) and being taken up as a burden (as in the assumption of an office). It is through the gap opened up by the hand between the body and itself that culture pours into nature and selfhood haunts the body.

Even if we did not have empirical evidence that tools preceded language – so that the latter is a secondary, not a primary, source of culture – there are reasons for giving the hand/tool priority. It is arguable that the sense of agency needs to be established in order that signs can be exploited actively to signify – so that shaped or determinate meaning can be produced as well as consumed. We need to look outside of language for the source of this sense, and we find it in the hand/tool.[45]

Notwithstanding the crucial contribution of language, general intelligence and increasing brain size, therefore, to the development of human culture, the hand remains the tool of tools, the agent behind agency. The hand and its tools lit the fuse that led ultimately to the cultural explosion that has lifted humans out of the evolutionary process.

So, we have a sense of agency and this is enhanced by the toolmaking and tool-use that the intuition of agency makes possible. Might not, however, this sense of agency be an illusion?

Is the Sense of Agency an Illusion?

7 The sense of agency cannot be 'wrong', 'factually incorrect', because it is rooted in the lived 'tautology' of the agentive self

This may seem counter-intuitive.[46] Surely, it will be argued, there is a difference between the proposition:

1. 'The special properties of the hand and of my relationship to it and, through this, my relationship to my body give me a *sense* of agency'

and the proposition:

2.   'I *am*, in fact, truly an agent.'

The sense that one is an agent does not, surely, entail the reality that one is an agent. So, while the sensorimotor hand may explain why one might feel that one is an agent (as opposed to being dissolved in the causal net and as passive as any other part of that net), this would not presumably count as evidence or proof that agency is liberated from mechanism.

Against this common-sense argument, I am inclined to offer the following bold (and just about thinkable) thought: that the sense that one is an agent – that one is an actor rather than being part of a wider scene of mere happening – is intrinsically true, that its truth is built into its existence,[47] that it is precisely the kind of thing about which one could not be wrong.

'I believe I am an agent, therefore I am an agent' – surely this is a non-sequitur. Granted, being an agent is not something one could be simply mistaken about – like not knowing the name of the British prime minister, or believing that the Morning Star and the Evening Star are different entities. But is it not possible that being an agent is still an illusion? The answer is that, if it is not an illusion that one is a self, then it cannot be an illusion that one is an agent; for the same thing that gives rise to the sense of being a self, a subject, is precisely that which gives rise to being an agent, as opposed to merely being dissolved in the ocean of causality. An entity that can be the bearer of the notion that it is a self – the lived tautology or existed identity that 'I am this thing'[48] – must also be an agent. For the lived tautology 'That I am this thing' carries with it the sense of responsibility for this thing: it is an office one is obliged to be. Awakening to the notion of freedom (or agency) and access to real freedom are the same thing because they are both mediated by the existed identity, the existed tautology of the embodied self. Now one cannot – for good Cartesian reasons – be mistaken that one is a subject, or has subjectivity, or that one is a self, of some minimal sort. Hence one cannot be mistaken that one truly is an agent.

What am I saying? Essentially, that subjectivity – which is the epistemological interior of our body captured in 'That I am this thing' – is inextricably linked with freedom and that it follows from this that the fact that one is a self and the fact that one is an agent are inseparable.[49] We enact our acts – rather than their simply happening to or within us – precisely because we are selves. The *fait*/intuition 'That I am this' makes me a point of origin in two (inextricably linked) senses: the centre of a world that is my world, the 0,0,0 point of lived space, and the source of certain events that will count as my actions. What makes my actions *actions* (as opposed to mere events) is connected with what makes them have their special kinds of meanings; and this is rooted in human selfhood, human personhood, which transcends the animal organism.

Might this appropriation of (some) events (ultimately traceable to the body) as our acts be an illusion? After all, our agency, and our powers as agents, are limited. More to the point, they are considerably more limited than we, in our everyday understanding of ourselves and our lives and destinies, are sometimes aware of, so we are in many individual cases mistaken as to the scope of our agency. Even those who do not consider it useful to think that we are driven to do what we do by our genes, our bodily chemistry or, more specifically, by the neurotransmitters in certain parts of our brains, will concede that our behaviour is shaped by the longstanding environment that has shaped us, by the historical accidents that flow from our being born and living in certain circumstances. No one, in short, can deny that we are constrained by the facticity of our circumstances, including the consequences of our past actions which have helped create the many frameworks within which we are enclosed. That is, of course, true. All that this proves, however, is that our freedom is conditioned, not unconditioned. And I have no trouble accepting this. It does not, however, prove that freedom, or agency, is an illusion.

Indeed, freedom has to be conditioned in order for it to have particular content, for it to be exercised. Agency has to act upon, and within, a framework composed of, states of affairs it has not chosen. At its deepest level, we have to be 'a given something' we have not chosen to be in order that we should act on choice. If we had no given characteristics (and it matters little for the present argument whether these are genetically, environmentally or otherwise determined), then there would be nothing in us to act and to express its freedom through action. Similarly, we need to be inside a framework in order for our free actions to have actual content, for us to have something to be free about. Givenness of the agent and givenness of his or her circumstances are consequently necessary conditions of an agency that is expressed in necessarily specific actions. There has, first, to be something unchosen that is accepted as myself in order that I may choose, in order that there should be a chooser. And secondly, there has to be an assumed or given framework within which the chooser chooses in order that that something in particular should be chosen out of the entire range of physical possibilities. The menu has to be finite. The frameworks are constraints, yes; but they are *enabling constraints* without which the agent would lack an agenda. The things that seem to determine us from outside the reach of our agency are also those things that make the notion of exercising agency meaningful. (That is why it is difficult to think of God as free because He has nothing to be free from, nothing to be free about, nothing to free Himself towards. No wonder He has such a dull history: he is little other than a crystal of frozen, abstract attributes.)[50]

From the necessarily conditioned nature of agency, it follows that passivity, and the experience of being powerless, and of being out of control, and of suffering (things that I, as a doctor, am particularly aware of), while they seem to be opposed to agency, are also derivatives of this primary sense of agency, of my expropriating an explicit self which has its body, and its world, and its plans, and its biography, and its pride, and its ambitions.

8 We can be wrong about the extent of our freedom and the extent to which we are free on a particular occasion

All right, it may be argued, the sense that one is an agent is not, and cannot, be overall an illusion. But still there are times when we are illuded in our belief that we did something freely and some of our actions are more or less free than others. And, if we can be deluded sometimes about our status as agents, and not know when those occasions are, then the relationship between the sense of agency and the reality of acting as a more or less free agent cannot be as internal or necessary as I have claimed. Moreover, even though we are only sometimes wrong, since we do not always know which times these are, this is as bad as always being wrong.

Worse still, there are times when one is factually wrong not only about why one is doing something, but even that one is doing it at all. For example, RT may dream that he is walking by a cliff when in fact he is sleeping safely in bed. These mistakes go deeper than the standard 'Freudian' cases in which the individual believes she is doing something for a conscious reason when she is actually doing it for an unconscious reason or, indeed, as a consequence of a biological/material cause; that she is acting as a reason-driven agent when her actions are merely the effects of causes unknown to her. In these cases, there are still reasons, even if they are wrong: there is still an important residue of agency in rationalisation.[51] In the cliff case, by contrast, there is no action at all and no reason, not even a mere rationalisation.

This evidence that we may be mistaken – that we are not, on certain occasions, actually the agents of what we believe to be our actions, that our agency is often mistaken as to itself – is not sufficient proof that we are never agents or that, as agents, we never really know what we are doing, never really wake up out of forces or mechanisms that have us in their thrall. The very fact that I have had to select certain (unusual) cases to illustrate how we may be illuded as to our status as agents implicitly demonstrates that there are other circumstances under which we are not illuded. For example, it is only under rare circumstances – identified as dreaming – that I am illuded as to the fact that I am walking. Most of the time when I am walking, I really am walking. And most of the time when I am walking to the pub in order to enjoy a looked forward to quiet hour reading and drinking in a pub, I really am walking to the pub and for the reason given. That is to say, despite all the cerebral and others mechanisms that are required to make it possible for me to go to the pub and to have the wish to do so, I am pulled by reasons – which project a possible future – rather than pushed by causes – which exist in an actual past.

To draw a wider conclusion, I do not have to be always, and completely, free for the belief that I am an agent to be true. Conversely, being mistaken as to the scope of my agency is not the same as being entirely mistaken that I am an agent at all. For the reasons already given, we must not think of agency as all or nothing, howsoever difficult it is to think of it as anything other than all or nothing. And the sense that one is an agent does not have to be a completely transparent one on all individual occasions. There is a necessary, general transparency which makes it impossible for the feeling that I am an agent to be untrue on all occasions, as awakening to the possibility that one is an agent and actually being an agent are internally connected, being two aspects of coming to the sense of self, of appropriating one's own body (and through it a world in relation to the body) for subjectivity and the sense that 'I am this thing'. It is difficult, none the less, to think of agency as other than all-or-nothing. Why is this so? Why do we resist the idea of 'conditioned' freedom and so feel uncomfortable with the notion of true agency as the emergent characteristic of humans arising out of the instrumentalisation of their bodies as a result of the possession of hands?

9 It is neither necessary nor appropriate to think dichotomously about agency and mechanism

We tend to think of freedom as something that we either have or do not have: you are either an agent or you are entirely assimilated into the causal net. The notion of degrees of agency, like that of degrees of consciousness, is one that is difficult to get clear about. And yet there is no doubt that there are degrees of both. I have argued so far that humans have a unique sense of agency and, uniquely among forms of matter, are free, choosing, beings, the originators of actions rather than the mere place where things, happenings, happen. But it is also true not only that we are not equally free, equally choosing, in all our actions, but also that we are not equally free, equally choosing, at all times in our lives. We are less free when we are asleep or drugged than we are when we are awake in broad living daylight. Moreover, we have all of us been helpless, seemingly unchoosing, infants; and some of us, before our death, will go through a period in which, because of dementia, we seem almost entirely devoid of the freedom to choose and act. There is no doubt that I am more plausibly an agent today as an adult than I was in my first year, or days, or minutes of life. And all of us will be returned at our death to the utter unfreedom of our own bodies when they are no longer haunted by a sense of agency. Liberation from the organic world is temporary: we gradually emerge into the light and then return to the darkness of the organism and the material physical world of which it is a part.

It seems as if our freedom exists only by permission of, or the happy accident of, certain conditions. Certainly; but this is something we have already dealt with: the conditionality of freedom is necessary to it, rather than a reason for doubting its reality. The fact, however, that agency should emerge at some time in our lives and pass through various stages of incompleteness before we reach our adult state is somehow more worrying. How can I be truly free if my freedom came only gradually and was itself not freely chosen?

This question is not as worrying as it may at first sight seem. For it is based upon an assumption that I (my self) and my freedom emerged independently. That I was once entirely unfree (as when I was an infant) and that subequently I was free. That there was a period (as when, for example, I was in nappies) when I was, my self existed, but my freedom wasn't, when my agency hadn't come into being.

To worry in this way is to have missed the point of the earlier discussion arguing the internality of the relationship between the sense that 'I am this thing' and the sense that I am an agent. 'I' and 'my freedom' emerge in parallel; as the 'I' develops – perhaps rather as a photograph develops in fixative – so its freedom develops. This being the case, there is no time at which the 'I' exists without, prior to, its freedom. The 'I' cannot be unfree because the 'I' and freedom – the sense of 'I' and the sense of agency – are born and grow as twins. The awakening of

freedom or the birth of agency is not, therefore, located at a time in the
history of the 'I' because the one cannot exist without the other: I cannot
precede its freedom. The assertion 'I really am free' is inextricably linked
to the assertion 'I really am I'. The 'I' may occultate – as when I am
asleep, or when I am drugged – but this does not make it unreal. Of
course 'I really am I' is closer to being an empty tautology than 'I really
am free', but it is not entirely empty and the fundamental presupposi-
tions behind both are essentially the same.

Similar considerations apply to the waning of agency. Even in quite
advanced states of dementia, the individual has some notion of his own
interest and some idea of pursuing it. Well after the long-range time
scales and overarching frameworks of ordinary life – which confer, and
are derived from, a sense of who (in the widest sense) and where (in the
widest sense) one is – have crumbled, there are still small-scale acts of
choosing, little achievements of deliberation and dexterity informed by
sense of purpose. Freedom has not entirely vanished until the self – the
sense that 'I am this thing' – has shrunk to nothing, like the spot on the
TV screen that used to fade at the end of the evening's viewing.
Choosing may be on a smaller and smaller scale, but it still remains
choosing in a way that is denied animals.[52]

The notion that agency is present to different degrees at different
times in our lives should be no more difficult to accept than that any self
emerges in the world at a particular time – that, for example, RT came
into being in 1946 and will have gone out of being (alas!) – or become
his posthumous fame – by 2064. That RT was not fully a self or an agent
until he was, say, one or five or ten or even twenty, also should not pose
difficulties. It simply means that RT's body came into being before his
self had fully developed. When RT is looking back on the helpless infant
RT in 1946, he is not looking at an earlier version of himself, but at an
earlier stage in his body, before it had fully graduated to the intuition
'That I am this thing' and the body had woken up to the possibility of
choice and hence to agency. This is no more shocking than the fact that
selves and their like emerged at some time in history – when *Homo
sapiens* first appeared.[53]

As agency develops, it takes into account more and more of the
world. The agent's implicit context of action includes wider time-scales
and space-scales. (Think of RT aged one year reaching for a dummy and
RT at fifty-five reaching towards the completion of this book.) This
widening scope of agency points towards the notion of an ideal agency
which brings together all one's wishes and takes account of the four
corners of one's self-world. This is achieved in a variety of ways –
perhaps in art (adumbrated in Paul Valéry's notion of the implex);[54]

perhaps in philosophy; perhaps in sexual love when world touches world and each world is the sun to the other and transfigures it with strange-familiar light.

10 The Sense of Agency is not an Illusion

The arguments given so far may cause more discomfort than carry conviction. For a start, the notion underpinning both the sense of agency and the truth of that sense – the hand-awoken intuition that I am this thing, the lived tautology or existential identity of the self in the appropriation of a shifting subsection of one's body and its world as the thing that one is – is one that is difficult to take hold of and retain. But the elusiveness of this notion should not be a matter of concern; for there is a huge body of evidence that the notion of agency, nutured in its earliest manifestations in the individual human being and the human race by the sensorimotor hand, is valid.

This body of evidence includes the incredible success of toolmaking man in gaining mastery over the forces of nature and creating within the natural world in which he first found himself a human world more suited to human tastes and more amenable to human needs. If agency is an illusion, it is an extraordinarily potent one! If the emerging human sense that we are agents, that we have the ability to seize hold of our personal and collective destiny with our decreasingly bare hands, could ever be described as a 'hypothesis', no hypothesis could have had richer and more gratifying consequences and have received, at an ever-increasing rate over the last 40,000 years, more abundant confirmation.

The emergence of the agent is associated with an ever-plumper sense of self – initially collective and opposed to nature and then (as society became complex and hierarchical and tools more remote from individual persons) more individual and opposed to society – and with progressive interiorisation of personhood. The individual experiences herself not only as an agent, but as one acting from within an inside that is outside of two outsides – the outside that is the natural or material world and the outside that is the social world that is the sum of the other selves' activities, traces and presences.

Summary

The origin of the sense of agency has been attributed to the special powers and virtues of the human hand. This organ makes possible the transformation of our relationship to our own bodies into an instrumental one, as opposed to one of 'dumb' suffering. To head off any misunderstanding, it is important to emphasise that the thesis does not depend upon denying consciousness, or even fleeting self-consciousness, to non-human animals. Nor does it require denying a modicum of manipulative indeterminacy and bodily self-addressing in other primates. What we are proposing is that the greatly enhanced freedom of choice, with an expanded manipulative indeterminacy constrained by a closer respect for the manipulandum, and an intensified self-addressing through 'meta-fingering' took hominids over a threshold that other primates were near – to progressive instrumentalisation of the body and the creation of tools and the instrumentalisation of the relationship to the world (and a world as a world of objective presences) – and that this ultimately led to the difference between the life that beasts live – suffer, endure, experience – to the life that humans *lead*. Just as the genius of manipulation was built on the genius of reaching, so opposability built on reaching and independent finger movement, to create the very special constrained, manipulative freedom that makes the hand a tool, the human body instrumental and the human being an agent. Opposability put the last coping stone in place that permitted humans to remain above nature long enough to create their own place outside of nature. By this means we moved from prehension to apprehension and then (but this is another story – for Volume 3) to comprehension. Through the gap that is opened up between the body and itself, a subject–object gap created in the first instance by the exploring, active hand, the distinctively human world enters the world of organic nature.

The unique instrumentality of the human body is of profound significance; for not only does it make possible an ever more explicitly instrumental relationship to the material world around our bodies, it also imbues us with a sense of ourselves as agency. This sense of agency is born, along with the sense of self: the self is 'assumed' in the irrefutable relationship to our own bodies. 'Assumption' is here meant in two senses: as in a logical precondition; and as in something taken up, as for example in the assumption of an office. The twin birth of agency and the self means that the self cannot be illuded in its intuition that it is an agent: that which creates the sense of agency is born at the same time as the agent and the possibility of agency. Fichte's assertion that 'The I is not a fact but an act' needs to be adjusted: the fully realised possibility of (deliberate) action and the emergence of the 'I' are internally connected. Selfhood and agency are two sides of the same coin.[55] How the organic living body becomes the humanly lived body – the focus of a human life, the centre of an infinitely complex egocentric space – remains profoundly unclear, but my insertion of the human hand into the debate has, I hope, contributed to clarifying the question and to suggesting the direction of future research.

At the very least, it may indicate new ways of addressing the problem of reconciling determinism – and the third-person view sees everything in the universe (including human behaviour) as being caught up in a web, of material causation which unfolds according to general laws unchosen by any individual, least of all the behaver – with our first-person sense of being free and responsible agents.[56] This incompatibility seems inescapable only if we begin with the notion of a subject physically located in the third-person world of physics (or, indeed, an impersonalised, society composed of quasi-physical forces). We need to step back further and recognise that there are no such things as actions until selves (which neither originate from nor can be explained by the material world) transform the world into 'circumstances', 'setting', 'substrates', 'bases', 'conditions' for there being action. Any approach to the mystery of the freedom of the will must begin with the question of how it is that the material world becomes something in, upon, against, and for the sake of which, we act.[57]

10.3 FROM BIOLOGY TO PHILOSOPHICAL ANTHROPOLOGY

The chiro-philosophical meditations to which the reader has just been exposed do not pretend to amount to a new theory of agency or even a new solution to the utterly perplexing problem of how agency could emerge in a world of tightly scripted causation. I hope, however, I have cast some light on how it is that, uniquely, human beings are agents and are self-choosing to a unique degree – in particular connecting the emergence of agency and the ever-increasing dabness of the human hand; and on the intimate relationship between the intuition of agency and the sense of self such that the sense that one is an agent cannot be illusory because being a self and being an agent derive from the same fundamental apprehension – that 'I am this thing'. At the heart of my position is the belief that the dawning of agency is a process of becoming, or assuming, the body that we *are* in a kind of lived tautology of selfness and that this assumption is made possible by the instrumental relation to our bodies awoken by the instrumentality of the hand. Once the idea of freedom is awakened, then true – relative, conditioned – factual freedom can start to develop and grow. Of all the animals, we alone are then able explicitly to be aware of, and try to break down, and develop a science of, the barriers to our freedom.

Some may be a little uneasy at the mixing of biology and philosophy. The lamentable example of so-called 'evolutionary epistemology'[58] justifies such unease. The indefensibility of 'evolutionary epistemology' that purports to explain human knowledge – and its truth and power – on the basis of its adaptive value is readily stated. We cannot explain the fact that there is knowledge (of all sorts) on the basis of a theory – the theory of evolution – that is itself an advanced piece of human knowledge. When we are trying to get at the fundamental basis of human knowledge, we cannot take Darwinism for granted. The suggestion that we are accurately aware of the world because we are adapted to have such knowledge (on pain otherwise of not being at all) rather puts the cart before the horse: the theory of evolution lies at the end of a very long chain of reason based upon a huge mass of knowledge and cannot be assumed when we are trying to found, or justify, or explain, that knowledge.

Importing biology into the origin of the sense of agency may seem equally dubious. There is, however, a difference. While evolutionary epistemology tries to biologise knowledge and invokes evolutionary theory to explain the (practical) truth of knowledge (indeed to support a pragmatist account of the nature of truth itself), my own chiro-philosophy does not appeal to biology to settle the question of the nature or reality of agency. That comes from an argument about the nature of the self and from evidence derived from the unique success of the human animal in mastering the planet. Nor do I pretend to prove that agency was an inevitable consequence of some biological process such as natural selection.

It was by no means inevitable that the intuition of agency would emerge in any particular species, even one that has to be provided with such marvellous luck as a hand. Agency and deliberate action do not necessarily better equip an organism for survival than would improved mechanisms – as I have argued at length elsewhere.[59] The pay-off for toolmaking man – in terms of increased survival – did not really come until tools had been around for over two million years – mainly in the last 40,000 years, and most particularly in last 6,000–7,000 of those 40,000 years, and most particularly of all in the last 500 years of those 6,000–7,000 years. Prior to that, more investment in 'better' instincts may have been wiser. When we compare the 'pseudo-tools' that nature produces, such as a spider's web, with the pebble chopper that was the sole product of toolmaking man for nigh on 1.5 million years, it is difficult to suppress a smile of amusement at human incompetence.[60] Of course, as we have seen (in section 9.3), even primitive tool-use brought other things in its wake – society, language, brain-enlargement[61] – but even so it is difficult to see why mutations that favoured better instincts, rather than persistence with low-tech tools, should have gained the upper hand. (It has, of course, been suggested that tool-use has been acquired and lost a few times during the course of primate evolution.) The intuition of agency, howsoever fruitful it has at last proved to be, was not, therefore, biologically foreordained. There is no biology of agency, though there is a biology of what makes it possible for an organism to act as if it were an agent.

If the hand was indeed the occasion of the awakening to agency (instrumentality of the body, technology, explicit principles, abstractions, reasons, moralities, etc.), then for one organism it has pointed the way out of biology into culture. This starts to address the seeming paradox by which we are part of nature and yet not assimilated into nature; what Kate Soper has described as 'the paradox of humanity's simultaneous immanence and transcendence'.

> Nature is that which Humanity finds itself within and to which in some sense it belongs, but also that from which it also seems excluded in the very moment in which it reflects upon either its otherness or its belongingness.[62]

We are creatures who, unlike any other, reflect upon nature, have theories about ourselves, do science and create art, speak in sentences and deal in abstract possibilities and in explicit general principles, find causes for things, appeal to reasons to explain events and to guide and defend our behaviour, and so on. We are the sole bit of Nature to nurse the Idea of Nature; and this alone measures how far we have travelled out of Nature.

Once we acknowledge the lack of biological foundation (in the sense of adequate justification or causal inevitability) for the intuition of agency – howsoever the ground may have been biologically prepared through the especial handiness of the hand – once we recognise that the initial intuition of agency was but a slow-burning fuse, which, over a long time, grew towards an explosion – we are spared the embarrassment of trying to stitch an epistemological, or metaphysical, or even ontological, account of our exceptional nature on to a small biological difference. The difference that lies at the root of our differences does not account for the million-petalled boughs that ultimately grew out of them. Nor does the biological origin of, and biological constraints upon, our sense of agency undermine or relativise its truth.[63]

It is interesting to consider how the initial 'point intuition' in which 'I am this thing' and 'I am this body' is not clearly separate from the 'I am able to control this body' has unfolded over time. How it is that something that emerges – as a sense or feeling – from the world becomes something that is true of the world; or becomes a source of truths about the world that are subsequently validated by the increasing self-efficacy made possible through ever-more powerful technology. The early technology – in which there begins to be made explicit certain general principles, and the links between needs and the actions that would serve them, in which implements are set out in extracorporeal space – is both exfoliated into specific rules and laws and is vindicated. The fundamental intuition that the world can be grasped and changed through myself as agent – and which cannot properly be described as true or false – subsequently gives rise to, or creates the context for the emergence of, specific ideas that may be true or false. The point-intuition thereby grows into an increasingly content-filled sense of self and self as agent that contains things that are true and things that are false. This point-intuition marks the moment at which the biological organism which simply lives in the natural world started to give place to the explicit human being who is in the natural world but is not entirely of it, being distanced from it by its many explicit truths and falsehoods and by being moved by reasons that take account of these truths and falsehoods, these possibilities, instead of being moved by instincts that are simply coupled into the way things materially are.[64] This last, however, is a theme for a later volume.[65]

NOTES

1. John Tooby and Irven DeVore, 'The reconstruction of hominid behavioural evolution through strategic modelling', in Warren G. Kinzey (ed.), *The Evolution of Human Behavior: Primate Models* (New York: State University of New York Press, 1987), p. 183.
2. Kathleen Gibson, 'General introduction: Animal minds, human minds', in Kathleen Gibson and Tim Ingold (eds), *Tools, Language and Cognition in Human Evolution* (Cambridge: Cambridge University Press, 1993), p. 8.
3. Like every other element of the story, this account of our expulsion from an original Eden – tree-covered, fertile and uniformly centrally heated – is disputed. Some writers (for example, Earnest Hooten [cited in Peter J. Bowler, *Theories of Human Evolution: A Century of Debate 1844–1944*, Oxford: Blackwell, 1986, p. 204]) somewhat romantically stressed the role of initiative in prompting our ancestors' descent from the trees. They left the trees in pursuit of a more varied and fuller diet: 'they wanted to live their lives more abundantly'. The crucial event was 'not the result of environmental accident, but rather a manifestation of that superior intelligence and initiative which, inherent in the proto-human stock, determined its evolutionary destiny'. This is a more uplifting explanation of the drivers to the emergence of modern humanity than a nasty turn in the weather, and more akin to the Genesis story, which places the blame for the Fall on intelligence and curiosity. At any rate, it does not affect the argument that follows. (The notion of the descent from the trees as expulsion from an initial Edenic state is counterbalanced by the

more attractive and equally popular idea that it was an escape from a green prison – an ecological niche in which primates were held in a state that fell short of human dignity and greatness. See ibid., p. 163.)

4. According to Bowler (ibid., p. 241), the evidence suggests that the upright posture preceded the major expansion of the human brain. Fossil records indicate that the brains of earliest mammals were no more advanced than those of the reptiles, consistent with the belief that the brain developed only in response to external pressures. The extraordinary size of the human brain, it has been hypothesised, reflects the number of times the organism had to adjust to new ways of life: three changes in mode of locomotion (from brachiation to quadrupedal locomotion in the forest; thence to quadrupedal locomotion in plains; and finally to bipedal locomotion in the plains) and the switch to a predominantly visual world. The final step unique to man was the rapid expansion of the brain after the acquisition of the upright posture (itself a stunning achievement). Implicit in the thesis of this book, the initial driver to brain growth was the greatly expanded range of possibilities opened up by the development of the hand.

5. The picture here is not very clear. It has been suggested that *Homo habilis* is a composite of an Australopithecine and an early form of *Homo erectus* – *Homo erectus habilis*. At any rate, *Homo habilis* appeared about 2,000,000 years ago, and was replaced by *Homo erectus* about 1.75 million years BP. *Homo sapiens* emerged about 500,000 years ago. (I have derived this information from Graham Richards, *Human Evolution: An Introduction for the Behavioural Sciences*, London and New York: Routledge & Kegan Paul, 1987, pp. 82 et seq.)

6. The literal-minded (among whom I number myself) might be tempted to think of the passage out of the forest into the open plain and the switch of emphasis from proximate to telereceptors as a great clearing of the collective primate mind. The notion of the 'clearing' is a key metaphor for *Da-sein*, or human being-there, in Martin Heidegger's philosophy.

7. Once hominids made artificial weapons, they could do without the great canine teeth which apes used for defensive purposes: armed to the teeth, they no longer required to be armed in their teeth.

8. This has been offered to account for the fact that the great apes did not take advantage of their large brains: there was no little additional survival value in becoming more cunning, more skilful, agile and, generally, more intelligent. In the absence of survival advantage, there was no driving force. Orthogenesis – the notion of evolution driven by internally programmed trends forcing variation along predetermined lines, as opposed to adaptive evolution based on natural selection – is now regarded as pre-scientific. It died with the modern synthesis of genetics and evolutionary theory.

It is consistent with the notion that cunning had survival value in group hunters that the first uses of intelligence and dexterity – hurling stone weapons – coincided with the replacement of instinct by strategy. The ballistic use of the arm and the weapon required a transformed sense of space and the ability to learn from experiences that one has brought about oneself. Hurling stones at a target one eventually learns to hit is a primitive form of experimentation. (See William H. Calvin, 'The unitary hypothesis: a common neural circuitry for novel manipulations, language, plan-ahead, and throwing', in Gibson and Ingold, *Tools, Language and Cognition in Human Evolution*.) It is no accident that the origins of science lie in the art of war.

9. John Napier, *Hands* (London, New York: Pantheon, 1980), p. 97.

10. It is noteworthy that the human hand is anatomically relatively primitive: it does not display the morphological specialisation seen in heavy non-human primates such as the great apes whose hands are subject to the biomechanical constraints of locomotion. This may have been because during hominid evolution hands were no longer required to provide bodily support at a time when humans were still relatively small and light. It is quite likely that the hand played a much more important evolutionary role with its fingers and palm acting as sense organs and touch agents than with its mechanical capabilities for gripping. As John Napier has put it, the most successful primates 'are those that have departed least from the ancestral pattern of structure but furthest from the ancestral pattern of behaviour' (*Roots of Mankind*, London: George Allen & Unwin, 1971), p. 9.

11. E. Trinkaus, 'Evolution of human manipulation', in S. Jones, R. Martin and D. Pilbeam (eds), *The Cambridge Encyclopaedia of Human Evolution* (Cambridge: Cambridge University Press, 1992).

12. The continual rewiring of the brain in response to the activity and associated experiences of end organs such as digits has been the subject of a huge research effort over the last few decades. The plasticity of the individual brain is well established. There is an extensive animal and human literature demonstrating the interaction between hand and brain, with both microscopic (synapses) and macroscopic (maps) changes occurring as a consequence of alterations in hand activity and in association with learning. Of the many recent reviews of this, Rita Carter's *Mapping the Mind* (London: Weidenfeld and Nicolson, 1998) is the most approachable. An authoritative account of the recent scientific literature is Dean V. Buonomano and Michael M. Merzenich, 'Cortical plasticity: From synapses to maps', *Annual Reviews of Neuroscience* 21, 1998, pp. 149–86.

One could imagine plasticity becoming fixed in the genome by natural selection of those animals with the most usefully plastic brains, with enormous consequences. As Paillard has put it:

> The liberation of the hand from the requirement of locomotion and its promotion to the rank of privileged interface between the organism and its material environment have profoundly remodelled the architectural landscape of the primate brain compared with that of other mammals. (Paillard, in *The Use of Tools by Human and Non-Human Primates*, A Symposium of the Fyssen Foundation, edited by Arlette Berthelet and Jean Chavaillon, Oxford Science Publications: Clarendon Press, 1993, p. 37)

13. Tooby and De Vore, 'The reconstruction of hominid behavioural evolution', p. 187. The interactions may be very complex and subtle. For example, we may envisage a sequence in which techniques embedded in procedures augment human intelligence and this augmented intelligence is then reflected back on to the techniques such that the understanding implicit in them is made explicit, and procedural 'know-how' is consequently in the form of declarative 'know-that', which is in turn exposed to critical examination and improvement.

Until quite recently in human history, the practice has preceded the theory and tools have embodied implicit rather than explicit principles. Now tools are often drawn up to a preordained specification: toolmaking is design-driven (the design including not only scientific principles but also certain implicit social principles such as are embodied in the law) rather than imitation– or intuition-driven. Science-based (or 'cognitive', 'top-down'), as opposed to practice- or artisan-based technological progress, is very recent, as Lewis Wolpert has pointed out. The early technological revolution 'owed more to the blacksmith's world than to the Royal Society' ('Science and anti-science', *Journal of the Royal College of Physicians* 21(2), 1987, pp. 159–65).

The consequence of this revolution in toolmaking and tool-use – most dramatically illustrated by the First Industrial Revolution – is the transition from hand-held tools directed by skilful operators to machines tended by unskilled operators. Tools uprooted from the eye and hand of the individual uproot tool-use from personhood, and from social identity, of the kind that a skilled craftsman would enjoy. Advanced tools embody abstract and general and generalisable (indeed globalisable) solutions to problems, so that identical tools may be used world-wide. (This rational standardisation is the opposite of the irrational, social standardisation of hand-axes and other palaeolithic tools.) According to Ingold (*Tools, Language and Cognition in Human Evolution*, p. 286), 'disembedding of technical from social relations' has led 'to the modern opposition between technology and society' – or, better (since technology is an expression of the collective genius and wishes of human society), of 'experienced sociality' or sociability. Of which more presently.

14. We could even attempt to explain, as Nicholas Humphreys does, why our intelligence is so much greater than it seems to need to be. Humphreys has argued that the intellectual capabilities of even non-human primates, as revealed in their ability to manipulate gadgets in the laboratory, are greater than would be required for dealing with the physical environment under natural conditions. This apparently unexplained spare capacity is actually required to read the minds of their fellow creatures, so that skill transmission can by-pass genes and occur culturally – which requires social skills including reading what is in the minds of others. (Nicholas Humphreys, 'The social function of the intellect', in *Growing Points in Ethology*, edited by P. P. G. Bateson and R. A. Hinde, Cambridge: Cambridge University Press, 1976, pp. 303–17.)

15. François Jouffroy, in Berthelet and Chavaillon, *The Use of Tools by Human and Non-Human Primates*, p. 29.

16. The distinctive features of human consciousness and the unsatisfactoriness of neural explanations of those features are addressed at length in Raymond Tallis *The Explicit Animal*, 2nd edn (London: Macmillan, 1999); and *On the Edge of Certainty* (London: Macmillan, 1999).

17. As John Maynard Smith (*The Theory of Evolution*, 3rd edn, London: Penguin, 1975, p. 313) has put it:

> What is characteristic of man is that this capacity of individuals to adapt has been so increased that it has led to a qualitatively new process, that of continuous historical change.

18. Elisabetta Visalberghi, 'Capuchin monkeys: A window on tool use in apes and humans', in Gibson and Ingold, *Tools, Language and Cognition in Human Evolution*).

19. Chimps are the only primates that use tools regularly in the wild. As William McGrew points out ('The intelligent use of tools: twenty propositions', in Gibson and Ingold, ibid.), animal tool-use is mainly for subsistence: outside of this use, it is mundane and obscure; weapon-use is of uncertain frequency and significance; and only chimps have toolkits, using different tools to solve the same problem or the same tool to solve different problems. Moreover, chimpanzees are alone among non-human primates in mobilising complementary manual functioning in tool-use – for

example, the tool being held in one hand in a precision grip and the object of the action being held in the other hand often in a power grip, as when a twig is used to pick the marrow out of a bone. Their range of tool-use, however, is still unimpressive.

McGrew also emphasises how tool-use in all non-human animals is separate from other attainments – vocal communication, degree of intelligence, etc. Laboratory measures of intelligence show no difference between tool-using chimpanzees and non-tool-using gorillas. While it may be possible to make animal tool-using comparatively impressive – and to seem to close the gap between humans and animals – by comparing the most advanced pongid technology with the most primitive human technology, this is to miss the point about human tool-use entirely, as we discussed in the previous chapter.

20. Huge efforts have been made to teach chimpanzees some kind of equivalent of human language or to persuade others that what they have learned is human language. The raptures that have greeted the occasional production of something that is interpreted as a new word or a grammatical construction seem rather disproportionate. It is all too easy to over-interpret the linguistic behaviour and to exaggerate the linguistic attainments of non-human animals. We can argue that some animals can string together sounds to form phrases, or to emit calls that have 'reference' (a term that should be used with considerable caution).

Such over-generous interpretations of animal behaviour are not confined to language. It is wise to be sceptical when one is informed of the supposed collapse of the hallmarks of humanity: lethal inter-group conflicts; long-term behavioural bonds among genetic relatives; symbolic capacities; use of syntax; emitting sounds of environmental reference; recognising self in mirrors (of which more presently); deliberate deception; cross-modal perceptions; and – using a tool to make a tool. These things may have been observed but only briefly and nothing sustained has been built on them; moreover, the observations may have actually been the product of misplaced explicitness.

At any rate, they should not be used to justify denying the obvious fact that our lives, and the things that motivate our lives, are unimaginably different from those of animals. There may not be qualitative uniqueness – in the simple sense in which we may say that we have this quality and they do not have even a scintilla of it – but uniqueness remains, if not in the activity, then in the level of accomplishment. More generally, we do not need absolute discontinuity to prove that there are real differences. These differences are there for everyone (but the theory-blinded) to see. We need 'hallmarks' and 'qualitative' differences only when people assert that real, enormous, differences are not real.

21. Visalberghi, in Gibson and Ingold, *Tools, Language and Cognition in Human Evolution*, p. 147.

22. McGrew, in ibid. There is a good deal of evidence to suggest that chimpanzees, unlike monkeys, have self-awareness. Some of the evidence is summarised in Raymond Tallis, 'Evidence-based and evidence-free generalisations: a tale of two cultures', in David Fuller and Patricia Waugh (eds), *The Arts and Sciences of Criticism* (Oxford: Oxford University Press, 1999). The point, however, is this reflexive awareness is transient and neither sustained nor elaborated into a self in the way that human self-awareness is.

23. Paillard, in *The Use of Tools by Human and Non-Human Primates*, p. 40.

24. Peter Reynolds, in Gibson and Ingold, *Tools, Language and Cognition in Human Evolution*, p. 419.

25. Alfred Wallace, *Culture and Personality* (New York: Random House, 1964), quoted in S. Jones, R. Martin and D. Pilbeam (eds), *The Cambridge Encyclopaedia of Human Evolution* (Cambridge: Cambridge University Press, 1992), p. 169.

26. Derek Bickerton, *Language and Species* (Chicago: University of Chicago Press, 1990), quoted in Gibson and Ingold, *Tools, Language and Cognition in Human Evolution*, p. 230.

27. Kathleen Gibson, in Gibson and Ingold, ibid., p. 3.

28. E. Sue Savage-Rambaugh and Duane M. Rambaugh, 'The emergence of language', in ibid., p. 87.

29. For a brilliant critical account of these trends, see Kenan Malik's *Man, Beast and Zombie: What Science Can and Cannot Tell Us About Human Nature* (London: Weidenfeld and Nicolson, 2000). I cover the same territory from a more purely philosophical point of view in *The Explicit Animal*. See also Raymond Tallis, 'Against Dr. Panglum', *Prospect*, January 2001.

30. See Ludwig Wittgenstein's *On Certainty* (Oxford: Blackwell, 1974) for a profound exploration of this notion of the interconnectedness of understanding.

31. This is spelt out in great detail in *The Explicit Animal*. It is, however, rather unsatisfactory to think of 'reason' as the distinctive feature of human beings. This is not because cynics feel duty-bound to break out into wild laughter when we talk about 'Man, the Rational Animal', but because reason (though it is much wider than rationality and what informs reasonable, temperate behaviour), seems too thin, and to capture too little of the density of the human presence and co-presence. 'Explicitness' is better because it encompasses reason, and language, future orientation, etc. We shall return to this issue in Volume 3, *The Knowing Animal: A Philosophical Inquiry into Knowledge and Truth*.

32. It should hardly be necessary to point this out, were not so many writers so determined to ignore what is in front of their nose in order to place humans – morally, intellectually, etc. – on all fours with animals. The commonest reason for wanting to do this rather odd thing is that it makes the world tidier and easier for the practitioners of scientism to make complete and unified sense of the world. Since Darwin, the exceptional nature of humans – who do things like writing *The Origin of Species* – has been a bit of an embarrassment. As Ruth Willats (personal communication) has pointed out, only some animals are singled out for special treatment; for example, whales have been lifted on a wave of sentiment – they were seemingly harmless (tell that to Captain Ahab) and faced extinction – and granted cognitive achievements their CVs hardly justify. She suggests that animal worship 'goes deeper than a revulsion at the horrors of the twentieth century or even a corrective to, say, Descartes' assertion that vivisection is OK as animals don't feel pain' and it is of relevance 'that polytheistic societies typically have *animal* gods. We've always, it seems, wanted to believe that animals are in some way our superiors.'

33. See my *Not Saussure*, especially Chapter 4, 'Reference restored'; and *The Explicit Animal*, especially Chapter 7, 'Recovering consciousness'.

34. This is the opposite of the tarsier's all-purpose 'grab' described by Napier in *Hands*, p. 97.

35. Quantum indeterminacy was frequently invoked in the twentieth century as a lifeline for the notion of human freedom because it seemed to offer a way out of the prison of causal determinism. There are several reasons for dismissing this as daft. First, quantum indeterminacy applies to the world of micro-physics, which is hardly the world of the macroscopic human agents. Secondly, quantum physics applies

indifferently to human bodies, to pebbles and to stars, while only humans are free. Thirdly, indeterminacy is not something that can be controlled or exploited by the entities that exhibit it: it is just as remote from active 'doing' as is linear or non-linear causation. Micro-physical randomness, in short, does not deliver macroscopic human freedom.

All that quantum mechanics has to offer to those seeking to understand the origin of agency in a world of causation is the suggestion that the universe is indeterminate in the absence of measurements – and hence of the observers who make the measurements. This seems to take the conscious subject into the heart of the material world. How to move forward from this, however, is not clear. We shall revisit this issue in Volume 2, *I Am: A Philosophical Inquiry into First-Person Being*.

36. See section 5.2, 'The Carnal Hand'.
37. The relationships we establish with another's body in lovemaking are founded on the relationships we have with our own bodies. This is perhaps less obvious than may appear at first sight. The haunted, owned, body, with its hierarchy of privacy and privilege access is the child of the complex instrumental relationship we have to ourselves through our bodies as a result of the special relationship to our hands. See also Raymond Tallis, 'Carpal knowledge: A natural philosophy of the caress', *Philosophy Now*, September/October 2001, pp. 24–7.
38. Perception and action cannot be extricated from one another except in the imaginary moment of purely passive contemplation. (Even the still fisherman holding himself ready for a bite or the still thinker refraining from all movement receives a steady report of the motor presence of his own body in the continuous corrective effort to maintain motionless posture.) And this integration is even more clearly evident when the hand is active. As Paillard points out, 'Manipulation is assisted by tactile information which the cortical projection map develops proportionately with the corresponding motor map' (in Berthelot and Chavaillon, *The Use of Tools by Human and Non-Human Primates*, p. 40). There are, however, separate pathways to deal with the palpatory hand 'concerned with the intake of sensory information' and 'the executive hand for grasping' (p. 40). Integration takes place only at the highest level, when the action of the knowing hand is assumed by a self.
39. It is important not to confuse this existential tautology – 'A *is* itself'; I *am* (this thing that I *am*) – with the mere logical form of the tautology: 'A = A'. 'Existential tautology' may be an unfortunate term and 'existed identity' or 'the existential intuition' may be better. For a detailed discussion, see Volume 2, *I Am: A Philosophical Inquiry into First-Person Being*.
40. 'If I use my teeth to eat with, no-one can consider my teeth as a tool. However, if I use them to work leather with, the question remains open to discussion' (Sigaut, in Berthelot and Chavaillon, *The Use of Tools by Human and Non-Human Primates*, p. 405).

Incidentally, animals' comparative lack of (discretionary) instrumental use of various parts of the body (as opposed to stereotyped instinctive uses, as when a goat butts, a cow kicks, two deer lock antlers) explains why it seems so funny when they make non-standard, instrumental uses of body parts; as when, for example, a dog stands on its hind legs and punches another dog.
41. The complex relationship we have with our own bodies – being, suffering, owning, using, pleasure, looking after them – will be discussed in the two volumes to come.
42. See Mircea Eliade (quoted in Berthelot and Chavaillon, ibid., p. 406):

tools are not a prolongation of the body organs. The most ancient stones that we know of were worked with an aim that did not prefigure in the human body. This is specifically the case in cutting (an action which is different from tearing with the teeth or scratching with nails).

43. Another manifestation of this is the emerging status of the body as an exhibit to be flaunted – as in dancing or simply self-exposure – and in adornment. The imperative to control our appearance – to make it clean-looking, smart, sweet-smelling – and, more generally, 'to prepare a face to meet the faces that we meet' – is a further development of this instrumental relationship to our bodies, so that we can conceive of it as an object of another's awareness and as something to be manipulated. The external appearance of the hand itself may be the object of our solicitude, as in manicure. (Only an evolutionary psychologist would need to have it pointed out that the instinctive modifications of appearance seen in, say, a cat puffing itself out when it meets an adversary is not the same as the image-consultant guided, magazine-advised modifications sought by contemporary humans.)

The very complex, mediated, instrumental relations humans have to their own bodies is manifested in the practice of medicine. Through the notion of professional physicians and their predecessors – healers, shamans, priests – certain forms of unpleasant bodily self-awareness (suffering, disability) are transformed into instances of general categories of sickness, for which there are a certain general kinds of explanation and to which there applies a body of knowledge and practices. The transition from the experience of illness to the notion that one is suffering from devil possession or renal failure is a huge step towards the instrumentalisation of one's body in which it is generalised and objectified. The first step – the era of shamanism – is a compromise: the illnesses are seen to be embedded in the kind of person one is; the second step – the era of scientific medicine – takes generalisation and objectification much further – to the point where the only personal aspect of illness (which otherwise is about the impersonal processes of the living matter of which the body is composed) is one's experience of 'it', the illness. (I discuss this in greater depth in *Hippocratic Oaths: Contemporary Medicine and Its Discontents*, Grove Atlantic, forthcoming.)

44. This general concern about the objective appearance and meaning of our body in another's gaze shades into the notion of the body as an asset, or as having assets (pause for schoolboy sniggers, etc.) and another's body as an asset, a trophy, a possession. The instrumental relation to one's own body is the founding intuition which underpins the instrumental relation to others, particularly of males in relation to females – women as chattels, as gifts, as a means of exchange. We note in passing that designation of the male sexual organ as a tool (with no comparable designation of a female sexual organ) reflects the relative power structures in the sexual relationship. The male tool is the instrument of his own pleasure and the servant of his desires, into which the female is incorporated. It is an instrument which acts upon material.

45. The active nature of sign-use is most apparent when signs are arbitrary. Arbitrariness, which permits signs to be used in combination and in syntactical and semantic cooperation – so that items which have no meanings by themselves may contribute to the meaning of a phrase or longer sequence which does have meaning by itself – is a distinctive feature of human language.

This very clear difference between animal communication and human discourse shows in what way Savage-Rumbaugh and Rumbaugh are incorrect when they assert that

By viewing language as the inevitable outcome of the social interaction of intelligent creatures, humankind may lose some sense of uniqueness, but gain in return a deeper understanding of itself. (in Gibson and Ingold, *Tools, Language and Cognition in Human Evolution*, p. 106)

The kind 'of social interaction of intelligent creatures' is precisely what is unique about humans. Human language is unique not only in what it is – how it works, what it achieves – but also in respect of the unique circumstances, the unique precursors, it requires to bring it into being.

46. The arguments briefly touched on here are set out in more detail in Raymond Tallis, 'Is human freedom a self-fulfilling illusion?', *Monist* (in press).

47. The superficial analogy with Descartes' argument for the existence of a Perfect or Infinite Being – if such a being did not actually exist imperfect and finite beings could not have conceived of it, consequently, since they do conceive of it, it must exist – is not entirely accidental.

48. For a more detailed discussion, see 'That I am this thing', in Tallis, *On the Edge of Certainty*.

49. I am inclined (for reasons that are not entirely clear to me) to quote Paul Valéry when he said that 'Desire *qua* desire cannot be an illusion. Like the God of St. Anselm, the idea of it and its existence are identical'. I am inclined, almost, to invoke Descartes' argument (alluded to in note 44) for the existence of God. A finite/ imperfect being (such as RT) could not conceive of an infinite/imperfect being, so the notion of such a being must have been implanted in her or him by a real Perfect or Infinite Being. I am most inclined, however, to underline the argument that the step by which we acquire an explicit identity, as being this (not-quite-bodily) thing, is the same as the step which makes us true agents. This will be further discussed in Volume 2.

50. Likewise angels or disembodied minds: they would have nothing to 'be about'. Their lives would be empty of content (not even Forms to contemplate or equations to mull over): undifferentiated, viewpointless, lackless, desireless, needless, stasis would be their daily fare.

    The argument that freedom needs to be relative or unconditioned in order that it should have content shows how wrong it is to think of embodiment (or belonging to a particular culture, or a particular era, or thinking in a particular language) as a prison. Without bodies (cultures, eras, languages) and their unsatisfactoriness that leaves unfinished business, there would be no particular agenda: we would have nothing to strive for, to lack, to be concerned about, actively to be in becoming. Discarnate humans would be agenda-less. (Etymologically speaking, there would be nothing 'to be moved' because there would be nowhere to move – no location, no distance – and nothing to be moved by or for.)

51. Even when we are doing things for reasons we know not, we are still doing them for reasons. And we still have to customise our actions to match the interface between general instincts and specific requirements of the situation. Choosing is still required. The person in the grip of so-called irrational forces has to deploy a considerable amount of rationality in order to act out his/her irrational wishes. Wars employ quartermasters as well as mobilising irrational passions. An *amour fou* requires a good deal of organisation: concealment, psychological games, bus timetables, etc. For more on this see Raymond Tallis, *Enemies of Hope: A Critique of Contemporary Pessimism*, 2nd edn (London: Macmillan, 1999).

52. The respect we do, or should, show to people even with quite advanced dementia is

not just respect to the person they have been – enough in itself – but also to the residual person they are. In a way, it is a respect for ourselves, for the kind of creature we are.

53. The dependence of our being full-blown agents upon our postnatal organic development – so that, for example, I can't be a true agent until myelination of the central nervous system has reached a certain stage – is no more shocking than the fact that I am not an agent in the womb. The increasing understanding we have of the complex (unconscious, unchosen) mechanisms that underpin our freely chosen actions also seems to put great pressure on the notion of agency. Agency, however, never is, nor ever can be, pure: it is always built on (and indeed built out of) bodily mechanisms – as we have noted at intervals in this book, in particular in section 2.3, organic happening is the very fabric of human doing.

54. See Paul Valéry, *Idée Fixe*. It is discussed in Raymond Tallis, *Newton's Sleep: Two Cultures and Two Kingdoms* (London: Macmillan, 1995). See 'The myth of enrichment'.

55. This may sound rather Kantian. And indeed it is, to the extent that it lifts the issue of freedom above the question of the properties of the material world and postulates an internal relationship between the self and its freedom: the assumption of the self and the assumption of agency are interlinked. It is Kantian also to the extent that the self and its freedom are assumptions that are not part of the empirical world. It is not Kantian inasmuch as it does not postulate a transcendental realm – equivalent to his noumenal realm – for this creates insuperable difficulties in connecting this undifferentiated realm with the specific realities of the empirical world of ordinary life. (We shall return to this in Volume 2.)

56. Mary Midgeley, in her recent book (*Science & Poetry*, London: Routledge, 2001), points out that the most worrying sense of 'determinism' is that of 'outside compulsion'. However, if what I am determines what I do, then I am not compelled from outside in what I do. We could develop this argument by saying that the more intimate the intrusion of outside forces, the more I am that which is intruding and the less, therefore, I am intruded upon and the more I am that which is doing the determining.

The insight, which the next volume develops, is that the emergence of the 'I', in virtue of which I appropriate (or 'assume') that which I am – a quasi-tautology that both presupposes and precedes its outcome – lifts us above the determinant-determined pairings of determinism. The emergence of the 'I' and its freedom seem to be simultaneous. If there is 'I' then there is freedom.

This still leaves a seriously unsolved problem: the emergence of an 'I' (out of nature) that makes nature its object does not change the rest of nature, in particular, the relationship between 'I''s body and the material world it interacts with. So the emergence of a free 'I' does not free us from nature. All it does is make nature the object and theatre of our freedom. Even so, although the initial awakening of agency is such a small event, it leads to large things; so large that, as a recent atlas shows us, half of the world's surface has been changed by man and 25 per cent of it has been ploughed or concreted over.

57. Incidentally, we shouldn't get too excited about what neuroscience has or has not to tell us about the freedom or otherwise of humans and the reality or unreality of agency. While recent discoveries about brain activity and higher mental functions may seem to some to suggest that our unfreedom and the grip of nature penetrates to the core of our being, in practice all they do is to focus the problem of the relative

freedom of the agent on a particular part of the causal net or the material world. It recasts the general challenge of getting clear about how agents can relate to the sea of causation as a more specific conundrum about how agents can arise out of a meshwork of bodily, more specifically cerebral, mechanisms. It neither adds to nor substracts from our ordinary understanding of the matter, in accordance with which we are entangled to a lesser or greater degree in material causes. The question still remains: How is our freedom entangled? How does it get disentangled so that we can operate upon the tangle of which we are a part?

58. See Tallis, *On the Edge of Certainty*; and Volume 3 of this trilogy.

59. This is discussed in more detail in Tallis, *The Explicit Animal*. See especially pp. 38–43.

60. And we have to remember that the hand itself was generated by unconscious mechanisms: the evolutionary processes that give rise to it phylogenetically and the developmental processes that enable it to self-shape in the womb. By contrast, attempts to produce deliberately something that approximates even a few of the features of the hand, using even the most advanced technology, fail dismally and look like doing so for the forseeable future.

61. We have sometimes talked in this chapter about the hand as if it operated, and we lived, in a language-less world. And, of course, for most of its history, 'manukind' has been language-less. I hope, however, that the previous chapter has pre-empted any impression that I have overlooked the role of language as a crucial engine in driving the more recent stages of the awakening of the cultured self out of the biological organism. All of these things – language, tools, sociality, larger brain and increased general intelligence – have interacted. For example, handly touch lies close to the the sense of possibility that lies around the cradle of linguistic consciousness. I award the palm to the hand only because it was in at the beginning. Our progressive differentiation began with the hand but it was soon reinforced by its own products and cerebral consequences.

62. Kate Soper, quoted in Malik (*Man, Beast and Zombie*, p. 53). Ingold (*Tools, Language and Cognition in Human Evolution*, p. 467) talks about

> a tension in Western thought between the thesis of man's absolute separation from, and domination over, the world of nature (including animals), and the counterthesis that all living forms (including humans) can be ranged in a single continuum or chain of being.

This is a tension reflected in my own thinking – that of a biologically trained, philosophically minded individual. Darwin's attempt to bypass this tension by suggesting that, instead of a chain, there was an ever-branching tree, doesn't really address our (well-founded) feeling that there is something unique and exceptional about human beings. Demoting us from the top of the tree to the tip of a branch on a bush doesn't really help: there may not be single chain of being but, while humans and chimpanzees are both different from, say, cats, the way the human is different from a cat is different from the way a chimp is. The way humans are different from all other animals is different from the way other animals are different from each other.

63. See the discussion of Nietzsche's biologisation of knowledge in *On the Edge of Certainty*, pp. 32–44; and Volume 3 of this trilogy.

64. The originating and abiding error of sociobiology – whose central notion is that social behaviour is shaped by gene-based instincts designed to ensure the replication of those very same genes – is that it fails, or refuses, to acknowledge this funda-

mental gap between instinct-driven organisms and reason-invoking, choosing humans. It tries to get biology to straddle both sides of this divide which has been getting deeper and wider for at least 500,000 years. Adaptive determinism as applied to organisms cannot encompass individual judgements and cultural choices. To put this another way: the little we understand about animals is not helpful to our understanding humans and neither undercuts nor supersedes the fantastic amount we know about humans, beginning with our unique knowledge of what it is like to be ourselves.

My position is not that we are not derived from animals. Of course we are: we did not fall from the sky. But the millions of years during which we have progressively deviated from animals is enough to make most organism-based explanation of our behaviour (as opposed to our kidneys' behaviour) totally useless. A description of the roots does not capture the rustling of the leaves.

65. In Volume 3, we shall discuss how the transition from sentience (which humans share with other beasts) to knowledge (which is unique to humans) uncouples humans from nature, permitting them to engage with it on more favourable terms than do other creatures.

CODA

CHAPTER 11

Waving Farewell to the Hand

11.1 INTRODUCTION

We have almost reached the end of our attempt to get a grip on the human hand, a structure whose manipulative skills have taken us humans to places, indeed to worlds, which are ours alone. Every aspect of our inquiry has generated more questions than it has discovered answers. The reader has been exposed to some fairly reckless speculation, especially in the last few chapters where we alighted upon such matters as the origin of human number sense and the interrelationships between hand and brain and between tools, language, intelligence and gesture. Most recklessly, I have endeavoured to bring biology to the very frontiers of metaphysics and to found a genetic anthropology upon the explosive consequences of a few accidents of biology. This is not, of course, to fall into biologism – which aims to explain present human nature exclusively in terms of our organic present or past; but rather to suggest how it was that we humans, alone among all species, in some respects escaped our biological destiny and were able to place greater and greater distances between ourselves and our organic heritage, distances that may be measured by comparing ourselves with our nearest animal cousins. How, in short, we extricated ourselves from nature.

My hostility to biological reductionism is connected with another purpose of this book, of equal importance as its explanatory ambitions – that of celebration. I want to say, and to justify saying, 'What a piece of work is man (or woman)!' While the latest chapters of this inquiry are argumentative and analytical, the earlier chapters, which are more descriptive, are, therefore, just as close to its mission. I have wanted to share my astonished admiration at the versatility of the hand – and of the manual creatures who possess and are possessed by it – at least as much to advance theories about its key role in lifting us out of total immersion in organic life. Although the (evolved, organic) hand may be the link between nature and culture, the distance between hands and paws – as lavishly demonstrated by what we humans do with our unaided and aided hands – is enormous. The harder we look at humans and at chimpanzees, the greater and more profound the differences we see between them. Even if we compare something relatively simple – for example, the chimpanzee's use of gesture with the human elaborations of gestures that were discussed in Chapter 3 – we still see vast differences between us and them. And if we compare a grown-up chimpanzee that has finally learned the use of a percussion hammer to crack open a nut – the highest expression of tool-using in the animal kingdom – with an engineer poring over the computer-generated plans for a factory making components for a piece of advanced technology, then we can see that our animal cousins are not even poor relations – or paw relations: they live in a different universe, albeit on the same planet.[1] Celebration, then, has been just as important as explanation, if only as a way making clear the enormity of what it is that has to be explained.

It might be thought unnecessary to labour the difference between humans and animals; that the scale and depth of the gulf between us and them is so obvious that no one needs to point it out. Alas, this is not so. Much of the thought of the twentieth century was dominated by utterly debased accounts of human nature and the belief that man, if not an empty zombie, was a beast – and of a particularly unpleasant kind.[2] A multitude of (often warring) sciences (molecular biology, neurology, neuropsychology, etc.) and pseudo-sciences (sociobiology, psychoanalysis, evolutionary psychology, etc.) have denied the distinctive nature of human beings.[3]

The attack on human exceptionalism is frequently presented as an inevitable consequence of Darwinism and the result of a mature understanding of our status arising out of the modern synthesis of molecular genetics (which has shown that amongst other things we share 99 per cent of our DNA with chimpanzees) and evolutionary theory.[4] Anyone who disagrees with omnicompetent fundamentalist Darwinism is liable to be accused of rejecting the findings of science, or of being anti-science itself, or of being in the grip of an explicit or dishonestly concealed religious agenda.[5]

That is why it has seemed necessary to labour the differences between humans and all other creatures in order to make them visible even to those who are bewitched by 'Darwinismus' – an inflamed state of Darwinian thought in which evolutionary theory is the only framework within which it is permitted to think about human nature. There is much, as we have seen, to make visible. The distances between humans and their nearest animal kin[6] are vast and they span many dimensions. For this reason, there is very little that one can say usefully about human psychology, or human behaviour or human society, on the basis of our presumed kinship with the animals. We share with them certain physiological requirements – for food, drink, shelter, regular bowel actions, etc. – but in this respect we are no closer to chimpanzees than to cats, mice or anteaters, which are rarely looked to as role models to help us understand our our own actual or desirable behaviour. We are closer to other primates with respect to certain instincts but these instinctive behaviours – for example, those relevant to mother–child interactions – are so utterly transformed by differences of context between humans and even the highest non-human primates that lessons learnt from animal behaviour are at best banal reinforcements of lessons learned from watching humans directly and at worst directly misleading, giving seeming additional authority to views that are based merely upon intuition.[7]

By using the human hand to increase the visibility of these differences, as well as to help us to understand how they came about, one of my aims has been to inhibit the excessive ease with which we seem to cross the human–animal boundary when we are seeking a better understanding of ourselves. It is far too tempting when we are looking out from within the human world to imagine that there is a continuum between human animals and non-human primates, the latter and lower mammals, and so on. We might be less inclined to imagine this if we envisaged the animals looking in and considered what, if any, sense they could make of most of the things we do. The analogy I offered in *Enemies of Hope*[8] was that of the ha-ha in a country house, which marks the boundary between culture (the garden) and nature (the parkland beyond) and is aimed at preventing animals from straying into the garden and causing damage. The ha-ha permits an uninterrupted view, spanning culture and nature if one looks outwards from the garden to the country park. The view, from the standpoint of an animal at the bottom of the ha-ha, however, is rather more restricted; far from seamless continuity, there is a formidable, indeed, insuperable, barrier: it is many hundreds of thousands of years deep and, like the Wall of Death in the circus, it is steepest at the top, matching the exponential rate of development of human culture.

11.2 THE PARADOX OF HANDYMAN: (1) PART OF AND SEPARATE FROM NATURE

It is one thing to emphasise the discontinuity between humans and the rest of the animal kingdom; quite another to understand it – especially for someone like myself: biological science has permeated the intellectual air I have breathed since childhood. (At the age of fifteen I declared myself to be 'a biochemical materialist'.) The challenge, for anyone trying to develop a philosophical anthropology that doesn't depend upon the assumption that we have fallen from the sky is that of turning one's back on biologism without at the same time turning one's back on biology and the biological facts about us; to take account of what science has told us about human nature without succumbing to scientism. In focusing on the special properties of the human hand – and its wide influence on the rest of the body (notably the brain) – I have tried to account at least in part for our uniqueness in terms of biological facts without leaving human beings entirely steeped in their organic nature. The hand, I have argued, has lifted us out of the state of nature over the threshold into an entirely different, a cultural, realm which cannot be understood in organic, or biological, terms.

Whereas collectively the passage from organic nature to human culture seems an irreversible step (unless some natural or manmade catastrophe destroys the fabric of our various civilisations), individually this is only temporary; indeed, slightly more temporary than the span of a human life. We begin as organisms; then, through organic development and cultural induction, rise above our organic state (though we are always kept in touch with it through our organic needs and the vulnerability of our bodies to accident and illness) into mature agents; and finally sink back into our organic state as we unravel or 'undevelop' towards the ending of our lives. Our brief arc through the light of the collective cultural life of humanity is enclosed between an organic beginning and an organic ending and the return of the organism is always at hand.[9] Throughout this arc, nature is both nurture and threat; there is consequently a profound ambivalence in our relationship to nature and in the manner in which we must conceive of it. In waving farewell to the hand, let us examine this first.

The puzzle of our relationship to nature is of particular concern to thinkers – increasingly predominant since the Enlightenment – for whom it is a matter of irrefutable fact that man is a piece of nature; that, far from being a spiritual child of God, *Homo sapiens* is an animal of sorts. For Enlightenment thinkers this was an essential underpinning of the progressive notion that human beings and their institutions could be approached using the same methods as scientists had used so successfully in extending their understanding of the natural world: the dispassionate gaze of the *philosophe*, unclouded by the priestly dogma of the past, could mobilise reason and empirical observation to discover principles that would inform the reformation of human society and erode the tyranny of traditional custom and practice upon which so much injustice and suffering was founded. Most Enlightenment thinkers, while accepting that man was a piece of nature, still held that he was set off from the natural world by his rationality, which enabled him to be pulled by reasons rather than simply pushed by causes, tropisms or instincts. Where that reason came from was not made clear and, indeed, not all Enlightenment philosophers were equally convinced of its existence as a distinct capacity: man could just as well be seen as a machine as a rational agent. Julien de la Mettrie's extreme vision of man as a carnal machine, a totally mechanistic and materialistic account of the human mind reduced to the functioning of the brain, was however unacceptable even to the most irreligious of his fellow *philosophes*. The notion of man as a piece of nature was softened by, as it were, keeping reason above the miasma of organisms interacting with one another and their environment.

It was Darwin who, by embedding human origins in the processes evident throughout nature, opened the way for the complete assimilation of man to Nature. The full implications of what Daniel Dennett has dubbed 'Darwin's Dangerous Idea' were not entirely apparent to himself and it has been left to his successors, especially in the second half of the twentieth century, to draw them out. Sociobiology and evolutionary psychology are but two strands in a complex nexus of intellectual currents whose collective tendency is to cancel the distance between man and Nature; between the human mind and human society on the one hand and natural processes on the other. Although there is no obligation even for a biological scientist to be a fundamentalist neo-Darwinian, it is difficult to maintain human exceptionalism without seeming to reject the spectacularly successful intellectual framework of contemporary biology; difficult to affirm human uniqueness without seeming to overlook, or even to deny, man's animal origins, his animal properties and organic needs. Even the notion that man has a special relationship to Nature of which he is a part seems to imply that one believes in something that is underwritten by a corresponding relationship to some kind of transcendent Being and brings one too close to the views of Bible Creationists.

Nevertheless, many post-Darwinian thinkers have felt the need for some kind of explanation of our exceptional status. As Bowler says:

> stories of human origins are told to emphasize how we came to differ from the rest of animals, or how we become separated from nature. Yet the most controversial aspect of Darwinism was that it insisted on 'man's place *in* nature'. It undermined the traditional distinctions between humans

and animals (possession of a soul) and forced us to think of ourselves as products of the natural process.[10]

There was the suggestion, put forward by the well-respected biologist Hugo De Vries, that a massive mutation could lead to the instantaneous production of a new species through the appearance of individuals with entirely new characteristics. J. Arthur Thompson similarly argued that 'primitive man expressed a mutation, a sudden uplift, separating him by a leap from the animal' (in Bowler, ibid., p. 49). As Bowler points out, 'mutations in this context could all too easily become an excuse for treating the appearance of the human mind as an unprecedented step into a new world, just as earlier thinkers such as Charles Lyell had appealed to a saltative origin for mankind to defend their belief in the human soul' (ibid.).

The gradualist view presented in this book – applicable to both the evolution of the unique versatility of the human hand and of the cultural consequences of this – would seem, *prima facie* at least, to be less vulnerable than these earlier attempt to preserve the exceptional status of human beings. A small but crucial biological difference leads to an increasingly wide divergence between man and his nearest animal kin. The margin of agency built into the proto-instrumental hand makes possible ever more elaborate tool-use. This initiates a process gradually leading to increasingly complex sociability and, eventually, linguistic communication. Sociability and language drive each other and shape a common neural substratum until there emerges a separate cultural sphere which is able to develop autonomously – once an 'escape velocity' has been reached and the gravitational field of purely organic life sufficiently attenuated. By this means, an accident of biology results in a concatenation of mutually reinforcing and enhancing developments from which there emerge human faculties, skills, preoccupations, etc. for which biological explanations and biological understanding are no longer appropriate.

This account of the biological origin of human culture does not require us to deny either that we are fundamentally different from animals or that we are derived from animals and that we are still organisms. It allows us to be rooted in nature, but not immersed in it, or even, in any helpful sense, explained by it, except in so far as our bodily being defines us. We have our roots in the natural world of the evolved organisms we are but these roots are not sufficient to give an account of the leaves of the human culture in which we live.[11] Or, less ambitiously, we can be partly part of nature and partly free of nature.

This long-term effect of our gradual, but importantly and manifestly incomplete, liberation from our organic state should be no less difficult to understand or to defend than the fact that, individually, we are both the site of (conscious and unconscious) mechanisms and, at the same time, agents of more or less chosen actions. Or that we should be the unchosen agents of chosen actions. (We shall revisit this in Volume 2.)

And yet there is something that remains deeply unexplained. It is the extent and profundity of the transformation of our relationship to nature: the completeness of an inversion whereby man's place in nature is replaced, or echoed, by nature's place in man; such that, by thought, humans collectively enclose the nature by which they are enclosed. We cannot, it seems, provide a satisfactory naturalistic explanation of the thing called mind which does this inversion.

This concern is captured in the passage cited in the previous chapter:

> That evolution, over all-but-infinite time, could change one physical organ into another, a leg into a wing, a swim bladder into a lung, even a nerve net into a brain with billions of neurons, seems remarkable, indeed, but natural enough. That evolution, over a period of a few million years, should have turned physical matter into what has seemed, in the most literal sense of the term, to be some kind of metaphysical entity is altogether another matter.[12]

Once mind starts to reflect upon nature – indeed to develop the notion of nature – not only does it cease to be comprehensible as being a part of nature; it comes to seem very odd that it had anything to do with nature at all. The strongest argument against the belief that Darwinism explains everything is that there is such a thing as a Darwinist. The idea of The Theory of Evolution as a little by-secretion of the material evolutionary process seems implausible.[13]

Here the hand can help us only to a degree, and here we must focus in the future. One thing is for sure; any solution to this problem will require us to be prepared to undertake a radical rethink of the kinds of things we believe the world to be made of.

11.3 THE PARADOX OF HANDYMAN: (2) SUBJECT TO AND YET MANIPULATING NATURE'S LAWS

We have assigned the hand a key role in lifting us out of our state of nature and liberating us from the organic condition in which all other animals are immersed. Culture and civilisation are built by the hand – and the tools it creates to augment its powers – and repose ultimately in the special versatility of human hands. Even if this thesis is not accepted in full – and the complementary or possibly more fundamental roles of language and/or general intelligence are highlighted instead – the central importance of the hand in transforming the conditions under which the human animal lives its life cannot be denied.[14] The question we have to ask ourselves is this: How did the hand pull it off? If the hand is the link between Nature and Culture, how did the hand lift us above our state of nature?

We have placed the intuition of agency, arising out of the manipulative indeterminacy of the self-addressing hand, at the heart of the matter. This intuition of agency has a built-in guarantee of truth because it is linked to the sense of self: 'That I am this [thing]' and 'That I bring things about' or 'That these events are my actions' or 'That I am these events' are bound together like conjoint twins. They lie at the origin of a process whereby a gathering sense of personhood, of 'I', and a progessively elaborated assumption of control – through the hand and its tools and through the cognitive and social spin-offs from these – spiral upwards together, like the two strands of a double helix, connected by numerous cross-bridges. The scope of agency is not, of course, unlimited; indeed, it may be more limited than the agent believes. But the constraints on agency, we have argued, are not to be understood simply as limitations: they are also necessary to give agency its specific content; the facticity that gives the agency something to be about, something to will. That was the story recounted in the last chapter. It aimed not only to explain how the human agent could break free of, and shape, the causal nexus of which he or she, as an organism, is a part, but also the role of the uniquely dexterous human hand in the passage of humans from Nature to Culture.

We have elaborated the story at some length, but there is an unanswered question at the root of it. It is a question that J. S. Mill tried, and failed, to answer in his essay on 'Nature'.[15]

Mill distinguished two meanings in the term 'Nature': in the first, 'Nature is a collective term for everything which is'; in the second, 'it is a name for everything which is of itself, without voluntary human intervention'. 'Nature' in this second sense is how things, left to themselves, will be. He uses this distinction to demonstrate the vacuity of the recommendation that one should 'act according to nature':

> To bid people to conform to the laws of nature when they have no power but what the laws of nature give them – when it is a physical impossibility for them to do the smallest thing otherwise than through the laws of nature, is an absurdity. (ibid., p. 152)

There is, however, the germ of an idea in this recommendation. 'Though we cannot emancipate ourselves from from the laws of nature as a whole,' Mill argues,

> we can escape from any particular law of nature, if we are to withdraw ourselves from the circumstances in which it acts. Though we can do nothing except through laws of nature, we can use one law to counteract another. According to Bacon's maxim, we can obey nature such as to command it. Every alteration of circumstances alters more or less the laws of nature under which we act; and by every choice which we make either of ends or of means, we place ourselves to a greater or lesser extent under one set of laws of nature instead of another. (ibid., pp. 152–3)

The 'useless precept' that we should follow nature could be rescued if it were changed to a precept to study nature:

> to know and take heed of the properties of the things that we have to deal with, so far as these properties are capable of forwarding or obstructing any given purpose. (ibid., p. 153)

Then 'we should have arrived at the first principle of all intelligent action, or rather at the definition of intelligent action itself'.

This is not as clear, or as reassuring, as it may at first seem. You cannot buck the laws of nature, Mill argues, even in order to conform to them deliberately, in order to obey the precept *Naturam sequi*. You are completely in their thrall. What you can do, however, is so to position yourself that you fall under, or have to conform to, one law – one that will promote your purposes – rather than another that will confound them. You cannot go against the grain of nature, but you need to align yourself with the grain that is compatible with your aims.

This sounds momentarily persuasive until we ask the next, obvious, question: By what natural law am I permitted to choose the natural law which will serve my purposes? *Nous sommes embarqués.* Indeed, we are more than embarked: we are immersed. The laws of nature are the very thread, and indeed the weaving, that makes the fabric of our being. How can I rise above the laws in which I am already immersed in order to arrange to fall under the law of my choice? By what means, precisely, can I, who am a part of nature, command nature through obeying it? If it seems absurd to imagine requisitioning the laws of nature to serve our purposes, is it any less absurd to imagine positioning oneself in order to choose one in preference to another? In both cases, we seem to have to lift ourselves up out of nature by our natural bootstraps and our natural arms. It seems impossible.

The key notions are that of 'positioning' oneself in order to conform to the law of one's choosing – and so to exploit that law – and that of the transcendence of the natural world that this seems to require. Where is this positioning going to come from? Whence this transcendence?

The answer perhaps lies in the account of agency given earlier. Bootstrapping will be made possible through the lived quasi-tautology of the agentive self: existed identity will plant the flag of deixis – of 'me', 'here', 'now' – in the impersonal vastness of objective nature. The 0,0,0 coordinates corresponding to the self's position at the exact (exact because logical) centre of egocentric space create the transcendent position from which it is possible to position and reposition oneself with respect to this law or that. (In fact, in the early, pre-scientific history of humankind and most of the history of most of us, it is nothing so grand as a Law of Nature that is at issue; more a question of this material opportunity or that, this strategy or another, this way round or an alternative. It is only when we develop technologies that laws of nature are suborned explicitly to our ends; and, for most of us – users rather than creators of technologies – the laws of nature are out of sight, embedded in our technologies.)[16]

The argument that lies at the heart of this book – beneath the equally important celebrations – is that the hand is the instrument of the transcendence required to bring us out of nature sufficiently to manipulate it beyond the kind of manipulations that are available to animals. The margin of indeterminacy in our choice of grasps – using an organ that is in unprecedented communication with itself – on the world is the model that awakens agency, the 'lived tautology' of the self: it is the microscopic harbinger of the macroscopic manipulations that technological man, working collectively, imposes on the natural world. Literal grasping and manipulation are not only the supreme metaphor, but the precursor of problem-solving. Ultimately, we owe to our wonderful hands our ability 'to obey nature in such a manner as to command it'. Our hands enable us to pull it off.

Out of the hand comes our self-fulfilling sense of agency and the derivative notion of blame and (even) of causation. At any rate, it lies at the origin of our sense of using natural forces to shape the world according to our (unnatural) wishes. We thumb a ride on the natural forces and by this means give way in order to get our own way. Deliberate action is an interaction between activity and passivity. Even seemingly continuous effortful action has to include passive yielding to natural forces; and that 'giving way' is itself made up of natural forces.[17]

The passivity at the heart of activity is illustrated by walking down hill, which is effectively a controlled and continuously corrected stumble.

As, indeed, is all walking, if less obviously so: the shifting of the centre of pressure, the rocking of the centre of mass from side to side, the swing phase of gait, all have seeds of passivity in their very interstices. And so also, perhaps even less obviously still, is all motor activity. In reaching out for an object, we propel our arms and they travel in accordance with Newtonian laws of motion,[18] notwithstanding that this ballistic phase is constantly being checked and, if necessary, interfered with to correct any deviation from the path of true agency. We have, in short, to rely on the material properties of our bodies and their subservience to the laws of physics in order to carry out even the most deliberate actitivies – never mind subconscious ones such as maintaining the standing position while we are busy talking. There is a constant intercutting between conscious intention, bodily mechanisms and the laws of physics. It is this that the grasping hand – as opposed to the groping paw or the alternating legs – first brings to consciousness.

The mystery of how it is possible that 'I do' can stand at the centre of some of 'This happens' gathers force as we become more and more aware of the continual presence of natural laws and of their particular manifestations in bodily mechanisms behind, before and within our actions. The manipulative indeterminacy available to a hand in intense commmunication with itself, which wakes us up out of the sleep of causation (all matter), tropism (all living matter) and instinct (higher living matter), wakens us up to causation, to laws of nature and to bodily mechanisms, has much to answer for.

11.4 THE BALANCE SHEET: (1) KNOWLEDGE. DOES THE HAND GRASP THE TRUTH?

The intuition of agency comes, we have argued, ultimately from the hand.[19] Clearly, it does not remain confined to the hand. The sense of agency assimilates many other kinds of things: the remainder of the agent's body – the hand instrumentalises our relationship to many other body parts; the tools the hand develops; the cognitive skills that interact with tools; the society that is implicit in the tools; the language that tools and society give birth to and/or are shaped by; and so on. If, however, we think of the origins of the sense of agency, we can return to the questions: Is this sense correct? Is it true? Is it valid? We have argued that agency could hardly be (generally, always) deceived about its own nature precisely because the sense of agency is born, assumed, at the same time as the sense of the self. Self and agency are internally linked. If there really are selves, if 'I' truly exists, then it is an agent. We can, however, still ask another question: not whether agency is true or real and the intuition that one truly is an agent is correct or valid, but whether the world as progressively revealed to the ever more powerful human agent – of which there can be no doubt – is the world as it truly is.

There is a short answer to this. The very fact that, collectively, human agents are getting ever more powerful must mean that man is getting something right; that humankind is accessing more and more truths about the world. The most obvious manifestation of this is the increasing effectiveness of technology based upon scientific laws of ever widening scope and predictive power. Does it really follow from this, however, that the passage from *Homo habilis* to Einstein is a journey ever deeper into truth? Is human knowledge of the world 'truer' than the chimpanzee's knowledge of the world? The answer to these questions must be yes, if we make certain (not unreasonable) assumptions about the nature of the connection between (true) knowledge and the power to change things as one wishes.

The relationship between knowledge and power has been the subject of a huge, confusing and often confused literature over the last few decades. The greater truth of science compared with the everyday understanding made available through personal experience has been challenged by (often envious) non-scientists, who claim that science is not objectively true about nature and that the truths that prevail in orthodox science are merely the truths that are promulgated by the most dominant, orthodox groups. Scientific truths moreover are human artefacts, if only because they are framed in symbolic systems (in, for example, sentences and formulae) that are human artefacts. The truths of physics belong to the human institution of the physics fraternity and the truths of astrology belong to the human institution of the astrology fraternity – and feminist relativisers of science emphasise the masculin- ity of the scientific communities – and neither is more objectively true of nature than any other. Truths, in summary, are relative to human discourse and, through the interaction of power and discourse, to the power structures of communities of discourse.

This is familiar territory, which I have explored elsewhere.[20] Suffice it to say that, if astrology and physics were equally 'true' or 'valid', it is difficult to see why the the latter is, and the former is not, a powerful tool for helping us to achieve our aims – for predicting and shaping the future. And if all truths, including scientific ones, were relative to discursive communities, why technologies based upon them – transport, medicine, information – are not confined in their effectiveness to such communities; why antibiotics produced according to science-based methods and based in the scientific understanding of bacteria and clinical trials are equally effective in all parts of the globe; and why telecommunications systems – which are a supreme expression of the science of the twentieth century – do not break down when they leave the places where the discoveries upon which they were based were made and validated. The arguments about the relationship between (true) knowledge and power, certainly as regards the natural sciences and the technologies derived from them, may be (temporarily) settled as follows. The power of technologies is the strongest evidence one could hope for of the objective truth of the knowledge underpinning of technologies. From which it follows that scientific knowledge no more boils down to the powers of human groups to impose their views on others than those powers themselves count as knowledge. Examples of power-imposed 'scientific' truths – the geocentric universe of the Church, Lysenkoist genetics – only underline the distance between objective truth and power.

While the universal applicability of scientific knowledge seems to refute the sociological argument that its truth is relative to particular communities,[21] it may not deal with the more fundamental epistemological questions as to whether the truths utilised by the human agent are relative not to particular human groups but to humanity as whole. Could it be that humanity achieved its unique mastery over the planet without its knowledge being in any objective sense true? Does the power of science-based technology really testify to the truth of science and really prove that we are more privy to the truth of nature than are our animal kin? I am inclined to say yes, for this reason: if we cannot read nature and know at least to some degree what nature is like in itself, then we shall not be able to anticipate the consequences of our actions upon natural processes. (Just as, by analogy, we cannot manipulate people without being able to read their minds and anticipate their actions and reactions.) We would not be able to manipulate nature so effectively if we had no idea what it was *in itself*. (The notion of the intrinsic nature of something needs to be clarified; we shall revisit this in Volume 3.)

This argument is strengthened by another consideration arising from the already alluded to separation between knowledge and power, or knowledge and its application, or know-how and know-that. Much of the scientific basis of current technology was established a long time before it could be put to practical application: a great deal of general know-that preceded the particular know-how made available by application of know-that. Conversely, much practical activity proceeded in advance of a full scientific understanding; for example, levers were used before the mathematical relationship between the mechanical advantage and the relative distances of the end being manipulated and the end applied to the object from the fulcrum was understood and made explicit. Once it was made explicit, of course, then more complex levers could be devised to produce more precisely controlled effects. This mutually reinforcing interaction between know-how and know-that, between independently arrived at declarative and procedural knowledge, supports the notion that both forms of knowledge are rooted in objective reality. The fact that the humans it serves are also rooted in nature and have natural needs – our great cultural developments and distances do not, as we have noted, cancel this – show that the complex activities that serve our needs must be rooted in some truths about nature. Indeed, we have to get nature right if we are to keep culture going: the most refined and abstract cultural activities depend upon a supply of food. A culture marches towards progress on its stomach.

We can, however, examine the issue at a greater depth and dig beneath the questions of whether 1) knowledge is relative to particular human groups (cultures, epochs), and 2) knowledge is relative to the human species as a whole and its collective needs. We can ask whether the ever-more powerful technology driven by our sense of agency really is based upon, and is an indirect revelation of, a more complete knowledge of how things (including ourselves) really are. In other words, we can look beyond the simple interaction between knowledge and power (truth is what I can force you to believe and which serves my particular interests) or the deeper pragmatism which asserts that truth is what 'works' (for us) and that what works is, by definition, most true or closer to the truth. We can ask whether the dabness of the hand that awoke us to the possibility of agency also woke us up to the true nature of things. Is Handyman truly awoken man? Does hand-awoken agency reveal truth? Is progressive mastery of the universe a progressive revelation of its essential character? Is the wakefulness embodied in tools, and the agency implicit in our instrumental body and its many instrumental servants, true of anything other than the inescapable truth of agency itself, along with the needs that furnish it with its agenda.

To ask these questions is to move into very difficult territory, where the notions of (propositional) truth, awareness arising out of sense experience, wakefulness and explicitness jostle for position with respect to the respective fundamentality of their relationships to what is really there. What is sensible in pragmatism asserts that the proof of the pudding is in the eating. If an action guided by a certain belief brings about the desired effect, then that belief is likely to be true. More generally, while the sense of oneself as an agent must be upheld by success in bringing about the effect one wants, there is no intrinsic truth revealed in a successful mechanism which is comprised of events that simply happen rather than being made to happen by a 'doing' or an 'action'. The world picture of the pragmatic philosopher does not allow for the difference between the 'truth' of a successful spider's web, and the truth of a successful prediction cast in the form of a proposition. Both get things 'right' in the sense of 'working', but they are 'right' in utterly different ways.

Are we then to conclude that we get things right in a way that no other animal – indeed no other form of matter – can match? Is the world revealed to the knowledge, in particular that which is explicitly based in science, that directs our successful agency the correlative of an enhanced wakefulness to what is really out there? The notions of the superior wakefulness of humans compared with animals and the complementary idea of all other beasts being (compared with us) obnubilated are difficult to sustain when we think of an exquisitely alert predator. And yet the notion, I would like to argue, is valid.

To grasp how it is true, it might be useful to approach the issue by going back to the place where, according to our argument, agency was born: in the grip applied by the human hand. The grips we apply to objects are utterly customised to them: we are able to 'respect' them in the way that animals cannot. (Whether this respect is sustained is open to question, as we shall discuss in the next section.) My precise grip that prehends the object – conforming to its outline, taking account of its texture, varying the pressure in response to perception of its weight and its fragility – in a sense also apprehends it. This apprehension is alert to the distinctive otherness of the object. Herein lies an important point of interaction between the development of dexterity and intelligence: the prehended object is explicitly there in itself. The customised grip is the opposite of the mechanical, mindless coupling of organism and environment, which characterises even the most exquisitely adapted non-human animal. It is a prehension that opens on to apprehension, which in turn opens on to comprehension.

This is the point of awakening out of mere adaptive fit (as embodied in the metabolic coupling of a lower organism and its environment, the tropisms of the more complex creatures and instinctive behaviour exhibited by higher organisms) into explicit awareness of truths about the environment and a wakefulness to the environment (as 'Other' to the 'Self') that is denied to animals. The material world has an explicit otherness, an explicit partial scrutability, that stimulates experimentation and deliberate inquiry – with grips and (eventually) with tools. The agentive self and the object of its agency are born of the act of distancing and fission. The subject–object pair creates the context in which truth (as well as explicit, correctable) falsehood is *able to emerge*.[22]

Apprehension – and the sense that the object exists in its own right and that there is something in it that has to be discovered, even if only as a preparation for an appropriation for purposes not intrinsic to it – is the basis for classification and (as we have noted), more importantly, for reclassification. Classification – and reclassification which is based upon the intuition that the first class does not exhaust what is in the object – delineates possibility and hence opens into the future tense: apprehension is like a cognitive antenna; it is a pre-set, incompletely shaped, partially indeterminate uncertainty. And it opens on to comprehension: classification succeeded by reclassification opens up the sense of an *intrinsic nature* of the object, which underpins the fundamental intuition behind scientific enquiry. The initial revelations of dexterity in turn drive, and are subsequently driven by, the ever-growing revelations of the mind.[23]

The dexterous hand, in other words, is not isolated. It soon interacts with an intelligence eventually co-driven by other factors, with language and sociability. Nor is it isolated in the literal sense of being separated from the arm: intelligence and wakefulness can creep back up the upper limb. The genius of reaching may learn much from the dazzle of dexterity. And, as Calvin has suggested, throwing may have a central role in driving the growth of intelligence and (in our terms, the sense of self and of agency).[24] Pro-jection has an etymologically satisfying relationship with the existentialist idea of a self which launches itself forward into a future – towards a goal that lies ahead in space, which also makes its 'aheadness' in time explicit.

So we assert that humans are not only more successful in achieving mastery of nature but that, unlike animals, they achieve mastery through objective explicit truths. They have a truer notion of what is there: they encounter the object at least in part on the latter's terms, conforming to the object. The grip is at the same time self-consciously a grope, imbued with the sense of the partly hidden, intrinsic nature, the otherness, of the object; with a sense that there is more to know; a sense of ignorance. The intuition of ignorance, of more to know, lies, of course, at the root of all human enquiry, informing the 'active uncertainty' (Dewey's beautifully apt phrase) of thinking.

In the beginning was the hand with its dexterity and its sensitivity and its indeterminacy; and out of the instrumental relationships the hand established within the body of the human primate arose the tools which then set out in visible space the notion of agency – of how we might control and take charge of and be responsible for events. This intuition eventually became unpacked into innumerable assertable propositions – truths and falsehoods. With the cumulative, collective experience that the sociality of tools permitted, individual awareness grew into a shared body of technical know-how and of explicit know-thats upon which our unique and progressive mastery over things is founded. (We could see tools – which exteriorise and to some extent freeze problem-solving – as generic claims, arguments, principles, set out in space; and the successful tools as precursors of accurate claims, valid arguments and true principles.) Thus did the daring, dim intuition of agency become a reality, and with it the self grew more complex and clearly defined and its relationship to the environment became not only that of an experiencing body but of a knowing mind, distanced from the world of actualities by possibilities that postulate and capture objective truths.

Bold claims are being made here; some of them bolder than I would wish to stake my reputation on. Am I really so literal-minded a realist as my arguments seem to suggest? Do I really believe that in us the natural world has woken up to what it in itself really is? If so, what has it woken up to? To matter? To the material in which we are thrown and of which we are composed? Is it true that, in the consciousness of animals, matter is comparatively unawoken; that it is dopy, even asleep, compared with its state in us? Does it make sense to think of some creatures more objectively awake than others? Does it even make sense to think of us inhabitants of the twenty-first century as more awake, conscious, aware, than were people living 2,000 years ago? Or 200,000 years ago? (Did Neanderthals miss out on the true nature and meaning of the world? Was their entire history tangential to the truths that we possess?)

More to the point, given that we have not yet reached the end of the cultural evolution of humans (indeed, we have only just picked up speed) are we – those humans alive at the beginning of the twenty-first century – only half-awake compared with a fuller, even full, conscious-ness, awakenness, to come? Is there progressive awakening? Does the future of wakefulness lie with us or with some other form of living matter? Is the true image of this awakening that of seeing something like a god face-to-face; or does it reside in the consciousness of that god, to which we shall approximate asymptotically?

The admittedly rather bizarre question as to whether matter – or the fundamental material of the universe – knows itself better in us than in a chimpanzee seems easy to answer in the affirmative, so long as we do not ask the further question of what it is that matter (or the fundamental material of the universe) would know if its self-knowledge were complete. This is a question that seems even more questionable if we doubt whether matter in itself – or the pristine stuff of the world – has any intrinsic properties, or ones, at any rate, that correspond to the kinds of experiences that we are able to have.[25] (Suppose, for example, there were no secondary qualities outside of consciousness.) And the

question as to whether human objective truths take them nearer to
wakefulness than the chimpanzee, which does not deal in such truths,
likewise seems easy to answer in the affirmative only so long as we
accept without question that living in, or with, or in access to, objective
truths is the form that definitive wakefulness would take. It seems less
clear what the answer should be if objective truths are simply one form
of wakefulness and less clear yet if they are seen as a diversion from the
wakefulness that is inherent in full-blooded immersion, enjoyed by
beasts, in the particulars of existence.

I circle round these questions not because I expect them to be
answerable, even though some writers such as Herder felt they had
answers to them.[26] I do so only to highlight the difficulties that arise
when we pass from the notion of agency – and the technology to which
it gives birth – as leading to more effective mastery of the universe on to
the idea that agency takes us deeper and deeper into truth and that we,
the bearers of those truths, step into an ever-brighter wakefulness. And
this question and uncertainty are appropriate, given that I am a member
of a species that is not only uniquely possessed of the notion of agency,
but also uniquely aware of its own impotence.[27]

We leave open the question of wakefulness – and of whether the
hand's grip reveals more of the essential nature of things as it becomes
firmer and more extensive, whether its increased mastery is based upon
more complete disclosure of the true nature of things – although we may
find it difficult to resist the belief that the cognitive balance sheet of the
hand is anything other than positive. These are deep waters and, as we
are far, perhaps too far, from the land as well as from the hand, we shall
leave their exploration to another occasion.[28]

11.5 THE BALANCE SHEET: (2) MORAL AND SPIRITUAL

Even if we accept that we know so much more than any other species,
are we any the better for it? Is (technologically self-transformed) handyman a boon to himself, quite apart from whether he is a boon to other
species or to the planet itself? In drawing up a moral and spiritual
balance sheet of the hand, we do not judge what man has achieved with
his bare hands – that, surely, must be admirable – but the impact on the
natural world and on himself of the technology that has grown out of
the dexterity of his hands and the dexterity of mind that it has fostered.
Getting this right and, in particular, being even-handed about this, is of
the utmost importance and presents the utmost difficulty. For it is
essential for thinking straight about where we humans are headed –
whether we are lumbering (if by indirection, with many setbacks and

major wobbles) towards some kind of state in which Adam's curse is rescinded and we are free fully to realise ourselves as human beings; or whether we are bound for Hell in a hand-cart.

There is, of course, no shortage of available views on this matter. There are Arcadian fantasies of a pre-technological past. Here a relaxed pastoral life, dominated by pliant nymphs and gentle shepherds playing the oaten stop and suffering mild pangs of love, is lived in a world in which keeping warm and avoiding disease and the getting of dinner seem to happen effortlessly, where conflict appears to have been pre-empted for lack of things to fall out over, and authority is replaced by fraternity. We may set such fantasies aside, though it is important to appreciate how potent an influence they have had upon thought about the place of technology in the world.[29] Even those less romantically inclined, who do not believe in a primordial state of easy happiness, may still question whether the material gains from advanced technology – comfort, security (outside of situations of conflict whose scale technology increases), increased prosperity and lengthened life expectancy – have been more than offset by losses, even if we overlook the possibility that the uneven distribution of the wealth created by technology may itself bring net suffering. The moral and spiritual consequences of advanced technology, it has been argued by many thousands of writers over the last 250 years, have been wholly negative. The roll call of those who believe that technological Handyman has a degraded relationship to the natural world (with potentially devastating consequences for the latter), to his fellow humans and to himself is impressive, encompassing figures as diverse as William Blake and Theodor Adorno.

For Heidegger, this degraded relationship to the natural world – indeed, to Being itself – was implicit in technology from its very beginnings. And technology itself reaches into the very beginning of Western civilisation; and the moral and spiritual damage it has caused, antedates the Scientific Revolution and the Industrial Revolution, with the application of power machinery to production, which followed from it. The essence of technology is 'enframing'[30] – that is, enclosing all of nature in its availability to, and manipulability by, us. Technology 'sets upon' nature, 'unlocking, transforming, storing, distributing, switching' – so that everything in nature is reduced to a 'standing-reserve'. It is revealed 'to stand by, to be immediately on hand, indeed to stand there just so it may be on call for a further ordering' (Heidegger 1977, p. 298). Technology, the distinctive contribution of Handyman to the order of things, reduces everything to something 'handy'. The adverse effect of this is very profound indeed: the continuous revelation of Being as 'handy beings' obscures other modes of revelation:

> The rule of enframing threatens man with the possibility that it could be
> denied to him to enter into more original revealing and to experience the
> call of a more primal truth. (ibid., p. 309)

Technology is, in short, in danger of becoming, or bringing, 'oblivion of
Being' and may usher in 'desolation of the earth'.

The object of Heidegger's concerns goes beyond the science-based
technology that came to prominence in the latter half of the eighteenth
century and informed the Industrial Revolution, reaching back to the
revolution of thought in Periclean Athens. He connects the 'oblivion of
Being' with the origin of 'metaphysics' and the domination of logos over
presence in the philosophy that succeeded the pre-Socratics. In this
respect, his concerns are not typical of most critics of technology; but he
shares with most critics of technology a failure to suggest an acceptable
alternative to the hand-powered transformation of the earth expressed
in technology and, in the absence of clear alternatives, even to indicate
how we might build on his arresting views in trying to formulate an
even-handed judgement on the works of the hand.

More typical than Heidegger are the enormously influential views of
Max Horkheimer and Theodor Adorno. Their *Dialectic of Enlightenment* may reasonably be taken to be representative of the anti-
technology views that came to such prominence in the twentieth
century.[31] In the famous opening of their book, they declare the Enlightenment to be the source of twentieth-century endarkenment:

> In the most general sense of progressive thought, the Enlightenment has
> always aimed at liberating men from fear and establishing their
> sovereignty. Yet the fully enlightened earth radiates disaster triumphant.
> (ibid., p. 1)

The pathologising of culture or technological civilisation is captured in
Adorno and Horkheimer's claim that

> every step in the progress of civilisation has so far been inseparable from
> a repression of the capacity of men and women to lead free and whole
> lives. (ibid.)

The replacement of myth and fancy by reason and fact, they argue,
sooner or later rebounds on demythologising humanity: the life of the
individual in a disenchanted world becomes empty. Nature, for example,
is reduced to defoliated objectivity: its happy mixture of qualities and
gods is displaced by naked quantities linked by mathematical laws.
'Men pay for the increase of their power with alienation from that over

which they exercise their power' (ibid., p. 9). The relationship to nature is the opposite of enchanted: man knows things only in so far as he can manipulate them. This eventually affects his relationship to his fellow men and ultimately to himself:

> The unity of the manipulated collective consists in the negation of each individual: for inviduality makes a mockery of the kind of society which would turn all individuals into the one collectivity. (ibid., p. 13)

When the animism 'which spiritualised the object' is supplanted by 'industrialism which objectifies the spirits of men' (ibid., p. 28), 'the individual is reduced to the nodal point of conventional responses and modes of operation expected of him'. World domination over nature 'turns against the thinking subject himself; nothing is left of him but the eternally same *I think* that must accompany all my ideas' (ibid., p. 26).

For Adorno and Horkheimer, this reduction of the individual to an instrument in a world of instruments, a means in an interlocking nexus of means, created the conditions for the mass slaughter of the world wars, total war being Taylorism conducted by other means. At any rate, reduction of the individual to a number is the result of processes set in motion by the rationalism and bureaucracy that invade every aspect of social life which is driven by the 'repressive equality' that derives ultimately from the Enlightenment ethos of the parity of all individuals. The religious faith that the Enlightenment had believed it had shown to be 'a swindle' is supplanted by 'an instrument of rational administration by the wholly enlightened as they steer society towards barbarism'.[32]

Toolmaking man – whose developing technology reached a culminating expression in industrial society and the application of power machinery to mass production[33] – interacting with a demythologised nature and despiritualised fellow men locked in rational relations, becomes imprisoned in an ever more nakedly instrumental relationship with nature, with other men and with himself. The consequences are dire: a natural world laid waste; mankind reduced to subservient tools of a dominant, but inscrutable whole, which preserves only itself; and an empty, weightless self. The work of hands has, ultimately, reduced Handyman to a hired hand. Many hands, joined through technology and the institutions it supports and by which it is supported, far from making light work, make darkness come.

This sounds utterly depressing. But the analysis of Adorno and Horkheimer is not decisive. Their negative attitude towards technology and industrialisation and their diagnosis and prognosis of civilisation raise more questions about technology than are answered. Here are a few.

1. If the life of *Homo technologicus* is so awful, would man have been better off without technology? What was life like before technology? The few facts we have suggest that it was short, hazardous and unpleasant, with little safety and less comfort. In the absence of direct evidence, the nature of personal relationships in pre-technological times has to be guessed at, but cold and hungry humans who pass their lives grubbing inefficiently in the dirt and in bloody hunting expeditions are unlikely to have been especially sensitive to each others' feelings and wishes and/or notably genteel.

2. Has technology brought material benefits? On the whole, it has. With the exceptions of some regrettable miscarriages and appalling misuses – not small, but not outweighing the overall, continuous gains – technology has brought benefits and made life materially better. Global changes in life expectancy – an increase in approximately twenty years in average life expectancy worldwide over the twentieth century (with a greater increase in developing countries than in developed countries) – is a crude but compelling indicator of increased prosperity; as is the continuous greater per capita consumption of nutriments in the developing as well as the developed world. There are still large-scale disasters and places where chronic destitution are the norm; but they are fewer than they were a hundred years ago. While material prosperity may not bring happiness, it is the ground floor of happiness. A full stomach and freedom from premature death and chronic illness are not in themselves sufficient conditions of happiness; but they are necessary conditions of happiness for most people.

3. Could there have been another way to ensure adequate material prosperity for large numbers of people? Perhaps there could have been, but no one has thought of it yet. Besides, it seems unlikely that alternative approaches, if they existed, would not have arisen in the hundreds of thousands of years of the life of *Homo sapiens* before the present modes of technology achieved dominance. One must assume that these alternative approaches, if they had been tried, did not become dominant because they failed to deliver what people needed. The history of technology in recent centuries has been story of the survival of the most effective.

Behind all these questions is the most fundamental of all: Is the state of nature, from which we have been led by the hand, and its techno-logical proxies, a desirable state? Would it have been better, spiritually and morally, for mankind if the opposability index and the saddle joint at the base of the thumb had not been such that man enjoyed unique manipulative powers? Is the nature from which our hands have delivered us beneficent?

We cannot, of course, answer this because we have even less idea about the quality of life of our pre-hominid ancestors than we do about that of our Stone Age forebears. The evidence suggests overwhelmingly, however, that nature is not beneficent. And even if it were better that hominids had never appeared on the planet, once they had appeared, it must surely have been better for them that they should have been increasingly able to improve on the state of nature in which they found themselves. For, as J. S. Mill, has expressed it:

> The scheme of Nature regarded in its whole extent, cannot have had, for its sole or even principal object, the good of human or other sentient beings.[34]

Life, for most sentient beings, is not good and the more developed the sentience the more aware beings are of this fact. What good it brings them 'is mostly the result of their own exertions':

> The order of nature, in so far as unmodified by man, is such as no being, whose attributes are justice and benevolence, would have made, with the intention that his rational creatures should follow it as an example. (ibid., p. 156)

The hand, as the great agent of the modification of nature and the servant of man's exertions is, therefore, a beneficent force.

While it is important not to exaggerate the horror of the natural world, it is even more important, if we are to think straight about the pluses and minuses of technology, not to sentimentalise it. And this applies just as much when we consider the moral status of animals as when we consider the moral status of mankind. The animal kingdom is not, on the whole, cuddly. Joseph de Maistre's vision of the natural world – though not the political position he uses to underpin it or his vision of human nature – has a compelling truth:

> In the whole vast dome of living nature there reigns an open violence, a kind of prescriptive fury which arms all creatures to their common doom: as soon as you leave the inanimate kingdom you find the decree of violent death inscribed on the very frontiers of life ... The whole earth, perpetually steeped in blood, is nothing but a vast altar upon which all that is living must be sacrificed without end, without measure, without pause, until the consummation of things, until evil is extinct, until the death of death.[35]

We must dissent from de Maistre's belief that man was the most relentless and successful killer of all. To assert this (and many in the twentieth century have echoed him) is to overlook the billion person-centuries of ordinary, often caring, behaviour and focus exclusively on war and persecution. The conditions under which man is, or would become, a wolf to man are not readily defined, but civilisation supported by technology and the direct work of hands is least favourable to violence. For all its frailty and its episodic descent into violence, and, indeed, the violence upon which it is sometimes founded, civilisation is most remote from the state of nature described by de Maistre and, indeed, by his political antithesis, Mill, who notes that

> If there are any marks at all of special design in creation, one of the things most evidently designed is that a large proportion of all animals should pass their existence in tormenting and devouring other animals[;]

and observes, with justified sarcasm,

> the apparent intention of Providence that throughout animated nature the strong should prey upon the weak. (Mill, 1885, pp. 158–9)

This indictment of nature – which still leaves out the physical threats posed by the natural world (drowning, freezing, dying of hunger and thirst, etc.) – and its implicit reminder of what human life is like in the state of nature, is an essential corrective to the sentimentalised views of those whose interactions with relatively untutored nature tend to be confined to Sunday outings, voluntary expeditions and browsings in the work of nature writers, rather than immersion in nature as an inescapable condition of existence.[36] Nature is not beneficent; at best it is even-handed between the claims of various life forms – bacteria and human children, helminths and loved parents. And those who live close to the state of nature are not necessarily more beneficent to one another than those distanced from it by the comforts of civilisation. The spiritual and ethical dimension of life is more likely to flourish in material prosperity than in destitution. 'Grub first and then ethics,' as Brecht remarked. 'Seek for food and clothing first, then the kingdom of God shall be added unto you,' Hegel said.[37] Well-fed people in warm rooms are likely to be more sensitively aware of one another than individuals starving in cold, unsheltered air. Suffering individuals tended to be isolated in and by their suffering; where all are suffering, even the most seemingly organic herd, is broken up into monads, each enclosed in his or her bubble of pain. Those who mourn the steps that have taken us further and further from the state of nature to the techno-civilisations of the present – the evolution of hominids, the emergence of *Homo habilis* and *Homo sapiens*, the development of complex societies based upon tool-use and cooperative interactions, the passage from 'organic' to 'contractual'[38] communities – should try living the (short, brutal) life of pongids, or of Neanderthals, or of pre-industrial man, or of humans with no recourse to justice or rights in pre-contractual, pre-Enlightenment societies. Whereas it may be saying too much to claim that moral and spiritual development (rather than the mere sentimental idea of it) come in the wake of the triumphs of technology, it is nonsense to assert that the uncomfortable life of man close to nature (starvation, thirst, disease) was an incubator for beneficence to one's fellows and a profound understanding of, and delight in, the given world.

This has been well expressed by Kenan Malik: 'Only through controlling nature, and transcending nature do we begin to realise ourselves as human beings, as creatures who make our history, rather than simply act it out' (2000, p. 388). 'As societies progress technologically, so the potential for moral and political progress becomes greater ... Without technological advance, without overcoming the tyranny of nature, then the scope for moral advance, for greater political freedom becomes restricted. No people enslaved to nature can achieve freedom; and the less enslaved they are, the more potential they possess to free themselves politically' (ibid., p. 368).

If we are going to be even-handed in our assessment of the work of the hand and the technology that issues from it, therefore, we must set aside inaccurate and sentimental notions: that nature is intrinsically beneficent; and that animals are morally and spiritually as beautiful as they sometimes look physically. We must acknowledge the misery inherent in living in a state of nature and the benefits of a technologically-based civilisation which, in the eye-blink between the Renaissance and the present, we have hardly yet begun fully to realise.

At the same time, however, we must also recognise that something is lost when dexterity is increasingly supplanted by tools and Handyman becomes a tender of machines. It brings with it, as so many commentators of the last two centuries have pointed out, the danger that with the progressive mechanisation of labour and the industrialisation of the fruits of labour as 'output', individuals will themselves be reduced to instruments, to components of man–machine–factory complexes. They will then be at risk not only of being themselves treated, but also of treating others, as mere instruments – as hired hands picked up or put down as one might pick up or put down a tool, agglutinated to a 'workforce' that is totally subservient to a narrowly defined end of producing ever more 'output'. Even white-collar workers may be reduced to mere instantiations of an office or (in an era of casualisation) transient expressions of a set of functions whose scope and name and provenance are forever changing.

For the anthropologist Tim Ingold, whose sentiments echo those of Heidegger, righting the wrong would involve taking back even more of the work of hands. The fundamental error, according to Ingold – and one of the basic premisses of Western thought – is the belief that 'the mission of man is to achieve mastery over nature'.[39] This error can be traced all the way back to the displacement of the presumed original mode of human existence – that of the hunter-gatherer – by a pastoralist way of life. The relationship of the hunter-gatherer to the natural world, Ingold claims, is epitomised by the relationship between the prey and hunters as reflected in the world picture of the hunters. According to this picture, the prey offers itself as a gift and it has to be wooed rather than coerced. This is in contrast to the farmer's relationship to nature, which has to be transformed (as when fields are ploughed and sown and crops harvested) or coerced (as when animals are domesticated and subordinated to the material needs of the farmer). The tools of the pastoralist are instruments of coercion, whereas those of the hunter-gatherer foster a revelatory and cooperative relationship between man and nature. The agricultural revolution, therefore, set us on a disastrous course in which nature has been reduced to and treated as an adversarial environment and there has been a shift from participation to 'a stance of contemplative detachment' in which the natural world is 'a world of physical objects confronting the isolated human subject'. The subjection of the planet by coercive technology is reflected in the development of complex coercive societies.

This, one may suppose, has many ramifying effects. Among them is the objectification of agency or its embedding in objects which Adorno and Horkheimer alluded to. People are reduced to the instruments of other people's purposes and those purposes, mediated through ever more complex technologies embedded in ever more complex social relations, are separated from individual agents. The individual human being, as a repository of skill and experience, becomes less and less important. The machine as 'the autonomous tool' (Hegel) increasingly separates human agency from the limits of the human body: there is a disembodiment of agency or a division within the agent who is divorced from his agency. The agent is also disenvironed: the efficacy of his actions is diffused and is remote from the locality of the agent, uprooted from deixis. The here-and-now preoccupations of the agent are irrelevant to his actions as a machine tender. Modern technology consequently places the human agent at odds with the machine: his moments of his own life, his own flickering cognitive skills, are as nothing compared with the accumulative or collective genius, the centuries of embedded cognitive activity, embodied in the complex machine. Man is no longer even an artisan; he is an operative. He is neither a hands-on, nor even a 'thoughts-on' – for the thoughts he is enacting are the collective thoughts of anonymous others – worker. The separation between the worker-as-operative, the agent, and his manipulative skills as tender of machines, widens and deepens. There is a division between knowledge – which is embedded in the machine and often hidden from the operator – and his actual practice. The 'hands-on' bit is small and does not reflect any special virtues – of skill or understanding – in the operative. The machine tender is hardly even a 'subject'; at any rate, from the point of view of the labour and its output, his subjectivity matters not at all.

The final outcome of the evolution of the work of the hands, therefore, is to both reduce the individual to a minimally skilled 'hired hand' and diminish the role of the hand itself. The technologically enhanced grip proves to be a stranglehold that places the collective hands round the neck of the individual. The objectivation of the world goes hand in hand with emptying or objectivation of the subject. The body is a subordinate instrument emptied of personhood. This disembodiment of the agent is dramatically illustrated by the difference between the hunter-gatherer directly killing his prey and the official in the abattoir signing the papers to authorise the slaughter of so many head of cattle or the slaughterman pressing the appropriate button.

According to Ingold – the lineage of whose views can be traced at least to Hegel and the Marx of the Paris Manuscripts and to the sentiments that informed the Romantic critique of the Enlightenment – the virtual extrusion of the agent from his labour as a result of ever more effective and elaborate automation, which reduces him to a simple instrument (designed to carry out the same narrow set of operations again and again and again) and reduces the natural world he works on to spiritless matter, creates an adversarial situation between the individual and the society of which he is a part, and potentially reduces human relationships to a degrading or even inhuman instrumentality.[40]

These dangers are real and one should not be prompted to deny them just because some writers – particularly those on the left such as Marx or Adorno and Horkheimer – have assumed apocalyptic postures in the face of the problem of the mechanisation and industrialisation of work. Nevertheless, one should still ask: What are the alternatives? The state of nature? Few would choose this, though they might be attracted by the notion of the simple life refracted through some Arcadian fantasy. Less advanced technology? What would this mean? In practice, it is likely to mean less effective technology, closer proximity to destitution for all except the wealthy, and, as a consequence, more direct oppression by one's fellow humans. Those who advocate less advanced technology and a rolling back of mass production should be obliged to make clear how much of the direct and indirect work of hands should be taken back. This, in turn, depends on how far back, and how deep, one feels the problem goes. For Heidegger, it is not merely the quantity, or the sophistication, of the technology that is at issue: the problem seems to lie with the stance towards Being that is implicit in *Homo technologicus*. The passage from ontology to metaphysics – and the resulting 'forgetfulness of Being' that lies at the root of technology – took place, so far as he was concerned, at the end of the pre-Socratic era. It was then that the hand and the eye become dominant and the relationship of *Da-sein* or human being to Being became one of objectification as well as manipulation and domination. Man, it would seem, was well set on his path to 'the desolation of the earth' by the time Archimedes was making the simple contraptions that he devised to support the arts of peace and war. A society acceptable to technophobes would therefore seem to be one not far from the state of nature.

It is also difficult to know how much of stories, such as those told by Ingold, one should accept; in particular the implicit comparison with a putative happier state antedating the increasing mastery of humans over the natural world. The notion that a cooperative, as opposed to a coercive, relationship with nature was ever on the cards seems fanciful. There are some bits of nature – scorpions, viruses, earthquakes, to name only the first three that come to mind – that one would not wish to cooperate with. Nor would much of nature wish to cooperate with us. The hunter-gatherers' idea that the animal offered itself as a gift does not seem likely to capture the animal's viewpoint: being torn to pieces and eaten is not usually the kind of thing that species (who, after all, survive largely because they are equipped to think of Number One – leaving aside a bit of intra-species altruism to permit group selection) are likely to welcome. As for non-transformative appropriation – hunter-gatherer rather than pastoralist style – this rather assumes that untransformed nature was intrinsically desirable.

At the risk of labouring the point, it is worth reiterating that the state of nature was unlikely to be a particularly happy one. Leaving aside early death, hunger, insecurity and the loss of children, one might imagine the unremitting anti-meaning of unrelieved discomfort from many sources – arthritis, infectious disease, infestations and unhealing wounds – would outweigh the attentuation of meaning by the emptying of subjectivity in advanced society.

11.6 HANDING ON

Whatever sum we write at the the bottom of the balance sheet – whether negative or positive – the world we live in will be a world largely shaped by human hands, unless we arrange to be bombed back beyond the Stone Age. (And it has to be remembered that, because technology is densely interconnected, taking back only a small part of it – say high-level quality control in mass production – will result in much more being taken back; for example, the safe treatment of infectious diseases with affordable antibiotics produced to an adequate standard. (See in this context the passage from Adam Smith cited in note 1.) We must, therefore, accept the work of hands and the instrumentalisation of (some aspects of) nature and (some aspects of) society and (some aspects of) our relationships to others and even ourselves as an inevitable consequence of this. This is the price of growing agency and control over some crucial elements in our experience and our destiny. The instrumental relationship to one's own body – underlined by modern medicine which paradoxically owes so much of its effectiveness and its limitations to viewing our individual bodies as a collection of general mechanisms – which lies at the root of the sense of agency, also opens up distances between the body and nature and to a greater or lesser degree instrumentalises one's relationships with others and one's place in society. The challenge for human beings who wish to retain and extend agency is not to adopt a non-instrumental relationship to the world – this would be impossible – but to mitigate its adverse consequences while retaining, and indeed maximising, its indubitable benefits.

There seem to be several ways of doing this. The first is to develop and to hold fast to a clear view of ourselves and our extraordinary nature. This – the celebration of our complexity and of the history of our collective massive achievements – is precisely the opposite of what much current thinking aims to do. In an attempt to make materialist, neurobiological and computational accounts of the human mind remotely plausible, the depth and complexity and uniqueness of the human self is routinely denied and a savagely impoverished of human consciousness is fostered.[41] History is treated ahistorically as a mere power-play, a class struggle, a narrative of iniquity and the massive achievements of the past are judged through ahistorical and cynical eyes. The stunning intellectual adventures of science and philosophy and the aesthetic achievements of art are taken for granted or belittled.

The profound mystery, the miracle, of the fact that, for one species, one form of matter, the universe is to an increasing degree intelligible, is simply overlooked. The overall tendency to denigrate human beings – to treat them as either dressed-up beasts, or as savages that have not moved on from the Stone Age or as zombies[42] – will itself exacerbate any damage caused by instrumentalisation of human life.

Conscious rejection of these negative accounts of human beings – as not merely one-sided but as deeply missing the point – will free us to develop a sense of possibility, of what has, and of what might be, achieved through art, through love and through contemplation. This will, in turn, provide necessary correctives to the world of increasing consumption that is driven by a sense of emptiness and a too purely instrumental attitude towards the world. If we were able truly to experience ourselves, and each other and the world – indeed, if we were better able fully to experience our experiences – then we might be liberated from the treadmill of spiralling consumption that, along with a rising population, not only condemns us all increasingly to being instruments of each other's purposes, but also threatens to bring about the very desolation of the earth that those hostile to technology believe is inherent in it.[43]

Humans are capable of creating unique experiences through the transformation of their appetites. Their appetites may be rooted in physiological need or some kind of biological function; but they grow into something utterly different. The complex institutions, discourses, traditions, customs that surround something as simple as eating dramatically illustrate this. We have hardly begin to experience these transfigured appetites – or not at least in this sense of experiencing them in full consciousness. We take our present extraordinarily complex relationships to our needs and appetites entirely for granted and ride on our present state without any regard to the distances we have travelled (which remain, as it were, coiled up inside them our dailyness). If we do look beyond the present state of our appetites, it is usually only to be scornful: to see the simple appetites beneath the complex activity as a way of deflating human pretension; to prove that human ceremony merely launders the animal essence. We have been so well schooled by the calumniators of humanity, for whom the essence of humanity is most truly reflected in the worst of which they are capable, that we find it much easier to say 'What a nasty piece of work is a man!' or 'What a jerk is a man!' than to echo Hamlet's awestruck cry. Our greatest achievements, our most generous sentiments, our most inspired visions, are dismissed as disguises for base instincts. The Bach 'B Minor Mass' is, when all is said and done, just another set of animal cries.

The profound possibilities that are open to human beings, and that are evident from what they have so far achieved, and the way in which they may be denied, are particularly dramatically illustrated by that most metaphysical of all human appetites, an appetite that, more than any other, is transformed into a distinctively human desire: the sexual appetite. It seems, superficially, to be unpromising – which is why those who have wanted to escape the supposed degradation of the human condition (holy men and women, contemplatives, mystics, philosophers) have treated it with suspicion, disdain or even terror. The direct interaction of naked bodies can seem like a regression to a pre-human condition. And the sexual exploitation of one person by another – where one is subjected to another's need for pleasure and, through this, for domination – can be a most brutal expression of the instrument-alisation of the relationship to others arising out of the work of hands. And yet it can also be the vehicle of the most transcendent experience of togetherness, of a transfiguring tenderness and mutual delight: out of the vertigo of the caress of The Carnal Hand (see section 5.2) new meanings can be made and the sense of the world transilluminated in a new way.

Those for whom human nature is essentially animality deceived as to its own character will see this as sentimental twaddle and self-deception and, if they concede that there is a distinctively human sexuality, will argue that it is to be found in the exploitative world of mass-produced pornography. The metamorphosis of animal appetites and biological needs into human desires can, of course, be degrading. The corruption of the sex instinct into the exploitation and degradation of others is a supreme example of this. The link between distinctively human desires and increased consumption, accumulation of wealth, the immiseration of others, the polluting of the planet, etc. is not denied. What is denied is that their corruption betrays their essence and that there can be no escape from the cycles of exploitation and ever-increasing consumption except into the (highly implausible) renunciation of desire or through reversion to the 'innocence' of the animal condition.

We must build on what has been achieved hitherto and move forward. The latest stage in the self-transformation of the work of the hand permits this. In the beginning was the supremely dexterous hand whose powers were amplified by precision. The precise hand created tools further to amplify its power and sharpen its precision. The power-ful, precise hand then discovered the power and precision of virtual digits. The world became mathematised, needs were quantified and the means to them enumerated. Virtual digits increasingly shaped the tools that the hand used to enhance its powers and its precision in order to

realise the agency it had discovered within and through itself. The work
of hands became ever more indirect as tools achieved increasing
autonomy in machines: numbers, the ghosts of the digits, manipulated
the machines. The work of hands became, as we have noted and some
thinkers have mourned, less 'hands on'. Machines combine the virtues
of hand-and-brain. As we progress into the latest era of the handy
world, machine technology advances towards the increasing autonomy
of robotics whose applications spreads out from the standardised universe of the mass production of goods to the messier needs of domestic
life. The work of the hands becomes less the shifting and shaping of
material things and more the processing of what is known as
'information'.[44] We may anticipate a world in which the hand finally
fades away as the main agent of productive labour – mission accomplished, apart from a little adjustment every now and then (the hand
that holds the mobile phone or gives the instruction or presses the
button).[45]

This, combined with a clear understanding of human possibility as
we have hinted at, will free the hand to be the agent of hands-on caring
or and of recreation – handicraft, music-making, sport, lovemaking.
The noisy, polluting world of the first generation of intelligent tools will
be replaced by the infinitely renewable quiet world of information
processors. There will still be a need for consumption – man does not
live or love by information alone – but this will diminish. The hand will
not fade: its warmth will seek out the warmth of others' hands. And art,
tenderness and love will be able to find their true place at the heart of
human life.

This, then, is the future our hands could grasp. The hand-story so far
has been one of incredible and wondrous achievement dappled with
setbacks, unforeseen horrors, natural disasters and the man-made
catastrophes of war and peace. There is much in the legacy of the hand
that is to be regretted; but there is much more to be applauded. The
work of hands has taken us to the place apart which we alone occupy
and in which enjoy and endure our unique status in the world of living
creatures. It is neither possible, nor is it desirable, to regress to a state of
nature or to some half-way house between animals and ourselves. We
must build on the legacy handed down to us.

And the future of this legacy, and the human beings who have created
it, will be bright, only if we get ourselves and our achievements clearly in
focus. This means breaking with a long tradition of self-contempt which
derives from a distorted piety in which our fear of nature and our sense
of our own frailty originally prompted mankind to postulate a Supreme
Being who had to be placated and who would be offended if we took

our destiny and our well-being into our own hands. Although many no longer believe in this Supreme Being, a displaced and distorted version of the humility and self-abasement this Being seemed to demand is expressed in our self-contempt and our seeing in every man-made disaster a just punishment for the original Promethean sin of trying to take hold of our own destiny.[46] We have to recognise that, although we are not ultimately self-created, we are increasingly the authors of our own nature, the products of our own handiwork, and living in a nature of our own making. While in the beginning there was animal biology, there is now human society. We have a unique destiny and, uninhibited by misplaced piety, we can seize this unique destiny with both our hands, so that our hands shall not lose their grip on the future of mankind, or on the very grip they have brought into their world.

11.7 A LAST WAVE FAREWELL

That, for the present, is as far as we can take our story of the contribution of the Ever-increasing Dabness of the Human Hand to The Great Awakening of Human Agency out of the Eternal Slumber of Mechanism that enfolds the Animal, Biological and Material Universe and of what it tells us about the future possibilities of mankind. The interacting developments of the bare and tooled hand, successively with the brain, general intelligence, society and language in driving the liberation of the human organism from the state of nature to one of culture and the transformation of the material world into a limitless nexus of the ready-to-hand is a huge theme for future explorations.

If I pause here, it is because I want to end not with analysis, explanation and argument, but with wonder and celebration at how much has grown out of so little. How the unfolding of the world has been steered in a new direction, along a path where we humans are unaccompanied by any other kind of being, by a seemingly slight difference. If we are alone in our place apart and are likely to remain so, this is due not to our being the terminus of an evolutionary process that has run out of possibilities or run through its entire repertoire – there is no predetermined repertoire, only the limitless varieties that may come out of accidental mutation and survival of the most adapted – but because the competition of the most developed species is with man and this overshadows competition with each other.

We are a totally new force in the evolution of life on the planet; for we, and the environment we create, are the most important environmental factor in the lives of an increasing number of other organisms. There is no genetic progression that can keep pace with our cultural progress; no evolution-driven arms race that can arm itself against humankind. So, increasingly, other species live courtesy of mankind – in whom the evolutionary process becomes aware of itself – and Man becomes (to use Heidegger's famous phrase) the shepherd of being, of all living creatures.

In just such a spirit of celebration, I look at my hand placed against a rock. Compared with this rock, the flesh, even the bones, of my hand are a mere thermal in the air, a shimmer in the daylight dispensed by the ten billion-year-old sun. And it is hands such as these that have changed everything: have gained (if only temporarily for individuals and perhaps temporarily for the human race as a whole) power over so much life and death, over so much of the living and non-living material of the universe. Hand-born, humanity is the most extraordinary upstart stuff in the universe. From the moment we were able to touch the tips of our fingers with the tips of our thumbs and to take hold of a pebble – cool against our warm grasp, insentient against its sentience, ignorant against our knowledge – and shape it into the first tool, our destiny, and that of our planet, was set.

By this small chance, the future of the world has come to lie in our hands. We owe it to ourselves, and indeed to the world, to think clearly about Handkind, building upon a grateful and wondering sense of how far humans have travelled notions of where they might yet travel in the future. Upon such clear thinking may depend the difference between a future that is bright with hope and one that is bright with conflagration; between Utopia and Apocalypse.

NOTES

1. One doesn't, of course, have to invoke high technology to find examples of tool-making remote from biological interactions and embedded in complex social relations. Adam Smith's account of the nexus of interactions underpinning the manufacture of a cheap coat would make the point just as well:

   The woollen coat, for example, which covers the day labourer, as coarse and rough as it may seem, is the product of the joint labour of a great multitude of workmen. The shepherd, the sorter of wool, the wool-comber or carder, the dyer, the scribbler, the spinner, the weaver, the fuller, the dresser, with many others, must all join their different arts in order to complete even this homely production. How many merchants and carriers, besides, must have been employed ... how much commerce and navigation ... how many ship-builders, sailors, sail-makers, rope-makers ...

   Were we to examine, in the same manner, all the different parts of his dress and household furniture ... the meanest person in a civilized country could not be provided even according to what we very falsely imagine, the easy and simple manner in which he is commonly accommodated. (*The Wealth of Nations*, New York: Modern Library, 1937, pp. 11–12)

Or, to go further back, the expeditions in ancient times in pursuit of luxury goods – spices from the East, etc. – with their long-term aims, deferred goals, numerous intermediary steps, documentation (bills of lading, etc.), and legal and institutional frameworks would also make this point.

2. See Kenan Malik's brilliant *Man, Beast and Zombie: What Science Can and Cannot Tell us about Human Nature* (London: Weidenfeld and Nicolson, 2001). Its arguments are summarised in Raymond Tallis, *Prospect*, February 2000, pp. 24–9. Reading Tallis, however, is no substitute for reading Malik.

3. This is one limb of the pincer movement attacking human dignity and the belief in the efficacy and virtue of the conscious human agent. The other component comes from anti-humanist intellectuals, who have done their best to displace the conscious human agent acting in accordance with reason and objective knowledge by unconscious mechanisms or systems. See Raymond Tallis, *Enemies of Hope: A Critique of Contemporary Pessimism*, 2nd edn (London: Macmillan, 1999).

4. A notable recent expression of this is Daniel Dennett's *Darwin's Dangerous Idea: Evolution and the Meanings of Life* (London: Allen Lane, 1995), which is devoted to promulgating Dennett's Daft Idea that anyone who cannot accept a materialistic account of the mind and a biologistic account of human beings is simply too stupid or too cowardly to see the true consequence of Darwinism. In order to support this view, he has to deny all sorts of things that are undeniable, including trivia such as qualia (the contents of consciousness), the intentionality of experiences and the deliberateness of actions.

5. Or all three, as I found to my cost when I criticised neurobiological theories of the mind in a recent article. See Raymond Tallis, 'Brains and minds: a brief history of neuromythology', *Journal of the Royal College of Physicians of London* 34(6), 2000, pp. 563–7 and the subsequent correspondence. 'Neuromythology' [Letter], *Clinical Science* 1(1), 2001, pp. 88–9.

6. Also spelt out in great (and perhaps wearying) detail in Raymond Tallis, *The Explicit Animal*, 2nd edn (London: Macmillan, 1999). See especially Chapter 6, 'Man, the explicit animal'.

7. I am thinking in particular of the way in which John Bowlby's theories of child care – which kept so many women at home and out of the workforce in the 1950s and 1960s – were based upon notions of bonding and attachment that acquired a spurious authority from anthropomorphic interpretations of the experiments of the Harlows on Rhesus monkeys brought up with dummy mothers.

8. Tallis, *Enemies of Hope*, Chapter 2 'Falling into the ha-ha'.

9. To vary the passage from *As You Like It* quoted in the Preface: 'These are counsellors that feelingly persuade me of part of what I am and what always awaits to become all of me.'

10. Peter Bowler, *Theories of Human Evolution: a Century of Debate 1844–1944* (Oxford: Basil Blackwell, 1986), p. 14.

11. Just as any ancestral connection we may have with palaeolithic hunter-gatherers is irrelevant to understanding the problems of contemporary man.

12. Derek Bickerton, *Language and Species* (Chicago: University of Chicago Press, 1990) quoted in Kathleen Gibson and Tim Ingold, *Tools, Language and Cognition in Human Evolution* (Cambridge: Cambridge University Press, 1993), p. 230.

13. And if we argue for the separate creation of the human mind (outside the evolutionary process), we may as well argue for the separation creation of the entire human being and that would never do.

14. The origin of agency and its link with the self will be examined in considerably more detail in Volume 2 of this trilogy.
15. Published posthumously in *Nature, the Utility of Religion, and Theism*, 3rd edn (London: Longman, Green and Co., 1885). I have drawn on the selections in Henry D. Aiken, *The Age of Ideology. The Nineteenth-Century Philosophers* (New York: Mentor Books, 1956).
16. I have not addressed fully all the problems thrown up by Mill's account of how we should deal with nature in order to achieve our ends. For example, the implicit notion that there is only one natural law applying to one set of circumstances is a strange one, as is the complementary idea that the laws have their own local spheres of operation – as if they were the laws of different lands. I will return to Mill's ideas in Volume 2.
17. This may connect with Benjamin Libet's suggestion that we do not initiate actions but rather select and control them. Actually, this negative freedom to delete possible actions is no more comprehensible than the positive account of freedom as the ability to initiate action. There is an excellent discussion of his reasons for suggesting this and a critique of Libet's experiments in Daniel Dennett, *Consciousness Explained* (London: Penguin, 1991), pp. 153–66. For a critique of Dennett's interpretation of Libet's experiments, see Volume 3 of this trilogy, *The Knowing Animal: A Philosophical Inquiry into Knowledge and Truth*.
18. Whether the initiation of movement can be understood in Newtonian terms, or indeed the laws of classical physics, is a question of immense interest. There may be another crack in the seamless web of physical nature and its immutable laws here.
19. The nature of knowledge and its relationship to truth will be the main theme of Volume 3, where we shall examine the question of the superior truth of scientific knowledge in more detail.
20. See, for example, Raymond Tallis, *Newton's Sleep* (London: Macmillan, 1995); and Raymond Tallis, *On the Edge of Certainty* (London: Macmillan, 1999).
21. The fact that there is a sequence – knowledge first, power later – also undermines the sociologist's case. For example, Newton's laws of planetary motion and James Clerk Maxwell's equations were validated long before they were found to have practical application.
22. See Volume 3 of this trilogy.
23. It is possible to see here the origins of human temporality – the explicit sense of being oriented towards a future with its revelations and experiences to come – and even of *Da-sein*, that being whose being is an issue for itself. It would be very satisfying if we could link the origin of the world of *Da-sein* – composed of the ready-to-hand – with the origin of *Da-sein* itself, in a way that is not dependent upon its world being the mere cognate of *Da-sein*. The question of whether *Da-sein* began in time is a vexed one and Heidegger himself would certainly have not welcomed the suggestion that *Da-sein* woke up when the creature with the opposable thumb started choosing his grips. He is not entirely happy with *Homo technologicus* anyway, as we shall discuss.
    The suggestion that the ready-to-hand emerged in response to specifically human hands also suggests that pre-human, objective presences, rather than beings ready-to-hand, are primordial; that we begin with something like 'matter' as the given, as the substratum of the Nature into which, and from which, we are born. For a further discussion, see Raymond Tallis, *A Conversation with Martin Heidegger* (Basingstoke: Palgrave, 2001).

24. See William Calvin, 'The unitary hypothesis: a common neural circuitry for novel manipulations, language, plan-ahead and throwing?', in Gibson and Ingold, *Tools, Language and Cognition in Human Evolution*.

25. This question becomes particularly pressing when we consider those neural theories of knowledge that claim that consciousness is the direct knowledge we have of neural activity in virtue of our *being* that neural activity. See Volume 3.

26. The Whiggish notion that human history is a story of progressive 'improvement' in consciousness – with human awareness becoming more truth-laden, for example – would, of course, be rejected by the tradition of cultural and cognitive relativism inaugurated by Johan Gottfried Herder's *Ideas on the Philosophy of the History of Mankind* (expounded with incomparable brilliance by Isaiah Berlin in *The Crooked Timber of Humanity*, edited by Henry Hardy, London: HarperCollins, 1991).

27. With respect to this point, it is astonishing to reflect that one animal alone – ourselves – should have such a pronounced idea of its finitude so that it should conceive of, and worship, the notion of an Infinite Being, with limitless power and limitless knowledge and limitless presence. Descartes' argument in *Discourse on Method* for the reality of God could be turned on its head. That a finite being can conceive of an infinite being does not prove that the infinite being exists; only that there is something very special about us, irrespective of our finitude.

28. See Volume 3 of this trilogy.

29. A recent expression of this was the romanticisation (by anthropologists such as Marcel Sahlins) of the hunter-gatherer life of the !Kung Bushmen who, it was suggested, were not rich in material goods but maintained a good standard of living on the basis of relatively little work. See Malik, *Man Beast and Zombie*, pp. 244–5. Romantic primitivism is subjected to a brilliant analysis and critique in Roger Sandall, *The Culture Cult. Designer Tribalism and Other Essays* (Boulder, CO: Westview Press, 2001).

30. See 'The question concerning technology', available in *Martin Heidegger. Basic Writings*, translated by David Farrell Krell (London: Routledge & Kegan Paul, 1977), pp. 284–317.

31. Theodor Adorno and Max Horkheimer, *Dialectic of Enlightenment*, translated by John Cumming (London: Verso, 1973).

32. The connection between instrumentalism and oppressive dictatorship is well captured by one of the many brilliantly sardonic asides in Albert Camus's *The Rebel*:
    The concentration camp system of the Russians has, in fact, accomplished the dialectical transition from the government of people to the administration of objects, but by confusing people with objects. (translated by Anthony Bower, London: Penguin Classics, 1971, p. 205)

33. Many elements went into the Industrial Revolution, as Krell (*Basic Writings*, p. 284) points out in his Introduction to Heidegger's essay on technology:
    Everything is jumbled together into inscrutable 'factors': revolutionary discoveries in the natural sciences, detection and extraction of energy resources, invention of mechanical devices and chemical processes, availability of investment capital, improved means of transportation and communication, land enclosures, mechanization of agriculture, concentration of unskilled labour, a happy combination of this-worldly and other-worldly incentives – and the age of modern technology is off and running before anyone can catch his breath and raise a question.

34. J. S. Mill, *Nature, the Utility of Religion, and Theism*, p. 160.

35. This passage is cited in Isaiah Berlin, 'Joseph de Maistre and the origins of fascism',

collected in *The Crooked Timber of Humanity*, edited by Henry Hardy (London: Fontana, 1991), p. 111.

36. For more on this, see Raymond Tallis, 'Anti-science and organic daydreams', 'The murderousness and gadgetry of this age', in *Newton's Sleep* (London: Macmillan, 1995).

37. Quoted by Walter Benjamin in his 'Theses on the philosophy of history', in *Illuminations*, edited by Hannah Arendt (London: Jonathan Cape, 1970).

38. Though, as Mary Midgeley has pointed out in *Science and Poetry* (London: Routledge, 2001), social contract thinking, which was a liberating force when it was initially advanced by Enlightenment thinkers, may no longer be so. Originally, it challenged the abuses of power as part of 'a political campaign against the use of religion to justify exploitation'; and its narrow contractual view of political obligations was 'a defence against the use of religiously-motivated loyalty by self-interested rulers'. Contractual and individualistic thought, however, had the unintended side-effect of making it difficult to understand, even less to accept, our wider responsibilities towards humans outside of our own society or even our immediate circle. This may ultimately threaten the planet.

39. Tim Ingold, 'Tool-use, sociality and intelligence', in Gibson and Ingold, *Tools, Language and Cognition in Human Evolution*, p. 441.

40. A connection encapsulated in Walter Benjamin's aphorism that 'Prostitution can lay claim to being considered 'work' the moment work becomes prostitution' (quoted in J. M. Coetzee, 'The marvels of Walter Benjamin', *New York Review of Books*, 11 January 2001).

41. Raymond Tallis, 'The poverty of neurophilosophy', in *On the Edge of Certainty*; *Enemies of Hope: A Critique of Contemporary Pessimism*, 2nd edn (London: Macmillan, 1999).

42. See Malik, *Man, Beast and Zombie*, passim.

43. See Raymond Tallis, 'The difficulty of arrival', in *Newton's Sleep*; 'The work of art in an age of electronic reproduction', in *Theorrhoea and After*; and 'The hope of progress', in *Enemies of Hope*.

44. A term it is almost impossible to avoid using rather carelessly. See the entry on 'Information', in Raymond Tallis, 'A critical dictionary of neuromythology', in *On the Edge of Certainty*.

45. Two caveats here. First of all, there are many parts of the world where work is still back-breaking – indeed body-breaking – where people literally groan with the effort of physical labour. There are many other parts of the world where the ordeal of precision is still very much the overwhelming experience of everyday: the sweatshops of medium technology mass production. Secondly, even where the ordeals of power and of precision are greatly alleviated, work has still retained one immemorial characteristic: repetition. Irrespective of whether one is a checker-out of an ever-forming and ever-reforming queue of shoppers in a supermarket, or a civil servant producing endless documents, or a general practitioner seeing thirty patients in the morning and thirty patients in the evening, day in day out, week in week out, repetition remains the key characteristic of work. We have a long way to go before we can say that Adam's curse has not yet been rescinded.

46. See Tallis, 'The murderousness and gadgetry of this age', in *Newton's Sleep*.

Index

and wrist, 23–4
thumb, fully opposable, 13, 22, 24, 157, 159
  and growth of intelligence, 35
  opposability index, 267
  and precision grips, 174
  and sensitivity of fingertips, 142–3
  unique to humans, 277
thumb-sucking, 134n
tickling, 139–40
Tolstoy, Leo, 15
Tooby, John and De Vore, Irven, 269–70, 302–3n
tool
  as classifying device, 240–1
  definitions, 222–3, 254n
  notion of, 196, 284
  as signifier, 230–1, 237, 255n
  see also tool-making; tool-use; tools
tool design, 223
  theory and practice and, 302–3n
tool development
  accelerating, 234–7, 238, 245–6, 249–50
  effect on individualism, 339–40
  and principles, 39, 227, 302–3n
  slowness of, 227, 233–4, 240, 253n
  see also precision
tool-making, 253n, 254n
  cooperative, 240
  by craftsmen, 234–5, 255n, 258n
  secondary, 226–9
  social context of, 231–2, 240, 253n
tool-use, 12, 22, 222, 253n, 265, 277
  by animals, 223–6, 252n
  and brain size, 271
  depersonalised, 236
  and evolution of intelligence, 38, 244–5, 256n, 298
  and instrumentality, 38, 283
  and intuition of agency, 283, 299
  and language, 237–41, 242, 288
  societal dimension of, 227, 231, 240, 245, 330, 348n
  see also tool-making
tools
  as autonomous, 285
  composite (polyliths), 229, 241, 253n
  compound, 39, 235–6

cutting, 252n
  with handles, 39, 228–9
  interliths, 229
  manufactured, 39, 40, 176
  modification of, 226, 253n
  multiplicity and variety of, 248–9
  relationship to hand and body, 231, 234, 235, 255n
  in ritual, 232, 234
  role in social development, 232–7, 258–60, 325
  standardisation of, 40, 227, 234, 240, 253n, 303n
  stored, 39, 176, 228
  see also machines
torque, 57
touch, 30–1, 144
  in gloves, 128
  and hand-holding, 111, 112
  invasive (as violation), 145
  and knowledge, 30, 141–2, 144–5
  lascivious, 146
  and reciprocity, 141, 279, 280
  sense of, 28–9, 103, 142–3
trade, and enumeration, 212, 216–17n
trajectory (reaching)
  adjustments to, 50, 57–8
  'bell-shaped velocity curve', 50, 54, 56
transport, 248
Trinkhaus, Eric, 26, 39, 179
truth(s)
  explicit awareness of, 329
  intrinsic, 328–9
  and knowledge, 326–7, 328–9
  objective, 332
  scientific, 326
typing, 61, 62, 186, 187, 193n

V-signs
  filthy, 94–5, 193n
  for Victory, 93–4, 95
Valéry, Paul, 294
van Vliet, Paulette, 1–2, 58
vision, 37, 216n
  effect of bipedalism on, 264–5
visual control, 27–9, 147
Voltaire, 49

UNIVERSITY OF WOLVERHAMPTON
LEARNING & INFORMATION SERVICES